Otto Hahn

The Philosophical magazine : comprehending the various branches of science, the liberal and fine arts, geology, agriculture, manufactures and commerce

Otto Hahn

**The Philosophical magazine : comprehending the various branches of science, the liberal and fine arts, geology, agriculture, manufactures and commerce**

ISBN/EAN: 9783742846297

Manufactured in Europe, USA, Canada, Australia, Japa

Cover: Foto ©Klaus-Uwe Gerhardt /pixelio.de

Manufactured and distributed by brebook publishing software (www.brebook.com)

Otto Hahn

The Philosophical magazine : comprehending the various branches of science, the liberal and fine arts, geology, agriculture, manufactures and commerce

# THE
## LONDON, EDINBURGH, AND DUBLIN
# PHILOSOPHICAL MAGAZINE
## AND
# JOURNAL OF SCIENCE.

### CONDUCTED BY
SIR DAVID BREWSTER, K.H. LL.D. F.R.S.L.&E. &c.
RICHARD TAYLOR, F.L.S. G.S. Astr.S. Nat.H.Mosc.&c.
RICHARD PHILLIPS, F.R.S.L.&E. F.G.S. &c.
SIR ROBERT KANE, M.D. M.R.I.A.

"Nec aranearum sane textus ideo melior quia ex se fila gignunt, nec noster vilior quia ex alienis libamus ut apes." Just. Lips. Polit. lib. i. cap. 1. Not.

## VOL. XXXII.
NEW AND UNITED SERIES OF THE PHILOSOPHICAL MAGAZINE, ANNALS OF PHILOSOPHY, AND JOURNAL OF SCIENCE.

### JANUARY—JUNE, 1848.

### LONDON:
RICHARD AND JOHN E. TAYLOR, RED LION COURT, FLEET STREET,
*Printers and Publishers to the University of London;*.
SOLD BY LONGMAN, BROWN, GREEN, AND LONGMANS; SIMPKIN, MARSHALL AND CO.; S. HIGHLEY; WHITTAKER AND CO.; AND SHERWOOD, GILBERT, AND PIPER, LONDON: — BY ADAM AND CHARLES BLACK, AND THOMAS CLARK, EDINBURGH; SMITH AND SON, GLASGOW; HODGES AND SMITH, DUBLIN; AND WILEY AND PUTNAM, NEW YORK.

"Meditationis est perscrutari occulta; contemplationis est admirari perspicua...... Admiratio generat quæstionem, quæstio investigationem, investigtio inventionem."—*Hugo de S. Victore.*

# CONTENTS OF VOL. XXXII.

## (THIRD SERIES.)

### NUMBER CCXII.—JANUARY 1848.

|  | Page |
|---|---|
| Sir D. Brewster on the Optical Phænomena, Nature, and Locality of *Muscæ volitantes*; with Observations on the Structure of the Vitreous Humour, and on the Vision of Objects placed within the Eye | 1 |
| Prof. J. R. Young on the Integral $\int \frac{dx}{x}$, and on some consequences that have been deduced from it | 11 |
| Mr. H. M. Noad on the Action of Nitric Acid on Cymol | 15 |
| Mr. C. Brooke's Account of the remarkable Magnetic Disturbance which continued from the 22nd to the 25th of October 1847. (With a Plate.) | 35 |
| Sir R. Kane's Note of the occurrence of a Deposit of native Earthy Carbonate of Manganese in Ireland | 37 |
| Mr. W. R. Birt on the Great Symmetrical Barometric Wave, November 1847, and other important undulations | 38 |
| Mr. J. Coekle on Algebraic Equations of the Fifth Degree | 50 |
| Mr. H. Watts on the Analysis of Hop-Ash | 54 |
| M. Plateau's Experimental Researches on Figures of Equilibrium of a Liquid Mass withdrawn from the Action of Gravity: Second Series | 61 |
| Mr. F. A. Abel on some of the Products of Oxidation of Cumol by Nitric Acid | 63 |
| Notices respecting New Books:—Recent Cambridge Works on Pure Mathematics | 69 |
| Phosphate of Iron, Manganese and Soda, by M. A. Damour | 74 |
| Analysis of Columbite from the Environs of Limoges, by M. A. Damour | 74 |
| On the Acids of Sulphur, by MM. Fordos and Gelis | 75 |
| On some Properties of Carbon, by M. Lazowski | 76 |
| Detection of free Sulphuric Acid added to Wines | 77 |
| On the Composition of Urano-Tantalite and Columbite | 77 |
| On the Fossil Vegetation of Anthracite Coal | 78 |
| Meteorological Observations for November 1847 | 79 |
| Meteorological Observations made by Mr. Thompson at the Garden of the Horticultural Society at Chiswick, near London; by Mr. Veall at Boston; by the Rev. W. Dunbar at Applegarth Manse, Dumfries-shire; and by the Rev. C. Clouston at Sandwick Manse, Orkney | 80 |

## NUMBER CCXIII.—FEBRUARY.

| | Page |
|---|---|
| Sir J. W. Lubbock on Shooting Stars | 81 |
| Mr. A. Claudet on different Properties of Solar Radiation producing or preventing a deposit of Mercury on Silver Plates coated with Iodine, or its compounds with Bromine or Chlorine, modified by Coloured Glass Media and the Vapours of the Atmosphere | 88 |
| Prof. J. R. Young on the Combination of the Theorems of Maclaurin and Taylor | 98 |
| Dr. J. W. Draper on the Production of Light by Chemical Action | 100 |
| Mr. J. Cockle's Account of the Method of Vanishing Groups | 114 |
| Dr. R. P. Cotton's Observations on the Geological Age of Bone-Caverns | 119 |
| Mr. J. Drinkwater on the Preparation of absolute Alcohol, and the Composition of " Proof-Spirit " | 123 |
| Mr. J. Glaisher's Remarks on the Weather during the Quarter ending December 31, 1847 | 130 |
| Mr. H. E. Strickland on the present state of Knowledge of the Geology of Asia Minor | 137 |
| Proceedings of the Royal Society | 139 |
| ———————— Cambridge Philosophical Society | 141 |
| ———————— Royal Astronomical Society | 144 |
| Analysis of a Hydrated Silicate of Alumina, by MM. Damour and Salvetat | 149 |
| On the Action of Chlorine on Benzoate of Potash, by M. Saint-Evre | 151 |
| Action of Chlorine on Cyanide of Mercury, by J. Bouis | 152 |
| Frigorific Mixture | 153 |
| Researches on Phosphorus, by M. P. Thenard | 153 |
| On Christianite—a New Mineral | 155 |
| On the Identity of Metacetonic and Butyro-Acetic Acids—Propionic Acid, by MM. Dumas, Malaguti and F. Leblanc | 156 |
| On the Composition and Properties of Nicotina | 158 |
| Meteorological Observations for December 1847 | 159 |
| ———————— Table | 160 |

## NUMBER CCXIV.—MARCH.

| | |
|---|---|
| Sir D. Brewster on the Distinctness of Vision produced in certain cases by the use of the Polarizing Apparatus in Microscopes | 161 |
| Prof. Faraday on the Use of Gutta Percha in Electrical Insulation | 165 |
| The Rev. J. Challis on the Course of a Ray of Light from a Celestial Body to the Earth's Surface, according to the Hypothesis of Undulations | 168 |
| Sir J. W. Lubbock's Note on Shooting Stars | 170 |

| | Page |
|---|---|
| Mr. J. Goodman's Researches into the Identity of the Existencies or Forces—Light, Heat, Electricity and Magnetism. | 172 |
| Sir D. Brewster on the Phænomena of Thin Plates of Solid and Fluid Substances exposed to Polarized Light. (With a Plate.) | 181 |
| Mr. A. Claudet on Photographic phænomena referring to the various Actions of the red and yellow Rays on Daguerreotype Plates when they have been affected by daylight | 199 |
| M. Niépce de Saint-Victor's Observations on some remarkable Properties of Iodine, Phosphorus, Nitric Acid, &c. | 206 |
| Mr. A. Claudet on the Question of Priority respecting the Discovery of the accelerating process in the Daguerreotype operation | 215 |
| Notices respecting New Books:—Daubeny on Volcanos, Earthquakes and Thermal Springs | 216 |
| Proceedings of the Royal Society | 219 |
| On a remarkable Solar Spot | 232 |
| On the Preparation and Chemical Constitution of Asparagin | 233 |
| On the Transformations of Asparagin | 235 |
| On Chrysammic Acid, by M. Mulder | 236 |
| Meteorological Observations for January 1848 | 239 |
| ———— Table | 240 |

## NUMBER CCXV.—APRIL.

| | Page |
|---|---|
| Prof. De Morgan's Account of the Speculations of Thomas Wright of Durham | 241 |
| Mr. R. Hunt on the supposed Influence of Magnetism on Chemical Action | 252 |
| The Rev. B. Bronwin on the Solution of a particular Differential Equation | 256 |
| M. Melloni's Researches on the Radiations of Incandescent Bodies, and on the Elementary Colours of the Solar Spectrum | 262 |
| The Rev. J. Challis's Theoretical Determination of the Velocity of Sound | 276 |
| Mr. S. Roberts on the Development of Functions of the form $F(z+x)$ | 284 |
| Notices respecting New Books:—Daubeny on Volcanos, Earthquakes and Thermal Springs | 287 |
| Proceedings of the Royal Society | 300 |
| On a late Solar Spot, by W. Pringle, Esq. | 308 |
| On a new Method of distinguishing the Protoxide of Iron from the Peroxide by the Blowpipe, by E. J. Chapman, Esq. | 309 |
| On the Existence of several Metals in the Human Blood, and the Fixed Salts it contains | 310 |
| On the Artificial Formation of Crystallized Minerals, by M. Ebelmen | 312 |
| On the Crystalline form of Metallic Zinc | 314 |

|   | Page |
|---|---|
| On the Crystallized Monohydrate of Zinc, by M. J. Nicklès | 315 |
| On the Hydrate of Cadmium, by M. J. Nicklès | 317 |
| Action of Acids and Alkalies on Asparagin and Aspartic Acid, by M. Piria | 317 |
| Meteorological Observations for February 1848 | 319 |
| ———— Table | 320 |

## NUMBER CCXVI.—MAY.

|   |   |
|---|---|
| Dr. T. Andrews on the Heat disengaged during the Combination of Bodies with Oxygen and Chlorine. (With a Plate.) | 321 |
| The Astronomer Royal's Remarks on Professor Challis's Theoretical Determination of the Velocity of Sound | 339 |
| Mr. G. G. Stokes on the Constitution of the Luminiferous Æther | 343 |
| Mr. J. P. Joule on Shooting Stars | 349 |
| Mr. J. Cockle's Analysis of the Theory of Equations, with a few Remarks on recent English Works on the subject. In a Letter to T. S. Davies, Esq., F.R.S., &c.: with Notes on some of the Topics, by Mr. Davies | 351 |
| Sir W. R. Hamilton on Quaternions; or on a New System of Imaginaries in Algebra (*continued*) | 367 |
| Prof. E. Wartmann on an easy method of measuring the distance and height of an elevated point, accessible or inaccessible, fixed or moveable, by means of a single instrument, and by taking the observation from only one station | 375 |
| Notices respecting New Books:—Herschel's Astronomical Observations made at the Cape of Good Hope | 378 |
| Proceedings of the Royal Society | 389 |
| Action of Nitric Acid on Brucia, by M. Aug. Laurent | 392 |
| On Cacothelin, by M. Aug. Laurent | 393 |
| On a new Method of estimating Arsenic, Antimony and Tin, by Prof. H. Rose | 394 |
| On a Reagent for Strychnia | 396 |
| On the Presence of Selenium in the Iodide of Potassium | 397 |
| On Transparent and Opake Arsenious Acid, by M. Bussy | 398 |
| Meteorological Observations for March 1848 | 399 |
| ———— Table | 400 |

## NUMBER CCXVII.—JUNE.

|   |   |
|---|---|
| Sir D. Brewster on the Decomposition and Dispersion of Light within Solid and Fluid Bodies. (With a Plate.) | 401 |
| Mr. G. Boole's Remarks on a Paper by the Rev. B. Bronwin on the Solution of a particular Differential Equation | 413 |

|  | Page |
|---|---|
| Mr. T. S. Davies on Geometry and Geometers | 419 |
| Mr. J. Cockle on certain Researches of Murphy | 421 |
| Mr. W. J. Henwood's Abstract of Meteorological Observations made during the year 1847 at Gongo Soco, in the interior of Brazil | 422 |
| Dr. T. Andrews on the Heat disengaged during the Combination of Bodies with Oxygen and Chlorine (*concluded*) | 426 |
| Mr. E. L. Garbett's Description of some Parhelia seen at Portsea on the 29th of March 1848; with some Remarks on these Phænomena generally. (With a Plate.) | 434 |
| Prof. De Morgan on the Additions made to the Second Edition of the *Commercium Epistolicum* | 446 |
| The Law of the Nutrition of Animals pointed out by Dr. R. D. Thomson, illustrated by Dr. F. Knapp | 456 |
| Dr. R. Hare's Objections to the Theories severally of Franklin, Dufay and Ampère, with an attempt to explain Electrical Phænomena by Statical or Undulatory Polarization | 461 |

## NUMBER CCXVIII.—SUPPLEMENT TO VOL. XXXII.

|  |  |
|---|---|
| Dr. R. Hare's Objections to the Theories severally of Franklin, Dufay and Ampère, with an attempt to explain Electrical Phænomena by Statical or Undulatory Polarization (*concluded*) | 481 |
| Sir D. Brewster's Observations on the Elementary Colours of the Spectrum, in reply to M. Melloni | 489 |
| The Rev. J. Challis on the Velocity of Sound, in Reply to the Astronomer Royal | 494 |
| Prof. E. Wartmann on some New Lines in the Solar Spectrum | 499 |
| Mr. J. Glaisher's Remarks on the Weather during the Quarter ending March 31, 1848 | 506 |
| Notices respecting New Books:—Herschel's Astronomical Observations made at the Cape of Good Hope; Bell's Elements of Plane Geometry; Tate's Principles of Geometry | 518 |
| Proceedings of the Royal Society | 537 |
| On the advantage of Electrotyping Daguerreotype Plates | 541 |
| On the Acids of Pines, by M. Aug. Laurent | 542 |
| Action of Zinc on Selenious Acid | 544 |
| Liebenerite—a new Mineral | 544 |
| Meteorological Observations for April 1847 | 545 |
| ———— Table | 546 |
| Index | 547 |

## PLATES.

I. Illustrative of Mr. Brooke's Account of the remarkable Magnetic Disturbance which continued from the 22nd to the 25th of October 1847.

II. Illustrative of Sir D. Brewster's Paper on the Phænomena of Thin Plates of Solid and Fluid Substances exposed to Polarized Light.

III. Illustrative of Dr. T. Andrews's Paper on the Heat disengaged during the Combination of Bodies with Oxygen and Chlorine.

IV. Illustrative of Sir D. Brewster's Paper on the Decomposition and Dispersion of Light within Solid and Fluid Bodies.

V. Illustrative of Mr. E. L. Garbett's Description of some Parhelia seen at Portsea on the 29th of March 1848.

*Erratum* in Mr. FARADAY's paper, vol. xxxi.
Page 416, line 12 from top, *for* equally *read* axially.

*Erratum* in Mr. J. Cockle's paper, vol. xxxii.
Page 363, line 15 from the bottom, *for* 64 *read* 62; *for* 83 *read* 77; and *for* 84 *read* 82.

Fig. 1.

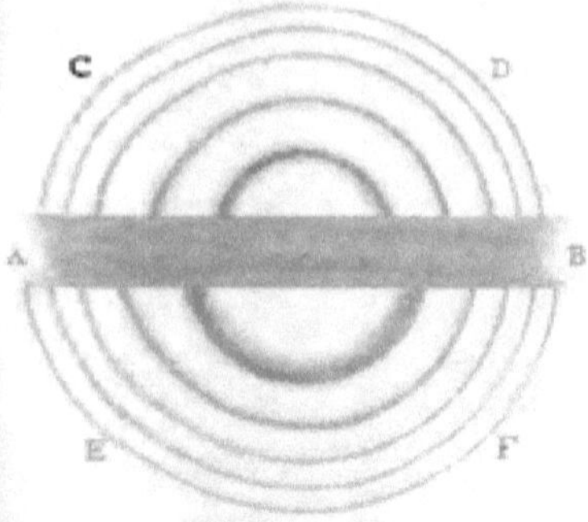


Fig. 2

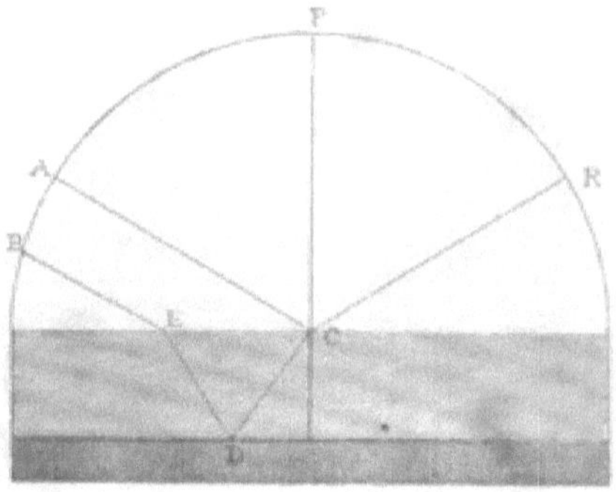


Fig. 3.

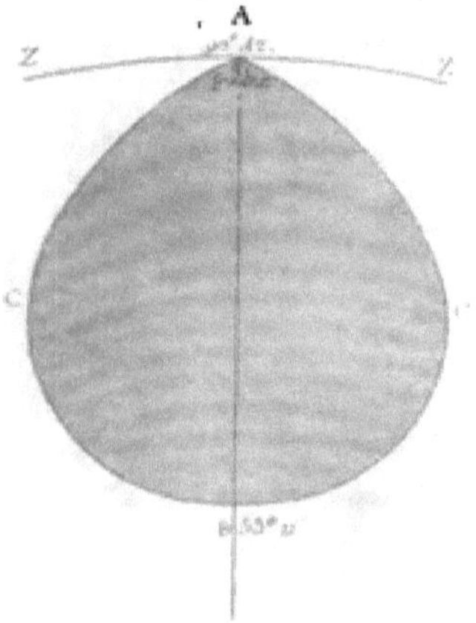


Glass & Water

Fig. 4.

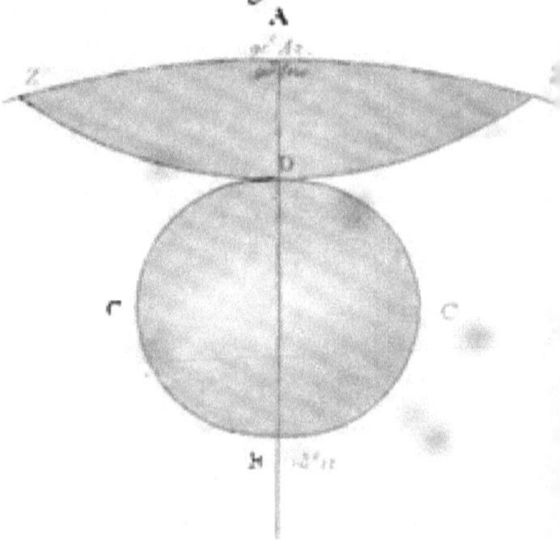


Fluor Spar & Water

J. Basire sc.

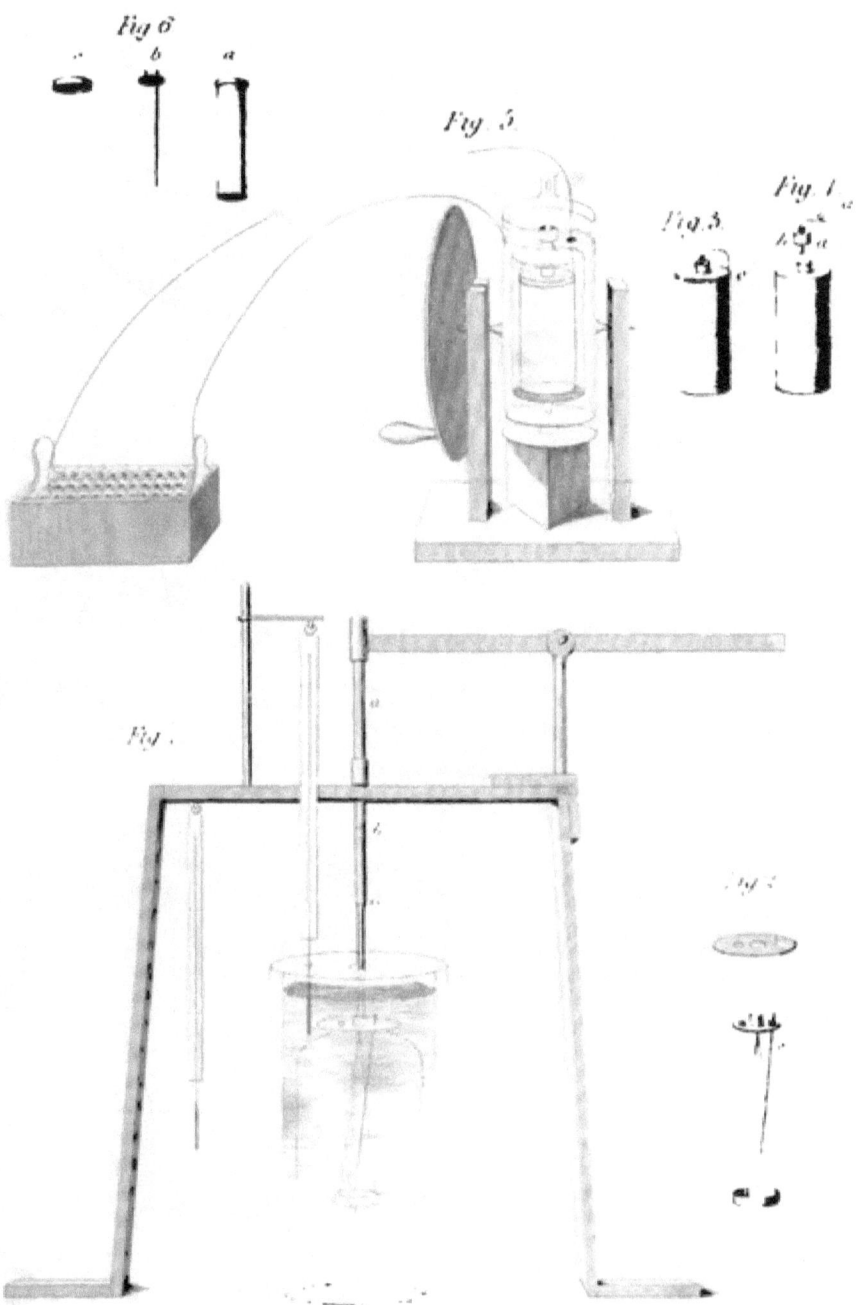

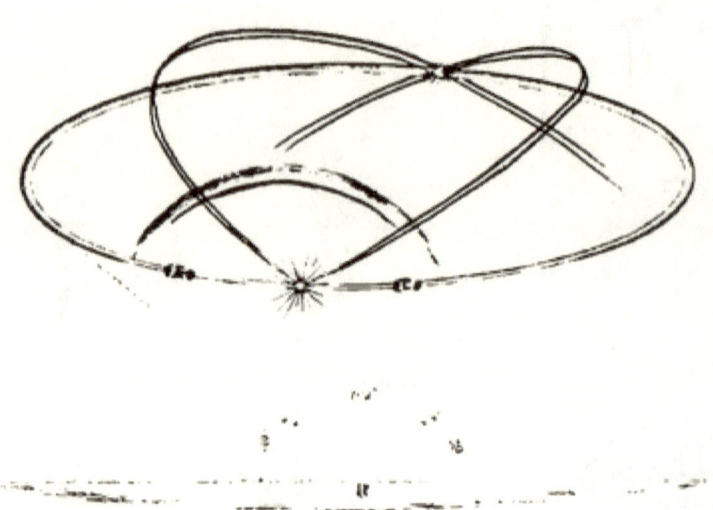

Fig 2.
½ past 10 A.M.

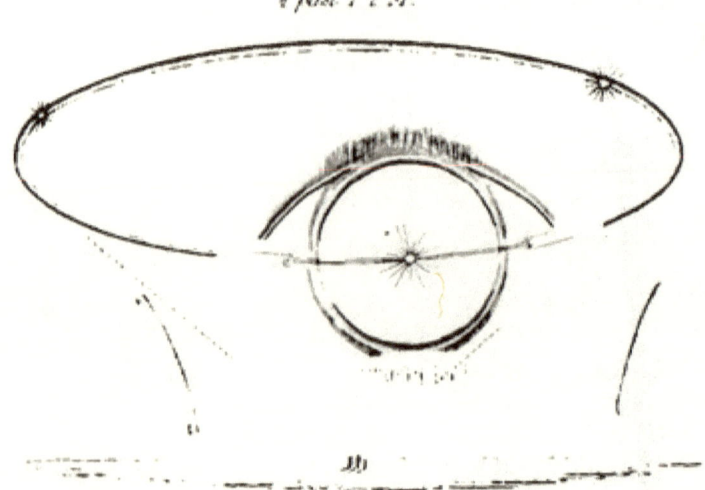

Fig 3.
½ past 1 P.M.

Parhelia seen at Portsea 29th March 1828.

Fig. 1.

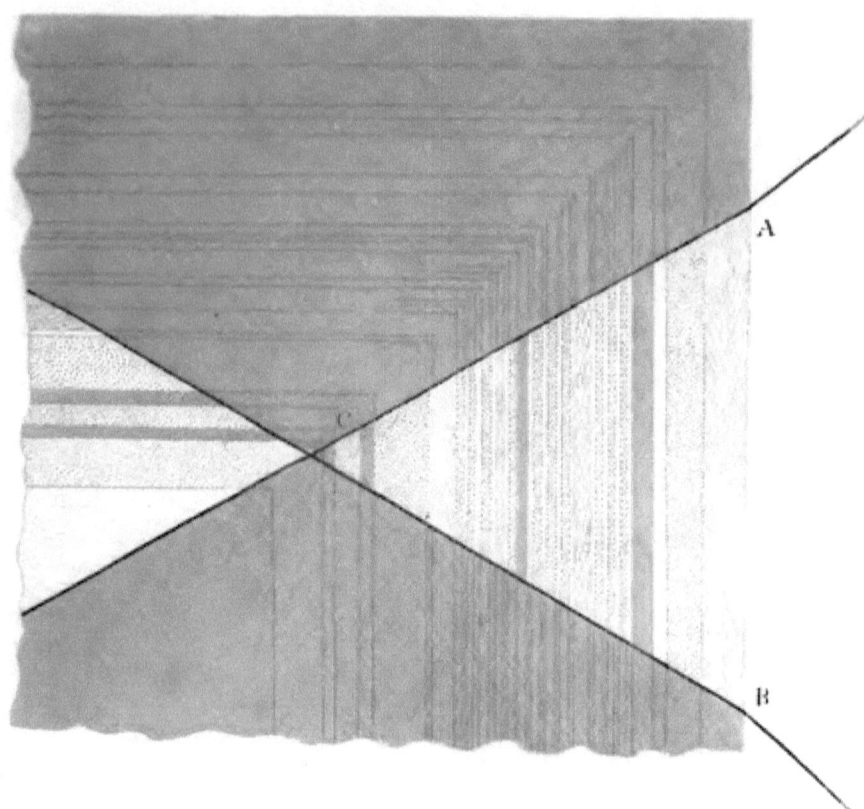

# THE LONDON, EDINBURGH AND DUBLIN PHILOSOPHICAL MAGAZINE AND JOURNAL OF SCIENCE.

[THIRD SERIES.]

*JANUARY* 1848.

I. *On the Optical Phænomena, Nature, and Locality of* Muscæ volitantes; *with Observations on the Structure of the Vitreous Humour, and on the Vision of Objects placed within the Eye.* By Sir DAVID BREWSTER, *K.H., D.C.L., F.R.S., and V.P.R.S. Edin.**

ALTHOUGH some of the phænomena of *Muscæ volitantes* may be seen by persons of all ages, and with the best eyes; and though those which are more peculiarly entitled to the name are exceedingly common beyond the middle period of life, yet no account has been given of them that has even the slightest pretension to accuracy. M. De la Hire, in his *Differens Accidens de la Vue*, describes these *Muscæ* as of *two* kinds; some permanent and fixed, which he ascribes to small drops of extravasated blood upon the retina; and others, as flying about, and changing their place, even though the eye be fixed. The *first* kind, he describes as like a dark spot upon a white ground; and the *second*, as like the knots of a deal board. Some parts of them, he says, are very clear, and surrounded with dark threads, and are accompanied with long fillets of irregular shapes, which are bright in the middle, and terminated on each side by parallel black threads.

In order to account for these knots and irregular fillets, De la Hire supposes that "the *aqueous humour* is *sometimes* troubled with some little mothery ropy substance, some parts of which, by the figures of their little surfaces, or by refractive powers different from the humour itself, may cast their distinct images upon the retina. He supposes them in the *aqueous* humour rather than in the *vitreous*, because of its greater fluidity for a freedom of descent, and because they will then

* From the Transactions of the Royal Society of Edinburgh, vol. xv. p. 377. Read March 6, 1843.

appear to descend, as being situated *before* the pupil, or, at least, *before* the place of intersection of the pencils*."

Dr. Porterfield, who has given a very inaccurate drawing of the filamentous *Muscæ*, considers them as produced by diaphanous particles and filaments, that swim in the *aqueous* humour before the crystalline; and he regards the distinct pictures of them upon the *retina* of *long-sighted* persons, as produced by the rays which pass *through* the dense particles, having suffered a greater refraction than those which pass *by* them, so as to be converged to *foci* upon the retina†.

The latest writer on this subject, Mr. Mackenzie of Glasgow, describes the *Muscæ* as resembling *minute, twisted, semi-transparent* tubes, partially filled with globules, which sometimes appear in motion; while another set are more opake, or perfectly dark, and follow the motions of the eye. The latter he considers as "of a more dangerous character than the former, and as occasioned, generally, by a partial insensibility of the retina," either from the pressure of some "irregular projecting point or points of the choroid, or from some other cause." Mr. Mackenzie regards the globules within the semi-transparent tubes, as probably "blood passing through the vessels of the retina, or of the vitreous humour;" and he remarks, "that neither these semi-transparent tubes themselves, nor any of the filamentous *Muscæ*, or black spots (which are so frequently complained of), possess any real motion, independent of the general motion of the eyeball;" and hence he concludes that they "must be referred either to the retina itself—including, of course, the three laminæ of which it is composed,—or to the choroid coat." "The probability is," he adds, "that the semi-transparent *Muscæ*, of a tubular form, are owing to a dilatation of the branches of the *arteria centralis retinæ* ‡."

Such was the state of our information on the subject of *Muscæ volitantes*, when my attention was specially directed to it, in consequence of finding in my own eye a good example of the phænomenon; and, having carefully investigated the facts as observed by other persons in their own eyes, I trust I shall be able to lay before the Society a correct description, and a satisfactory explanation, of the general phænomena.

Although the bodies which are within the eyeball, and give rise to the phænomena under consideration, are often seen under ordinary circumstances, yet, in order to see them with

* Smith's Optics, vol. ii. Rem. p. 5.
† Treatise on the Eye, vol. ii. p. 74–80.
‡ Practical Treatise on the Diseases of the Eye, 1830, pp. 748, 750.

distinctness, we must look at the sky, or a luminous object, either through a very minute aperture, or, when the light is limited or feeble, through a lens or microscopic doublet, of very short focus, held close to the eye. By this means we shall observe a luminous ground, covered, more or less, with transparent filaments or tubes, transparent circles, exceedingly minute, and (when they do exist) with *Muscæ*, or black spots like flies.

In examining the transparent filaments, I have observed them of *four* or *five* different sizes, the smallest of which are the most distinct. These distinct filaments are bounded by two sharp black lines, and the space between them is more luminous than the general ground on which they are seen. In the larger filaments, the black lines are coloured at their edges, and, on the outside of each of them, are one or more coloured fringes.

The minute transparent circles, when smallest, have a luminous centre, with a sharp black circle round it. In the larger ones, this circle is coloured at its edges; and, on the outside of it, are one or more circular coloured fringes. These spherical bodies sometimes exist singly, and sometimes in groups, partly connected by small filaments, and partly by an invisible film, to which they seem attached. They sometimes adhere to the outside of the filaments, and very frequently occur *within* the filaments, so as to prove that these filaments are *tubular*. These spherical bodies have, like the filaments, *four* or *five* different sizes.

In making observations on these spherical bodies, the observer will sometimes see luminous spots pass through the field; but as these arise from the state of the lubricating fluid on the outside of the cornea, they have no connexion with the phænomena under our consideration.

The transparent filaments, already described, are seldom seen single. Two or three are united, like threads crossing one another; and sometimes a great number are united, like a loose heap of thread, in which case obscure spots appear at the places where the crossings of the filaments are most numerous.

In some cases a single long filament is once or twice doubled up upon itself, and sometimes a *knot* is, or appears to be, tied upon it, consisting of several folds, as it were, of the filament. This *knot* has several *very dark spots* at the places where the different portions of the filament are in contact; and this accumulation, as it were, of black specks, constitutes the real *Muscæ*. In many, indeed in almost all of these *Muscæ*, when distinct, a little bright yellow light accompanies the black specks.

All the bodies which we have now described have two different motions; one arising from the motion of the head or eyeball, and the other when the eyeball is absolutely fixed. By a toss of the head they are thrown into different absolute and relative positions, sometimes ascending and descending in succession, sometimes oscillating between two limits, and generally with different velocities. When the eye is first applied to the lens or aperture, the field of view is tolerably free of these moving bodies; but the light seems to stir them up, as it were, and, to a certain extent, the longer we view them, the more numerous do they become.

If the centre of motion of the eyeball coincides with the centre of visible direction, the *Muscæ* will *ascend* when the eye looks *upward*, and *vice versâ*, whether they are placed before or behind that common centre. If the eyeball remains fixed, the *Muscæ* in *front* of the above centre will have the *direction* of their *real* and *apparent* motions the same, and those *behind* that centre will have these two directions *different*. Hence the appearance of two opposite currents when the eyeball is turned quickly from one extreme of its range, either vertically or horizontally, to its mean position; and so rapid is their motion through the luminous field, that it seems covered with continuous lines parallel to the direction in which the eyeball has been moved,—an effect arising from the duration of the impression of light upon the retina.

If we mark individual filaments, or groups, or knots, we shall find that they change their shapes, one part of a filament doubling itself over another, and again resuming its elongated form. The minute spherical bodies separate and approach one another; but I have not been able to satisfy myself that those within the tubular filaments change their place. They often *appear* to do so; but as this necessarily arises from the bending of the filament, and from the varying obliquity of different parts of it owing to its change of form or place, we are not entitled, from this apparent motion, to consider them as moveable within the tube. It is certain, however, that they have no progressive motion, as supposed by Mr. Mackenzie.

In order to obtain a correct knowledge of the phænomena of the real *Muscæ*, I confined my attention to one in my own eye, of which I first made a drawing in October 1838. It is represented in the annexed figure, and consists of four filaments, ABC, BDE, FGH, and AK. Between BC and BDE there is a sort of transparent web containing a great number of minute spherical specks, and something similar, though less extensive, below FGH. The real *Musca* exists at A, and has obviously been produced by the accidental overlapping of the different filaments which are united with it.

In four and a half years, the *Musca* at N has perceptibly increased in size, and the length of the associated filaments has diminished. It is distinctly seen without any of its accom-

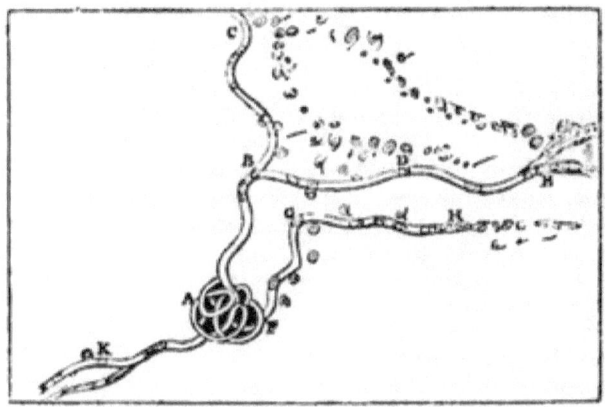

paniments in ordinary light, but is in no respects injurious to vision, as it is never stationary in the axis of the eye. When seen by means of the lens, the long branch FGH takes various positions, sometimes falling below the knot or *Musca* A, and sometimes crossing the main branch AB, below B. The branch BDE has often a loop at D, and FGH another at G.

Having had occasion to study the phænomena of the *diffraction* of light, as produced by transparent fibres and films of different forms, I could not fail to observe that the phænomena above described were the shadows formed on the retina by divergent light passing by and through transparent filaments and particles placed within the eyeball. They are indeed perfectly identical, and may be accurately imitated in various ways. If we crush a crystalline lens in distilled water, or macerate some very thin laminæ of it, and dry a drop of the fluid on a piece of glass, we shall perceive, with a fine microscope a little out of focus, or with an ill-adjusted illuminating apparatus, a number of minute fibres, single and in groups, and knots, with minute spherical particles, which display the very same phænomena of *diffraction* as the analogous bodies within the eyeball.

Hence it follows, that the filaments and spherical particles, whose diffracted shadows have four or five different sizes, have the same magnitude, and are placed at four or five different distances from the retina; those which give the sharp, black, and minute shadows, being placed near the retina, and those which are large and ill-defined at a distance from it.

These various bodies, though they change their place, still preserve their general distance from the retina, thus clearly indicating that the vitreous humour is composed of cells within which the filaments and *Muscæ* are lodged. That they do not exist in the aqueous humour is very obvious, because if they did, they would either rise to the top or sink to the bottom of the aqueous chamber when the eyeball was at rest, and thus withdraw themselves entirely from the field of view, which they never do.

In order to obtain further information respecting these *Muscæ*, I fixed the eyeball in different positions*, and looking at a sheet of white paper, I marked upon it the various positions on the paper where the *Musca* rested. It never withdrew itself from the field of view, and suffered no sensible change in its size; but it rested in positions at different distances from the axis of vision. In one position of the head I could bring the *Musca* into the optic axis so as to obtain the most perfect vision of it, but in all other positions of the head it rested at a distance from the optic axis; though in these it could, by a toss of the head, be made to cross the axis of vision. In making these experiments, we must recollect that, as the *Musca* is generally seen by oblique vision, it will very frequently disappear, though it has not withdrawn itself from the field of view. In all positions of the head the *Musca* appears to descend, so that it must actually *ascend* in the vitreous humour, and be specifically lighter.

Now, it is obvious that, if we determine the visible position of the *Musca* when at rest in different positions of the head, we determine the direction of lines passing from the centre of visible direction through the points in the vitreous humour where the *Musca* rested, and thus obtain a general notion of the *form of the cell* in which it is contained. But we may go still further, and determine with considerable accuracy the diameter of the *Musca* or its filaments, and also their distance from the retina, and thus obtain a knowledge of its locality, and of the form of the cavity by which its excursions are limited.

In order to do this, I place before the eye two bright sources of light, so as to obtain from them, by the method already described, two divergent beams of light, and I thus obtain double images on the retina of all objects placed within the eyeball. The filaments or *Muscæ* in the anterior part of the vitreous humour will have their double images very distant:

* In order to do this, the observer must place himself on his back, on his face, on his right side or on his left side, or he may place the vertical axis of his eyeball at any angle to a vertical line.

those in the middle of it will have their double images much nearer: those near the retina will have their two images close or perhaps overlapping each other; while any object on the retina itself, any black spot arising from defective sensibility, will have only one image, as it were. Now, if we measure the distance of the two sources of light from each other, and also their distance from the centre of visible direction, when the two images of the filaments, &c. are just in contact, we may determine the size of the filament and its exact position, as well as its distance from the retina. In making this experiment, I first found that the angle of apparent magnitude of the shadow of the filament ABC was eight minutes, and consequently that it subtended this angle at the centre of visible direction*. Now, if we take the radius of the retina as 0·524 of an inch, the diameter of the shadow of the filament will be 0·0122, or $\frac{1}{820}$th of an inch, and its distance from the retina 0·018, or $\frac{1}{55}$th part of an inch.

When we use a small aperture alone for producing a divergent pencil, the centre of divergency must necessarily be without the eyeball; but we may throw the centre of divergency within the eyeball, and place it at any distance from the retina, by using a lens of the proper focus. If we wish to place this centre near the retina, a lens of considerable focal length must be used, and as the light collected by it will be powerful, it will extinguish all the smaller filaments and minute spheres, and allow only the larger *Muscæ* to be seen. We must therefore reduce its aperture by looking through a pin-hole or other minute opening. When we wish to have a clear field of view for examining the larger *Muscæ*, we may extinguish all the smaller ones by increasing the luminosity of the field. If we wish to study the filaments or *Muscæ* that may be placed about the middle of the vitreous humour, we must use a lens of such an aperture as will obliterate all those more remote from the retina.

It is very obvious, from the preceding observations, that objects placed within the eyeball are not seen, as Dr. Porterfield believes, by rays *which pass* THROUGH *dense particles having suffered a greater refraction than those which pass* BY *them*. A fibre or particle of glass of nearly the same refractive power as the vitreous humour will be seen distinctly by means of its image formed on the retina by diffracted pencils. If the light is not sufficiently divergent, or is too intense to produce and exhibit the diffracted image, the object will be

* This may be done by projecting it upon a luminous surface, and marking its apparent size; or by comparing it with the images of objects of known dimensions seen with a fine microscope.

invisible, unless it be of such a size, and so near the retina, as to show itself by its ordinary shadow. But in whatever way the image of the object is formed, the mind takes cognizance of it, or gives it an external locality, by means of the same law of visible direction which regulates the vision of objects placed without the eyeball.

While these results exhibit the true physical cause of all the optical phænomena and limited movements of the filaments and *Muscæ*, they lead also to some important and useful conclusions of a more general nature. It had been conjectured that the vitreous humour of animals was inclosed in separate bags or cells connected with the hyaloid membrane by which the vitreous mass is enveloped. The preceding experiments not only appear to demonstrate that this is the structure of the vitreous humour in man, but to show that there are at least *four* or *five* cells between the retina and the posterior surface of the crystalline lens. The limited motion of the *Muscæ* indicates that the cell in which they float is of very limited extent. When the vertical diameter of the eyeball, in its natural position, is placed, by the inclination of the head, 30° to the right-hand of a vertical line, and the optic axis of the eye directed 20° below a horizontal line, the *Musca* is seen along the optic axis, and consequently in the most perfect manner. One point of its cell must therefore touch the optical axis.

I have endeavoured, with the assistance of my eminent colleague Dr. Reid, to discover cells in the vitreous humour of quadrupeds and fishes by the aid of the microscope and other means, but we have not succeeded: and unless some chemical substance shall be found which acts differently upon the albuminous fluid and the membranous septa, it is not likely that they will be otherwise rendered visible*.

Mr. Ware, in a paper on the *Muscæ volitantes of nervous persons*†, describes some as "globules twisted together, and others as like the flue that is swept from bed-rooms," and he considers it "probable that they depend on a steady pressure on one or more minute points of the retina which are situated near the axis of vision‡." In the cases described by Mr. Ware, the *Muscæ* were liable to great and sudden changes in intensity and number, particularly from causes affecting the nervous

* The vitreous humour, when slowly dried, either by itself, or along with parts of the septa in which it may be contained, shoots into beautiful crystalline ramifications proceeding from the four angles of a quadrilateral crystal. Thin six-sided plates frequently occur, but they seem to exercise no action upon polarized light, probably on account of their thinness. The same effects were produced when the vitreous humour from a fresh eye was well-washed in distilled water.

† Medico-Chirurgical Trans., 1814, vol. v. p. 255.   ‡ Ibid. p. 266.

system, and hence they cannot be regarded as of the same character as the *Muscæ* described in this paper, unless we suppose that *Muscæ*, invisible under ordinary circumstances, become visible in consequence of an increased sensibility of the retina.

This supposition, however, is by no means probable, because the *Muscæ* are not visible by any light of their own, and an increase of sensibility in the retina would affect equally the luminous field on which they are seen. But as this point is of some importance both in a physiological and a medical aspect, I have submitted it to direct experiment. With this view, I examined the *Muscæ* in the morning before the sensibility of the retina had been diminished by exposure to daylight, and found that they were neither increased in number or intensity. I varied this experiment by diminishing the sensibility of the retina. This was done by holding a bright gas flame close to the eye, and near the axis of vision, till the retina lost its sensibility to all the rays of the spectrum, except a few of the more refrangible ones[*]. In this case, too, the *Muscæ* were as numerous and distinct as before, and we may therefore consider it as certain, that the *Muscæ* described by Mr. Ware, in so far as they were of the same character as those in the healthy eye, are not affected by any variation in the sensibility of the retina. I am disposed to think that they consisted of the ordinary *Muscæ* seen simultaneously with others produced by the pressure of the blood-vessels on the retina, and that it was the latter only which underwent the variations which he describes.

It is not easy to form any rational conjecture respecting the cause and purpose of the numerous filaments by which the *Muscæ* are produced; for as they exist in all eyes, whether young or old, they are neither the result of disease, nor do they indicate its approach. Were they fixed or regularly distributed, we might regard them as transparent vessels which supply the vitreous humour; but existing, as they do, in detached and floating portions, they resemble more the remains of those vessels, or of others whose functions are no longer necessary. But though these filaments have no morbid character, they may nevertheless obstruct and even destroy vision. They certainly interfere with nice microscopical observations, and in observing the minute and almost imperceptible lines in the solar spectrum, I have found them to be occasionally injurious. It is quite possible that some of the cells behind the lens or even near the retina and around the optic axis might be filled up with accumulated *Muscæ*, and produce a consider-

[*] Lond. and Edin. Phil. Mag., 1832, vol. i. p. 172; vol. ii. p. 188.

able degree of blindness; but this is an effect of them which there is little occasion to apprehend.

Mr. Mackenzie* informs us, "that few symptoms prove so alarming to persons of a nervous habit or constitution as *Muscæ volitantes*, and they immediately suppose that they are about to lose their sight by cataract or amaurosis." Professor Plateau of Ghent, to whom I had communicated, at his own request, some of the preceding results, mentions to me, that few physicians are able to distinguish between the *Muscæ* described above, and those appearances which indicate amaurosis, and that they often, without cause, alarm patients who consult them for the first time respecting such affections of the eye. He assures me that the results contained in this paper have already been the means of freeing from alarm many persons with *Muscæ volitantes*, and that they had even done this to a distinguished physician†.

The details in the preceding pages may, therefore, be considered as establishing the important fact, that *Muscæ volitantes* have no connexion whatever either with Cataract or Amaurosis, and that they are nearly altogether harmless. This result has been deduced by the aid of a recondite property of divergent light, which has only been developed in our own day, and which seems to have no bearing whatever of an utilitarian character. And this is but one of numerous proofs which the progress of knowledge is daily accumulating, that the most abstract and apparently transcendental truths in physical science will sooner or later add their tribute to supply human wants, and alleviate human sufferings. Nor has science performed one of the least important of her functions when she enables us, either in our own case, or in that of others, to dispel those anxieties and fears which are the necessary offspring of ignorance and error.

St. Leonard's College, St. Andrews,
March 4, 1843.

*Postscript.*—The *Muscæ* described in the preceding paper increased slightly during the years 1843, 1844, and 1845, in consequence of the overlapping of the filaments ABDE and

---

* Practical Treatise, &c., p. 751.

† Professor Plateau mentions in his letter to myself, that he had been led to suppose that the *Muscæ* had their seat in the vitreous humour rather than in the aqueous; but that he had been stopped by the difficulty of reconciling this opinion with the viscosity of the vitreous humour. As the vitreous humour is *perfectly fluid* within each cell, the viscosity here supposed, being only apparent, no longer presents any difficulty.

FGH; but as the length of these filaments was then considerably reduced, their tendency to twine themselves round A, from any sudden motion of the eyeball, was diminished, and there has been no enlargement of the black spot or *Musca* during the years 1846 and 1847.

St. Leonard's College,
December 11, 1847.

---

II. *On the Integral* $\int \frac{dx}{x}$, *and on some consequences that have been deduced from it.* By J. R. YOUNG, *Professor of Mathematics in Belfast College*[*].

IT is the object of the present short paper to remove some obscurities connected with the ordinary treatment of the simple integral $\int \frac{dx}{x}$. It will be anticipated therefore that the remarks which I have to offer are of a very elementary character: too much so indeed to entitle them to a place in a Journal of this kind, were it not that such obscurities, in the first elements of science, as experience has often shown, are frequently the source of important errors in its more recondite applications.

The integral just adverted to is a particular case of the more general form $\int x^n dx$, of which the value, disregarding correction, is known to be $\frac{x^{n+1}}{n+1}$. In the particular case noticed, that namely in which $n = -1$, this expression for the value is said to *fail*; though it is admitted to be valid in every other case, whether $n$ be whole or fractional, positive or negative.

It may possibly be remembered by some of the readers of this Journal, that such an isolated failing case, in a general algebraic formula, is an occurrence that I have endeavoured to show can never happen; and that if any such formula hold for all values between $a$ and $b$, it must equally hold for the extreme limits $a$ and $b$ themselves.

In the instance before us, the particular information, which the general form is supposed to fail in supplying, is obtained from other considerations; and the value of the wanting integral affirmed to be log $x$. And the reason sometimes assigned for the inefficiency of the general form, in the particular case, is "that the equation $\int \frac{dx}{x} = \log x$, supposes the function of

---

[*] Communicated by the Author.

12 Prof. J. R. Young *on the Integral* $\int \frac{dx}{x}$, *and on*

$x$ denoted by $\int \frac{dx}{x}$ to vanish when $x=1$, whilst the equation $\int x^n dx = \frac{x^{n+1}}{n+1}$ supposes $\int x^n dx$ to vanish when $x=0$." It appears to me that this explanation is by no means sufficient to justify the assertion that the general form *fails*. Every student of the calculus knows that, by integrating the same expression by different methods, different functions of the variable will often arise, which can only become identical, in particular applications of the results, when each is connected with its own supplementary constant. One method may lead us to logarithmic functions, another to circular; and though they both arise from one and the same differential, they cannot, in general, be equated till each has received its own peculiar correction. In such instances it appears to me that it would be just as proper to say that one of these methods *fails*, as in the instance before us. The fact is, that in all cases of general integration, where the supplementary constant is suppressed, the process is really performed between limits, one of which is fixed, and the other arbitrary. To be strictly accurate, $\int \frac{dx}{x} = \log x$ should be written $\int_1^x \frac{dx}{x} = \log x$.

Introducing this accuracy of expression, let us now return to the general form, which in the case under consideration is $\int_1^x x^{-1} dx$; or, for convenience, changing $x$ into $1+z$, $\int_1^{1+z} x^{-1} dx$. By the general form, the value of this is $\frac{(1+z)^0 - 1^0}{0}$. Developing by the binomial theorem, we have

$$(1+z)^0 = 1^0 + 0z + \frac{0(-1)}{2} z^2 + \frac{0(-1)(-2)}{2.3} z^3 + \&c.,$$

and consequently

$$\frac{(1+z)^0 - 1^0}{0} = z - \frac{1}{2} z^2 + \frac{1}{3} z^3 - \frac{1}{4} z^4 + \&c.,$$

the known development of $\log(1+z)$, or $\log x$; so that the general form really gives us $\int_1^x x^{-1} dx = \log x$, without any failure at all. And we thus get moreover the interesting symbolical result,

$$\frac{(1+z)^0 - 1}{0} = \log(1+z),$$

or rather
$$\infty(1+z)^{\frac{1}{\infty}} - \infty = \log(1+z); \therefore \log x = \infty\, (x^{\frac{1}{\infty}} - 1),$$
from which the exponential theorem, and thence the whole theory of logarithms, may be readily derived.

In Liouville's well-known memoir on General Differentiation, in the thirteenth volume of the *Journal de l'Ecole Polytechnique*, the distinguished author has, I think, fallen into error, in consequence of being governed by the prevailing views respecting the failure of the general form here discussed. He is led (page 84) to the formula
$$x^p = \frac{-p}{\Gamma(1-p)} \int_0^\infty (e^{-zz} - 1) z^{-p-1} dz,$$
which, in accordance with those views, he affirms (page 85) to be "*absolument fausse lorsque $p=0$.*" In justification of this, he maintains that the definite integral
$$\int_0^\infty (e^{-zz} - 1) \frac{dz}{z}$$
is *a finite quantity*.

Now since
$$\int \frac{e^{-zz} dz}{z} = \int \frac{dz}{z} - xz + \frac{x^2 z^2}{1.2^2} - \frac{x^3 z^3}{1.2.3^2} + \&c.,$$
$$\therefore \int_0^\infty \frac{e^{-zz} dz}{z} = \int_0^\infty \frac{dz}{z} - x\infty + \frac{x^2 \infty^2}{1.2^2} - \frac{x^3 \infty^3}{1.2.3^2} + \&c;$$
and consequently the proposed integral, namely,
$$\int_0^\infty \frac{e^{-zz} dz}{z} - \int_0^\infty \frac{dz}{z} = -x\infty + \frac{x^2 \infty^2}{1.2^2} - \frac{x^3 \infty^3}{1.2.3^2} + \&c.$$

How this can be pronounced to be *zero*, I am at a loss to conceive. That it is infinite, instead of zero, necessarily follows from its interpretation in the left-hand member of the original equation, even if there were no internal evidence of the fact. In the particular or extreme case considered, that left-hand member becomes $x^0 = 1$; and the right-hand member is the series here exhibited multiplied by 0, the limiting value of $p$: the form therefore is merely a particular instance of $0 \times \infty$; interpretable, as all the cases which this terminates are interpretable, by the unambiguous form on the left. Several errors of like kind occur in Liouville's memoir; all traceable to the same oversight respecting fundamental principles.

It may not be superfluous to remark, in reference to the foregoing series for $\log(1+x)$, that whenever that series is not convergent, a supplementary correction is considered to be comprehended under the "&c." In the various transformations which this series is made to undergo, in order that it may serve the purpose of the actual construction of logarithmic tables, it will be found on examination that they are always such as to preserve throughout the convergency of the series, so that the correction adverted to disappears. If however we replace $a$ by $a-1$, $a$ being the base of the system, we then render the series necessarily divergent; and it is common in writings on this subject (see for instance Miller's Diff. Calc., p. 10) to apply to it in this state certain transformations, by which it is said to be converted into a converging series. But no diverging series can admit of such conversion; and whenever this appears to be accomplished, it will always be found that the original series is taken, not by itself, but in conjunction with its correction; and thus the change apparently brought about independently of this correction, is, in reality, a new development of the function generating the original series.

There is a well-known theorem of Lagrange, which, in the case of Taylor's series, enables us to assign the limits within which must lie the error we commit by taking any finite number of terms of the series as an equivalent for the undeveloped function. In the form in which Lagrange delivered it, the theorem is

$$f(z+x) = fz + xf'z + \frac{x^2}{2}f''z + \frac{x^3}{2.3}f'''z + \ldots \frac{x^n}{2.3\ldots n}f^{(n)}(z+u),$$

in which he says "$u$ désigne une quantité inconnue, mais renfermée entre les limites 0 et $x$" (*Théorie des Fonctions*, p. 68); and the same conditions are always said to be necessary whenever the theorem is announced. It is certainly of little or no practical moment to correct this statement; yet in order that extreme cases even may not be improperly excluded, it is necessary to widen the limits so as actually to include 0 and $x$. For it is plain that if the series be finite, and we stop at the last term, which it is conceivable we might sometimes do without knowing that the final term was reached, $u$ would be actually 0; and if we stop at the first term, then in every case $u$ would be equal to $x$; so that, leaving the term at which we stop entirely unrestricted, the generality of the theorem requires that the limits 0 and $x$ be included. From an examination of this theorem, I am inclined to think that it is capable of greater definiteness and precision than is at present given to it, the range between the limits depending in general upon the place of the term at which we stop: but the discussion of this point must be reserved for a future occasion.

I may perhaps be permitted to add in conclusion, for the information of those interested in such elementary matters, that the statement in the former part of this paper, in reference to the ease with which the exponential theorem may be derived from the above expression involving $\infty$, is confirmed in a communication to the Mechanics' Magazine; in which also will be found a short algebraical investigation of the development of the important function $\frac{x}{t^x-1}$. The Part of the Magazine containing the communication here alluded to, will appear simultaneously with the present Number of this Journal. It is a publication which has of late devoted considerable space to mathematical speculations, and is enriched with interesting papers by Professor Davies, Mr. Cockle, and other distinguished contributors to the Philosophical Magazine.

Belfast, Nov. 19, 1847.

III. *On the Action of Nitric Acid on Cymol. First Part.* By H. M. NOAD, *Esq.**

*Formation of Toluylic and Nitrotoluylic Acids.*

WE possess in benzoic acid and its derivatives a well-defined group of substances connected in a variety of ways with a large number of organic families. These interesting bodies have been made subjects of investigation by several chemists. The study has been a fascinating one, and has resulted in a thorough development of their history, and of the products of their decomposition.

This group may be considered the prototype, as it were, of several parallel groups, presenting a very close relation with the composition of the benzoyle family. The careful study of the former has gradually made these known to us, in the same manner as the study of alcohol and its derivatives made us acquainted with several corresponding classes of bodies.

The methyle compounds, with which we have become familiar through the experiments of Dumas and Peligot† on pyroxylic spirit, and the amyle series, the origin of which we owe to the investigations of Cahours‡ on fusel oil, form two groups, the analogy of which with the alcohol series can be traced in every direction; they differ in composition from the former only by a multiple of $C_2 H_2$, thus—

$HO, C_2 H_3 O =$ hydrated oxide of methyle.
$HO, C_4 H_5 O =$ hydrated oxide of ethyle.
$HO, C_{10} H_{11} O =$ hydrated oxide of amyle.

* Communicated by the Chemical Society; having been read June 7, 1847.
† Liebig's *Annalen*, xv. 1.   ‡ Ibid. xxx. 288.

The same relation is likewise observed in the acids resulting from the oxidation of these bodies, and these acids are perhaps even better adapted to point out this interesting regularity, as the gaps existing between the different alcohols are filled up in the series of the acids, which may be formed in a great variety of ways. A glance at the following table will render the regularity above alluded to at once obvious:—

| Alcohols. | Acids. |
|---|---|
| $HO, C_2 H_3 O$, pyroxylic spirit. | $HO, C_2 HO_3$, formic acid. |
| $HO, C_4 H_5 O$, alcohol. | $HO, C_4 H_3 O_3$, acetic acid. |
| | $HO, C_6 H_5 O_3$, metacetonic acid. |
| | $HO, C_8 H_7 O_3$, butyric acid. |
| $HO, C_{10} H_{11} O$, fusel oil. | $HO, C_{10} H_9 O_3$, valerianic acid. |
| | $HO, C_{12} H_{11} O_3$, caproic acid. |
| | $HO, C_{14} H_{13} O_3$, œnanthylic acid. |
| | $HO, C_{16} H_{15} O_3$, caprylic acid. |
| | $HO, C_{18} H_{17} O_3$, pelargonic acid. |
| | $HO, C_{20} H_{19} O_3$, capric acid. |
| &c. | &c. |

Now it seems that benzoic acid is a member of a similar series of acids, distinguished from each other by the same amounts of carbon and hydrogen, and that we may expect to find a representative of every single term of the benzoyle series in these other families. An examination of cumin oil by MM. Gerhardt and Cahours[*] has brought to light a new acid,—cuminic acid, $HO, C_{20} H_{11} O_3$, which exhibits a perfect analogy with benzoic acid, not only in its physical properties, but also in the metamorphoses which it undergoes when acted on by chemical agents. This acid is distinguished from benzoic, $HO, C_{14} H_5 O_3$, by containing $3(C_2 H_2)$ more; it stands to benzoic acid as valerianic acid stands to acetic acid, and when distilled with lime it is converted into cumol, $C_{18} H_{12}$, which represents benzol, $C_{12} H_6$, in the benzoyle series. The same investigation of cumin oil has made us acquainted with another carbo-hydrogen cymol, $C_{20} H_{14}$, which is also a representative of benzol in another series; but up to the present time the acid from which this carbo-hydrogen derives, and which would contain $4(C_2 H_2)$ more than benzoic acid, has not been discovered.

By the investigations of Pelletier and Walter[†] on the products of the distillation of resinous substances, of Deville[‡] on the distillation of tolu balsam, and of Boudault and Glenard[§] on the dry distillation of the dragon's blood, an addi-

---

[*] Liebig's *Annalen*, xxxviii. 67.
[†] Ibid, xxviii. 295.
[‡] *Ann. de Chim. et Phys.* 3 sér. t. iii. p. 168.
[§] *Journ. de Pharm. et de Chim.* 3 sér. t. vi. p. 250.

tion has been made to the number of carbo-hydrogens, and we have obtained knowledge of a new body, which was described by the first chemists under the name of retinaphtha, by the second under that of benzoëne, and by the last under that of dracyle; for all three Berzelius* has proposed the more appropriate name of toluol† ($C_{14} H_8$); this body, which differs from benzol in containing $C_2 H_2$ more, also represents that carbo-hydrogen in a new family, a number of members of which has already become known. Thus Deville has shown that on treating his toluol with sulphuric and nitric acids, the corresponding terms of hypo-sulphobenzolic acid, nitrobenzol, and dinitrobenzol are obtained. Investigations of the action of nitric acid on oil of anise by Cahours‡, and on Oleum dracunculi by Laurent §, have led to the discovery of anisylic, nitranisylic acids, and anisol (draconic, nitrodraconic acids and dracol), corresponding respectively to salicylic, nitrosalicylic acid and phenol; more recently Cahours‖ has found in hydride of anisyle even the term corresponding to hydride of salicyle, and Drs. Muspratt and Hofmann¶ have produced the organic base corresponding to aniline; in the paper in which this new and remarkable substance is described, these gentlemen have given a table, in which the analogy between the anisyle and salicyle groups has been pointed out.

In order to render this parallelism complete one principal term of the new series has hitherto been wanting, viz. the acid corresponding to benzoic acid. In the following paper will be pointed out the formation and properties of this substance, and the corresponding nitrogenous acid, both arising amongst the products of the oxidation of cymol.

---

* *Jahresbericht*, xxii. p. 354.

† On comparing the properties which Pelletier and Walter ascribe to retinaphtha with those of benzoëne given by Deville, it is nearly certain that both substances are identical, though Deville seems to be inclined to establish a difference. A comparative study is however still wanting. Regarding dracyle, I may mention here that when engaged in the investigation of toluidine with Dr. Muspratt, we prepared a portion of this body according to the directions of Glenard and Boudault. The dracyle obtained possessed all the properties of toluol; we converted the body thus prepared into nitrodracyle (nitrotoluol), from which, by treatment with reducing agents, beautiful crystals of toluidine were obtained. In our paper on this organic base an analysis of the sulphate is given, and on referring I find that we forgot to mention that the salt analysed was prepared with the very toluidine obtained from the carbo-hydrogen arising with the distillation products of dragon's blood. This experiment removes any doubt that might have remained as to the identity of toluol and dracyle.—*Dr. A. W. Hofmann*.

‡ Liebig's *Annalen*, xli. 56. § Ibid. xliv. 313.

‖ Ibid. lvi. 307. ¶ Mem. of Chem. Soc. vol. ii. p. 367.

## Preparation of Cymol.

The experiments of Gerhardt and Cahours have shown that cumin oil (*oleum cumini*) is a mixture of two distinct oils,—cuminol ($C_{20} H_{12} O_4$), a body corresponding closely to oil of bitter almonds, and cymol ($C_{20} H_{14}$); by treatment with potash, the oxygen oil is converted into cuminic acid, while the carbo-hydrogen distils over unaltered. As, for the experiments about to be detailed, it was the latter of these two oils that was required, the mode of separation which I found it most convenient to adopt was the following:—The oil was first submitted to distillation alone, and about two-thirds of it drawn over; this portion was then repeatedly distilled with sticks of caustic potash, until the alkali remained unaltered; fresh potash was introduced after every third or fourth distillation, and the oil was regarded as pure when it ceased to lose anything after two or three distillations; latterly I found it advantageous to employ a retort of copper in this operation, the heated alkali proving exceedingly destructive to vessels of glass. The quantity of cymol obtained averaged about 7 oz. for every pound of cumin oil; and here I must be allowed to express my thanks to my friend Mr. Warington for having kindly undertaken to furnish me with a supply of oil obtained directly from the seeds by distillation: without his assistance I should scarcely have been able to have followed out my investigation, on account of the high price and varying quality of the oil obtained in commerce; from three-quarters of a hundred weight of seed Mr. Warington obtained at four distillations 2 lbs. 12 oz. of oil, which yielded me 18 oz. of beautiful and pure cymol.

To render cymol perfectly anhydrous, it was left for some time in contact with pieces of fused chloride of calcium and again distilled; in this state it is a limpid, colourless, highly refracting oil, of a very agreeable odour; its specific gravity I found to be 0·8576 at 16°, and its boiling-point, as a mean of two determinations with two specimens of the oil obtained at different periods, and which agreed closely with each other, 171°·5 C.

Cymol has been identified with camphogene, a substance previously obtained by Dumas[*], by the action of anhydrous phosphoric acid on camphor, and lately studied by Delalande[†]. At the commencement of my experiments I thought that this might probably be a useful practical method of procuring the carbo-hydrogen; from the difficulty however of obtaining anhydrous phosphoric acid in sufficient quantities,

[*] Liebig's *Annalen*, vi. 249.   [†] Ibid. xxxviii. 343.

and from the small amount of camphogene obtained, I found it otherwise, and I merely prepared a sufficient supply to enable me to obtain an additional proof of the identity of the two oils, which I did in a manner hereafter to be described. I may remark that even after repeated distillations with renewed quantities of anhydrous phosphoric acid I was unable to procure camphogene quite free from the peculiar smell of camphor, nor was there to be discovered in it the slightest approach to that fragrant odour by which cymol is characterized.

### Action of Nitric Acid on Cymol.

The action of nitric acid on cymol or camphogene has never hitherto been the subject of minute examination. Gerhardt and Cahours in their paper only mention that nitric acid of moderate concentration does not attack cymol when cold; that on heating nitrous acid is disengaged, and the carbohydrogen gradually passes into a peculiar acid, which on cooling is precipitated as a curdy mass; that this acid is rather soluble in water, alcohol and æther, crystallizing only with difficulty, and decomposed by heat, partially subliming in fine light needles or woolly flakes; and that fuming nitric acid decomposes cymol with the formation of the same acid and a yellow resin; none of these substances were however submitted by these chemists to elementary analysis. Delalande states that on treating camphogene with boiling fuming nitric acid it is converted into a white solid matter, becoming crystalline in the acid, and containing nitrogen. From these statements it seemed evident that the action of nitric acid on cymol gives rise to a variety of bodies, a supposition which experiments have completely verified; indeed, by a careful examination of this reaction, I have ascertained that not less than five or six different substances are produced; these bodies, some of which are acid, and some of a neutral character, are separated with considerable difficulty. In the present memoir I propose to confine myself to the acids only, reserving the regular substitution products of cymol, with the basic bodies arising therefrom, the substances representing nitrobenzol, aniline, &c., in the cymol series for a future paper.

I commenced with fuming nitric acid of the highest degree of concentration, the action of which on cymol is exceedingly violent; to avoid explosions it was necessary to keep the vessel cool by immersion in water; the oil was added gradually, drop by drop, to the acid, which speedily became of a dark red colour; by repeated distillations I obtained a beautiful crystalline acid, the analysis of which, leading to the formula

$HO, C_{16} H_6 NO_7$, rendered it evident, from the mode of its formation, that it must be considered as a substitution product of a corresponding non-nitrogenous acid, $HO, C_{16} H_7 O_3$, the very acid that is wanting in the toluol series, to the production of which acid my attention was now particularly directed.

Many attempts were made to oxidize the oil without having recourse to nitric acid; long-continued distillations with chromic acid, or with peroxide of manganese and sulphuric acid proved quite ineffectual, but after a great number of tentative operations, I at length succeeded, by the following method, in obtaining the wished-for substance, for which I propose the name of *toluylic acid*:—Ordinary nitric acid was diluted with about six times its bulk of water, and cymol added in the proportion of about 2 oz. of the oil to 1 lb. of the acid; the mixture was then introduced into a capacious retort and the distillation continued for two or three days; with acid of this strength there is no fear of a violent action; the oxidation of the oil proceeds slowly and quietly; it first becomes of a bright blue colour from the absorption of nitric oxide gas, then yellow, and after having been ten or a dozen times poured back into the retort, it begins to change more and more its physical character; it becomes heavier and more tenacious, and finally sinks to the bottom of the vessel; the process is known to be completed by a portion of the newly-formed acid passing over with the vapour of water, and condensing in the receiver, and if the whole operation has been successfully conducted, the contents of the retort become nearly solid on cooling from the crystallization of the acid; the weaker the nitric acid employed, and the longer the time consumed, the whiter and purer is the resulting acid; if a much stronger acid than that above prescribed be employed, violent action takes place when the boiling-point is reached, nearly the whole of the contents of the retort is projected into the receiver, and the new acid is found at the close of the operation to be contaminated with a considerable quantity of the nitrogenous acid, from which it is impossible afterwards entirely to free it; even when the operation has been slowly and carefully conducted with a very weak acid, it still contains a certain quantity of this acid, as numerous analyses proved, from which it is only to be freed by a series of troublesome operations; and it was only after a careful study and comparison of the salts formed by the respective acids that I was enabled to lay down a precise method for their separation. This method is founded on the great solubility of toluylate of baryta in cold water, and the very sparing solubility of the corresponding salt of the nitrogenous acid in the same menstruum. The crude acid is thrown on a filter, and the adhering nitric acid removed by washing with cold water; it is then boiled with hydrate of lime, and the resulting lime-salt, filtered when quite cold, afterwards decomposed by nitric or hydrochloric acid; if the acid does not precipitate tolerably white, the same operation is repeated, and the well-washed acid is then dissolved in baryta water and carefully evaporated to dryness on the water-bath; it is redissolved in cold water, filtered, reprecipitated by hydrochloric acid, washed, and the process repeated until the dry baryta salt dissolves completely in cold water; it should then be once or twice crystallized, after which it is generally quite pure.

The quantity of pure acid as thus obtained from 2 oz. of cymol is very small, but I have not hitherto been fortunate enough to discover a better or less circuitous method of procuring it; could an oxidizing action be effected on the oil without the use of nitric acid a great saving would undoubtedly be achieved, but, as before stated, all my attempts in this direction proved unavailing; it is not impossible that the object may be obtained by permanganate of potash. I made one experiment with this salt, and there was evidently a reduction of the permanganic acid, but no trace of toluylic acid could be discovered, from which it seems evident that the oxidation had in this case proceeded too far and the cymol become converted into carbonic acid; this reaction has not however as yet been sufficiently studied.

### Composition of Toluylic Acid.

On submitting toluylic acid to elementary analysis in the usual manner, by burning it with oxide of copper, I obtained the following results:—

I. Acid obtained by sublimation, not having been previously treated with baryta:—0·2225 grm. gave 0·569 grm. carbonic acid and 0·1190 water.

II. Acid obtained as before from a new preparation:—0·2105 grm. gave 0·540 grm. carbonic acid and 0·1130 water.

III. Acid obtained from the lime salt:—0·160 grm. gave 0·415 grm. carbonic acid and 0·085 water.

IV. Acid obtained from the baryta salt:—0·3120 grm. gave 0·803 grm. carbonic acid and 0·161 water.

V. Acid obtained as before from a new preparation:—0·320 grm. gave 0·825 grm. carbonic acid and 0·1715 water.

These numbers correspond to the following per-centages:—

|          | I.    | II.   | III.  | IV.   | V.    |
|----------|-------|-------|-------|-------|-------|
| Carbon   | 69·74 | 69·96 | 70·09 | 70·19 | 70·31 |
| Hydrogen | 5·94  | 5·96  | 5·98  | 5·98  | 5·95  |

and with consideration of the atomic weight as deduced from the analysis of the silver and baryta salts, lead to the following formula, $HO, C_{16} H_7 O_3$, as may be seen by the following comparison:—

|   |   |   | Theory. | Mean of the three last experiments. |
|---|---|---|---|---|
| 16 equivs. | Carbon | 96 | 70·58 | 70·20 |
| 8 ... | Hydrogen | 8 | 5·88 | 5·97 |
| 4 ... | Oxygen | 32 | 23·54 |  |
| 1 ... | Toluylic acid | 136 | 100·00 |  |

This acid thus becomes isomeric with hydride of anisyle and benzoate of oxide of methyle.

### Properties of Toluylic Acid.

From an aqueous solution of any of its salts toluylic acid is precipitated by nitric or hydrochloric acid as a snow-white curdy mass, which under the microscope resolves itself into a great number of small acicular crystals: it is soluble to a considerable extent in boiling water, out of which it crystallizes on cooling in small needles; in alcohol, æther and pyroxylic spirit it is soluble almost to any extent; when heated it fuses and sublimes without decomposition in beautiful needles: in its state of perfect purity it is inodorous and tasteless, but the impure acid has a peculiar and sickening smell, somewhat resembling that of oil of bitter almonds. When boiled for some time with concentrated nitric acid, it loses an atom of hydrogen, in the place of which an atom of hyponitric acid enters, nitrotoluylic acid being formed; and when heated with caustic lime or baryta it is decomposed into carbonic acid and toluol.

In the formation of toluylic acid from cymol four equivalents of carbon and six equivalents of hydrogen are eliminated in the form of oxalic and carbonic acids and water. In several preparations large quantities of oxalic acid were found. There exists a striking similarity in the manner in which nitric acid acts upon cymol and oil of anise, an oil in its composition closely connected with cymol, and which gives rise to anisylic acid, between which and toluylic acid there is also a marked resemblance. The composition of oil of anise being $C_{20} H_{12} O_2$, we may consider it as cymol which has lost two equivalents of hydrogen and taken two of oxygen. The composition of the acids formed by the action of nitric acid on these two oils is as follows:—

Toluylic acid . . . . . $HO, C_{16} H_7 O_3$
Anisylic acid . . . . . $HO, C_{16} H_7 O_5$.

## Compounds of Toluylic Acid.

From the extreme difficulty of obtaining this acid in a state of purity in any quantity, I have not been able to examine as many of its salts as I could have wished; the following will however serve to confirm its composition and establish its atomic weight.

*Toluylate of Baryta.*—The formation of this salt has been already described; I was unable to obtain it in a well-defined crystalline form. Its analysis yielded the following result:—

0·7955 grm. gave 0·453 sulphate of baryta = 37·37 per cent. baryta, agreeing very closely with the formula

$$BaO, C_{16} H_7 O_3,$$

as indicated by the subjoined comparison:—

|  | Theory. | Experiment. |
|---|---|---|
| 1 equiv. Anhydrous acid 127 |  |  |
| 1 ... Baryta ... 76 | 37·44 | 37·37 |

*Toluylate of Silver.*—This salt was formed by dropping nitrate of silver into a perfectly neutral solution of toluylate of ammonia; it fell as a white curdy mass, which was washed on a filter with cold water and purified by two or three crystallizations out of boiling water: it crystallizes in small needles. On analysing this salt the following numbers were obtained:—

I. 0·3785 grm. burned with oxide of copper gave 0·544 grm. of carbonic acid and 0·1045 water.

II. 0·334 grm. ignited gave 0·1485 silver.

III. 0·1725 grm. from another preparation gave 0·0767 silver.

IV. 0·1705 grm. from a third preparation gave 0·0757 silver.

These numbers correspond to the following per-centages:—

|  | I. | II. | III. | IV. |
|---|---|---|---|---|
| Carbon | 39·198 |  |  |  |
| Hydrogen | 3·03 |  |  |  |
| Silver |  | 44·46 | 44·46 | 44·4 |

and lead to the formula $AgO, C_{16} H_7 O_3$, as may be seen by the following comparison:—

|  |  | Theory. | Experiment. |
|---|---|---|---|
| 16 equivs. Carbon | 96 | 39·51 | 39·198 |
| 7 ... Hydrogen | 7 | 2·88 | 3·03 |
| 4 ... Oxygen | 32 | 13·17 |  |
| 1 ... Silver | 108 | 44·44 | 44·44 |
| 1 ... Toluylate of silver | 243 | 100·00 |  |

*Toluylate of Copper.*—This salt was prepared by dropping a solution of sulphate of copper into a perfectly neutral solution of toluylate of potash; it fell as a bright blue precipitate closely resembling the corresponding benzoate. It is very soluble in ammonia, forming a dark blue solution, and soluble to a slight extent in boiling water, separating on cooling as a granular precipitate: its analysis gave the following result.

0·3385 grm. ignited, the residue treated with nitric acid and again ignited gave 0·0822 grm. of oxide of copper = 24·28 per cent., agreeing with the formula $CuO, C_{16} H_7 O_3$.

|  |  | Theory. | | Experiment. |
|---|---|---|---|---|
| 1 equiv. | Anhydrous acid | 127·0 | 76·19 | |
| 1 ... | Oxide of copper | 39·7 | 23·81 | 24·28 |
|  |  | 166·7 | 100·00 | |

*Toluylate of Oxide of Ethyle.*—This compound was formed by transmitting a stream of dry hydrochloric acid gas through a solution of the acid dissolved in strong alcohol, until the latter fumed strongly; it was then distilled, about two-thirds drawn over, and the residue in the retort mixed with water; the new æther precipitated in the form of a dark heavy liquid; it was digested with ammonia to remove any uncombined toluylic acid, well-washed with distilled water, dried, by being allowed to remain for some time in contact with pieces of fused chloride of calcium, and then distilled: it passed into the receiver nearly colourless, but on standing it deposited a small quantity of crystalline matter, which proved to be the æther of the nitrogenous acid, the acid employed not having been obtained from the baryta salt. By a second distillation, collecting only the first portions, the whole of the other æther was removed and a pure substance obtained.

*Analysis.*—0·223 grm. gave 0·596 carbonic acid and 0·151 water. Centesimally,—

Carbon . . . . . 72·9
Hydrogen . . . . 7·52

agreeing closely with the formula $C_4 H_5 O, C_{16} H_7 O_3$, as the following comparison of the theoretical with the experimental numbers shows:—

|  |  | | Theory. | | Experiment. |
|---|---|---|---|---|---|
| 20 equivs. | Carbon | . . . | 120 | 73·17 | 72·90 |
| 12 ... | Hydrogen | . . | 12 | 7·31 | 7·52 |
| 4 ... | Oxygen | . . . | 32 | 19·52 | |
| 1 ... | Toluylic æther | . | 164 | 100·00 | |

When perfectly pure this compound is a colourless, fragrant liquid, having an odour closely resembling that of cinnamic or benzoic æther, and a pungent and slightly bitter taste. It boils at 228° C., which temperature may perhaps be one or two degrees too high, the determination having been made before the last traces of the nitrogenous æther had been removed; still it exhibits a new confirmation of the observation of H. Kopp, that the difference in the boiling-points of two analogous compounds, which differ by two equivalents of carbon and two of hydrogen, is 19° C. Benzoic æther, the composition of which is $C_4 H_5 O, C_{14} H_5 O$, boils at 209°. Unfortunately I had not a sufficient quantity of the liquid after purification for a second determination.

The following salts I have examined qualitatively only, considering the composition and atomic weight of the acid well-enough established by the preceding analyses.

*Toluylate of Potash*, formed by exactly neutralizing the acid with caustic potash, is a very soluble salt, crystallizing with great difficulty in small needles.

*Toluylate of Soda* is still more soluble than the preceding. I could not obtain it in the crystalline state.

*Toluylate of Ammonia* crystallizes in small prisms.

*Toluylate of Lime* crystallizes out of a concentrated aqueous solution in long shining needles.

### Products of the Decomposition of Toluylic Acid.

*Nitrotoluylic Acid.*—I have already observed that on treating cymol with concentrated and fuming nitric acid violent action ensues, and that by repeated distillations a crystalline acid containing nitrogen is obtained. I must now describe this action more in detail. The nitric acid employed should be concentrated and fuming, otherwise there will be a considerable formation of another crystalline substance, which is in its chemical character neutral, and which is not easily converted into nitrotoluylic acid. The properties and composition of this new product will be fully considered hereafter. The distillation must be continued as long as nitrous fumes continue to be evolved, and the retort then allowed to cool, upon which a considerable quantity of crystalline matter is deposited, and on adding cold water a copious precipitate takes place. The whole is now thrown on a filter and washed with cold water till all the nitric acid is removed; the precipitate is then digested with ammonia, the greater part dissolves; a portion however collects at the bottom of the vessel in the form of a red oil, which is to be separated. The ammoniacal salt is next decomposed by hydrochloric acid, the acid collected on a filter and well-washed with cold water, in

26   Mr. Noad *on the Action of Nitric Acid on Cymol.*

which it is very sparingly soluble; it is then dissolved in hot alcohol, boiled for a few minutes with animal charcoal, and filtered; by spontaneous evaporation the new acid crystallizes out in beautiful rhombic prisms of a pale yellow colour.

### Composition of Nitrotoluylic Acid.

The powdered crystals by combustion with oxide of copper yielded the following numbers:—

 I. 0·330 grm. gave 0·640 carbonic acid and 0·1205 water.
 II. 0·382 grm. gave 0·7396 carbonic acid and 0·136 water.
 III. 0·4145 grm. gave 0·806 carbonic acid and 0·152 water.
 IV. The nitrogen was determined by Dumas' method in an atmosphere of carbonic acid. The particulars of the experiment are as follows:—

0·600 grm. gave 41·5 cubic cent. of moist nitrogen. Barometer 0$^m$·7973; Thermometer 18°·5 C.

These numerical results correspond with the following per cents.:—

|          | I.    | II.   | III.  | IV.  |
|----------|-------|-------|-------|------|
| Carbon   | 52·89 | 52·80 | 53·03 |      |
| Hydrogen | 4·06  | 3·95  | 4·07  |      |
| Nitrogen | ...   | ...   | ...   | 79·6 |

and lead to the formula $HO, C_{16} \left\{ \begin{matrix} H_6 \\ NO_4 \end{matrix} \right\} O_3$, as the following comparison of the calculated numbers with the mean of analysis shows:—

|                          | Theory. |        | Mean of expt. |
|--------------------------|---------|--------|---------------|
| 16 eqs. Carbon           | 96      | 53·03  | 52·90         |
| 7  ... Hydrogen          | 7       | 3·86   | 4·00          |
| 1  ... Nitrogen          | 14      | 7·74   | 7·96          |
| 8  ... Oxygen            | 64      | 35·37  |               |
| 1  ... Nitrotoluylic acid| 181     | 100·00 |               |

By the following analyses of some of the salts of this acid the above formula is fully confirmed, and the atomic weight of the acid proved.

*Nitrotoluylate of Baryta.*—This salt was formed by adding chloride of barium to a neutral solution of nitrotoluylate of ammonia. A white curdy precipitate was determined, soluble to a considerable extent in boiling water, out of which it crystallized on cooling in beautiful stellated tufts, having a shining appearance when dry: after two or three recrystallizations it was submitted to analysis, and yielded the following results:—

0·738 grm. gave by ignition 0·290 grm. of carbonate of

baryta = 30·54 per cent. baryta, corresponding with the formula $BaO, C_{16}\{^{H_6}_{NO_4}\}O_3$, as may be seen by the following comparison:—

|  | Theory. |  | Experiment. |
|---|---|---|---|
| 1 equiv. Anhydrous acid | 171·50 | 69·24 |  |
| 1 ... Baryta . . . | 76·66 | 30·76 | 30·54 |
|  | 218·16 | 100·00 |  |

*Nitrotoluylate of Silver.*—This salt was formed by dropping nitrate of silver into a neutral solution of nitrotoluylate of ammonia; it fell as a white curdy mass resembling chloride of silver. It is soluble to a considerable extent in hot water, and by long boiling becomes partially decomposed; it crystallizes from a hot aqueous solution in beautiful feathery tufts; it is only sparingly soluble in alcohol.

By combustion with oxide of copper the following results were obtained:—

I. 0·3505 grm. gave 0·424 grm. carbonic acid and 0·070 water when ignited alone.

II. 0·3385 grm. gave 0·127 grm. of silver.

III. 0·230 grm. gave 0·086 grm. silver. Centesimally:—

|  | I. | II. | III. |
|---|---|---|---|
| Carbon . . | 33·0 |  |  |
| Hydrogen . | 2·12 |  |  |
| Silver . . . ... |  | 37·52 | 37·38 |

corresponding with the formula $AgO, C_{16}\{^{H_6}_{NO_4}\}O_3.$

|  |  | Theory. |  | Experiment. |
|---|---|---|---|---|
| 16 equivs. Carbon . . | 96 | 33·33 | 33·00 |
| 6 ... Hydrogen . | 6 | 2·08 | 2·12 |
| 1 ... Nitrogen . . | 14 | 4·86 |  |
| 8 ... Oxygen . . | 64 | 22·22 |  |
| 1 ... Silver . . . | 108 | 37·51 | 37·45 |
| 1 ... Nitrotoluylate of silver . | 268 | 100·00 |  |

I have already mentioned that I prepared a small quantity of camphogene by the action of anhydrous phosphoric acid on camphor; in order to obtain an additional experimental proof of the identity of this substance with cymol, I have studied the action of concentrated nitric acid on it. I found it most convenient to prepare a silver salt of the acid thus obtained, the analysis of which yielded me the following numbers:—

I. 0·396 grm. gave 0·486 carbonic acid and 0·85 water.
II. 0·372 grm. gave 0·139 silver.
III. 0·2935 grm. gave 0·110 silver.
These numbers correspond in per cents. to—

|          | I.    | II.   | III.  |
|----------|-------|-------|-------|
| Carbon   | 33·46 |       |       |
| Hydrogen | 2·38  |       |       |
| Silver   | ...   | 37·36 | 37·47 |

And by comparing them with the preceding they will be found sufficiently near to warrant the conclusion that the two carbo-hydrogens are identical. On treating the acid formed by the action of fuming nitric acid on camphogene with ammonia, the same heavy oil which was observed in the case of cymol separated, and after a while crystallized; but from the small quantity of camphogene at my command, I was unable to procure sufficient of this substance for a comparative experiment, or to bring forward any additional proof of the identity of the two oils.

*Nitrotoluylate of Lime.*—This salt was prepared by decomposing nitrotoluylate of ammonia by chloride of calcium. It fell as a granular crystalline mass, much more soluble in water than the corresponding baryta salt, and crystallizing out of its aqueous solution in small clustering groups of oblique rhombic prisms; it was obtained perfectly pure by two or three recrystallizations.

*Analysis.*—0·6965 grm. gave by ignition, treatment with carbonate of ammonia, and a second gentle ignition, 0·1775 grm. carbonate of lime = 14·27 per cent. of lime, agreeing exactly with the formula $Ca, OC_{16}\left\{{H_8 \atop NO_4}\right\}O_3$.

|                            | Theory. | | Experiment. |
|----------------------------|---------|-------|-------|
| 1 equiv. Anhydrous acid    | 171·50  |       |       |
| 1 ... Lime                 | 28·5    | 14·25 | 14·27 |
|                            | 200·00  |       |       |

*Nitrotoluylate of Oxide of Ethyle.*—A solution of the pure acid in strong alcohol was submitted to a current of dry hydrochloric acid gas till copious fumes were evolved; it was then distilled; the first portions that passed into the receiver consisted of a mixture of alcohol and hydrochloric æther; the distillation was continued until a few drops collected on a watch-glass gave a milkiness when mixed with water; it was then stopped, and the retort allowed to cool; a considerable quantity of the yellow heavy oil collected at the bottom of the vessel, which was poured off into a beaker; in a few minutes it solidified into a yellow crystalline mass. This impure æther was next treated with carbonate of potash, by which all adhering undecomposed acid was removed; it was then thrown on a filter, well-washed with cold water, and dried by pressure between folds of bibulous paper; it was now of a pale amber colour, and possessed a very agreeable odour; it was redissolved in hot alcohol and filtered, the alcoholic solution on cooling solidified into a light lemon-coloured crystalline mass; this was dried between folds of blotting-paper, transferred to a watch-glass, and, placed in the water-bath, it immediately liquefied: after remaining about an hour it was removed, and on cooling it gradually crystallized into a mass of needles radiating from a common centre and having a very beautiful appearance.

It was analysed by combustion with oxide of copper, and furnished the following results:—

0·362 grm. gave 0·760 grm. carbonic acid and 0·175 grm. water. Centesimally—

$$\begin{array}{lr} \text{Carbon} & 57\cdot26 \\ \text{Hydrogen} & 5\cdot37 \end{array}$$

agreeing with the formula $C_4 H_5 O, C_{16} \begin{Bmatrix} H_6 \\ NO_4 \end{Bmatrix} O_3$, as shown by the following comparison:—

|  |  |  | Theory. |  | Experiment. |
|---|---|---|---|---|---|
| 20 eqs. Carbon | . . . . | 120 | 57·42 | | 57·26 |
| 11 ... Hydrogen | . . . . | 11 | 5·26 | | 5·37 |
| 1 ... Nitrogen | . . . . | 14 | 6·69 | | |
| 8 ... Oxygen | . . . . | 64 | 30·63 | | |
| 1 ... Nitrotoluylic æther | . | 209 | 100·00 | | |

The remainder of the æther was dissolved in a strong alcoholic solution of ammonia and set aside with the view of procuring nitrotoluylamide: this substance, however, which it would have been interesting to have compared with the corresponding term of the benzoyl series lately obtained by Mr. Field*, I have not yet been able to obtain.

*Nitrotoluylate of Oxide of Methyle.*—To prepare this substance, nitrotoluylic acid was dissolved in pure pyroxylic spirit, and the solution subjected to a long-continued stream of dry hydrochloric acid gas, as in the corresponding ethyle compound. On distilling the fuming acid liquid, a considerable quantity of a dense, black oily substance collected at the bottom of the vessel: this was evidently the methyle compound contaminated with results of the decomposition of the

---

* Philosophical Magazine, vol. xxxi. p. 459.

pyroxylic spirit by the hydrochloric acid gas. On cooling the acid liquid was poured off and the oil repeatedly washed with water; in a few hours it solidified into a confused crystalline mass, still however black and having a peculiar vinous smell: an attempt was made to purify it by distillation with water; in consequence, however, of its high boiling-point, very little passed over into the receiver after two or three hours' distillation. It was then heated with strong nitric acid, and after boiling for a few minutes, water added; the æther now readily separated in clear, light yellow oily drops: ammonia was then added to remove any nitrotoluylic acid that might have been present, and the oil collected on a watch-glass; in a few minutes it solidified into a crystalline mass, which was dissolved in æther, filtered and recrystallized, and then exposed for some time to the heat of the water-bath; on cooling it solidified as before, and was then considered sufficiently pure for analysis.

0·376 grm. gave by combustion with oxide of copper 0·756 grm. of carbonic acid and 0·164 grm. of water, corresponding in per cents. to

Carbon . . . . 54·84
Hydrogen . . . 4·83

and agreeing with the formula $C_2 H_3 O, C_{16} \left\{ \begin{array}{c} H_8 \\ NO_4 \end{array} \right\} O_3$.

|  | Theory. |  | Experiment. |
|---|---|---|---|
| 18 eqs. Carbon . . . . | 108 | 55·38 | 54·84 |
| 9 ... Hydrogen . . . | 9 | 4·61 | 4·83 |
| 1 ... Nitrogen . . . | 14 | 7·18 |  |
| 8 ... Oxygen . . . . | 64 | 32·83 |  |
| 1 ... Nitrotoluylate of oxide of methyle . | 195 | 100·00 |  |

After standing two or three days, beautiful colourless stellar crystals were deposited on the sides of the vessel containing an aqueous solution of this æther; it is probable, therefore, that this as well as the last-described compound is, when perfectly pure, colourless. The two æthers closely resemble each other in their physical characters, the smell of the latter is, however, less agreeable than that of the former; both are decomposed by potash into nitrotoluylic acid and alcohol or pyroxylic spirit.

The following salts of this acid I merely examined qualitatively.

*Nitrotoluylate of Potash* is a very soluble salt crystallizing with great difficulty in small needles.

*Nitrotoluylate of Soda*, like the corresponding salt of toluylic acid, I could not obtain in any definite crystalline form.

*Nitrotoluylate of Ammonia* crystallizes out of its aqueous solution in long needles; it is very easily decomposed, losing the whole of its ammonia when boiled with animal charcoal. I intend to return to the study of this salt, and hope to obtain from it the body which I failed to procure from nitrotoluylic æther, viz. nitrotoluylamide.

*Nitrotoluylate of Strontia.*—This salt, which in appearance is not to be distinguished from the corresponding baryta salt, was formed by dropping chloride of strontium into neutral nitrotoluylate of ammonia: it is rather more soluble in boiling water than the baryta compound, and the crystals deposited on cooling are rather larger.

*Nitrotoluylate of Copper.*—On adding solution of sulphate of copper to perfectly neutral nitrotoluylate of ammonia a basic salt is formed. I have not yet obtained a definite copper salt of this acid.

### Action of a mixture of Sulphuric and Nitric Acids on Nitrotoluylic Acid.

When nitrobenzol is boiled repeatedly with the strongest nitric acid it loses an atom of hydrogen, in the place of which another atom of hyponitric acid enters. The transformation proceeds very slowly. The new substance (dinitrobenzol) is however obtained very speedily, as Drs. Muspratt and Hofmann[*] have shown, by dropping benzol or nitrobenzol into a mixture composed of equal parts of fuming nitric acid and concentrated sulphuric acid as long as the liquid remains homogeneous. This method has lately been employed with great success by M. Cahours, who, amongst many other interesting products, has obtained trinitranisic acid, $C_{16} \left\{ \begin{array}{c} H_5 \\ 3(NO_4) \end{array} \right\} O_6$; dinitrocuminic acid, $C_{20} \left\{ \begin{array}{c} H_{10} \\ 2(NO_4) \end{array} \right\} O_4$; and dinitrobenzoic acid, $C_{14} \left\{ \begin{array}{c} H_4 \\ 2NO_4 \end{array} \right\} O_4$. It appeared interesting to submit nitrotoluylic acid to a similar treatment, but after digesting the acid with the mixture for several days the anticipated transformation had not taken place, the numbers obtained by analysis being those given under III., "composition of nitrotoluylic acid." I intend however to repeat this experiment.

### Distillation of Toluylic Acid with Baryta—Toluol.

Although the preceding analyses of toluylic and nitroto-

---

[*] Mem. Chem. Soc. vol. iii. p. 111.

luylic acids have established the composition of these two compounds in a perfectly satisfactory manner, there still remained one experiment to be made in order to prove that toluylic acid occupies in the toluyle series the same place which benzoic acid has in the benzoyle series; in order to prove that the acids analysed are really the true toluylic and nitrotoluylic acids, and not merely bodies having the same composition, being isomeric with them: this experiment was to attempt the transformation of toluylic acid into toluol under the same circumstances by which benzoic acid becomes converted into benzol. I devoted the acid from four ounces of cymol to this experiment, and by distillation with caustic baryta, which I found to answer much better than lime, I obtained some grammes of a beautiful limpid colourless liquid, having the precise smell of the carbo-hydrogen sought for. By distillation from a fresh portion of baryta the oil was rendered perfectly anhydrous; in this state its boiling-point was taken. It began to boil at 109°, the thermometer gradually rose to 110°·5, barometer $0^m \cdot 763$ (30·1 inches).

It was burned in the ordinary manner with oxide of copper and yielded the following results:—

0·2410 grm. gave 0·809 grm. of carbonic acid and 0·196 grm. of water, corresponding in per cents. to

Carbon . . . . 91·50
Hydrogen . . . 9·03

and agreeing exactly with the formula of toluol, $C_{14} H_8$, as the following comparison shows:—

|  |  | Theory. | | Experiment. |
|---|---|---|---|---|
| 14 eqs. Carbon | . . . | 84 | 91·3 | 91·50 |
| 8 ... Hydrogen | . . | 8 | 8·7 | 9·03 |
|  |  | 22 | 100·0 | 100·53 |

The formation of toluol from toluylic acid is perfectly analogous to the production of benzol from benzoic acid.

$$\underbrace{C_{16} H_8 O_4}_{\text{Toluylic acid.}} + 2 BaO = \underbrace{C_{14} H_8}_{\text{Toluol.}} + 2(BaO, CO_2).$$

The remainder of the carbo-hydrogen was converted into nitrotoluol by the action of fuming nitric acid: the well-washed oily fluid was then dissolved in alcohol, saturated with ammoniacal gas and treated repeatedly with sulphuretted hydrogen, the whole being distilled after each saturation with hydrosulphuric acid, to facilitate the deposition of the sulphur; the dark red solution was evaporated to expel the alcohol, water added, and then submitted to distillation with potash, in addition to ammonia and aqueous vapour, a yellow oil passed into the receiver, which did not however solidify on cooling, probably in consequence of the presence of ammonia; it was therefore saturated with oxalic acid, evaporated to dryness in the water-bath, redissolved in boiling alcohol and filtered; on cooling, oxalate of toluidine separated in fine white needles, these were washed, dissolved in boiling water, and decomposed by potash; the toluidine, which separated in colourless oily drops, was taken up by æther, on the evaporation of which it remained in the form of a crystalline mass. Although the nature of this substance was sufficiently obvious, nevertheless, to remove all doubt respecting it, I converted it into the double platinum salt by mixing it with hydrochloric acid and bichloride of platinum. The beautiful orange-yellow spangular mass was washed with æther and dried on the water-bath. Its analysis gave the following result:—

0·930 grm. gave by ignition 0·292 grm. of platinum = 31·398 per cent.

This determination agrees with the formula for chloride of platinum and toluidine—$C_{14} H_9 N, H Cl, PtCl_2$.

|  |  | Theory. |  | Experiment. |
|---|---|---|---|---|
| 14 eqs. Carbon | . . | 84·00 |  |  |
| 9 ... Hydrogen | . . | 9·00 |  |  |
| 1 ... Nitrogen | . . | 14·00 |  |  |
| 3 ... Chlorine | . . | 106·50 |  |  |
| 1 ... Platinum | . . | 98·68 | 31·6 | 31·398 |
|  |  | 312·18 |  |  |

By the production of toluylic and nitrotoluylic acids there is not only filled up a gap which has hitherto existed in the toluyle series, but an important step has been made in the series of acids to which I have alluded at the commencement of this paper, of which indeed at the present time a few scattered members only are known. The following table presents a general view of some of the most important members of the different groups, and exhibits the gaps which remain to be filled up by future experiments.

| I. | II. | III. | IV. | V. |
|---|---|---|---|---|
| $HO, C_{12}H_3O_3$ unknown | Salicylic acid ... $HO, C_{14}H_3O_5$ | Anisylic acid ... $HO, C_{16}H_7O_5$ | $NO_2, C_{16}H_6O_2$ unknown | $HO, ? = H_3O_2$ unknown |
| | Nitrosalicylic acid ... $HO, C_{14} \begin{Bmatrix} H_2 \\ NO_4 \end{Bmatrix} O_5$ | Nitranisylic acid ... $HO, C_{16} \begin{Bmatrix} H_6 \\ NO_4 \end{Bmatrix} O_5$ | | Hydrated Cinnamic... |
| | Phenol ... $HO, C_{12}H_5, O$ | Anisol ... $HO, C_{14}H_7, O$ | | Cuminic acid |
| | Oil of bitter almonds $H_2, C_{14}H_5O_2$ | | | |
| | Benzoic acid ... $HO, C_{14}H_5O_3$ | Cuminic acid ... | | |
| | Nitrobenzoic acid ... $HO, C_{14} \begin{Bmatrix} H_4 \\ NO_4 \end{Bmatrix} O_3$ | Nitrocuminic acid, $HO, C_{16} \begin{Bmatrix} H_6 \\ NO_4 \end{Bmatrix} O_5$ | | Nitrocuminic acid |
| | Dinitrobenzoic acid, $HO, C_{14} \begin{Bmatrix} H_3 \\ 2NO_4 \end{Bmatrix} O_3$ | | | Dinitrocuminic acid |
| | Benzonitrile ... $C_{14}H_3N$ | | | Cuminitrile |
| | Benzol ... $C_{12}H_6$ | Toluol ... $C_{14}H_8$ | | |
| | Nitrobenzol ... $C_{12} \begin{Bmatrix} H_5 \\ NO_4 \end{Bmatrix}$ | Nitrotoluol ... $C_{14} \begin{Bmatrix} H_7 \\ NO_4 \end{Bmatrix}$ | | Nitrocumol |
| | Dinitrobenzol ... $C_{12} \begin{Bmatrix} H_4 \\ 2NO_4 \end{Bmatrix}$ | Dinitrotoluol ... $C_{14} \begin{Bmatrix} H_6 \\ 2NO_4 \end{Bmatrix}$ | | Dinitrocumol |
| Seminaph-thalidine $C_{10}H_3N$ | Aniline ... $C_{12} \begin{Bmatrix} H_7 \\ N \end{Bmatrix}$ | Toluidine ... $C_{14}H_9N$ | | Cumidine |
| | Nitraniline ... $C_{12} \begin{Bmatrix} H_6 \\ NO_4 \end{Bmatrix} N$ | | | |
| | Bromaniline ... $C_{12} \begin{Bmatrix} H_6 \\ Br \end{Bmatrix} N$ | | | |
| | Dibromaniline ... $C_{12} \begin{Bmatrix} H_5 \\ Br_2 \end{Bmatrix} N$ | | | |
| | Tribromaniline ... $C_{12} \begin{Bmatrix} H_4 \\ Br_3 \end{Bmatrix} N$ | | | |

* This beautiful base has lately been prepared by Mr. Nicholson in the laboratory of the Royal College of Chemistry.

The preceding table shows that there are indeed a great number of substances still to be discovered. In the first series it will be seen that as yet we have only one member, semi-naphthalidine*, the base corresponding to aniline and toluidine, and obtained by Zinin in a very curious reaction of sulphide of ammonium on dinitronaphthalol. The second series is best known; it is closely connected with the indigo series by salicylic acid, nitrosalicylic acid and aniline. As however the term of indigo is as yet not represented in any of the other families I have omitted to connect them. The third is the toluyle series, which has become enriched by the present investigation with two of the principal terms: of the following no term whatever is known. The next contains a series of interesting compounds arising from oil of cumin, and of the last group we have at present only cymol. In a future paper I hope to introduce some of the substances deriving from this carbo-hydrogen.

This investigation was conducted in the laboratory of the Royal College of Chemistry, and I cannot bring it to a conclusion without acknowledging the great obligation I am under to Professor Hofmann for the constant advice and assistance which he afforded me during its prosecution, and expressing my warmest thanks to him for his valuable instructions in the method of conducting organic investigations generally.

---

IV. *An Account of the remarkable Magnetic Disturbance which continued from the 22nd to the 25th of October* 1847. *By* C. Brooke, *M.B., F.R.S.*†

[With a Plate.]

DURING this period, which was marked by the appearance of the unusually splendid Aurora Borealis described in the November Number of this Journal, a greater amount of consecutive disturbance of the magnetic instruments took place at the Royal Observatory than has ever been noticed since the establishment of the magnetic department.

A continuous record of the great and incessant changes of declination and horizontal force has been obtained by the self-registering photographic apparatus designed by the writer, and described in the Philosophical Transactions, part 1, 1847. The vertical element of magnetic force was not subjected to any corresponding amount of variation. By permission of the Astronomer Royal, a fac-simile of one of the most remarkable portions of the register of the declination magnet is annexed,

* Erdmann's Journal, xxxiii. 29.
† Communicated by the Author.

as a favourable specimen of the present state of magnetic registration.

The scale of time is marked on the photographic base-line, and is about 1·2 inch to one hour; the hours denote Göttingen mean astronomical time. The scale of angular space is 5 inches to 1° in azimuth, and is measured in a direction perpendicular to the base-line, the position of which corresponds nearly to 23° 41′ of W. declination.

During $22^d$ and $23^d$ the W. declination ranged between 22° 17′ and 23° 37′, but the greatest change is that which is represented in Plate I. This comprises the variations of declination from $24^d$ $11^h$ to $22^h$. The declination is observed to decrease rapidly from 23° 14′ at about $11^h$ $40^m$, to 21° 53′ at about $12^h$ $5^m$; and after several considerable fluctuations, to increase to 23° 35′ at about $13^h$ $13^m$, indicating a variation of 1° 42′ in little more than one hour. The breaches of continuity in the line during these large excursions, indicate that the magnet has not rested at any one point long enough to mark the paper. The least time during which the tracing pencil of light will produce a visible impression is probably about $4^s$.

Between $16^h$ and $19^h$ the excursions of the magnet are so incessant and considerable, that periodic observations, even at the least periods at which an observer could continuously record them, would scarcely give an adequate idea of the progress of the disturbance. This vibratory movement of the magnet probably corresponds with the "peculiar mechanical agitation" mentioned by Captain Lefroy in an account of the disturbance of the 24th of September at Toronto, published in the November Number of this Journal, and is quite distinct from mere oscillation of the magnet about its mean place. The secondary vibrations accompanying the larger excursions of the magnet are very well shown between $18^h$ and $21^h$. These have very rarely been observed in the photographs thus obtained during the last two years. They would appear to indicate the simultaneous existence of two distinct disturbing causes; of which that producing the larger and more gradual excursions is far more frequently in operation.

The register has been disconnected at $18^h$ for the convenience of the Plate; and the register of the bifilar magnetometer, obtained on the same paper, in order to avoid confusion, has been altogether omitted. It may however be remarked, that at the time when the variation of horizontal force was most considerable, amounting to more than one-tenth of the whole force, the northern hemisphere was brilliantly illuminated with coruscations, as described by Mr. Glaisher, and at this period the disturbance of the declination was not proportionably great; but shortly afterwards, when the streamers shot up to the zenith, and the arch of light was formed, the great changes of declination took place, the disturbance of horizontal force being at the same period comparatively inconsiderable.

After the period represented in the Plate, the disturbances were diminished both in amount and frequency; and after $25^d\ 12^h$ they entirely ceased.

---

V. *Note of the occurrence of a Deposit of native Earthy Carbonate of Manganese in Ireland.* By Sir ROBERT KANE[*].

THE place where this substance has been found is in the townland of Glandree, parish of Tulla, in the eastern portion of the county of Clare. The precise locality is near the top of a mountain, about 900 feet above the level of the sea, on the side of a new road connecting Scariff with Gort.

The rock of the locality is the old red sandstone, from under which the clay-slate rises close by. The surface is, however, very much covered by boulders of sandstone and by bog, and broken into hummocks, separating little basins, in which deposits of marl, very rich in lime and of much value for agricultural purposes, are usually found. The extensive employment of these marls made me very anxious to find additional localities of them; and I took advantage of a new road being opened through the district during last year by the Board of Works, to have collected for me specimens of all such materials as in any way resembled marl, as could be found in the cuttings along the line of road. Amongst them, and from the precise locality already stated, was one fawn-coloured earthy matter which effervesced strongly with acids, especially when heated, and which, on more exact examination, turned out to be not carbonate of lime, but carbonate of manganese.

This substance forms a layer of several inches thick, lying under a stratum of bog of about two feet thick, and resting on the partially decomposed surface of the underlying sandstone and slate rocks. It is of a brownish-fawn colour generally; but the parts that are quite free from admixture of peat are much lighter, and indeed undistinguishable in colour from the carbonate of manganese artificially prepared. On being dried carefully, it is found not to be quite amorphous, but to consist of nodules of a purer packed in a mass of less pure material; but these nodules are so friable and soft, that few of them now remain in the specimens that have been deposited in our museums.

The composition of two different specimens of this mineral was found to be—

* Communicated by the Author.

|                                  | A.    | B.    |
|----------------------------------|-------|-------|
| Protocarbonate of manganese      | 74·55 | 79·94 |
| Carbonate of lime                | a trace | 2·43 |
| Protocarbonate of iron           | 15·01 | 11·04 |
| Clay and sand                    | ·33   | ·37   |
| Organic matter, moisture and loss| 10·11 | 6·22  |
|                                  | 100·00 | 100·00 |

The carbonate of manganese is known to be one of the rarest forms in which that metal occurs; and so far as I am aware, it has been hitherto found only in a compact and crystallized form. The condition of the substance now described may therefore possibly be quite new to science; but certainly it has not been found constituting a kind of marly deposit spread extensively under bog, nor is it known at all as an Irish mineral.

It is highly probable that the study of the action to which this material is subjected under its native condition, may throw some light on the theory of the impregnating and cementing of rocks by the peroxide, and indeed perhaps to the mode of generation of the native earthy peroxides of manganese. I shall however not at present enter on that question, but merely indicate to philosophical geologists the fact of this mineral certainly influencing, by its chemical actions, the rocky masses with which it is associated.

Museum of Irish Industry,
51 Stephen's Green, Dublin.

VI. *On the Great Symmetrical Barometric Wave, November 1847, and other important undulations.* By WILLIAM RADCLIFF BIRT[*].

IN the engraving illustrating this article (p. 45), fig. 2 indicates the *form* of the great symmetrical wave of November, as it passed London in the present autumn. It is placed under the great wave of November 1846, fig. 1, for the purpose of exhibiting the points of similarity and difference. The most casual glance of the eye will detect a considerable similarity with a much greater range in 1847; also a larger development of the individual waves.

In 1846 the wave commenced on the 2nd, culminated on the 9th, and terminated on the 17th.

In 1847 the wave commenced on the 8th, culminated on the 14th, and terminated on the 21st.

Previous to offering some remarks on the last return of the great symmetrical wave, it will be desirable to solicit the attention of the reader to the *type* of the barometric oscillations during the middle portion of November, as ascertained in

[*] Communicated by the Author.

1845[*]; viz. "that during fourteen days in November, more or less equally disposed about the middle of the month, the oscillations of the barometer exhibit a remarkably symmetrical character; that is to say, the fall succeeding the transit of the maximum or highest reading is to a great extent similar to the preceding rise. This rise and fall is not continuous or unbroken; in three out of four of the occasions on which it has been observed, it has been found to consist of five distinct elevations. * * * * At the setting in of the great November wave the barometer is generally *low*, sometimes below twenty-nine inches. This depression is succeeded by *two* well-marked undulations, varying from one to two days in duration. The central undulation, which also forms the apex of the great wave, is of larger extent, occupying from three to five days; when this has passed, two smaller undulations corresponding to those at the commencement of the wave, make their appearance, and at the close of the last the wave terminates." On the last two returns, the great wave presented features that require the preceding *type* to be somewhat modified. The symmetrical character on both occasions was distinct, but the crown or central apex was not the *highest*. In 1846, the wave on the posterior slope, which is bisected by the last vertical line in the engraving, was the highest at the northern and north-western stations; and on the last return the subordinate waves on both the anterior and posterior slopes were higher than the central. With this exception, there appears to be nothing to militate against the general *accuracy* of the *type* as above expressed. It appears that on all occasions on which the writer has observed the great symmetrical wave, it has been completely separated from all the preceding and succeeding barometric movements,—an *individuality* has been attributed to it in consequence of this separation; and the movements between the epochs marking its commencement and termination have more or less been referable to the foregoing type. On most occasions the barometric movements *preceding* the great wave have occurred at a considerable altitude, while those *succeeding* it have been observed at lower altitudes.

The individuality of the great symmetrical wave consists more in the *character* of the barometric movements than either in the *form*, as given by the curve, or the *absolute measurement* of the atmospheric pressure, as observed by means of the barometer. Both the curve and the altitude of the mercurial column vary very considerably, while the symmetrical character is much more constant. This consists (in most cases) in the initial and terminal minima being very distinct, and the inflexions of the curve as the barometer approaches its terminal

---

[*] Phil. Mag. S. 3. vol. xxix. p. 357.

minimum, being to a great extent similar to those marking the barometric rise to the central apex. From this it follows that great difficulty must exist in the observation of the wave. If, for instance, any particular curve is expected to return, the observer in most cases will be disappointed; he will also meet with disappointment if he expects that on certain days the barometer will attain certain altitudes. The surest way is to prepare a paper of engraved squares, and for a few days before the expected return of the wave, to project the altitudes of the barometer in a curve. While this is going on, uncertainty will often attach to the proceeding until the wave is just approaching its termination, when the symmetry will become apparent, provided the observer is situated near the locality of greatest symmetry. Should he be removed even a short distance *in some directions* from the area or line of greatest symmetry, the curve will not be *fully* referable to the foregoing type: one portion may be thrown *higher* than another, with which at the point of greatest symmetry it is of equal altitude. It is very desirable to mark out distinctly the localities of these departures from symmetry, and to determine the *directions* in which the *greatest excursions* take place; especially as another important feature of the wave appears to be intimately connected with them, viz. the barometric range from the lowest minimum to the highest maximum, which increases in some directions very considerably. In order therefore to observe the wave satisfactorily, and to be certain of its return, three features require to be fully apprehended:—the symmetrical character of the curve, as expressed in the foregoing type, with the modification alluded to; the departure from this symmetry in certain localities, which may be noticed in barometric movements, evidently referable, by the nature of the curve and the period elapsing between the initial and terminal minima, to the great wave; and the barometric range during this period, which will be found to vary in certain directions.

The reader will readily see from this enunciation of phænomena appertaining to the great symmetrical barometric wave, that the *phases* of the wave, as exhibited at any given locality, *bear* a considerable analogy to certain phænomena presented during a solar eclipse. The *line* of terrestrial surface on which the barometric wave presents the most perfect symmetry, corresponds to the line of country on which the eclipse is central; and the spot at which the wave is observed to be most strongly developed, may be regarded as corresponding to the spot at which the sun is eclipsed centrally on the meridian. This line of greatest symmetry, referring to the barometric wave, extends a considerable distance over central Europe; on each side the symmetry *is departed from*, some points, as we have before observed, being thrown higher than others with which they were on a level. This displacement presents very regular gradations, and may be considered as corresponding to the deviations from totality or annularity observed during the progress of a solar eclipse at stations removed from the line at which it is central. The further the observer is situated from the *central line*, the smaller the eclipse, and the greater the deviation either from totality or annularity. In like manner, the further the observer is removed from the *line of greatest symmetry* of the barometric wave, the *greater* will be the deviations from symmetry in the curve representing the observations. The analogy just noticed not only holds good for one eclipse and one barometric wave, but as the same eclipse presents at the same stations different *phases* on the occasions of its successive returns, sometimes appearing only as a slight obscuration of the solar disc, at others as a great and central eclipse, so the barometric wave presents a different *phase* on each of its returns; the *curve* representing the observations during its transit exhibits a different *form*, the symmetrical arrangement of its parts constituting its distinguishing characteristic\*. From the assemblage of curves representing the great symmetrical wave on its successive returns, the lines of greatest symmetry appertaining to each return may be determined, and from these the *mean* line of greatest symmetry may be traced over Europe. It will be more difficult to trace in connexion with this line mean lines of *deviation* on each side, owing to the erratic character of the subordinate waves forming the *inflexions* of the symmetrical curve; but this may be done with great ease on the occasion of each successive return, provided there are a sufficient number of stations of observation judiciously placed over the surface of Europe, from which such a chart may be constructed. In the present instance we may take the two apices of the 10th and 18th. It is highly probable that at some station to the south-east of London *both* attained the *same* altitude: this station would be at least near to, if it was not, the station of greatest symmetry. The departure from symmetry would not only be indicated, but the numerical value of it given by the depression of one apex below the other. Thus at London this value is ·051; but at Weston in Somersetshire it is ·161, and at Halifax in Yorkshire it appears to be ·250; and there is very little doubt that it will be found to increase, especially towards the north-west. When these values of deviation from symmetry are determined year after year, and combined so as to obtain the

---

\* By referring to the phænomena of a solar eclipse as analogous to those of a barometric wave, it is not intended to convey the idea that there is any necessary connexion between them.

mean value for each station, then a chart representing to the eye the line of greatest symmetry with the lines of deviation on each side, could readily be constructed. The following table is intended to illustrate these remarks. The values of the most prominent points of the wave are given, from which the departure from symmetry may easily be deduced. The same may be done for other stations.

Barometric readings of the most prominent points of the Great Symmetrical Wave of November 1847.

| Phase. | Epoch. | London. | Weston. | Halifax.* |
|---|---|---|---|---|
| Central apex .......... | Nov. 14 | 30·328 | 30·270 | 29·900 |
| Two interior minima { | 12 | 30·062 | 30·018 | 29·700 |
|  | 17 | 30·115 | 30·188 | 29·800 |
| Two exterior maxima { | 10 | 30·351 | 30·210 | 29·850 |
|  | 18 | 30·402 | 30·410 | 30·100 |
| Two exterior minima { | 8 | 29·579 | 29·449 | 29·075 |
|  | 21 | 29·516 | 29·446 | 29·060 |

My attention has been called by Mr. Chalmers of Weston-super-Mare, Somersetshire,—to whom I am indebted for the readings in the fourth column of the foregoing table,—to the similarity existing between the great wave of 1798 and 1847 at London. The observations in 1798 were made by Luke Howard, Esq. A chart of the barometric movements during the entire year, illustrates an article on the influence of the sun and moon on the barometer, published in the Philosophical Magazine for 1800. In this chart the movements during November are seen to be greatly in accordance with the *type* as expressed above. Fig. 3 in the engraving, illustrating this article, is the projection of these movements on a similar scale to the curves of 1846 and 1847. The similarity between the curves of 1847 and 1798 is very considerable. The vertical lines passing through the principal points of these curves clearly indicate that the epochs of these points in 1798 and 1847, especially the two interior minima and the two exterior maxima, *differed from each other but an hour or two*: in this respect the resemblance is very close. The horizontal lines are intended to show the *deviation from symmetry*, supposing the two interior minima, being at the same altitude, to represent perfect symmetry. [The equal altitudes of the two exterior maxima is a much better general expression of this element.] The highest horizontal line in fig. 1, just touching the second interior minimum, indicates a reading of 30·299; the lowest

---

* These numbers have been taken from a curve with which I have been furnished by John Youd, Esq. of Halifax. Those at London and Weston are given as read off from the scale.

horizontal line in this figure just touches the first interior minimum value 30·198, diff. ·101. The same lines in fig. 2 are respectively 30·115 and 30·062, diff. ·053, and in fig. 3 29·650 and 29·600, diff. ·050: it is likely the *true* difference was less. The above numbers relative to fig. 3 are those taken from the curve of 1798. It is to be remarked that the second interior minimum in that year was the lowest. The principal difference between the curves of 1798 and 1847 consists in the greater elevation of the central portion of the curve of 1798. The curve of 1846 appears to exhibit the greatest deviation from symmetry.

The preceding remarks refer more particularly to the *phase* presented by the *curve* in any given locality, and also to the *deviations in certain directions* from a well-recognised *type*, embodying the essential characteristics of the curve during a definite period; and although this period is *variable* within certain limits, yet the similarity of the curves (such similarity consisting, as before noticed, in a peculiarity of character, by which the individuality of the curve is readily recognised) appears to be confirmatory of the idea suggested by the observations of 1845, namely, that we have obtained the *type of the barometric oscillations during the middle portion of November*. The occurrence of the *curve* in the year 1798, its appearance at Dublin in twelve out of seventeen years' observations between 1829 and 1845, together with the regularity of its return at London from 1841 to 1847, must certainly place this matter beyond a mere hope, as expressed in 1845, and lead to the conviction that a careful study of these curves will enable us to make out some of their *laws*. At all events, the attentive meteorological observer has already been so far successful as to recognise the last in its earliest stage, confirming, to a certain extent, the view of Sir John Herschel, expressed in his Report on Meteorological Reductions\*, 1843. " And it would be no small meteorological discovery, if, by the study of the character and progress of barometrical fluctuations, we could either make out any law of the greater ones which would enable us even roughly to predict them, or any peculiarity in their physiognomy by which we could recognise them in their earlier stages, as by this we might possibly be led to the prediction of great storms."

This remark of Sir John's clearly indicates the *two* directions in which this interesting study is to be prosecuted,—the *characters* of the barometric fluctuations and also their *progress*. The reader will find each of these branches amplified

\* Reports of the British Association for the Advancement of Science, 1843, p. 99.

in my Report on Atmospheric Waves, presented to the British Association in 1846*. "First, the determination of the *phases* of the larger undulations, with the smaller secondary waves superposed on their slopes, forming the *types* of the various seasons of the year; and second, the absolute extent of each atmospheric wave in space, the direction of its crest, its amplitude in miles, the altitude of its crest above, and the depression of its troughs below the surface of general repose of the atmosphere, the place of its formation, the manner in which it is propagated, the precise direction and extent of its motion, the force with which it is translated from place to place, and the locality of its final extinction."

In addition to the determination of the type of the middle portion of November, now generally known as the great symmetrical barometric wave of November, we are, I apprehend, on the eve of ascertaining the type for November during its whole extent. I have now before me a chart of the barometric movements at Halifax during the last November; and if I mistake not, the *characters* of the entire oscillations closely agree with those of preceding Novembers. The annual depression on or about the 28th † is most distinctly marked; and the opposite character, that of a high barometer at the commencement of the month, is as distinct. 1842 presented us with an elevated mercurial column at the commencement of November: the same order of things occurred in 1845 and 1846; and there is a high probability that the movements preceding the great wave occur at a much greater altitude than those succeeding it. Figs. 4 and 5 are curves of the annual depression on or about the 28th, as it passed London in 1847 and 1798. In 1798 the epoch was a day earlier. The horizontal line in fig. 4 represents an altitude of 30·000, in fig. 5 its value is 29·500. It is worthy of remark that this depression in 1847 was succeeded by an enormous wave, which passed its maximum on the night between the 1st and 2nd of December, value 30·397. This maximum forms the December boundary of the depression of the 28th, see fig. 4. Upon the passage of this maximum the barometer commenced falling rapidly, and continued thus falling, with one or two interruptions, until early on the morning of the 7th, when at 5·35 A.M. the reading of the barometer at London was 28·573. Thus the depressions of the 28th of November and the 7th of December form the anterior and posterior troughs of this immense wave, its altitude from the

* Reports of the British Association for the Advancement of Science, 1846, p. 163.
† Phil. Mag. S. 3. vol. xxix. p. 359.

Curves of the Great Symmetrical Barometric Wave, and the depression of the 28th Nov. 1846, 1847, and 1798.

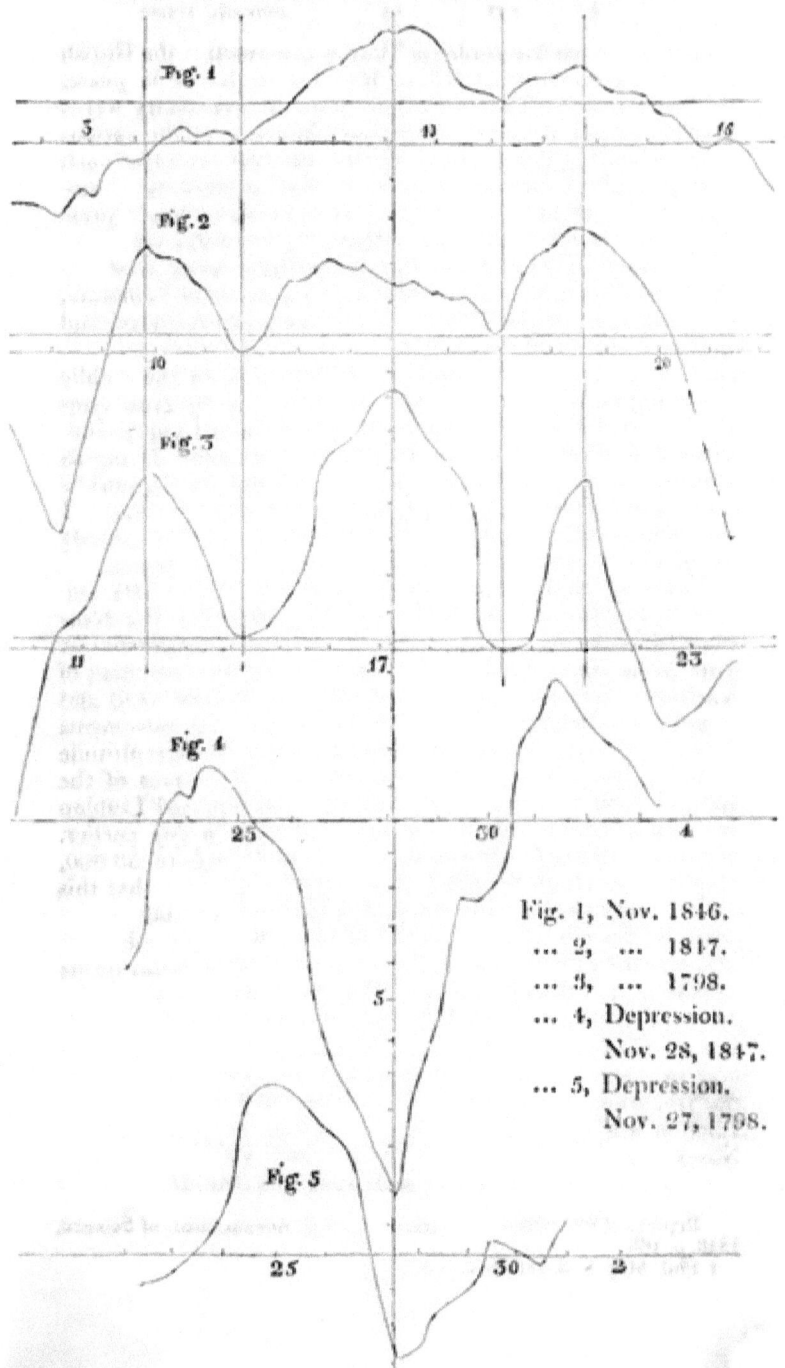

Fig. 1, Nov. 1846.
... 2, ... 1847.
... 3, ... 1798.
... 4, Depression. Nov. 28, 1847.
... 5, Depression. Nov. 27, 1798.

posterior trough to the apex being 1·624 inch\*. The depression of the 7th of December appears to have been an *extraordinary* depression, somewhat of the character of the depressions on December 25, 1810, and 1821. (See Phil. Mag. vol. xxx. p. 18.) The vast magnitude of this wave, its amplitude in time, stretching over nine days, fifteen hours and twenty minutes, during the whole of which the barometer was rapidly changing, the acuminated character of its troughs and crest, connected with the unusual epoch of its posterior trough, will render it a most interesting subject for investigation. The *phase*, as exhibited at London, is so well-marked, that every deviation from it in other localities can be readily ascertained, the depression of the December minimum below that of November clearly and distinctly assigned, and, I apprehend, with such precision, that a chart of deviation from symmetry—regarding perfect symmetry as indicated by the equal altitudes of the two minima—easily constructed, and the rate of progress and direction of motion correctly deduced from the epochs of maximum and minima. I am not aware that an instance has fallen under my notice so suitable for carrying on the inquiry with success, as the wave which transited on the 1st of December 1847.

In taking up the investigation of this wave with an especial view to the second branch of the inquiry, as noticed above, it must be borne in mind that *the curve of the barometric movements from November 28 to December 7 is* not likely to exhibit a *section* of an atmospheric wave, properly so called. It has already been determined that "the barometric curve, including a complete rise and fall at any one station, is *not* the curve resulting from the transit of any *one* wave; it does *not* represent the *form* of any *reality* in nature; but it *does* represent, and is an exponent of, the effects resulting from the contemporaneous transits of waves, or systems of waves†." The first step is to ascertain the absolute *difference* of pressure existing between any two or more stations‡. For this purpose all the observations must be corrected and reduced to the *level of the sea*, and then the slopes of the individual waves will become apparent, and the directions of the crests and troughs determined. From such an investigation, some notion may be

\* The true altitude of this wave, as determined from the Greenwich observations, appears to have been 1·855 inch; the epoch of the minimum of the 7th was 2·35 A.M., value 28·381; and the amplitude rather less than here stated.

† Reports of the British Association for the Advancement of Science, 1846, p. 138.

‡ The more numerous the stations the more accurate will be the results obtained.

formed of the vast extent these waves generally cover. The transference of the points or lines of maxima and minima, as existing in space and as determined by this mode of discussion, will give the directions in which the waves are moving, and also the rate of their progress. A new field of view opens upon the mind in thus studying barometric phænomena. The types forming the first branch of the inquiry become inlets to the knowledge of movements of vast extent, and of realities, which although *unseen* by us, produce the most terrific commotions in the atmosphere. The wave of which we have been speaking has not passed over the United Kingdom, nor has it swept the shores of sea-girt Britain, without leaving melancholy traces of its progress. Could we ascend in our inquiries from the contemplation of the rotatory storm, as determined by Redfield and Reid, to the production of such storm by the crossing of two large long waves, as suggested by Sir John Herschel in his Report on Meteorological Reductions, from which we have already quoted, an important step would be gained. Sir John states\*, " There is certainly one point of view in which some of the phænomena of revolving gales would seem capable of explanation \* \* \* \*, and in which they would become traced up, not to 'funnel-shaped revolving depressions' in the nature of water-spouts, but simply to the crossing of two large long waves running in different directions. The way in which a rotary movement in an ellipse or circle, or in some other partly oval and partly rectilineal figure, may result from the combination of two rectilineal movements of advance and recess, will easily be understood by the analogy of the circular and elliptic polarization of light, where rectilinear movements of the ætherial molecules are conceived to be similarly combined. Some features in such storms are strongly in harmony with this view; viz. the fact, that in them the direction of the wind at a given locality never makes more than one rotation, and not always that; and that in the central line of the storm's progress, there is a simple and sudden reversal of direction. On the other hand, it must not be concealed that some features militate against it; for instance, the fact that such gales are stated always to 'revolve' in one direction; whereas on this view of their origin, the changes of wind ought to be in opposite directions, on opposite sides of the medial line."

In an article which the writer communicated to Mr. Lowe of Highfield House near Nottingham, and which is inserted in that gentleman's work on Atmospheric Phænomena, an attempt has been made to exhibit the connexion, which there

\* Reports of the British Association for the Advancement of Science, 1843, p. 100.

is great reason to believe exists, between the atmospheric wave and the rotatory gale: the direction of the wind in both cases is the same. With respect to the atmospheric wave, it is shown in my Third Report*, "that the direction of the aërial current on the anterior slope (the barometer *rising*) is at right angles to the axis of translation directed towards the *left-hand*; while on the posterior slope (the barometer *falling*) it is the reverse, still at right angles to the axis of translation, but directed towards the *right-hand*." In the article alluded to, it is shown that the same holds good in the case of the revolving storm. As the first half of the storm approaches, the wind rushes by the observer towards the *right-hand* with a *falling* barometer; as the second half of the storm passes off, the direction of the wind is reversed,—it rushes past towards the *left-hand* with a *rising* barometer. The great point, however, is to establish the existence of a rotatory storm in connexion with the crossing of two large waves. To this there appears at present a considerable *drawback*, on account of the immense size of the waves, and the great dearth of observations in certain localities and directions, especially on the surface of the ocean, which prevents the clear apprehension of the waves in the complete totality of their existence. This might be obviated to a great extent by the establishment of observations at all civil, military and naval stations, and on board all Her Majesty's vessels, government steamers, merchants' ships, &c.; and if these observations were collected and preserved in an office appointed for their reception, where they might undergo a searching and rigorous discussion, our knowledge of these movements would speedily be greatly increased, and their connexion or nonconnexion with the rotary gale finally determined. It appears from a letter addressed by Prof. Loomis to Colonel Sabine, and inserted in a late Number of this Magazine, that an extensive system of meteorological observations is likely to be set on foot in the United States, *provided the co-operation of the British Government can be obtained*. "What I propose," says the Professor, "is that at every *government station* a register should be kept for a period of one, two, or three years." Should this plan be carried out for Canada, it would greatly contribute to the complete solution of any problem that might be suggested, at once to make the system *general*, and include every portion of the terrestrial surface subject to the authority of the British Government, and obtain observations from every portion of the oceanic surface accessible to our vessels. Under these circumstances, any results obtained from the American

* Reports of the British Association for the Advancement of Science, 1846, p. 136.

observations would receive considerable elucidation from observations made on the Atlantic, the West Indies, and the western shores of Europe.

I cannot close these remarks without referring to the preservation of H.M.S. Vernon, last July, in consequence of a knowledge of the law of storms, by which she was enabled to avoid a typhoon while sailing in the China seas. In the Illustrated News of November 20th, a letter with a diagram is inserted, exhibiting the altered course of the ship *to allow the typhoon to pass*. In introducing the subject, the writer observes, " that among the many *things unseen* by which we are surrounded, high winds are subjected to fixed laws, affecting their motions and durations, and directed in their courses by the same unerring hand that regulates in wisdom the more *visible things* of creation." A note is also added, which we give entire. ["The 'circular theory of storms' is strongly recommended to the notice of sailors; and they will find much assistance also from *daily observations of the barometer*, and of the dry- and wet-bulb thermometer. We will take this opportunity of recommending meteorologists more fully to investigate the subject of the theory of storms. The writer of this has been in a locality where the air has been in a calm state, while at the same time (as he has learned from letters addressed to him) a gale of wind has been blowing around him, the direction of the wind in some places being due east, in others due west, and blowing from different points at other places at the same time."—J. G.] In the above extracts we find the results of a practical application of the knowledge derived from the investigation of such subjects as we have been treating of; and if Sir John Herschel's suggestion is correct, that the circular storm results from the crossing of two large atmospheric waves, then not only is it desirable that meteorologists should more fully investigate the theory of storms, but they should extend their inquiries, and look beyond the storm to those vast movements which sweep over the entire continent of Europe, stretching from its extreme south-western to its extreme northern point, and follow them as they majestically roll over the surfaces of our oceans and continents, and endeavour to detect in the points of their intersections the gyrative tornados which every spring and autumn visit our coasts, and spread devastation and death wherever their destructive influence is felt. A knowledge of the laws of atmospheric waves must greatly contribute to our knowledge of the circular storm.

Let

$$x = A_1, x^4 - A_2 x^3 - A_3 x^2 - A_4 x - A_5 = 0$$

be the general equation of the fifth degree. Also let

$$y = x - a = x - r.$$

and represent the transformed equation in $y$ by

$$y^5 - B_1 y^4 - B_2 y^3 - B_3 y^2 - B_4 y - B_5 = 0;$$

then this last equation may be put under the form

$$\left(y - \tfrac{1}{5} B_1\right)^5 - B'_2 y^3 - B'_3 y^2 - C_4\left(y - \tfrac{1}{5} B_1\right) - C_5 = 0,$$

where

$$B'_2 = B_2 - \tfrac{2}{5} B^2_1; \quad B'_3 = B_3 - \tfrac{4}{5^2} B^3_1;$$

$$C_4 = B_4 - \tfrac{1}{5^3} B^4_1; \quad C_5 = B_5 - \tfrac{1}{5} B'_1 - \tfrac{1}{5} B_1 C_4;$$

now, making

$$z = y + \tfrac{1}{5} B_1,$$

we shall have transformed the given equation in $x$ into the following:

$$z^5 + C_4 z + C_5 = 0, \quad \ldots \ldots \quad (1.)$$

provided that $x$, $y$, and $z$ satisfy the conditions

$$B'_2 = 0, \text{ and } B'_3 = 0.$$

* Communicated by the Author.

Since these conditions are equations involving three undetermined quantities $x$, $y$ and $z$, they may with propriety be denoted by

$$\varphi(x, y, z) = 0, \quad \ldots \ldots \quad (2.)$$

and

$$\psi(x, y, z) = 0 \quad \ldots \ldots \quad (3.)$$

respectively; and, since two dimensions of $x$, $y$, $z$ appear in (2.), and three in (3.), the former condition will in general represent a surface of the second, and the latter a surface of the third order.

I have in this work (S. 3. vol. xxviii. pp. 132, 133) already adverted to my own process for reducing equations of the fifth degree to a trinomial form. With what facility such reduction may be performed, at least so far as the decomposition of (2.) into linear factors is concerned, will be seen on referring to my papers on analytical geometry in the last and in the current volume of the Mechanics' Magazine.

It would not be difficult to show that when (2.) represents a hyperbolic paraboloid, a hyperboloid of one sheet, a cone, a cylinder, a pair of planes, a single plane, or a single straight line, then (2.) and (3.) can be satisfied simultaneously by real values of $x$, $y$, and $z$. In this case $C_4$ and $C_5$ will be real.

When (2.) represents a hyperboloid of two sheets, an elliptic paraboloid, an ellipsoid, a point, or an unreal surface, (2.) and (3.) cannot be so satisfied, and $C_4$ and $C_5$ will be in general both unreal.

Should $C_4$ and $C_5$, or either of them, prove to be unreal under the above assumption for $v$, it might be a question whether both those quantities would not take real values under some other assumption, such as

$$v = xu^\alpha + yu^\beta + zu^\gamma + u^\delta;$$

but I am very strongly of opinion that they would not, and I am inclined to think that the reality of $C_4$ and $C_5$ depends upon the nature of the roots of the given equation in $u$. [There is perhaps some analogy between the question before us and that of the irreducible case in cubic equations.] If this be the correct view, no change of process can affect the final result; and we may apply, not only to Mr. Jerrard's, but to the above, and to every possible method of effecting this transformation, the remark of Sir W. R. Hamilton, that the coefficients of the transformed equation will often be unreal when those of the given one are real.

II. This appears to be the proper place for explaining an error into which I fell at page 132 of a previous volume of this work (vol. xxviii. just cited). I there omitted to notice that the quantities $l'$ and $l''$, being perfectly arbitrary, may be supposed to satisfy not only the equation (c.) but also the following,

$$\Lambda'''x_a^{\lambda'''} + \Lambda^{iv}x_a^{\lambda^{iv}} = l'x_a^{\lambda'} + l''x_a^{\lambda''}, \quad \ldots \quad (d'.)$$

where $x_a$ is a root other than $x_s$. Let $x_a$ be $x_{n-1}$, then

$$l_{n-1} = 0; \quad \ldots \quad \ldots \quad \ldots \quad (e'.)$$

and we must write $[l_1 \ldots l_{n-2}]^2$ instead of $[l_1 \ldots l_{n-1}]^2$ in equation (f.). But in this case, in order that we may satisfy

$$[l_1 \ldots l_{n-2}]^2 = 0 \quad \ldots \quad \ldots \quad (g'.)$$

without making the $l$'s vanish, we have the condition

$$n - 2 > 1,$$

or $n = 4$ at least; and $_aY$ may be of such a form as to render it necessary that $n$ be not less than 5, which is the case in the transformation above considered. As to this, see page 395 of the last-mentioned volume, where I have pointed out the error here discussed, but not in such a manner as to make the foregoing explanation superfluous.

III. As connected with, and by way of concluding, this part of the subject, let

$$w = \frac{w'}{b};$$

then (1.) gives

$$w'^5 + b^4 C_4 w' + b^5 C_5 = 0,$$

which will be of the form

$$w'^5 + Dw' + D^5 = 0, \quad \ldots \quad \ldots \quad (4.)$$

provided that

$$b = \left(\frac{C_5}{C_4^5}\right)^{\frac{1}{4}}.$$

Now let

$$w' = \chi(D)$$

be a solution of (4.), then

$$D = \chi(w')$$

will also be a solution: by combining these solutions we obtain the functional equation

$$\chi^2(w') = w', \text{ or } \chi^2(D) = D;$$

and the same result might be obtained from any trinomial equation of the fifth degree—as I have already noticed (vol. xxviii. p. 133, note).

IV. At pages 190, 191 of the same (28th) volume of the present work, there occur errors resembling those at pages

132, 133, and which may be corrected in a similar manner. For this purpose let

$$L_a^m = \Lambda^m \left( x_a^{\lambda^m} - \frac{\gamma_2}{\gamma_3} x_a^{\lambda'''} \right);$$

then it is, in substance, assumed (p. 190) that the equation

$$L_a^{iv} + L_a^v + \ldots L_a^{xi} = l' x_a^{\lambda'} + l'' \left( x_a^{\lambda''} - \frac{\gamma_2}{\gamma_3} x_a^{\lambda'''} \right) \quad . \quad (5.)$$

is only true for $a = n$, that is to say, for the root $x_n$. But the two quantities $l'$ and $l''$ may be taken so as to render this relation true, not only for $a = n$, but also for another value of $a$, which we may select at pleasure from among the suffixes of the roots. Let this other value be $n-1$, then (5.) will hold for the root $x_{n-1}$, and we have

$$l_{n-1} = 0;$$

so that it becomes necessary in the group ($\alpha$) to write $l_{n-2}$ instead of $l_{n-1}$, and consequently to change ($\alpha$.) into

$$\begin{array}{l}[l_1 . l_{n-2}]^2{}_1 = f_1{}^2(n-2) = 0 \\ [l_1 . l_{n-2}]^2{}_2 = f_2{}^2(n-2) = 0 \\ [l_1 . l_{n-2}]^3 = f^3(n-2) = 0 \end{array} \Bigg\} \quad \ldots \quad (\alpha'.)$$

where $f^a(b)$ denotes a *homogeneous* function of the $a$th degree and of $b$ undetermined quantities. Hence we have

$$n - 2 > 3, \text{ or } n > 5, \quad \ldots \quad (\nu'.)$$

whence the least admissible value of $n$ is 6, or, in critical cases, 7, and the equation of the fifth degree cannot (to say nothing of the additional difficulty occasioned by the occurrence of critical functions) be solved by means of the processes under our consideration, although those processes enable us to effect certain transformations of equations of degrees higher than the fifth (vol. xxviii. p. 395).

2 Church Yard Court, Temple,
 November 18, 1847.

*Postscript.*—I venture to hope that the time is now approaching when we may expect a discussion of the physico-mathematical problem connected with the Spheroidal Condition of Liquids. I regret that I have not had an opportunity of making an attempt, however humble, at its solution; and I would add that the enunciation of it, contained in a letter (signed S.X.) which I addressed to Mr. Taylor from Great Oakley some two years since, and which will be found at pp. 568, 569 of vol. xxvii. of this work, may be advantageously modified.—J. C.

## VIII. *On the Analysis of Hop-Ash.* By HENRY WATTS, B.A., *Assistant in the Laboratory of University College, London.**

THE hops, the ash of which forms the subject of the following analysis, were of the variety called "the Grape." They were grown last year at Hawkhurst in Kent, on a good soil, being a stiff clay loam resting on the Hastings sand. The produce was 12 cwt. per acre, which is rather above the average produce of the district, the quantity being ascertained after the hops had been taken from the kiln, cooled and bagged.

The hops in this state lost $11\frac{1}{2}$ per cent. by drying at 212°.

1000 grs. of the hops in the same state burnt in an earthen crucible yielded in four experiments, 62, 65, 67 and 64 grs. of ash. The mean of these is 64·5; hence the quantity of ash is about $6\frac{1}{2}$ per cent.

The appearance of the ash was highly ferruginous.

### *Qualitative Analysis.*

A portion of the ash was exhausted with water, and the soluble and insoluble portions separately examined.

The soluble portion of the ash was found by the usual reagents to contain carbonic, sulphuric, phosphoric and silicic acids and chlorine. The bases were potash and a little soda.

The insoluble portion, in like manner, was found to contain lime, magnesia, alumina and peroxide of iron, in combination with carbonic and phosphoric acids, together with a considerable quantity of siliceous sandy matter insoluble in acids, and a little unburnt charcoal. This after ignition was further examined by fusion with carbonate of soda, and found to consist of silica, with traces of alumina, oxide of iron and lime. The presence of phosphate of alumina being unexpected, great pains were taken in this part of the analysis to place the matter beyond question.

### *Quantitative Analysis.*

#### A. *Proportions of soluble and insoluble matter.*

1. 100 grs. of the ash (recently ignited) were boiled in water. The insoluble portion was collected on a weighed filter and thoroughly washed.

  Insoluble matter dried at 300° weighed 64·72 grs.
  Therefore soluble matter   ...  35·28 ...

---

* Communicated by the Chemical Society; having been read May 3, 1847.

2. 50 grs. of ash treated in the same manner gave—
  Insoluble matter $=31\cdot87=63\cdot74$ per cent.
  Soluble matter $=18\cdot13=36\cdot26$ ...

3. These results differ by about 1 per cent.; the difference probably arises from the slow decomposition of an alkaline silicate by continued digestion in hot water.

Taking the mean of the two results, we have—
  Matter insoluble in water $=64\cdot23$ per cent.
  ... soluble ... $=35\cdot77$ ...

B. *Matter soluble in water.*

I. *Acids and Chlorine.*—1. Alkaline liquid from 100 grs. of ash (A. 1) concentrated by evaporation to the bulk of 1000 water grain-measures, then divided into four equal portions.

2. First portion decomposed by sulphuric acid in flask-apparatus gave $0\cdot54$ gr. of carbonic acid $=2\cdot16$ per cent.

3. Second portion treated with chloride of barium and nitric acid gave $6\cdot03$ grs. of sulphate of baryta: therefore $2\cdot07$ grs. of sulphuric acid $=8\cdot28$ per cent.

4. Third portion treated with [nitrate of silver and nitric acid gave $2\cdot29$ grs. of chloride of silver: therefore $0\cdot564$ gr. of chlorine $=2\cdot26$ per cent.

5. Fourth portion mixed with solution of pernitrate of iron made by dissolving $3\cdot68$ grs. of good iron wire (harpsichord wire) in nitric acid, and therefore containing $5\cdot26$ grs. of peroxide of iron. The liquid being then treated with excess of ammonia, the precipitate washed, dried and ignited, was found to weigh $5\cdot47$ grs.; and deducting $5\cdot26$ grs. of peroxide of iron, there remains $0\cdot21$ gr. of phosphoric acid, or $0\cdot84$ per cent.

II. *Silica and Alkalies.*—1. Alkaline liquid from 50 grs. of ash (A. 2) acidulated with hydrochloric acid and evaporated to dryness; residue digested in dilute hydrochloric acid, silica collected on filter, washed, dried and ignited, weighed $1\cdot22$ gr. $=2\cdot44$ per cent.

2. Filtered solution treated with baryta-water to separate sulphuric and phosphoric acids; excess of baryta removed by carbonate of ammonia; filtered liquid evaporated to dryness, and ammoniacal salts driven off by ignition; the residue consisting of chlorides of fixed alkalies, weighed 16 grs. $=32$ per cent.

3. $2\cdot25$ grs. of these mixed chlorides dissolved in water and treated in the usual manner with $3\frac{1}{2}$ times their weight of sodio-chloride of platinum, gave $7\cdot06$ grs. of chloride of platinum and potassium, corresponding to $2\cdot157$ grs. of chloride of potassium. Now $2\cdot25:32::2\cdot157:30\cdot68$; we have therefore

Chloride of potassium 30·68 p. c. = 19·41 p. c. of potash.
... sodium 1·32 ... = 0·70 ... of soda.
———— ————
32·00 20·11

### C. *Matter insoluble in water.*

I. *Siliceous sandy matter.*—Insoluble matter from 100 grs. of ash (A. 1) boiled in hydrochloric acid; liquid evaporated to dryness to render silica perfectly insoluble; residue digested in dilute hydrochloric acid; undissolved matter, consisting of silica and charcoal, collected on weighed filter, washed and dried at 300°.

Silica and charcoal weighed . 18·26 grs.
Silica (after ignition) . . . 15·44 ...
therefore Charcoal . . . . . . . . 2·82 ...

II. *Earthy Phosphates.*—1. Filtered solution (C. I.) treated with excess of ammonia yielded a precipitate which being washed, dried and ignited, gave of earthy phosphates 27·26 grs.

2. Phosphates, after ignition, dissolved in hot hydrochloric acid and reprecipitated by ammonia; precipitate digested in warm acetic acid to dissolve phosphates of lime and magnesia; the insoluble portion consisting of phosphates of iron and alumina weighed 8·25 grs.

3. Phosphates of iron and alumina redissolved in hot hydrochloric acid; solution boiled with excess of caustic potash, undissolved portion collected on filter, washed, dried and ignited, gave

Weight of phosphate of iron . = 4·57 grs.
Therefore phosphate of alumina = 3·68 ...
————
8·25 ...

4. Alkaline solution (C. II. 3) boiled with sal-ammoniac, gave a precipitate of phosphate of alumina, which weighed only 1·8 gr. instead of 3·68; but the liquid filtered from this precipitate gave, when treated by Berthier's process, a quantity of phosphoric acid weighing 1·91 gr., which, added to 1·80 gr., gives 3·71 grs. for the quantity of phosphate of alumina, differing by only 0·03 gr. from 3·68 grs. We may infer from this that the quantity of phosphoric acid in combination with alumina is about 2·5 per cent.

5. To determine the quantity of phosphoric acid in combination with oxide of iron, the 4·57 grs. of phosphate of iron (C. II. 3) were redissolved in hot hydrochloric acid, and the solution treated with ammonia and sulphuret of ammonium:

the sulphuret of iron, after washing, was oxidized by nitric acid and the oxide of iron precipitated by ammonia. The result was

|  | Oxide of iron | 2·71 grs. |
|---|---|---|
| therefore | Phosphoric acid | 1·86 ... |
|  |  | 4·57 ... |

6. Acetic acid solution (C. II. 2) containing the phosphates of lime and magnesia treated with oxalate of ammonia; oxalate of lime washed, dried and ignited, gave 14·23 grs. of carbonate of lime = 7·97 grs. of lime.

7. Liquid filtered from lime, treated with excess of ammonia, gave

Pyrophosphate of magnesia 4·37 = $\begin{cases} 2·77 \text{ phosphoric acid.} \\ 1·60 \text{ magnesia.} \end{cases}$

8. The quantity of phosphoric acid in combination with lime was determined by difference; thus

Total quantity of earthy phosphates = 27·26 grs.

| Phosphates of iron and alumina | 8·25 grs. |  |
|---|---|---|
| Phosphate of magnesia | 4·37 ... |  |
| Lime | 7·97 ... |  |
| Making together | ——— | 20·59 ... |
| Therefore phosphoric acid | | 6·67 ... |

This is very nearly the quantity required to form the tribasic phosphate; for the combining number of lime being 28, and that of phosphoric acid 71·38, we have

$$84 : 71·38 :: 7·97 : 6·77,$$

which result differs by 0·1 from 6·67.

The quantity of phosphate of lime is 7·97 + 6·67 = 14·64.

9. If we reckon as above (C. II. 4) the quantity of phosphoric acid in the phosphate of alumina at 2·5 per cent., we have for the total quantity of phosphoric acid in the insoluble part of the ash 6·67 + 2·77 + 1·86 + 2·50 = 13·80. Adding to this the quantity contained in the soluble portion (B. I. 5), viz. 0·84, the total amount of phosphoric acid will be 14·64 per cent.

III. *Carbonates of Lime and Magnesia.*—1. Liquid filtered from precipitated phosphates (C. II. 1), boiled with oxalate of ammonia, precipitate washed, dried and ignited, gave carbonate of lime 11·04 grs., containing 6·18 grs. of lime and 4·86 grs. of carbonic acid.

2. Filtrate containing magnesia evaporated to dryness; residue ignited to drive off ammoniacal salts and redissolved in hydrochloric acid. Solution mixed with carbonate of soda

in excess, boiled briskly for half an hour and filtered; filtrate evaporated quickly to dryness, residue digested in boiling water, and undissolved portion added to precipitate on filter; precipitate of carbonate of magnesia washed, dried and ignited, gave 3·74 grs. of magnesia.

To determine the quantity of carbonic acid in combination with this, we have 20·67 : 22 :: 3·74 : 3·99, this added to 3·74 grs. of magnesia, gives 7·73 grs. of carbonate of magnesia.

3. From this it appears that the total quantity of carbonic acid in combination with lime and magnesia is 4·86 + 3·99 = 8·85 grs.

To verify this, the carbonic acid was determined directly from the insoluble portion of 50 grs. of ash (A. 2). This insoluble matter weighed 31·87 grs. or 63·74 per cent. Of this, 14·27 grs. decomposed by hydrochloric acid in flask apparatus, gave 2·07 grs. of carbonic acid. Now

$$14·27 : 63·74 :: 2·07 : 9·24.$$

This quantity differs by 0·39 from 8·85, the calculated quantity. The excess is probably due to the escape of a little hydrochloric acid during the boiling of the liquid in the flask apparatus. The estimation of the lime and magnesia is more to be depended upon than that of the carbonic acid.

### Summary.

The phosphoric, carbonic and silicic acids exist both in the soluble and insoluble portions of the ash.

The total quantity of phosphoric acid has been already estimated approximately at 14·64 per cent. (C. II. 9).

The quantity of carbonic acid in the soluble portion is 2·16 (B. I. 2), and in the insoluble 8·85 (C. III. 3), making together 11·01 per cent.

The quantity of silica in the soluble part is 2·44 (B. II. 1), and in the insoluble part 15·44 (C. I.), making together 17·88 per cent.

The total quantity of lime is 14·15 per cent., viz. 7·97 in the phosphate, and 6·18 in the carbonate (C. II. 6, and C. III. 1).

The magnesia amounts to 5·34 per cent., 1·60 being in the state of phosphate (C. II. 7) and 3·74 in that of carbonate.

The total quantity of alkaline bases (potash and soda) is 20·11 per cent. (B. II. 3). From this we must deduct the quantity of oxygen corresponding to 2·26 of chlorine (B. I. 4), viz. 0·51, because portions of the potassium and sodium are in the state of chlorides.

Finally, then, we have for the constituents of the hop-ash,—

I. *Acids.*

|  |  |
|---|---|
| Phosphoric acid | 14·64 |
| Sulphuric acid | 8·28 |
| Silicic acid | 17·88 |
| Carbonic acid | 11·01 |
| Chlorine | 2·26 |
|  | ——— 54·07 |

II. *Bases.*

|  |  |
|---|---|
| Potash | 19·41 |
| Soda | 0·70 |
| Lime | 14·15 |
| Magnesia | 5·34 |
| Alumina | 1·18 |
| Peroxide of iron | 2·71 |
|  | 43·49 |
| Deduct oxygen | 0·51 |
|  | ——— 42·98 |
| Charcoal and loss | 2·95 |
|  | 100·00 |

These materials we may suppose to be arranged as follows:—

I. *Matter soluble in water.*

|  |  |
|---|---|
| Chloride of sodium | 1·32 |
| Chloride of potassium | 3·09 |
| Carbonate of potash | 6·79 |
| Sulphate of potash | 18·05 |
| Phosphate (tribasic) | 2·50 |
| Silicate of potash | 3·83 |
|  | ——— 35·58 |

II. *Matter soluble in acids.*

|  |  |
|---|---|
| Carbonate of lime | 11·04 |
| Carbonate of magnesia | 7·73 |
| Phosphate of lime | 14·64 |
| Phosphate of magnesia | 4·37 |
| Phosphate of alumina | 3·68 |
| Phosphate of iron | 4·57 |
|  | ——— 46·03 |

III. *Insoluble matter.*

|  |  |
|---|---|
| Silica, &c. | 15·44 |
| Charcoal | 2·82 |
|  | ——— 18·26 |
|  | 99·87 |

The sum of the soluble ingredients thus determined, viz.

35·58, differs by only 0·19 from 35·77, the amount of the same directly determined (A. 3).

The sum of the components which are insoluble in water, viz. 46·03 + 18·26 = 64·29, differs by 0·06 from the quantity of the same directly determined, viz. 64·23.

The loss on the whole analysis is 0·13 per cent.

*Quantities of materials removed from an acre of land by the crop.*

The produce, as stated at the commencement of the paper, was 12 cwt. per acre, and the amount of ash is 6½ per cent. This gives 87 lbs. 6 ozs. of ash to the produce of an acre. Hence it is easy to calculate the quantities of the several mineral ingredients of the hops removed from an acre. In this estimate no account need be taken of the bines, since they are rotted and returned as manure to the soil.

The quantities of the several constituents are as follows:—

|  | lbs. | oz. |
|---|---|---|
| Phosphoric acid | 12 | 13 |
| Potash | 17 | 0 |
| Lime | 12 | 6 |
| Magnesia | 4 | 11 |
| Sulphuric acid | 7 | 4 |
| Silica | 15 | 10 |
| Alumina, oxide of iron and common salt | 6 | 15 |
|  | 76 | 11 |

By way of comparison the following statement of the inorganic materials removed by a heavy crop of grain (not including straw or chaff) of the estimated yield of 42 bushels to an acre*, extracted from the excellent report of Messrs. Way and Ogston in the Agricultural Journal, vol. vii. part 2, may prove interesting.

From each acre were removed,—

|  | lbs. | oz. |
|---|---|---|
| Phosphoric acid | 21 | 4 |
| Potash | 13 | 1 |
| Magnesia | 5 | 5 |
| Silica, sulphuric acid, oxide of iron, and soda | 3 | 7 |
|  | 43 | 1 |

It is well-known that the cultivation of hops is carried on by a most lavish application of farm-yard manure to the ruin

* Specimen No. 41, p. 631.

of every other crop, the rest of the land being defrauded of its due share of nourishment to supply the increasing demands of the hop-garden: and further, that in this cultivation there is no relief by alternating crops or fallows, unless the occasional failures from blight and other causes may be so termed. The quantity of alkali thus removed every year exceeds that of a very heavy crop of grain, while the phosphoric acid amounts to more than half that of the latter. It is probable also that the quantities of phosphoric and sulphuric acids present in the ash do not indicate the total quantities of sulphur and phosphorus removed from the soil, inasmuch as portions of these elements may exist in the plants as proteine-compounds.

---

IX. *Experimental Researches on Figures of Equilibrium of a Liquid Mass withdrawn from the Action of Gravity: Second Series.* By M. PLATEAU[*].

THE theory of capillary action, as established by the labours of Laplace, Poisson, &c., is not limited to the explanation of the cause of the ascension or the depression of liquids in narrow spaces, and the determination of the laws which regulate this phænomenon; it also permits, as is well known, of our arriving at the differential equation which represents the free surface of a liquid, in circumstances where the form of that surface is influenced by molecular attraction, as for example at the summit of the raised or depressed column in a capillary tube, along the sides of a solid body in part immersed, &c. But this equation cannot be integrated but by approximation, so that it is impossible to determine strictly the forms of the surface in question. On the other hand, on account of the preponderating action of gravity, the influence of molecular attraction can only become observable on surfaces, or portions of surfaces, which present but a small extent either in all directions or at least in one direction, such as the surface which terminates a capillary column, that of a liquid drop placed on a solid plane which it cannot moisten, the portion of the surface of a liquid raised along the sides of the vessel which contains it, &c. It would consequently be very difficult to verify by accurate admeasurements this important part of the theory; and it has hitherto remained almost without any other confirmation than that deduced from the simple aspect of the phænomena.

Now it will be remembered that in his preceding memoir

[*] From an abstract by M. Quetelet, published in the *Bulletin de l'Académie Royale de Belgique*. The First Series of these interesting investigations appeared in the 13th Part of the Scientific Memoirs.

(Taylor's Scientific Memoirs, part xiii. p. 16) M. Plateau described a simple process, by means of which he succeeded in completely neutralizing the action of gravity upon a liquid mass of considerable volume, at the same time leaving this mass perfectly free to obey the molecular forces. If, therefore, as in the case of ordinary capillary phænomena, the attraction of a solid system is interposed, the form which the free surface of the mass will assume will be identically the same as if the liquid had been in reality deprived of all gravity. But then the equation relative to the surfaces of equilibrium is reduced to a very simple form, which allows, in several cases, of omitting the integration, and, on the other hand, nothing any longer limits the extent which may be given to surfaces, so that the results of experiment are susceptible of exact admeasurements. We are thus able to submit the theory to numerous and perfect verifications. This is one of the objects which M. Plateau proposed to himself in his researches, starting from the second series now laid before the Academy.

But his ingenious experiments, besides the support they give to the theory of capillary action, have another kind of interest, in so far as they exhibit the curious spectacle of figures of equilibrium suitable to a liquid deprived of gravity; the theoretical and experimental study of these figures forms a second object of research. The equation representing these figures shows at once that the sphere, the plane, and the cylinder must be found among them; now, the author has shown, in his preceding memoir, that when the liquid mass of his experiments is not adherent to any solid system, it always assumes precisely the spherical form. With respect to plane and cylindrical surfaces, as they are from their nature indefinitely extended, the first in all directions, and the second in the direction of its axis, it is evident that they cannot be assumed by a finite and entirely free mass; but the author obtains portions of them by causing the liquid mass to adhere to suitable solid systems.

The results at which he arrives on this subject lead him to realize polyhedrons entirely liquid, with the exception of their angles, which are formed of thin iron wires. He produces the cylinder by attaching the liquid mass to two rings of iron wire placed parallel one to the other.

The observation of certain peculiar facts relative to these liquid figures leads the author to several important consequences, among which we may mention the indication of a mode of experiment which would perhaps allow of arriving at the determination of a limit above which must be found the length of the radius of sensible activity of molecular attraction.

Lastly, the author deduces from a property of the liquid cylinder the complete theory of the constitution of liquid veins discharged through circular orifices,—a constitution so completely investigated experimentally by Savart, the cause of which, however, has remained without any satisfactory explanation. Although such a vein be formed of a liquid freely submitted to the action of gravity, M. Plateau shows that we may apply to it, somewhat modified, the considerations relative to a liquid upon which this force does not act.

The author announces, in conclusion, that in the following series he shall direct his attention to other figures of equilibrium of revolution than the sphere and the cylinder, and to figures not included in that class for which the equation may be interpreted in a strict manner.

---

X. *On some of the Products of Oxidation of Cumol by Nitric Acid.* By Mr. F. A. ABEL.[*]

FROM the investigations on the action of nitric acid upon organic bodies, *one* result, in reference to the manner in which this acid acts, has been undoubtedly established. We know that in most cases the carbon of the organic substance remains untouched; that according to the degree of concentration of the acid a smaller or larger number of equivalents of hydrogen are expelled, and that the remaining part of the organic body combines with the remainder of the nitric acid. Thus is produced that innumerable class of neutral compounds considered by some chemists to be combinations of nitrous acid with organic oxides, and by others to be products of the substitution of hyponitric acid for hydrogen. It is indifferent which of these views is adopted, the fact having been established by hundreds of experiments, and we are enabled by analogy to predict with tolerable certainty the result of any new experiment.

The case is quite different when the oxidation is not confined to the hydrogen, but is extended to the carbon. The numerous experiments made on this subject do not as yet afford any general conclusion; we are far from being able to form an opinion, previous to experiment, of the nature of the product formed. This will be obvious if we examine the action of nitric acid on a class of bodies which are very nearly related to each other, both by the manner in which they are formed and in their general chemical behaviour. Benzol, to-

[*] Communicated by the Chemical Society; having been read June 21, 1847.

luol, cinnamol (styrol), cumol, naphthalol, cymol, are acted upon by nitric acid, the corresponding products of substitution are formed.

Benzol . . $C_{12}H_6$   Nitrobenzol . . $C_{12}\begin{Bmatrix}H_5\\NO_4\end{Bmatrix}$   Dinitrobenzol . . $C_{12}\begin{Bmatrix}H_4\\2NO_4\end{Bmatrix}$

Toluol . . $C_{14}H_8$   Nitrotoluol . . $C_{14}\begin{Bmatrix}H_7\\NO_4\end{Bmatrix}$   Dinitrotoluol . . $C_{14}\begin{Bmatrix}H_6\\2NO_4\end{Bmatrix}$

Cinnamol . $C_{16}H_8$   Nitrocinnamol . $C_{16}\begin{Bmatrix}H_7\\NO_4\end{Bmatrix}$

Cumol . . $C_{18}H_{12}$   Nitrocumol . . $C_{18}\begin{Bmatrix}H_{11}\\NO_4\end{Bmatrix}$   Dinitrocumol . . $C_{18}\begin{Bmatrix}H_{10}\\2NO_4\end{Bmatrix}$

Naphthalol $C_{20}H_8$   Nitronaphthalol $C_{20}\begin{Bmatrix}H_7\\NO_4\end{Bmatrix}$   Dinitronaphthalol $C_{20}\begin{Bmatrix}H_6\\2NO_4\end{Bmatrix}$

Cymol . . $C_{20}H_{14}$   Nitrocymol . . $C_{20}\begin{Bmatrix}H_{13}\\NO_4\end{Bmatrix}$ *

In the above two columns of combinations the number of equivalents of carbon will be found the same as in the carbo-hydrogens. We have however succeeded with most of these bodies, by the continued action of the acid upon them, or by the observation of particular conditions, in oxidizing also a portion of their carbon, bodies with acid properties being produced which contain a smaller number of equivalents of carbon than the carbo-hydrogens from which they were derived. The composition of these acids does not however bear any constant relation to the carbo-hydrogens, such as observed in the above-mentioned products of substitution.

By the continued action of nitric acid on naphthalol, naphthalic acid, discovered by Laurent and Marignac†, is produced, the composition of which is expressed by the formula

$$2HO, C_{16}H_4^fO_6.$$

The action of nitric acid on cinnamol (styrol) has been studied by Drs. Hofmann and Blyth‡. They have shown that cinnamol may in this manner be converted into benzoic acid.

The products obtained by the action of nitric acid on toluol have been studied by Deville§. He found that the two above-mentioned products of substitution were easily formed. He moreover believes to have converted toluol, by a long treatment with oxidizing agents, into benzoic acid; he is however in doubt about the result of his experiment, as he could not always succeed in the transformation, and his method of preparing toluol did not exclude the possibility of its containing benzoic æther in admixture. If benzoic acid can in reality be obtained from toluol, we have here an instance

---

\* This substance is now under investigation by Mr. Noad.
† Liebig's *Annalen*, xli. p. 98, and xlii. p. 215.
‡ Phil. Mag. 3. S. vol. xxvii. p. 97.
§ *Ann. de Chim. et de Phys.* 3d Ser. t. iii. p. 168.

of the formation of an acid without the original number of equivalents of carbon in the carbo-hydrogen being diminished.

In the paper lately read before this Society by Mr. Noad, he has shown that cymol is converted by the continued action of dilute nitric acid into toluylic acid.

It will be seen from these examples that we are unable to determine anything beforehand regarding the nature of these products of oxidation. The manner in which nitric acid or any other oxidizing agent acts is evidently closely connected with the constitution of the body exposed to their influence. Aided by the manner in which nitric acid acts on naphthalol, Marignac has in fact founded a view of the constitution of this body. He considers the carbo-hydrogen in question to be a combination of two others, namely, $C_{16}H_4$ and $C_4H_4 = C_{20}H_8$, naphthalic acid, $C_{16}H_4O_6$, being formed by the action of nitric acid on the first, while the other is converted by the influence of the oxygen into water and oxalic acid or carbonic acid. By this view many of the reactions of naphthalol may be explained in a very satisfactory manner. It is possible that similar views may be applied to the other carbo-hydrogens, by which their behaviour with oxidizing agents may be similarly explained; a great number of investigations are however required before we can arrive at any general result.

The following experiments, which I have instituted at the suggestion and under the direction of Dr. Hofmann, may, I hope, be considered as a slight contribution to this subject.

It is known that when cumol is treated with concentrated nitric acid it yields the usual products of substitution of the carbo-hydrogens. Gerhardt and Cahours have observed further, that by the continuous action of dilute nitric acid on cumol a crystalline acid is produced*. This acid has not, however, been more closely investigated. According to the experiments on toluol, cinnamol and cymol before mentioned, this acid might be of three different kinds, according to the analogy of cumol with any one of these carbo-hydrogens. If the number of equivalents of carbon were to remain the same as in toluol, the acid obtained might be HO, $C_{18}H_9O_3$, until now unknown (differing from toluylic or cuminic acid in containing $C_2H_2$, more or less). Should two equivalents of carbon be eliminated, as is the case with cinnamol, the formation of toluylic acid might then be expected; and lastly, should cumol be analogous to cymol, that is, should it lose four equivalents of carbon, the acid must then be benzoic acid.

In the preparation of cumol I proceeded in the manner described by its discoverers, Gerhardt and Cahours. Pure

* Liebig's *Annalen*, xxxviii. p. 67.

cuminic acid was distilled with four times its weight of caustic lime in a copper retort placed in a deep sand-bath, the temperature of which was gradually raised to a red heat. The distillate obtained was colourless, possessing however an empyreumatic odour, which it did not lose on being rectified over hydrate of potash to free it from any cuminic acid that might have come over with it. I afterwards found that this peculiar odour was immediately removed on distilling the oil with a concentrated solution of chromic acid, which leaves the cumol of its agreeable aromatic smell without affecting its composition. This is a method that might perhaps prove useful in many cases where the peculiar odour of a carbohydrogen is disguised by the presence of a small quantity of some foreign substance.

When dried over chloride of calcium this body possessed exactly the same properties as described by Gerhardt and Cahours. Its boiling-point was found by them to be $144°$ C.; a later experiment of Gerhardt gave $153°$ as the boiling-point. The cumol that I prepared boiled at $148°$ C. Its analysis gave me the following results:—

0·2029 grm. burned with oxide of copper gave 0·6725 grm. of carbonic acid and 0·1804 grm. of water; corresponding to

|  |  |  |
|---|---|---|
| Carbon | . . . . | 90·34 |
| Hydrogen | . . . | 9·88 |

which numbers agree with the composition of cumol.

|  |  | Theory. | Found. |
|---|---|---|---|
| 18 eqs. Carbon . . | 108 | 90·0 | 90·34 |
| 12 ... Hydrogen . | 12 | 10·0 | 9·88 |
|  | 120 | 100·0 |  |

On boiling cumol with concentrated nitric acid it is quickly converted into a heavy oil, which is the analogue to nitrobenzol. If the boiling is continued this oil disappears, and is gradually converted into a yellow crystalline mass, soluble in ammonia with the exception of a slight fixed residue (dinitrocumol). The ammoniacal solution gives with hydrochloric acid a white precipitate, difficultly soluble in cold water, but more easily so in hot water, from which it crystallizes on cooling. These crystals are generally somewhat coloured; recrystallization after treatment with animal charcoal removes this colouring matter.

Several combustions of the acid dried at $100°$ C. showed me that my substance must be a mixture. I therefore distilled another portion of cumol with fuming nitric acid for several days, and obtained a crystalline body similar to the former, which was purified in the usual manner. A combustion of this body gave me the following results:—

0·2628 grm. of substance yielded 0·4890 grm. carbonic acid and 0·0743 grm. water.

Or in 100 parts,—

    Carbon . . . . 50·73
    Hydrogen . . . 3·18

These numbers correspond to the composition of nitrobenzoic acid, $HO, C_{14} \left\{ \begin{matrix} H_4 \\ NO_4 \end{matrix} \right\} O_3$, as is seen when compared with the theoretical numbers.

|  |  |  |  | Theory. | Found. |
|---|---|---|---|---|---|
| 14 equivs. | Carbon | . . | 84 | 50·30 | 50·73 |
| 5 | ... Hydrogen | . | 5 | 3·00 | 3·18 |
| 1 | ... Nitrogen | . . | 14 | 8·38 |  |
| 8 | ... Oxygen | . . | 64 | 38·32 |  |
|  |  |  | 167 | 100·00 |  |

On addition of nitrate of silver to the ammoniacal salt of this acid a white precipitate was formed, sparingly soluble in hot water, from which it crystallized on cooling. I had not sufficient substance to recrystallize the salt, and could therefore only purify it by washing.

Its analysis gave me the following result:—

0·1657 grm. of substance left, on being burnt, 0·0650 grm., or 39·24 per cent. of silver; which agrees sufficiently well with the composition of nitrobenzoate of silver.

|  |  | Theory. | Found. |
|---|---|---|---|
| Nitrobenzoic acid | . 158 | 57·67 |  |
| Oxide of silver | . . 116 | 42·33 | 42·14 |
|  | 274 | 100·00 |  |

In order to be perfectly certain, the small quantity remaining of the silver salt was submitted to distillation. There sublimed a portion of the acid, mixed with a few drops of an aromatic oil. The product of the distillation was therefore submitted to Dr. Hofmann's process for detecting nitrobenzol; it was dissolved in a mixture of alcohol and sulphuric acid, and reduced by means of a piece of metallic zinc. After the disengagement of hydrogen had ceased, the liquid was neutralized with potash and agitated with æther. A few drops of the ætherial solution gave, on evaporation with hypochloride of lime, the beautiful violet colour characterizing aniline.

These experiments were sufficient to identify nitrobenzoic acid, and it seemed more than probable that the excess of carbonic acid obtained in the first analysis arose from the presence of benzoic acid.

I therefore distilled a fresh quantity of cumol with nitric acid, and recollecting the difficulty Mr. Noad experienced in the preparation of toluylic acid, I employed my acid so dilute that even on boiling the mixture no disengagement of red fumes was visible. Having continued the distillation for four or five days the cumol was converted into a crystalline mass, which was strained off from the mother-liquor and recrystallized from water. The properties of this acid distinguished it immediately from nitrobenzoic acid; it was much more soluble in cold and hot water, and might be easily recognised as benzoic acid. Not having sufficient substance for a combustion, I converted the acid into an ammoniacal salt, and precipitated this with nitrate of silver. A white flocculent precipitate was obtained, much more easily soluble in water than nitrobenzoate of silver. On cooling, beautiful crystals separated, having all the properties of benzoate of silver.

The analysis of this salt gave me the following results:—

I. 0·1837 grm. of substance yielded 0·1138 grm. chloride of silver, corresponding to 0·0857 grm. or 46·65 per cent. of silver.

II. 0·1658 grm. yielded 0·0780 grm., or 47·04 per cent. of silver, which numbers correspond with the formula $AgO, C_{14} H_5 O_3$, as may be seen when compared with the theoretical numbers.

|  | Theory. |  | Found. |  |
|---|---|---|---|---|
|  |  |  | I. | II. |
| Benzoic acid | 113 | 49·35 |  |  |
| Oxide of silver | 116 | 50·65 | 50·08 | 50·50 |
|  | 229 |  |  |  |

These results were sufficiently near, considering the small amount of substance employed.

From these experiments we see that cumol on being boiled continuously with nitric acid is converted into benzoic and nitrobenzoic acids. The oxidation of cumol is therefore analogous to that of cymol.

$$\underbrace{C_{20} H_{14}}_{\text{Cymol.}} + 18O = \underbrace{HO, C_{16} H_7 O_3}_{\text{Toluylic acid.}} + 4CO_2 + 6HO.$$

$$\underbrace{C_{18} H_{12}}_{\text{Cumol.}} + 18O = \underbrace{HO, C_{14} H_5 O_3}_{\text{Benzoic acid.}} + 4CO_2 + 6HO.$$

The behaviour of cumol under the influence of the continued action of dilute nitric acid induced me to submit benzol, so nearly related to cumol, to a similar treatment. After having however continued the distillation for about a week I could not obtain an acid from benzol. On employing highly diluted acid, the benzol was gradually converted into nitrobenzol.

Neither benzol nor nitrobenzol is attacked by pure chromic acid, or the oxidizing mixture of bichromate of potash and sulphuric acid. Results quite as unsatisfactory as these were obtained on boiling a solution of hyposulphobenzolic acid with chromic acid or peroxide of manganese.

## XI. *Notices respecting New Books.*

### RECENT CAMBRIDGE WORKS ON PURE MATHEMATICS.

1. *Euclid's Elements of Geometry*, &c. By ROBERT POTTS, M.A. Trinity College. 8vo. Parker, 1845.
2. *School Edition of Potts's Euclid*, &c. 12mo. Parker, 1846.
3. *Appendix to the larger edition of Potts's Euclid*. Parker, 1847.
4. *Solutions of the Trigonometrical Problems proposed at St. John's College from 1829 to 1836.* By THOMAS GASKIN, M.A., late Fellow and Tutor of Jesus College. Deightons, 1847.
5. *Solutions of Geometrical Problems, consisting chiefly of examples in plane coordinate Geometry, proposed from Dec. 1830 to Dec. 1836, by the same.* Deightons, 1847.

THESE two sets of works, though as opposite in their manner as if they had been written for the sake of contrast, are yet so far related in respect to their subject as to be properly analysed under the same heading. The object of Mr. Potts is to develop the pure principles of the ancient geometry; that of Mr. Gaskin to display the powers of the modern to the greatest advantage. Each too has been eminently successful in his undertaking; and has shown the most admirable mastery over his respective subject. We are indeed glad to see this; as for many years the elementary productions of the Cambridge press had been gradually diminishing in value, originality, and adaptation to educational purposes. We shall give a brief account of them in the order of their appearance, beginning with Mr. Potts's Euclid and Appendix.

The Elements of Euclid, it may be supposed, cannot differ materially in one edition from another; especially when, as is the case with most of them as well as this, the text of Simson is professedly adopted. This is true in the main: but it is not true in respect to the business of actual instruction, as every tutor too well knows. In using the older editions of Simson nothing is so embarrassing to a student or so troublesome to the tutor, as the parcelling out the syllogisms (or rather, generally, the enthymemes) of which a long demonstration is composed. Many tutors had recourse to marking them in pencil in the pupils' copies of the book. Then again came the separation of each syllogism into its separate members. All this created not only intolerable labour for the tutor, but disgust in the student's feelings, and confusion in his comprehension and remembrance of the argument. One attempt to remedy this inconvenience was made by Mr. Williamson in his "Symbolical Euclid," which was in a great degree successful as far as this particular class of difficulties was concerned; but on the other hand it was attended with incalculable injury, by removing from geometry that distinctness of conception, both as regards fundamental ideas and the nature of geometrical demonstration, which has from time immemorial been the *peculiar charm and value* of this science. Mr. Potts, however, has literally maintained the very text of Simson and secured the very spirit of Euclid's geometry, by means which are simply mechanical. It consists in printing the syllogism in a separate paragraph, and the members of it in separate subdivisions, each, for the most part, occupying a single line. The divisions of a proposition are therefore seen at once without requiring an instant's thought. Were this the only advantage of Mr. Potts's edition, the great convenience which it affords in tuition would give it a claim to become the geometrical text-book of England. This, however, is not its only merit.

Prefixed to the work is an elaborate history of geometry,—too elaborate in respect to the early geometry, perhaps, and too sketchy in respect to the modern. In its general character it resembles the prefaces of Bonnycastle and Butler, but is in many parts much more amplified than either. We would recommend the author to recast this in a second edition—to omit some of the details respecting mediæval geometry, and to give an ample analysis of the researches of the continental geometers of the last half-century. This part of the work, indeed, satisfies us less than any other; although it is not without considerable merit.

The "notes" appended to each book of Euclid in succession (and a few additional ones in the "Appendix") are partly critical as regards turns and expressions in the original text of Euclid, but principally geometrical as regards difficulties of conception or imperfections of demonstration. They bespeak an acute mind and a judicious teacher; and they will be of very great service to the solitary student and careful thinker.

Then follows a dissertation on the "Ancient Geometrical Analysis," somewhat incomplete it is true; the subject is, however, resumed in the "Appendix," and treated with a fulness and perspicuity that is very unusual (perhaps unprecedented) in treatises even professedly composed on the subject—such as those of Lawson and Leslie. This, with the judiciously chosen illustrations of the method, cannot fail, we think, in reviving amongst Cambridge men a taste for that most interesting department of the Greek geometry; and, if not amongst the older members of the University, yet amongst its coming race of men, from the facility and ease with which Mr. Potts has put it in their power to master both the method and its application, this subject will regain something of the respect which was paid to it in the bygone brightest days of geometry.

In the "Appendix" is inserted a short tract on the "Theory of Transversals"—a subject almost totally unknown in this country.

Indeed Mr. Potts tells us that there is only one single work published in England where it is fully discussed, or even mentioned at all; and we believe the first use even of the *term* in any English book was made in this Magazine in 1826 by the author to whom Mr. Potts refers, in a paper on Pascal's Mystic Hexagram.

We come in the last place to a series of "Geometrical Exercises," above a thousand in number. These are collected *exclusively* from the Cambridge University papers—either those given in the Senate House or in the different Colleges during the present century. Opinions will be divided as to the wisdom shown by Mr. Potts in confining himself to those sources from which to draw his "problems" —as it is the somewhat fanciful practice of the University to denominate all propositions whatever. We shall offer no opinion on this question; but assume that Mr. Potts had reasons satisfactory to his own mind for this act of deference to his University predecessors. At all events we have here a vast mass of "Exercises" of all degrees of difficulty, from the most simple to the most transcendent; and certainly a great number of them are as remarkable for their elegance as for their difficulty.

The practice of "problem-solving" is much and very properly insisted on in the Cambridge course of reading. Possibly the study of problems which have been set in former years may be the best means of preparing the men to solve those which may be set hereafter. It may be under such a supposition that Mr. Potts so limited his grounds of selection. After all, as the Euclid is for the most part confined to the "Freshman's year," these exercises would have far transcended the powers of the men without occasional, indeed frequent, suggestions from a tutor. Many of them would embarrass even an expert geometer, if placed before him suddenly in the course of his tutorial duties—and some of them, under the same circumstances, the ablest geometers of the present century. To obviate this objection, Mr. Potts has published in his Appendix, a series of "Hints" more or less full as the occasion seemed to demand. To use the language of a respected cotemporary, in which we fully concur, we should describe them thus:—"In some cases references only are made to the proposition on which a solution depends; in others we have a step or two of the process indicated; in one case the analysis is briefly given to find the construction or demonstration; in another case the reverse of this. Occasionally, though seldom, the entire process is given as a model; but most commonly, just so much is suggested as will enable a student of average ability to complete the whole solution—in short just so much (and no more) assistance is afforded as would, and *must be*, afforded by a tutor to his pupil. Mr. Potts appears to us to have hit the 'golden mean' of geometrical tutorship."

In order to render his work more extensively useful, Mr. Potts has printed a smaller edition for the use of schools, containing the first six books of Euclid with the principal notes on each, and a selection from the Exercises sufficient for all the purposes of school-education. Being printed on the same arrangement as the larger edition, and published at a price lower, we believe, than any other edition of Euclid, it cannot fail to meet the wants of a large class of schools in this country at the present day. It is used, we understand, in all our great Grammar Schools, in the Royal Military Academy, and many other public institutions, as well as in a large number of private schools.

The works of Mr. Gaskin all tend to show the power of what is vulgarly in modern times called "analysis" to deal with geometrical propositions. As far as his books can give any insight into his thoughts, it would appear to be his aim to supersede the Greek geometry. This may arise however from the circumstance of the other ground being already occupied by Mr. Potts, and his honourable unwillingness to interfere with the objects of his *collaborateur*; and we are the more disposed to think so from some speculations in his "Third Appendix to the Solutions of Geometrical Problems," which prove him to possess a considerable share of geometrical power as well as a more than usual share of algebraical. Whatever view be taken of this, we can most cordially award him our praise for the masterly manner in which he has applied algebra to many of the problems in both his volumes; and in cases too where he had great difficulties to contend against from the unsuitability of his instrument for its intended operation. It is a remarkable circumstance that those problems which are most easily resolved by pure geometry give rise to the greatest difficulty and complexity by every method of algebraical treatment; and *vice versâ*. An authority of no mean weight has indeed asserted that in such cases "the fault is not in the analysis, but in the analyst:" but we may say with the same propriety on the other side, that "the fault is not in the geometry, but the geometer." Be this as it may, in the *present state* of geometry and algebra, we believe our position will not be generally disputed. Mr. Gaskin, then, has imposed upon himself many artificial difficulties; whilst on the other hand he has mastered them more completely than we believe any one of his University cotemporaries could have done—more completely, it is certain, than they had ever before been mastered. There are, indeed, isolated exceptions, but these are few; whilst the great address and ability displayed in the majority of the solutions place Mr. Gaskin amongst the most successful and effective writers on the application of Algebra to Geometry of our age and country.

Mr. Gaskin's selection of the "problems" given in the "College Papers of St. John's" (containing the "Trigonometrical Problems from 1829 to 1846," and the "Geometrical Problems from 1830 to 1846") is apparently founded on an assumed superiority of the papers given in that College over those given in any other. Upon this point we have no means of judging: but we know that the papers of St. John's are much sought after by the undergraduates (especially on the more elementary subjects), upon which to exercise themselves. Mr. Gaskin's choice is, therefore, in all probability a judicious one; and as it is a University question rather than a public one, Mr. Gaskin is himself the better judge in such a case. The idea under which the solutions are constructed is well expressed in the preface to the Trigonometrical papers:—"The time allowed for the solution of each paper being limited to about three hours, the author has adopted the method which each example most naturally suggested, in preference to the employment of analytical artifices by which many of the results might have been obtained more concisely. In every case he has endeavoured to point out the form in which the student would be expected to present the solution to the examiner." The geometrical papers are also evidently solved on the same principle; and we feel bound to say that under such conditions, a better set of solutions could not have been produced. They are everywhere marked by a perfect knowledge of the broad principles of the science, and by an address in the management of his symbols, which is almost peculiar to Mr. Gaskin. We are not offering any opinion as to whether Mr. Gaskin's plan be the best that could have been adopted; but we merely affirm that, having selected a plan, he has fulfilled his objects with consummate ability.

The gem of Mr. Gaskin's two volumes, however, in the eyes of a mathematician, will be the three "appendices" to the geometrical problems. The first and third of these are upon a problem which has received much attention both from English and foreign geometers, in one form or other:—" In a given conic section to inscribe a polygon all whose sides (produced if necessary) shall pass through given points." Much as this problem has been discussed (for a pretty complete list of these discussions, we must refer to Mr. Potts's "Appendix," p. 98), we believe that Mr. Gaskin has not been anticipated in his method by any one whatever; and certainly of all the attempts to solve this difficult problem by algebraic methods, his process is the most direct and elegant. We are glad to see such *models* of investigation laid before the men; and especially by an author whose name carries that weight in the University which his does.

To the second "Appendix" we must award less praise. It is mainly composed of a discussion of the equation of the second degree between $x$ and $y$. It is complete, but complex and cumbrous: and is is inferior in all respects but completeness, to many others that we could easily point out; whilst even in respect to its one good quality, it is not superior to several of them. We have not room, however, to particularise.

The remaining part of this Appendix is devoted to the deduction of a considerable number of properties of the conic sections, references for which are made to different papers set either in the Senate House or in the various Colleges. In these solutions a mixed method is pursued. Certain cardinal propositions are established by coordinate methods; and from these, by geometrical considerations, the others are deduced. Great difference of opinion exists among geometers as to the propriety of this mode of investigation; and we shall not offer ourselves either as dictators or umpires on the question. It is sufficient to say, that granting these cardinal properties (as Pascal's Hexagram, for instance) to have been established in a manner to satisfy any given geometer, he will find the deductions from them to have been effected with great brevity, clearness and elegance.

On the whole, then, we cannot but congratulate the University on the appearance of the works of Messrs. Potts and Gaskin; and we trust they will be speedily followed by others as valuable, either by those authors themselves, or by other men possessing an equal amount of learning and soundness of judgement.

## XII. *Intelligence and Miscellaneous Articles.*

### PHOSPHATE OF IRON, MANGANESE AND SODA.
#### BY M. A. DAMOUR.

THIS mineral was recently found among the pegmatites of the environs of Chanteloub, near Limoges, by M. Mathieu, a mineral-dealer.

When viewed in mass, its colour is clove-brown; its fracture lamellar and shining; and in some places, which appear altered, it is chatoyant like diallage. It possesses three rectangular cleavages, which leads to the conclusion that the mineral crystallizes in right rectangular prisms. This mineral scratches fluor spar, and is scratched by a steel point; its density is 3·468. When heated by the blowpipe on platina, it melts into a non-magnetic globule. With fluxes it gives the reactions of manganese, and gives water when heated in the tube. Hydrochloric acid dissolves it readily, a little chlorine being evolved.

A qualitative analysis showed that the mineral is composed essentially of phosphoric acid, peroxide of iron, and oxide of manganese and soda, combined with a small quantity of water.

The mean of six analyses gave—

| | |
|---|---|
| Phosphoric acid | 41·25 |
| Peroxide of iron | 25·62 |
| Oxide of manganese | 23·08 |
| Soda | 5·47 |
| Water | 2·65 |
| Silica | 0·60 |
| Peroxide of manganese | 1·06 |
| | 99·73 |

The physical characters and chemical composition of this mineral distinguish it from all previously known phosphates, and show that it should be classed as a distinct species.—*Comptes Rendus*, Novembre 1847.

### ANALYSIS OF COLUMBITE FROM THE ENVIRONS OF LIMOGES.
#### BY M. A. DAMOUR.

This mineral species, which has hitherto been found in a few places only, has been met with in a quarry near Chanteloub. The specimen, below described, was confounded with specimens of wolfram and triplite, which M. Mathieu had collected. Its colour, hardness and great density, induced M. Damour to believe that it contained columbic acid. It occurs in the form of nuclei imbedded in yellowish-white felspar. It is of a tarnished bluish-black colour on the surface; the fresh fracture is shining and glossy; its powder is black, approaching gray. It scratches glass, and its density is 7·651. It does not fuse by the blowpipe; but when heated on charcoal with tartrate of potash, it yields globules of tin. Acids do not act upon it. Analysis gave—

| | |
|---|---:|
| Columbic acid | 82·98 |
| Oxide of tin | 1·21 |
| Oxide of iron | 14·62 |
| Oxide of manganese | traces |
| Silica | ·42 |
| | 99·23 |

Its composition is therefore similar to that of the mineral from Finland.—*Comptes Rendus*, Novembre 1847.

### ON THE ACIDS OF SULPHUR. BY MM. FORDOS AND GELIS.

All the chlorides of sulphur yield, with the aqueous solution of sulphurous acid, the same compounds. The principal product of this reaction is a new oxygenated compound of sulphur, in which five equivalents of sulphur are combined with an equal number of equivalents of oxygen, and form a molecule which saturates only one equivalent of base, and which is consequently represented by the formula $S^5O^5$, MO.

This acid differs from all the acids of sulphur hitherto known. It is not to be confounded either with that to which M. Wackenroder has assigned the same formula, without having analysed it, the formation of which he observed during the reaction of hydrosulphuric acid on the aqueous solution of sulphurous acid; for M. Wackenroder states positively, in his memoir, that the barytic salt which he obtained is soluble in alcohol and in æther, and is not precipitable from its solution in water by them, whereas it is by these very means that MM. Fordos and Gelis isolate their acid.

The new acid $S^5O^5$, MO is the isomeric of hyposulphurous acid $S^2O^2$, MO. Both have the same composition in 100 parts, but they differ completely in all their characters. Mineral chemistry does not present any case of isomerism comparable to that of these two acids. To discover analogous cases, the compounds of carbon must be referred to; and this fact supports the approximation, which M. Berzelius was the first to establish, between the composition of the acids of sulphur recently discovered, and that of the compounds of organic chemistry.

The authors divide all the acids of sulphur into two perfectly distinct classes: in one the sulphur remains invariable, and the quantity of oxygen increases; in the other, the number of equivalents of oxygen remaining five, the sulphur varies as the numbers 2, 3, 4 and 5. The acid now particularly described is the last of this class.

The name of *sulphuric series* is given to the first: it includes all the acids anciently known; and the name of *thionic series*, from θεῖον, *sulphur*, is given to the four acids more recently discovered. They are distinguished from each other by prefixing to the generic name the Greek particles which represent the numbers 2, 3, 4 and 5.

Thus we have the following acids:—

Dithionic $S^2O^5$, hyposulphuric acid of Gay-Lussac and Welter.

Trithionic $S^3O^5$, sulphhyposulphuric acid of Langlois.

Tetrathionic $S^4O^5$, bisulphated hyposulphuric acid, discovered by Fordos and Gelis in 1842.

Pentathionic $S^5O^5$, the acid which is the subject of the present memoir.

The pentathionic acid in the free state greatly resembles the other acids of the series. The solution is not rendered turbid by acids; it does not absorb iodine, and it forms soluble salts with the alkaline and earthy oxides. These characters prevent this acid from being confounded with hyposulphurous acid. The pentathionate of barytes was most particularly examined; it may be obtained combined with one equivalent of alcohol or two equivalents of water. Its formula in the state of hydrate is $S^5O^5$, BaO, 2HO; the hydrate is very alterable; the alcoholic compound keeps better.

The spontaneous decomposition of the pentathionate of barytes is extremely curious; it may, by losing sulphur, become successively tetrathionate and then trithionate.

$$S^5O^5=S^4O^5+S;$$
$$S^4O^5=S^3O^5+S^2.$$

Sometimes the deposit of sulphur is accompanied with sulphate of barytes, and in this case the solution acquires the smell of sulphurous acid. These products, which are formed in larger quantity as the temperature is higher, are the results of the ultimate decomposition of the trithionate,

$$S^3O^4, BaO=SO^3, BaO+SO^2+S.$$

These decompositions, which give rise to many products, and which continue during the whole time of the preparation, render the procuring the pentathionic acid extremely difficult, and serve to explain all the various results which the reaction of the chlorides of sulphur may occasion in the aqueous solution of sulphurous acid.—*Comptes Rendus*, Novembre 1847.

---

### ON SOME PROPERTIES OF CARBON. BY M. LAZOWSKI.

The properties of carbon are numerous; they have been partly studied, but every day produces new facts: when it is in a state of ignition, it possesses some very remarkable properties.

When a piece of ignited charcoal, which is very clean and free from ash, is immersed into a solution of a metallic salt, it reduces the metallic salt which is contained in it, and the metal itself is deposited with all its natural brilliancy on the piece of charcoal. Thus the salts of tin, copper, platina, palladium, mercury, silver and gold, &c. furnish most brilliant deposits.

M. Lazowski has remarked, he says, that when the salts are too acid or too much concentrated, no effect is produced. The dilute solutions of the salts of copper often yield, by covering the charcoal, the most varied shades of colour, from the finest azure blue to that of metallic copper. The parts of the charcoal upon which certain metals are deposited in preference, are the extremities; whilst other metals cover equally all the surface of the reducing body; at other times, and this occurs with the protochloride of tin, the metal appears in very brilliant crystals, disseminated on the periphery of the charcoal.—*Journ. de Chim. Méd.*, Decembre 1847.

### DETECTION OF FREE SULPHURIC ACID ADDED TO WINES.

The detection of a small proportion of sulphuric acid added to red wines, cannot be effected by means of barytic salts, for all wines contain greater or smaller quantities of the sulphates of potash and lime.

M. Lassaigne states that in an examination undertaken by him and MM. Ossian Henri and Bayard, they found that it was not possible to separate, by the action of pure sulphuric æther, four or five thousandths of sulphuric acid added to red wine, and consequently that this method did not always answer in proving the existence of this acid in the free state.

After many attempts, the authors ascertained a simple reaction, which allows of determining the presence of this acid, even when it exists in wines, in the proportion of a thousandth and a half.

When a piece of paper which has been touched with pure wine is dried at a gentle heat, the spotted portion is unaltered; whereas paper which has been moistened with wine, to which a very small quantity of sulphuric acid has been added, reddens, and becomes brittle and friable between the fingers when slightly rubbed, before the white paper becomes at all coloured.

Pure wine to which nothing has been added, leaves by spontaneous evaporation a violet-blue spot; whereas wine to which a very small quantity of sulphuric acid has been added (two to three thousandths), gives by drying a rose-coloured spot.

On examining into the sensibility of this simple process, the authors found that they were able to detect by its means one thousandth $\frac{1}{4}$ of sulphuric acid in red wine.

The paper most proper for the experiment is common glazed paper, containing starch or fecula. This kind of paper is well-known in commerce; and it is easy to discover it by the blue colour which it assumes when moistened with an aqueous solution of iodine.—*Ibid.*

### ON THE COMPOSITION OF URANO-TANTALITE AND COLUMBITE.

According to a notice published in the *Comptes Rendus Mensuels de l'Académie de Berlin*, Avril 1847, p. 131, by M. Henri Rose, the yttéro-ilménite of M. Hermann is merely the urano-tantalite described by M. Gustave Rose. M. Henri Rose has satisfied himself of their identity, by means of some specimens of yttéro-ilménite which had been sent to him; his new experiments confirm his first results; and he has found it impossible to extract any ilmenic acid from the mineral in question, which he considers to be merely niobic acid, mixed with a certain quantity of tungstic acid.

As the urano-tantalite (the yttéro-ilménite of M. Hermann) contains no columbium, M. Henri Rose proposes to give it a new name, that of *Samarskite*, in honour of M. Samarski, Director of the Mines of Siberia.

This mineral contains a little yttria and protoxide of manganese besides niobic and tungstic acids, oxide of uranium and protoxide of iron.

Many of the specimens of samarskite are mixed with columbite, the crystalline form of which is such as it has been described by M. Hermann.

The columbite of Siberia has been examined by M. Th. Bromeis: the acid which it contains is niobic acid nearly pure, with mere traces of pelopic and tungstic acids.—*Journ. de Ch. et de Phys.*, Nov. 1847.

### ON THE FOSSIL VEGETATION OF ANTHRACITE COAL.

Mr. J. E. Teschemacher, at the recent meeting of the American Association of Geologists and Naturalists, read a paper on this subject, confining his observations to the remains of vegetation found in the *body* of the coal, apart from that in the accompanying shales. The principal points of the memoir were, that the remains of the larger forms of the coal epoch, as well as of the smaller plants, were abundant in the coal, contrary to the usual opinion. Specimens were exhibited from the interior of the coal, showing the external and internal parts of plants—the vessels, the leaves, the seeds, &c.

Since the meeting, Mr. Teschemacher has continued his investigations, and has communicated in a letter to one of the editors the following results:—

1st. What I considered as vessels were said to be mere marks of sliding of the coal. Prof. Bailey prepared a specimen of this by his method, and told me that if I found vessels there, my proposition was correct. Examined by Agassiz and myself, with his large Oberhauser, it turns out to be *nothing* but a *mass* of perforated vessels, as clear and distinct as if they were recent. M. Agassiz observed, "One moment suffices to remove every doubt on the subject."

2nd. What I considered as fossil seeds were said to be mere peacock-eye coal; the dark carbonaceous centres of these seeds, which I held to be carbonized cellular matter, was thought to be a mere mistake and the seeds imaginary. I have since discovered them with distinct and clear apparently spinous appendages. M. Agassiz thinks the seed a Samara, and I have found sufficient quantity to pick out the carbonaceous matter from the interior with a fine needle—decarbonize it in a clean platina crucible over a spirit-lamp, with every possible precaution to prevent any foreign substance mixing therewith. On examining this with the Oberhauser, 700 diameters, M. Agassiz showed to Dr. Gould and myself the cells as clear and plain as possible; it is a mass of cellular matter, as I stated. You may of course imagine the extreme tenuity of the parietes of cells of seeds when decarbonized, and the difficulty of those less experienced than M. Agassiz in the microscope in managing the subject—he feels quite convinced of their being fossil seeds. The nature of the genus of plants must require further examination.

3rd. The smooth glossy surfaces, which I considered the external parts of large plants rendered smooth by intense pressure, were said to be nothing more than slickensides. My position here is proved much more easily than in the other cases, by specimens passing gradually from the smoother through different degrees of protuberance (all still smooth and polished), until we arrive at the full form of the Lepidodendron. Nay more, I have found the parallel lines (channels) which are on the slickens ides, also on the perfectly-formed Lepidodendra. The correctness of my views here I could prove to the most sceptical.

The discoveries still to be made on this subject are numerous and important; and I doubt not that the investigation of the coal itself will soon solve the doubts hitherto existing in the comparison of the coal fossils with recent plants.

I will merely add, that I have found quite distinctly the impression of the cellular cuticle of some of these plants, which of course cannot be seen in an impression on shale, the grains of the sedimentary matter being as large as the surface of the cells; but on the pasty mass of coal the impression is perfect.—Silliman's *Journal*, Nov. 1847.

### METEOROLOGICAL OBSERVATIONS FOR NOV. 1847.

*Chiswick.*—November 1. Overcast: very fine: clear. 2—4. Foggy. 5. Densely overcast: very fine. 6. Very fine: rain. 7. Cloudy. 8. Fine. 9. Exceedingly fine: clear. 10. Frosty: fine: clear. 11. Fine: cloudy. 12. Rain: fine. 13. Clear and fine: overcast. 14. Overcast: slight rain. 15. Fine. 16. Rain. 17. Fine: clear: sharp frost. 18. Frosty: clear. 19. Frosty: hazy. 20. Dense fog. 21. Foggy: hazy and damp. 22. Overcast: exceedingly fine. 23. Cloudy: rain. 24. Very fine. 25. Cloudy. 26. Constant rain. 27. Foggy: rain. 28. Overcast: rain: barometer very low. 29. Very fine. 30. Rain: cloudy and mild.

Mean temperature of the month .............................. 44°·61
Mean temperature of Nov. 1846 .............................. 43 ·73
Mean temperature of Nov. for the last twenty years ...... 42 ·88
Average amount of rain in Nov. ................................ 2·56 inches.

*Boston.*—Nov. 1, 2. Fine. 3. Foggy. 4, 5. Cloudy. 6. Cloudy: rain P.M. 7—10. Fine. 11. Rainy. 12. Rainy: rain early A.M. 13. Fine. 14. Fine: beautiful morning. 15, 16. Cloudy. 17. Fine: at noon thermometer 43: stormy P.M. 18. Fine: snow early A.M.: first ice this morning. 19. Fine. 20. Foggy. 21. Cloudy. 22. Rain. 23. Rain: rain early A.M. 24. Fine. 25. Windy: six o'clock P.M. therm. 52·5: rain P.M. 26. Cloudy: three o'clock P.M. therm. 48·0: rain P.M. 27. Rain: rain P.M.: half-past six P.M. therm. 48. 28. Rain. 29. Fine. 30. Rain: rain early A.M.

*Sandwick Manse, Orkney.*—Nov. 1. Cloudy: drops. 2. Cloudy: clear. 3. Showers: clear. 4. Cloudy. 5. Rain. 6. Cloudy: drops. 7. Cloudy: rain. 8. Damp: rain: cloudy. 9. Showers: cloudy. 10. Showers. 11. Bright: clear. 12. Clear. 13. Bright: damp. 14. Rain: cloudy. 15. Bright: showers. 16. Hail-showers. 17. Snow-showers: hail-showers. 18. Drizzle. 19. Drizzle: cloudy: aurora. 20. Clear: cloudy. 21, 22. Cloudy: rain. 23. Showers: sleet-showers. 24. Bright: showers. 25. Cloudy: showers. 26. Showers: cloudy. 27. Clear: frost: rain. 28. Clear: frost: cloudy: frost. 29. Bright: cloudy. 30. Showers.

*Applegarth Manse, Dumfries-shire.*—Nov. 1. Showers: heavy rain A.M. 2. Very fine. 3. Fair: frost A.M. 4. Dull: slight drizzle. 5. Threatening. 6. Occasional showers. 7. Heavy rain. 8. Heavy rain: flood. 9. Fair and fine. 10. Dull A.M.: rain P.M. 11. Rain all day. 12. Rain A.M.: cleared. 13. Raw: frost A.M. 14. Dull, but fine. 15. Showers A.M.: heavy P.M. 16. Fine A.M.: showers P.M. 17. Frost: ice on pools. 18. Hard frost. 19. Dull: fair. 20. Dull: slight drizzle. 21. Dull: rain P.M. 22. Fine A.M.: rain P.M. 23, 24. Heavy showers. 25. Rain: heavy. 26. Fine A.M.: rain P.M. 27. Fine: frost A.M. 28. Frost: fair. 29. Rain early A.M. 30. Showery.

Mean temperature of the month .............................. 45°·7
Mean temperature of Nov. 1846 .............................. 44 ·4
Mean temperature of Nov. for twenty-five years............ 40 ·4
Rain in Nov. 1847 ................................................. 3·79 inches.
Average rain in Nov. for twenty years ..................... 3·60 „

*Meteorological Observations made by* Mr. Thompson *at the Garden of the Horticultural Society at* Chiswick, *near London; by* Mr. Veall, *at* Boston; *by the* Rev. W. Dunbar, *at Applegarth Manse*, Dumfries-shire; *and by the* Rev. C. Clouston, *at Sandwick Manse*, Orkney.

| Days of Month. 1847. Nov. | Barometer. Chiswick. Max. | Barometer. Chiswick. Min. | Barometer. Boston. 8½ a.m. | Barometer. Dumfries-shire. 9 a.m. | Barometer. Dumfries-shire. 9 p.m. | Barometer. Orkney, Sandwick. 9¼ a.m. | Barometer. Orkney, Sandwick. 8¾ p.m. | Thermometer. Chiswick. Max. | Thermometer. Chiswick. Min. | Thermometer. Boston. 8½ a.m. | Thermometer. Dumfries-shire. Max. | Thermometer. Dumfries-shire. Min. | Thermometer. Orkney, Sandwick. 9¼ a.m. | Thermometer. Orkney, Sandwick. 8¾ p.m. |
|---|---|---|---|---|---|---|---|---|---|---|---|---|---|---|
| 1. | 30·286 | 30·024 | 29·79 | 29·97 | 29·92 | 29·80 | 29·70 | 65 | 36 | 53 | 56 | 48 | 50½ | 53½ |
| 2. | 30·343 | 30·305 | 29·83 | 30·03 | 30·28 | 29·80 | 30·09 | 55 | 43 | 50 | 56 | 52 | 50 | 50 |
| 3. | 30·325 | 30·270 | 29·88 | 30·25 | 30·19 | 30·21 | 30·28 | 50 | 44 | 50 | 50 | 30 | 48 | 41½ |
| 4. | 30·216 | 30·138 | 29·77 | 30·04 | 29·96 | 30·11 | 29·96 | 50 | 44 | 49 | 51 | 46 | 46 | 47 |
| 5. | 30·010 | 29·941 | 29·62 | 29·79 | 29·54 | 29·73 | 29·56 | 56 | 42 | 43 | 55 | 44 | 50 | 49½ |
| 6. | 30·021 | 29·904 | 29·57 | 29·71 | 29·66 | 29·58 | 29·54 | 57 | 47 | 51 | 56 | 52 | 51 | 51½ |
| 7. | 29·988 | 29·796 | 29·44 | 29·51 | 29·25 | 29·32 | 29·10 | 61 | 52 | 52·5 | 54 | 52 | 52½ | 50½ |
| ● 8. | 29·596 | 29·492 | 29·12 | 29·17 | 29·11 | 29·38 | 29·08 | 61 | 33 | 56 | 58 | 53 | 43½ | 51 |
| 9. | 30·176 | 29·820 | 29·33 | 29·50 | 29·95 | 29·50 | 29·83 | 55 | 27 | 47 | 52½ | 47 | 47½ | 47 |
| 10. | 30·281 | 29·963 | 29·80 | 29·88 | 29·79 | 29·53 | 29·61 | 56 | 32 | 47 | 54 | 41 | 51 | 49½ |
| 11. | 30·220 | 30·095 | 29·74 | 29·91 | 29·93 | 29·95 | 30·07 | 55 | 48 | 47·5 | 53½ | 45 | 46 | 44 |
| 12. | 30·118 | 30·012 | 29·55 | 30·04 | 30·10 | 30·07 | 30·09 | 55 | 29 | 51 | 47 | 41½ | 41 | 41 |
| 13. | 30·231 | 30·222 | 29·83 | 29·99 | 30·09 | 29·92 | 29·98 | 54 | 37 | 41 | 51 | 35 | 47 | 48½ |
| 14. | 30·265 | 30·242 | 29·84 | 30·04 | 29·98 | 29·96 | 29·98 | 55 | 44 | 46·5 | 54 | 44 | 50 | 48 |
| ☽ 15. | 30·220 | 30·201 | 29·70 | 29·92 | 29·84 | 29·86 | 29·66 | 59 | 46 | 57 | 56 | 53½ | 47½ | 46 |
| 16. | 30·197 | 30·157 | 29·69 | 30·00 | 30·00 | 29·72 | 29·86 | 53 | 33 | 51 | 56½ | 40½ | 41½ | 38½ |
| 17. | 30·217 | 30·061 | 29·68 | 30·08 | 30·30 | 30·20 | 30·36 | 43 | 30 | 37 | 42 | 32½ | 37½ | 37 |
| 18. | 30·372 | 30·316 | 30·00 | 30·30 | 30·20 | 30·14 | 29·95 | 42 | 19 | 34 | 41½ | 26½ | 43 | 50 |
| 19. | 30·369 | 30·296 | 30·00 | 30·16 | 30·12 | 29·93 | 30·00 | 42 | 23 | 35 | 48½ | 36 | 52 | 51 |
| 20. | 30·215 | 29·444 | 29·80 | 30·00 | 29·82 | 29·90 | 29·67 | 42 | 36 | 43 | 47½ | 44 | 48 | 49 |
| 21. | 29·836 | 29·593 | 29·50 | 29·53 | 29·14 | 29·53 | 29·21 | 42 | 37 | 41 | 48 | 45 | 45½ | 45 |
| ○ 22. | 29·646 | 29·570 | 29·21 | 29·37 | 29·04 | 29·40 | 28·81 | 50 | 35 | 41·5 | 57 | 40 | 41 | 43 |
| 23. | 29·964 | 29·534 | 29·23 | 29·28 | 29·48 | 29·01 | 29·20 | 56 | 28 | 46·5 | 50 | 38 | 42 | 43 |
| 24. | 30·126 | 30·037 | 29·61 | 29·53 | 29·63 | 29·41 | 29·56 | 54 | 44 | 41 | 50 | 39 | 42 | 42 |
| 25. | 30·069 | 29·925 | 29·61 | 29·59 | 29·50 | 29·47 | 29·38 | 52 | 43 | 48 | 53½ | 43 | 45½ | 40 |
| 26. | 29·861 | 29·483 | 29·48 | 29·55 | 29·44 | 29·44 | 29·39 | 45 | 39 | 43 | 46½ | 38½ | 40½ | 39 |
| 27. | 29·226 | 29·145 | 28·96 | 29·25 | 29·19 | 29·40 | 29·21 | 49 | 41 | 47·5 | 42 | 33½ | 38 | 40½ |
| 28. | 29·141 | 28·908 | 28·75 | 28·91 | 28·90 | 29·04 | 29·00 | 50 | 29 | 47 | 38 | 29 | 34 | 36½ |
| ☾ 29. | 29·699 | 29·342 | 28·93 | 29·05 | 29·38 | 29·06 | 29·22 | 50 | 31 | 40 | 45 | 33 | 42½ | 41½ |
| 30. | 29·826 | 29·720 | 29·28 | 29·29 | 29·58 | 29·13 | 29·32 | 56 | 35 | 51 | 52 | 41 | 46 | 43 |
| Mean. | 30·035 | 29·865 | 29·55 | 29·722 | 29·710 | 29·650 | 29·622 | 52·33 | 35·90 | 46·1 | 50·5 | 41·4 | 45·35 | 45·21 |

| Days of Month. 1847. Nov. | Wind. Chiswick. 1 p.m. | Wind. Boston. | Wind. Dumfries-shire. | Wind. Orkney, Sandwick. | Rain. Chiswick. | Rain. Boston. | Rain. Dumfries-shire. | Rain. Orkney, Sandwick. |
|---|---|---|---|---|---|---|---|---|
| 1. | sw. | s. | s. | s. | ·01 | ...... | ...... | ·06 |
| 2. | sw. | s. | w. | w. | ·02 | ...... | ...... | ·07 |
| 3. | s. | calm | ne. | w. | ·01 | ...... | ...... | ·20 |
| 4. | e. | ese. | e. | se. | ...... | ...... | ...... | ...... |
| 5. | s. | s. | se. | sse. | ...... | ...... | ...... | ·11 |
| 6. | s. | s. | s. | ssw. | ·24 | ...... | ...... | ·22 |
| 7. | sw. | s. | s. | sw. | ...... | ·07 | ...... | ·01 |
| ● 8. | sw. | s. | se. | s. | ·10 | ...... | 0·97 | ·31 |
| 9. | nw. | sw. | w. | ssw. | ...... | ...... | ...... | ·15 |
| 10. | sw. | wsw. | s. | w. | ...... | ...... | ...... | ·03 |
| 11. | s. | sse. | nne. | w. | ·10 | ...... | ...... | ·15 |
| 12. | w. | calm | n. | s. | ·02 | ·11 | ...... | ·04 |
| 13. | w. | calm | n.–w. | wsw. | ...... | ...... | ...... | ...... |
| 14. | sw. | calm | sw. | w. | ·01 | ...... | ...... | ·11 |
| ☽ 15. | sw. | calm | sw. | wnw. | ...... | ...... | ...... | ·01 |
| 16. | n. | calm | w. | nnw. | ·09 | ...... | 1·17 | ·25 |
| 17. | n. | n. | nnw. | nnw. | ·01 | ...... | ...... | ·39 |
| 18. | n. | calm | sw. | w. | ...... | ...... | ...... | ·08 |
| 19. | nw. | calm | sw. | wsw. | ...... | ...... | ...... | ·02 |
| 20. | nw. | calm | sw. | sw. | ...... | ...... | ...... | ...... |
| 21. | n. | calm | se. | sse. | ·01 | ...... | ...... | ·06 |
| ○ 22. | w. | calm | sw. | s. | ·01 | ...... | ...... | ·61 |
| 23. | nw. | calm | sw. | sw. | ·18 | ·27 | 0·08 | ·50 |
| 24. | sw. | w. | sw. | sw. | ...... | ·19 | ...... | ·30 |
| 25. | sw. | sw. | sw. | ssw. | ·04 | ...... | ...... | ·07 |
| 26. | s. | calm | sw. | s. | ·54 | ·09 | ...... | ·16 |
| 27. | e. | sw. | ne. | ssw. | ·17 | ·04 | ...... | ...... |
| 28. | s. | calm | n. | ...... | ·04 | ·53 | ...... | ·09 |
| ☾ 29. | sw. | w. | wnw. | s. | ·02 | ...... | ...... | ...... |
| 30. | sw. | w. | w. | w. | ·04 | ·02 | 1·60 | ·15 |
| Mean. | | | | | 1·66 | 1·32 | 3·79 | 4·15 |

# THE LONDON, EDINBURGH AND DUBLIN PHILOSOPHICAL MAGAZINE AND JOURNAL OF SCIENCE.

[THIRD SERIES.]

*FEBRUARY* 1848.

XIII. *On Shooting Stars.* By Sir J. W. LUBBOCK, Bart.*

AS I am not aware that any attempts have as yet been made to explain the cause of the sudden disappearance of shooting stars, I venture to offer the following remarks.

A minute brilliant spot of light is seen to traverse a portion of the heavens with great rapidity, it then disappears, often very suddenly.

Three hypotheses may be used to account for this most curious phænomenon.

1. The body shines by its own light, and then explodes like a sky-rocket, breaking into minute fragments too small to be any longer visible to the naked eye.

2. Such a body having shone by its own light, suddenly ceases to be luminous.

"The falling stars, and other fiery meteors which are frequently seen at a considerable height in the atmosphere, and which have received different names according to the variety of their figure and size, arise from the fermentation of the effluvia of acid and alkaline bodies which float in the atmosphere. When the more subtle parts of the effluvia are burnt away, the viscous and earthy parts become too heavy for the air to support, and by their gravity fall to the earth."—Keith's Use of the Globes. According to Sir Humphry Davy, in the Philosophical Transactions for 1817, "the luminous appearances of shooting stars and meteors cannot be owing to any inflammation of elastic fluids, but must depend upon the ignition of solid bodies."

3. The body shines by the reflected light of the sun, and

* Communicated by the Author.

I do not here pretend to treat of such a meteor as that I described in the Philosophical Magazine, vol. xxx. p. 4; see also vol. xxxi. p. 368. The phænomena which it presented were very different from those usually presented by shooting stars, and may have arisen from its meeting with the resistance of the earth's atmosphere.

ceases to be visible by its passing into the earth's shadow, or, in other words, is eclipsed.

Upon the two former suppositions, the fact of the star's disappearance conveys to us no knowledge of its position or of its distance from the earth; and all that can be said is, that if it be a satellite of the earth, the great rapidity of its motion involves the necessity of its being at no great distance from the earth's surface,—much nearer than the moon; while the resistance it would encounter in traversing the air would be so great, that it is probably without the limits of our atmosphere.

But although the two first suppositions leave us without instruction as to the orbit or position in space of the body in motion, the case is far different on the third hypothesis: for knowing the time when and the place in the heavens where the star disappeared, the elements of the geometry of three dimensions furnish the means of determining the exact distance of the body from the place of the spectator or from the centre of the earth. Nor is this observation difficult; for if seen on a starlight night, by attending to the configuration of the neighbouring stars, a close approximation may be found to the place of disappearance, which, in the event of such bodies existing, will be most valuable in the interval which must probably elapse before any orbits will have been determined with sufficient precision to enable us to anticipate their arrival, and to make preparations for obtaining more accurate data.

I propose to consider the third hypothesis.

Let $R'$ = sun's semidiameter,

$D$ = the distance of the sun's centre from that of the earth,

$R$ = earth's semidiameter,

$a$ = azimuth of the moving body at the instant of disappearance,

$\zeta$ = zenith distance of the moving body,

$\rho$ = the distance of the moving body from spectator.

$x, y, z$ the rectangular coordinates of the moving body, and also at the instant of disappearance, of a point on the surface of shadow.

$\theta$ = depression of sun's centre, so that $90° + \theta$ = sun's zenith distance, the sun being supposed to have set, the equation to the cone limiting the shadow of the earth is

$$\{-x\cos\theta + (z+R)\sin\theta\}\left\{\frac{R'-R}{D}\right\}$$
$$= R - \left\{\{x\sin\theta + (z+R)\cos\theta\}^2 + y^2\right\}^{\frac{1}{2}}, \quad (1.)$$

if $R' = 883000 \quad R = 7916 \quad D = 95{,}000{,}000$

$$\log \frac{R'-R}{D} = 7\cdot 66330.$$

Let

$$\frac{R'-R}{D} = q = \cdot 004605$$

$z^2(\sin^2 \theta - q^2 \cos^2 \theta) + 2xz\{\sin \theta \cos \theta + q^2 \sin \theta \cos \theta\} + y^2 + z^2\{\cos^2 \theta - q^2 \sin^2 \theta\}$
$+ 2R\{x(\sin \theta \cos \theta + q^2 \cos \theta \sin \theta - q \cos \theta) + z(\cos^2 \theta - q^2 \sin^2 \theta + q \sin \theta)\}$
$= R^2\{\sin^2 \theta(1+q^2) - 2q \sin \theta\}.$

The origin being at O the place of the spectator, the axis O$z$ being drawn from O to the zenith, and the axis $x$ having the same azimuth as the sun, if the azimuth of the moving body be reckoned from that point in the horizon,

$$x = \rho \sin \zeta \cos \alpha \quad y = \rho \sin \zeta \sin \alpha \quad z = \rho \cos \zeta;$$

and putting these values in equation (1.),

$\rho^2 \Big\{ \{\sin^2 \zeta \cos^2 \alpha (\sin^2 \theta - q^2 \cos^2 \theta) + 2 \sin \zeta \cos \alpha \cos \zeta \{\sin \theta \cos \theta + q^2 \sin \theta \cos \theta\}$
$\qquad + \sin^2 \zeta \sin^2 \alpha + \cos^2 \zeta \{\cos^2 \theta - q^2 \sin^2 \theta\} \Big\}$
$+ 2\rho R \Big\{ \sin \zeta \cos \alpha \{\sin \theta \cos \theta + q^2 \cos \theta \sin \theta - q \cos \theta\}$
$\qquad + \cos \zeta \{\cos^2 \theta - q^2 \sin^2 \theta + q \sin \theta\} \Big\}$
$= R^2\{\sin^2 \theta(1+q^2) - 2q \sin \theta\}.$

Hence it is evident, that if the place and time of disappearance of the moving body are known, the distance $\rho$ from the spectator can always be determined by a quadratic equation. Moreover, as the cone limiting the earth's shadow envelopes the spectator after the sun has set on all sides, wherever the shooting star disappears, a value of $\rho$ can be found which will satisfy the problem as far as the disappearance alone is concerned.

If, as a first approximation, we consider the earth as a sphere, and the shadow of the earth as limited by a cylinder, such that the axis of the cylinder is a line drawn from the centre of the earth to that of the sun, the equation to the cylinder is

$$\{x \sin \theta + (z+R) \cos \theta\}^2 + y^2 = R^2, \quad . \quad . \quad (2.)$$

$\rho^2\{\sin^2 \zeta \cos^2 \alpha \sin^2 \theta + 2 \cos \alpha \cos \zeta \sin \zeta \sin \theta \cos \theta$
$\qquad + \cos^2 \zeta \cos^2 \theta + \sin^2 \zeta \sin^2 \alpha\}$
$+ 2\rho R\{\sin \zeta \cos \alpha \sin \theta \cos \theta + \cos \zeta \cos \theta^2\} = R^2 \sin^2 \theta$

When $y = 0$, that is, when the *shooting star* disappears,

having the same azimuth as the sun, $\rho$ is given by a simple equation

$$\rho = \frac{R(1-\cos\theta)}{\sin\zeta\cos\alpha\sin\theta + \cos\zeta\cos\theta}.$$

If $R+c$ be the distance of the moving body from the earth's centre,

$$x^2 + y^2 + (z+R)^2 = (R+c)^2$$
$$x^2 + y^2 + z^2 = \rho^2$$
$$\rho^2 + 2\rho R\cos\zeta = 2cR + c^2,$$

from which equation $c$ and $R+c$ may be found.

The azimuth of the body reckoned from the meridian, or the angle SZP, must be found by adding to $\alpha$ the azimuth of the sun at the time of observation. If we consider the spherical triangle ZPS as seen from the centre of the earth, the angle SZP is the same as the azimuth of the body at the place of the observer; ZS the zenith distance is given by the equation

$$\tan ZS = \frac{\rho\sin\zeta}{\rho\cos\zeta + R}$$

sin dec. $= \cos$ az. $\times \sin$ ZS $\times \cos$ geogl. lat.
$\qquad + \cos$ ZS $\sin$ geogl. lat.

$$\sin\text{ hour angle} = \frac{\sin ZS \sin az.}{\cos \text{dec.}} = \sin(\text{sid. time} - \text{R.A.}).$$

By help of these equations, and the distance of the body from the centre of the earth, the position of the body in space is known. If, therefore, all the observations of the disappearance of meteors on any given night were examined, they might be discussed in two ways; either upon the hypothesis of their accompanying the earth in its orbit as satellites, or upon the hypothesis of their moving round the sun, by changing the origin of co-ordinates to the sun's centre.

A body just skimming the earth's surface would revolve round the earth in $1^h\ 26^m$. This, therefore, is a lower limit; and I find that if the semi-axis major of satellite

$$=2,\text{ the period } = 2^h\ 56^m$$
$$=3, \quad\ldots\quad = 3\ 40$$
$$=4, \quad\ldots\quad = 4\ 50$$

the period of the moon's revolution being $27^d\ 7^h\ 46^m$, and her mean distance $60\frac{1}{3}$.

If $\xi\lambda$ is a small motion in longitude, as seen from the centre of the earth during the time $\delta t$, $e$ the eccentricity, $\mu$ a constant depending on the mass of the earth, which may be eliminated by means of the moon's period, $a$ the semi-axis major,

$$\delta\lambda = \frac{\sqrt{\mu}\sqrt{a(1-e^2)}}{(R+c)^2}\delta t.$$

We cannot however determine the quantity $\delta\lambda$ from the angular motion, as seen by the spectator.

If fortunately the disappearance be observed by two spectators on the same night at different times, we should then obtain all the elements of its orbit. For as the satellite moves in a plane passing through the earth's centre, the equation to the plane of its orbit referred to the same coordinates as before is

$$A\rho\cos\alpha\sin\zeta + B\rho\sin\alpha\sin\zeta + C(\rho\cos\zeta + R) = 0,$$

where $A, B, C$ are constants, which express the cosines of the inclination of the plane of the orbit to the planes $yz$, $xz$, and $xy$.

If we possessed another complete observation,

$$A\rho'\cos\alpha'\sin\zeta' + B\rho'\sin\alpha'\sin\zeta' + C(\rho'\cos\zeta' + R) = 0,$$

such equations would determine completely the position of the orbit in space, and two points in the orbit. Hence $\delta\lambda$ would be known, and $a(1-e^2)$. The two places would also furnish $e$ and $\pi$, the longitude of the perihelion. After the interval of days or weeks, the orbit of a satellite might have become materially altered by disturbances, but not in a few minutes, separating independent observations by spectators at different points of the earth's surface.

The perturbations of satellites may be very considerable, and hence their motions, as seen from any place on the earth's surface, may be very irregular; for while the mass of Jupiter, the planet which produces the greatest perturbations in the solar system, is only about $\frac{1}{1000}$ of that of the sun, the primary, the moon, which produces the perturbations of satellites, is probably at least $\frac{1}{70}$ that of the earth or fourteen times greater. It will be recollected also that the magnitude of the perturbations depends upon the mass of the disturbing body, and scarcely at all upon that of the disturbed body, when minute. The deviation of the figure of the earth from that of a sphere may also have a considerable effect, and even perhaps the irregularities of its surface and the unequal density of its substance. These circumstances, taken together, may account for the great irregularity of their appearance, even if their orbits are nearly circular. If their orbits are eccentric, we have another cause of irregularity, to which may also contribute that their period is not nearly the aliquot part of a day. Their numbers may be considerable, even allowing for the shortness of their periodic times, for *shooting stars* are seen so frequently that they scarcely excite attention or even a passing remark. The question of their origin seems to have excited more controversy than any other; but for the solution of this difficulty, I apprehend we possess no data which do not apply equally to the moon and to the other bodies of the solar system.

The motion of the shooting stars is so rapid, that, supposing them to shine by the reflected light of the sun, their relative position to that of the sun may change considerably, even during the short time in which they are visible, and therefore not only they may become larger and more brilliant because their distance from the spectator is diminished, but also because the visible portion of their illuminated disc is increased. Or, on the other hand, their distance from the spectator increasing, and the visible portion of their illuminated disc decreasing, they may cease to be perceptible to the naked eye without being eclipsed. But in this case it seems probable that their disappearance would not be so sudden; and it is therefore desirable that the observer should particularly notice and record whether the shooting star disappears suddenly or otherwise.

If $\delta\lambda'$ is the angular velocity in a circle at the same distance $r$ from the centre of the earth,

$$\delta\lambda' = \sqrt{\mu} r^{-\frac{3}{2}} \delta t$$

$$\delta\lambda = \sqrt{1-e^2} \sqrt{\frac{a}{r}} \lambda'.$$

This is greatest in the same orbit when $r$ is least; $r$ is least when $r = a(1-e)$; therefore $\delta\lambda$ is greatest when

$$\delta\lambda = \sqrt{1+e}\, \delta\lambda';$$

$e$ cannot exceed unity, therefore $\delta\lambda$ cannot exceed $\sqrt{1+e}\, \delta\lambda'$.

If $\delta\lambda''$ is the angular motion of the moon in $\delta t$, and if $r'$ is the distance of the centre of the moon from the centre of the earth,

$$\delta\lambda' = \frac{r'^{\frac{3}{2}}}{r^{\frac{3}{2}}} \delta\lambda''.$$

As the moon revolves in 27·322 days, if $\delta t = 1''$, and if

$r' = 237000 \quad r = 4000$ (in miles), $\delta\lambda'' = \cdot 55''$ (sex.).

This gives 250″ for the angular motion of a satellite in a second of time, as seen from the centre of the earth, and moving at a distance of 4000 miles from the centre. Suppose the satellite to be about 100 miles from the spectator, and to be so situated that the angular velocity, as seen by the spectator, is inversely as this distance compared with the former distance, the apparent angular velocity would be 170′ per second of time, or

170° per minute. This is equivalent to a velocity of about five miles per second; according to M. Quetelet, their observed velocity is, on the average, about twenty miles per second.

If the body move in space round the sun, and is not to be considered as a satellite of the earth,

$$\delta\lambda = \sqrt{\mu}\sqrt{1-e^2}\frac{\sqrt{a}}{r^2}\delta t.$$

If $\delta\lambda'$ is the angle described by the earth in $\delta t$,

$$\delta\lambda' = \sqrt{\mu}\, r'^{-\frac{3}{2}}\delta t,$$

$$\delta\lambda = \sqrt{1-e^2}\frac{\sqrt{a}\, r'^{\frac{3}{2}}}{r^2}\delta t.$$

If the body move in a circle $\delta\lambda = \delta\lambda'$, if $\delta t = 1''$, this gives $\delta\lambda' = [3 \cdot 03491]\frac{1}{\rho}$ (in degrees, $\rho$ being in miles), the number between brackets being a logarithm. If $\rho = 100$, this gives $\delta\lambda'$ about 10°, and the velocity about eighteen miles per second, agreeing with the observed velocity.

The angular velocity in this case, as seen by the spectator, would depend partly upon the motion of the earth in its orbit, and upon its direction relatively to that of the other moving body.

Perhaps it may be found upon investigation, that some *shooting stars* belong to one class and some to the other. The periods of satellites would necessarily be so short, that the appearances might be satisfied by a small number of such bodies, because their apparitions would recur so frequently. But if the *shooting stars* are bodies revolving in space, the same body would be seen so seldom, that the conclusion seems in that case unavoidable, that the number of such bodies must be very great. Experience leads to the conclusion, that, under favourable circumstances, there is scarcely a night in which several are not visible. Nor is there any reason *à priori* for supposing that such bodies abound more in orbits nearly intersecting the orbit of the earth than in any other part of the planetary system. It seems natural to suppose, that, coming so very near the earth, the attraction of the earth would in some cases overcome the attraction of the sun, and cause the body to revolve in future as a satellite. If we adopt the following data,

Distance of the sun = 95,000,000 miles,

Distance of the moving body from the centre of the earth = 4000 miles,

Mass of the earth $\frac{1}{354936}$, the attraction of the earth would be about 3000 times greater than that of the sun.

The interesting calculations of M. Petit\*, Director of the Observatory of Toulouse, not only render probable the existence of small satellites, but tend to establish the identity of a body revolving round the earth in about 3 hours 20 minutes.

I have endeavoured in this paper to point out the importance of marking the exact time and place of disappearance; for although if the place is found at any point of the path by two different observers, theoretically the parallax could be ascertained, in practice this method is beset with great difficulties.

It seems to me that the *splitting* of the falling stars, like a rocket and the *trains of light*, a phænomenon often witnessed, might, if other circumstances were favourable to the explanation, be accounted for by supposing the star to graze the surface of the shadow before absolute immersion.

Close to the earth's surface, the linear distance traversed in the penumbra must be small; but at greater distances this will increase, and perhaps render the disappearance less sudden. If the distance comes out large, it will of course be necessary to recalculate it, supposing the surface of the shadow to be conical and not cylindrical.

23 St. James's Place, Jan. 10, 1848.

---

XIV. *On different Properties of Solar Radiation producing or preventing a deposit of Mercury on Silver Plates coated with Iodine, or its compounds with Bromine or Chlorine, modified by Coloured Glass Media and the Vapours of the Atmosphere.* By A. CLAUDET, *Esq.* Communicated by Sir DAVID BREWSTER, *F.R.S. &c.*†

FROM the commencement of photography it has been known that the red, orange, and yellow rays exert but a very feeble photogenic influence on the Daguerreotype plate. The experiments of several philosophers, especially those of Sir J. Herschel on photogenic papers, published in February 1840, prove that this action is more particularly confined to the most refrangible part of the prismatic spectrum, commencing from the space found covered by the blue rays and extending to the extremity of the violet, and sometimes even beyond it.

In 1839, Sir J. Herschel observed that the red rays exercised on several photogenic papers an antagonistic action to the photogenic rays, modifying their effect. Contrary to this, in 1841, M. Ed. Becquerel presented to the Paris Academy of Sciences a memoir, in which he announced that the red,

\* See the *Comptes Rendus*, October 12, 1846, and August 9, 1847.
† From the Philosophical Transactions for 1847, part ii.; having been received by the Royal Society June 10, and read June 17, 1847.

orange, and yellow rays were endowed with the property of continuing the action commenced by the photogenic rays; these latter he called *exciting rays*; to the first he gave the name of *continuing rays*.

M. Ed. Becquerel made his experiments on photogenic papers, and added that he had observed the same effects on the iodized silver plate.

Dr. Draper of New York published in the Philosophical Magazine for November 1842, some remarks on a class of rays which he supposed to exist in the light of the brilliant sun of Virginia, and which had the property, when separated, of entirely suspending the action of the diffused light from the sky; these antagonistic rays extended from the blue to the extremity of the red, and appeared to be almost as active in preventing the decomposition of the iodide of silver as the blue rays were in producing it.

In January 1845 a memoir was read by me at the Society of Arts, London, in a part of which I recommended opticians to construct object-glasses in which they should particularly correct the chromatic aberration of the long photogenic space of the solar spectrum, even at the cost of the achromatism of the less refrangible rays. This, however, had been already indicated, without my being aware of it at the time, by Sir J. Herschel; but I added that the greater separation of the visual and photogenic focus which might result from such a combination, according to the quality of the glass employed, would be an advantage, by dispersing, at the focus or on the plate, beyond the photogenic lines, the red, orange or yellow rays; for the reason, that if they were brought to the same point they would tend to neutralize and destroy the effect of the photogenic rays.

In October 1846, M. Lerebours announced to the Paris Academy of Sciences that the red rays prevented the action of the photogenic rays; this announcement induced Messrs. Foucault and Fizeau to publish immediately similar results, which they had previously consigned to the Academy in a sealed memoir, bearing date May 1846.

These communications of Messrs. Lerebours, Foucault and Fizeau, led Dr. Draper to write a letter, published in the Philosophical Magazine of February last, repeating his observations on the spectrum of Virginia, adding several other analogous facts confirming the theory of a protecting and even destroying action exercised by the least refrangible rays. Dr. Draper, in the same letter, said that the rays which protect the plate from ordinary photogenic action are themselves capable, when isolated, of producing a peculiar photogenic effect.

Soon after the publication of M. Ed. Becquerel's memoir, M. Gaudin made some analogous researches on the Daguerreotype plate; and he succeeded in developing an image as perfect as that produced by mercury, by submitting the plate, when taken from the camera obscura, to the action of light alone under a yellow glass, and without any subsequent exposure to mercury.

This curious discovery gave some hope that, from the supposed continuing action of the red and yellow glasses, by submitting the plate alternately, or simultaneously, to the action of the mercury and of these glasses, an accelerated development of the image would result; but all the researches made to arrive at this point have been fruitless; and, until the present time, the labours of Messrs. Becquerel and Gaudin have received no satisfactory explanation or useful application.

My own experiments, which are the object of this memoir, seem to prove that M. Ed. Becquerel was mistaken as regards the Daguerreotype plate, in so far as he attributed to the red, orange, and yellow glasses a continuing action of the effect of the photogenic rays.

In the Daguerreotype, when we speak of the *photogenic effect*, we cannot understand any other than that which gives to the surface an affinity for mercurial vapour.

In the case of photogenic papers, it is true that the red, orange, and yellow rays render the parts previously affected by the photogenic rays black or of a darker colour. It is the same with the Daguerreotype plate, which after it has been feebly impressed, darkens rapidly to a violet colour under the radiation of a red or yellow glass. This is the only continuing effect I have observed, and this effect is not *continuing* in a Daguerreotype sense, it has no relation to the property of attracting the mercurial vapour; on the contrary, it will be seen from the experiments which I am about to describe, that the radiations of red, orange and yellow glasses entirely destroy this property. There exists then a certain analogy between the action of the red, orange and yellow glasses upon the photogenic papers and the Daguerreotype plate; and this continuing action is probably due to the distinct photogenic action possessed by these rays, as I am able to prove by facts of a very positive nature.

These two photogenic actions result from two different principles, nevertheless producing similar effects, as to the colour obtained, on the iodide, bromide or chloride of silver, whether it be found isolated, as is the case on the photogenic paper, or it be found in the presence of metallic silver, as happens upon the Daguerreotype plate; but they produce quite an opposite effect upon the silver plate, whatever may be the colour previously given to the surface by these two radiations, endowing it with a property, the one of attracting, the other of repelling the mercurial vapours. We must take care not to confound these two results; we can conceive two different actions giving the same colour to the iodide of silver, and we can also conceive that these two actions may be endowed with contrary properties as regards the fixation of mercurial vapour.

The facts pointed out by M. Gaudin are the results of an action which does not belong to the Daguerreotype, since they are manifested without the aid of mercury; for we must not lose sight of the fact, that the production of the Daguerreotype image is due only to the affinity for mercury of the parts previously affected by the photogenic rays. It does not then follow from the production of an image without mercury, by crystallization or some peculiar arrangement of the molecules, that the red, orange and yellow rays exert a continuing action analogous to that which determines the fixation of mercurial vapour.

The experiments of Sir J. Herschel, of Dr. Draper, of M. Lerebours, and of Messrs. Foucault and Fizeau, to prove the protective and destructive action of the red rays, were made with the prism.

These philosophers have thus operated with the isolated rays in all their natural purity, and after them it would have been useless to seek to confirm or to contradict experiments so ably conducted and so conclusive.

Sir J. Herschel, in a memoir published in the Philosophical Magazine for February 1842, approves only of experiments made by means of the prism, as they are less subject to error from the foreign rays, which the coloured glasses never entirely exclude. This observation is perfectly just in theory, but in practice, in the particular case of the photogenic power of different rays and of their different actions, it will be found that these phænomena can be studied with greater facility by using coloured glasses, and that the feeble quantity of foreign rays which they admit, far from interfering with the deductions of the experimenter, serve only to confirm and to render them more conclusive. We shall presently see that these foreign rays are completely neutralized in this class of experiments, and it would have been unfortunate not to have added these tests to those of the solar spectrum, since by the aid of coloured glasses I have been enabled, not only to confirm certain properties of the pure spectrum, but also to discover some others which had escaped my predecessors.

Having examined with a prism the light transmitted through the glasses used in these experiments, I found that the red absorbs two-thirds of the prismatic spectrum, from the space covered by the green to the extremity of the violet, leaving the red, orange, and a little yellow, followed by a very slight trace of green. The orange glass gave more yellow, the green being more decided. The light yellow glass intercepted the half of the spectrum; the red was less intense than in the preceding; the yellow occupied two-thirds of its total length, and the green became very distinct; but as far as my sight allowed me to judge, I could not discover any portion of blue in either case: certainly in the spectrum of the red glass there was not the least trace of it.

I will now detail the series of observations I have made upon light transmitted through certain media—the vapours of the atmosphere, and red, orange, and yellow glasses. These experiments have brought forth some results which will I hope contribute to lay the foundation of a more complete theory of the photographic phænomena.

Having noticed, one densely foggy day, that the disc of the sun was of a deep red colour, I directed my apparatus towards it. After ten seconds of exposure I put the prepared plate in the mercury box, and I obtained a round image perfectly black. The sun had produced no photogenic effect. In another experiment I left the plate operating for twenty minutes. The sun had passed over a certain space of the plate, and there resulted an image seven or eight times the sun's diameter in length; it was black throughout, so that it was evident, wherever the red disc of the sun had passed, not only was there a want of photogenic action, but the red rays had destroyed the effect produced previous to the sun's passage. I repeated these experiments during several days successively, operating with a sun of different tints of red and yellow. These different tints produced nearly the same effect: whereever the sun had passed there existed a black band.

I then operated in a different manner: not content with the slow motion of the sun, I moved the camera obscura from right to left, and *vice versâ*, lowering it each time by means of a screw. In this manner the sun passed rapidly over five or six zones of the plate. Its passage was marked by long black bands of the diameter of the sun, whilst the intervals were white. It was then evident that the red and yellow rays, which alone were capable of piercing the fog, had destroyed the action produced by the little photogenic light which came from the zenith.

I then operated with coloured glasses. After exposing a

plate covered with a piece of black lace to daylight, I covered one half, and submitted the other to the radiation of a red glass: the mercury developed an image of the lace on the part which had been acted on only by the white light; the other, which had afterwards received the action of the red rays, remained black. The red glass had destroyed the photogenic effect in the same manner as it had been done by the red light of the sun.

I made the same experiment with orange and yellow glasses, and obtained analogous results, but in different times.

Then, having exposed a plate to daylight, I subsequently covered it with a piece of black lace, and exposed it again under a red glass: this produced a negative image. The red had destroyed the effect of the white light in the intervals of the lace, the threads of which preventing the action of the red glass, produced a white image upon a black ground. In operating in this manner upon one-half of the plate, exposing the other half covered only by the same lace to the light of the day, I obtained by the first a negative, and by the second a positive image. The orange and yellow glasses give the same result, paying regard to the difference of time in their respective actions.

All these experiments prove what has been already observed by others before me, but in a different manner, that the red, orange, and yellow rays destroy the effect of the photogenic light, whether these rays be produced by the prism or by the action of coloured media; but, I believe, it has not been observed by any one before me, that after the destruction of the photogenic effect the plate is perfectly restored to its former sensitiveness to white light.

After exposing a plate to daylight, and then submitting it to the destructive action of red, orange or yellow rays, it will be found again sensitive to the same white light.

I have obtained plates which present an equal and uniform image, although the one-half had been exposed to light, and then restored by the red, orange, or yellow glass, while the other half had received only the single and final radiation. We may then expose a plate to light, destroy this effect by the action of red or yellow glass, which renders it again sensitive; then expose it again to light, destroy this second effect by the same coloured glass, and so on for many times, without changing the properties of the surface; so that if we stop after any of the exposures to white light, the plate will receive mercury; but if we stop after any of the exposures to red, orange or yellow light, we shall obtain no fixation of mercurial vapour.

Having exposed a plate to the two actions alternately, first, once upon one zone, twice upon another, and so on until the last zone had been exposed and destroyed six times, I covered the plate with a piece of black lace or an engraving, finally exposing the whole to white light; the result was an equal deposit of mercury upon the whole surface of the plate. The impression of the lace or engraving seemed to be the result of a single exposition to light, as would have been the case with a normal plate; therefore the action of the red, orange, or yellow glass upon a plate previously affected by light, produces the same effect as a fresh exposure to the vapours of iodine or bromine, when we wish to restore the plate to its first sensitiveness.

This restoring property of the coloured glasses may be of great use in the Daguerreotype manipulation. Instead of preparing the plates in the dark, it may be done with impunity in the open light. To give sensitiveness, we have only to place the plate for some minutes under a red glass before putting it in the camera obscura. The frame or box used to hold the plate, if furnished with a red glass at the bottom, will serve for this restoration. I have obtained in this manner images equal in effect to those produced on plates prepared in the dark.

This possibility of preparing plates in open day offers a great advantage to those who wish to take views or pictures abroad, and who cannot conveniently obtain a dark room. Again, in the case of a plate which has been left too long in the camera obscura, or accidentally exposed to the light, instead of rejecting it, we can restore its sensitiveness by placing it under a red glass. There is still another useful application of this property: if after one or two minutes' exposure to the mercury we perceive the image is too rapidly developing, or presenting signs of solarization, which a practised eye discovers before it is too much advanced, we have only to stop this accumulation of mercury by exposing the plate for a few seconds to the red light, and again place it in the mercury box, to complete the modifications, which give the image all its tones and the most favourable tint. In truth, we may complete all the operations of the Daguerreotype in the open air, in the middle of a field if necessary. We can introduce the plate into the mercury box, in the same manner that we did in the camera obscura, by means of the same frame and red glass, which also serves to protect it when we take it from the mercury to rapidly view its development. I say rapidly, for if we expose it too long to the red light, the photogenic effect will be neutralized. We shall presently see that the time required to observe the state of the image is not sufficient to affect its affinity for mercury, if it be found requisite to replace it in the mercury box. The exposure under red glass necessary to destroy the effect produced by white light, must be a hundred times longer than has been the exposure to white light, that of the orange glass fifty times, and that of the yellow glass only ten times; thus a plate exposed to white light for a second will be restored to its former sensitiveness in ten seconds by the yellow glass, in fifty by the orange, and in a hundred by the red. As soon as the sensitiveness of the plate affected by white light is restored by the coloured glasses, it may be affected again by the photogenic light. It is not even necessary that the restoration should be complete; at each degree of restoration the plate is capable of receiving an accumulation of photogenic effect. If the red rays have not acted more than fifty times longer than the daylight, only half of the effect will be destroyed; if twenty-five times longer, one-fourth; and so on in proportion.

Besides the destructive action of the red, orange and yellow glasses, these same radiations are endowed with a photogenic power, that is to say, they have, like the blue and violet rays, the power of causing the fixation of mercurial vapour. Therefore these radiations are endowed with two contrary actions; the one destructive of the effect of the photogenic light, and the other analogous to the effect of this light.

If the red, orange, and yellow radiations of the prism had not also the power of operating photogenically, it might be supposed that this action of the coloured glasses was due to some of the most refrangible rays transmitted by these coloured media. But this cannot be; for if the photogenic action of the red, orange, and yellow rays were the same as that of the more refrangible rays, it could never develope itself under the destructive action which the same glasses carry with them.

But there is yet more; each ray of the spectrum has its own photogenic action, and they are in this respect independent of each other, and of a different kind; so that the one cannot continue the effect commenced by the other, whether it be for the production or for the destruction of the photogenic effect. I would again observe, whenever I speak of a photogenic effect, I mean that which gives to the Daguerreotype plate the property of attracting the vapours of mercury.

If we expose a plate covered by an engraving to the red light 5000 times longer than is required to produce an effect by white light, we obtain by the fixation of mercury a feeble image, the lights of which are of a gray tone. I could never go beyond this feeble image, which appeared to be the maximum of effect for the red glass. It is impossible to attribute this effect to some feeble quantity of rays, properly called photogenic, passing through the coloured glasses, for we have seen that the blue and violet rays cannot operate under the destructive action of the red rays; this fact proves then evidently, that if the red radiation has a photogenic effect, it cannot be due to the same principle which produces the photogenic effect of the rays situated at the other extremity of the spectrum. The yellow glass has also a peculiar photogenic action of its own, it is a hundred times slower than that of white light, whilst its destructive action is not more than ten times as slow. We can obtain by the photogenic action of the yellow glass an image almost identical, as to force and colour, with an image produced by daylight; with this difference, that the excess of action does not give the blue solarization which we observe upon plates strongly affected by daylight.

The different nature of the photogenic action of red, orange, and yellow glasses, from that of the daylight, is also proved by the fact, that the photogenic action produced by these coloured glasses cannot be destroyed by their own reversing action, although the red will destroy the photogenic action of the yellow, and both of these will destroy the action of daylight.

The double property of producing and destroying a photogenic effect is manifested upon a specimen which offers on one-half of the plate a negative image, and upon the other half a positive image, produced at the same time by the same radiation. The length of time necessary to operate with the red glass has not allowed me to obtain a good impression, but I have succeeded perfectly with the yellow glass. The experiment is especially beautiful, and has been thus made:—

I exposed one-half of the plate to daylight for one second, keeping the other half in the dark. The entire plate was then covered with an engraving and exposed under a light yellow glass during ten seconds for the part previously affected by white light, and during a hundred seconds for that which had been kept in the dark. The yellow glass destroyed on the first half the effect of the daylight wherever the plate was not protected by the black lines of the engraving, and the parts only which under these lines had been protected from the destructive action, received the mercury, producing a negative image; while the same radiation of the yellow glass had operated photogenically upon the other half, developing a positive image by the fixation of mercury upon the parts corresponding to the lights of the engraving.

Having exposed a plate with an engraving under the red glass for sixty minutes, I replaced the red by a yellow glass, without the engraving; after exposing the half of this plate for five minutes under this yellow glass, the other half being kept in the dark, the mercury produced a negative image on the half exposed to yellow light, while the other gave no trace of either positive or negative action. This result can only be explained in the following manner:—

First. That sixty seconds had not sufficed for the apparent action of the red upon the half not exposed to the following radiation of the yellow glass.

Secondly. That nevertheless there had been the commencement of an action upon which the yellow glass had to exercise its destructive action.

Thirdly. That while the yellow glass was occupied in destroying the photogenic action of the red glass, restoring the surface to its primitive state, it was exercising a photogenic action upon the parts protected by the engraving from the red rays, and in five minutes this photogenic action of the yellow glass had produced a negative image by operating upon the shadows of the drawing.

It results from the experiments I have described, that the solar radiation, when modified by coloured media, is in the Daguerreotype process endowed with several different photogenic actions, corresponding with various rays of the spectrum.

The various photogenic actions of the modified solar radiation have distinct characters; each of these modifications is endowed with a photogenic power peculiar to itself, and which gives an affinity for mercurial vapour to the Daguerreotype plate. These various actions are so different, that we cannot mix them artificially to assist each other, as they are antagonistic. The effect commenced by the blue rays is destroyed by the red and yellow; that which was produced by the red is destroyed by the yellow; the effect of the yellow rays is destroyed by the red; and the effect of the two latter is destroyed by the blue; each radiation destroys the effect of the others. Thus it appears that each radiation changes the state of the surface, and each change produces the sensitiveness to mercurial vapour when it does not exist, and destroys this sensitiveness when it does exist.

The alternate change of the state of the plate by these various radiations seems to prove that the chemical compound remains always the same under these different influences; that there is no separation or disengagement of the constituent elements.

If the blue radiation or white light liberates iodine or bromine, these elements would evaporate or combine with the silver surface immediately beneath. If we take the first idea, how comes it that the red radiation re-establishes the compound in its primitive proportions; and, in the second case, how does it happen that these rays are capable of decomposing the surface beneath, liberating the iodine or bromine, and then combining them again with the upper surface? It is impossible to admit that the red radiation is endowed at the same time with the property of separating and the property of reuniting the same elements. We must then attribute it to a particular force—electricity perhaps, which might accompany each radiation, and which, under the influence of the one, would act positively, and negatively under the other, without changing the chemical compound. In one case this influence would give the affinity for mercury, and in the other destroy it.

At all events, we must look for another explanation of the phænomenon than the one which has hitherto been received, viz. the decomposition of the iodide of silver by the action of light. It is true that light decomposes iodide of silver, forming a subiodide, but this seems to require a longer time than that during which the surface is endowed with the property of attracting the vapours of mercury. In fact, the last property is communicated nearly instantaneously, which is not the case for the decomposition of the iodide by the action of light.

---

XV. *On the Combination of the Theorems of* Maclaurin *and* Taylor. *By* J. R. Young, *Professor of Mathematics in Belfast College*[*].

IN the application of Maclaurin's theorem to the development of a function $F(a+x)$ in a series proceeding according to the powers of $x$, we are always directed to differentiate the function F in reference to $x$, and then to put zero for $x$ in the several results. There is an unnecessary expenditure of symbolical work, and therefore of time in following this direction; for it is an axiomatic principle, which I have elsewhere announced[†], that whether we differentiate $F(a+x)$ in reference to $x$, and afterwards make $x$ zero, or make $x$ zero first, and then differentiate in reference to $a$, the results are identical; that is,

$$\left[\frac{d^n F(a+x)}{dx^n}\right] = \frac{d^n F(a)}{da^n},$$

[*] Communicated by the Author.
[†] Mechanics' Magazine, Jan. 15, 1848.

the brackets indicating what the expression between them becomes when $x=0$.

In writing down Maclaurin's theorem, authors differ considerably as to the notation employed for the coefficients. I have thought it would be well, for the sake of uniformity in this respect, if the plan generally adopted for distinguishing the coefficients of Bernoulli, and which, indeed, are only those of Maclaurin in a particular case, were universally followed. Maclaurin's theorem would thus be written

$$F(a+x) = M_0 + M_1 x + M_2 \frac{x^2}{2} + M_3 \frac{x^3}{2.3} + \&c., \quad . \quad (1.)$$

and Taylor's,

$$F(x+a) = T_0 + T_1 a + T_2 \frac{a^2}{2} + T_3 \frac{a^3}{2.3} + \&c. \quad . \quad . \quad (2.)$$

Applying the first of these theorems to the function $y = \log (a+x)$, in order to illustrate the foregoing principle, we have, making $x=0$,

$$\log a = M_0, \quad \frac{dy}{da} = \frac{1}{a} = M_1, \quad \frac{d^2y}{da^2} = -\frac{1}{a^2} = M_2,$$

$$\frac{d^3y}{da^3} = \frac{2}{a^3} = M_3, \quad \frac{d^4y}{da^4} = -\frac{2.3}{a^4} = M_4,$$

&c. &c.

$$\therefore \log(a+x) = \log a + \frac{x}{a} - \frac{x^2}{2a^2} + \frac{x^3}{3a^3} - \frac{x^4}{4a^4} + \&c.$$

And, from the process by which the coefficients have here been deduced, it is plain that Taylor's development of $\log (x+a)$ is got from this by simply changing the places of $a$ and $x$; and that the one development is always convertible into the other, by thus interchanging the two terms of the binomial under F. There is therefore no necessity for considering (1.) and (2.) as distinct theorems: nor is it correct to do so, since they are both comprehended under the same form ; for whichever be the term according to whose powers the development is to proceed, the coefficients are always to be derived from the function *after that term is made zero*. Hence, calling either term, indifferently, $t$; and denoting the differential coefficients derived, as here explained, by $D_1$, $D_2$, &c., the following theorem comprehends both (1.) and (2.):

$$y = D_0 + D_1 t + D_2 \frac{t^2}{2} + D_3 \frac{t^3}{2.3} + \&c.$$

Even when the function is not that of a binomial, but of a simple monomial, as $a^x$, $\log x$, &c., still it will be advisable, in seeking the development, to take the more general form $a^{x+h}$, $\log(x+h)$, &c., and to proceed as above, afterwards making $h=0$; for we shall thus always be led to true developments, and thence to the cases in which the sought developments are impossible, these being indicated by the hypothesis of $h=0$ causing the coefficients to become infinite. And it is obvious, from the method above described, that the coefficients of the development of $F(x+h)$ are just as readily obtained as those derived from $F(x)$ in the usual way.

In thus recommending that $x$ be replaced by $x+h$, when the development of $F(x)$ is required in powers of $x$, it will be observed, from what is said above, that it is merely proposed to deduce $D_0$, $D_1$, $D_2$, &c. from $F(h)$. If these are infinite when $h=0$, the inference will be, that, *with finite coefficients*, the development is impossible. But if we leave $h$ undetermined, and put, in the series, $x-h$ for $x$, we shall then get the development of $F(x)$, with finite coefficients, in powers of $x-h$; and as $h$ is arbitrary, we may thus approach as near to the proposed development as we please. And although for the purposes of actual numerical computation, the coefficients would become more and more unmanageable, from their increasing magnitude, as $h$ approaches to zero, yet even in this extreme case—in which the coefficients actually become infinite—the development, regarded as the last of the series of developments here spoken of, will still be analytically true.

Belfast, Jan. 5, 1848.

XVI. *On the Production of Light by Chemical Action.* By JOHN WILLIAM DRAPER, *M.D., Professor of Chemistry in the University of New York*[*].

THE production of light and heat by the combustion of various bodies is, of all chemical processes, that which ministers most to the comfort and well-being of man. By it the rigour of winter is moderated, and night made almost as available for our purposes as the day.

One would suppose that, of a phænomenon on which so much of our personal and social happiness depends, and which must have been daily witnessed by every man that has ever lived, all the particulars ought to have been long ago known. Among scientific men its importance has been universally recognized. The early theories of chemistry, such as those of Stahl and Lavoisier, are essentially theories of combustion.

It is nevertheless remarkable how little positive knowledge we still possess on this subject. Some chemists believe that

[*] Communicated by the Author.

the light emitted by flames is due to electric discharges; others, regarding light and heat as material bodies, which can be incorporated or united with ponderable substances, suppose that they are disengaged as chemical changes go on. In this confusion of opinions, a multitude of interesting and hitherto unanswered questions present themselves. It is known that different substances when burning emit lights of different colours: thus sulphur and carbonic oxide burn blue, wax yellow, and cyanogen lilac. What are the chemical conditions that determine these singular differences? How is it that, by changing the circumstances of combustion, we can vary the nature of the light? We turn aside the flame of a candle by means of a blowpipe, and a neat blue cone appears; why does it shine with a blue light?

Such inquiries might be multiplied without end; but a little consideration shows that their various answers depend on the determination of a much more general problem; viz. *can any connexion be traced between the chemical conditions under which a body burns, and the nature of the light it emits?* It is to the discussion of that problem that this memoir is devoted.

Sir H. Davy has already furnished us with two important circumstances in relation to the nature of flame:—1st. All common flames are incandescent shells, the interior of which is dark; 2nd, the relative quantity of light emitted depends on the temporary disengagement of solid particles.

It is only by a very general examination of the light arising from various solids, vapours and gases, when burning, that we can expect to obtain data for a true theory of combustion. This is what I shall endeavour to furnish on the present occasion.

As was foreseen by all the older chemists, the true theory of combustion, whatever it may prove to be, must necessarily be one of the fundamental theories of chemistry. It must include the nature of all chemical changes whatsoever. The subject is therefore not alone interesting in a popular sense, but of great importance in its scientific connexions.

1. *Prismatic analysis of the flames of various vapours and gases; proving that they yield all the colours of the spectrum.*

I commenced this investigation of the nature of flame, and of combustion generally, by an optical examination of various bodies in the act of burning. Some authors have asserted that certain flames yield monochromatic lights. It is necessary to verify this assertion if true, or set it aside if false.

The instrumental arrangement which I have employed is as follows:—The rays of the flame, of which the examination is to be made, pass through a horizontal slit $\frac{1}{50}$th of an inch wide and one inch long in a metallic screen, and are received at a distance of six or eight feet on a flint-glass prism, the axis of which is parallel to the slit. After passing the prism they enter a small telescope, which has a divided micrometer, and also parallel wires in its eye-piece. Through this telescope the resulting spectrum is viewed.

If it be the flame of a lamp of any kind that is to be examined, by using a moveable stand we are able to raise or lower it, and thus analyse different *horizontal elements* in its lower, its middle, or its upper part at pleasure. If, instead of a horizontal, we wish to examine a *vertical element* of the flame, the slit and the prism must of course be set vertically. The former mode possesses great advantages, as will be presently pointed out. It is to be understood, in all cases, that the eye-piece of the telescope is adjusted to give a sharp image of the slit, and the prism is at its angle of minimum deviation.

By this arrangement I have examined a great number of different flames; as those of oil, alcohol, solution of boracic acid and nitrate of strontian in alcohol, phosphorus, sulphur, carbonic oxide, hydrogen, cyanogen, arseniuretted hydrogen, &c. Among these it will be noticed different colours occur. Oil gives a yellow flame, alcohol a pale blue, boracic acid green, strontian red, phosphorus yellowish-white, sulphur and carbonic oxide blue, hydrogen pale yellow, cyanogen lilac, arseniuretted hydrogen white, &c.

Notwithstanding this diversity of colour, all these flames, as well as many others I have tried, yield the same result : *every prismatic colour is found in them*. Even in those cases where the flame is very faint, as in alcohol and hydrogen gas, not only may red, yellow, green, blue, and violet light be traced, but even bright Fraunhoferian lines of different colours.

This observation holds good for those flames reputed to be monochromatic; for example, alcohol burnt from a wick imbued with common salt. It is not alone a yellow light which is evolved; the other colours plainly, though more faintly, appear.

All flames, no matter what their primitive colours may be, evolve all the prismatic rays. Their special tints arise from the preponderance of one class of rays over another; thus in cyanogen the reds predominate, and in sulphur the blues.

The production of light, in the case of flames, is thus proved to be a very complex phænomenon. The chemical conditions under which their burning takes place are likewise very complex. The combustible vapour is surrounded on all sides by atmospheric air: diffusion occurs, and rapid currents are established by the high temperature. Such circumstances complicate the result; and it is only by observing the burning of an elementary solid, in which most of these disturbances are cut off, that we can hope to effect a proper resolution of the problem.

II. *Prismatic analysis of the light of an elementary solid burning at different temperatures; proving that as the temperature rises the more refrangible rays appear.*

I took from the fire a mass of anthracite coal, the fuel ordinarily used in domestic œconomy in New York, and which from its compactness, the intense heat it evolves, and other properties, appears to be well-fitted for such investigations as the present. This coal was placed on a support, so as to present a plane surface to the slit in the metal screen. The rays coming from it and passing the slit were received on a flint-glass prism, and viewed through the telescope.

When the coal was first taken from the fire, and was burning very intensely, on looking through the telescope I saw all the coloured rays of the spectrum in their proper order. I had previously passed through the slit a beam of sunlight reflected from a mirror, that I might have a standard spectrum with fixed lines. Now when the coal was burning at its utmost vigour, the spectrum it gave did not seem to me to differ either as respects length or the distribution of its colours from the spectrum of sunlight; but as the combustion declined, and the coal burnt less brightly, I saw that its spectrum was becoming less and less, the shortening taking place at the more refrangible extremity, one ray after another disappearing in due succession. First the violet became extinct, then the indigo, then the blue, then the green, until at last the red, with an ash-gray light occupying the place of the yellow was alone visible, and presently this also went out.

From numerous experiments of this sort, I conclude that *there is a connexion between the refrangibility of the light which a burning body yields, and the intensity of the chemical action going on; and that the refrangibility always increases as the chemical action increases.* It may perhaps be objected by some, that, in the form of experiment here introduced, two totally different things are confounded; and that the burning coal not only gives forth its rays as a combustible body, strictly speaking, but also as an incandescent mass.

To avoid this objection as far as possible, and also to reach a much higher temperature than could have been otherwise obtained, I threw a stream of oxygen gas on that portion of the anthracite which was opposite the slit; but my expectations were disappointed; for instead of the combustion being increased, the coal was actually extinguished by the jet playing on it. I therefore replaced the anthracite with a flat piece of well-burnt charcoal, kindled at the part opposite the slit, and throwing a stream of oxygen on this part, the combustion was greatly increased; and through the telescope I saw a spectrum rivalling that of the sunbeams in brilliancy, all the colours, from the extreme red to the extreme violet, being present.

Now on shutting off the supply of oxygen the combustion of course declined; and whilst this was going on, I looked through the telescope and saw the violet, the indigo, the blue, the green, &c. fade away in succession. By merely turning the stopcock, through which the oxygen came, I could re-establish the original colours or witness their decline. And it was very interesting to see with what unerring regularity, as the chemical action became more intense, the more refrangible colours were developed; and how, as it declined, they disappeared in due succession; the final tint being red, and that ash-gray in the position of the yellow, which I have described in my former memoir. (Phil. Mag. May 1847, p. 349.)

In the form of experiment here made the combustion is of course merely superficial; and the rays come from the charcoal, not as an incandescent, but as a burning body.

### III. *Of the constitution of flames; proving that they consist of a series of concentric and differently coloured shells.*

I regard the foregoing experiments as affording the means of explanation of the much more complicated phænomena of flames; and proceed to inquire whether the principle I have just brought forward, of the co-ordinate increase of refrangibility and chemical action, will hold good, premising the experiments now to be detailed with the following considerations.

All common flames, as is well-known, consist of a thin shell of ignited matter, the interior being dark, the combustion taking effect on those points only which are in contact with the air. From the circumstances under which the air is usually supplied, this ignited shell cannot be a mere mathematical superficies, but must have a sensible thickness. If we imagine it to consist of a series of strata, it is obvious that the phænomena of combustion are different for each. The outer stratum is in absolute contact with the air, and there the combustion is most perfect; but by reason of the rapid diffusion of gases into one another, currents, and other such causes, the atmospheric air must necessarily pervade the burning shell to a certain depth; and in the successive strata, as we advance inwards, the activity of the burning must decline. On the exterior stratum oxygen is in excess, at the interior the combustible vapour, and between these limits there must be an admixture of the two, which differs at different depths. Admitting the results of the foregoing experiments with anthracite coal and charcoal to be true, viz. that as combustion is more active rays of a higher degree of refrangibility are evolved, it follows that *each point of the superficies of every flame, no matter what the combustible may be, must yield all the colours of the spectrum*, the violet coming from the outer strata, the yellow from the intermediate, and the red from those within. If we could isolate an elementary horizontal section of a flame, it should exhibit the appearance of a rainbow-ring; and when those compound rays are received on the face of a prism, the constituent colours are parted out, by reason of their different refrangibility, and the eye thus made sensible of their actual existence.

When thus, by the aid of a prism, we analyse the light that comes from any portion of the superficies of a flame, we in effect dissect out in a convenient manner, and arrange together side by side, rays that have come from different strata of the burning shell. These, without the prism, would have pursued the same normal path, and produced a commixed effect on the eye, but with it are separated transversely, and each becomes perceptible.

It might be supposed that, in the familiar instance of an oil-lamp, if we put any check on the supply of the air and thereby check the intensity of combustion, we ought to have the flame emitting rays of light, the refrangibility of which becomes less and less, and which, from their being quite white, should pass through different shades of orange, and end in a dull red. But the compound nature of the burning vapour interferes with that result; for when a certain point is gained, the hydrogen for the most part alone burns, the carbon being set free as smoke, and such a flame cannot support itself in strict accordance with the principle given.

We must then search for other conditions under which carbon is found which are free from this difficulty. Two at once present themselves; they are carbonic oxide and cyanogen gas. In the former the carbon is already united with half the quantity of oxygen required for maximum oxidation, its complete combustion can therefore be carried on with a limited supply of atmospheric air; in the latter the carbon is united with nitrogen, which during combustion is set free, and interferes with the process by cutting off the more complete access of the atmosphere.

In place of the burning coal of the former experiments I

substituted a jet-pipe, through which the various gases might be made to pass, and the rays emitted by their flames enter the telescope after passing through the slit and prism. In this arrangement the slit should be horizontal and not vertical. So far from its being immaterial which of the two positions is selected, very great advantages arise from the former. If the slit be vertical, the prism it is true will separate the constituent colours from one another, but it fails to show their relative position. If it be horizontal, the relative positions of the different colours can be demonstrated; and it can be proved that a horizontal section of a flame is in reality, as has been already remarked, a coloured ring, the red being the innermost colour and the violet outside; for if this is the order in which the colours occur, the red ring must necessarily have a less diameter than the green, and the green than the violet; and when the prism, set in a horizontal position, separates those colours from each other, the sides of the resulting spectrum ought not to be parallel but inclined to one another, the breadth being least in the red, and increasing as we pass to the violet end. This increasing breadth proves that the constituent coloured shells of the flame envelope each other, the violet being outermost and therefore broadest. This valuable indication would be wholly lost if the slit was vertical.

This being understood, I may illustrate the facts now to be brought forward by an example of the prismatic analysis of a horizontal element of the flame of a spirit-lamp; it being understood that the prism is at its angle of minimum deviation, and the spectrum seen through the telescope. All the prismatic colours in their proper order are visible, the sides of the spectrum not being parallel, the inclination being quite rapid toward the red extremity, the rays of which come from the interior of the flame where the diameter is less. Mere inspection is sufficient to show the rapid approach of the red sides to each other; and I satisfied myself that, even in the more refrangible regions, there is the same want of parallelism, by rotating the telescope on its vertical axis, so that the vertical wires in its eye-piece might coincide with first one and then the other side of the spectrum. It will be understood that I took the proper precaution not to be deceived by a partial want of achromaticity in the telescope, which might have led to a mistake.

But, further, the yellow space of such a spirit-flame spectrum is crossed by a bright fixed line,—Sir David Brewster's monochromatic ray. It is a beautiful example of the principles just pointed out in this method of horizontal analysis, being of much greater width than the rest of the spectrum, and recalling to the imagination the appearance of Saturn's ring when nearly closed and seen through a telescope of moderate power. This ray, from its superior breadth, must necessarily come from that pale tawny light which invests the bright part of the flame. This, which is readily seen when the flame is large, envelopes the middle and upper parts, but cannot so easily be detected low down. It is to be attributed to the carbonic acid and steam that have risen at a high temperature in the burning shell, and are escaping at a degree above that of incandescence into the air, and are mingled with oxygen diffusing from the air into them. A similar tawny cloak surrounds the upper part of the flame of a candle; it answers to the oxidizing flame of the blowpipe, and yields Brewster's monochromatic yellow light.

IV. *Explanation of the nature of coloured flames; showing, for example, why carbonic oxide burns blue, and cyanogen red.*

To return now to carbonic oxide and cyanogen. Fig. 1. No. 1 represents the solar spectrum with its fixed lines; No. 3

*Spectra of various flames.* Fig. 1.

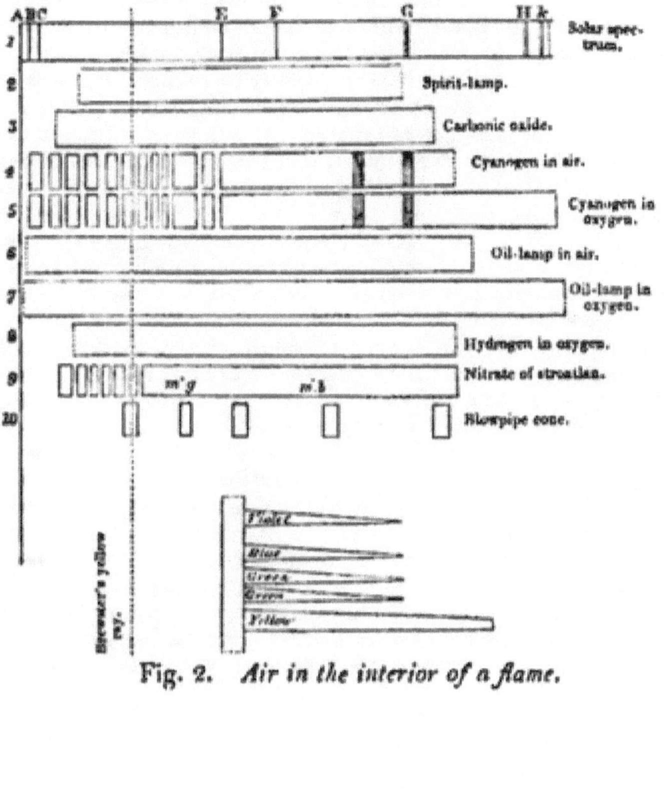

Fig. 2. *Air in the interior of a flame.*

represents the spectrum of carbonic oxide burning in the air. It begins in the red region short of the fixed line C, and terminates between the lines G and H. It yields therefore rays of every colour; and this is in accordance with the principles I have laid down; but when the relative quantity and force of the rays are estimated, in comparison with the sunlight spectrum, the red and orange are deficient, and the more refrangible colours predominate, and indeed it is the excess of these that gives the flame its characteristic blue tint. This agrees with what has been observed as to anthracite and charcoal; for with carbonic oxide a very limited supply of oxygen can bring about the maximum chemical action, and therefore liberate in abundance rays of maximum refrangibility.

This condition of things is inverted in the case of cyanogen gas. It is the nature of its flame to be enveloped, as it were, in a sheet of nitrogen arising from its own burning; and this necessarily impedes the access of air, and checks the intensity of the chemical change; a check which is at once betokened by the emission of a predominant number of rays of low refrangibility, or of a red colour.

But there is a striking difference in the chemical conditions under which carbonic oxide and cyanogen burn. In the case of the former the whole gas is combustible, in the latter the carbon alone; and we have in reality introduced an incombustible element into the flame; for as the carbon burns, the incombustible nitrogen is set free. It occurred to me, in selecting this gas for experiment, that this condition should impress a physical characteristic on the flame. I thought it was not impossible that dark lines in its spectrum might be the result; because there must be a peculiar arrangement of the burning strata, which together make up the shell of the flame, every two atoms of carbon setting free one of nitrogen. I did not know until subsequently that this flame had already been examined by Mr. Faraday. Having therefore confined some cyanogen, made from the cyanide of mercury, in a glass gasholder, which was filled with a saturated solution of common salt, I burnt it from the jet-pipe, and found that what I had surmised was actually the fact. There was a spectrum so beautiful, that it is impossible to describe it by words or depict it in colours. It was crossed throughout its extent by black lines, separating it into well-marked divisions. I could plainly count four great red rays of definite refrangibility, followed by one orange, one yellow, and seven green; whilst in the more refrangible spaces were two extensive groups of black lines, recalling somewhat from their position, but greatly exceeding in extent, Fraunhofer's lines marked G and H in the sun rays. I shall return to the consideration of this spectrum and to the nature of fixed lines presently; here only making the remark, that the burning of cyanogen, both as respects the colour of the light and the occurrence of fixed lines, is a direct consequence of the principle I am establishing.

The unassisted eye detects two well-marked regions in the cyanogen flame; a greenish-gray stratum on the outside, and a lilac-coloured nucleus within. Decomposed by the prism, a horizontal element of this flame shows that the exterior shell contains all the prismatic colours, except perhaps the yellow; but the green, the blue, and the violet greatly predominate. The interior lilac flame is the source of the bright spectrum with fixed lines just described.

V. *Continuation of the same principle in the case where combustion is carried on in oxygen gas instead of atmospheric air.*

If the principle that high refrangibility is connected with intense chemical action be true, it must hold good when the nature of the atmosphere in which the burning is carried forward is changed. If instead of being the common air it is oxygen gas, we ought to be able to foresee the result. Carbonic oxide, when made to burn in that gas, should not change its tint; because if the air can carry on the process to its maximum effect, oxygen can do no more. But the result should be just the reverse with cyanogen, which, if made to burn in oxygen, should be capable of emitting rays of higher refrangibility.

Foreseeing this result, I proceeded to submit the two gases to the test of experiment, and first arranged the carbonic oxide that its spectrum might be examined in the telescope as already described; then causing a clean bell-jar full of oxygen to be inverted over it, the flame diminished somewhat in size, emitted a slight crackling sound, *but retained its colour unchanged.* Its spectrum appeared precisely the same, both as respects extent and the distribution of colour, whether the burning took place in oxygen gas or in the atmospheric air.

If cyanogen be made to burn in oxygen, we should expect that it would lose to a great extent its characteristic lilac tint, and emit a whiter light. It was therefore very interesting to find, that the moment the flame was immersed in oxygen it lost much of its pinkish colour, and became of a dazzling brilliancy: and on examination through the telescope, though all the colours had increased in brightness, the most remarkable effect took place among the extreme refrangible rays. Far out of the limits of the ordinary spectrum, a ray of great purity and force was developed, as represented in fig. 1, No. 5. Its colour is violet.

I have made similar experiments on many other flames besides those here mentioned. It is not necessary to relate them in detail, for they give the same results. In every instance of combustion in the air, when the flame is bright enough, all the colours are visible; and when the combustion takes place in oxygen, they are increased in intensity. With hydrogen gas and alcohol, the light is so feeble that the eye cannot catch the terminal rays; but as soon as the combustion is made in oxygen, the red and the violet both appear, the latter however predominating. Several of these spectra, both in air and oxygen, are represented in fig. 1. In No. 9, the letters $mg$ and $ml$ indicate a maximum of green and of blue light in the form of bright lines.

It does not require the use of a prism to satisfy oneself of the change of tint that flames exhibit when the chemical action increases. In reality it is only necessary to contrast the colour of the light emitted in air and oxygen gas. In the latter case rays of a higher refrangibility uniformly arise.

On the evidence furnished by the foregoing experiments, I regard all flames as consisting of a shell of ignited matter in which combustion is going on with different degrees of rapidity at different depths, being most rapid at the exterior where there is a more perfect contact with the atmosphere, and diminishing inwards. In a horizontal section, the interior space, consisting of unburnt vapour, is black; this is surrounded by a ring where the combustion is incipient, and from which red light issues; then follow orange, yellow, green, blue, indigo, and violet circles in succession, the production of each of these tints being dependent on the rapidity with which chemical action is going forward, that is, on the amount of oxygen present; the tints gradually shading off into one another, and forming, as I have already said, a circular rainbow. An eye placed on the exterior of such a flame, sees all the colours conjointly, and from their general mixture arises the predominant tint.

An examination of the flame of a candle *vertically* confirms this conclusion; for the red projects on the top of the flame, and the blue towards the bottom.

From this, which may be regarded as the normal flame, the flame of cyanogen differs. It must consist of as many concentric shells as the prism separates it into regions of definite refrangibility. The interior part is therefore divided into four red layers, followed by one of orange, one of yellow, seven of green, &c. There are two great inactive spaces towards the outside of the flame, corresponding to the two great groups of fixed lines. Perhaps through all these inactive parts the incombustible nitrogen chiefly escapes.

VI. *Effects of the introduction of air into the interior of a flame, producing the destruction of the red and orange strata, and converting them into violet.*

It now becomes a curious subject of inquiry to determine what must take place when an ordinary flame is disturbed by the introduction of air into its interior. When a blowpipe jet is thrown through the flame of an oil-lamp, the sharp blue cone which forms, indicates, on the principles here set forth, that the combustion is much more active. But if the colours of a common flame come from different depths, the red being the innermost, it is clear that the introduction of a jet of air by a blowpipe should make the combustion rapid where before it was slowest, and the less refrangible colours ought to be destroyed. A prismatic analysis should exhibit the spectrum of a blowpipe flame without any red or orange.

In this examination no slit is required, as in the former experiments, for the cone itself when at a distance of six or eight feet is narrow enough for the purpose: it yields a very extraordinary spectrum. As was anticipated, I found that all the red rays were gone, and not a vestige of either them or the orange could be seen. But the spectrum was divided into five well-marked regions, separated from one another by inactive spaces; in short, I saw five distinct images of the blue cone, one yellow, two greens, one blue, and one violet. In fig. 1, No. 10, this result is represented.

This experiment may be verified without a telescope. On looking through a prism set horizontally at its angle of minimum deviation, at the blowpipe cone some six or eight feet distant, there will be seen a spectrum of that part of the flame which does not join in the production of the blue cone. It contains of course all the prismatic colours. But projecting from this are five coloured images of the cone; one yellow, two greens, one blue, and one violet. They are entirely distinct from one another, and are parted by dark spaces, fig. 2. (p. 107.)

Such is the effect of introducing air into the interior of a flame and destroying those strata that yield the red and orange colours. The effect of a blowpipe is to produce a double stratum of blue light, one being external, the other internal; also two strata of green, one again external, the other internal; and the escaping products of combustion, steam and carbonic acid, mingled with atmospheric air, constitute the oxidizing flame which envelopes the blue cone and emits Brewster's monochromatic yellow light. That the yellow light comes from this flame is proved by the greater length of its image.

VII. *Physical cause of the production of light by chemical action.*

Do not the various facts here brought forward prove that all chemical combinations are attended by a rapid vibratory motion of the parts of the combining bodies, which vibrations become more frequent as the chemical action is more intense?

The burning particles which constitute the inner shell of a flame are executing about four hundred billions of vibrations in one second; those in the middle about six hundred billions, and those on the exterior, in contact with the air, about eight hundred billions in the same time. The quality of the emitted light, as respects its colour, depending on the frequency with which those vibrations are accomplished, increases in refrangibility as the violence of the chemical action becomes greater.

The parts of all material bodies are in a state of incessant vibration: that which we call *temperature* depends on the frequency and amplitude of those vibrations conjointly. If by any process, as by chemical agencies, we increase that frequency to between four and eight hundred billions of vibrations in one second, ignition or combustion results. In the case of the former of these numbers the temperature is $977°$ F. At this temperature or epoch the waves propagated in the æther impress the organ of vision with a red light. *This also is the temperature of the innermost shell of a flame.* If the frequency of vibration still increases, the temperature correspondingly rises, and the light successively becomes orange, yellow, green, blue, &c., and this condition obtains in the successive strata of a flame as we pass from its interior to its exterior superficies.

The general principle at which I thus arrive, as the final result of this experimental investigation, viz. that there is a connexion between the vehemence with which chemical affinity is satisfied and the refrangibility of the resulting light, assumes the position of a simple consequence of the undulatory theory. Is it not very natural, if all chemical changes are attended by vibratory motions in the particles of the bodies engaged, that those vibrations should increase in frequency as the action becomes more violent? But an increased frequency of vibration is the same thing as an increased refrangibility.

I think that in this manner the theory of ethereal undulations is on the point of including many of those fundamental facts in chemistry which until now have been believed to be adverse to it, or at all events as standing apart from it. I recall the admirable remark which Mr. Whewell has made, in his History of the Inductive Sciences, how this theory, like that of universal gravitation, has exhibited all the aspect of a great physical fact, advancing to the explanation of things that seemed to have no necessary connexion with it, and converting what at first sight was regarded as contradictory into the firmest arguments for its truth.

VIII. *On the physical cause of Fraunhofer's dark lines.*

Although I have extended this memoir to so great a length, I have omitted many facts which have been made the subject of experiment. I cannot however conclude without offering some remarks on the artificial production and cause of Fraunhofer's fixed lines.

It has already been related how I was led to expect the production of these lines in the flame of cyanogen, from considering the circumstances under which its combustion takes place. Returning to this phænomenon, I shall here point out a very remarkable numerical relation existing among the fixed lines of the solar spectrum.

The following table contains Fraunhofer's determination of the wave-lengths corresponding to the seven great fixed lines of the spectrum, which are designated by the capital letters of the alphabet from B to H. I have added the wave-length of A from my own experiments.

*Table of wave-lengths corresponding to the eight great fixed lines of the solar spectrum, the Paris inch being supposed to be divided into one hundred millions of equal parts.*

$$A = 2660$$
$$B = 2541$$
$$C = 2422$$
$$D = 2175$$
$$E = 1945$$
$$F = 1794$$
$$G = 1587$$
$$H = 1464$$

An examination of this table proves that

the wave length of B is 119 parts less than A
............ C 238 ............
............ D 485 ............
............ E 715 ............
............ F 866 ............
............ G 1073 ............
............ H 1196 ............

and these differences of length are obviously very nearly as the whole numbers 1, 2, 4, 6, 7, 9, 10. This coincidence is far too striking to be merely accidental. Moreover, it must not be forgotten that the observed numbers, as determined by Fraunhofer, are wholly independent of any hypothesis.

If the relation of whole numbers was rigorously true, the numbers in the foregoing table would stand as follows: 119, 238, 476, 714, 833, 1071, 1190.

The wave-length of the most luminous portion of the spectrum, the centre of the yellow space, is 2060 parts. If we take this as an optical centre, it will be found that the great lines are situated symmetrically in relation to it. E and D are equidistant above and below it; the same observation applies to G and B, and also to H and A. The only departure from this symmetry is in the case of F, which is not symmetrical with C. It will be understood that I am here speaking of one of those spectra which are formed when a grating or ruled surface is used. In this the colours are arranged side by side, according to their wave-lengths; the centre of the spectrum, which is its most luminous portion, is occupied by the centre of the yellow space, and the light terminates at equal distances in the violet and red.

Do not these observations lead us to conclude, that the cause, whatever it may be, that produces these fixed lines is *periodic in its action?*

What that cause in reality is, we have not now facts sufficient to determine. I would not affirm that the disengagement of incombustible matter by a flame will always give rise to dark lines. But this is very clear; that in all those cases, as cyanogen, alcoholic solutions of nitrate of strontian, of boracic acid, &c., in which these lines are developed, incombustible matter is uniformly disengaged.

University, New York,
Dec. 25, 1847.

---

XVII. *An Account of the Method of Vanishing Groups.* By JAMES COCKLE, *Esq., M.A., of Trinity College, Cambridge; Barrister-at-Law, of the Middle Temple*[*].

IN a paper On certain Algebraic Functions just published in the Cambridge and Dublin Mathematical Journal, I have given a more detailed and connected view than I had previously done of the analysis which I have, since writing that paper, proposed to term the Method of Vanishing Groups. I have employed this analysis, perhaps not altogether without success, in the theory of equations and in analytical geometry; and I indulge a hope that the following little account of the

[*] Communicated by Dr. Nathaniel Lister, late Physician to St. Thomas's Hospital, &c.

manner in which, to the best of my recollection, the method occurred to my mind, may, as well as the subsequent portion of this article, prove to be not entirely uninteresting to some of the readers of the present Journal.

I was engaged upon the subject of the transformation of the general equation of the fifth degree into another of the same degree, in which the second, third, and fourth terms should be wanting. This transformation had already been effected by the peculiar processes of Mr. Jerrard; but another method of arriving at it had occurred to me, suggested as follows.

In analytical geometry of two dimensions, when we desire to ascertain whether or not a given equation of the second degree between two variable quantities $x$ and $y$ represents a system of (in general) two straight lines, our object may be attained thus: multiply the given equation by four times the coefficient of $x^2$; add to and subtract from the equation, as it will now stand, the square of the coefficient of $x$ in the equation as it originally stood; the right-hand side of the equation being supposed zero, the left will then consist of the square of a linear function of $x$ and $y$, together with a quadratic function of $y$ only; now if four times the coefficient of $y^2$ in this quadratic function be multiplied into the part free from $y$, and this product be found to equal the square of the coefficient of $y$ in the quadratic function, that function is a square, and the given equation represents two straight lines, if the latter square be negative (or one only if the quadratic function disappears in the first instance, or a point if both the squares be positive).

This part of my studies at the University of Cambridge flashed across my mind in connexion with the problem respecting the equation of the fifth degree. The problem in question requires the solution of a linear, a quadratic, and a cubic equation; or rather, in the point of view from which I was considering it, of a quadratic and a cubic only. I now saw that there might exist a quadratic equation between two unknown quantities, which yet should involve us in no elevation of degree when one of those quantities was, by means of such quadratic, eliminated from another equation involving them. This favourable case of the quadratic occurs when that equation consists, or may be reduced to the form, of one or two squares, which, or one of which at least, involve both the unknown quantities.

Now whenever the quadratic function of $y$ vanishes, or is a perfect square, the given quadratic is of one of the forms just alluded to. In the latter case, which alone attracted my attention, the last-mentioned equation may be exhibited as the sum or difference of two squares, one of which will involve two, and the other one, of the undetermined quantities. And this sum or difference may be decomposed into linear factors, by equating one of which to zero we might eliminate $x$ or $y$ from any other given equation involving those quantities. No elevation of degree would ensue from such elimination. I reflected on this in considering the quadratic, which presented itself in the question of the before-mentioned transformation of the equation of the fifth degree.

But—how to impress this form on that quadratic? to render the quadratic function of $y$ a square? And here Mr. Jerrard's indeterminate method afforded me a useful suggestion—the answer was obvious. If we can render the system of given equations indeterminate, and so introduce an undetermined quantity into the coefficient of $y$ and into the term free from $y$ in the quadratic function of that quantity which remains after we have obtained a square by adding to and subtracting from the given quadratic (multiplied by four times the coefficient of $x$) the square of the original coefficient of $x$—then by the aid of this undetermined quantity, can we not reduce the given quadratic to the required form, and so avoid elevation of degree in eliminating $x$ or $y$ between it and any other given equation? On trying this method I found it succeed. The result, which bears traces of the manner in which I obtained it, will be found at page 114 (art. 3) of the first volume of the Mathematician, although the notation used in this paper is different from that employed there. I have however here given the notation in which the idea is most likely to have suggested itself to my mind, and in which, if my memory serves me aright, it actually suggested itself.

Had I to discuss the same problem again, I should probably employ a homogeneous function of four undetermined quantities, and, by successive operations of the same kind as those which I have indicated at page 267 of the current number of the Cambridge and Dublin Mathematical Journal, reduce it to a sum of four squares, and then make the sum of the first and second equal zero, as also that of the third and fourth. The fundamental principle of the whole method, according to the view which I now take of it, is, for homogeneous functions of the second degree, this reduction by a uniform process to squares as many in number as the undetermined quantities.

Investigations of very different classes may yet present features of resemblance in their results, their principles, or their processes. And wherever such resemblance exists,—be it in result, principle or process,—it can never, in a philosophic point of view, be valueless to indicate its traces. Regarded in this light, it is the solution of a quadratic by the ordinary process of completing the square that affords a first glimpse of the general process of the reduction of a general quadratic function of any number of variables to the form of a sum of squares. For, disregarding, as for this purpose we should do throughout, the signs of the squares, and considering as an algebraic square every numerical quantity, the usual solution of a quadratic is effected by reducing a certain quadratic function to the form of a sum of two algebraic squares.

Starting then from the solution of the quadratic as its cradle, we next see the same process occurring in analytical geometry of two dimensions, and availing us in inquiring into the conditions requisite in order that a given function of the second degree, and of two variable quantities, may be susceptible of reduction to the form of a sum of two algebraic squares (in which case the function represents a straight line or lines, or a point). In the present instance, by continuing the process with which we commence, we might reduce the given function to the form of a sum of three algebraic squares, the "algebraic square" last arrived at being obtained by subtracting the square of half the coefficient of $y$ in the quadratic function of that quantity alluded to in the third paragraph of this paper, from that part of the function which is free from $y$. As I have already stated, it was by combining a suggestion derived from the process of ascertaining the reducibility of a quadratic function of two variables to the sum of two squares, with an idea suggested by a contemplation of the indeterminate methods of Mr. Jerrard, that I devised the method of vanishing groups; and I take this opportunity of mentioning, with befitting sentiments, that it was my friend Dr. Nathaniel Lister of St. Thomas's Hospital, who, some ten years since, first directed my attention to Mr. Jerrard's Mathematical Researches, and induced me to undertake their perusal,—a pursuit to which I applied myself ardently during my second term's residence at Cambridge. The necessity, however, or at least the propriety, of devoting myself to other sciences and branches of science, prevented me from giving my exclusive attention to the theory of equations, ever a favourite study with me; but in the spring of 1844 I arrived at the method which forms the subject of this article, and it was published in the Mathematician for July of that year. It is different from a process which I gave in a preceding volume (xxvi.) of this Journal, and to which I have elsewhere (Mechanics' Magazine, vol. xlvi.) given the name of the "method of symmetric products;" but I have employed it in this Magazine (see vols. xxvii. *et seq.*).

It was the opinion of an illustrious analyst, now no more, that the actual solution of the quadratic equation in general algebraical symbols contributed, in a greater degree than the solution of the cubic and of the biquadratic, to the advancement of algebra as a science (Murphy, Theory of Equations, page 1). And we may regard such solution under an aspect which did not meet the view of that great writer,—we may regard it as containing the germ of a process which enables us to exhibit far more general functions than those involved in the quadratic in the form of sums of powers, and which, combined with the indeterminate method when occasion requires, is capable of most extensive application in analysis. But it must never be forgotten that it was in the solution of a cubic that this indeterminate method—this great device of making a determinate problem algebraically indeterminate, and so solving it—was probably first elicited: and this circumstance ought to influence us materially in estimating the rank which the first discoverer of the solution of cubic equations is entitled to hold in scientific history. I consider the method of vanishing groups, when applied to the theory of equations, as the combination (accompanied by full developments) of the principle involved in the solution of the cubic with the process employed in that of the quadratic. Suggested, as it were, by a question in analytical geometry of two dimensions, that method admits of application in the analytical geometry of three dimensions; and I have in fact so applied it in my Chapters on Analytical Geometry, now in course of publication in the Mechanics' Magazine. Its processes would evidently be capable of a similar extension to an analytical geometry of $n$ dimensions, had we any knowledge of an entity possessed of more than three dimensions. Were such things within the bounds of our faculties, there would be functions of their dimensions, linear ones for instance, which would bear an analogy to the corresponding ones of the three-dimensioned entity space (and the one-dimensioned entity time), and which would by this method be discussed in a manner similar, or at all events but slightly different from, that of space (or time).

In conclusion, I may mention a point in which our results so closely resemble those deduced in another department of science, as to have suggested to me the name "Diophantic" as one which would be appropriate to our processes. I mean, that as in the Diophantine algebra we seek to form an equation, of which, if one side be zero the other shall consist of powers (squares, cubes, &c.) of numerical quantities connected by the signs plus and minus, so in our analysis the object is in general to obtain an equation, of which, one side being zero, the other shall consist of powers of algebraical quantities (numerical or not) similarly connected. I say in general, because perhaps the preferable view of the problem, which is the object of our method, is to consider it as that of reducing certain algebraic functions, whether they be supposed equal to zero or not, to the form of a sum of algebraic powers.

Should it be thought that in the present article I have dwelt at unnecessary length on certain points, I should urge by way of apology, that before it can be fairly estimated all knowledge must be systematized. And I would add, that all knowledge is probably capable of being so dealt with, to an extent of which we can as yet form no idea.

2 Church-yard Court, Temple,
November 8, 1847.

XVIII. *Observations on the Geological Age of Bone-Caverns.* By RICHARD PAYNE COTTON, *M.D.*, *Member of the Royal College of Physicians, London*\*.

THE geological period during which the caves of England formed the residences of wild beasts and cemeteries for the bones of their victims as well as themselves, is a subject of great interest, and can be best, if not exclusively ascertained, by comparing their animal remains with those of sedimentary deposits.

If a cabinet collection of cave specimens be contrasted with one of the Pleistocene freshwater formations, so great will appear the excess in the former, of small animals allied to, or identical with, those of our own times, that a date even more modern than "Pleistocene" might reasonably be given them. With a view of making a more just comparison, the following table has been constructed, showing the living and extinct animals common to both, and peculiar to each.

| Peculiar to sedimentary deposits. | | Peculiar to caverns. | | Common to both. | |
|---|---|---|---|---|---|
| Extinct. | Living. | Extinct. | Living. | Extinct. | Living. |
| Macacus pliocenus. | Castor Europæus. | Ursus priscus. | Vespertilio Noctula. | Ursus spelæus. | Felis catus. |
| Palæospalax magnus. | | Machærodus latidens. | Rhinolophus ferrum-equinum. | Hyæna spelæa. | Arvicola amphibia. |
| Trogontherium Cuvieri. | | Lagomys spelæus. | Meles Taxus. | Felis spelæa. | Cervus Elaphus. |
| Rhinoceros leptorhinus. | | Equus plicidens. | Putorius vulgaris. | Elephas primigenius. | Cervus Tarandus. |
| | | Strongyloceros spelæus. | Putorius erminius. | Rhinoceros tichorhinus. | Capra Hircus. |
| | | | Canis Lupus. | Equus fossilis. | Bison priscus. |
| | | | Canis Vulpes. | Asinus fossilis. | Aves (?) |
| | | | Arvicola agrestis. | Hippopotamus major. | |
| | | | Arvicola pratensis. | Sus scrofa. | |
| | | | Mus musculus. | Megaceros Hibernicus. | |
| | | | Lepus timidus. | Cervus Bucklandi. | |
| | | | Lepus Cuniculus. | Cervus Capreolus. | |
| | | | | Bos primigenius. | |
| | | | | Bos longifrons. | |

\* Communicated by the Author.

Thus of forty-two distinct Mammalia, twenty are found in both positions, seventeen are limited to the caverns, and five are found exclusively in freshwater strata.

From a mere survey of such a table, conclusions as to the relative age of the two series would be inaccurate; and it becomes necessary to consider the various circumstances under which each may have arisen, and the influence which the habitats of the various animals may have exercised upon the position of their remains.

The valley of the Thames, in many places so abundant in animal remains that a metropolitan churchyard could hardly boast of a greater collection of bones, presents some peculiarities worthy of attention, and bearing closely upon the point. The bones are in general in a good state of preservation, and often make up nearly the entire skeleton; but occasionally some fragments are met with, not resulting from original violence when deposited (as they are often surrounded by the most delicate freshwater shells) or careless removal, but apparently broken before carried to their place of interment. The frequency of animal remains appears to be just in proportion to their size, the small bones of large mammalia being much more uncommon than the larger ones, and the young of such animals as the Mammoth, Rhinoceros, and Hippopotamus being rarely met with, whilst all indications of the smaller genera so common in caverns are altogether absent. I have collected from these Pleistocene beds, chiefly at Ilford, remains of the following animals:—Mammoth, Rhinoceros, Ox, Auroch, Horse, Irish Elk, Deer, Bear, Sheep, Pig and Bird; but the first four only can be called abundant, and of these the Mammoth and Rhinoceros are at least ten times more frequent than the other two—the rest are but seldom met with. The Bear is the only representative of Carnivora, and of it only one specimen has been found; and the only evidence of a Bird consists of an ulna, of which more will be said hereafter.

Upon looking at such a collection, it is impossible to suppose that it can represent the whole creation of any geological period, or that such a mass of Mammalia can have been without an ample number of destroyers; for although the Tiger and Hyæna have been found in deposits of the same age, they are rare, and bear a very insignificant proportion to the Herbivora.

The bone-caverns reveal a set of circumstances exactly the opposite of the above. In these, several genera of Carnivora are abundantly preserved; and the bones with which they are associated belong either to a class of smaller animals or the young of the larger ones, and a collection of these remains equally fail in presenting us with representatives of an entire race. But if the two be united, an intelligible system is established—the young Mammoth and Rhinoceros meeting with their parents—Herbivora and Carnivora mixing for the first time perhaps in undreaded society, form a natural series of animals of all habits and sizes.

All this may appear but a coincidence, unless it can be shown why there should have been this separation in the position of their remains; but the habits of the various animals will yield the explanation.

Upon the approach of natural death or any catastrophe, the wary and active Carnivora would generally retire to, and die in, their dens; whilst the larger Herbivora would be more likely to leave their bones upon the plains, to be subsequently swept away and entombed by natural operations. But it was not by any sudden or violent action that the great accumulation of remains in either position took place. For ages Tigers and Hyænas did their office, and thousands became their victims. Animals of all sizes were exposed to their attacks; but the smaller ones, and the younger and weaker individuals of the larger class, were their most common prey; and it would rarely happen that such died a natural death, or if they did, their bones would seldom fail to become the property of Hyænas, hence they are almost exclusively found in caverns; but the larger and more formidable Mammoth and Rhinoceros must have less frequently met with violent death; or when this did occur, their bulk and weight would be against their finding their way into the dens of Hyænas, and their skeletons, more or less mutilated, would be left to be swept away and interred in fluviatile deposits, where they are now so abundantly found. The broken bones to which I have alluded may have had such an origin; they exhibit no teeth marks, but otherwise, in appearance, would bear out such an idea. Of six bones of Birds found by Dr. Buckland at Kirkdale, the ulna occurred four times, which led him to the ingenious observation that the strong quill-feathers attached to that bone may have prevented it being devoured. It is singular that the same bone should be the only one preserved at Ilford; especially as a row of strong tubercles proves it to have belonged to some powerful bird of flight, consequently with a strong set of wing-feathers; and if a similar explanation of its preservation be admitted, it affords additional strength to such an inference.

The accumulation in caverns may in reality have occupied more than one geological period; and long after the last hyæna ceased to exist, have been added to by the Wolf and Fox, to whose operations may be attributed the introduction of such animals as the Hare and Rabbit; whilst the Bat, Mouse, and Vole may have been at some other time not unwilling tenants of the same caves. But even assigning to all the same antiquity, for reasons given above, it is not surprising that these should be found only in caverns. The *Equus plicidens* and *Strongyloceros*, perhaps the only animals whose sole existence in caverns is difficult to account for, may yet find their representatives in sedimentary deposits: the latter is so uncommon that but one specimen has been met with, and that in Kent's Hole, and at Ilford remains of gigantic deer, too fragmentary to declare their affinities, are frequently found.

The remains peculiar to freshwater strata are such as might be expected to appear there. The Monkey would be an unlikely prey to Tigers and Hyænas; and the Water-Mole, Castor and gigantic Trogontherium, from their amphibious and wary habits, would rarely become the prey of land Carnivora; and if preserved at all, would mix with deposits continually going on from the element in which the greater part of their lives was passed. The occurrence of *Rhinoceros leptorhinus* exclusively in these formations does not appear so remarkable, when it is recollected that the genus itself is comparatively rare in caverns; and some peculiarity may have existed in this species, rendering it less liable than the other to become the prey of carnivorous contemporaries; and it is well-known that several living species, differing less from each other than the extinct ones did, have very different habits.

It must not be forgotten, that future discoveries may considerably alter inferences derived from our present knowledge on this subject. It is impossible to predict what may hereafter be revealed by chance or the labours of the geologist; and each year brings with it an increase to the number of fossil mammalia. But as the matter remains at present, there is nothing against the possibility, whilst many things tend to make it highly probable, that animals from the newer tertiary deposits were the contemporaries of those found in caverns; and that whilst the Mammoth and Rhinoceros, from their powers of defence, enjoyed a comparative immunity from attack, and left their bones in the slowly-forming aqueous strata, their younger and weaker associates frequently became victims to the appetites of fierce Carnivora, and were finally carried to the dens of Hyænas.

4 Bolton Street, Piccadilly,
December 1847.

XIX. *On the Preparation of absolute Alcohol, and the Composition of "Proof-Spirit."* By Mr. JOSEPH DRINKWATER. (*Communicated by* Professor Graham.)*

THE following experiments were undertaken, principally, with a view to determine the relative proportions of anhydrous alcohol and water in revenue proof-spirit, for which purpose it was necessary to procure alcohol in its absolute or pure state.

The processes employed were as follows:—

Carbonate of potash was exposed to a red heat to deprive it of water, and when sufficiently cool was pulverized, and added to ordinary alcohol of specific gravity ·850 at 60° F. till it ceased to dissolve any more; the whole was then allowed to digest twenty-four hours, being frequently agitated, when the alcohol was carefully poured off.

As much fresh-burnt quicklime as was considered sufficient when powdered to absorb the whole of the alcohol, was introduced into a retort, and the alcohol added to it; after digesting forty-eight hours, it was slowly distilled in a water-bath at a temperature of about 180° F.

The alcohol thus obtained was carefully redistilled, and its specific gravity at 60° F. was found in two experiments to be ·7946 and ·7947; agreeing very nearly with the determination of Rudberg, which has been adopted by Gay-Lussac and others, viz. ·7947 at 59° F.

It may be proper to state that the specific gravity was taken with a stoppered bottle, which was always counterpoised by another empty bottle of the same glass and form, placed in the opposite pan of the balance; the capacity of the weighing bottle at 60° F. was exactly 1000·01 grains of distilled water; and it was found on trial that this bottle could be repeatedly filled with the same liquid with no greater variation than one or two hundredths of a grain.

The temperature of the room in which these experiments were made was always brought to 60° F.; and the thermometer used was a standard instrument by Newman, and extremely sensitive (being graduated to one-tenth of a degree); on being plunged into the weighing bottle filled with alcohol it displaced about $4\frac{1}{2}$ grains of that fluid; this portion was replaced from the stock quantity (brought at the time to the proper temperature) by means of a pipette.

With a view however to discover whether it were possible by means of lime to abstract any more water from the alcohol, the retort was again filled with fresh-burned and pulverized

* Communicated by the Chemical Society; having been read June 21, 1847.

quicklime and the same alcohol mixed with it; the mixture was then allowed to digest a whole week at the ordinary temperature of the laboratory, about 60° F. After this time the alcohol was distilled off as before, but was redistilled very slowly, at first at the rate of about one drop in ten seconds (heat of water-bath 165° F.); this was continued till about one-twentieth of the whole had distilled over, the object being to allow any minute quantity of water which the alcohol might still retain to evaporate or diffuse itself into the atmosphere of absolute alcohol above it; the redistillation was then continued rapidly, the heat of the bath being increased to 180° F. till about one-twentieth more had passed over; the receiver was then changed and the remaining part slowly distilled off.

The specific gravity of this alcohol taken twice was ·7944 at 60° F. As a further test of its purity it was divided into two equal parts; one part was again digested on quicklime, and the other on sulphate of copper deprived of water by heat, the method of operation being as follows:—

1st. Some lumps of fresh-burnt quicklime were heated to a red heat, and in that state quickly pulverized and introduced into the tin boiler of a small still, which was partly immersed in water to prevent the melting of the solder.

This vessel was completely filled with quicklime, and was kept corked till sufficiently cool, when the alcohol was added, but it being comparatively small in quantity the lime appeared perfectly dry; the vessel was then securely corked.

2nd. A quantity of sulphate of copper was exposed to a red heat till completely deprived of water; it was then quickly pulverized and introduced into a small tin boiler, and when cold the alcohol (which was insufficient to cover it) was added, and the vessel closely corked.

These vessels with their contents were kept at the ordinary temperature of the laboratory (about 60° F.) for four days; they were then partly immersed in a water-bath, and kept at a temperature of about 150° F. for forty-eight hours, after which the alcohol was distilled and redistilled with all the precautions before-mentioned; the temperature of the water-bath on the redistillation never exceeded 172° F., and the first tenth part was put aside in each case as possibly impure.

The specific gravities of the alcohol thus obtained were as under:—

|   | Alcohol distilled from desiccated sulphate of copper. | Alcohol distilled from quicklime. |
|---|---|---|
| I. . . . | ·79470 | ·79409 |
| II. . . . | ·79472 | ·79412 |

From these experiments it would appear that sulphate of copper, when deprived of water, is not so effective as quicklime in removing the last traces of water from alcohol.

It was observed, however, that in general the specific gravity of the alcohol gradually increased, probably from its hygrometric property, by which it absorbed a minute quantity of moisture from the air on being transferred from one bottle to another; and thinking consequently that a small quantity of moisture might have been abstracted from the atmosphere during the distillation (which was conducted in the usual way), and the specific gravity thus slightly increased, I considered it desirable to make another experiment in which this source of error should be guarded against, by conducting the distillation as much as possible out of contact with the external air, and proceeded as follows.

The different portions of alcohol before obtained were mixed together, when the specific gravity was found to be ·7947; this alcohol was again digested at a temperature of about 150° F. for fourteen days with quicklime, previously heated to redness, as in the former experiment; it was then slowly distilled out of contact with the external atmosphere by means of a tube which passed from the condenser through a cork into the bottle in which it was to remain (the temperature of the water-bath was 175° F.), and the first tenth part was put aside as possibly containing a minute quantity of water; the remainder was then distilled off at 178° to 180° F.

This alcohol was quickly transferred to a dry retort and redistilled in a similar way (heat of water-bath 172° F.); the first tenth part was put aside, and the remainder kept as being pure anhydrous alcohol, or as free from water as it is possible to obtain it by this process. The specific gravity was taken the next day with all the precautions before mentioned, the alcohol being also kept during the time of transference as much as possible out of contact with humid air, when the results of four trials were as follow:—

Temperature of room 60° F.   Barometer 29·810.

|  |  |
|---|---|
| I. | ·793836 |
| II. | ·793806 |
| III. | ·793798 |
| IV. | ·793804 |
| Mean | ·793811 |

A portion of this alcohol was subsequently digested with quicklime for three months, it was then distilled, and its specific gravity was found to be exactly the same as before.

We may therefore conclude with considerable certainty

that the number ·79381 expresses the specific gravity of absolute alcohol at 60° F., within a very close degree of approximation.

My attention was next directed to the best method of determining the relative proportions of absolute alcohol and water which exist in legal or revenue proof-spirit.

There is some ambiguity in the wording of the act of parliament 58 Geo. III. c. 28, which defines proof-spirit to be " such as shall at the temperature of fifty-one degrees by Fahrenheit's thermometer weigh exactly twelve-thirteenth parts of an equal measure of distilled water," but the temperature of the water is not stated: there is no doubt however that the temperature of 51° F. was intended to apply to the water as well as to the spirit; therefore taking water at 51° F. as unity, the specific gravity of proof-spirit at that temperature will be ·92308; or raising the temperature of both to 60° F., the specific gravity will be ·91984—the expansions being calculated from Gilpin's Tables *.

It was found by a few preliminary experiments that the specific gravity ·91984 would lie between a mixture of 49 absolute alcohol + 51 water, and a mixture of 49½ absolute alcohol + 50½ water, all by weight. Mixtures were therefore made in these proportions in an apparatus procured for the purpose, consisting of two light flasks each capable of containing about 2200 grains of water. The alcohol and water were weighed separately in these flasks with the greatest care; after which the flasks were joined without mixing the liquids, the neck of one being ground into the neck of the other for that purpose; the liquids were then thoroughly mixed by transferring them alternately from one flask to the other. The flasks were disconnected when the mixed contents became cool, which were then transferred to a clean and dry well-stoppered bottle, and further secured by tying a piece of caoutchouc over the stopper.

It may also be proper to mention, that when placed in the balance, these flasks were always counterpoised by other empty flasks of the same material, and of very nearly equal size and shape; and to prevent loss from evaporation, a ground glass cap was placed over the mouth of each flask as soon as the exact weight was obtained. The errors of observation could not, I believe, in any case exceed one-hundredth of a grain, as the balance used in these experiments was one of Robinson's best instruments, which was previously adjusted by Newman expressly for the purpose; it was turned with its greatest load by less than one-hundredth of a grain.

* Philosophical Transactions for 1794.

The proportions of absolute alcohol and water mixed were as under, all by weight. Temperature of room 60° F. Barometer 29·832.

*First mixture.*—588 grs. alcohol + 612 grs. water, being in the proportion of 49 grs. alcohol + 51 grs. water.

*Second mixture.*—594 grs. alcohol + 606 grs. water, being in the proportion of $49\frac{1}{2}$ grs. alcohol + $50\frac{1}{2}$ grs. water.

After twenty-four hours, the bottles having been frequently shaken, the specific gravities of both mixtures were taken, with all the precautions detailed in the experiments on absolute alcohol: and in order to observe if the full condensation was gradual and required time for its completion, the mixtures were allowed to stand, with occasional agitation, for a further period of twenty-four hours, when the liquids were again weighed. The results were as follows:—

At 24 hours, temperature of room 60° F., barometer 29·630.
At 48 hours, temperature of room 60° F., barometer 29·550.

*First Mixture.*

I. ·920361 } after standing
II. ·920358 }   24 hours.
III. ·920361 { after standing
            {    48 hours.

Mean ·920360

*Second Mixture.*

I. ·919297 } after standing
II. ·919297 }   24 hours.
III. ·919307 { after standing
            {    48 hours.

Mean ·919300

It thus appears that both liquids attained a fixed specific gravity within the first twenty-four hours.

If we now express the preceding results by measure, and make the proportion of alcohol a constant quantity in the two mixtures, we have—

| Alcohol and water by weight. | | Alcohol and water by measure. | | Spec. gravity of the mixtures. |
|---|---|---|---|---|
| Alcohol. | Water. | Alcohol. | Water. | |
| 49 + 51 | } in the pro- | 100 + 82·62105 | | ·92036 |
| $49\frac{1}{2}$ + $50\frac{1}{2}$ | } portion of | 100 + 80·98470 | | ·91930 |
| | | Difference | 1·63635 | ·106 |

Dividing the difference of the quantities of water by the difference of specific gravity, we get ·015437, the mean quantity of water corresponding to each unit of difference in the specific gravities. But the difference between the specific gravity of proof-spirit and ·91930, one of the observed specific gravities, is 54; therefore we have $54 \times ·015437 = ·8336$, the quantity of water to be added to the spirit of that specific gravity to form proof-spirit, as follows:—

|            | Alcohol.     | Water.   | Specific gravity. |
|------------|--------------|----------|-------------------|
|            | 100 +        | 80·9847  | ·91930            |
| Add water  | 100          | ·8336    | 54                |
| Proof-spirit = | 100 +    | 81·8183  | ·91984            |

From the foregoing data the following results have been calculated:—

*Composition of Proof-Spirit.*

| Alcohol and water. | | Specific gravity at 60° F. | Bulk of mixture of 100 measures of alcohol +81·82 water. | Strength per cent. above proof of absolute alcohol. |
|---|---|---|---|---|
| By weight. | By measure. | | | |
| Alcohol. Water. 100 + 103·09 or in 100 49·24 + 50·76 | Alcohol. Water. 100 + 81·82 | ·91984 | 175·25 | 75·25 |

It is remarkable that Dr. A. Steel * arrived at almost the same composition for proof-spirit, namely, 49·2 and 50·8, partly by experiment and partly by calculation.

The table of M. Lowitz, showing the quantity of alcohol in spirits of different specific gravities (which is to be found in most chemical works published in this country), also agrees with these experiments at this particular point, although from some experiments which I have had occasion to make, I have found that at other points this table is incorrect; and as it is frequently consulted by chemists, it was considered desirable to make a few mixtures of pure alcohol and water, from which to calculate a more correct table for estimating the quantity of alcohol in mixtures containing not more than 10 per cent. of that liquid.

Eleven mixtures were therefore made, containing exactly ½, 1, 2, 3, 4, 5, 6, 7, 8, 9 and 10 per cent. by weight of absolute alcohol. These mixtures were made in the same apparatus, and with all the precautions described in the former experiments. They were allowed to stand at least 24 hours with occasional agitation before the specific gravities were taken, and several of them were again taken after a period of 48 and 72 hours, without any sensible variation.

The particulars are set forth in the following table:—

* Dr. Steel's papers, which contain much valuable information on the specific gravity of spirits, are contained in the 'Records of General Science,' vol. i. pp. 222-255.

## absolute Alcohol, and the Composition of "Proof-Spirit." 129

| No. of mixtures. | When the mixtures were made. | | | | | When the specific gravities were taken. | | |
|---|---|---|---|---|---|---|---|---|
| | Alcohol and water mixed. | | Quantity of alcohol per cent. by weight. | Temperature of room. | Height of barometer. | Specific gravity of mixture at 60° F. | Temperature of room. | Height of barometer. |
| | Alcohol. | Water. | | | | | | |
| | grs. | grs. | | | | | | |
| 1. | 5·5 + 1094·5 | | 0·5° F. | 60 | 29·700 | ·99905 | 60° F. | 29·690 |
| 2. | 11·0 + 1089·0 | | 1·0 | 60 | 29·700 | ·99813 | 60 | 29·690 |
| 3. | 22·0 + 1078·0 | | 2·0 | 60 | 29·690 | ·99629 | 60 | 29·500 |
| 4. | 33·0 + 1067·0 | | 3·0 | 60 | 29·718 | ·99454 | 60 | 29·610 |
| 5. | 44·0 + 1056·0 | | 4·0 | 60 | 29·690 | ·99283 | 60 | 29·500 |
| 6. | 55·0 + 1045·0 | | 5·0 | 60 | 29·718 | ·99121 | 60 | 29·610 |
| 7. | 66·0 + 1034·0 | | 6·0 | 60 | 29·742 | ·98963 | 60 | 29·644 |
| 8. | 77·0 + 1023·0 | | 7·0 | 60 | 29·742 | ·98813 | 60 | 29·644 |
| 9. | 88·0 + 1012·0 | | 8·0 | 60 | 29·670 | ·98668 | 60 | 29·800 |
| 10. | 99·0 + 1001·0 | | 9·0 | 60 | 29·670 | ·98527 | 60 | 29·800 |
| 11. | 110·0 + 990·0 | | 10·0 | 60 | 29·800 | ·98389 | 60 | 29·566 |

From the above data the following table has been calculated:—

Table of the quantity of absolute Alcohol by weight contained in mixtures of Alcohol and Water of the following specific gravities:—

| Specific gravity at 60° F. | Alcohol, per cent. by weight. | Specific gravity at 60° F. | Alcohol, per cent. by weight. | Specific gravity at 60° F. | Alcohol, per cent. by weight. | Specific gravity at 60° F. | Alcohol, per cent. by weight. | Specific gravity at 60° F. | Alcohol, per cent. by weight. |
|---|---|---|---|---|---|---|---|---|---|
| 1·0000 | 0·00 | ·9967 | 1·78 | ·9934 | 3·67 | ·9901 | 5·70 | ·9869 | 7·85 |
| ·9999 | 0·05 | ·9966 | 1·83 | ·9933 | 3·73 | ·9900 | 5·77 | ·9868 | 7·92 |
| ·9998 | 0·11 | ·9965 | 1·89 | ·9932 | 3·78 | ·9899 | 5·83 | ·9867 | 7·99 |
| ·9997 | 0·16 | ·9964 | 1·94 | ·9931 | 3·84 | ·9898 | 5·89 | ·9866 | 8·06 |
| ·9996 | 0·21 | ·9963 | 1·99 | ·9930 | 3·90 | ·9897 | 5·96 | ·9865 | 8·13 |
| ·9995 | 0·26 | ·9962 | 2·05 | ·9929 | 3·96 | ·9896 | 6·02 | ·9864 | 8·20 |
| ·9994 | 0·32 | ·9961 | 2·11 | ·9928 | 4·02 | ·9895 | 6·09 | ·9863 | 8·27 |
| ·9993 | 0·37 | ·9960 | 2·17 | ·9927 | 4·08 | ·9894 | 6·15 | ·9862 | 8·34 |
| ·9992 | 0·42 | ·9959 | 2·22 | ·9926 | 4·14 | ·9893 | 6·22 | ·9861 | 8·41 |
| ·9991 | 0·47 | ·9958 | 2·28 | ·9925 | 4·20 | ·9892 | 6·29 | ·9860 | 8·48 |
| ·9990 | 0·53 | ·9957 | 2·34 | ·9924 | 4·27 | ·9891 | 6·35 | ·9859 | 8·55 |
| ·9989 | 0·58 | ·9956 | 2·39 | ·9923 | 4·33 | ·9890 | 6·42 | ·9858 | 8·62 |
| ·9988 | 0·64 | ·9955 | 2·45 | ·9922 | 4·39 | ·9889 | 6·49 | ·9857 | 8·70 |
| ·9987 | 0·69 | ·9954 | 2·51 | ·9921 | 4·45 | ·9888 | 6·55 | ·9856 | 8·77 |
| ·9986 | 0·74 | ·9953 | 2·57 | ·9920 | 4·51 | ·9887 | 6·62 | ·9855 | 8·84 |
| ·9985 | 0·80 | ·9952 | 2·62 | ·9919 | 4·57 | ·9886 | 6·69 | ·9854 | 8·91 |
| ·9984 | 0·85 | ·9951 | 2·68 | ·9918 | 4·64 | ·9885 | 6·75 | ·9853 | 8·98 |
| ·9983 | 0·91 | ·9950 | 2·74 | ·9917 | 4·70 | ·9884 | 6·82 | ·9852 | 9·05 |
| ·9982 | 0·96 | ·9949 | 2·79 | ·9916 | 4·76 | ·9883 | 6·89 | ·9851 | 9·12 |
| ·9981 | 1·02 | ·9948 | 2·85 | ·9915 | 4·82 | ·9882 | 6·95 | ·9850 | 9·20 |
| ·9980 | 1·07 | ·9947 | 2·91 | ·9914 | 4·88 | ·9881 | 7·02 | ·9849 | 9·27 |
| ·9979 | 1·12 | ·9946 | 2·97 | ·9913 | 4·94 | ·9880 | 7·09 | ·9848 | 9·34 |
| ·9978 | 1·18 | ·9945 | 3·02 | ·9912 | 5·01 | ·9879 | 7·16 | ·9847 | 9·41 |
| ·9977 | 1·23 | ·9944 | 3·08 | ·9911 | 5·07 | ·9878 | 7·23 | ·9846 | 9·49 |
| ·9976 | 1·29 | ·9943 | 3·14 | ·9910 | 5·13 | ·9877 | 7·30 | ·9845 | 9·56 |
| ·9975 | 1·34 | ·9942 | 3·20 | ·9909 | 5·20 | ·9876 | 7·37 | ·9844 | 9·63 |
| ·9974 | 1·40 | ·9941 | 3·26 | ·9908 | 5·26 | ·9875 | 7·43 | ·9843 | 9·70 |
| ·9973 | 1·45 | ·9940 | 3·32 | ·9907 | 5·32 | ·9874 | 7·50 | ·9842 | 9·78 |
| ·9972 | 1·51 | ·9939 | 3·37 | ·9906 | 5·39 | ·9873 | 7·57 | ·9841 | 9·85 |
| ·9971 | 1·56 | ·9938 | 3·43 | ·9905 | 5·45 | ·9872 | 7·64 | ·9840 | 9·92 |
| ·9970 | 1·61 | ·9937 | 3·49 | ·9904 | 5·51 | ·9871 | 7·71 | ·9839 | 9·99 |
| ·9969 | 1·67 | ·9936 | 3·55 | ·9903 | 5·58 | ·9870 | 7·78 | ·9838 | 10·07 |
| ·9968 | 1·73 | ·9935 | 3·61 | ·9902 | 5·64 | | | | |

XX. *Remarks on the Weather during the Quarter ending December 31, 1847.* By JAMES GLAISHER, *Esq., of the Royal Observatory, Greenwich*\*.

THE quarterly meteorological returns for the past quarter, furnished to the Registrar-General, have been obtained from twenty-eight different places in England and one in Ireland. Upon every subject of investigation in these reports, and with almost every gentleman from whom they have been received, I have been in frequent correspondence; I know therefore, in most cases, the character of the instruments, and the circumstances under which the observations have been made.

Every return has been examined by myself, and each result checked by comparison with others made in neighbouring places; and in every case where suspicion seemed to rest, I have immediately had the observations examined; and in all cases where the numbers did not stand this examination, they have not been printed.

The whole of the observations were then reduced to mean places and discussed by myself, and the results form a body of meteorological facts of which I can speak with much confidence. In the course of their reduction, the character of the period over which the observations extend came forcibly under my notice; and I found it to be one remarkable in many respects, and such as would interest many of the readers of the Philosophical Magazine, who would not otherwise see the account in the Registrar-General's report itself; and its publication in the Philosophical Magazine will have the effect of bringing these valuable reports to the notice of persons interested in meteorology.

The daily temperatures of the air, evaporation and dew-point, during the whole quarter, with the exceptions of the period between Nov. 17 and Nov. 21, and between Dec. 20 and Dec. 31, have been above the average for the season, and at times these departures have been very great.

It perhaps may tend to clearness if I speak of each subject of investigation separately.

*The mean temperature of the air at Greenwich*—

For the month of October was $52°·9$, which is $4°·1$, $7°·5$, $4°·9$, $3°·4$, $2°·7$, and $2°·4$ *above* that in the years 1841 to 1846 respectively. The high temperature in this month is very remarkable.

For the month of November was $46°·9$, which is $4°·2$, $4°·1$, $3°·1$, $2°·9$, $1°·1$, and $0°·9$ *above* that of the years 1841 to 1846 respectively.

\* Communicated by the Author.

For the month of December was 42°·8, which is 2°·3 *above* that of 1841, 2°·2 *below* that of 1842, 1°·1 *below* that of 1843, 9°·8 *above* that of 1844, 1°·1 *above* that of 1845, and 9°·9 *above* that of 1846; or it is 3°·3 above that of the average for these six years.

The mean value for the quarter was 47°·5; that for 1841 was 44°·0; for 1842 was 44°·4; for 1843 was 45°·2; for 1844 was 42°·2; for 1845 was 45°·9; and for 1846 was 43°·1; so that the excess for this quarter above the corresponding quarter in the six preceding years are 3°·5, 3°·1, 2°·3, 5°·3, 1°·6, and 4°·4 respectively; or it is 3°·4 above the average for these six years. This difference is very large indeed, considering that it extends over so long a period of time as one-fourth part of a year.

*The mean temperature of evaporation at Greenwich—*
For the month of October was 50°·9, which is 3°·6 *above* that for the preceding six years.

For the month of November was 45°·6, which is 2°·6 *above* that for the preceding six years.

For the month of December was 41°·6, which is 3°·3 *above* that for the preceding six years.

The mean value for the quarter was 46°·0, which is 3°·2 *above* that for the six preceding years.

*The mean temperature of the dew-point at Greenwich—*
For the month of October was 49°·1, which is 4°·0, 6°·7, 4°·4, 3°·1, 2°·6, and 1°·9 *above* that for the years 1841 to 1846 respectively; or it is 3°·7 *above* the average for these years.

For the month of November was 44°·1, which is 4°·3, 3°·7, 3°·2, 2°·2, 1°·3, and 1°·0 *above* that for the years 1841 to 1846 respectively; or it is 2°·6 *above* the average for these years.

For the month of December was 39°·8, which is 4°·6 *above* that for 1841, 3°·4 *below* that for 1842, 2°·2 *below* that for 1843, 9°·8 *above* that for 1844, 2°·2 *above* that for 1845, and 10°·4 *above* that for 1846; or it is 3°·6 *above* the average for these years.

The mean value for the quarter was 44°·3, which is 3°·3 *above* that for the six preceding years.

*The mean weight of water in a cubic foot of air for the quarter* was 3·2 grains, which is 0·4 grain *above* that for the preceding six years.

*The additional weight of water* required to saturate a cubic foot of air was 0·4 grain; the average for the preceding six years was 0·3 grain.

*The mean degree of humidity of the atmosphere for the quarter* was 0·900, which is the same as that for the six preceding years.

*The mean elastic force of vapour for the quarter* was 0·310 inch, which is 0·030 inch *above* that for the average of the six preceding years.

*The mean reading of the barometer* at Greenwich for the quarter was 29·829 inches, which is 0·111 inch *above* that for the six preceding years.

*The average weight of a cubic foot of air* under the average temperature, humidity and pressure, was 540 grains; the average for the six preceding years was 543 grains.

*The rain fallen* at Greenwich within the quarter was six inches in depth; this quantity is two inches *less* than the average for the six preceding years. The total amount of rain fallen in the year 1847 was 17·6 inches, which is nearly eight inches *less* than the average amount for the six preceding years.

*The temperature of the Thames water* was 48°·2 by day, and 47°·6 by night. The water on an average was nearly of the same temperature as the air.

*The horizontal movement of the air* was about 950 miles weekly, being somewhat less than the average amount.

*The highest and lowest readings of the thermometer in air* at the height of four feet above the ground, and protected as much as possible from the effects of radiation and rain, were 73°·2 and 24°·5.

The average daily range of the readings of thermometers in air at the height of four feet was 11°·7, which is 3°·8 *greater* than the average range from the six preceding years.

In October the reading of the thermometer on grass was at or below 32° on five nights, and the lowest reading was 26°·5. In November it was below 32° on thirteen nights, and the lowest reading was 18°. In December it was below 32° on sixteen nights, and the lowest reading was 19°·3. The periods of time, however, during which these readings have continued have been very short, owing to the very cloudy state of the sky during the nights. The amount of heat radiated from the earth at night during the past quarter has been very small indeed.

*The mean amount of cloud* during the quarter was such as to cover upon the average a little more than three-fourths of the whole sky. The month of December was more clouded than any month since January 1845.

It is a fact well worthy of notice, that from the beginning of this quarter till the 20th of December, *the electricity of the atmosphere* was almost always in a neutral state; so that no signs of electricity whatever were shown for several days together by any of the electrical instruments. During this period, I myself several times minutely examined the whole of the electrical apparatus, and found it to be in a satisfactory state at all times. On the above day, and on every day afterwards till the end of the quarter, active electricity was shown.

The approximate mean monthly temperatures for other places besides Greenwich were found to differ but little in each month from those at Greenwich. In the comparison between places situated at different elevations, there is one leading difference in respect to temperature which we must expect to find, viz. that at the places of a higher level, a lower mean temperature, and a greater range of temperature take place, than at places situated at a lower level. These conditions are very clearly shown in the tables.

The monthly mean temperatures of those places in Cornwall and Devonshire in each of these three months were somewhat *above* those at other places. At Exeter, however, the difference in this respect from those in other counties is small; in fact the weather at this place during the past quarter more nearly resembled that of places out of these counties, than that of places situated within them.

The remarkable cold period referred to above, which happened between November 17 and November 21, between periods of so different temperatures, deserves particular notice. As far as I can infer from the meteorological returns from the country, it seems to have been general. Snow to a considerable depth fell within this period in Suffolk; but it is not noticed as having fallen elsewhere. The particulars of the changes of temperatures in the months of November and December I have detailed in the Registrar-General's weekly reports in December. I may here remark, however, that during these two months the usual diurnal rise and fall of the temperatures of the air and of the dew-point very frequently did not take place; and they were often reversed; a nocturnal rising temperature and a daily falling temperature were of frequent occurrence.

From the circumstance of these anomalous changes of temperatures, as might be expected, the usual diurnal difference in the readings of the barometer did not take place. The readings at times constantly *increased* for several days together, and then *decreased* for several days together. In December, on the seventh day, at 3 A.M., the remarkably low reading of 28·383 inches took place at Greenwich; and this low reading was general over the country; but it first took place at northern places and then at southern. Thus the minimum occurred at Durham on December 6, at 6 P.M., and it was 27·89 inches; at Stonyhurst during the evening, and it was 27·841 inches; at Liverpool at $10^h$ P.M., and it was 28·184 inches; at Cambridge on December 7, at $1^h 10^m$ A.M., and it was 28·382 inches; and at Greenwich on December 7 at 9ʰ A.M., and it was, as stated above, 28·383 inches. A reading so low as this is of rare occurrence. The previous instances at Greenwich are as follows:—In 1783, on March 6, the reading was 28·12 inches; in 1809, on December 17, the reading was 28·20 inches; in 1821, on December 25, the reading was 27·89 inches; in 1824, on November 23, the reading was 28·37 inches; and in 1843, on January 13, the reading was 28·10 inches.

During the quarter there were eight exhibitions of the aurora borealis, which occurred on the following days:—Oct. 15, 23 and 24; Nov. 1, 2, 19; Dec. 2 and 19. That on Oct. 24 was one of the finest I have seen. (See the Philosophical Magazine for November, and the Athenæum for November.) At every one of these times the magnets were much disturbed. The magnetic disturbance connected with the aurora of October 24 exhibited a greater amount of consecutive disturbance than had been before experienced at Greenwich since the establishment of the magnetic observatory in 1840. (See the Philosophical Magazine for January 1848; and a forthcoming account of the aurora seen in Cambridge, by Mr. Morgan, of the Cambridge Observatory.)

From the preceding remarks, it will be seen that the weather during the past quarter has been very unusual indeed. I have searched all meteorological records at my command, which have been made in the previous fifty years, and I have failed to find any season of similar character. In the year 1806 the average temperature for the last quarter of the year was $50°·1$ (see Philosophical Transactions for that year); and this result nearly agrees with that found by Luke Howard, Esq. (see his Climate of London), which was $50°·3$; but although this value is greater than that of the past three months, yet I am inclined to think that the temperature of this period in 1806 did not really exceed that of 1847, as at this time all mean temperatures depended solely on uncompared self-registering thermometers; and it is found that even with good self-registering thermometers, a subtractive correction is always required to deduce from them the true mean for the month. The only October in this century whose temperature seems really to have exceeded that of the past October, is that of 1811; so that whether we compare the weather of the past quarter by longer or shorter periods with that of similar periods in past years, it has evidently been of a very remarkable character, and of rare occurrence.

To the report of the Registrar-General are appended the monthly values at every station, from which the average values for the quarter have been determined, and which are contained in the following table:—

## Meteorological Table for the Quarter ending December 31, 1847.

| Names of the places | Mean pressure of the atmosphere of dry air reduced to the level of the sea. | Mean temperature of the air. | Highest reading of the thermometer. | Lowest reading of the thermometer. | Mean daily range of temperature. | Range of thermometer. | Mean estimated strength 0–6. | Wind (General direction). | Mean amount of cloud 0–10. | Number of days on which it fell | Rain. Amount collected. | Mean weight of vapour in a cubic foot of air. | Mean additional weight required to saturate a cubic foot of air. | Mean degree of humidity. | Mean whole amount of water in a vertical column of atmosphere. | Mean weight of a cubic foot of air. | Height of observer above the level of the sea. |
|---|---|---|---|---|---|---|---|---|---|---|---|---|---|---|---|---|---|
| | in. | ° | ° | ° | ° | ° | | | | | in. | gr. | gr. | | in. | gr. | feet |
| Helstone | 29.570 | 49.6 | 63.0 | 29.0 | 9.0 | 36.0 | 1.2 | s.w. | 6.8 | 55 | 17.6 | 4.0 | 0.2 | 0.925 | 5.1 | 535 | 106 |
| Truro | 29.629 | 49.7 | 62.0 | 30.0 | 8.0 | 32.0 | 0.8 | s.w. | 7.3 | 61 | 18.6 | 3.8 | 0.4 | 0.890 | 4.7 | 538 | 129 |
| Torquay | 29.606 | 49.4 | 61.0 | 31.0 | 7.3 | 33.0 | 2.4 | s.w. | 7.3 | 43 | 13.7 | 3.7 | 0.3 | 0.887 | 4.5 | 528 | 140 |
| Exeter | 29.694 | 46.7 | 67.0 | 25.0 | 10.0 | 42.0 | 0.8 | s.w. | 7.8 | 58 | 14.3 | 3.6 | 0.2 | 0.947 | 4.4 | 543 | 60 |
| Brighton | | 46.4 | 64.0 | 29.0 | 6.2 | 42.0 | | n.c. | 6.9 | 49 | | | | | | | |
| Chichester | | 45.9 | 67.0 | 26.0 | 10.9 | 41.0 | | | | | | | | | | | |
| Uckfield | 29.799 | 46.5 | 71.0 | 24.0 | 12.6 | 47.0 | 1.4 | s.w. | 6.7 | 29 | 8.8 | 3.5 | 0.3 | 0.872 | 4.4 | 542 | 189 |
| Beckington | 29.669 | 42.9 | 69.0 | 14.0 | 12.7 | 55.0 | | s.w. | 7.6 | 47 | 6.2 | 3.4 | 0.1 | 0.892 | 4.4 | 529 | 265 |
| Royal Observatory, Greenwich | 29.712 | 47.5 | 73.2 | 21.5 | 11.7 | 48.7 | | a.s.w. | 7.6 | 42 | 12.7 | 3.6 | 0.4 | 0.863 | 4.2 | 540 | 159 |
| Maidenstone Hill, Greenwich | 29.677 | 46.7 | 63.7 | 26.9 | 9.4 | 38.8 | | s.w. | 7.6 | 34 | 6.0 | 3.4 | 0.4 | 0.913 | 4.3 | 542 | 167 |
| Lewisham | | 46.6 | 69.0 | 24.0 | 11.7 | 45.0 | 2.9 | s.w. | 6.3 | 53 | 6.1 | 3.4 | 0.4 | 0.883 | 4.2 | | |
| Walworth | 29.527 | 44.9 | 70.0 | 27.0 | 11.7 | 43.0 | | var. | 7.4 | 39 | 5.8 | 3.1 | 0.5 | 0.860 | | 539 | 32 |
| Latimer Rectory | 29.641 | 44.2 | 68.0 | 23.0 | 13.2 | 45.0 | 0.5 | e. | 7.1 | 48 | 4.7 | 3.4 | 0.3 | 0.925 | 4.4 | 539 | 290 |
| Aylesbury | 29.624 | 45.2 | 72.0 | 21.0 | 12.2 | 51.0 | 1.2 | s.w. | 7.4 | 54 | 8.8 | 3.0 | 0.5 | 0.897 | 4.4 | 529 | 290 |
| Hartwell House | 29.575 | 44.6 | 68.5 | 25.0 | 15.1 | 45.5 | 1.3 | s.w. | 7.4 | 34 | 7.0 | 3.4 | 0.2 | 0.941 | 4.4 | 537 | 300 |
| Stone Observatory | | | | | 11.5 | | | | | 43 | 8.0 | 3.5 | | | | | |
| Pool Cottage, Hereford | | 45.6 | | | | | | a.s.w. | 6.8 | 58 | 13.8 | | | | | | |
| Cardington | | 44.3 | 66.0 | 25.0 | 11.2 | 41.0 | | s.w. | 6.8 | 39 | 6.3 | 3.1 | 0.4 | 0.896 | 4.2 | 539 | |
| Thwaite | | | 72.0 | 29.0 | 13.3 | 43.0 | 0.6 | a.w. | 7.7 | 40 | 6.7 | 3.4 | 0.3 | 0.904 | 4.2 | 511 | 290 |
| Cambridge Observatory | 29.705 | 45.6 | 70.0 | 26.2 | 13.3 | 43.0 | 1.0 | calm. | 3.3 | 40 | 5.4 | 3.0 | 0.6 | 0.864 | 3.9 | 558 | 88 |
| Saffron Walden | 29.712 | 46.3 | 69.0 | 26.2 | 9.7 | 44.7 | 2.6 | s.w. | 6.4 | 40 | 6.0 | 3.4 | 0.4 | 0.897 | 4.0 | 541 | |
| Norwich | 29.670 | 45.6 | 64.0 | 31.0 | 8.0 | 33.0 | | var. | 6.6 | 40 | 6.4 | 3.4 | 0.4 | 0.858 | 4.0 | 528 | 29 |
| Derby | | 45.2 | 65.0 | 26.0 | 10.8 | 39.0 | | s.w. | 7.1 | 49 | 8.5 | 3.3 | 0.6 | 0.863 | 4.0 | 538 | 105 |
| Highfield House | 29.608 | 46.6 | 64.5 | 32.0 | 9.0 | 33.5 | 1.1 | s.w. | 7.1 | 43 | 7.8 | 3.3 | 0.5 | 0.855 | 3.9 | 539 | 57 |
| Liverpool Observatory | 29.575 | 47.7 | 64.6 | 29.4 | 6.6 | 35.2 | 1.1 | s.w. | 7.1 | 47 | 10.7 | 3.3 | 0.7 | 0.916 | 3.8 | 537 | 381 |
| Stanyhurst Observatory | 29.609 | 43.8 | 62.7 | 25.8 | 10.6 | 36.9 | 0.5 | var. | | 41 | 11.4 | 3.3 | 0.7 | 0.944 | 3.8 | 538 | 340 |
| Durham | 29.389 | 43.9 | 62.0 | 28.1 | 8.5 | 36.9 | 2.0 | a.s.w. | 7.2 | 33 | 7.1 | 3.2 | 0.2 | 0.941 | 3.9 | 539 | 121 |
| Newcastle | 29.536 | 43.4 | 64.0 | 29.3 | 10.2 | 32.5 | | var. | | | 10.3 | 3.5 | | 0.968 | 4.3 | | |
| Drummargal House, Scarva, Ireland | | 44.5 | 64.0 | 23.3 | 10.2 | 40.7 | 1.4 | s.w. | 6.9 | 50 | 12.4 | 3.4 | 0.2 | 0.943 | 4.1 | | 17 |
| Number of column | 1 | 2 | 3 | 4 | 5 | 6 | 7 | 8 | 9 | 10 | 11 | 12 | 13 | 14 | 15 | 16 | |

From the numbers in the first column it appears that the volume of dry air was very nearly the same at all parts of the country. The mean of all the results in the first column is 29·640 inches, and this may be considered as the pressure of dry air for England during the quarter ending December 31, 1847.

From the numbers in the second column we find, for the quarter ending December 31, 1847, that the mean temperature of the air for the counties of Cornwall and Devonshire was 48°·9, and for the remaining counties, excepting those north of latitude 54°, was 45°·7, and that the mean temperature of Durham and Newcastle was 44°·8.

The average daily range of the temperature of the air in Cornwall and Devonshire was 8°·6; at Brighton and Liverpool was 6°·4, and the mean value for all other places was 10°·5. The greatest mean daily ranges took place at Hartwell, Cambridge, Latimer Rectory, Uckfield, &c., and the least occurred at Brighton, Liverpool, Torquay, Truro, Norwich, &c.

The highest reading during the quarter was at Greenwich, which was 73°·2, and the lowest was at Beckington, which was 14°. The extreme range of temperature in England during the quarter was therefore 59°·2.

The average quarterly range of the thermometer-readings in Cornwall and Devonshire was 35°·7; at Brighton and Liverpool was 33°·6; at those places situated between the latitudes of 51° and 52½°, was 44°·7; and between the latitudes of 52½° and 55° was 36°. The ranges at those places situated at a high elevation, were in all cases much greater than at those places situated in the same parallel of latitude but at a lower elevation.

The mean direction of the wind for all places was S.W., except at Brighton, where it was N.E.

From the numbers in the ninth column it would seem that the distribution of cloud has been nearly the same at all parts of the country, and such as to cover three-fourths of the whole sky.

The fall of rain has been the largest in Cornwall and Devonshire; the average amount for the quarter was 16 inches; and it has fallen on a greater number of days in those counties than in any others; the average number was 54, but this number was exceeded by 7 at Truro. At Torquay the number was 43 only. At Walworth the fall seems to have been the least in amount, but this value is not confirmed by those at neighbouring places; the next in order is Cambridge, Lewisham, Saffron Walden, Greenwich, Uckfield, Cardington and

Norwich. [The construction of the several gauges is different, and many of them have not been tested either by weighing the collected water, or by accurately measuring the vessels in which it is received. At Walworth Crosley's self-registering gauge is used, which, after being in use a short time, does not truly register the fall, and it should not be depended upon solely in any case.]

Columns 12 to 16 contain the mean hygrometrical results, and they are nearly identical at most places; at Beckington, however, the air seems to have been very nearly in a state of saturation during these three months, if the instruments be good by which the observations were made; they have not however been compared with standards. The degree of humidity in the Vale of Aylesbury is greater than that due to its latitude, and this seems to be decided, as the results at three different stations agree very well together.

Those results from the station in Ireland, depending on the temperature of the air, the direction and strength of the wind, and the amount of clouds, agree with those in England at the same latitude, but those depending on humidity of the air, and on the amount of rain, exhibit an excess over those in England.

January 27, 1848.

XXI. *On the present state of knowledge of the Geology of Asia Minor.* By H. E. STRICKLAND, F.G.S.[*]

IN the last Number of the Journal of the Geological Society, part 2, p. 74, is a letter from M. von Tchihatcheff, extracted from Leonhard and Bronn's *Neues Jahrbuch*, 1847. I rejoice to find from it that this gentleman is about to undertake a systematic geological survey of Asia Minor, a country which, from the magnificent scale on which its secondary and tertiary rocks are displayed, and the wonderful diversity of its volcanic phænomena, is probably inferior to none of equal area in geological interest. Our knowledge of the geology of Asia Minor is, in truth, comparatively limited, and we may therefore look for results of the highest value from M. Tchihatcheff's researches. But although much remains to be done by the geologist in Asia Minor, yet we are not wholly without information on this subject; and as it might be inferred from M. Tchihatcheff's silence as to the labours of others that such was the case, I have thought it desirable to give a brief summary of the progress that has already been made in this branch of inquiry.

[*] Communicated by the Author.

The existence of a tertiary marine formation on the shores of the Dardanelles was made known nearly half a century ago by Olivier, a scientific zoologist, who recognised in this pliocene deposit many existing species of Mediterranean shells, the names of which he has enumerated.

The slaty rocks of the Thracian Bosphorus, flanked by volcanic rocks on the north and by tertiary beds on the southwest, have long been known. The occurrence of fossils in the former rocks was noticed by Fontanier (*Voyages en Orient*). In 1836 Mr. W. J. Hamilton and myself proved, by means of these fossils, that the formation was Silurian; and in a paper by myself in the Transactions of the Geological Society, vol. v., On the Geology of the Thracian Bosphorus, the district between the sea of Marmora and the Euxine is described in some detail. In the following year the same region was explored by M. de Verneuil, whose researches (published in the *Bull. Soc. Géol. de France*) entirely confirm those which we had previously made.

The vicinity of Smyrna was geologically explored by Mr. Hamilton and myself during the winter of 1835-36, and the results are given in my memoir on that district (Geol. Trans., vol. v.). In this paper will be found the first attempt at a *classification* of the geological formations of Asia Minor.

This classification is further carried out in a joint memoir which we published in the Geol. Trans. vol. vi., On the Geology of the western part of Asia Minor, in which we described the southern shores of the sea of Marmora, the valleys of the Macestus, the Rhyndacus, the Hermus, the Cayster and the Meander, besides giving short notices of Erythræ, Boodroom, Cnidus and Rhodes. The most interesting of the districts here described is unquestionably the Catacecaumene, the volcanic phænomena of which were illustrated by coloured maps, sections and landscapes.

After my return to England Mr. Hamilton penetrated to Armenia, and returned through the interior of Asia Minor to Smyrna, during the whole of which lengthened journey he kept careful notes of all the geological phænomena which came in his way. These facts will be found duly recorded in his work entitled " Researches in Asia Minor, Pontus and Armenia, with some Account of their Antiquities and Geology." The same journey supplied him with the materials for his memoir in the Geol. Trans., On the Geology of part of Asia Minor between the Salt Lake of Kodj-hissar, and Cæsarea of Cappadocia, with a description of Mount Argæus. The latter mountain was ascended by Mr. Hamilton, and its height ascertained by the barometer.

The geological survey of the neighbourhood of Smyrna was extended westward along both shores of the Gulf, and over the peninsula of Karabournou, by Lieut. Spratt, and the fossils which he collected have been described by Prof. E. Forbes (Journ. Geol. Soc., vol. i. p. 156).

The same gentlemen have given a short notice of the geology of Lycia in the Journ. Geol. Soc., vol. ii. p. 8; and in their joint "Travels in Lycia" their observations are to be found in greater detail, and are embodied in the beautiful map of Lycia which accompanies the work.

The geology of Rhodes and of Samos has been described by Lieut. Spratt (Proc. Geol. Soc., vol. iii. p. 774, and Journ. Geol. Soc., vol. iii. p. 65).

Mr. Warington W. Smyth has described the mining districts of the Eastern Taurus in Journ. Geol. Soc., vol. i. p. 330.

And lastly, Dr. Daubeny, in his work on Volcanos just published, has devoted an entire chapter to the volcanic phænomena of Asia Minor.

Besides these more elaborate treatises, a variety of scattered hints and notices on Anatolian geology may be collected from the works of Fontanier, Andreossy, Beaufort, Texier, Ainsworth, Fellows, and others. From these multifarious sources I commenced three or four years ago to construct for my own use a general geological map of Asia Minor. Of course it is a very fragmentary production; and the numerous blank spaces in it show how much we have yet to learn as to the geology of that country.

I trust however that I have now shown that the geology of Asia Minor is not so completely untrodden a field as M. Tchihatcheff's letter would seem to imply; and having thus briefly vindicated the labours of others, I shall look forward with lively interest to the valuable additions to our knowledge which we may expect from that traveller's researches.

## XXII. *Proceedings of Learned Societies.*

### ROYAL SOCIETY.

[Continued from vol. xxxi. p. 376.]

"ABSTRACT of a Thirteenth Series of Tide Researches." By Dr. Whewell.

The first part of this paper, "*On the Tides of the Pacific,*" forms a sequel to former papers by the same author, especially to his first memoir on this subject, printed by the Royal Society in 1833 ('Essay towards a first approximation to a map of Cotidal Lines'), and to the *Sixth Series* published in 1836 ('Results of an extended series of Tide Observations made on the coasts of England and

America in June 1835'). Among the results obtained in the latter paper, it appeared that all the "cotidal lines" which have been most exactly traced, meet the coast at a very acute angle; and for that and for other reasons stated in other memoirs, the drawing of cotidal lines across wide oceans is a very precarious process. In addition to this consideration, the scantiness of our materials has hitherto made it impossible to trace the tides of the Pacific in a connected form; and the absence of lunar tides in the central parts of that ocean (as at Tahiti) makes it difficult to represent the course of the tides by means of cotidal lines at all. We are thus led to consider in what other way the course of the tides over wide spaces may be represented : and it is stated by the author, that either a *stationary undulation*, or a *rotatory undulation*, of the central parts of an ocean, with a border of cotidal lines proceeding outwards from the central undulation into bays and arms of the sea, would represent, in a great measure, the tidal phenomena of the Atlantic and Pacific, as far as they are known. The *rotatory undulation* here spoken of need not be understood to be a *rotatory motion* of the water, but a geometrical rotation of the cotidal line, such as takes place in the German Ocean ; the tide in the central part (that is, the rise and fall of the surface) vanishing, as was shown by the observations of Capt. Hewett, though the tidal currents at that point alternate regularly. Such a movement of the cotidal line may perhaps represent the phenomena of the North Pacific.

The author has collected materials for a Tide Map of the Pacific from various navigators;—Cook, Flinders, King, Captains FitzRoy, Sir E. Belcher, Sir James Ross, Stokes, Kellet, and others of our own countrymen; Malaspina, Freycinet, Du Petit-Thouars, Wrangel and Admiral Lütke, and other Spanish, French and Russian navigators. The result of these appears to be, that on the eastern coast of the Pacific, the tide comes from the west; arrives first at the coast near Acapulco and Nicoya, and is later and later both to the north and to the south of this point; passing to the eastward round Cape Horn, as observed by King, and to the northward along the coast of North America, and then to the westward along the Aleutian Isles, and so to Kamtschatka, as stated by Admiral Lütke.

The tides in the centre of the Pacific are too small and anomalous to allow us to trace the connection among them. At Tahiti, according to the observations of Sir Edward Belcher, the solar and lunar tides appear to be equal.

The tides have been traced along the coasts of New Zealand and Australia by Cook, Flinders, and other succeeding navigators. They come from the east; and the cotidal lines which mark their progress appear to have a north and south range, except when deflected by passing round promontories and the like. When we pass westward from the eastern coast of Australia, the cotidal lines are too much broken and complicated by the intervention of islands, to be traced with our present materials of knowledge.

The second part of the memoir, "*On the Diurnal Inequality*," treats of the difference of the two tides of the same day, which has also been discussed in former memoirs by the author, and its laws so fully made out, that this inequality has been introduced into the tide tables for Liverpool and for Plymouth. This inequality depends mainly on the moon's declination. In England it is small: it is very marked on the coasts of Spain, Portugal and North America, as was shown by the observations of 1836: but in the North Pacific and in the Indian seas, it reaches an enormous amount, and shows itself with curious differences. In many places in those seas, the diurnal inequality is much larger than the differences of spring and neap tides, and is so large as utterly to confound the usual modes of estimating the "establishment" of a place.

This inequality affects the tides of various parts on the coast of Australia to a very great amount, and with very remarkable differences. It is seen at Adelaide on the south, and Port Essington on the north coast; and at each place it produces a difference of several feet between every two successive tides, when it is at its maximum: but this difference affects mainly the *high waters* at Adelaide and the *low waters* at Port Essington*. Also on the west coast of Australia, near Swan River, the diurnal inequality appears with another peculiarity, affecting the times of high water rather than the heights. These differences, the author remarks, show that the diurnal wave travels separately from the semidiurnal wave; but our materials do not at present enable us to analyse the compound tide into these two waves, and to trace the course of each.

The author observes, in conclusion, that our knowledge of the tides is not likely to be completed, nor even much advanced, by tide observations made by navigators and surveyors voyaging with other main objects. The later observations of the Pacific, though made with great industry, have added little to the knowledge derived from Cook, Flinders and King, because they were not geographically connected with each other: and the great discrepancies of the observations at the same place show how little correctness the mean of them, or the result, however obtained, can pretend to.

The results of the recent observations, with which the author has been furnished by various navigators and by the Hydrographer's Office, have been obtained by throwing the observations into curves, according to methods formerly used and described by the author. This labour has been carefully performed by Mr. D. Ross of the Hydrographer's Office.

---

CAMBRIDGE PHILOSOPHICAL SOCIETY.
[Continued from vol. xxxi. p. 380.]

May 3, 1847.—On the Internal Pressure to which Rock Masses may be subjected, and its possible influence in the Production of the Laminated Structure. By W. Hopkins, M.A., F.R.S.

If a plane of indefinitely small extent pass through any proposed

---

* These results follow from a series of tide observations made at Adelaide by Mr. Bealten, and at Port Essington by Sir Gordon Bremer.

point in the interior of a continuous solid mass in a state of constraint, the resultant pressure or tension on this plane will vary with the angular position of the plane, and its direction will not, as in fluid masses, be generally perpendicular to the plane. There are, however, three angular positions in which the direction of the pressure does coincide with a perpendicular to the plane. These are called *principal directions*, and are at right angles to each other; the corresponding pressures are called *principal pressures*. In these particular positions of the plane there will be no *tangential* action upon it; but generally the whole pressure or tension may be resolved into two parts, of which one is *normal* and the other *tangential*. In certain positions of the plane these forces assume their maximum or minimum values. The normal action is a maximum, when a perpendicular to the plane coincides with one of the three principal directions; and a minimum, when it coincides with another, the third of those directions, not corresponding either to a maximum or minimum value. These conclusions have been established by Poisson, Cauchy and others. In this paper the author has investigated the positions of the small plane, when the *tangential force* upon it is a maximum. There are two of these positions perpendicular to each other, in each of which the plane passes through that principal direction which does not correspond to either the maximum or minimum value of the normal force, and bisects the corresponding right angle between the other two principal directions—those of the maximum and minimum normal forces. Having established the relative positions of the planes of greatest normal and of greatest tangential action, the author proceeds to examine how far the evidence afforded by the distorted forms of organic remains may justify the conclusion that these forces have had an influence in determining the position of the planes of cleavage in the rocks containing those remains.

Conceive one stratified bed placed on another, and acted on by forces tending to give the upper a small sliding motion along the surface of the lower one. A considerable *tangential force* will be called into action between the beds; and if any object be placed between them, its lower part will be pushed in one direction by the action of the lower bed, while its upper part will be equally pushed in the opposite direction by the action of the upper bed, and thus the object will be *twisted* from its original form. For example, suppose the object be an equilateral shell lying between the two beds, with the plane of junction of the two valves parallel to the surfaces of the beds, and suppose the median line of either valve to be perpendicular to the direction in which the one bed tends to move along the other. The shell in its distorted form will no longer be equilateral; one half of each shell will be crumpled into a smaller space, while the other half will be extended into greater breadth; so that if there be longitudinal folds on the valve, those on the former half will be pressed together, and those on the latter will be dilated into greater breadth. An exactly similar effect will be produced on both shells; but the compressed half of one will be opposite to the dilated half of the other.

Again, suppose the beds to be acted on by forces tending to compress them equally in a direction parallel to their surfaces. The shell will then be *compressed* in the same direction, so that, generally, the ratio of the length to the breadth of the shell will be altered, but without that *twisting* which will characterize the distorted form in the former case. In the case of this paragraph, the direction of compression will coincide with what has been above termed a *principal direction*, and it will also be that of *maximum normal pressure*. In the previous case, the common surface of the two beds will be the plane of *maximum tangential action*.

If, then, in any stratified mass, we observe the organic remains to be regularly distorted, and *twisted* from their original forms, as above described, we may conclude that the planes of stratification have nearly coincided with those of *maximum tangential action*; but if, on the contrary, the distortion consists only in compression of the shells in a given direction along the surface of the bed where they are found, we may conclude that the direction of *maximum normal pressure* has nearly coincided with this direction of compression, and was consequently parallel to the planes of stratification. The masses in which distorted remains have been found, are generally those which have been much disturbed. The disturbing forces are those to which the distortions are to be referred; and it may be remarked, that in such cases the directions of maximum and minimum pressure at any point would probably lie in a plane perpendicular to the strike of the elevated beds, and that consequently the planes of maximum tangential action, which bisect the angles between those directions, will have approximately the same strike as the beds themselves.

The bearing of these conclusions on the question of laminated structure is easily seen. Suppose the planes of lamination are observed to be nearly coincident with those of stratification, and that the distortion of the organic remains consists in their being *twisted* from their primitive forms. Then, if the position of the planes of lamination has been due to the internal pressures to which the mass has been subjected, it is to *tangential action*, and not to *direct pressure*, that the effect is attributable. Again, if the planes of lamination have nearly the same strike as the beds, and are inclined to them at an angle of about 45°, while the organic remains have been distorted only by *direct compression*, the planes of lamination must in this case also have coincided with those of maximum tangential action, and we shall have the same conclusion as in the former case. The direction of compression of the organic forms ought, according to this view, to be perpendicular to the intersections of the planes of lamination and those of stratification.

Mr. Sharpe, in a paper recently published in the Journal of the Geological Society, has stated nearly all the evidence hitherto collected on this subject; and it appears that the organic bodies are most *twisted* from their original forms in those cases in which the planes of lamination coincide most nearly with those of stratification, and that they have generally suffered most *direct compression* without twisting in those cases in which the planes of lamination are inclined to those of stratification at an angle of 40° or 50°. We must therefore conclude, according to the last paragraph, that *the planes of lamination approximately coincide with those which were formerly the planes of greatest tangential action.*

The author does not regard this mechanical action as the probable primary cause of the laminated structure, but rather as a secondary cause, which may have had its influence in determining the positions of the planes of lamination. He trusts that further evidence will be collected on the subject.

---

ROYAL ASTRONOMICAL SOCIETY.

[Continued from vol. xxii. p. 533.]

Dec. 10, 1847.—Annular Eclipse of October 8–9, 1847. Captain Jacob writes that "the eclipse was observed at Bombay.

|                    | Bombay M. T.        |
|                    | h  m   s            |
|--------------------|---------------------|
| Eclipse begins     | 1   7  36           |
| Annulus forms      | 2  53  43           |
| Annulus breaks     | 3   1  15·5         |
| Eclipse ends       | 4  28   6           |

"From the place of observation the lighthouse bears S. 18° 40′ W., and Malabar Point flagstaff, S. 88° 55′ W.: these two are points in the trigonometrical survey; but I have not the survey data, with the exception of the latitude, 18° 53′ 40″, and longitude, 72° 51′ 12″ of the lighthouse. From these and a good map of Bombay, I get for my position, latitude 18° 56′ 14″, and longitude 72° 52′ 07″. The survey longitudes are believed to be erroneous in defect rather more than 1′. The bearings were determined by measurement with a pocket sextant from the setting sun, and are probably within 2′ of the truth. The times of the beginning and end of the eclipse are uncertain; the former to 4$^s$ or 5$^s$, the eye having been withdrawn from the telescope at the moment; the latter to 2$^s$ or 3$^s$, from the sun's limb being tremulous. The times of the annular phase were considered exact, and the resulting longitude of the place comes out $\left\{ \begin{array}{c} 4^h\ 51^m\ 37^s\cdot5 \\ 37\ \cdot 8 \end{array} \right\}$ or $\left\{ \begin{array}{c} 72°\ 54′\ 22″ \\ 27 \end{array} \right\}$ from these two times.

"The day was remarkably clear for the season, not a cloud having passed until near the end of the eclipse. Shortly before the annular phase, a faint ray or brush of light was seen issuing from the sun's northern cusp, which soon after extended in both directions as a tangent to the sun's limb: nothing of the kind was visible at the other cusp; possibly it arose from a passing film of vapour.

"When the annulus was about forming, the first thing noticed was the light running rapidly round on the south side, leaving a break of considerable extent, which seemed to arise from a projecting table-land in the moon. This was soon withdrawn, and at the same instant a kind of ligament, or stalk, of about 1′ in breadth, was seen attaching the moon's limb to that of the sun, which was now quite clear, this small spot only excepted; the moon's limb was also perfectly well-defined except in this point. The ligament lasted for 3˙ or 4˙, perhaps more, elongating as the moon advanced, and was at length suddenly retracted into her circumference, the end appearing broken or toothed. At the breaking of the annulus the phænomenon was different; the moon's limb continued to approach that of the sun, till, when very close, a portion of the former, about 30° in extent, suddenly flowed over in dark lines, with bright spaces between, which almost immediately vanished, the whole appearance not lasting above 2˙. The first appearance was like that shown in plate 1, fig. 10 of the Society's Memoirs, vol. x., and the last more resembled figs. 1 and 3 of the same plate, but the lines were more numerous though they could not be counted. The telescope used was a $3\frac{1}{2}$ foot by Dollond, with a power of 40.

"Not being in good health, I was unable to make any further observations of importance, except that the temperature of the air fell during the eclipse from 87° to 84°·5, and rose again to 85°·5 at the termination; and that, while the annulus lasted, the sun's rays had scarcely a perceptible effect on the thermometer.

"The time of the retraction of the ligament was noted as that of the formation of the annulus; and the time when the lines began to run across as the time of the end of the same. No light could be seen round the moon's limb when *off* the sun, either before or after the annulus."

Beads in Annular Eclipses. By the Rev. Professor Baden Powell.

The author considers the fact of the existence of the phænomenon in question as sufficiently well-established, notwithstanding the equally admitted discrepancies in the accounts given of the appearance of the beads by different observers. Observers differ as to such points as the stationary or fluctuating character of the beads and the degree of their changes into threads; and they have sometimes been seen by one observer and not by another when the circumstances have been in some degree different. These discrepancies the author thinks due in some cases to the different coloured glasses employed, and in others to the loss of light, as, for example, when the images are projected on a screen. He thinks Mr. Caldecott's explanation of the tremulousness of the beads (as being due to atmospheric mirage) unsatisfactory, and is rather inclined with Mr. Airy to attribute it, in part, to the rapid decrease of the intensity of the sun's light near the borders.

The author considers the whole of the phænomena that have been observed to be due to two causes, viz. to the rapid decrease of light at the sun's edge, and to the acknowledged law of irradiation, that it increases with the increase of the intensity of the light.

This being allowed, he imagines that "any small opening or notch on the moon's edge will give rise to an enlarged image or patch of light by irradiation; and that this will be *much greater* as the part occasioning it is further advanced on the sun's disc;" thus the formation of *beads* is accounted for, and their elongation.

"Again, when the junction is broken, the same causes will account for the *widening* of the separation, and that in a *greater degree towards the sides* which are more remote from the circumference."

The author then proceeds to illustrate his explanation by means of diagrams applying to the different phases of the phænomenon; and he considers the principles laid down in explanation to possess the character of a *vera causa*, though they may not suffice to explain all the phænomena.

Differences in the appearances of the beads as described by different observers must also be expected, both from the preceding theory, and from the circumstance that there are differences in the *power* and *aperture* of the *telescopes* employed. The author hopes shortly to be able to offer to the Society some contributions towards the better elucidation of this subject.

It is perhaps questionable whether the same principles will afford an explanation of certain apparently analogous phænomena observed in the transits of Venus; but, in general, the adherence of the planet to the limb of the sun by a neck at the point of junction, and the protuberance of the disc towards the same part of the separation, are appearances which agree sufficiently with the cause above assigned.

In a note appended to Professor Powell's paper, he alludes to the observations of the eclipse of October 9 of the present year, in which small beads were observed, with waving in the limb, but without increase or elongations of the shadows into threads, or any other change. In the case of M. Schaub's observations, the complementary combination employed might, by the loss of light, have destroyed any effects of irradiation. Also, as the ring formed was very thin, the difference of the intensities of the sun's light for the breadth of the band would be very small; and thus the causes above referred to might not act to a perceptible extent: the whole of the phænomena might be simply accounted for, as M. Mauvais observes, by the mere consideration of the irregularities of the moon's limb as it just touched that of the sun.

Results deduced from the Occultations of Stars and Planets by the Moon, observed at Cambridge Observatory from 1830 to 1835. By the Astronomer Royal.

These occultations were reduced at the time in the most complete manner which was then practicable. A very approximate place of the star having been assumed, the apparent place of the point of the moon's limb at which the occultation took place was known, and by the application of the proper correction for parallax, the geocentric place of the same point for the instant of occultation was also known. The geocentric place of the moon's centre was computed for the instant of occultation, according to the lunar tables. From the spherical coordinates of these two points, their distance was computed, which ought to be equal to the tabular semidiameter of the moon. Any discordance must arise from some of the following sources:— an error in the assumed R.A. or N.P.D. of the star, an error in the tabular R.A. or N.P.D. of the moon, an error in her parallax or semidiameter, or in the time of observation. The effects of errors of all these kinds (except that of the moon's semidiameter) upon the computed distance between the moon's centre and the point on her limb, were calculated and expressed symbolically; and finally, the computed distance, with the addition of these symbolical terms, was made absolutely equal to the tabular diameter, with the addition of a symbolical term: thus the final equation contains one numerical term derived from the observation, and seven symbolical terms. This is essentially the simplest and most complete result which can be derived from the observation of an occultation; and if the numerical values of any one of the symbols shall become known, such symbols may, by numerical substitution, be removed from the equation.

The equations, in the form just described, are published in the various volumes of the Cambridge Observations from 1830 to 1835.

The form can now be simplified for the following reasons:—

1st. The stars have been carefully determined, hence the symbols for their errors in R.A. and N.P.D. can be got rid of in all cases. The same may be said, with few exceptions, of the places of the occulted planets.

2nd. Mr. Henderson's investigation of the value of the horizontal parallax of the moon (Mem. Roy. Ast. Soc., vol. x.) enables us to remove the corresponding symbol.

3rd. An error had been committed in the computation of the symbolical factor respecting the correction to be made to the time of observation. The change in the place of the moon's centre had been correctly computed; but the change in the correction for parallax, consequent on a change in the hour angle depending on a correction for time, had been omitted. The equations are now cleared of this fault.

To facilitate the application of the results to lunar theories, the form of the equations has been changed; and they now depend on errors of longitude and ecliptic north polar distance, and not on errors of R.A. and N.P.D.

It was not thought advisable to introduce into the equations the numerical correction of the moon's semidiameter, as deduced from transit and circle observations, as it would be hazardous to assume that this semidiameter is necessarily the same as the semidiameter of the opake body behind which the occultations occur.

To the year 1833 inclusive, the lunar elements are computed from the *Berliner Jahrbuch*: for 1834 and 1835, they are derived from the Nautical Almanac. The computations have been partly made by Mr. Glaisher, partly by Mr. H. Breen, Jun.; and the Astronomer Royal places great reliance on the accuracy of the results.

The memoir is divided into three sections.

Sect. I. Places of the occulted stars adopted for computation.

Sect. II. Correction of the assumed value of horizontal parallax, and correction of the factor of the error of time, depending on the change of parallax during the error of time.

Sect. III. Transformation of the final equations, from the form depending on errors of the moon's place in R.A. and N.P.D. to a form depending on errors of the moon's place in longitude and ecliptic north polar distance; and exhibition of the final results.

Letter from the Rev. W. R. Dawes.

"On the first of the last month, while tracing the southern limits of the great nebula in Orion, my attention was attracted by the appearance of the star which stands on the point of the *proboscis major*. With my 8½-foot equatoreal, power 195, the star was distinctly separated into two, whose magnitudes were carefully estimated to be the eighth and ninth. I have since searched in vain for any notice of the duplicity of this star; yet it must have come under the eye of every observer who has scrutinized the ramifications of this most extraordinary of the nebulæ. In the map of the regions and stars of the nebulæ, presented by Sir John Herschel to the Astronomical Society in 1826, and contained in vol. ii. of the Memoirs, this star is inserted and denominated *A*. The same designation is given to it in the catalogue of the stars in the nebula given by Sir John in page 28 of his Results of Astronomical Observations made at the Cape, in which it stands as No. 135. It is there called 6·7 magnitude, which is far brighter than it appears in *this* latitude: yet its identity is unquestionable. Though one of the most conspicuous stars in that part of the nebula, and inserted with perfect accuracy, from micrometrical observations in the beautiful plate in Sir John's volume of Results, yet no intimation is given of its being double. Neither does it appear in the catalogue of double stars, observed with the 20-foot reflector. It seems scarcely probable, that if, ten years ago, it presented its present appearance, it should not have been recognized under the power of the 20-foot reflector, and within 30° of the zenith. This would perhaps be more extraordinary than that it should have escaped detection by Mr. Cooper with his gigantic refractor, or by Dr. Lamont with the large telescope of 11¼ inches aperture at the Royal Observatory at Munich (whose observations of the nebula are specially referred to by Sir John Herschel), or by Struve at Dorpat, or finally by De Vico at Rome, who seems to have paid great attention to this object, and in whose picture the star in question appears as of the eighth magnitude, which is also assigned to it by Lalande, in whose catalogue it stands as No. 10567. The unavoidable inference would seem to be, that the star must have emerged from a single state within the last ten years. But if its change has been so rapid, it is surprising that it was never observed to be double *previously to its closing*, either by Struve in his sweeps for double stars, or by the scrutinizing eye of Sir W. Herschel, who brought some of the largest and most perfect of telescopes to bear upon it. If, on the other hand, the star has always been as distinctly double as it is now, then it would be difficult to say what amount of non-observation may be received as conclusive evidence of non-existence. The object is, at any rate, one of peculiar interest; and I would earnestly request attention to it by such observers as possess instruments competent to its satisfactory measurement. Its mean place for 1848·0 is R.A. $5^h$ $28^m$ $27^s$; N.P.D. $95°$ $43'$ $47''$."

The star Weiss xx. 122, supposed to be missing, is inserted in the Berlin Map, Hora xix. published in 1840.—(R. W. R.)

## XXIII. *Intelligence and Miscellaneous Articles.*
### ANALYSIS OF A HYDRATED SILICATE OF ALUMINA.
### BY MM. DAMOUR AND SALVETAT.

THIS mineral is found in the environs of Montmorillon (Vienne). It occurs in cavities in a brownish argil; it is very soft and saponaceous to the feel, perfectly amorphous, and may be readily broken down between the fingers; its colour is bright rose-red. Without possessing the plastic properties of clay, it very readily diffuses through water; it is infusible by the blowpipe; it is also infusible in the high temperature of a porcelain furnace, but assumes the whiteness and appearance of biscuit, and is hard enough to scratch glass.

When heated in a tube, it yields much water, loses its rose colour, and becomes grayish-white; from $60°$ F. and upwards it loses water gradually, and when heated to $212°$, it still obstinately retains $0·1512$ of combined water. With microcosmic salt it partially dissolves, and leaves a bulky skeleton of silica; solution of caustic soda separates from it a small portion of gelatinous silica.

Hydrochloric acid partially attacks it, without producing the slightest effervescence, and dissolves some lime, magnesia, potash, alumina, oxide of iron, and traces of manganese; the greater part of the mineral remains insoluble, and retains its rose colour. If, after this treatment with acid, the insoluble portion be boiled in a solution of caustic soda, a considerable quantity of silica is dissolved; the insoluble portion being again treated with hydrochloric acid, it is completely decomposed; the silica separates in a flocculent state, and the solution contains the rest of the alumina.

Sulphuric acid, when heated till it begins to vaporize, completely decomposes the mineral, within about one-hundredth; on pouring water on the substance thus acted upon, the alkali and the other bases are dissolved, and pure silica is deposited. The solution, separated from the silica, gives with ammonia a precipitate coloured with a little oxide of iron; the solution, separated from the alumina, is rendered turbid by oxalate of ammonia, and phosphate of soda afterwards produces an appreciable degree of turbidness.

Examination showed that the mineral contained no sulphuric acid; and the various tests indicated that the mineral is essentially composed of silica, alumina and water, and also contained small quantities of lime, magnesia, potash, oxide of iron, and manganese; the peculiar rose colour appeared to be owing to combustible matter.

The different analyses of this mineral were performed by various processes; and in all of them at least one gramme was used.

A. The mineral was fused with four times its weight of very dry carbonate of soda; the residue was treated with water and hydrochloric acid; the silica was separated by evaporation twice to dryness; heated to redness and weighed, it was totally soluble in a solution of caustic soda.

The solution, separated from the silica, was precipitated by ammonia, and suffered to remain at rest during twenty-four hours. The deposit of alumina and peroxide of iron was redissolved on the filter by dilute hydrochloric acid.

The solution was supersaturated with soda, which redissolved the alumina, and left the peroxide of iron with a small quantity of lime and magnesia, which the alumina had taken down with it. These matters were redissolved in hydrochloric acid, and the oxide of iron precipitated by ammonia, the filtered liquor being added to that which contained the greater part of the lime and magnesia.

The alkaline solution of alumina was decomposed by hydrochloric acid, and this last separated by hydrosulphate of ammonia; the peroxide of iron was dried and weighed; it dissolved totally in boiling hydrochloric acid.

Lastly, the lime and magnesia were successively precipitated by oxalate and phosphate of ammonia; the ammoniaco-magnesian phosphate was washed with slightly ammoniacal water.

B. The decomposition of the mineral by means of hydrofluoric acid, admitted readily of ascertaining the quantity of alkalies which it contained. The operation was performed in a platina crucible, and the solution evaporated to dryness with sulphuric acid; the residue was treated with water, the solution was filtered, the oxide of iron and alumina separated by ammonia, and the lime then thrown down by oxalate of ammonia.

The liquor filtered after the separation of the lime was evaporated to dryness, and the residue, heated to redness, consisted of alkaline sulphates, mixed with sulphate of magnesia; the sulphates were dissolved in water and precipitated by acetate of barytes; the solution was filtered, evaporated to dryness, and calcined to decompose the acetates and convert them into carbonates; these were treated with water; the alkaline carbonates dissolved, and the magnesia remained insoluble with the carbonate of barytes.

The alkaline carbonates were converted into chlorides and weighed, the potash precipitated by chloride of platina. The magnesia was separated by sulphuric acid from the carbonate of barytes, with which it was mixed, and estimated in the state of sulphate.

C. The employment of excess of boiling sulphuric acid and evaporation to dryness, is a very simple method of analysing minerals of this description. The substance decomposed by this method was treated with water; the deposit separated by filtration, and which consisted of silica, readily dissolved in excess of caustic soda, except a minute quantity of sand, which did not amount to more than 0·0140 of the weight of the substance submitted to analysis. The alkaline liquid, saturated by an acid, gave pure silica, which was separated by the usual processes, after the evaporation to dryness had been twice repeated.

The mean of four analyses performed by M. Salvetat (I.), and of three by M. Damour (II.), gave the following results:—

|              | I.    | II.   |
|--------------|-------|-------|
| Silica       | 49·40 | 50·04 |
| Alumina      | 19·70 | 20·16 |
| Peroxide of iron | ·80 | ·68 |
| Lime         | 1·50  | 1·46  |
| Potash       | 1·50  | 1·27  |
| Soda         | traces |      |
| Magnesia     | ·27   | ·23   |
| Oxide of manganese | traces | traces |
| Water        | 25·67 | 26·00 |
|              | 98·84 | 99·84 |

*Ann. de. Ch. et de Phys.*, Novembre 1847.

## ON THE ACTION OF CHLORINE ON BENZOATE OF POTASH.
### BY M. SAINT-EVRE.

When a continuous current of chlorine is passed into a solution of benzoate of potash rendered strongly alkaline, there is produced, after the lapse of some time, an abundant disengagement of carbonic acid; and chloride of potassium is also formed. The character of this reaction is, then, a combustion of a part of the carbon of the benzoic acid, and consequently a substance must be formed, the molecule of which is more simple. Analysis fully confirms this conclusion. The new substance is an acid which is precipitated in the state of a potash salt; this salt purified, and then decomposed by sulphuric acid, yields the acid in question; this last, in its turn, after purification by several crystallizations, constitutes a volatile substance fusible at $176°$ to $181°$ F. Its analysis by the salt of silver yielded numbers which indicated the formula $C^{24}H^{10}Cl^2O^4$.

Subtracting the chlorine and going back to the primary substance, it will be seen that it differs from the hydrate of phenyle of M. Laurent only by the fixation of two molecules of oxygen, and it is well known that this is the relation of an acid to aldehyde which corresponds to it. The author therefore proposes provisionally to call the new substance *monochloruretted phenylic acid*. If we had phenylic acid $C^{16}H^{12}O^4$, the hydrocarburet formed at a high temperature in presence of the caustic alkalies, would be necessarily phenylen $C^{20}H^{12}$. This last, in its turn, treated with fuming nitric acid, would yield the nitrogenous body $C^{20}\begin{pmatrix}H^{10}\\N^2O^4\end{pmatrix}$. Lastly, this dissolved in ammoniated alcohol, and submitted to the action of a current of sulphuretted hydrogen, as happily suggested by M. Zinin, ought to yield, by the fixation of hydrogen, the body $C^{20}H^{14}N^2$, that is to say, nicotina.

This is exactly what happens in the present case; except that instead of having the preceding bodies, a parallel series is obtained, in which one equivalent of chlorine is substituted for one equivalent of hydrogen.

The author has successively obtained the substances represented by the formulæ $C^{20}\begin{pmatrix}H^{10}\\Cl^4\end{pmatrix}$ (monochloruretted phenyle), $C^{20}\begin{pmatrix}H^8\\Cl^2\\N^2O^4\end{pmatrix}$,

and lastly $C^{20} H^{19} Cl^2 N^2$, which is merely chlorinated nicotina, or perhaps a polymeric of this alkaloid.

The author states, that cinnamic acid, and even margaric acid, have already given him results comparable to the preceding. Suberic acid, under the same circumstances, gives rise to two new bodies, one of which is liquid and the other solid.

M. Saint-Evre states that he is now engaged in submitting to the same kind of reaction the anisic, cinnamic, nitrobenzoic, and hippuric acids.—*Comp. e. Rendus*, Decembre 13, 1847.

ACTION OF CHLORINE ON CYANIDE OF MERCURY. BY J. BOUIS.

When bottles of chlorine are exposed to the solar rays with a saturated and boiling solution of cyanide of mercury, there are produced, after a certain time, some drops which fall to the bottom of the water, in the form of a heavy yellow oil. The chlorine is absorbed with rapidity, and it must be supplied till the colour ceases to disappear. During the reaction there are formed chloride of mercury, hydrochloric acid, and hydrochlorate of ammonia, which remain dissolved in the water; chloride of cyanogen, nitrogen, and carbonic acid are disengaged.

M. Jules Bouis has examined this reaction. The yellow oil A which is produced has an extremely strong and irritating odour, and occasions a great flow of tears. It is more dense than water, and insoluble in it; but it is decomposed by it, and acquires an acid reaction. It is soluble in æther and in alcohol. Whether moist or dry, it deposits after a long time crystals of sesquichloride of carbon $C^2 Cl^6$. It explodes when heated.

This very changeable substance gave by analysis, carbon 10·47 to 10·92; nitrogen 8·34 to 8·43; chlorine 78·49 to 78·89. M. Bouis deduces from these results the formula $[C^6 N^4 Cl^{14}]$, which requires carbon 11·6; nitrogen 8·9; chlorine 79·5.

It is to be observed that the coincidence is not perfect; according to this formula, there would even be a loss of 2 per cent. on the sum of the elements obtained by experiment. But it is to be remembered that the substance is very difficult to operate with, and a nearer approximation is perhaps impossible. M. Bouis does not say whether he collected any water by the combustion of this substance; and M. Gerhardt observes, that the formula $C^3 N^6 H Cl$ would require, carbon 11·4; nitrogen 8·9; hydrogen 0·3; chlorine 79·4.

When this compound is exposed to the action of a moderate heat it boils, gives out nitrogen mixed with carbonic acid, and there distils a colourless liquid B, which, on standing, deposits crystals of sesquichloride of carbon $C^2 Cl^6$.

This new liquid is colourless, limpid, heavier than water, and has a strong irritating odour. It is insoluble in water, but soluble in alcohol, and more so in æther. It boils at about 185° F.; but this point is not fixed, and rises gradually. M. Bouis found this liquid, cleared as much as possible from chloride of carbon, to consist of, carbon 12·36—11·57—12·35; chlorine 81·80—80·42—81·63; nitrogen 4·9—5·1. M. Bouis deduces the formula [$C^{10} N^4 Cl^{14}$], which appears to M. Gerhardt to be rather complicated.

Lastly, when nitric acid is added to the liquid A, and the mixture is slightly heated, it boils and emits torrents of gas, which cause the apparatus to fly to pieces. Nitrogen and carbonic acid are disengaged, and much nitrous vapour is formed, mixed with yellowish vapours of a very strong odour. Distillation gives sesquichloride of carbon $C^2Cl^6$, and also a very volatile colourless liquid C, the odour of which is more irritating than that of the preceding products. M. Bouis found in the liquid C, carbon 10·26—10·9; chlorine 75·86—75·74; nitrogen 8·21—7·85. He represents these numbers by the formula [$C^5 N^4 Cl^{14} O^1$], which require carbon 10·9; nitrogen 75·5; oxygen 4·9.

M. Gerhardt observes that, supposing hydrogen to exist in this compound, the formula would be $C^5 N^4 H Cl^9 O$; carbon 10·9; hydrogen 0·2; nitrogen 8·1; chlorine 75·5.

M. Gerhardt remarks that the preceding formulæ are not deducible in a simple manner from the composition of cyanides and water; the substance B appears to be specially inadmissible. M. Bouis supposes sesquichloride of carbon to pre-exist in these compounds, and sets out from this hypothesis to explain the formation of it.—*Journ. de Pharm. et de Ch.*, Octobre 1847.

## FRIGORIFIC MIXTURE.

It is stated by M. B. F. Jourdan, that when a mixture is made of equal weights of commercial hydrochloric acid and finely-powdered sulphate of zinc, the cold produced sinks the thermometer from 50° to 20° F.—*Ibid.* Janvier 1848.

## RESEARCHES ON PHOSPHORUS. BY M. P. THENARD.

The author states that in the last researches which he presented to the Academy, he announced that by passing hydrochlorate of methylene over phosphuret of calcium at a high temperature, five different products were obtained, all of which were new, and all phosphorized, and which vaporized and condensed in receivers, three in a solid state and two liquid; that the three solid products, entirely formed of phosphorus, hydrogen and carbon, were especially worthy of particular attention; that one of them is a powerful alkali, the properties and probable composition of which he had described; and that the most remarkable of the three, which is spontaneously inflammable, and has an odour analogous to that of cacodyl, is converted, under the influence of acids, into a certain quantity of the two others.

The author also added, that if it were true that the alkali was represented in its composition by 1 equivalent of phosphorus, 9 of hydrogen, and 6 of carbon, $PH^1C^6$, it was probable that the two other liquids were represented, one by 1 equivalent of phosphorus, 6 of hydrogen and 4 of carbon, $PH^6C^4$, and the other by 2 equivalents of phosphorus, 3 of hydrogen and 2 of carbon, $P^2H^3C^4$; that is to say, that the three compounds of phosphorus and hydrogen, $P^2H$, $PH^2$, $PH^3$, combine, the first with one equivalent of methylene, the second with 2, and the third with 3.

M. Thenard states, that being desirous of submitting his views to the test of experiment, he prepared, not without danger, the new products which he wished to examine.

The analysis of the new alkali was frequently repeated, as also of the inodorous and non-alkaline matter, into one of which the spontaneously inflammable substance is transformed : the formula of the first is $PH^3$, $3C^2H^2$, and of the second $P^2H$, $C^2H^2$. After having thus verified his first conjectures, the author was occupied exclusively with the spontaneously inflammable liquid. The examination was beset with difficulties, owing to the disagreeable qualities of the compound, and its unstable and inflammable nature.

The formula of this compound was found to be $PH^2$, $2C^2H^2$. Its properties are, that it is a transparent liquid, colourless and slightly viscid, insoluble in water, and has an excessively disagreeable odour; it boils at about 482° F. When exposed to the air it inflames spontaneously; but when kept in a bottle into which air is gradually introduced, it absorbs oxygen slowly, and is converted into a beautiful, very acid crystalline product.

With hydrochloric acid gas it exhibits the most important phænomena. It forms at first a solid monohydrochlorate, which is crystallized and very permanent, and afterwards passes to the state of bihydrochlorate, which is liquid and of slight stability; and if the action of the acid continues, it is uniformly transformed into hydrochlorate of the alkali $PH^1 3C^2 H^2$, and into a yellow substance $P^2HC^2H^4$.

The monohydrochlorate when put into water at 32° F. dissolves without alteration; but if the temperature be gradually raised, it decomposes at the same time as the water, so as to give rise to a new acid, which the alkali produces by oxidizement, and to a new gas which gradually combines with its volume of oxygen, and produces a liquid of strongly marked acid properties; and it also absorbs either one or two volumes of hydrochloric acid gas, and forms fine crystals, from which water instantly disengages the new gas.

M. Thenard concludes from his experiments,—

1. That phosphorus combines with hydrogen and carbon in several proportions.

2. That the three phosphurets of hydrogen at present known unite,—

The solid phosphuret $P^2 H$ with one equivalent of methylene;

The liquid phosphuret $PH^2$ with two equivalents of methylene;

The gaseous phosphuret $PH^3$ with three equivalents of methylene; that is to say, with as many equivalents of methylene as there are of hydrogen in the phosphurets.

3. That the first of these three new compounds is solid, yellow, inodorous, insipid, insoluble in water, and inert, at least at common temperatures; that the second is liquid, extremely noxious, spontaneously inflammable, and susceptible of forming a new acid when gradually exposed to oxygen; that the third is alkaline, non-inflammable, and susceptible, like the preceding, of absorbing oxygen gas, and giving rise to a totally different acid.

4. That the spontaneously inflammable compound may be converted into the two others under the influence of a great excess of acid; but in the state of monohydrochlorate it is decomposed by the action of water and of heat, producing a new gas $PH^3 C^6 H^6$, or probably $PH C^6 H^6 H^6$.

5. That this same compound is analogous to cacodyl; and confirms by this analogy the natural relations which exist between arsenic and phosphorus.

The author concludes with the following considerations:—

Is it not probable that, with other hydrochlorates of carburetted hydrogen and phosphuret of calcium, a series of products would be obtained analogous to those which are yielded by hydrochlorate of methylene?

May we not hope that the arseniurets of hydrogen will produce similar combinations; and is it going too far to presume that it will probably be the same with nitruret of hydrogen?

There would thus be formed a great number of new compounds which ought to be assimilated to organic compounds, and of which theory now indicates the composition and properties.

It is even probable that phosphorus occurs in cerebral matter, the nerves, &c., in which it has been discovered in this state of combination; but the phosphuret of hydrogen in them must be combined with much carburetted hydrogen.

The author has already procured a new series of products resulting from the reaction of hydrochloric æther, or hydrochlorate of ethyle and phosphuret of calcium: they are such, that the series which they constitute is to that which the author has described, as alcohol is to pyroxylic spirit.—*Comptes Rendus*, Decembre 13, 1847.

---

ON CHRISTIANITE—A NEW MINERAL.

M. Descloizeaux states that in the month of July 1846, he found in the cavities of an amygdaloidal trap which forms the bay of Dyrefiord, on the western coast of Iceland, some small translucent colourless crystals, which scratched glass readily, were fragile, and of sp. gr. 2·201.

These crystals are very closely aggregated together, and, grouped in the mammillary form or that of cock's-combs, analogous to some varieties of prehnite, have as their primary form a right rhombic prism of 111° 15′, in which one of the sides of the base is to the height as 537 to 786.

The prevailing form consists of the faces $b^1$ placed on the edges of the base of the prism, of the base and of the modification $g^1$ parallel to the small diagonal of this base.

The inclinations of the faces are as follow:—

$b^1$ on the face $m$ of the prism.... 147°·30′
$b^1$ on the base of $p$ ............. 122°·30′
$b^1$ on $b^1$ adjacent.............. 123°·07′
$m$ on $g^1$ .................... 124°·22′

The low specific gravity of the small crystals from Dyrefiord, their crystalline form, and the analyses which M. Damour has published in the ninth volume of the *Annales des Mines*, show that they agree perfectly with the species long since separated from harmotome by MM. Gmelin and Nepel, and since by M. Köbler, under the name of harmotome with a base of lime, or harmotome of Marburg.

The crystals of this mineral, which are met with in the ancient volcanic rocks of Annerode near Giessen, of Stempel near Marburg, and Habichtswald near Cassel, possess, besides the faces stated to belong to the Iceland variety, a modification also placed on the edges of the base of the primary form, and the crystallographical sign is $b^{\frac{3}{5}}$.

This modification, which is not known in common harmotome, the primary and prevailing forms of which are almost identical with those of lime harmotome, makes with the base of the prism an angle of 138° 54′, and with the face $b^1$ an angle of 163° 35′.

The great external resemblance of the Marburg mineral and the small crystals of Capo di Bove near Rome, and Aci-Reale in Sicily, long since described by M. Lévy under the name of *phillipsite*, induced M. Köhler to suppose that these two substances constituted only one species; but the recent analyses of phillipsite, published by M. Marignac in the 14th volume of the *Annales de Chimie et de Physique*, demonstrate that this arrangement cannot take place.

The Iceland and Marburg minerals form therefore a distinct species, inasmuch as they possess a peculiar form and composition; M. Descloizeaux proposes the name of *Christianite* for this mineral.—*Comptes Rendus*, Novembre 15, 1847.

---

ON THE IDENTITY OF METACETONIC AND BUTYRO-ACETIC ACIDS—PROPIONIC ACID. BY MM. DUMAS, MALAGUTI AND F. LEBLANC.

M. Gottlieb obtained some years since a new acid by oxidizing sugar by means of potash, which he called *metacetonic acid*, on the supposition of the possibility which the formulæ indicated, and which experiment has confirmed, of obtaining it by subjecting metacetone to the action of oxidizing bodies. M. Redtenbacher has since found that glycerine, under the influence of ferments, also yields metacetonic acid; and he has since succeeded in separating considerable quantities of it from the product obtained by oxidizing oleic acid with nitric acid.

The authors now cited have found this same acid as one of the results of the destruction of hydrocyanic æther, by means of potash. M. Nœllner had also observed in the matters to which the fermentation of tartrate of lime gave rise, a peculiar acid, resembling acetic acid, which on this account he named *pseudo-acetic acid*. M. Nicklès has submitted this acid to rigid experiments, which show that it possesses the same composition as metacetonic acid; and some inferences induce him to suppose that it has a certain tendency to separate into butyric and acetic acid; hence the name of *butyro-acetic acid*, by which he proposes to distinguish it. M. Nicklès insists in his memoir on some facts which he regards as sufficient to constitute an essential difference between his acid and metacetonic acid; he mentions several properties which he thinks sufficient to separate them; but these properties are evidently owing to the still imperfect history of metacetonic acid. On comparing metacetonic acid extracted from metacetonate of potash, with that prepared by means of hydrocyanic æther and butyro-acetic acid derived from fermented tartrate of lime, the authors ascertained that they were identical, having the same composition expressed by $C^6 H^6 O^4$; they have the same odour and appearance; they both crystallize at common temperatures in laminæ analogous to those which are yielded by acetic acid. They combine with water in all proportions, the compound floating in the form of an oily stratum on a solution of phosphoric acid or of chloride of calcium; they both boil at about 284° F.; their salts act in the same manner; when distilled with arsenious acid they yield products which have the odour of alcarsine; the salts of silver which the two acids form, are identical both in appearance and in composition.

M. de la Provostaye determined that the crystals of the metacetonate and butyro-acetate of barytes were similar in form, and that all the angles which could be compared were identical.

From the collection of facts now stated, the authors think they are entitled to conclude that metacetonic acid, pseudo-acetic acid, and butyro-acetic acid constitute the same and one only acid.

This acid, they further remark, is the first which exhibits the fatty character, setting out from formic or acetic acid, towards the fatty acids properly so called; it is the first which separates from solution in the form of an oily stratum; it is the first which gives, with the alkalies, salts that are unctuous to the touch, similar to alkaline soaps. These characters have induced the authors to give to this substance the name of *propionic acid*, a name which indicates its place in the series of fatty acids; it is the first of them.

When one of the authors indicated, six years since, the existence of a group of acids having the general formula $C^n H^n O^4$, he could cite only eight acids which were susceptible of being referred with certainty to this general formula; they were the formic, acetic, valerianic, œnanthylic, lauric, myristic, ethalic and margaric. To reduce the butyric, caproic and capric acids to this general formula, it was requisite to admit a slight inaccuracy in the explanation of the generally correct analyses of M. Chevreul. Recent researches on these three acids have perfectly confirmed this supposition.

As however there must exist between margaric and formic acid fifteen intermediate acids, six remained to be discovered. These gaps were almost entirely filled up by the metacetonic, caprylic, pelargonic, cocinic and benic acids, recently discovered by a more attentive study of fatty bodies. There may now be reckoned, including anamirtic acid, eighteen acids forming a continuous series, in which only a single term is wanting.

It is proper to add that the unpublished researches of M. Brodie prove that the general formula $C^8 H^8 O^4$, far from stopping at margaric acid, includes a new acid, the composition of which is $C^{14} H^{34} O^4$, and even acids which reach still higher formulæ. We are therefore certain that there are, confining ourselves to the first among them, eight fatty acids to discover between margaric acid and that the formula of which has just been given, and that these acids will be less fusible, more solid, and consequently more proper for certain uses, as for example of giving light, even than margaric acid itself, provided abundant sources of them should be discovered. It is therefore a subject of the greatest interest to collect and to analyse with care fatty matters of vegetable origin. Everything induces the belief that by them the gaps will be occupied. We are however so little advanced in knowledge respecting the fatty matters which exist in insects, that it would not be surprising if an attentive study of their materials should furnish some of the terms which sooner or later may enrich the series by completing it.

Everything induces the hope that the twenty-six acids which we are entitled to nominate are not the only ones, and nothing authorises us to foretell to what point the simple formula $C^n H^n O^4$ will extend or where its application may stop.—*Comptes Rendus*, Novembre 29, 1847.

## ON THE COMPOSITION AND PROPERTIES OF NICOTINA.

M. Barral finds that nicotina consists of—

| | | |
|---|---|---|
| 40 eqs. of carbon | = 240 | 74·07 |
| 28 eqs. of hydrogen | = 28 | 8·64 |
| 4 eqs. of azote | = 56 | 17·29 |
| | 324 | 100·00 |

Nicotina combines with water in all proportions, and is also hygrometric. In an atmosphere saturated with the vapour of water, 100 parts are capable of absorbing 177 parts of water in three weeks, and this it loses completely in an atmosphere dried by potash.

When nicotina is thus hydrated it becomes entirely a crystalline mass, when exposed to a refrigerating mixture of salt and ice. It is unquestionably owing to the presence of water in nicotina, that MM. Posselt and Reimann have stated that this alkali may be solidified: this does not occur with anhydrous nicotina.

Chlorine acts energetically on nicotina. When a few drops of it are let fall into a bottle of chlorine, the combination may be so vivid as to emit light; hydrochloric acid is disengaged, and a liquor of a blood-red colour is obtained. If the bottle be then exposed to the action of light for some days, the liquor is decolorized; and if the external air is below 46° F. it crystallizes in long needles, which disappear when the temperature rises. The product when treated with alcohol is decomposed, and a whitish deposit is formed which may be separated by the filter, and being dissolved in alcohol, crystals are obtained by spontaneous evaporation. The filtered water is strongly acid; and when concentrated by a gentle heat it becomes of a brownish-red colour. Phosphorus is insoluble in nicotina, but sulphur dissolves in it. At 212° F. 100 of nicotina dissolve 10·58 of sulphur, the greater part of which is deposited in small needles on cooling; the nicotina becomes of a deep brown tint.—*Ann. de Ch. et de Phys.*, Juillet 1847.

---

## METEOROLOGICAL OBSERVATIONS FOR DEC. 1847.

*Chiswick.*—December 1. Very fine: clear. 2. Frosty: overcast and mild. 3. Densely overcast: rain. 4. Clear: overcast: boisterous. 5. Fine. 6. Boisterous, with rain; lightning at night. 7. Rain: cloudy and boisterous: clear and windy at night. 8. Clear and cold. 9. Rain: overcast. 10. Rain: cloudy. 11. Densely clouded: fine. 12—14. Very fine. 15. Very fine: slight rain. 16. Cloudy. 17. Slight rain. 18. Rain. 19. Fine: cloudy. 20. Cloudy. 21—23. Overcast. 24. Foggy. 25, 26. Overcast. 27, 28. Cloudy. 29. Hazy. 30. Rain. 31. Hazy and damp.

    Mean temperature of the month .................................... 41°·09
    Mean temperature of Dec. 1846 .................................... 31 ·26
    Mean temperature of Dec. for the last twenty years .......... 39 ·59
    Average amount of rain in Dec. .................................... 1·58 inch.

*Boston.*—Dec. 1. Fine. 2. Fine: 8 o'clock P.M. thermometer 54°. 3. Cloudy: rain P.M. 4. Fine: rain P.M. 5. Cloudy: rain early A.M. 6. Rain. 7. Rain: stormy A.M. and P.M. 8. Fine: rain A.M. 9. Rain. 10. Fine. 11, 12. Cloudy. 13—15. Fine. 16. Rain. 17. Fine: rain early A.M. 18. Rain: rain A.M. and P.M. 19. Fine. 20. Rain. 21. Fine. 22—29. Cloudy. 30. Snow: rain and snow A.M. and P.M. 31. Rain: rain A.M.

*Applegarth Manse, Dumfries-shire.*—Dec. 1. Wet A.M.: cleared and was fine. 2. Wet A.M.: damp all day. 3. Damp A.M.: cleared: fine. 4. Heavy rain and high wind. 5. Rain: unsettled weather. 6. Shower of snow: frost. 7. Heavy rain: frost A.M. 8. Fair, but cloudy. 9. Rain early A.M.: fine. 10. Showers. 11. Rain all night and morning. 12. Fair and fine. 13. Fair A.M.: rain and wind P.M. 14. Fine A.M.: rain P.M. 15. Mild and fair A.M.: rain P.M. 16. Rain nearly all day: flood. 17. Fair and mild: slight rain P.M. 18. Fair, but cloudy. 19. Frost A.M.: dull and cloudy. 20, 21. Frost, slight. 22. Frost, hard: clear. 23. Fine: slight frost. 24. Fine. 25. Frost: fine and clear. 26. Fine: clear. 27, 28. Frost: fine. 29. Heavy fall of snow. 30. Snow lying: frost, hard. 31. Frost, very keen: thermometer 11½°.

    Mean temperature of the month .................................... 40°·2
    Mean temperature of Dec. 1846 .................................... 33 ·5
    Mean temperature of Dec. for twenty-five years ............. 38 ·19
    Mean rain in Dec. for twenty years ............................... 2·94 inches.

Meteorological Observations made by Mr. Thompson at the Garden of the Horticultural Society at CHISWICK, near London; by Mr. Veall, at BOSTON; by the Rev. W. Dunbar, at Applegarth Manse, DUMFRIES-SHIRE; and by the Rev. C. Clouston, at Sandwick Manse, ORKNEY.

| Days of Month. | Barometer. | | | | | | Thermometer. | | | | | | | Wind. | | | | Rain. | | |
|---|---|---|---|---|---|---|---|---|---|---|---|---|---|---|---|---|---|---|---|---|
| | Chiswick. | | Boston 8½ a.m. | Dumfries-shire. | | Orkney, Sandwick. | | Chiswick. | | Boston. 8½ a.m. | Dumfries-shire. | | Orkney, Sandwick. | | Chiswick. 1 p.m. | Boston. | Dumfries-shire. | Orkney, Sandwick. | Chiswick. | Boston. | Dumfries-shire. | Orkney, Sandwick. |
| | Max. | Min. | | 9 a.m. | 2 p.m. | 9½ a.m. | 8½ p.m. | Max. | Min. | | Max. | Min. | 9½ a.m. | 8½ p.m. | | | | | | | | |
| 1847. Dec. | | | | | | | | | | | | | | | | | | | | | | |
| 1. | 30·353 | 30·188 | 29·75 | 29·87 | 30·00 | | | 51 | 25 | 42 | 47 | 36 | | | w. | w. | w. | | | | | |
| 2. | 30·269 | 30·173 | 29·83 | 29·90 | 29·80 | | | 55 | 51 | 42 | 54 | 40 | | | sw. | calm | w. | | ·11 | ·12 | | |
| 3. | 30·113 | 29·992 | 29·60 | 29·84 | 29·73 | | | 57 | 36 | 55 | 54 | 45 | | | sw. | calm | sw. | | ·28 | ·50 | | |
| 4. | 29·943 | 29·445 | 29·49 | 29·50 | 29·00 | | | 51 | 41 | 40·5 | 50 | 42½ | | | sw. | w. | w. | | ·12 | ·38 | | |
| 5. | 29·486 | 28·287 | 28·88 | 28·98 | 29·10 | | | 53 | 31 | 43 | 45 | 36 | | | sw. | w. | w. | | ·17 | ·13 | | |
| 6. | 28·837 | 28·550 | 28·42 | 28·43 | 28·19 | | | 53 | 40 | 48 | 53 | 35 | | | sw. | w. | nw. | | ·04 | ·94 | | |
| 7. | 29·202 | 28·611 | 28·27 | 28·80 | 28·40 | | | 53 | 31 | 42·5 | 45 | 35½ | | | nw. | nw. | nw. | | ·16 | ·26 | 1·67 | |
| 8. | 29·725 | 29·528 | 29·20 | 29·29 | 29·36 | | | 43 | 28 | 33·5 | 35½ | 29 | | | sw. | w. | w. | | ·03 | ·03 | | |
| 9. | 29·707 | 29·538 | 29·11 | 28·98 | 29·05 | | | 57 | 51 | 48 | 51 | 32 | | | sw. | sw. | sw. | | ·01 | ·03 | | |
| 10. | 29·835 | 29·778 | 29·34 | 29·50 | 29·59 | | | 55 | 49 | 53 | 52½ | 36 | | | sw. | w. | w. | | | | | |
| 11. | 29·872 | 29·730 | 29·32 | 29·30 | 29·49 | | | 53 | 29 | 51 | 44 | 42 | | | sw. | w. | sw. | | | | | |
| 12. | 30·018 | 29·937 | 29·56 | 29·60 | 29·73 | | | 53 | 38 | 44 | 47½ | 36 | | | w. | w. | wsw. | | | | | |
| 13. | 30·028 | 29·992 | 29·65 | 29·65 | 29·74 | | | 53 | 35 | 44 | 49 | 42 | | | w. | w. | sc. | | | | | |
| 14. | 30·056 | 30·032 | 29·69 | 29·79 | 29·79 | | | 51 | 32 | 41 | 49 | 42 | | | w. | w. | sc. | | | | | |
| 15. | 30·018 | 29·972 | 29·65 | 29·62 | 29·66 | | | 54 | 47 | 45·5 | 50 | 42 | | | w. | w. | sc. | | ·03 | ·03 | 1·37 | |
| 16. | 29·885 | 29·806 | 29·48 | 29·52 | 29·45 | | | 52 | 46 | 45½ | 52½ | 42 | | | w. | w. | esc. | | | ·02 | | |
| 17. | 29·772 | 29·538 | 29·37 | 29·30 | 29·08 | | | 55 | 46 | 48·5 | 53 | 43 | | | w. | sw. | sc. | | ·03 | ·29 | | |
| 18. | 29·462 | 29·339 | 29·12 | 29·19 | 29·24 | | | 49 | 26 | 48 | 54 | 45 | | | w. | sw. | sw. | | ·34 | ·65 | | |
| 19. | 29·520 | 29·388 | 29·13 | 29·22 | 29·48 | | | 47 | 32 | 38 | 43 | 43 | | | w. | sc. | nne. | | ·01 | | | |
| 20. | 29·675 | 29·667 | 29·41 | 29·70 | 29·69 | | | 41 | 31 | 39 | 43 | 42½ | | | ne. | sc. | ne. | | | | | |
| 21. | 29·619 | 29·579 | 29·34 | 29·59 | 29·52 | | | 35 | 34 | 35·5 | 39 | 32½ | | | ne. | ne. | ne. | | | | | |
| 22. | 29·948 | 29·732 | 29·47 | 29·66 | 29·85 | | | 36 | 31 | 33·5 | 36 | 33½ | | | ne. | sc. | sc. | | | | 1·92 | |
| 23. | 29·910 | 29·658 | 29·58 | 29·74 | 29·36 | | | 39 | 32 | 34 | 38½ | 33½ | | | ne. | sc. | sc. | | ·05 | | | |
| 24. | 30·045 | 29·786 | 29·59 | 29·83 | 30·08 | | | 39 | 35 | 38 | 38½ | 29 | | | ne. | ne. | ne. | | | | | |
| 25. | 30·185 | 29·990 | 29·90 | 30·10 | 30·24 | | | 40 | 35 | 37·5 | 38½ | 35 | | | ne. | calm | ne. | | | | | |
| 26. | 30·190 | 30·141 | 29·90 | 30·10 | 30·16 | | | 41 | 35 | 41 | 42 | 37½ | | | ne. | ne. | ne. | | ·01 | | | |
| 27. | 30·225 | 30·204 | 29·93 | 30·18 | 30·10 | | | 37 | 30 | 39 | 36 | 29 | | | nw. | ne. | ne. | | | | | |
| 28. | 30·195 | 30·182 | 29·92 | 30·15 | 30·10 | | | 37 | 25 | 35·5 | 37 | 32 | | | ne. | calm | ne. | | ·17 | | | |
| 29. | 30·094 | 29·732 | 29·75 | 29·78 | 29·38 | | | 38 | 35 | 36 | 35½ | 32 | | | ne. | nsw. | ne. | | ·20 | | 0·12 | |
| 30. | 29·856 | 29·712 | 29·45 | 29·64 | 29·84 | | | 40 | 32 | 34 | 35 | 33 | | | sc. | sc. | n. | | | | | |
| 31. | 29·854 | 29·817 | 29·60 | 29·83 | 29·72 | | | 37 | 30 | 34·5 | 24 | 11½ | | | ne. | sc. | e-sw. | | ·61 | | | |
| Mean. | 29·867 | 29·685 | 29·42 | 29·570 | 29·577 | | | 47·00 | 35·19 | 41·4 | 44·4 | 36·5 | | | | | | | 1·81 | 3·06 | 4·18 | |

# THE LONDON, EDINBURGH AND DUBLIN PHILOSOPHICAL MAGAZINE AND JOURNAL OF SCIENCE.

[THIRD SERIES.]

*MARCH* 1848.

XXIV. *On the Distinctness of Vision produced in certain cases by the use of the Polarizing Apparatus in Microscopes.* By Sir DAVID BREWSTER, K.H., D.C.L., F.R.S. and V.P.R.S. Edin.*

HAVING lately had occasion to examine some very minute crystals, and also some animal and vegetable fibres that possessed the doubly-refracting structure, I was surprised to find that, by the use of the polarizing apparatus, I could eliminate two kinds of indistinctness which affect the vision of microscopic objects. The interposition of a Nicol's prism, or of an analysing rhomb of calcareous spar, however skilfully formed, between the eye and the object, has always been considered as deteriorating the microscope, and the observer is justified in removing it in ordinary cases when he wishes to obtain the most perfect definition which his instrument can give. When the object, however, has a doubly-refracting structure of the slightest kind, so as to act upon polarized light, the polarizing apparatus is of vast service in developing its form and structure, not merely its doubly refracting structure, but that form and structure which it exhibits in common light.

In order to illustrate this use of the polarizing apparatus, let us take the seed of the *Collomea grandiflora*, which, when steeped in water, throws out hundreds of spiral fibres like corkscrews, with the spires sometimes elongated by pressure into waving lines, and sometimes compressed almost into contact†. If we now place these spirals between two plates of glass and in castor-oil which has nearly the same refractive power as the fibres, we shall obtain a tolerably distinct view

* Communicated by the Author.
† This elongation and compression of the spirals was produced by pressing the spirals out of the seed when steeped in castor oil.

of them without the polarizing apparatus; but we shall find it very difficult, if not utterly impracticable, to trace the fibres through their circumvolutions and obtain a satisfactory definition of them. This difficulty arises from the *diffraction* of light; the rays which pass the edges of the fibres interfering not only with one another, but with the rays which pass through the fibres, and producing great indistinctness of vision.

If we now expose the spiral fibres to polarized light, and apply the analysing rhomb, we shall see them beautifully delineated on a dark ground in the light which they depolarize and transmit. Spirals which were imperfectly seen before will be seen distinctly now; and the minute points or duplications of the fibre which mark each spire, when the whole is drawn out nearly into a straight line, will be beautifully defined, though they were entirely invisible in common light. By turning round the analysing rhomb and making the field of view alternately dark and luminous, we shall be able to compare the two modes of vision which I have described.

The cause of the superior definition thus obtained it is not difficult to discover. I have elsewhere shown that the imperfect definition obtained by microscopes arises from the diffraction of light; and I have pointed out the method of illuminating microscopic objects so as to reduce the diffraction to a minimum, if not to remove it. In the present case, however, the *diffraction is entirely removed*. As no light whatever passes by the edges of the fibres, there can be no interference, and consequently no diffraction and no fringes, and therefore the fibre must be seen with the most perfect definition.

In making these observations, I discovered another advantage arising from the employment of polarized light. In many cases we cannot use a second plate of glass between the object and the object-glass of the microscope, so as to have the object placed in a stratum of fluid with parallel sides: we are therefore obliged to allow the rays from the object to suffer refraction through the irregular surface of the fluid in which it lies. There are cases, too, where the object is imbedded in a refracting medium, upon which we can neither grind, if it is solid, nor obtain, when it is fluid, a flat surface. The irregularities therefore of surface around the object to be viewed, refract the transmitted light in such a manner as always to injure vision, and often to obliterate the object altogether. By using polarized light we get rid entirely of this irregularly refracted light, with the exception of that minute portion which corresponds with the surface directly interposed between the object and the object-glass. In order to witness this effect, we have only to place some of the spirals of the *Collomea* on a plate of glass and cover them with a thin film of castor-oil, which of course cannot be made parallel. By viewing them in the polarizing apparatus, and making the field of view alternately dark and luminous, we shall see the superior distinctness of vision which is obtained by the use of polarized light. In getting rid of the second plate of glass we get rid of its imperfections, both of surface and of substance, and we get rid also of the spherical aberration which it introduces, and for the removal of which we are obliged, when using high powers, to make an adjustment in the object-glass.

The preceding observations are of course applicable only to those microscopic objects which depolarize light; but there is scarcely an animal or a vegetable fibre which does not possess this property. The minutest hair of the smallest animal which I have been able to procure depolarizes light; and if a case should occur where the depolarizing structure exists, and could be rendered visible by doubling the thickness of the fibre, we might obtain this effect by making the polarized light pass twice through the fibre by reflexion, and thus exhibit itself luminously on a dark ground.

When microscopic objects have no action upon polarized light, we can only remove the indistinctness produced from diffraction by such an illumination as will cause the light to diverge from the object as if it were self-luminous. The method of doing this was first described in the Edinburgh Journal of Science, and afterwards more fully in my Treatise on the Microscope; but as this method has been confounded with Dr. Wollaston's[*] method of illuminating microscopic objects by a celebrated optician, M. Chevalier of Paris, I shall embrace the present opportunity of showing that the two methods have no resemblance whatever.

In proposing a method of illuminating microscopic objects, Dr. Wollaston's object was to get rid of the superfluous light which gave indistinctness to microscopic vision, and not to remove the evils arising from *diffraction*. He never even mentions *diffraction*, or any other cause but that of *superfluous light*, as the origin of imperfect vision, arising from the usual modes of illumination. He was, indeed, not aware that the *diffraction* of the light used for illuminating objects was the evil to be corrected; and he has accordingly neither corrected it by his method, nor attempted to correct it. "In the illumination of microscopic objects," he says, "*whatever light is collected and brought to the eye beyond that which is fully commanded by the object-glasses, tends rather to impede than assist distinct vision.* My endeavour has been, to collect as much

[*] Philosophical Transactions, 1829, p. 9.

of the admitted light as can be done by simple means, to a focus in the same place as the object to be examined. *For this purpose* I have used with success a plane mirror to direct the light, and a *plano-convex lens* to collect it." In describing the apparatus itself, he enjoins that this "plano-convex lens, or one properly crossed, so as to have the least aberration, should be about *three-quarters of an inch focus*, having its plane side next the object to be viewed; and at the bottom is a circular perforation A, of about three-tenths of an inch in diameter, for limiting the light reflected from the plane mirror, and which is to be brought to a focus at *a*, giving *a neat image of the perforation* A at the distance of about eight-tenths of an inch from the lens ET (the plano-convex lens) and in the same plane as the object which is to be examined. * * * * The lens ET, or the perforation A, should have an adjustment by which *the distance between them* may be varied, and *the image of the perforation be thus brought* into the same plane with the object to be examined." * * * "For the *perfect performance* of this microscope," Dr. Wollaston adds, "it is necessary that the axes of the lenses and the centre of the perforation should be in the same right line. This may be known by the image of the perforation being illuminated throughout its whole extent, and having *its whole circumference equally well-defined*. For illumination at night, *a common* bull's-eye lanthorn *may be used with great advantage*."

In the APPENDIX to this paper, Dr. Wollaston gives the following directions for the adjustment of his illuminating lens. "The position of the lens may be varied so as to bring *the image\* of the perforation into the same plane* with the object to be viewed. * * * Supposing the plano-convex lens (the illuminating lens) to be placed at its proper distance from the stage, *the image of the perforation* may be readily brought into the same plane with the object, by fixing temporarily *a small wire across the perforation* with a bit of wax, viewing any object placed upon a piece of glass upon the stage of the microscope, and varying the distance of the perforation from the lens by screwing its tube *until the image of the wire is seen distinctly at the same time with the object upon the piece of glass*."

From these extracts we do not say it is manifest, but we say it is demonstrable, that Dr. Wollaston was not in the least degree acquainted with the method which I subsequently published, of illuminating microscopic objects, and which is now in

---

\* That is, the *well-defined* circular image in the conjugate *focus* of the perforation considered as a circular object, from which the rays diverge,—not certainly in the conjugate focus of the rays which pass through the perforation.—D. B.

universal use. The object of that method is to remove the indistinctness produced by diffraction, by converging the illuminating rays upon the object, so that they may again radiate from the object as if it were self-luminous. This effect can only be obtained by furnishing the microscope with an illuminating apparatus as perfect as its magnifying apparatus. In Dr. Wollaston's method there is no convergency of the rays upon the object. The rays do not diverge from the margin of the aperture, but from the source of light; and even if Dr. Wollaston had directed that the illuminating rays should be converged accurately to foci coincident with the points of the object to be viewed, a lens *three-quarters of an inch* in focal length was quite useless for any such purpose. To try to make light radiate from an object seen in a microscope with any reasonable magnifying power by means of such a lens, would be as absurd as to attempt to see the satellites of Saturn through an opera-glass; but it would be still more absurd to make such an attempt by an optical arrangement, under which the object is illuminated by rays which diverge from a great or an infinite distance, while the object itself is in the conjugate focus of a perforation within two or three inches of the lens!

Dr. Wollaston was too sagacious an observer, and had too much knowledge of optics to make any such proposition. His apparatus accomplishes perfectly the purposes which he contemplated; and it is no error of his, but only an error of his commentators, that we have now been endeavouring to correct.

St. Leonard's College, St. Andrews,
February 14, 1848.

---

XXV. *On the Use of Gutta Percha in Electrical Insulation.* By MICHAEL FARADAY, *F.R.S., Foreign Associate of the Academy of Sciences, &c.*

Royal Institution,
Feb. 9, 1848.

MY DEAR PHILLIPS,

I HAVE lately found gutta percha very useful in electrical experiments; and therefore, that others may take advantage of its properties if they have occasion or are so inclined, give you this notice for insertion in the Philosophical Magazine. Its use depends upon the high insulating power which it possesses under ordinary conditions, and the manner in which it keeps this power in states of the atmosphere which make the surface of glass a good conductor. All gutta percha is not however equally good as it comes from the manufacturer's hands; but it does not seem difficult to bring it into the best state: I will describe the qualities of a proper specimen, and refer to the differences afterwards. A good piece of gutta percha will insulate as well as an equal piece of shell-lac, whether it be in the form of sheet, or rod, or filament; but being tough and flexible when cold, as well as soft when hot, it will serve better than shell-lac in many cases where the brittleness of the latter is an inconvenience. Thus it makes very good handles for carriers of electricity in experiments on induction, not being liable to fracture: in the form of thin band or string it makes an excellent insulating suspender: a piece of it in sheet makes a most convenient insulating basis for anything placed on it. It forms excellent insulating plugs for the stems of gold-leaf electrometers when they pass through sheltering tubes, and larger plugs supply good insulating feet for extemporary electrical arrangements: cylinders of it half an inch or more in diameter have great stiffness, and form excellent insulating pillars. In these and in many other ways its power as an insulator may be useful.

Because of its good insulation it is also an excellent substance for the excitement of negative electricity. It is hardly possible to take one of the soles sold by the shoemakers out of paper or into the hand, without exciting it to such a degree as to open the leaves of an electrometer one or more inches; or if it be unelectrified, the slightest passage over the hand or face, the clothes, or almost any other substance gives it an electric state. Some of the gutta percha is sold in very thin sheets, resembling in general appearance oiled silk; and if a strip of this be drawn through the fingers, it is so electric as to adhere to the hand or attract pieces of paper. The appearance is such as to suggest the making a thicker sheet of the substance into a plate electrical machine for the production of negative electricity.

Then as to inductive action through the substance, a sheet of it is soon converted into an excellent electrophorus; or it may be coated and used in place of a Leyden jar; or in any of the many other forms of apparatus dependent on inductive action.

I have said that all gutta percha is not in this good electrical condition. With respect to that which is not so (and which has constituted about one-half of that which, being obtained at the shops, has passed through my hands), it has either discharged an electrometer as a piece of paper or wood would do, or it has made it collapse greatly by touching, yet has on its removal been followed by a full opening of the leaves again: the latter effect I have been able to trace and refer to a conducting portion within the mass covered by a thin external non-conducting coat. When a piece which insulates well is cut, the surface exposed has a resinous lustre and a compact character that is very distinctive; whilst that which conducts has not the same degree of lustre, appears less translucent, and has more the aspect of a turbid solution solidified. I believe both moist steam-heat, and water-baths are used in its preparation for commerce; and the difference of specimens depends probably upon the manner in which these are applied, and followed by the after process of rolling between hot cylinders. However, if a portion of that which conducts be warmed in a current of hot air, as over the glass of a low gas flame, and be stretched, doubled up, and kneaded for some time between the fingers, as if with the intention of dissipating the moisture within, it becomes as good an insulator as the best.

I have soaked a good piece in water for an hour; and on taking it out, wiping it, and exposing it to the air for a minute or two, found it insulate as well as ever. Another piece was soaked for four days and then wiped and tried: at first it was found lowered in insulating power; but after twelve hours' exposure to air under common circumstances it was as good as ever. I have not found that a week's exposure in a warm air cupboard of a piece that did not insulate made it much better: a film on the outside became non-conducting; but if two fresh surfaces were exposed by cutting, and these were brought into contact with the electrometer and the finger, the inside portion was still found to conduct.

If the gutta percha in either the good or the bad condition (as to electrical service) be submitted to a gradually increasing temperature, at about 350° or 380°, it gives off a considerable proportion of water; being then cooled, the substance which remains has the general properties of gutta percha, and insulates well. The original gum is probably complicated, being a mixture of several things; and whether the water has existed in the substance as a hydrate, or is the result of a deeper change of one part or another of the gum, I am not prepared to say. All I desire in this note is to make known its use in the arrangement of extemporary or permanent electrical apparatus for the advantage of working philosophers, both juvenile and adult.

I am, dear Phillips,
Yours,
M. FARADAY.

XXVI. *On the Course of a Ray of Light from a Celestial Body to the Earth's Surface, according to the Hypothesis of Undulations.* By the Rev. J. CHALLIS, *M.A., F.R.A.S., Plumian Professor of Astronomy in the University of Cambridge*[*].

THE question I am about to consider arises out of the explanation of the aberration of light which I gave in the course of a discussion in the pages of this Journal, of which Professor Powell has given an account in vol. xxix. p. 425, and vol. xxx. p. 93. That explanation was based on the fact, that *the measured direction of a body not partaking of the earth's motion is necessarily referred to the direction of a body partaking of the earth's motion.* From this principle, combined with the known velocity of the earth, and the velocity of light deduced from observations of the eclipses of Jupiter's satellites, not only does aberration result (Phil. Mag., vol. xxvii. p. 321, and vol. xxviii. p. 91), but the calculated amount agrees also as closely as possible with that ascertained by astronomical measurement (Phil. Mag., vol. xxviii. p. 394). There is therefore no residual phænomenon to be accounted for. The explanation requires no consideration of the way in which the eye is acted upon by light, it rests on no hypothesis whatever, being a strict deduction from facts, it remains the same whether we adopt the emission theory of light or the undulatory, whether there be æther or no æther, whether the æther be in motion or at rest. I make this statement, lest it should be supposed that the aberration of light depends for its explanation in any degree upon the answer to the theoretical question I now proceed to consider. The truth of the undulatory theory of light depends very materially upon it.

The aberration of light being accounted for in the manner referred to above, it follows as a necessary consequence, that the course of light from a celestial object to the eye of the spectator is *rectilinear*. This is easily conceivable on the emission theory of light; but is the fact consistent with the undulatory theory? The ætherial medium must be put in motion, first, by the earth's rotation about its axis, next by its motion in its orbit, and lastly, by the motion in space which it partakes of in common with the other bodies of the solar system. Is it probable that through the æther thus disturbed a wave can be propagated in a rectilinear course? It has, in fact, been proved by Mr. Stokes (Phil. Mag., vol. xxvii. p. 9), that the normal to the front of the wave will be bent through a certain small angle in a certain direction, inclining towards that in which the earth is moving; and if nothing further

[*] Communicated by the Author.

could be said on the subject, a curvilinear motion of light would result, and thus the undulatory theory would be found to be inconsistent with fact. I have, however, shown (Phil. Mag., vol. xxvii. p. 323–326, and again in Phil. Mag., vol. xxviii. p. 92), that in consequence of the motion of translation of the wave caused by the motion of the æther, the direction of propagation *in space* of a given point of the wave deviates from the normal to the front by exactly the above-mentioned angle, and in exactly the opposite direction. It follows that the propagation in space is rectilinear; and thus the transmission of light through the perturbed æther, without suffering aberration from the motion of the æther, is accounted for on the hypothesis of undulations. Mr. Stokes has acquiesced in this view (Phil. Mag., vol. xxix. p. 8), and there is consequently no longer any point in dispute between us.

The above solution of the proposed question rests however on an assumption. The resolved parts of the motion of the æther at any point $xyz$ caused by the earth's motion being $u, v, w$ in the directions of the axes of co-ordinates, it is assumed that $u dx + v dy + w dz$ is an exact differential. Is this assumption allowable? Does it not restrict too much the kind of motion? This is the only point relating to this subject which remains to be cleared up. Mr. Stokes has given it consideration in the communication last quoted. The following solution of the difficulty, derived very simply from known hydrodynamical equations, occurred to me very recently; and it is mainly for the purpose of bringing it under the notice of mathematicians that I have returned to this subject. Let the pressure at any point $xyz$ at the time $t$ be $a^2(1+s)$, $s$ being a small quantity whose powers above the first are neglected. Then, as is known,

$$a^2 \frac{ds}{dx} + \frac{du}{dt} = 0, \quad a^2 \frac{ds}{dy} + \frac{dv}{dt} = 0, \quad a^2 \frac{ds}{dz} + \frac{dw}{dt} = 0.$$

Hence by integration,

$$u = C - a^2 \int \frac{ds}{dx} dt = C - a^2 \cdot \frac{d \cdot \int s\, dt}{dx},$$

$$v = C' - a^2 \int \frac{ds}{dy} dt = C' - a^2 \cdot \frac{d \cdot \int s\, dt}{dy},$$

$$w = C'' - a^2 \int \frac{ds}{dz} dt = C'' - a^2 \cdot \frac{d \cdot \int s\, dt}{dz},$$

where C, C', and C'' are functions of $x, y, z$ which do not contain the time. The above are general values of $u, v, w$, for every instance of motion in which powers of the velocities above the first may be neglected. Now in the case before us it is clear that no part of the velocity can be constantly the same at a given point for any length of time; for in proportion as the earth recedes from the point, the velocity will become less and less and ultimately vanish. This is true whether the æther be disturbed by the earth or its atmosphere. Hence we shall have

$$C = 0, \quad C' = 0, \quad C'' = 0.$$

Consequently, substituting $\varphi$ for $-a^2 \int s\, dt$, we have

$$u = \frac{d\varphi}{dx}, \quad v = \frac{d\varphi}{dy}, \quad w = \frac{d\varphi}{dz},$$

and $u\,dx + v\,dy + w\,dz$ an exact differential.

Cambridge Observatory, Feb. 8, 1848.

## XXVII. *Note on Shooting Stars.* By Sir J. W. Lubbock, Bart.[*]

I WISH here to correct an oversight in p. 85 of the last Number, where it is implied that the same *shooting star* may be observed to disappear at different instants of time by different observers. It is obvious that if the moving body cease to shine by reason of its entering the shadow of the earth, this event is entirely irrespective of the position of the observer; and therefore if it should be observed by more than one person, such observations will furnish the parallax, and may determine whether this mode of accounting for the disappearance of the star is correct or not. If it has been attempted to determine the difference of terrestrial longitude by such observations, probably the materials exist somewhere by which the accuracy of the hypothesis can at once be tested. It may possibly however be again observed on the same night, either by the same or different observers, after an entire revolution.

It has been the subject of speculation whether such bodies can owe their origin to violent action at the moon's surface. But observers are, I believe, agreed that the surface of the moon offers no evidence of great agitation. The indentations of the surface remain unchanged, and no phænomena have, I

[*] Communicated by the Author.—The calculation in p. 83 of $q$ should stand thus:—

if $R' = 441500 \quad R = 3958 \quad D = 95,000,000$

$$\log \frac{R' - R}{D} = 7{\cdot}36227 \quad \frac{R' - R}{D} = q = {\cdot}002302.$$

believe, been seen which indicate the existence of volcanos, which might discharge small bodies with great force, and thus give rise to satellites of the earth.

The case is widely different as regards the sun. Changes of enormous magnitude are continually witnessed on its surface, which indicate the action of forces agitating the mass probably in a state of fluidity. Recently I have observed spots which were even visible to the naked eye, and of which, on the following and succeeding days, not a trace could be found by a good telescope.

If a body were thrown up from the sun's surface, it must, omitting all consideration of the planets, describe an ellipse having the centre of the sun in one of the foci; and thus, however great the force by which the body may be supposed to have been discharged, it must return to the sun, and, impinging upon it, would not perform even one entire revolution. If however we consider the action of the other planets, and especially of Jupiter, it seems by no means impossible that in returning, a body so discharged might *clear* the sun, and perform many complete revolutions round the primary, that is, it might become a comet (or *shooting star*). It would be interesting to ascertain how much the perihelion distance of such a body might be lengthened under given circumstances by the action of Jupiter; or whether, under any hypothesis of the configuration of the planets, the perihelion distance of any known comet could be brought under ·004647. Le Verrier suggests that some of the comets may have become fixed to our system and retained by the action of Jupiter; and that in consequence of the same action, they may again wander in space and cease to belong to this system[*]. But may not such bodies owe their origin to the same forces, of which the existence is indubitable, which operate on the surface at any rate of the sun's mass? and if so, it is by no means impossible that by calculating the perturbations of some comet for the past, especially one whose perihelion distance is small, it may be traced back to its origin, and the very year ascertained when it left the solar mass.

The phænomena of *shooting stars* may possibly throw light upon the question of the extent to which an atmosphere extends capable of affording any sensible resistance to the mo-

---

[*] " Dans un certain nombre de siècles toutefois, elle atteindra de nouveau l'orbite de Jupiter, dans une direction opposée à celle par laquelle elle a pu arriver dans le système planétaire : et son cours sera certainement encore une fois altéré. Peut-être même Jupiter la rendra-t-il aux espaces auxquels il l'avait dérobée."—Le Verrier, *Comptes Rendus*, Dec. 20, 1847, p. 925.

tion of such bodies, and may thus afford an interesting illustration of the connexion which exists between different branches of physical science. In my Treatise on the Heat of Vapours, p. 48, I have given a table, showing, upon the hypothesis I there adopted, the density and temperature for a given height above the earth's surface. According to that hypothesis, at a height of fifteen miles the temperature is $240°\cdot6$ F. below zero, the density is $\cdot03573$, and the atmosphere ceases altogether at a height of $22\cdot35$ miles. In the *Comptes Rendus des Séances de l'Académie des Sciences*, tom. viii. p. 95, M. Biot has verified a calculation of Lambert, who found from the phænomena of twilight the altitude of the atmosphere to be about eighteen miles. The constitution of the higher regions of the atmosphere, according to the hypothesis adopted by Ivory, is very different, and extends to a much greater height. See p. 3 of the Supplement to my Treatise on the Heat of Vapours, where I have given a table showing the constitution of the atmosphere according to Ivory. Such a table for the constitution due to Laplace's hypothesis is still wanted.

---

XXVIII. *Researches into the Identity of the Existencies or Forces—Light, Heat, Electricity and Magnetism.* By JOHN GOODMAN, *Esq.*[*]

### On Thermo-Electricity.

IT was discovered some years ago by Mr. Sturgeon, that thermo-electricity does not require more than one metal for its development.

In confirming this discovery, I have found that the current was developed only by the more *crystalline* metals, bismuth, antimony, iron, steel, zinc, &c., as will appear on inspecting the accompanying table.

I found also that each metal possessed its own distinctive and peculiar amount of current, as indicated by the galvanometer, and that always in the same direction: that when two opposing metals were united in producing a thermo-current, the minor current would be found to neutralize the opposing current, precisely to the amount of its own powers, and with as much exactitude as if it had been done by arithmetical calculation.

Thus iron alone gave $7\frac{1}{2}°$ current. Conjoined with zinc $5°$; zinc alone $2\frac{1}{2}°$ in the opposite direction.

It was also discovered that a minor current conjoined to one

[*] From vol. viii. of the Manchester Literary and Philosophical Society's Memoirs, and communicated by the Author.

| Metal or disc employed. | Tool or opposing metal. | Mechanical Electricity. Current, and its direction, as seen at the galvanometer. | Simple affinity. | Thermo-electric nature. | Thermo-electricity. Currents and direction. | Voltaic condition, with acids, &c. |
|---|---|---|---|---|---|---|
| Bismuth disc | Copper wire | 40° from the copper towards the bismuth | B. electro-negative | B. electro-negative | 35° to 40° given out at its heated extremity; to the copper from its heated end. | B. In nitric acid with platina or copper, pos. |
| Ditto | Steel tool | 40° to 45° from the tool | B. negative | B. negative | In all cases ditto. | |
| Ditto | Bismuth rod | 10° to 15° from the rod | Disc negative | | 42½° towards B. | |
| Ditto | Antimony rod | 45° from the rod | B. negative | B. negative | | |
| Ditto | Silver sharpened | 40° from the silver | B. negative | B. negative | | |
| Ditto | Gold | 35° from the gold | B. negative | B. negative | | |
| Ditto | Lead | 27½° from the lead | B. negative | B. negative | | |
| Iron disc | Steel tool | 10° from the iron | I. positive | I. positive | 7° towards the heated end. | |
| Large disc | Steel tool | 20° from the tool | I. negative | I. negative | * | |
| Iron rod | Steel file | 7½° from the iron | I. positive | I. positive | 7°; as above. | |
| Zinc disc | Copper wire | 3° from the zinc | Z. positive | Z. positive | 2½° to 3° from the cold extremity. | In acid sulph. dilute zinc pos. As in electro-motion. |
| Ditto | Sharp edge of copper | 3° from the zinc | Z. positive | Z. positive | Ditto | |
| Ditto | Turning-tool | 3° (by steam power) from the tool | Z. negative | Z. negative | 3°. The zinc current opposed that of the iron. | In sulphuric acid, zinc pos. iron neg. |
| Ditto | Iron sharpened | 4° to 5° from the iron | Z. negative | Z. negative | | |
| Ditto | Bismuth rod | 12° from the zinc | Z. positive, | | | |
| Ditto | Bismuth rod | 15° from the copper | Z. positive | C. positive | 33° see above. | |
| Copper disc | Rod of zinc | 2½° to 4° from the zinc | Z. negative | Z. rubs copper | 2½° as above | As in electro-motion. |
| Ditto | Sharp iron | 8° from the iron | C. positive | C. negative | 5° to 7½° see above. | |
| Ditto | Steel tool | 2½° to 3° from the steel | C. negative | C. negative | | |
| Ditto | Copper rod | 0° simply a conductor | | | 0° simply a conductor. | |
| Brass disc | Steel tool | 3° from the tool | | | | |
| Silver | Copper disc | simply a conductor | S. positive | S. positive | 1° to 1½° towards the heated end. | |
| Gold | Ditto | simply a conductor | | G. positive | ½° to 1°. | |
| Lead | Ditto | 0° from the lead | | L. negative | 2° towards its cold extremity. | |

* By *first* heating the steel in conjunction with iron, and giving it the greater influence of the flame, the current was reversed.—Iron neg. steel pos.

of a more powerful nature, does not generally augment, but rather diminish the amount of the latter*.

I found that the uncrystalline metals, gold, silver, copper, lead, &c., were unable to develope currents of any appreciable amount (as seen also in the Table), although the heating process was continued to a considerable degree of intensity. (See 37, 38.)

The experiments adduced show that these latter metals may be simply regarded as conducting media to thermo-electricity, that they offer no specific resistance to the flow of current, and may therefore be employed either in conjunction with electro-positive or electro-negative metals.

The results thus arrived at resemble much those evinced by the experiments of Dr. Franklin and others on the tourmaline, in which ordinary electricity was developed by heat alone, save that in this instance the electricity resembles the voltaic fluid, owing no doubt to the want of that complete insulation among the molecules of the metals which is afforded by the tourmaline.

It is remarkable that no polar fluid, or electricity of any kind, is ever developed without the employment of a crystalline, insulating, or imperfectly conducting body; for in voltaic arrangements the *electrolyte is this non-conducting medium*; in the cases just cited, the tourmaline was the intermediate polar body; in ordinary electricity, the glass cylinder is the non-conducting body, or "electric;" and in thermo and mechanical electricity (hereafter to be mentioned), the crystalline metals, bismuth, iron, steel, antimony, zinc, &c., are found to be the intervening polar structures, giving rise to these forms of electric fluid.

The same remarks hold good also with regard to the polar condition and *insulating* properties (witnessed by the author) of high-pressure steam in the generation of hydro-electric, and to the polarizable quality of steel and iron in electro-magnetic, magneto-electric, and magnetic phænomena.

In contemplating the known electrical phænomena which occur by the contact of dissimilar metals, and the processes of friction, pressure, fracture, vaporization, &c., and witnessing the effects which heat thus produces upon bismuth, &c., I devised the friction of this metal in a lathe, as a preparatory experiment to some hereafter contained, in hopes of being able to manifest *the continuous transmission of electricity from*

* It was found that the crystalline metals, bismuth and antimony, which form the best combination for thermo-electric purposes, are naturally mutually reciprocal metals. Bismuth negative, 45°; antimony positive, current 22¼°; and yet conjoined, they only produced a current of 48°.

*the one surface to the other*, as evinced by a current passing through the galvanometer from or towards the other extremities of the metals employed. This, to my mind, would evince the *origin of radiant heat*, the *result of friction*, in the mechanical processes, drilling, turning, filing, &c., and which on its discovery I named "*mechanical electricity*."

In the printed report of the British Association for 1845, which met at Cambridge, I find that M. Paul Erman of Berlin presented a paper containing one or two experiments of a somewhat similar nature to the Association, but of which I was not aware until the publication of the report, and the completion of many of my experiments.

April 2, 1846, I made the following experiment:—

Upon a mandril of copper a cylinder of bismuth was cast. One end of the mandril was fixed in dry wood, and arranged in a turning lathe; the other revolved against the point of the "following up head stock," as is usual: the surface of the cylinder or disc was turned smooth, the mandril having been previously soldered to the bismuth, so as to ensure full metallic communication.

Instead of a metal rest a wood one was now used, and afterwards a small piece of wood placed under the ordinary rest; to insulate this and the tool from the other portion of the lathe, was found to be *all that is necessary* in these experiments. A spring of brass wire was made to press firmly against the turning mandril, so as to ensure metallic contact, and its other extremity was in communication with the northern extremity of the galvanometer[*].

In the following experiments, the direction of the current is simply stated *as seen at the galvanometer*, which will be found in all cases to be the reverse of what takes place between the opposing metals. Thus, in the experiments in which *the zinc robs the copper*, as seen at the galvanometer, the current is progressing *towards the copper* (see 31, &c.); and yet the actual transfer at the surfaces is from the copper to the zinc.

*Exp.* 21. On applying the smooth surface of the end of a piece of *thick rod copper* to the turned surface of the cylinder, producing friction, a current was observed from the copper towards the bismuth. The rod copper was soldered to a wire in connexion with the southern extremity of the galvanometer.

*Exp.* 22. By accident the rod copper was torn away, and I

---

[*] The galvanometer in these experiments was not of the highest sensibility. It consisted of forty-six turns of copper wire, the 1/25th of an inch in diameter. The needle was single, and had therefore a northern tendency to counteract.

applied merely the extremity of the connecting wire against the revolving cylinder. The galvanometer was deflected many degrees, and considerably more *than by the friction with the larger surface*. A large surface *appeared to induce complex results, and to destroy elementary or simple indications*.

Exp. 23. By means of a set-screw I connected the galvanometer S wire to a turning-tool, and slightly turning or shaving off ribbons of bismuth, a considerable current was indicated *from the tool towards the bismuth*. This experiment with the bismuth disc and steel tool was afterwards repeated by steam power,—current 40° to 45° constant, vibrated to 80° or 90° at first.

Exp. 24. With a bismuth rod against the bismuth cylinder, a current of 4° and afterwards of 10° to 15° towards the cylinder was observed *.

Exp. 25. The bismuth disc and an antimony rod gave a current of 45° in the usual direction for bismuth, the antimony robbing the bismuth. Antimony positive, bismuth negative.

Exp. 26. Silver with bismuth 40°. The usual bismuth current.

Exp. 27. Gold with bismuth 35°. The usual bismuth current.

Exp. 28. Lead with bismuth $27\frac{1}{2}°$. The usual bismuth current from the lead to the bismuth.

Exp. 29. *With an iron disc* rotating under similar conditions, I obtained, by a turning-tool of steel, *a current of* 10° *from the iron towards the tool*.

I tested the galvanometer by a voltaic pair to see the direction of the current, and found the direction as stated to correspond.

I repeated afterwards the same experiment by steam power, with a much larger cylinder of cast iron, apparently harder than before, and the needle vibrated from 15° to 30°, stationary at 20°; the current in that instance, *from the tool towards the disc*, tested by voltaic pair.

Exp. 30. *With a zinc disc* and steel tool, at first no certain indication of current. Repeated afterwards, with and without steam power, current 3°, and afterwards 5°, constant, from the tool towards the zinc.

Exp. 31. With the extremity of the copper connecting wire, current $2\frac{1}{2}°$ from the zinc towards the wire. Repeated with steam power, 3° towards the copper.

May 1, 1846. With a sharp cutting edge of copper against

---

* It is here seen that a preponderance is given in favour of the rod or tool, both metals being alike; the rod is positive, the disc negative.

the zinc disc, 3° to 5° towards the copper. These experiments *correspond with the phænomena of electro-motion*—zinc robbing copper.

Exp. 32. With a bismuth rod against the zinc cylinder, a current of 12° was evinced from the zinc towards the bismuth.

Exp. 33. With a piece of iron sharpened, current 4° to 5° from the iron towards the zinc, iron positive, zinc negative.

Exp. 34. May 2. *A copper disc* rubbed by a rod of bismuth, current produced vibrating to 30°, stationary at 15° *towards the bismuth from the copper*.

Exp. 35. *A rod of zinc* against the same copper, the edges of the disc being made sharp, $2\frac{1}{2}°$ towards the copper, with a good cutting edge, 4° constant; the zinc by this means being well cut. Repeated 4°. Zinc robbing copper, as in exp. 31.

Exp. 36. A piece of iron made sharp with filing, when used with a large copper disc $3\frac{1}{2}$ inches in diameter, gave a current of 8° stationary, while the edge remained good and removed shavings from the iron towards the copper, iron positive.

Exp. 37. Employed a piece of rod *copper* in friction against the revolving *copper* disc, and not the least indication of current was observed.

Exp. 38. Silver thus employed against the copper disc, gave a slight current of 1° from the silver towards the disc.

Exp. 39. With a steel tool, a constant current of $2\frac{1}{2}°$ *towards the copper*.

Exp. 40. A brass rod turning instead of a disc, and steel tool, current 5° from the tool towards the brass.

*Magnetism.*

Exp. 41. By filing iron with a steel file, a current of $7\frac{1}{2}°$ is produced from the iron towards the file, and the two metallic bodies become oppositely magnetic, as shown by the following experiments.

The steel surface becomes positive and the iron negative, which are electro-polar conditions.

It will be immediately seen, that not only does the friction of a file upon a piece of soft iron induce two oppositely electrical conditions of surface, but that this *electrical state is also a truly magnetic condition*, and offers an explanation how, or in what manner the various mechanical operations, screw-tapping, drilling, filing, &c. evince magnetic phænomena. An attempt to establish the opinion of magnetism being a *static electro-polar condition*, was by the author of this paper brought forward, and published in the Report of the British Association for 1842, page 17.

Exp. Having selected a steel file and piece of fine iron wire free from magnetic polarity, I proceeded to draw the file several times over the surface of the wire, when, by holding them on each side the north pole of a suspended magnetic needle, it was found that the wire attracted, and the file repelled, this pole with considerable force.

Exp. A new file attracted both poles of a magnetic needle, or was unmagnetic. A piece of iron wire slightly *repelled* the pole. After rubbing the wire along its surface, and holding the wire on one side of the north pole and the file on the other, the needle was *attracted by the wire and repelled by the file*.

Exp. A new file attracted the north pole of a magnetic needle 10°; a piece of iron wire repelled the same. After filing the same and placing this pole of the needle between them, the file repelled and the wire attracted the needle. This experiment was repeated with the same result.

A thick file and a thick piece of soft iron did not produce any change, the process not being sufficiently powerful to induce magnetic polarity in any considerable mass of metal*.

Exp. Another file was neutral, rather attractive. The repulsive end of a piece of magnetic iron wire was employed. After filing briskly around the surface of its extremity, the *file repelled* and the *wire attracted* the north pole.

Exp. Took the opposite extremities of the file and wire; the wire repelled, the file attracted; but on rubbing them together, an instant change took place; the *file repelled, and the wire attracted the needle*.

Repeated with the same results. These operations were performed when the metals pointed southward. It was discovered, however, that an opposite result took place when the filing was performed towards the north. The file then attracted, and the wire repelled the north pole; but the evinced trifling difference of affinity between iron and steel, as shown in (15.), may tend to produce this uncertainty, which subjects them to the government of the earth's polarity.

Is the current induced by mechanical operations simply thermo-electric, or not?

Exp. 42. Immersed the lower half of the bismuth cylinder in water at 55°. By turning it with a steel tool about one minute (the water revolving around the cylinder the whole period), a current was constantly maintained, at length from 35° to 40°, fine turnings being produced.

The water, 9 oz. and 2 drs., in which the bismuth disc was immersed, and which would derive the principal part of the

* The finer the materials employed, the more highly developed were the magnetic effects; and on this account iron wire was used.

heat from the whole process, being heated only to 57° or 2°\*, and the tool immersed in a like quantity of water, was found to increase it only half a degree.

Exp. 43. A conducting wire, made to press against the revolving bismuth disc slightly, produced a current of $2\frac{1}{2}°$ to $5°$; but on using a disconnected turning-tool to the same side and near the wire, the current was still $2\frac{1}{2}°$ to $5°$; and yet the tool could have induced a current of $30°$ or $40°$. On increasing the pressure of the wire against the cylinder, current $6°$ to $9°$; on using the turning-tool as before, no increase of current could be perceived; yet on applying a lighted taper at the junction of the wire to the cylinder, current $35°$.

The turning-tool does not, therefore, *augment the heat of surface of the disc,* so as by heat to produce a current of thermo-electricity.

Exp. 44. Attached the two galvanometer wires to the piece of bismuth used in the experiments for the production of thermo-electricity, one at each end. Rubbed *one extremity of the bismuth* with force against the revolving copper disc for one minute, and yet *no current* was indicated, which would have been the case, if the heat developed by friction in these cases had been the source of development of the fluid; for instantly on applying the *same end to the flame of a spirit-lamp,* the galvanometer began to deflect. Repeated the experiment with like results; and on removing the wire at the end of the bismuth next to the copper disc, and attaching it to the spring which connected the mandril with the galvanometer for mechanical electricity, a current *was instantly produced by the same friction.* Repeated, and with like results†.

Exp. 45. Repeated a similar experiment with iron. The sharp iron of exp. 36 was attached to the two galvanometer wires, one at each end: on turning with its sharp extremity the copper disc for some time, which produced an instantaneous current in exp. 36, no deviation of the needle was at all observed; but by holding the same end of the iron for a few moments in the spirit flame, a constant deviation commenced, which gradually progressed to $7\frac{1}{2}°$.

Repeated the experiment with like results: yet when the end adjoining the disc was disconnected and attached to the spring in contact with the mandril, i. e. *the ordinary connexion for mechanical electricity* being made (as in 36), *an instanta-*

---

\* Observe, the *turnings alone* which were made, would, as will be hereafter shown, heat the water nearly to this amount, and the *tool* would in this instance heat the water more than the disc; therefore the heat derived from the disc would be less than $\frac{1}{2}°$.

† The metals here employed are the crystalline, which have been shown to be the only bodies evolving the phænomena, copper being only a simple conducting body.

neous current of 8° (*stationary*) *was the result*. Thus it is seen, that with the *same heat developed* in each case, by the mechanical arrangement, is given an immediate current, which heat will not give a current at all by the thermo-electric process, and it is therefore evident *that thermo- and mechanical electricity are not derived from the same source.*

These experiments appear very decisive. The fact of the current invariably *pursuing the course of that in electro-motion, or contact of dissimilar metals*, in all cases where metals illustrative of this phænomenon are employed, speaks in favour of the dissimilarity of the source of these two modifications.

It is also to be remarked here, that if mechanical electricity were the result of the heat applied to the extremity of the metal, *the friction of flat surfaces, which is known to produce much more heat than simply cutting or turning with a sharp edge*, would produce the greatest deflection of the needle; but by this means it is found that none, or scarcely any current is developed, even with a disc of bismuth. (See 22, 23.)

Exp. 46. Is mechanical or thermo-electricity conductible by water? A rod of bismuth was arranged for thermo-electricity in this experiment, and the voltaic decomposition apparatus was employed; it was discovered that the thermo-electric current is utterly *inconductible by water or acidulated water*; the heat was carried on to fusion, but the galvanometer did not deflect in any appreciable manner. It is also inconductible by a strong solution of sulphate of copper.

Exp. 47. The thermo-electric current from bismuth passed through a *large piece of bismuth*, deflecting the galvanometer gradually up to 15°, by the steady heat of a spirit-lamp.

Exp. 48. Mechanical electricity is not conducted at all by *solution of sulphate of copper.*

Exp. 49. And is also *inconductible by acidulated water*, in the ordinary decomposition apparatus.

Exp. 50. But is readily transmitted by an intervening *piece of bismuth* of equal temperature.

### Remarks.

The *direction* of the current from every individual metal, and from one metal relatively with another, is at all times *invariable*, both in mechanical and thermo-electricity.

The *quantity of force* circulating through the galvanometer, and proceeding from any given metal or specific pair of metals, is constantly about the same in amount, proportional to the intensity of the developing process, in both modifications. Each metal *evinces an amount* of force *comparatively proportional* with that of every other metal employed, both in the mechanical and in the thermo-electricity.

XXIX. *On the Phænomena of Thin Plates of Solid and Fluid Substances exposed to Polarized Light.* By Sir DAVID BREWSTER, K.H., D.C.L., F.R.S., and V.P.R.S. Edin.[*]

[With a Plate.]

HAVING received from Dr. Joseph Rende one of his beautiful instruments called the *Iriscope*, and made several experiments with it, I soon perceived that it might be advantageously employed in various investigations in physical optics. This instrument consists mainly of a plate of highly polished black glass, having its surface smeared with a solution of fine soap, and subsequently dried by rubbing it clean with a piece of chamois leather. If we breathe upon the glass surface, thus prepared, through a glass tube, the vapour is deposited in brilliant coloured rings, the outermost of which is black, while the innermost has various colours, or no colour at all, in proportion to the quantity of vapour deposited. The colours in these rings, when seen by common light, correspond with Newton's *reflected rings*, or those which have *black centres*, the only difference being, that in the plate of vapour, which is thickest in the middle, the rings in the iriscope have black circumferences[†]. By using a large system of rings, or depositing the vapour in straight lines in the plane of incidence, we can at once observe the phænomena of the coloured rings or bands at various angles of incidence.

The first person who investigated the modification of Newton's rings in reference to polarized light was M. Arago, who has given an account of his observations in a beautiful and highly interesting memoir, in the third volume of the *Mémoires d'Arcueil*, published in 1817. Without knowing what had been done by M. Arago, Professor Airy entered upon the same inquiry in 1831 and 1832; but the phænomena which he observed were the same as those which had been previously discovered by M. Arago, with the exception of the modification of the rings when formed by a lens pressed against the surface of a diamond.

When Newton's rings are formed by a lens pressed against

[*] From the Philosophical Transactions, 1841, part 1. p. 43.

[†] These rings may be formed upon almost all transparent bodies with more or less brilliancy, though I have found several substances, and occasionally pieces of glass, that will not absorb the soap. The rings are produced upon natural as well as artificial surfaces, that is, upon transparent surfaces produced by fusion or crystallization, as well as upon those polished by art. The soap being gradually dissolved by the vapour, requires to be frequently renewed. I find that other substances, particularly some of the oils, produce the same effect as soap. The rings disappear quickly by evaporation, and their brilliancy and purity of colour depend on the relative temperature of the vapour and the glass.

a surface of glass, M. Arago observed that they were black centred, as usual; and whether viewed with the eye or with a doubly refracting rhomb of Iceland spar, that the single or the double system of rings had the same colours and the same diameters, the rings being completely polarized at the polarizing angle of the glass.

When the lens, however, was pressed against a metallic mirror, and examined with a doubly refracting rhomboid, two images perfectly similar appeared between a perpendicular incidence, and that of $55°$ or the polarizing angle of glass. One of the images disappeared entirely at this angle of $55°$, when the principal section of the rhomboid was perpendicular or parallel to the plane of reflexion; but reappeared at greater incidences, with this remarkable peculiarity, that the colour of each of the rings which composed it was complementary to that of the corresponding rings in the image which had disappeared.

M. Arago likewise remarks that we may easily perceive with the eye, naked and without the assistance of any crystal, that at a certain angle near $55°$ the rings are composed of two distinct sets having unequal diameters, the rhomboid separating in a great measure the two sets of rings, because they are very unequally polarized. He likewise found that these phænomena were not produced when the rings were formed upon *native sulphur* and *diamond*.

"If the presence of a metallic mirror," says M. Arago, "is necessary for the production of the phænomenon in question when the rings are formed upon a plate of air, the case is otherwise when the thin body has much more density, and is in contact by one of its faces with another medium of sufficient refractive power. Thus *coal* presents often in its cleavages very bright colours, produced by an extremely thin substance, and which are decomposed into two complementary images when they are examined with a rhomboid under sufficiently oblique incidences. The colours which are formed artificially by the progress of evaporation, on thin films of alcohol or oil of sassafras, deposited upon coal or any other analogous substance, give rise also to two images, dissimilar, and of opposite tints*."

In order to investigate the phænomena of the rings of vapour in the iriscope, I illuminated them with light polarized in an azimuth of $90°$, or perpendicularly to the plane of incidence, and examined them by a magnifying glass, when the centre of the rings was seen by light reflected at about $53° 11'$,

* *Mémoires de Physique et de Chimie de la Société d'Arcueil*, tom. iii. p. 363. Paris, 1817.

the polarizing angle of water. The effect, which was very striking, is shown in Plate II. fig. 1. The central part, AB, of the system of rings, CDEF, was without rings and colours of any kind: the upper half, CD, was part of a system of rings with *white* circumferences, and was formed by polarized light incident on the film at an angle *greater* than the polarizing angle of water; while the under half, EF, was part of a system of rings with *black* circumferences like those seen by common light, and was formed by polarized light incident on the film at an angle *less* than the polarizing angle of water.

The absence of rings in the middle portion, AB, was of course owing to there being no light reflected from the *first* surface of the film with which that reflected from the *second* surface could interfere; and the reason of there being light reflected from the second surface was, that the light reflected from it was not incident at its polarizing angle.

I have elsewhere shown[*], that when a film of water is laid upon glass whose refractive index is above 1·508, there is no angle of incidence upon the first surface of the film which will allow the refracted ray to fall upon the glass at the polarizing angle; and hence at every angle of incidence on the film, the refracted light is reflected from the glass *at angles less than the polarizing angle of the united media*, or less than an angle whose tangent is equal to $\frac{m}{m'}$, $m$ being the refractive index of the glass, and $m'$ that of the water. When the refractive index of the glass is 1·508, the angle of incidence on the film must be 90° exactly, in order that the refracted ray may fall upon the glass at the polarizing angle whose tangent is equal to $\frac{m}{m'}$.

Now as the portion of the coloured rings at CD, fig. 1, is formed by the interference of two pencils, CA, DEB, fig. 2, one of which, CA, is reflected at an angle, PCA, *above* the polarizing angle of water, and the other, EB, at an angle *below* or *less* than that angle; while the portion EF, fig. 1, is formed by the interference of two pencils, which are both reflected at angles *below* or *less* than that angle, we may suppose that in the formation of the rings with a white circumference, analogous to those with a white centre, there is a loss of half an undulation, while that loss takes place in the interference of common light, or of two pencils reflected on the same side of the polarizing angle.

When the rings are seen at angles between 0° of incidence and 53° 11′, the polarizing angle of water, they are *black* in

[*] Philosophical Transactions, 1815, p. 138.

the circumference, like the portion shown at EF, fig. 1; and when they are seen at incidences between $53° 11'$ and $90°$, they are *white* in the circumference, like the portion shown at CD, fig. 1.

If the rings of vapour are formed upon a polished surface of *fluor spar*, additional phænomena will be exhibited. At all incidences, from $0°$ to about $78°$, rings of the same character will be seen as already described; but the ratio of the refractive powers of water and fluor spar is such, that at an incidence of $78° 4'$ upon the surface of the vapour, the light incident on the spar will be reflected at the polarizing angle of the united media. Thus if $m = 1·437$, the refractive index of fluor spar, and $m' = 1·336$, the refractive index of water, then $\frac{m}{m'} = 1·0716$, the refractive index of the united media, or of their separating surface. The polarizing angle for this surface will therefore be an angle whose tangent is $1·0756$ or $47° 5'$, and the angle of incidence on the first surface of the watery film corresponding to the angle of refraction $47° 5'$, which is the angle of incidence on the second surface, is $78°·4$.

At an incidence of $78° 4'$, therefore, the rings will disappear altogether, as at $53° 11'$, because the pencil incident on the spar will not be reflected. At incidences greater than $78° 4'$ the system of rings with the black circumference will again appear as at incidences below $53° 11'$, and will be visible up to $90°$ of incidence, the interfering pencils being now both reflected at angles above the polarizing angle of the surfaces which reflect them.

This experiment with vapour and fluor spar I have not made; and it may be difficult to see the rings at such an oblique incidence. If the rings are formed by soap upon *plate glass*, or by *alcohol* upon *fluor spar*, the second disappearance of the rings may be seen:

$$\frac{\text{Plate glass}}{\text{soap}} \quad \frac{m}{m'} = \frac{1·510}{1·487} = 1·0154.$$

Polarizing angle at second surface of the soap    $45° 26'$
Angle of incidence on the first surface . . . $71° 45'$

$$\frac{\text{Fluor spar}}{\text{alcohol}} \quad \frac{m}{m'} = \frac{1·437}{1·370} = 1·049.$$

Polarizing angle at second surface of alcohol    $46° 22'$
Angle of incidence on the first surface . . $82° 32'$

If we call $m$, $m'$ the indices of refraction of the two substances, viz. the *film* and the *surface* upon which it rests, $m$ being the larger index, then a ray incident at $90°$ will fall upon the common surface of the two media at the polarizing angle of that surface, when the angle of refraction at the first surface is equal to the tangent, or cotangent of the polarizing angle, according as the refractive power of the film is less or greater than that of the body upon which it rests.

Hence we have

$$\sin i' = \frac{1}{m} \text{ or } \frac{1}{m'},$$

and

$$\tan i' = \frac{m}{m'}, \text{ or } \cot i' = \frac{m}{m'},$$

and

$$m = \frac{m'}{\sqrt{m'^2 - 1}}, \text{ and } m' = \frac{m}{\sqrt{m^2 - 1}},$$

when a ray incident at 90° is polarized at the second surface, or falls upon it at the polarizing angle.

These formulæ enable us to discover between what limits of refractive power the second disappearance of the rings can take place, and consequently what substances we should employ in order to observe it. In this manner we obtain the following results for the mean rays of the spectrum:—

| Values of $m'$. | Values of $\frac{m'}{\sqrt{m'^2-1}}$, or $m$. |
|---|---|
| 3·000 | 1·061 |
| 2·500 | 1·090 |
| 2·000 | 1·154 |
| 1·900 | 1·176 |
| 1·800 | 1·202 |
| 1·700 | 1·236 |
| 1·600 | 1·281 |
| 1·554 | 1·307 |
| 1·508 | 1·336 |
| 1·500 | 1·341 |
| 1·400 | 1·428 |
| 1·336 | 1·508 |
| 1·307 | 1·554 |

The limits, therefore, between which the *second* disappearance of the rings can take place are 1·554, the index for *quartz* and *flint glass*, and 1·307, the index for *ice*. But though the range is very limited, it nevertheless includes a considerable variety of solid and fluid bodies. I have omitted the indices of Tabasheer, and the fluids produced by the compression of gaseous bodies, because, though their refractive powers are beneath 1·307, they cannot be used in the present inquiry.

When $m$ and $m'$ are thus related, the *white-centred rings* will just disappear when $i = 90°$, the light being then incident on the second surface at its polarizing angle. But if we use a film of still less refractive power in relation to the second body, the refracted rays will fall on the second surface at an angle *greater* than the polarizing angle ($i$ being still $90°$), and consequently *the black-centred rings will reappear*, and there will be some angle of incidence I on the film, less than $90°$, at which the angle of refraction $i'$ will be equal to the polarizing angle of the second surface. This angle will be found from the expression

$$\sin I = \frac{m\,m'}{\sqrt{m^2 + m'^2}}.$$

When $m = m'$ no rings whatever will be formed, as no light is reflected at the common surface; but if $m = m'$ only for a particular colour in the spectrum of each substance, and if these indices differ considerably for another colour, rings will be formed in which that colour predominates, in which $m > m'$, or $m < m'$. This takes place in a remarkable manner with *oil of cassia* and *flint glass*, in which $m = m'$ for the *red* rays, but $m > m$ for the *blue* rays. The consequence of this is, that a quantity of *blue* light is reflected from the separating surface of the oil and the glass; and hence if a sufficiently thin film of oil of cassia is laid upon the glass, *blue* would greatly predominate in the system of rings.

Hitherto the azimuth of the polarized light has been $90°$, or perpendicular to the plane of reflexion. Let us now suppose that its azimuth is gradually changed from $90°$ to $0°$ by the rotation of the polarizing surface or crystal.

At all azimuths, from $90°$ to $0°$, the rings with the black circumference are seen, between the angles of $0°$ and $53°\ 11'$, and at the incidence of $53°\ 11'$. But at incidences between $53°\ 11'$ and $90°$, in the case of the iriscope, very interesting phænomena appear. We shall first describe what takes place at $56°\ 45'$, the polarizing angle of the black glass. At this angle none of the polarized light is reflected when the azimuth is $90°$, and the rings with the *white* circumference are beautifully seen on the dark ground of the glass, which now reflects no light. As the azimuth is changed to $87°$, $88°$, &c., the black glass reflects a little light, and the two surfaces of the film a little more light, the rings gradually become fainter and fainter, till at an azimuth of about $79°\ 0'$ they disappear exactly as they did at $53°\ 11'$, and in the azimuth $90°$. When this disappearance takes place, the light reflected from the glass seems to be exactly equal to the light reflected from both surfaces of the film. At other angles of incidence the rings disappeared at different azimuths, varying from 90° to about 45°, as the angle of incidence varied from 53° 11′ to 90°. I found it difficult, however, to measure these azimuths with any accuracy, as the rings were not permanent; and I was therefore obliged to form the colours of thin plates upon highly refracting substances, such as *diamond*, *chromate of lead*, *artificial realgar*, and *greenockite* (the most refractive of all bodies), which had high polarizing angles. A solution of fine soap gave brilliant colours when dried, and in this way I obtained the following results with the surface of a very fine diamond. The index of refraction of the soap was 1·475, and that of the diamond 2·44, and their respective polarizing angles 55° 52′, and 67° 43′.

| Angle of incidence of the polarized light. | Azimuth of the plane of polarization at which the rings disappear. | |
|---|---|---|
| | Observed. | Calculated. |
| 55 52 | 90 0 | 90 0 |
| 60 | 73 0 | 74 27 |
| 65 | 68 30 | 67 49 |
| 67 43 | 66 20 | 65 10 |
| 70 | 63 30 | 63 14 |
| 75 | 59 15 | 58 23 |
| 90 | | 46 30 |

As the disappearance of the rings was not owing to the extinction of one of the interfering pencils, as at 55° 52′, for a sufficient quantity of polarized light was reflected from both surfaces of the film, there was reason to believe that it might arise from the two pencils being polarized at right angles to each other, in conformity with the law relating to the action of the second surfaces of plates which I have given in a former paper*.

Calling $x$ the azimuth of primitive polarization, $i$ the angle of incidence on the *first* surface of the film, $i'$ the corresponding angle of refraction, and consequently the angle of incidence on the *second* surface, $i''$ the angle of refraction at the *second* surface, and

$\varphi =$ the inclination of the plane of polarization of the reflected pencil CA, fig. 3,
$\varphi' =$ that of the refracted pencil CD,
$\varphi'' =$ that of the reflected pencil DE, and
$\varphi''' =$ that of the refracted pencil EB, with which CA interferes; then by Fresnel's formula we have for the ray CA,

$$\tan \varphi = \tan x \cdot \frac{\cos(i+i')}{\cos(i-i')};$$

* Philosophical Transactions, 1830, pp. 148, 149.

and by my formulæ* we have

$$\cot \varphi' = \cot x \cos(i-i')$$

$$\tan \varphi' = \tan x \cdot \frac{1}{\cos(i-i')}$$

$$\tan \varphi'' = \tan x' \cdot \frac{\cos(i'+i'')}{\cos(i'-i'')}.$$

But, after one refraction,

$$\tan x' = \tan \varphi = \tan x \cdot \frac{1}{\cos(i-i')};$$

hence

$$\tan \varphi'' = \tan x \cdot \frac{1}{\cos(i-i')} \cdot \frac{\cos(i'+i'')}{\cos(i'-i'')}$$

and

$$\cot \varphi'' = \frac{1}{\tan x} \cdot \cos(i-i') \cdot \frac{\cos(i'-i'')}{\cos(i'+i'')}.$$

And multiplying this by $\cos(i-i')$ for the change of plane produced by the second refraction at E, we have for the ray EB,

$$\cot \varphi''' = \cot x \cos^2(i-i') \cdot \frac{\cos(i'-i'')}{\cos(i'+i'')}.$$

Now the two pencils which interfere, viz. CA and EB, have their planes of polarization inclined at angles $\varphi$ and $\varphi'''$ to the plane of reflexion; but in order that these angles may be complementary to each other, or may together make 90°, we must have $\tan \varphi = \cot \varphi'''$, or

$$\tan x \frac{\cos(i+i')}{\cos(i-i')} = \cot x \cos^2(i-i') \cdot \frac{\cos(i'-i'')}{\cos(i'+i'')};$$

and consequently

$$\tan^2 x = \cos^2(i-i') \cdot \frac{\cos(i-i')}{\cos(i+i')} \cdot \frac{\cos(i'+i'')}{\cos(i'-i'')};$$

and

$$\tan x = \cos(i-i') \cdot \sqrt{\left( \frac{\cos(i-i')}{\cos(i+i')} \cdot \frac{\cos(i'-i'')}{\cos(i'+i'')} \right)}.$$

When the angle of incidence is 90°, $\cos(i+i') = \sin i'$, and $\cos(i-i') = \sin i'$, and hence

$$\tan x = \frac{1}{m} \sqrt{\frac{\cos(i'-i'')}{\cos(i'+i'')}}.$$

If we now calculate by these formulæ the values of $x$ for the different angles of incidence in the preceding table, and subtract them from 90°, we shall have the numbers in the third

* Philosophical Transactions, 1830.

column of the table, which agree with those observed within the limits of the errors of observation. In the case of *water* and *glass*, too, where the azimuth of disappearance was observed to be about 79° or 11°, the formula gives 79° 28′, or 10° 32′, at an incidence of 56° 45′.

In order to ascertain the relation between the mutual inclination of the planes of polarization of the interfering pencils when they produced *black-centred* or *white-centred* rings, I have computed the following table for an incidence of 56° 45′.

| Azimuth of polarized light. | $+\varphi$ | $-\varphi'''$ | Film of *water* and *glass*. Inclination of planes $\varphi$ and $\varphi'''$. | |
|---|---|---|---|---|
| 90  0 | 90  0 | 90  0 | 180  0 | *White*-centred rings. |
| 87 30 | 74 43 | 82 45 | 157 28 | |
| 85  0 | 49 30 | 75  4 | 124 34 | |
| 79 28 | 28 26 | 61 34 | 90  0 | *No rings.* |
| 70  0 | 15 28 | 43 19 | 58 47 | |
| 45  0 |  5 45 | 18 57 | 24 42 | *Black*-centred rings. |
| 35  0 |  4  3 | 13  3 | 17  6 | |
| 20  0 |  2  6 |  7  7 |  9 13 | |
|  0  0 |  0  0 |  0  0 |  0  0 | |

By taking $\varphi$ *positive*, or on the *right*-hand side of the plane of reflexion, then $\varphi'''$ must be *negative*, or on the left-hand side of that plane\*; hence $+\varphi$, $-\varphi'''$ will be the mutual inclinations of the planes of polarization of the interfering pencils, and we obtain the important law,

*That when two polarized pencils reflected from the surfaces of a thin plate lying on a reflecting surface of a different refractive power interfere, half an undulation is not lost, and* WHITE-*centred rings are produced, provided the mutual inclination of their planes of polarization is greater than* 90°; *and that when this inclination is less than* 90°, *half an undulation is lost, and* BLACK-*centred rings are produced; when the inclination is exactly* 90°, *the pencils do not interfere, and no rings are produced.*

At an incidence of 45° upon water and glass, where the signs of $\varphi$ and $\varphi'''$ are the same, the maximum difference in the planes of polarization is 23° 12′, which takes place in azimuth 70° 30′; and at an incidence of 10° the greatest difference is 2° 16′, which takes place at an azimuth of about 45°.

In the case of *soap* and *plate glass*, where the black-centred rings appear beyond the incidence of 71° 45′, the difference of inclination in the planes of the two pencils is also less than 90°.

I was now desirous of examining the phænomena of a per-

\* See Philosophical Transactions, 1830, p. 70, fig. 1.

fect system of rings when the film had a greater refractive power than the substance upon which it was laid; after many ineffectual attempts to obtain such a system, I succeeded by laying a very small portion of *oil of laurel* upon *water* placed in a black vessel, or on the surface of diluted or real ink. The rings thus produced are splendid beyond description, and exhibit the various phænomena with singular beauty. As the polarizing angle of the oil *exceeds* that of the water, the *black*-centred rings are seen at the polarizing angle of the water, when the reflected light disappears. They continue to be seen till we reach the polarizing angle of the oil, when the rings disappear, and the white-centred ones commence, and continue till we reach the incidence of $90°$ *.

In forming thin films upon metallic surfaces, I employed many of the metals, and found the phænomena nearly the same upon them all, and differing very little from those produced upon transparent bodies. On a fine specimen of *specular iron ore*, I found a system of rings ready-formed, with three orders of colours. The azimuth of the polarized light being inclined $90°$ to the plane of reflexion, the system of rings disappeared wholly at an angle of incidence of $58° 36'$, which is therefore the polarizing angle of the unknown substance of which it was formed: consequently its index of refraction is about $1·638$. Between this angle and $90°$ of incidence, the *white* centred rings appeared; but at $72° 39'$, the polarizing angle of the iron (which gives its refractive power for the *red* rays $3·200$), the rings were singularly fine, being seen on a beautiful blue ground, produced by the disappearance of the *red* light, which is polarized at that angle. I now measured the azimuth of the plane of polarization when the rings disappeared, which was $59° 25'$, whereas by the formula it is $57° 59'$; a discrepancy not to be wondered at, when we consider that the index of refraction for the red rays, viz. $3·200$, was used, in place of that for the mean ray, which is not known. The inclination of the planes of polarization of the two interfering pencils, when calculated by the previous formulæ, is $+32° 7'$, and $-57° 53'$; so that these planes being

* These thin plates of oil of laurel exhibit some curious phænomena, which I believe have not been noticed. If we wet with water, alcohol, or the oil of laurel itself, the extremity of a short piece of wire, such as a large pin, and hold the pin in the hand, so that its head may be above, and almost touching the film, the film will recede in little waves of a circular shape, which form a new system of coloured rings; and they become covered with the vapour from the fluid on the head of the pin in such small particles that they reflect no light, and the rings appear to be blackened. By withdrawing the pin, the film is restored to its former state. The same effect is produced by heating the pin, or the fluid upon it, to promote evaporation.

inclined 90° to each other, as in the case of soap and diamond, no interference takes place, and the rings disappear.

In the fine specimens of *oligist iron ore* from Elba, I have found crystals covered with the most beautiful coloured films, both of uniform and variable thickness. These films are not acted upon by the ordinary acids, like the coloured films upon steel, and appear, from their optical properties, to be of a metallic nature. When they are exposed to a polarized ray, they exhibit generally the same phænomena as the films already described; but there is no angle of incidence at which the colours disappear, either in the azimuth of 90°, at the polarizing angle of the first surface of the film, or in those azimuths where the pencils, from the first and second surface, have their planes of polarization inclined 90° to each other. This, no doubt, arises from the high dispersive power of the film, in consequence of which the different homogeneous rays are polarized at angles considerably different from each other.

The phænomena of transparent films of low refractive power, when laid upon the polished surfaces of metals, and exposed to polarized light, are not very different from those which are exhibited when the film rests upon a transparent surface. I at first used a solution of soap, which produced pretty good tints on speculum metal; but at last I fell upon a method of laying down the most beautiful systems of coloured rings upon all surfaces of all forms, whether metallic, transparent or opake. For this purpose I used the *oil of laurel*, which, when placed upon the surface of water, expands into a film, which gives the finest system of coloured rings. Having laid the plate of polished metal in a small porous wooden tray, such as is used for holding minerals, I poured water into it, so as to cover the metallic surface to the depth of the fiftieth part of an inch. I then formed a film of the oil upon the water, immediately above the metallic surface. In a short time the absorption of the water by the porous tray allowed the film of oil to descend and rest upon the metallic surface*. When the adhering moisture was removed by evaporation, the film was extremely beautiful; and if protected from dust may be preserved for any length of time.

Having laid a film of this kind upon *speculum metal*, I obtained the following results. The coloured rings disappeared almost completely at 56°, the polarizing angle of the oil. The *black-centred* rings appeared at all angles less than 56°, and the *white-centred* rings at all angles above it. Both the systems of rings were exceedingly distinct at the greatest angles

* The same effect is produced more slowly by evaporation; or the water may be sucked out of the tray by a tube, or run off by an aperture.

of incidence, whereas on transparent surfaces of low refractive power, they can scarcely be seen at such angles. When the azimuth of the polarized ray varies from 90° to 0°, the rings disappear at different angles of incidence; or when the angles of incidence vary, the rings disappear in different azimuths. I measured these azimuths when the polarized ray was incident upon speculum metal, and obtained the following numbers:—

| Angles of incidence. | Azimuth in which the rings disappear. | | Difference. |
|---|---|---|---|
| | Observed. | Calculated. | |
| 90° 0′ | | 40° 23′ | |
| 71 50 | 56° 25′ | 57 22 | − 0 57 |
| 60 0 | 65 45 | 65 4 | + 0 41 |
| 56 5 | 90 0 | 90 0 | |

In computing column third from the formula in p. 168, I used 1·49 as the index of refraction of *oil of laurel*, and 4·011 as the index of refraction for *speculum metal*, as deduced from my experiments on its elliptic polarization*.

I have made similar experiments when the rings were transferred to *silver*, whose elliptical polarization approaches nearest to circular polarization; and to *grain tin*, which appears to have the highest refractive power of any of the metals; but I found it very difficult to ascertain with any accuracy the azimuths in which the rings disappear.

If we use common in place of polarized light in the preceding experiments, and analyse the reflected light by a rhomb of calcareous spar, the very same phænomena will be exhibited.

When the films or thin plates are not laid upon the surfaces of fluid or solid bodies, the phænomena are of an entirely different kind. At all angles of incidence, and in all azimuths, the colours and character of the rings are the same, whether we use common or polarized light. In obtaining this result I stretched thin films of various oils, such as *oil of laurel, oil of cassia, oil of turpentine*, and many others, across circular apertures, and examined them in light polarized in different azimuths. The rings of course vanished at the polarizing angle of the oil, and the brilliancy of the colours varied with the angles of azimuth and incidence, but the complementary rings never appeared, the rings being always those with the black centre†.

* Philosophical Transactions, 1830, p. 324.
† The physical phænomena exhibited in these attenuated films are very remarkable. A current of fluid is projected from the margin and centre of the ring of fluid across the fluid surface, resembling the top of a pine apple. This movement makes the film thinner at some places than others, and

In order to understand the cause of this, we must inquire into the state of polarization of the interfering pencils. The ratio of refraction being the same at both surfaces of the film, we have

$$\tan \varphi = \tan x \cdot \frac{\cos(i+i')}{\cos(i-i')}, \text{ and } \cot \varphi''' = \cot x \cdot \frac{\cos^3(i-i')}{\cos(i+i')};$$

and when $\tan \varphi = \cot \varphi'''$, which is the case when $\varphi + \varphi''' = 90°$, we have

$$\tan x = \frac{\cos^2(i-i')}{\cos(i+i')}.$$

When $i = 90°$, $\tan \varphi = A$, or the azimuth of the polarized ray, and $\cot \varphi''' = \frac{\cos^3 i'}{\sin i'}$.

If we now compute the values of $\varphi$ and $\varphi'''$ at different angles of incidence and in different azimuths of the polarized light, we shall obtain the results in the following Table. In azimuths 0° and 90°, $\varphi$ and $\varphi''' = 0$.

Inclination of the planes of polarization of the two pencils, $\varphi$ and $\varphi'''$.

| Angles of incidence. | Azimuth 22° 30'. | | Azimuth 45°. | | Azimuth 67° 30'. | | Azimuth 90°. | |
|---|---|---|---|---|---|---|---|---|
| | Pencil from first surface. | Pencil from second surface. | Pencil from first surface. | Pencil from second surface. | Pencil from first surface. | Pencil from second surface. | Pencil from first surface. | Pencil from second surface. |
| 0    | 22 30 | 22 30 | 45 0  | 45 0  | 67 30 | 67 30 | 80 0  | 80 0  |
| 10   | 21 42 | 22 5  | 43 51 | 44 24 | 66 40 | 67 4  | 79 36 | 79 48 |
| 20   | 19 11 | 19 34 | 40 13 | 40 38 | 64 13 | 64 14 | 78 13 | 78 23 |
| 30   | 15 25 | 15 55 | 33 40 | 34 33 | 58 7  | 58 58 | 75 10 | 75 38 |
| 40   | 10 18 | 11 1  | 23 41 | 25 11 | 43 21 | 48 37 | 68 6  | 68 6  |
| 50   | 4 18  | 4 52  | 10 18 | 11 37 | 23 41 | 26 24 | 45 52 | 49 23 |
| 56 in 45 | 0 0 | 0 0 | 0 0 | 0 0 | 0 0 | 0 0 | 0 0 | 0 0 |
| 60   | 2 6   | 2 35  | 5 4   | 6 13  | 12 5  | 14 44 | 26 42 | 31 42 |
| 70   | 7 54  | 11 52 | 18 32 | 26 53 | 39 0  | 50 45 | 62 16 | 70 49 |
| 80   | 15 11 | 24 41 | 33 13 | 47 58 | 57 41 | 69 32 | 74 56 | 80 58 |
| 85   | 18 40 | 33 34 | 39 12 | 58 2  | 63 5  | 75 30 | 77 48 | 83 43 |
| 90   | 22 30 | 43 57 | 45 0  | 66 44 | 67 30 | 79 54 | 80 0  | 85 40 |

The results in this Table, which may be considered as those of

hence arises an irregular system of coloured bands, with an incessant play of varying tints, as if the fluid were animated. The bands of colour are serrated with salient points, from which the fluid seems to shoot across the film. In the oils of cinnamon, naphtha, spearmint, wormwood, rapeseed, nutmegs, bergamot, savine, rosemary, &c., the phænomena are peculiarly beautiful. With poppy oil, the red and green tints of the 4th, 5th, and 6th orders were also seen.

observation\*, exhibit at one glance the general phænomena at all angles of incidence and azimuth.

The two interfering pencils are in every case reflected at angles either *both above* or *both below* the polarizing angle, and hence their planes of polarization are always on the same side of the plane of reflexion and in the same quadrant, and consequently they never can be at right angles to each other so as to prevent interference. For the same reason the inclination of the planes never can exceed 90°, so as to produce the complementary white-centred rings, in conformity with the law previously given.

If, for example, we compute the value of $x$ in the preceding formula at an incidence of 70°, we shall find it 66° 25′, at which azimuth the inclinations $\varphi$ and $\varphi'''$ of the planes of polarization are 40° 47′, and 49° 53′; but though the sum of these angles is 90°, yet the real inclination of the planes is $\varphi''' - \varphi = 9° 6'$.

This property of parallel transparent films, of giving by reflexion pencils polarized in planes at various inclinations, when the incident light is polarized in different azimuths, enables us to obtain two pencils of polarized light, inclined at any angle, varying from 0° to 21° 44′ in glass, and to study the phænomena which such pencils exhibit, either in their mutual action, or in their relations to other properties of light.

But the phænomena become more varied and interesting when the second surface of the plate is *inclined* to the first. In this way we may produce effects analogous to those produced by a change in the refractive power of the second surface by contact with another refracting surface, and obtain pencils inclined 90° to each other, and therefore exhibiting the white-centred rings. The phænomena will in this case resemble those of a film of oil upon water.

When the refractive index of a parallel film exceeds 1·508, the ray is incident on the second surface at an angle less than the polarizing angle; but by inclining the second surface we can make it fall upon it at a greater angle than the polarizing angle. The phænomena may be still more varied by inclining the surface of emergence to the surface of incidence†; but as it is not easy to obtain films with faces suitably inclined to each other, it is unnecessary to pursue this branch of the subject any further.

Such are the phænomena of *thin* and *thick* plates when viewed by polarized light, or by common light subsequently analysed by a doubly refracting rhomb. But if we use polar-

\* See Philosophical Transactions, 1830, pp. 74, 138.
† Ibid. p. 147, fig. 3.

ized light, and subsequently analyse the light transmitted through the thin plates, we shall obtain a series of very interesting and instructive phænomena, analogous to those produced by plates of doubly refracting crystals which exhibit the polarized tints. In both these cases, the film is interposed between a polarizing plate and an analysing rhomb. If the film is too thick to produce colours, it will depolarize the polarized ray, in a manner analogous to that of a crystallized plate, which is not thin enough to give the polarized tints; and if the film is sufficiently thin to produce uniform tints, a coloured band or system of rings, with black or white centres. Their action is analogous to that of thin crystallized plates, which either produce uniform tints like the laminæ of sulphate of lime, or uniaxal or biaxal systems of rings.

It would be unprofitable to describe minutely the great variety of phænomena which thin plates thus exhibit, as they vary with the refractive power of the fluid or solid upon which they are laid, so that I shall confine myself to the case in which a thin plate of oil of laurel rests on the surface of a specimen of *artificial realgar*. In common light, the colours of this film are very beautiful, but when examined in polarized light by an analysing rhomb, they are brilliant beyond description.

1. *When the azimuth of the polarized light* is 90°, and the incidence of the polarized ray 56° 5', the polarizing angle of oil of laurel.

When the film is viewed without the polarizing rhomb, no rings are seen, as there is no light reflected from the first surface of the film, and consequently no interference.

When the film is viewed with the polarizing rhomb, having its principal section in the plane of incidence, no rings appear, either in its ordinary or extraordinary image. But if the plane of polarization is less or more than 90°, by even a small quantity, then after the rhomb has been turned round nearly 90° towards the right, a system of *black-centred* rings is seen for an instant, and these, after disappearing, are followed by a system of *white-centred* ones, the white-centred rings appearing first if the rhomb is turned to the left. The same phænomena are repeated in every quadrant of the circular motion of the rhomb.

2. *When the azimuth of the polarized light varies* from 90° to 0°, the incidence being 56° 5', as before.

At 90° azimuth the phænomena are as above described.

At $67\frac{1}{2}$°. Rhomb 0°, no rings.

Rhomb turning to the right, the white-centred rings appear, then vanish, when the azimuth of the rhomb is less than $67\frac{1}{2}$°; then black-centred rings appear, which vanish at 180°; then succeed the white-centred ones, which vanish at about 210°; then the black-centred, which continue to 360°.

At 45°, 22½°. The very same phænomena appear at these and other azimuths, the azimuths of the rhomb at which the rings disappear out of the plane of incidence being a little less than the azimuths of the polarized light.

At 0°. The evanescence of the rings takes place when the azimuths of the rhomb are 0°, 90°, 180°, and 270°, the *white-centred* rings appearing in the *first* and *third*, and the *black-centred* ones in the *second* and *fourth* quadrant.

3. *Azimuth of polarized light* 90°.

Incidence of polarized light 68° 3′, the polarizing angle of realgar.

At this angle all the light reflected from the realgar has disappeared, excepting a dark bluish purple, in the middle of which is seen, without using the rhomb, a splendid system of richly-coloured rings, with a *white centre*. When the rhomb is applied as before, and performs a complete revolution, the white-centred rings are seen all round, disappearing at 90° and 270°.

4. *When the azimuth of the polarized light varies from* 90° *to* 0°, *the incidence being* 68° 3′, *as before.*

At 90° azimuth, the phænomena are as above described.

At 80°, and all other azimuths, the *white-centred rings* are seen when the rhomb is at 0°; but they disappear at azimuths of the rhomb a little less than the azimuths of polarization, and are then succeeded by the *black-centred rings*.

At 0° azimuth, the rings disappear when the rhomb is at 0° and 180°, and are *black-centred* all round.

Without using the rhomb, the rings always disappear at the azimuth $x$, at which the planes of polarization of the interfering pencils are rectangular.

At incidences above 68° 3′, the phænomena are of the same character. The rings are *white-centred* in 90° of azimuth, and when the rhomb is at 0°. They become very brilliant about 45°. Near 90° of rotation the rings vanish, and immediately the black-centred system appears, which quickly vanishes, and is succeeded by the white-centred system.

5. *Angles of incidence less than* 56° 5′.

In 90° of azimuth of the polarized ray, and the rhomb being at 0°, the black-centred rings are seen, and continue to be seen during a complete revolution of the rhomb. In all azimuths, from 90° to 0°, the rings disappear by turning the rhomb to the left, the arch diminishing from 90° to 0°; but in azimuths of an intermediate magnitude, the disappearance of the rings is followed by the appearance of the *white-centred system*, which quickly disappears, and is succeeded by the *black-centred system*. This phænomenon is seen best near 45° of azimuth.

When the plates or films are too thick to give the coloured rings, the phænomena of the differently polarized pencils may be finely seen by using *coloured glasses*, in which the pencils reflected from both surfaces may be observed. If the glass is *green*, for example, the pencil or image of a small aperture or luminous body will be *green*, while that reflected from the first surface, though in reality colourless, will appear *red*, from the physiological action of the green light upon the retina. Hence the two differently polarized pencils will have different colours, as if they were the tints of polarized light. If these coloured glasses are laid upon, or cemented on one side to, metals or highly refracting substances, the polarization of the coloured pencils which they reflect will be modified according to the principles already explained, and they will exhibit many interesting phænomena, varying with the colours of the glasses, as if the colours were produced by the absorption of polarized light.

In order to convey a general idea of the different classes of phænomena described in the preceding paper, I have represented two of the most important in figs. 4 and 5.

1. *Glass and Water.*—When a film of aqueous vapour is laid upon glass whose index of refraction is 1·508, the rings disappear at 53° 11', the polarizing angle of the water, and also in the various azimuths where the two interfering pencils are polarized in planes at right angles to each other. At all azimuths greater than these, and at angles of incidence above the polarizing angle, the *white-centred* rings appear; and at all azimuths less than these, and at all incidences (except those at which the white-centred rings are seen), the *black-centred* rings appear.

The following Table shows the values of $x$, or the azimuths of disappearance of the rings, as computed from the formula in p. 49:—

| Angles of incidence. | Azimuths. | Complements. |
|---|---|---|
| 53° 11' | 90° 0' | 0° 0' |
| 55   0 | 82  8 | 7 52 |
| 60   0 | 76 52 | 13  8 |
| 65 | 75 15 | 14 45 |
| 67 | 75 10 | 14 50 |
| 70 | 75 30 | 14 30 |
| 73 | 76 18 | 13 42 |
| 74 | 76 42 | 13 18 |

| Angles of incidence. | Azimuths. | Complements. |
|---|---|---|
| 75° | 77° 9′ | 12° 51′ |
| 76 | 77 36 | 12 24 |
| 80 | 80 0 | 10 0 |
| 85 | 84 15 | 5 45 |
| 90 | 90 0 | 0 0 |

If we now conceive AB, fig. 3, to be the section of the plane of incidence, having the different incidences marked upon it from 90° to 53° 11′, and if round a centre in AB prolonged, where 0° of incidence falls, we describe the azimuthal circle ZAZ, then the complements of the azimuths of the polarized light being set off from the corresponding angles of incidence on each side of AB, the curves ACB, ACB passing through these points will show at what angles of incidence and azimuth the rings disappear, in consequence of the planes of polarization of the two pencils being at these places rectangular.

At all incidences, and in all azimuths within the shaded space ACBC, the *white-centred rings* are seen, and at all other azimuths and incidences the *black-centred rings* are seen.

2. *Fluor Spar and Water.*—I have taken this combination as a specimen of the phænomena which take place at some incidences less than 90°, when the refracted ray falls on the second surface of the film, at angles greater than its polarizing angle. The following Table shows the values of $x$ and their complements:—

| Angles of incidence. | Azimuths. | Complements. |
|---|---|---|
| 53° 11′ | 0° 0′ | 0° 0′ |
| 55 | 82 35 | 7 25 |
| 60 | 77 47 | 12 13 |
| 63 | 76 54 | 13 6 |
| 65 | 76 41 | 13 19 |
| 67 | 77 6 | 12 54 |
| 70 | 78 9 | 11 51 |
| 75 | 82 0 | 8 0 |
| 78 | 88 41 | 11 9 |
| 78 4 | 90 0 | 0 0 |
| 80 | 83 28 | 6 32 |
| 85 | 77 31 | 12 29 |
| 90 | 74 14 | 15 46 |

By projecting these values, as is done in fig. 4, we obtain a double set of curves which unite at D, where the angle of incidence is 78° 4′, at which the refracted ray falls upon the second surface at its polarizing angle.

At all incidences, and in all azimuths within the shaded portions of the figure ZAZD, DCBC, the *white-centred rings* are seen. At all azimuths and incidences corresponding with the outlines of the curves ZDZ, DCBC, the *rings disappear*; and at all azimuths and incidences without the shaded portions of the figure, the *black-centred rings* are seen*.

St. Leonard's College, St. Andrews,
April 8, 1841.

---

XXX. *Photographic phænomena referring to the various Actions of the red and yellow Rays on Daguerreotype Plates when they have been affected by daylight.* By A. CLAUDET, *Esq.*

To the Editors of the Philosophical Magazine and Journal.

GENTLEMEN,

HAVING made on the 24th of October 1847, a communication to the Académie des Sciences of Paris similar to that I sent on the 10th of June to the Royal Society, On different Properties of Solar Radiation acting on Silver Plates coated with Iodine, or its compounds with Bromine or Chlorine, a discussion ensued, in which Messrs. Ed. Becquerel and Gaudin (see *Comptes Rendus*, Oct. 31 and Nov. 2) controverted the accuracy of some part of my experiments. I had stated that the red and yellow glasses had the property, as well as the pure red and yellow rays of the spectrum, of destroying the photogenic action produced by daylight on silver plates coated with iodine, or its compounds with bromine and chlorine; Messrs. Ed. Becquerel and Gaudin asserted that the red and yellow glasses had not the property of destroying, but of continuing the action commenced by daylight on the simply iodized plate.

As soon as I was apprised of the remarks made by Messrs. Becquerel and Gaudin, I repeated the experiments, and to my great surprise I found that the destructive action of the red and yellow glasses did not appear, on this trial, to extend to the simply iodized, but only to the bromo-iodized plate. I lost no time in communicating to the Académie des Sciences the result of these experiments; and at the meeting of the 22nd of November my letter stating the apparent contradiction was read.

This led me to continue the experiment, in order to examine the question more attentively, and fortunately enabled me to discover some new properties so interesting that I made

* No reference is made in these figures to the phænomena which are seen by using both polarized light and the analysing rhomb.

a new memoir on the subject, at the same time trying to explain the anomaly existing between Messrs. Ed. Becquerel and Gaudin's experiments and my own.

As persons interested in these questions might only read my paper to the Royal Society, which you have inserted in full in the last Number of the Philosophical Magazine, I consider it my duty to publish immediately what has passed before the Académie des Sciences in reference to my communication; and I shall be much obliged if you will allow me a place in your pages for the insertion of the following translation of my new memoir to the Académie des Sciences, which has been read at the meeting of the 20th of December. (See *Comptes Rendus*.)

I have the honour to be, Gentlemen,
Your most obedient Servant,
A. CLAUDET.

---

I have again examined my former experiments, and I find some specimens which show that red and yellow glasses have destroyed the effect of the photogenic light on plates simply iodized. How can this fact be reconciled with Messrs. Ed. Becquerel and Gaudin's experiments, and those I had just made in consequence of these philosophers' observations? Had I made any mistake in the classification of my former specimens, or had I erred in my mode of operating? This might be, and I feared such was the case, as I just obtained quite different results. I then questioned my assistant, and he recollected well that we had repeatedly experimented upon plates simply iodized, and that we had then found that red and yellow glasses did destroy the action of daylight, as well on iodized plates as on those which had been submitted to the compound vapour of iodine and bromine.

I then recollected a curious fact mentioned by Dr. Draper of New York (see Phil. Mag., Feb. 1847, pages 89 and 90), which at the time of its publication I had found so inexplicable that I did not pay much attention to it, and which I had totally forgotten during the course of my experiments.

Dr. Draper said, " Such are the facts I observed, and they seem to have been reproduced by MM. Foucault and Fizeau; but there are also others of a much more singular nature. In these Virginia specimens *the same protecting action reappears beyond the violet.*

" The only impressions in which I have ever seen this protecting action beyond the violet, are those made in Virginia in 1842; they were made in the month of July. Struck with this peculiarity, on my return to New York the following August I made many attempts to obtain similar specimens, but in no instance could the extra-violet protecting action be traced, though the analogous action of the red, orange, yellow, green and blue, was perfectly given. Supposing, therefore, that the difference must be due either to impurities in the iodine or to differences in the method of conducting the experiment, I tried it again and again in every possible way. *To my surprise I soon found that the negative effect was gradually disappearing*; and on Sept. 29 it could no longer be traced, except at the highest part corresponding to the yellow and green rays. In December it had become still more imperfect, but on the 19th of the following March the red and orange rays *had recovered their original protective power*. It seemed, therefore, that in the early part of the year a protective action had made its appearance in the red ray, and about July extended over all the less refrangible regions, and as the year went on it had retreated upwards.

"Are there then periodic changes in the nature of the sun's light?" &c.

From these experiments of Dr. Draper it would appear that, according to the months of the year in which we operate, the red and yellow rays either do or do not exercise a destructive action. It must be remarked that Dr. Draper mentions only iodized plates, that he always speaks of iodine alone, and that he never alludes to bromine or chlorine, which were hardly in use at the time of his experiments.

Dr. Draper adds (page 91), "I further found that when different rays are brought to act upon each other, the result does not alone depend upon their intrinsic differences, but also on their relative intensities. Thus the green and lower half of the blue rays, when of a certain intensity, protect the plate from the action of the daylight; but if of a less intensity, they aid the daylight.

"The red and orange rays, when of a certain intensity, increase the action of daylight on the plate; but if of a less intensity, they restrain it."

It would result from this last observation of Dr. Draper, that when the red and orange rays are not endowed with the destructive action, they, on the contrary, have the property of continuing or assisting the action of daylight.

Is it not then possible, that, like Dr. Draper, I may have made my first experiments on the iodized plate during the period when the red and yellow rays were endowed with their destructive action, and that Messrs. Becquerel and Gaudin may have made theirs when these rays had lost their destructive and had acquired their continuing action, at a period corresponding to the present?

Having made my experiments with the greatest care, I seize with satisfaction this manner of explaining phænomena apparently contradictory. It would indeed be curious and interesting to find that neither myself nor the other experimenters are in error, and that we differ only as regards conditions and circumstances, which, without our knowledge, have exercised an influence upon our experiments. But there can be no doubt as regards the iodized plate, when it has been subsequently submitted to the vapour of bromine alone, or of bromine and chlorine united. I have operated with these substances during the various periods of the year, and I have invariably found that the red, orange, and yellow glasses destroy the action of daylight*.

This arises perhaps from the high degree of sensitiveness of all the coatings containing bromine. During the periods of the year when, by the intensity and purity of daylight, the simple iodide of silver has acquired the maximum of sensitiveness, it may be affected like the bromo-iodide, which, being about 100 times more sensitive, is always capable of receiving the destructive action of the less refrangible rays. Then it would appear that the destructive action of these rays require a highly sensitive coating to become manifest.

This manner of viewing the question is corroborated by a curious phænomenon, in other respects very interesting, and which I think has hitherto escaped the researches of photographers. I intended to treat this subject at some length in a separate paper, but I cannot do better than make use of this fact on the present occasion, and I shall therefore not defer its publication.

There exists a coating of iodide of silver which is twenty-five times more sensitive than the coating of Daguerre. Daguerre did not imagine that his process was susceptible of such a degree of sensitiveness. What an unexpected result at the time of his discovery! It is to be regretted that it escaped the inventor of the Daguerreotype, and that it did not precede

* I must here state, that considering the Daguerreotype plate as now exclusively prepared with bromine in addition to iodine, I have paid much more attention to this combination than to the original and now obsolete preparation of Daguerre containing only iodine; and I have had the opportunity of experimenting on plates prepared with iodine and bromine, and with iodine, bromine, and chlorine during a whole year, in all seasons; so that if there might exist any uncertainty as to the destructive effect of red and yellow glasses on silver plates simply iodized, there can be no doubt as to the permanency of the destructive effect on the bromo-iodized plate with or without chlorine, in every season and in all circumstances.

the discovery of the accelerating action of bromine and chlorine, which we have found to be 100 times more sensitive*.

When the plate is prepared with this coating of iodine, the red and yellow glasses destroy the effect of daylight produced on that coating, in the same manner as when the iodized plate has been subsequently submitted to the vapour of bromine.

There are, then, certainly some cases when the red and yellow glasses are not endowed with the property of continuing the action commenced by daylight on the simply iodized plate, but when they are endowed with the property of destroying that action. This highly sensitive coating of iodine is obtained in the following manner:—

When a plate of silver is submitted to the vapour of iodine, it assumes at first a yellow tint, and afterwards becomes successively rose, red, violet, blue and blue-green; all these various tints constitute what I shall call the simple coating; they are all sensitive nearly in the same degree.

In continuing to iodize, a second coating is formed in a series of the same tints as the first. The plate becomes yellow a second time, and it passes successively through the rose, red, violet, blue, and blue-green tints: this second coating is twenty-five times more sensitive than the first. But the most sensitive point is about the rose tint.

A third coating with the same tints can be obtained by a longer exposure to the vapour of iodine; but it is less sensitive than the second; the surface of the silver begins to be attacked by the strong action of the iodine; and after the washing with hyposulphite it appears milky, which injures the purity of the image.

If a silver plate be submitted to the vapour of iodine in such a manner as to give it gradually, by horizontal zones, all the tints of the first and second coatings, and in that state entirely affected by daylight, then exposed only on one vertical half during a few minutes under a red glass, so that the action of the red glass be exercised only on one half of each zone of the various tints of the two coatings, the mercurial vapour affects the surface in such a manner, as to show that the red glass has destroyed the action of daylight on the second coating of iodine, and has continued the same action on the first. The red glass has brought back the half of the more sensitive coating to the same degree of effect produced on the less sensitive, which has not received the action of the red glass. It

---

* I made the discovery of the accelerating property of chlorine, bromine and iodine combined in certain proportions in May 1841, and I communicated a paper on the subject to the Royal Society, which was read the 10th of June following.

has therefore destroyed the action of daylight on the more sensitive coating, and has continued the effect commenced on the less sensitive, to the same degree of intensity as the part of the more sensitive coating which has not received the action of red glass; so that each half of the plate has an effect perfectly equal and identical, in every point, to that of the other half, but in an inverted manner. A remarkable result is, that the horizontal zone, which is precisely in the middle of the plate, has the same intensity of photogenic effect in all its length. This proves that there has been neither destruction nor continuation on the space, where the coating by its thickness had the mean state of sensitiveness.

In putting aside the question of the influence of the various periods of the year on the destruction or continuation of the effect of daylight by the red and yellow rays, until we may have been able to verify the exactness of the facts mentioned by Dr. Draper, it is not possible to say in a general way that the red and yellow glasses are endowed with the property of continuing the effect of daylight on iodide of silver; for I have just proved that there are cases in which the contrary always takes place, according to the thickness of the coating of iodine.

Since the vapours of the atmosphere as well as the coloured glasses render the action of light negative, in absorbing certain rays and allowing only certain others to pass, it would not be surprising that, from the simultaneous action of the vapours of the atmosphere and of the coloured glasses, some contradictory effects might result; that when light has to pass through two different kinds of absorbing media, a certain effect could be produced; and that when the atmosphere is pure and free from all kinds of vapour, the absorption of coloured glass only might produce an effect of quite an opposite nature.

According to the position and density of the vapours of the atmosphere, all the points of the luminous space are not endowed with the same photogenic properties. So that in some circumstances a plate, first exposed to the blue light of the zenith, loses the property of receiving the mercurial vapour, if it be exposed a second time to the horizontal light of the south, when there exist some vapours, although not sufficiently dense to render the sun decidedly yellow. I have obtained specimens in which this curious result is manifest. One of them exhibits a negative image. This effect was produced by exposing a plate, first to the blue light of the zenith, and afterwards, covered with an engraving or a piece of black lace, to the light of the south.

The possible simultaneous existence of two antagonistic

lights reflected from the atmosphere explains those anomalies which are so annoying to photographers; for example, those circumstances under which it seems impossible to obtain any image, whatever may be the length of exposure in the camera. This difficulty is imputed to the preparation of the plates, the state of the accelerating solutions, &c.; and after all it only exists in the light. As much effect is often obtained in 30 seconds as in 120 seconds, for it is possible to have obtained a first effect which has been afterwards destroyed; and that must inevitably be the case if, during the latter part of the exposure in the camera obscura, any clouds or vapours have suddenly rendered the light of the sun yellow; in this case the object which had first reflected white light, becoming capable of reflecting only yellow light, this last must destroy the effect produced by the first.

If the object reflects at the same time blue light from the zenith and yellow light from the southern horizon, the two lights may be neutralized and destroy each other, so that no photogenic effect can be obtained. Sometimes, when the sky is cloudless, the space at the zenith is of a particularly deep blue colour; whereas the vapours produced by the heat of the sun make the sky appear slightly tinted with yellow, from the horizon to a certain height. In those circumstances all photographers must have observed that the operation in the camera obscura is excessively slow.

This may probably explain those dark specimens *, which were so weak in effect, obtained some years ago on the Alps during clear and cloudless weather, by an operator sent to Italy by M. Lerebours to take Daguerreotype views. M. Lerebours' operator was an experienced photographer, and he found, to his great surprise, that on the summit of the Alps he could not obtain any effect in less than five or six times what he considered to be the necessary exposure. He was surrounded with snow, the sun was shining in all its brilliancy, the sky was pure and cloudless, of a deep blue colour, whereas the horizon was without doubt slightly tinted yellow, on account of the vapours produced by the melting of the snow and ice of the glaciers.

Mr. Lerebours' operator was using at that time (in 1840) plates only iodized; and this fact would confirm the neutralization of the photogenic effect upon plates of iodide of silver, by the less refrangible rays acting simultaneously with white light, according to Dr. Draper's observations.

It would be interesting if M. Lerebours could state the

* I have one of these curious specimens in my possession, for which I am indebted to M. Lerebours' kindness.

period of the year in which his artist operated on the Alps; although it might be that from the high elevation of those regions the operator was precisely in those atmospheric conditions which exist on less elevated grounds during only certain months, on account of the density of the atmosphere that the sun's rays have to penetrate.

I shall not conclude this paper without expressing a wish that M. Ed. Becquerel, M. Gaudin, Messrs. Foucault and Fizeau, as well as Dr. Draper, will continue their researches, and that we shall abstain from all discussion on this subject until we have been able to verify the facts under all possible circumstances. Time and only a few experiments will suffice to settle the question. We are all animated with the wish of arriving at the truth, and facts alone must now decide between us. Whatever may be the result, we all can individually congratulate ourselves on having contributed by our separate labours to the explanation of the phænomena of photography, and to the advancement of this new and interesting science.

XXXI. *Observations on some remarkable Properties of Iodine, Phosphorus, Nitric Acid, &c.* By M. NIÉPCE DE SAINT-VICTOR[*].

### On Iodine and its action.

I BELIEVE that I first discovered a property of iodine which we should least expect it to possess, viz. that of being attracted by the black parts of an engraving, manuscript, &c., leaving the white parts untouched. Thus, an engraving is submitted to the vapour of iodine for about five minutes at a temperature of from 60° to 70° F.; fifteen grammes of iodine are required for each square decimeter (a longer exposure is requisite at a lower temperature); this engraving is then laid upon paper "sized" with starch, care being taken to moisten it previously with water acidulated to 1° with sulphuric acid. This is the only substance which as yet has been found to give the impressions any degree of permanency: however, they ultimately disappear on exposure to the air and light; but by pasting them beneath a plate of glass, they may be preserved for a very long time. The proofs just after having been pressed with a ball of linen exhibit remarkably distinct impressions, which on drying, however, become cloudy. But what is still more remarkable is, that several copies of the

[*] Translated from the *Annales de Chimie et de Physique* for January 1848, having been communicated in two parts to the Académie des Sciences the 22nd of June 1846, and 11th of January 1847.

same engraving may be taken without subjecting it to the renewed preparatory process, and the last impressions are always the most distinct; for on leaving the engraving exposed for a very considerable time to the vapour of the iodine, the white parts ultimately become impregnated with it, if the paper has been starched; but the dark parts always predominate, however long the exposure may be continued.

The engraving is in no way altered by the process, and it may be copied an indefinite number of times.

I have discovered a means of copying every kind of drawing by the same process, whether made with printer's or common ink (provided gum does not enter into its composition), or with Indian ink or black-lead; in short, any kind of lined drawing may be copied, but they must be previously subjected to the following process:—they are first immersed for a few minutes in a weak solution of ammonia, then in water acidulated with sulphuric, nitric, or hydrochloric acid, and allowed to dry; they are then exposed to the vapour of iodine, and the process above described repeated. By this method, tracings of designs may be produced which hitherto could not be done in any other way, even when they existed in the substance of the paper. Moreover, when there are two images, one on the face and the other on the back of the same sheet of paper, they can easily be copied separately.

I have pointed out the necessity of the paper which is to receive the impression of an engraving being sized with starch, because the real colouring matter of the copy is the iodide of starch; it afterwards occurred to me to coat the surface of plates of porcelain, opaline glass, alabaster and ivory, with starch-paste, and then to act upon them in the same manner as I had acted upon the paper: the result, as I had anticipated, was incontestably superior, as compared with the impressions upon simple paper sized with starch. When the impression obtained by this process is perfectly dry, it is coated with picture-varnish; and when placed under glass, it acquires such stability, that I have preserved some of them for more than eight months without their undergoing any perceptible change.

When I wish to copy an engraving, I prefer using opaline glass, behind which I paste a sheet of paper to render it less transparent: a reversed impression is obtained upon this plate; but in using a plate of common glass which is subsequently reversed, the proof appears non-inverted, and it is only requisite to place a sheet of paper behind it to make the impression more apparent. It may also be kept as a window-pane; but in this case the impression must be placed between two plates of glass, so as to preserve it from injury and secure its permanency. The latter application would be very advantageous for the magic lantern.

The impressions may be obtained of various colours, such as blue, violet and red, according as the starch is more or less boiled; in the former case it inclines to red. A more or less deep bistre colour is obtained by exposing the impression to the vapour of ammonia; but it acquires its primitive colour when varnished after this operation; consequently an impression thus modified by ammonia cannot be varnished.

I shall now speak of the impressions which may be obtained upon different metals. Thus, by exposing an engraving to the vapour of iodine (for a few minutes only, so as to avoid impregnating the white parts), subsequently laying it (without wetting) upon a plate of silver and then placing it in a press, in five or six minutes we have a most faithful copy of the engraving; on subsequently exposing this plate to the vapour of mercury, we obtain an image resembling the Daguerreotype impressions.

Copper is operated upon as we have just stated for silver, and the plate is subsequently exposed to the action of the vapour of solution of ammonia, which is gently heated to produce a more copious disengagement; but care must be taken not to expose the plate of copper until the first vapours have escaped from the box, for this operation requires such an one as is used for mercury. The same plate is subsequently cleaned with water and a little tripoli. After this operation, the image is developed and appears black like the preceding; and moreover, the modification produced by the contact of ammonia extends to such a depth in the plate, that it is not obliterated until the metal itself is sensibly worn.

The latter process will facilitate the labour of tool-engraving.

The copying can also be effected on iron, lead, tin and brass; but I know no means of fixing the impressions.

I shall only enumerate here, from among the many and new experiments which I have made on iodine, those the results of which are certain. Thus, I oiled an engraving printed with printer's ink (*encre grasse*), and when dry, exposed it to the vapour of iodine. The impressions were analogous to the preceding, except that they were less distinct. I subsequently made some sketches upon a sheet of white paper (sized with starch) with black crayon, common ink (without gum) and lead; all were copied, and with still greater distinctness when traced on paper prepared for oil-painting. I afterwards took an oil-painting (unvarnished) and copied this also, with the exception of certain colours composed of substances which do not absorb the iodine. The same applies to coloured engravings.

This will be understood when I state, that an engraving exposed to the vapour of mercury or sulphur no longer takes the iodine; the same occurs when it is immersed in nitrate of mercury diluted with water, nitrate of silver, the sulphates of zinc, copper, &c.; oxide of copper, minium, ultramarine, cinnabar, orpiment, white lead, gelatine, albumen, and gum produce the same effects. However, drawings made with these substances may be copied, by subjecting them, with some modifications, to the preparation previously described. I may say that I have not found any drawings which could not be copied, except those made with the iodide of starch.

I shall now speak of a second property which I have discovered in iodine, and which is quite independent of the former; it is that of being attracted by designs in relief, and by all bodies which present ridges, of whatever colour or composition. Thus all embossed impressions on white paper are copied perfectly.

The edges of a strip of glass or marble produce also an impression. The same effects occur with other elastic fluids, gases or vapours, as the fumes of phosphorus exposed to the air, and the vapour of nitric acid. But iodine also exerts the property of which I spoke at the commencement, as I obtained the following results.

I joined a piece of white wood to a piece of ebony; after having glued them I planed them both, by which means I obtained a perfectly flat black and white block: this was next exposed to the vapour of iodine and then placed upon a plate of copper; the black portion only was copied. I made similar combinations with chalk and a black stone, white and black silk, and always obtained the same results.

All these phænomena are manifested both in the most perfect darkness as also *in vacuo*. I may repeat here, that if the objects are exposed for too long a time to the vapour of the iodine, the white portions ultimately become impregnated, but the black parts are always strikingly distinct upon the plate of metal.

On making the same experiments with chlorine and bromine, the same results were obtained with the former as with iodine; but the impression is so indistinct, that it is requisite to blow upon the metal to perceive it, or rather to expose the plate of copper to the vapour of ammonia, and the plate of silver to the vapour of mercury, to render it distinctly visible.

The results with bromine were unsuccessful; all my experiments were made with either plates of silver or copper. There is one experiment which I think worthy of mention, as being of theoretical interest; it is this: after having put a layer of starch-paste upon a Daguerreotype silver plate and upon one of copper, the impression of a drawing which I had thought to copy on the layer of starch became fixed upon the metal without leaving any sensible trace on the layer of starch. It was thus evident that the iodine had passed to the metal, in consequence of a superior affinity to that which it has for the starch.

## On Phosphorus.

I found that the product of the slow combustion of phosphorus exposed freely to the air possesses the same property as iodine, of being absorbed by the black parts of an engraving or any kind of drawing, whatever may be the chemical nature of the black substance.

Thus on exposing an engraving to the vapour of phosphorus burning slowly in the air, and subsequently laying it upon a plate of copper, placing it in a press for a few minutes and exposing it to the vapour of solution of ammonia, we obtain a perfectly distinct and thoroughly fixed impression. The impression is quite invisible when the drawing is separated from the plate of copper, and it is absolutely necessary to have recourse to the ammonia to render it visible; just as, if we require to take it upon a plate of silver, this must be exposed to the vapour of mercury. I drew some black and white lines with oil-paints upon picture-canvas; on exposing them to the same vapour, the black portions only were copied on the metallic plate; that is to say, the black parts being impregnated with the vapour, and having been placed in contact with the copper, the vaporized substance acted upon the metal, and the white bands which did not contain any of it left the copper untouched. When this plate was exposed to the vapour of ammonia, the image became very distinct. However long an engraving may be exposed to the vapour of phosphorus, the black parts alone become impregnated with it; but when it has remained a considerable time, the impression becomes slightly visible upon the plate, as if figures had been drawn upon it with a piece of phosphorus; and on exposing it to the vapour of ammonia, the impression appears as if in relief.

A plate of silver or copper exposed to the same vapour reproduces by contact all kinds of drawings, and yields a positive impression. It must be understood, that to render the impressions visible they must be exposed to mercury or ammonia.

The vapour of the yellow sulphuret of arsenic (orpiment) heated in the air imparts to an engraving, when exposed to it for about five minutes, the property of impressing its own image upon a plate of copper or polished silver, upon which it is pressed without any other preparation. This operation is very readily effected, and will therefore be very useful to the tool-engraver.

### On Nitric Acid.

With nitric acid I obtained the following results. On exposing an engraving (whatever may be the composition of the black parts) to the vapour which is evolved by pure nitric acid, afterwards laying it upon a plate of silver or copper, and leaving it there for some minutes, we obtain a distinctly visible negative impression. The white parts are coated with a white mist, the black are the pure copper.

An oiled engraving, and figures drawn with charcoal or black crayon upon white paper, yielded the same results. I subsequently exposed a block made of white wood and ebony, and found that the white band alone was copied.

If an engraving is left exposed to the vapour of this acid for a long time, the black parts are ultimately impregnated like the white; and the plate of metal upon which the engraving has been applied is then covered with a uniform layer, which presents no further trace of the drawing.

An engraving will only serve to make one or at the most two impressions; after this it must be left exposed to the air for twenty-four hours before it can be again used, and frequently it ceases to reproduce its image. We thus see that the action is not characterized in the same manner as in the case of iodine and phosphorus. This vapour is deposited equally upon the parts in relief and upon the depressions: thus an oil-painting and embossed impressions or stamps without ink are easily copied by this means. The same effects occur with dry chloride of lime, but it requires to be gently heated before exposing the engraving to the vapour which is evolved from this substance, and which gives a negative impression, like nitric acid.

### Appendix to the preceding Memoirs*.

On exposing the black and white feathers of birds (as those from the wings of a magpie or the tail of the lapwing) to the vapour of iodine, the black differed sensibly from the white; and with the same feather I have made eight or ten impressions upon copper, all of which presented a well-marked line of demarcation between the black and the white parts. I afterwards immersed an engraving in tincture of iodine, and after having produced several successive impressions upon starched

* Communicated to the Academy, October 25, 1847.

paper, I ultimately obtained a positive and perfectly distinct impression, just as if I had used the vapour of iodine: the same occurs if the engraving be immersed in an aqueous solution of iodine.

I must not omit to mention, that in copying an engraving all the black or coloured points which almost always exist in the substance of the paper are copied in the same manner as the lines of the engraving; in such cases they must be removed by touching them with ammonia, or some other means.

Before leaving the positive impressions to pass to the negative, I may state that I obtained the same results with iron pyrites as with the sulphuret of arsenic; the latter is however preferable on account of the facility of execution of the process, and because it leaves no mark upon the engraving. These impressions resist the action of nitric acid.

I have also obtained a positive impression with the bichloride of mercury. If the design on the copper be exposed to the vapour of ammonia, it appears much more distinct, and is well-fixed.

I shall now allude to the negative impressions which are obtained by means of substances possessing the power of being deposited upon the white parts of an engraving in preference to the black, as nitric acid. The new results obtained were as follows:—I immersed printed characters in pure nitric acid (taking care to withdraw them immediately); I laid them upon a plate of copper, and on removing them after a certain time, found the characters in relief resembling a page of type.

If an engraving is immersed in water acidulated with nitric acid, and allowed to dry until but little moisture is left, and is subsequently laid upon a metallic plate, we almost always obtain a very evident negative impression; and when this is not the case, simply blowing upon the plate is sufficient to make it visible. A black and white feather treated in the same way, also yielded an impression in which the white part only was copied; a result the reverse of that obtained by impressing upon the metal a feather after exposure to the vapour of iodine. Hydrochloric acid produces almost the same effect as nitric acid; but the latter is much preferable.

I have already stated that chloride of lime (hypochlorite of lime) produces a negative impression when an engraving is exposed to the vapour evolved from it, an opposite result to that obtained with chlorine. The impression is also negative if we plunge an engraving into solution of chloride of lime, whilst it is positive when immersed in pure chlorine. When an engraving is placed in contact with chloride of lime dissolved in water or the vapour which it exhales by its heat, on subsequently laying it upon blue litmus paper, the white parts of the engraving are copied in white; whilst if the engraving is placed in contact with solution of chlorine or the vapour which it exhales, the black parts are copied in red. But to obtain these results, especially with chloride of lime, the temperature must be raised to about 104° F. The same effects are produced upon silver and copper.

## On Photography upon Glass.

Although this essay is merely preliminary, I publish it in its present state, not doubting that it will make rapid progress in more practised hands than mine, and by those who will be enabled to experiment under better circumstances than I have been enabled to do.

I shall point out the means which I have employed, and which have yielded satisfactory although not perfect results: as everything depends upon the preparation of the plate, I shall describe the best method of preparing the starch.

I take five grammes of starch, which are mixed first with five grammes of water and afterwards diluted with ninety-five grammes, and lastly thirty-five centigrammes of iodide of potassium dissolved in five grammes of water. The whole is placed upon the fire: when the starch is dissolved, it is allowed to cool, next strained through linen, and then allowed to flow upon the plates of glass, taking care to cover the entire surface as equally as possible. After wiping them beneath, I place them upon a perfectly horizontal plane, so as to dry them as quickly as possible in the sun or by means of a stove, in order to obtain a layer which is not fissured; that is to say, to prevent the glass from being covered with circles in which the coating is thinner than elsewhere (which are produced, in my opinion, by the iodide of potassium). The starch should always be prepared in a porcelain vessel, and the quantity, five grammes, which has been mentioned, is sufficient to coat ten plates, of the size known in commerce by the name *d'un quart*[*]. It is thus seen that a large number of plates are easily prepared at once. Moreover, bubbles of air must be excluded, as these would make so many small holes in the impressions. The plate being thus prepared, when we wish to proceed, it is merely requisite to apply the *aceto-nitrate* to it, by means of a piece of paper plunged several times into this compound; a second piece of paper moistened with distilled water is subsequently laid upon the plate. A second method consists in previously impregnating the layer of starch with distilled water, before laying on the aceto-nitrate; in the latter case the image is much

[*] Of about 4½ inches by 3½.

blacker, but the exposure to the light should be continued a little longer than in the method first indicated. The plate is afterwards placed in the camera obscura, and retained there perhaps a little longer than when paper prepared by Blanquart's process is used*. However, I have obtained very black impressions in twenty or twenty-five seconds in the sun, and in a minute in the shade†.

The operation is then conducted as for the process on paper, *i. e.* gallic acid is used to bring out the impression and bromide of potassium to fix it.

This is the first process which I used; but having tried albumen (white of egg), I obtained a remarkable superiority in every respect, and I believe the preference must be given to the latter substance. The plates were prepared as follows:— I took the most transparent part of the white of egg‡ (the liquid portion), in which I placed some iodide of potassium; then, having allowed it to flow upon the plates, I left it to dry at the ordinary temperature (if this was too high, the layer of albumen cracked). When about to use it, the aceto-nitrate is applied by pouring it upon the plate, so as to cover the entire surface at once; but it is better to plunge it into this composition so as to obtain a perfectly uniform layer. The aceto-nitrate renders the albumen insoluble in water, and makes it strongly adherent to the glass. With albumen, rather longer exposure to the light is required than when starch is used. The action of the gallic acid is also slower; but by way of compensation, we obtain remarkable distinctness and delicacy of the lines, and which, in my opinion, will some day be brought to the perfection of an image upon a plate of silver.

I tried gelatinous matters: they also yield very distinct impressions (especially if filtered, which is essentially requisite for all substances), but they are too readily dissolved by water. If starch is employed, the finest should be chosen; my experiments were made with that manufactured by Groult.

By employing the means which have just been pointed out, negative impressions are obtained. I have not made any positive impressions; but I presume that they can be obtained as on paper, or by placing the substances in starch, and not in albumen, which it is not even necessary to immerse in the solution of common salt. With the latter substance, the plate must be plunged into the silver-bath.

* Mr. Blanquart's process is no other than the Calotype invented by Mr. H. F. Talbot.—EDIT.
† By slightly heating the plate, less time is required.
‡ The fresher the white is, the more viscid it is.

If the use of paper should continue to be preferred, I would advise the coating of it with one or two layers of starch or albumen, and then we should have the same distinctness of the impression as in the proofs made with iodine; but I believe that, with regard to photography, paper will never be equal to a hard and polished body covered with a sensitive layer. I may add that very beautiful positive impressions may be made upon opaline glass.

May we not hope by this method to take impressions from lithographic stones, even if the copied impression had to be drawn in chalk, if it cannot be done with any other kind of inking? I have obtained very beautiful impressions upon a *schist* (hone-stone) coated with a layer of albumen. By this means, engravers upon copper and wood will be able to obtain impressions, which it will be very easy for them to work upon.

XXXII. *Question of Priority respecting the Discovery of the accelerating process in the Daguerreotype operation.* By A. CLAUDET, *Esq.*

*To the Editors of the Philosophical Magazine and Journal.*

GENTLEMEN,

I HAVE lately heard that Mr. Goddard knew as far back as the year 1840 that bromide of iodine was more sensitive to light than iodine alone in the Daguerreotype process; and that a short letter merely mentioning the fact written by him was inserted at the time in the Literary Gazette, 12th Dec., 1840.

Having myself until now had all the honour of the discovery of the accelerating properties of chlorine and bromine combined with iodine, I am happy to be the first to bring Mr. Goddard's claim before the public, who will have to bestow on him the share of merit for what he has done prior to my communication to the Royal Society, which was read at the meeting of the 10th of June 1841. I have acted openly. After having made my communication to the Royal Society, I made the same to the Académie des Sciences the 22nd of the same month, and my discoveries have been mentioned in all the treatises on photography; and until now, neither Mr. Goddard nor any other person has yet contested publicly that I was the first inventor of the accelerating process in the Daguerreotype operation.

It is strange that Mr. Goddard's letter should have been unknown and unnoticed by all writers on photography either English or foreign. If Mr. Goddard had found the means to avail himself with certainty of the properties of bromide of iodine, if he did not wish to make a secret of it, he should have written at the time a full and explicit paper on the subject, and published it through the medium of some scientific society or journal. In question of priority, it is not enough to have stated that we have made the discovery of a new agent; we must prove it by enabling others to test it and to apply its properties.

It must be observed that bromide of iodine is a compound very little known in chemistry, that its real proportions have not yet been accurately established, that it is excessively difficult to form the mixture of the two elements in the proper relation to each other, which gives the increase of sensitiveness to the Daguerreotype plate, and that excess of one of the two elements destroys that sensitiveness. Mr. Goddard should have stated these proportions, and the mode of applying the coating on the plate. Bromide of iodine alone is not sufficient in the preparation of the Daguerreotype plate; its vapours must be applied when the plate has already been coated with pure iodine. This was an important feature in my discovery, which rendered it at once most valuable to photographers.

Nevertheless the name of Mr. Goddard should be honourably mentioned in the history of the progress of photography; not only for the discovery to which I have just alluded, but also for having been one of the first in England who investigated with zeal, enthusiasm, and scientific abilities, all the phænomena connected with this admirable invention.

I have the honour to be, Gentlemen,
Your most obedient Servant,
London, Feb. 23, 1848.    A. CLAUDET.

## XXXIII. *Notices respecting New Books.*

*A Description of Active and Extinct Volcanos, of Earthquakes, and of Thermal Springs, with remarks on the causes of these phænomena, the character of their respective products, and their influence on the past and present condition of the Globe.* By C. DAUBENY, M.D., F.R.S. Second Edition, greatly enlarged. London: Simpkin, Marshall and Co.

THERE is no department of terrestrial physics (we speak not of astronomy) which gives us a more exalted view of the grandeur of Nature's operations, than the phænomena of volcanos. The endless diversities of organic life, past and present, the marvels of chemistry, of optics, of crystallography, of acoustics, of electricity, and the other sensible properties of matter, captivate the observer by their beauty rather than by their sublimity. But in the volcano and its concomitants, the eruption, the lava-stream, the earthquake, the thermal spring, we are allowed a glimpse into the very workshop of Nature;

we behold Creative Power evolving and modifying the raw material, which is afterwards to be invested with form and life, and the sense of awe predominates over our admiration. Volcanic geology also differs from all other branches of natural history, in not being limited to the bounds of our terrestrial prison. We know nothing, and we never can know anything in this life, of the zoology, or the botany, or the mineralogy of other celestial bodies; but the forms and configurations of our own satellite, and in some degree of the planets also, enable us to study volcanic geology in other spheres, and thus to add to the proofs, which gravitation supplies, of the uniformity of Nature's laws.

The occurrence in almost every region of the earth's surface of volcanic products, ancient or modern, and their general uniformity of character, prove how essentially they are connected with the internal structure of the globe; while the minor variations in their phænomena afford an endless source of interest to the geologist, the physical geographer, the mineralogist and the chemist. Innumerable observations of volcanic phænomena have been made in recent times, and are widely scattered over the field of literature; but some *resumé* of the whole subject was required to generalize these erratic facts, to condense their substance, and to guide the more ardent student to the original sources of knowledge. Such an object is incidentally aimed at in most modern treatises on geology; but Dr. Daubeny was, we believe, the first, in this country at least, to devote an especial work to the whole subject of volcanos. His treatise, published more than twenty years ago, has been long and deservedly esteemed; but from the lapse of time, had fallen much in arrear of the present state of science. The work now before us, which he modestly terms a second edition, is so greatly extended, both in the amount of its information and in the maturity of its reasonings, that it might well have been designated by an original title.

The first and largest portion of the work contains an admirable summary of the *facts* of volcanic geology, arranged according to the regions of the earth's surface where they occur. The wonderfully extensive diffusion of volcanic phænomena, and the diversities which they exhibit in each district, render any other than a geographical arrangement of them almost impracticable. The many personal examinations which Dr. Daubeny has made of volcanic regions, and the length of time that his attention has been given to the subject, have enabled him to render the descriptive portion of his work very complete; and the many reflected lights which he has thrown upon it from historians and classic poets, make it interesting to other classes of readers besides geologists. The chapters upon the volcanos of France, Italy, Greece, Asia Minor, and Syria, are particularly instructive in this respect. The many authentic accounts of the activity of volcanic foci in historic times, now slumbering for awhile, now bursting forth in some unexpected locality, prove the vast extent of the fiery lake on which the lovely lands and seas of Southern Europe tranquilly float.

In his chapter on Syria, Dr. Daubeny shows the great probability that the destruction of the plain of Siddim was effected by a volcanic eruption, which caused a subsidence of the valley of the Jordan, and buried the guilty cities with its ashes. This is a most interesting question, and one which theologians and geologists should unite to solve; but strange to say, the materials for its solution are still very incomplete. Will not one of the many travellers, who annually flock to the Holy Land in quest of excitement, make an *accurate* levelling from the Mediterranean to the Dead Sea, give us a good orographical and geological map of the region round it, or tell us how far the *submarine* depression extends up the valley of the Jordan, and whether this depressed area is wholly due to subsidence, or has been subsequently extended by aqueous *denudation?*

We cannot attempt to follow Dr. Daubeny through the mass of curious details and philosophic generalizations which he has collected on the volcanos of all countries. We will therefore proceed to the second part of the work, which speaks of earthquakes and thermal springs, as incidental phænomena supposed to be connected with volcanos.

In treating of the unquestionable connexion which often subsists between earthquakes and volcanic operations, Dr. Daubeny seems too much disposed, we think, to consider this connexion as universal. Geologists are apt to forget, what would otherwise be a truism, that an earthquake is merely a quaking of the earth; they seem to infer from the terrific accompaniments of these events, that the earthquake itself is a *vera causa*, and speak, for instance, of the upheaval of land being due to an earthquake, when in fact the earthquake is due to the upheaval of the land. Now an earthquake ought to be simply defined "a vibratory movement of part of the earth's surface;" and in ascending towards its cause, we may attribute it *immediately* to a sudden snapping asunder or rubbing together of two adjacent rocky masses in the focus whence the vibration proceeds. This act of disruption or of friction is the result of internal movements in the body of the earth, and these movements are probably due to a plurality of causes. Volcanic explosions no doubt form one of these causes; but we will not venture to say that they form the chief, far less the only source of these hypogene concussions. Giving volcanic eruptions full credit for the sudden upheavals of land which they have occasioned, we cannot go the length of attributing to their mechanical action the slow and gradual elevations and depressions which unquestionably take place.

These chronic changes of level are much more easily explained by the contraction or expansion caused by a subterranean change of temperature. And this may be due either to a cosmical change in the temperature of the space through which the solar system moves, or to a slow cooling of the earth's interior from radiation, or to superficial changes, such as the increase or diminution of ice, or of forests, or of hot or cold marine currents, or to the convection of caloric by thermal springs. It is also, no doubt, often due (as in the Puzzuoli case) to changes of temperature connected with volcanic agency; but this is a very different operation from the mechanical thrusts caused by igneous eruptions. Elevation by thermal expansion is only due to volcanos, in the same sense that the rise of the mercury in a thermometer, when placed on a hot lava-stream, is due to them.

Another probable cause of earthquakes is the *settling* of parts of the earth's crust from the long-continued action of gravitation. As in a house with a bad foundation, the walls continue to settle and to crack, long after the building has been finished, which crackings often startle the inmates by their sudden vibration and noise, so we may suppose that certain parts of the earth's surface may have a *bad foundation*, either from cavities caused by diminution of temperature, or by the elevation of land in neighbouring districts, or from the yielding or compressible nature of the substratum. In such a case the surface-beds will slowly and imperceptibly subside, till from the increasing pressure they suddenly give way at some weak point, and this fracture causes an earthquake. Such a process of *settling* is no doubt one of the causes of those *faults* which are so common in all rocks, even when far removed from volcanic agencies.

[We will resume next month the consideration of some other points contained in this important and valuable work.]

## XXXIV. *Proceedings of Learned Societies.*

### ROYAL SOCIETY.

[Continued from p. 141.]

*Anniversary Meeting*, November 30, 1847.

THE Marquis of Northampton in the Chair.

The President delivered his Address to the Meeting, of which the following are extracts:—

GENTLEMEN,

Since our last Anniversary, your Council have been much occupied with anxious deliberation on many subjects of great importance to our Society: among these, the one that chiefly interests science is perhaps the question, how we may most completely secure the proofs of priority in the communication of scientific discovery. For this purpose we have framed rules which I hope may be found sufficient for the attainment of our object.

During the last year, an important alteration has been made in our Statutes with reference to the election of new Fellows, as you must be well aware. This change was made with the approbation of a large majority of your Council. As I was one of those who entertained considerable doubts of its prudence and expediency, I cannot claim any praise if it prove advantageous to the Society, nor must I be considered responsible in case of its failure. Having been adopted, however, it appears to me that it ought not hastily to be either rescinded or modified; that it ought to have a fair trial, for the experience of many years can alone decide whether it be injurious or beneficial.

Many of you, Gentlemen, must be aware that a much more stringent regulation was at one time in contemplation, which would have affected your privileges. Had not that proposition been abandoned, I should have felt it my duty to urge strongly on the Council the propriety of bringing the whole question before the Society at large, and I have little doubt that that course would have been readily adopted. As, however, the limitation of the number fifteen applies alone to the number to be recommended by the Council, leaving to you the power to elect more candidates, should you think fit to do so, there seemed to me to be no necessity for calling you together in a Special General Meeting.

Having stated to you my doubts as to the expediency of the limitation of the number of Candidates recommended by the Council, it is right to add that those doubts do not at all extend to the change in the manner of our election. I am convinced that considerable advantage must accrue from its being attended with greater solemnity, and from the participation of a larger number of our Fellows in its exercise. This change has also the further recommendation, that the reading of our papers will not be perpetually interrupted by the circulation of the ballot-box.

I now come to the most grateful part of my address—that of the presentation of the Royal and Copley Medals. The two subjects proposed for the former this year were the sciences of Chemistry and Mathematics. As in the latter there was no paper coming within the Royal regulations to which we could properly give the medal, we were obliged by the same regulations to turn to the subjects of Physics and Geology. We have, in consequence, awarded the Medal in Physics to Mr. Grove, for the paper which constituted the subject of the Bakerian Lecture; and to Mr. Fownes, for papers which, as Mr. Grove's, appear in the Philosophical Transactions.

The Copley Medal was presented to Sir John Herschel for his long, and arduous, and valuable labours in the service of astronomy at a very distant part of our globe.

Among the deceased Members are the following:—

Hugh, Third Duke of Northumberland.
Nicholas Carlisle.
William Dealtry, D.D.
The Right Hon. Sir Edward Hyde East.

Mr. Macvey Napier was born in the year 1777, and descended from an ancient family in the West of Scotland. After successful studies in the two Universities of Glasgow and Edinburgh, he became a member of the Society of Writers to the Signet. His talents would probably have led him to great success in the legal profession, had not his taste for literary and philosophical pursuits led him to other avocations. He was, however, the object of so much respect and regard, that he was at an early age elected by the Society to the honourable office of their librarian; an office for which he seems to have been admirably qualified. At a later period, they selected him from many able competitors to deliver lectures on Conveyancing. The University of Edinburgh subsequently evinced their sense of the merits of these lectures by converting the lectureship into a professorship, with a handsome endowment, and permitting Mr. Napier to become the professor without ceasing to be librarian.

In the year 1814, Mr. Napier edited the Supplement to the Encyclopædia Britannica, and at a later period, he superintended a new edition of the same important work, and by so doing conferred a great benefit on the science of his country and of the world.

In the year 1830, Mr. Napier was appointed to the situation of principal Clerk of Session, and resigned that of librarian to the Writers to the Signet, having the year before succeeded Mr. Jeffery as the editor of one of the most influential of those quarterly journals whose publication is of the greatest importance to the literary and scientific interests of the country. He had been a contributor to the Edinburgh Review previously, and was therefore the better able to manage it with success. A memoir that has been published on his life, evidently written by one well-acquainted with his merits, remarks, "He was in all respects perfectly trustworthy: all secrets confided to him were sacred; and the most distinguished of his contributors were farther ready to admit the value of his suggestions and the justice of his criticisms."

He continued to attend to the duties of his class at the University very nearly to the time of his death.

He married young, and left a large family at his death, which happened in the 71st year of his age.

During the latter years of his life his health had been declining; but his intellectual powers were unimpaired to the last. By those with whom he was intimate even a higher estimate of his talents is entertained than what is felt by those who merely look to the important share that he took in literature and science as the editor of the Encyclopædia Britannica and the Edinburgh Review. So at least says the author of the memoir alluded to already. This seems difficult; but they alone can judge of the merits of his confidential correspondence and his part in domestic society: it is perhaps more important to say, that he was "a pious, an intelligent and an honest friend." He became a Fellow of the Royal Society in the year 1817.

The Rev. JOHN HAILSTONE was born on the 13th of December, 1759, and received his early education at Beverley School in Yorkshire. From thence he went to Cambridge, where he pursued his mathematical studies with so much success that he took the high degree of Second Wrangler at the examination in the year 1782. The same course of study was followed by him in after-life.

In the year 1784, he became a Fellow of Trinity College, and in 1788, he was appointed to the office of Woodwardian Professor of Mineralogy. After holding this Professorship for the long period of thirty years, he married and retired to the vicarage of Trumpington, near the University; a village interesting to the lover of literature as having been the residence of Anstey, the author of the Bath Guide, and at a subsequent period, of Mr. Hailstone's brother professor, the celebrated traveller, Edward Daniel Clark.

Here Mr. Hailstone died on the 9th of last June, at the very advanced age of 87, retaining his faculties till the last. After his election to the Woodwardian Professorship he went to Germany to profit by the lectures of Werner. To Mr. Hailstone the University is indebted for additions to her collection of minerals and fossils. He published a syllabus of Lectures, but did not succeed in bringing together a class, as he received little or no encouragement from the heads of the University. He published little: one paper in the Geological Transactions, and a few short notices in the Transactions of the Cambridge Philosophical Society. In politics he was a whig. He was a friend to education, as he showed by the endowment of a day-school, and the expenditure of several hundred pounds in improving a parish school.

The Rev. WILLIAM PEARSON, LL.D.

Professor MACCULLAGH was born in the year 1809. The place of his birth was the townland of Loughlindhuhussey, then possessed by his grandfather, a man of considerable acquirements, and a scholar of some pretensions. This place is in the parish of Upper Badoney, in the county of Tyrone, about ten miles from Strabane.

Shortly after his birth, his father removed from the mountain farm he occupied to Strabane, principally that he might have the means of educating his son, it not being possible to do so in the secluded glen in which he lived. In Strabane he was, while very young, placed at the only respectable school at that time in the town. Here his genius soon displayed itself. After school hours he was almost constantly employed in solving mathematical problems; yet, it is remembered that when Euclid was first put into his hands he was dissatisfied with the task. He was only required to get the solution of a problem by heart, like a copy of verses, and repeat it. There was no attempt made at explanation. This did not suit the character of his mind, which even then could not rest until it thoroughly understood the nature of everything that came before it. For some days he was restless, unhappy and puzzled, wandering about with his Euclid in his hand. In his perplexity he met a neighbour, a working carpenter, a man of cleverness and talent, who, seeing the boy evidently unhappy, was good enough to ask him what was the matter. He immediately told his good-natured friend that he was obliged to get by heart a set of strange words, the meaning of which he wanted to understand; at the same time showing him the proposition he was committing to memory for the next day's task. The carpenter instantly sat down with the puzzled boy, and in a short time showed him what a proof was. This was the way in which Professor MacCullagh first learned to prove a proposition in Euclid. He was afterwards, when commencing his classical studies, sent to Lifford to the school of the Rev. John Graham, and subsequently to that of the Rev. Thomas Rollestone. He entered Trinity College, Dublin, as a pensioner in November 1824, being then in the fifteenth year of his age. In the following year, he became a candidate for Sizarship, and was successful. Throughout his under-graduate course he carried away every Honour both in Science and Classics.

In 1827, he obtained a Scholarship, and in 1832, (the year when his Scholarship expired) he was elected a Fellow. In 1835, he became Professor of Mathematics, Dr. Sadleir (the present Provost) having resigned expressly to make way for him. In 1843, he was chosen to fill the Chair of Natural Philosophy, in the room of the present Dr. Lloyd, who, by becoming a Senior Fellow, was incapacitated from continuing to hold it. In 1830, his first paper on Refracted Light was read in the Royal Irish Academy, and shortly after he became a Member of it, and contributed largely to place it in that position which it now holds among the learned Societies of the world. In 1838, he obtained the Conyngham Gold Medal from the Academy for his paper " On the Laws of Crystalline Reflexion and Refraction," which was presented to him, with an Address (since printed in the Proceedings) respecting the then existing state of science in that department, by Sir Wm. Rowan Hamilton, who was at that time President of the Academy. In 1839, Professor MacCullagh may be regarded as having laid the foundation of the highly valuable Museum of Irish Antiquities, now in Dublin, by presenting to the Royal Irish Academy the celebrated Cross of Cong. In presenting the Cross to the Academy, Professor MacCullagh stated, that his motive for doing so was, by putting it in the possession of a public body, to save it from that shameful process of destruction to which everything venerable in Ireland had been exposed for centuries, and to contribute at the same time to the formation of a national collection, the want of which, he had been told, was regarded by Sir Walter Scott as a disgrace to a country so abounding in valuable remains. He afterwards assisted in enlarging the Museum, which he had thus (it may be said) commenced, by munificent subscriptions. His contributions to the Academy were not confined to scientific subjects; they embraced matters of general literature, especially some connected with ancient Egyptian chronology. In 1842, he was awarded the Copley Medal for his investigations on the Theory of Light. Among the competitors were Bessel, Dumas, and Murchison. On this occasion he was much indebted to Dr. Lloyd's excellent report.

In the following year, he was elected a Fellow of the Royal Society, but was not a contributor to its Transactions. The reason frequently assigned by him for this was, that he felt bound to do as much as in him lay to raise and elevate the literary and scientific institutions of the country of his birth. This with him was ever a paramount object; and in connexion with that object, in the summer of the present year, he resolved, at great inconvenience to himself, to make an effort to free the University with which he was so closely connected from what he considered a disgrace, namely, its being represented in Parliament by men not educated within its walls. He was influenced, too, by what he considered a public want, that the interests of science and literature should be represented in the Imperial Parliament.

He was not successful; but his personal bearing throughout the contest was such as to secure to him the admiration and the good-will of all opponents as well as friends. This remarkable contest was, as might be expected, commenced and carried on by Professor Mac-Cullagh, without his ever accepting that pecuniary assistance which was frequently and warmly offered by others, but by him was gratefully declined.

About the middle of September, he commenced working at a subject which he was anxious to free his mind from as soon as possible. The heading of the paper remains: it is, "A Theory of Total Reflexion of Light. By James MacCullagh, Fellow of Trinity College, Dublin. Read May 24th, 1841."

Confinement and over-work gradually produced disease, mental as well as bodily; and after a few days' illness, an end was put to his career on the night of the 24th of October, in the 38th year of his age.

As it is understood that there will be given at the stated Meeting of the Royal Irish Academy, in March next, a more lengthened memoir of Professor MacCullagh's life than could conveniently be offered to the Royal Society now, I have contented myself with the few facts and dates which have been thus rapidly stated; and as I am led to believe that there will be given to the public on the same occasion an accurate and detailed account of his scientific labours and discoveries, which it has been found difficult (through want of time) to put together in a satisfactory manner for our Meeting this night, I will merely glance at some of the things done by him since this Society awarded to him the Medal already mentioned, being the highest honour in their power to bestow. My information is derived chiefly from gentlemen who have attended to and profited by his official teaching in the University of Dublin, and who, having since attained distinction and station in that University, speak now with a natural enthusiasm of their lost preceptor and friend.

Since Professor MacCullagh obtained the Copley Medal, in addition to the different papers which he published in the Proceedings and in the Transactions of the Royal Irish Academy, he has given seven courses of lectures in different branches of Natural Philosophy, in his capacity of professor of that subject, having for about eight years previously filled the Chair of Mathematics in a manner which those alone can fully appreciate who know what was the state of mathematical knowledge in the Dublin University previous to his election and what it is now, and who can compare the state in which he found it with that in which he left it. I allude to these Lectures, because it was in the delivery of them, that is, in the conscientious and due performance of the proper duties of his calling, that Professor MacCullagh is reported to have ever appeared to the greatest advantage. It was there that he used to display the extensive information, the elaborate research, and the vast acquired treasures of his highly cultivated mind; and it was there that he most delighted to turn to account the noble faculty of inventive genius with which he was so eminently gifted, in improving, by means of it, every subject he ever handled. There is no one capable of appreciating such subjects, and who enjoyed the privilege of attending the courses above referred to, but will admit, that during the several years of his purely mathematical lectures, nothing could exceed the depth or surpass the exquisite taste and elegance of all his original conceptions, both in analysis and geometry. Nor will it be denied by any who were so happy as to possess the opportunity of judging, that during the last three years and a half in which he filled the Chair of Natural Philosophy, his earnest endeavour was ever to instil sound and accurate physical conceptions into the minds of his hearers, and to array them, when stated in mathematical language, in all the charms which arises from true taste and appropriate refinement.

In his first course of Lectures—on the rotation of a solid body round a fixed point—he completely solved the case of a body abandoned to its own motions on receiving a primitive impulse in any direction, and under the action of no external accelerating forces. This problem he had finished several years before, and was preparing it for publication, when he found that he had been just anticipated, in many though not in all respects, by Poinsot, who published about that time a very elegant little tract on the subject. During the same course of Lectures he gave some interesting and original theorems respecting the rotation of surfaces of revolution moving freely in space, and acted on by any external accelerating forces, directed to any number of fixed centres.

In his course of Lectures on attractions, he gave some very beautiful theorems respecting the attraction of a body of any nature and form on a point distant a long way in comparison of its own dimensions. And he gave some most simple and elegant geometrical methods for finding the attraction of an homogeneous ellipsoid on any internal point. The subject of attractions seems indeed to have been a favourite one with him; and he on several previous occasions gave new and beautiful theorems in it, and in many important respects improved the existing theories, keeping always in advance of the knowledge of the time. He delivered also courses of Lectures on part of Sir Isaac Newton's Principia, and on Heat, Electricity and Magnetism.

I now come to Professor MacCullagh's great course of Lectures on "The Dynamical Theory of Light," which was on his part (whatever other researches on that subject may have been elsewhere made) the unaided creation of his own genius; and was founded on one single and simple hypothesis, on which as a basis (to borrow the language of Dr. Lloyd when speaking of Fresnel's beautiful theory of double refraction), he " has reared the noblest fabric which has ever adorned the domain of physical science, Newton's system of the Universe alone excepted." If we now venture to say that Professor MacCullagh ranks as a philosopher higher than Fresnel in the region of Light (and if that be admitted, he will certainly rank inferior to none on that subject), it is not thereby designed to institute any comparison between labours so different in their nature as those of these two great men. Professor MacCullagh may be regarded as standing to Fresnel in the same relation as Newton to Kepler. Fresnel undoubtedly discovered all the elegant laws of the propagation and double refraction of light in crystallized media, as well as in ordinary, with some of those of total reflexion at the bounding surfaces of ordinary media, but he did not account for them on any correct mechanical principles; with respect to propagation, the very first principles from which he sets out are such as cannot now be admitted: with respect to ordinary reflexion, he partly accounted for them on correct principles, in the particular case of ordinary media, which was the only one for which he had ever given them. Professor MacCullagh, on the contrary, not only deduced the known laws in all the three cases from mechanical principles of a nature so simple and probable, that they cannot but bear conviction of their truth to any mind reflecting on them, with anything like the attention they deserve, but he also gave the general equations of the propagation of light not only for all known media, but also for all media which could ever be discovered or even conceived. And with these he gave also the general conditions which must be fulfilled at the common bounding surface of every two, not only known, but conceivable media, and which in every case give all the laws of reflexion and of refraction, whether ordinary or total.

Thus did he deliver to his hearers and to posterity a perfect and complete mechanical theory; that is to say, analytically complete: so that any one who in future may attempt to discover in this region of science, can only do so by treading in his steps, and adopting his principles, but can never supersede them. In fact, he has discovered and handed down the general principles which must hold in all cases. It remains for future investigators only to apply them. He himself applied them to the two most general cases of propagation, viz. of polarized waves of undiminishing intensity in a crystalline medium, and of that peculiar species of propagated vibrations which take place in the rarer medium in every case of total reflexion at the surface either of an ordinary or of a crystalline medium. In the former case he arrived at all the laws of propagation in crystalline media which were discovered by Fresnel, with one single variation, and that the very one on which he himself had long previously corrected Fresnel, viz. the vibrations of the æther, in place of coming out to be perpendicular to the plane of polarization, as Fresnel had supposed, came out on the contrary to be parallel to that plane, as MacCullagh himself had supposed.

He was enabled by discoveries of his own, to deduce again in a far easier manner, all the beautiful geometrical laws of crystalline reflexion and refraction, which he had formerly laid before the Royal Irish Academy in 1837, and for which that body awarded him the honorary distinction of the Conyngham Medal, which I have before alluded to. And they fully confirmed the acute prophecy then made by his sagacious mind, on finding to his astonishment, that a law of reflexion depended for its existence on the existence of a law of propagation; when he said that the law of vis viva which he had assumed at the outset could not be a fundamental but rather a secondary law, and remarked that perhaps the next step in physical optics would be the deduction, as parts of one system, of all the laws both of propagation and reflexion from some higher and more general law, containing them both as particular cases: anticipations which were singled out for special attention, in the Address delivered by Sir W. Rowan Hamilton, on the occasion already referred to. How little perhaps did Professor MacCullagh then know that both of his own prophecies were destined to be so soon fulfilled, and both by the powers of his own mighty and creative mind!

In the general case of total reflexion at the surface of a crystal, he afterwards showed, by a most ingenious employment of imaginary quantities, that the refraction was still double, and never more than double; and he showed that the directions of the refracted rays remained always the same, whatever were the incidence, provided it gave total reflexion. Again, as he had done for the case of ordinary reflexion by means of his beautiful theorem of the polar plane, so in the case of total reflexion he determined the two directions of polarization, in a given incident plane polarized wave, which would give uniradial refracted rays, by means not of a polar plane, but of a polar cylinder, which he succeeded in showing was the analogous surface in the more difficult cases.

In the particular case of total reflexion at the surface of an ordinary medium, the whole theory of total reflexion became exceedingly simple, and that case is left by him completed. He showed that whatever were the incidence, the refracted wave was always perpendicular to the intersection of the plane of incidence, and of the surface of the crystal; he showed that the axes of the ellipse of vibration, projected on the plane of incidence, were parallel and perpendicular to that line; he gave a beautiful construction, by means of an equilateral hyperbola touching with its vertex the section of the index sphere at the point where it intersects the same right line, for determining the velocity of the refracted wave, and the ratio of the axes of its elliptic vibrations corresponding to any given incidence; he determined at once the limiting angle of total reflexion: and, finally, he got out the two empirical formulæ of Fresnel, for the acceleration of the refracted phase over the incident, and the subsequent equal acceleration of the reflected phase over the refracted; the one for the case of the incident light polarized in the plane of incidence, and the other for the same polarized in the perpendicular plane. For all cases, whether of propagation or of reflexion, ordinary or total, the whole theory, as he has left it, is analytically complete: but the geometrical interpretations in the general case of total reflexion at the surface of a crystal present very great difficulties. Many of these his acute intellect had with great labour surmounted; he had been working hard at the subject for the last four weeks of his life, and with so much success, that he had actually commenced a new paper for the Irish Transactions, embodying the results of his latest investigations. The heading of this paper, which I have already mentioned, remains in his own handwriting. It is believed that several of his manuscripts on other subjects are in the possession of his family, although it was not his custom to preserve many written papers.

ALEXANDER BRONGNIART, the son of a distinguished architect, was born at Paris in the year 1770. In early youth he derived his love of science, not only from his father, but also from his father's friends, Franklin, Lavoisier, and other eminent men of the day. He received his earliest lessons in science at the École des Mines, and afterwards at the École de Médecine. At the age of twenty, he came to England, and visited the mines of Derbyshire. On his return to his own country, he published a memoir on enamelling, which induced M. Berthollet, several years later, to recommend his appointment to the office of Director of the manufactory of Sèvres. At the time of the French Revolution, he had the misfortune to be suspected of the offence of favouring the escape of M. Broussonet, and was thrown into prison. More fortunate however than so many others who were arrested in that terrible time, he escaped with his life, and, after his release, returned to Paris and became a Mining Engineer. He subsequently was appointed Professor of Natural History at the École Centrale des Quatre Nations; and in the year 1800, commenced his superintendence of the manufactory of porcelain at Sèvres, an office filled by him for the long period of nearly half a century.

In the year 1807, appeared M. Brongniart's 'Traité Élémentaire de Minéralogie,' a work of great importance and merit.

M. Brongniart did not confine his scientific researches to mineralogy. Zoology also attracted his attention and profited by his labours, and a community of pursuit brought him into close relation with the illustrious Cuvier.

In the year 1808, he revisited this country and studied its freshwater formations, a study of great importance with reference to a work published by him, in conjunction with M. Cuvier, after his return to France, on the Geology of the Environs of Paris.

In consequence of the great service he had rendered to science, he was elected a member of the French Academy in the year 1815. Two years later, he visited Switzerland, the Alps and Italy, where he extended his geological fame by fresh observations; and in 1822, he published the second and enlarged edition of his Geology of the neighbourhood of the capital of France.

In the year 1824, he made a journey in Norway and Sweden, and in the course of it studied the more early fossiliferous deposits, and brought together the materials for a memoir on erratic blocks.

Other geological questions occupied his thoughts, and among them were the interesting phænomena of volcanos, and especially of Vesuvius.

Such is a brief account of the scientific career of this zealous and active philosopher, as exhibited in the touching address delivered after his death by his friend M. Elie de Beaumont. Science was not however his only, or perhaps his principal occupation, though it might be supposed that he had little leisure for any other. On the contrary, he diligently discharged for forty-seven years the duties of the director of a great national manufactory, and during the later years of his life, he published two important works on the potter's art; an art which, dating from very early periods of human existence, so eminently unites the beautiful with the useful; an art assuming a very different appearance at Nola or Pekin, at Firenze or Dresden; an art which seems to mark out the kind as well as degree of civilization of the different nations in which it has flourished or declined.

We should be mistaken, again, were we to imagine that natural science on the one hand and the care of the establishment of Sèvres on the other absorbed the whole thoughts and time of M. Brongniart. He took an active part in the affairs of the Institute, a zealous share in the advancement of knowledge by scientific association, and a lively interest in the pursuits of other inquirers after truth. He was, says M. de Beaumont, "non seulement le savant éminent, l'esprit supérieur, mais encore l'homme aimable, l'homme excellent, l'honnête homme, l'homme profondement dévoué aux plus nobles devoirs."

He became a Foreign Member of the Royal Society in the year 1815, and died at the advanced age of seventy-seven, admired, respected, beloved and lamented. He has left behind him a son inheriting his love for science and devotion to its cause.

The following Noblemen and Gentlemen were duly elected Officers and Council for the ensuing year, viz.—

*President.*—The Marquis of Northampton.
*Treasurer.*—George Rennie, Esq.
*Secretaries.* { Peter Mark Roget, M.D.
{ Samuel Hunter Christie, Esq., M.A.
*Foreign Secretary.*—Lieut.-Col. Edward Sabine, R.A.
*Other Members of the Council.*—Thomas Bell, Esq.; Robert Brown, Esq., D.C.L.; Sir James Clark, Bart., M.D.; Samuel Cooper, Esq.; Sir Henry De la Beche; Edward Forbes, Esq.; John P. Gassiot, Esq.; Thomas Graham, Esq., M.A.; John Thomas Graves, Esq., M.A.; Sir John F. W. Herschel, Bart., M.A.; William Hopkins, Esq., M.A.; Sir Robert H. Inglis, Bart., LL.D.; Charles Lyell, Esq., M.A.; the Duke of Northumberland; George Richardson Porter, Esq.; Lieut.-Col. Sykes.

Jan. 27, 1848.—"On Galvanic Currents existing in the Blood." By James Newton Heale, Esq., Licentiate of the Royal College of Physicians, and Fellow of the Royal College of Surgeons of England. Communicated by P. M. Roget, M.D., Sec. R.S.

The following abstract of this paper has been drawn up by the author.

The author endeavours to prove, by inductive reasoning and by historical considerations of the earliest indication of vitality in the egg, that motion of a fluid in a certain definite circle constitutes the first link in the chain of causes by which vitality is perfected; that all the other phenomena of living structure are supplementary and superinduced upon this primary and indispensable condition; and that, although it might be possible to maintain this primary circulation under certain circumstances, even though all the other functions of life were suspended or destroyed, they, on the contrary, cannot exist independently of that circulation. He shows it to be necessary to circulation, that two fluids, or a fluid in two different states, should communicate by two points or extremities with each other, and that these extremities should present such a resistance to their mutual connexion and commixion, that the transfer of conditions of each, from one to the other, must take place, otherwise the uniformity of both would speedily put an end to the process; and it is indicated that the forces in operation in these two places would be reverse to each other; in the one it would be from arterial to venous, and in the other from venous to arterial.

The blood-vessels containing the two kinds of blood are compared by the author to two bar-magnets placed side by side, the pulmonary and systemic capillaries representing the armatures placed at their extremities; with this limitation, that as the changes in the blood take place only in the two opposed sets of capillaries, the force is necessarily generated only in them, and therefore the intermediate blood contained in the larger blood-vessels merely represents conducting wires completing the circuit. The left side of the heart is viewed as being placed in the largest ampulla of the arterial circulation, and the right side of the heart as being in the like position with respect to the venous current.

The portal circulation is alluded to, in order to prove that a propelling force is not essential to produce circulation of blood. An account is given of numerous experiments on various animals, in which the ends of two similar wires (in some cases of copper and in others of platinum) were inserted; that of the one into a vein, and that of the other into an artery, the free ends of both wires being brought into connexion with a delicate galvanometer; and it was found that during life a galvanic current was indicated, passing along the artery and returning by the vein; that this current became more feeble in proportion as the vitality of the animal declined, and again more strong as the effect of the chloroform, which was administered for the purpose of preventing pain, subsided.

The author also observed, that the strong action of a muscle (the sterno-mastoid) between the two blood-vessels tended to discharge the galvanic force as it was generated; and that when that muscle was divided, the galvanic force became much stronger. When the connexion of the current with the lungs was severed by a ligature placed on the vein between the insertion of the wire and the heart, the current was instantly reversed, passing up the vein and returning by the artery. The same reverse current was indicated when the wires were inserted into portions of the blood-vessels which had been isolated, each by two ligatures, placed the one above and the other below the insertion of the wires. A similar effect was also obtained, as long as the blood continued to coagulate, when the two kinds of blood were drawn from the blood-vessels into separate cups, and brought into connexion with the galvanometer; the blood in the cups being connected together by the ends of a piece of copper or of a strip of muscle dipping into each.

Several experiments are related, tending to prove that the power which fluids, differing chemically from each other in however great a degree, were supposed to possess of acting chemically upon the copper wire, and thus generating currents, had been greatly exaggerated; and that much which had been attributed to this cause deserved rather to be ascribed to the polar forces, which the fluids had a tendency to assume, being discharged through the copper as a conductor, since the same effect was produced when platinum was used, and in an appreciable degree even when no metal was in contact with those artificial compounds, cotton moistened with water being only used to make the different connexions with the fluids.

The author then traces the course of the blood in the fœtus, showing that the blood passes in it, throughout the body, in the direction wholly from artery to vein; the upper half constituting one segment, and the lower half of the body the other segment of the circle; and pointed out that, thus far, there was no antagonism of forces, and therefore no power of generating a galvanic current, which he indicated was supplied by the smaller circle, through the placenta, joining the larger circle at the vena cava, and leaving it at the hypogastric arteries; the smaller circle inducing the current in the larger, in the same manner as the larger circle in the adult may be supposed to induce lesser secondary circles, as the hepatic, &c.

The author then dilates on the importance of the galvanic current in physiological and pathological inquiry; pointing out the peculiar significance of the fact of the reverse current being established as soon as the direct current is impeded; the systemic capillaries being endowed with the power of generating a force exactly the reverse to that set up in the lungs; the rapidity of the circulation thus being, *cæteris paribus*, the measure of the excess of the primary force over the resistance. He infers, that the galvanism found in the muscles owes its origin to the opposed condition of the blood in the capillary network which supplies each; the anastomoses of the arterial capillaries with each other increasing their galvanic surface, while their limited anastomoses with the veins supply the conditions necessary for the passive current. The office of conductors, for the active discharge of the accumulated force, is assigned to the nerves of the voluntary muscles; the author believing that the circuit by which this is effected is, in them, prolonged up to and from the nervous centres; which centres are, in their turn, shown to be liberally supplied with blood-vessels capable of influencing the galvanic equilibrium. The accelerated respiration caused by increased muscular exertion is attributed to this cause. It is inferred, that the involuntary muscles are provided with apparatus within themselves, adapted to regulate their periodical galvanic discharge. The mutual reaction of distant parts is attributed to the fact of the whole body being included in one galvanic circle, which cannot be disturbed in a part without the whole participating proportionally in the effects.

## XXXV. *Intelligence and Miscellaneous Articles.*

### ON A REMARKABLE SOLAR SPOT.

*To the Editors of the Philosophical Magazine and Journal.*

GENTLEMEN,

AS I believe the perception of a solar spot by the naked eye is of very rare occurrence, and has even been doubted, I take the liberty to state to you in corroboration of its truth, that I distinctly observed a large obscuration or spot on the sun's disc with the naked eye, appearing like a good-sized bean in shape and size, on Tuesday last, January 25. The observation took place at $1^h 30^m$ P.M., the sun's disc being of a blood-red colour at the time, owing to the intervention of a haze or fog, which enabled the eye steadily to gaze on it. The obscured part, viewed with telescopic powers of 60 and 120, resolved itself into two large central spots, stretching in a direction apparently parallel with the sun's equator, surrounded by a great number of smaller spots, particularly on the north side. This mass of maculæ melted into the elliptical appearance seen by the naked eye.

Perhaps in my ignorance I am overrating the rarity of this occurrence; but as Herschel only once saw a similar spot with the naked eye (in 1779), and I have not met with any recent accounts of such observations, I have ventured to proffer my testimony to the truth of the circumstance. Probably if the solar orb was more frequently examined during a fog, more of these maculæ might have been noticed. Sunset or sunrise would also be favourable times for such observation.

The earliest account we have of the observation of solar spots (at least in modern times) appears to be that given by Hakluyt, from the log-book of a ship on the coast of Africa in December 1590, when a spot appeared to the naked eye at sunset and sunrise, no doubt owing to the denseness of the atmospheric strata diminishing the sun's rays. The extract from the log is as follows:—"The 7th at sunset we saw a great black spot on the sun; and on the 8th, both at rising and setting, we saw the like, the spot appearing about the size of a shilling." This was before the telescopic discovery of maculæ by Galileo and others; and the spot so seen might have consisted of a collection of spots like that now visible. Trusting that you will excuse my addressing you for the reasons given,

I remain, Gentlemen,
Your obedient Servant,
W. PRINGLE.

Edinburgh, Jan. 27, 1848.

P.S. Perhaps I may be allowed to add, that a very striking aurora borealis occurred here on the night of Sunday, January 16, about twenty minutes from 10 P.M., which though not so playfully varied in its motions or hues as that of the 24th of October, presented a very imposing appearance from its mass and the intensity of its glare. It arose suddenly from the north-east, shooting rapidly up like a majestic pyramid of flame. The redness resembled the reflexion of a vast conflagration. The Great Bear appeared nearly in its centre, occupying about half its diameter in that point, the apex reaching to Capella, then culminating south of the zenith, round which it left a red spot after receding towards its base. Several lighter columns of red and orange shot up north of it. The whole gradually melted into the usual milky haze, in about a quarter of an hour.

18 Scotland Street, Edinburgh,<br>Feb. 9, 1848.

Having obtained, since my last communication, corroborative testimony on the subject of the solar spot, I beg leave to transmit it to you, by way of postscript. It was elicited by my having inserted in an Edinburgh paper a paragraph stating the circumstance, and requesting corroboration from any one who might have observed the spot. I give it in the words of the editor :—

"We have received several communications fully corroborating the observations of our correspondent, published on Saturday. The same phænomenon was distinctly observed by John Wauchope, Esq. of Edmonstone, who has kindly communicated to us particulars, similar to those already noted."—*Edinburgh Evening Post*, Feb. 2, 1848.

The great point of interest and importance deducible from the fact established, is the extraordinary enlargement of the solar spot, thus rendering it distinctly and palpably visible to the unprotected eye at the distance of ninety-five millions of miles. More than the usual tremendous agencies must have been in force to have produced so great an obscuration. Without a micrometrical observation it is, of course, impossible to approximate to its exact dimensions; but if the calculation be correct which assigns about 50,000 miles as the minimum diameter required for a spot to be visible to the unaided eye, I should feel strongly inclined, from the space obviously occupied by the obscuration on the solar disc, to consider it, at a rude guess, to have been in diameter at least one-twelfth part that of the sun.

This, however, I submit with necessary diffidence, leaving the point to be determined by more experienced and more scientific inquirers, some of whom may have observed the spot and measured its dimensions. Placing these slight observations at your disposal,

I remain, Gentlemen,<br>Your obedient Servant,<br>W. Pringle.

### ON THE PREPARATION AND CHEMICAL CONSTITUTION OF ASPARAGIN.

M. Piria, in order to obtain this substance, caused vetches to vegetate in the dark, expressed the juice and evaporated it. As soon as the liquor was near the boiling-point, an abundant deposit of coagulated albumen was formed; the filtered liquor was evaporated to an almost syrupy consistence, and after standing twenty-four hours, an abundant crystalline deposit was formed, possessing the aspect and properties of asparagin.

To purify these crystals they were washed with a little cold water, then dissolved in boiling water, and on cooling, crystals were formed.

To render these crystals perfectly white, they were again dissolved and treated with animal charcoal, and were thus rendered extremely fine. Forty pounds of vetches yielded about five and one-third avoirdupois ounces of asparagin, and consequently this plant is the most advantageous that can be employed.

By analysis there were obtained—

|  | Experiment. | Calculation. |
|---|---|---|
| Carbon | 31·80 | 32·00 |
| Hydrogen | 6·85 | 6·67 |
| Nitrogen | 18·84 | 18·67 |
| Oxygen | 42·51 | 42·66 |
|  | 100·00 | 100·00 |

To determine whether growth without the presence of light was requisite to produce asparagin in vetches, some green plants were treated in the same way; and M. Piria found, contrary to his expectations, that they yielded as much asparagin as those which grew in the dark.

The seeds were found not to contain any asparagin, and the plants were also examined at the commencement of flowering and during fructification; in the former case an inappreciable trace only of asparagin was obtained, and in the latter none whatever.

M. Piria observes, that all the authors who have treated of asparagin have regarded it either as an alkaloid, or as a neutral substance, and no one as an acid. Notwithstanding the previous opinions on the subject, the author considers asparagin as an acid. He found that the expressed juice had an acid reaction, which became stronger as it was evaporated, and that it acted upon the copper vessel in which it was evaporated; and he found also that when asparagin was heated with water and oxide of copper, that an azure-coloured solution was formed, which yielded a crystalline deposit of the same colour. This compound is more readily and abundantly formed by adding a hot concentrated solution of asparagin to one of acetate of copper, also strong and hot. If no immediate reaction takes place after mixture, the liquid must be heated; and by this there will be immediately formed a precipitate of a fine ultramarine-blue colour, and this continues to deposit during the cooling.

This compound is nearly insoluble in cold water, but is slightly soluble in hot, and very soluble in acids and in ammonia; when long kept at 248° F. in a current of dry air, it loses no water; when more strongly heated, it is decomposed with the disengagement of torrents of ammoniacal gas. Its analysis indicated as its formula, $C^8 H^7 N^2 O^5$, CuO.

It follows from this, that asparagin dried at 212° F., $C^8 H^8 N^2 O^6$ and considered as anhydrous, contains one equivalent of water capable of being replaced by one equivalent of oxide of copper. The analysis of this compound gave—

|  | Experiment. | | | Calculation. |
|---|---|---|---|---|
| Carbon........ | 29·30 | 29·43 | 29·35 | 29·50 |
| Hydrogen .... | 4·41 | 4·51 | 4·36 | 4·30 |
| Nitrogen ...... | 17·25 | 17·25 | 17·25 | 17·21 |
| Oxygen ...... | 24·64 | 24·43 | 24·65 | 24·58 |
| Oxide of copper | 24·40 | 24·38 | 24·39 | 24·41 |
|  | 100·00 | 100·00 | 100·00 | 100·00 |

To determine whether asparagin in combining with oxide of copper undergoes any change, a portion of the copper compound was decomposed by sulphuretted hydrogen. The liquor from which the sulphuret of copper was deposited possessed a decidedly acid reaction; when concentrated by a water-bath, the liquor deposited fine white brilliant crystals of asparagin. The external characters of these were such as to remove all doubt. They were analysed, and found to be crystallized asparagin.

It will then be observed that asparagin, in combining with oxide of copper, yields a saline compound, from which, by means of sulphuretted hydrogen, asparagin possessing its usual characters may be separated. Reckoning the copper to be in the state of oxide in this compound, it follows that dry asparagin contains one equivalent of hydrogen and one of oxygen more than combined asparagin. The formula of asparagin dried at 212° F. is then $C^8 H^7 N^2 O^5$, HO, and that of the salt of copper $C^8 H^7 N^2 O^5$, CuO.—*Ann. de Ch. et de Phys.*, Fevrier 1848.

## ON THE TRANSFORMATIONS OF ASPARAGIN.

M. Piria having, as shown in the preceding notice, determined the formula of asparagin, proceeded to investigate the production of substances derived from it.

*Action of ferments.*—A solution of asparagin when exposed undergoes no change if it be pure; if, on the contrary, the crystals are coloured, the solution undergoes a kind of fermentation, giving rise to the following phænomena.

The liquid loses its acid reaction and becomes feebly alkaline. In this state it exhales the disagreeable smell of animal matter undergoing the putrid fermentation; the surface becomes covered with a white mucilaginous pellicle, which, examined by the microscope, is shown to contain numerous infusoria. After a certain time the asparagin completely disappears, and succinate of ammonia is found in its place; or at any rate, a substance which, treated with acids, is decomposed into succinic acid and ammonia. In fact, if excess of hydrochloric acid be poured into the fermented liquor, and if it be evaporated by the water-bath, there remains a saline mass, which, treated with æther, separates into two portions, one of which is soluble and the other insoluble in it; the latter is entirely sal-ammoniac. The æthereal solution, properly evaporated, deposits an acid brown-coloured substance; this dissolved in water and saturated with ammonia, and decomposed by acetate of lead, gives a crystalline precipitate from which a white crystalline substance, possessing all the properties of succinic acid, may be separated by the action of sulphuretted hydrogen. This on analysis gave by—

|  | Experiment. | | Calculation. |
|---|---|---|---|
| Carbon | 40·27 | 40·40 | 40·68 |
| Hydrogen | 5·28 | 5·16 | 5·08 |
| Oxygen | 54·45 | 54·44 | 54·24 |
|  | 100·00 | 100·00 | 100·00 |

It appears, then, that impure asparagin dissolved in water and left to itself for some time is totally converted into succinate of ammonia. To explain this transformation, it is necessary only to compare the two formulæ—

 if from $C^8 H^{13} N^2 O^8$, succinate of ammonia,
 we subtract $C^8 H^8 N^2 O^6$, asparagin,

there remains $H^4 O^2 = 2HO + H^2$.

When then asparagin is converted into succinate of ammonia, it assimilates two equivalents of water and two equivalents of hydrogen, produced under the reductive influence of the putrefaction which occurs in the liquid.

This metamorphosis exhibits an important peculiarity, which has not been observed hitherto in other transformations of organic matter. The succinate of ammonia, which results from the reduction of the asparagin, does not return to the state of asparagin under the influence of oxidizing agents: thus it undergoes no alteration by the most concentrated nitric acid or by chromic acid.

M. Piria, to determine whether the nitrogenous bodies, which, by fermentation, converted the asparagin into succinate of ammonia, existed in the vetches themselves, added a quantity of the juice of etiolated vetches to a moderately strong and very pure solution of asparagin, and exposed the mixture to the air. In a few days the same phænomena appeared as already described as occurring with the impure asparagin. On examining the liquor at the expiration of about a fortnight, a considerable quantity of perfectly white crystals of succinic acid had separated.—*Ann. de Ch. et Phys.*, Fevrier 1848.

## ON CHRYSAMMIC ACID. BY M. MULDER.

The author states that he has examined chrysammic acid produced by the action of nitric acid on aloes; his results differ both from those obtained by M. Schunck and M. Robiquet. The pure acid, yielding a potash salt nearly insoluble in cold water, and of a greenish-gold colour, yielded (C = 75·12):—

|  | Experiment. | | Atoms. | Calculation. |
|---|---|---|---|---|
| C | 39·7 | 39·9 | 14 | 40·1 |
| H | 1·0 | 1·1 | 4 | 0·9 |
| N | 13·0 | | 4 | 13·3 |
| O | 46·3 | | 12 | 45·7 |

This result differs, especially as to the nitrogen, from that of M. Schunck, who found the formula $C^{13} H^4 N^4 O^{15}$. The analysis of the potash salt confirmed the composition of the hydrated acid. Dried at 248° F., at which chrysammate of potash gives a large portion of water, but the author has not yet determined the quantity, this salt gave—

|   | Experiment. | Atoms. | Calculation. |
|---|---|---|---|
| C | 34·1 | 14 | 33·9 |
| H | 0·8 | 2 | 0·4 |
| N | 11·2 | 4 | 11·3 |
| O | 35·2 | 11 | 35·4 |
| KO | 18·6 | 1 | 19·0 |

M. Schunck gives 17·88 KO in 100, which is sensibly too low.

Chrysammate of barytes, dried at 230° F. for several hours in a current of dry air, retains two equivalents of water. This salt yielded—

|   | Experiment. | Atoms. | Calculation. |
|---|---|---|---|
| C | 28·80 | 14 | 28·5 |
| H | 1·41 | 6 | 1·0 |
| N | .. | 4 | 9·5 |
| O | .. | 13 | 35·1 |
| BaO | 25·91 | 1 | 25·9 |

which represents $C^{14} H^6 N^4 O^{11}$, BaO, 2 Aq.

Chrysammate of copper, after being dried at 248° F., yielded—

|   | Experiment. | Atoms. | Calculation. |
|---|---|---|---|
| CuO | 16·45 | 1 | 16 |
| Anhydrous chrysammic acid | 83·55 | 1 | 84 |

A salt of lead obtained by means of chrysammate of potash and neutral acetate of lead, yielded a basic salt, which, like the barytic salt, was of a very fine red colour; it yielded,—

|   | Experiment. | Atoms. | Calculation. |
|---|---|---|---|
| C | 20·28 | 14 | 19·8 |
| H | 0·61 | 2 | 0·2 |
| N | 6·20 | 4 | 6·6 |
| O | 21·31 | 11 | 20·8 |
| PbO | 51·60 | 2 | 52·6 |

M. Robiquet examined the reaction of ammonia on chrysammic acid. He states that at 212° F. the resulting compound is $C^{10} H^{12} N^{10} O^{25}$; M. Mulder did not obtain a similar result. The atomic weight and oxygen of chrysammic acid do not agree with this formula: with 1 equivalent of hydrated chrysammic acid, that is to say with $C^{14} H^4 N^4 O^{12}$, there is an elimination of $H^2O$, and an addition of $N^2 H^6$.

M. Mulder has also stated that 100 parts of hydrated chrysammic acid lose, after being well-dried at 212° F. in a current of dry ammoniacal gas, 4·8 parts of water, and gain 4 of ammonia.

Then $C^{14} H^4 N^4 O^{12} + N^2 H^6 - H^2O$ gives—

| Hydrated chrysammic acid. | Water. |
|---|---|
| 2626·64 | 112·48 = 100 : $x$ ; |

$x = 4·3$ Aq.

Experiment gave 4·8 parts of water.

In another experiment,—

| Hydrated chrysammic acid. | Water. | Ammonia. |
|---|---|---|
| 2626·64 | —112·48 | +212·44 = 2726·60, |
| 2626·64 : 2726·64 = 100 : $x$ ; | | $x = 103·8$. |

Experiment gave 104.

The amide which is formed, and which the author calls *chrysammide*, is then composed of $C^{14} H^6 N^6 O^{11}$.

According to M. Robiquet, we have—

Before the experiment, $C^{30} H^8 N^4 O^{26} = 5603 \cdot 5$;

After the action of ammonia, $C^{30} H^{12} N^{10} O^{43} = 5703 \cdot 5$.

Then—
$$5603 \cdot 5 : 112 \cdot 48 = 100 : x;$$
$$x = 2 \text{ Aq.}$$

And, on the other hand,
$$5603 \cdot 5 : 5703 \cdot 5 = 100 : x;$$
$$x = 102.$$

It is then clear that $C^{14} H^4 N^4 O^{12}$ loses $H^2O$ and gains $N^2 H^4$, and that the composition of chrysammide, which M. Robiquet calls *chrysammanic acid*, is actually $C^{14} H^4 N^4 O^{11} + N^2 H^4$. Analysis confirmed these results.

Chrysammide, dried at 212° F., yielded M. Mulder,—

|   | Experiment. | Atoms. | Calculation. |
|---|---|---|---|
| C........ | 38·00 | 14 | 38·6 |
| H........ | 2·08 | 8 | 1·8 |
| N........ | 19·15 | 6 | 19·3 |
| O........ | 40·77 | 11 | 40·3 |

According to the composition of rectified chrysammic acid, there should be obtained, according to M. Robiquet,—

|   | Atoms. | Calculation. |
|---|---|---|
| C........ | 28 | 39·4 |
| H........ | 12 | 1·4 |
| N........ | 10 | 16·3 |
| O........ | 23 | 42·9 |

Chrysammide combines with bases and exhibits many important reactions, the examination of which is continued by M. Mulder.

The chrysolepic acid of M. Schunck is merely nitropicric acid. It is a substance the examination of which is very dangerous, on account of the violence with which its compounds with bases explode.

The above-stated analyses of chrysammic acid associate this substance to anilic, nitropicric and nitrophenic acids.

| Anilic acid. | Chrysammic acid. |
|---|---|
| $C^{14} H^8 N^4 O^9$, | $C^{14} H^4 N^4 O^{11}$, |
| $H^6 O^3$, | $N^2 O^2$, |
| $C^2 \quad O^3$, | $C^2 \quad O^1$, |
| $C^{12} H^4 N^2 O^2$, | $C^{12} H^2 N^4 O^7$. |

Nitropicric acid:
$$C^{14} H^4 N^6 O^{13} = C^{12} H^4 N^2 O^3 + N^2 O^1, N^2 O^4, H^2O.$$

Hephninic acid:
$$C^{12} H^4 N^6 O^{14} = C^{12} H^4 N^2 O^3 + 2 N^2 O^4, H^2O.$$

Nitrophenic acid:
$$C^{12} H^6 N^4 O^{13} = C^{12} H^6 N^2 O^3 + 2 N^2 O^4, 2 H^2O.$$

Chrysammide, prepared in the humid way, in the cold, and dried at 212° F., has the same composition as when prepared in the dry way. It yielded on analysis 38·7 per cent. carbon, 2·1 hydrogen, 18·6 nitrogen, and 40·6 oxygen.

An excess of ammonia decomposes chrysammic acid when heated in the same manner as the fixed alkalies, and renders it brown.—*Ann. de Ch. et de Phys.*, Jan. 1848.

METEOROLOGICAL OBSERVATIONS FOR JAN. 1848.

*Chiswick.*—January 1. Foggy: hazy: sleet-showers. 2. Very fine. 3. Densely overcast: cloudy and mild. 4. Exceedingly fine: clear. 5. Overcast: rain: clear. 6. Slight frost: clear: fine. 7. Slight frosty haze: heavy rain: clear. 8. Hazy. 9. Frosty: overcast. 10. Overcast: dusky clouds and cold. 11. Uniformly overcast, with dusky haze. 12. Overcast: slight rain. 13. Clouds tinged with red: overcast: rain. 14. Hazy: drizzly. 15. Cloudy: exceedingly fine, with bright sun: frosty. 16. Sharp frost: very fine: clear and frosty. 17. Rain. 18. Fine. 19. Cold easterly haze. 20—22. Densely overcast. 23. Slight snow. 24. Low fleeting clouds from N.E. 25. Cold dry easterly wind: densely overcast. 26. Dusky haze: clear and frosty. 27. Frosty. 28. Snowing: clear and frosty: snow in the evening. 29. Foggy: fine: clear. 30. Overcast: rain. 31. Densely and uniformly overcast: sleet.

Mean temperature of the month .......................... 33°·62
Mean temperature of Jan. 1847 .......................... 34 ·26
Mean temperature of Jan. for the last twenty years ...... 36 ·51
Average amount of rain in Jan. ........................... 1·59 inch.

*Boston.*—Jan. 1. Cloudy: rain early A.M. 2. Cloudy: rain A.M. and P.M. 3. Cloudy. 4. Fine. 5. Cloudy. 6. Fine. 7. Cloudy: snow A.M. 8. Cloudy: snow on the ground. 9. Fine: snow on the ground. 10, 11. Cloudy: snow on the ground. 12. Fine. 13, 14. Cloudy. 15. Fine: rain early A.M. 16, 17. Fine. 18. Fine: rain early A.M. 19, 20. Fine. 21. Cloudy: snow early A.M. 22, 23. Cloudy. 24—27. Fine. 28. Cloudy. 29. Cloudy: snow A.M. and P.M. 30. Cloudy: snow and rain P.M. 31. Fine: rain P.M.

*Applegarth Manse, Dumfries-shire.*—Jan. 1. Frost: cloudy P.M. 2. Thaw and rain. 3. Thaw and rain: snow gone. 4. Rain A.M.: cleared: rain P.M. 5. Heavy rain all night: flood. 6. Frost: cloudy P.M. 7. Frost, slight: sprinkling of snow. 8. Frost, slight: drizzle P.M. 9. Frost, slight: harder P.M. 10. Frost, rather hard: snow. 11. Frost: fog all day. 12. Thaw: soft wind: snow gone. 13. Remarkably fine: frost P.M. 14. Air moist: rain P.M. 15. No frost: showers and wind P.M. 16. Showery early A.M.: cleared. 17. Frost, severe: slight snow. 18. Frost: clear: keen. 19. Frost: clear and fine. 20. Frost, severe: clear. 21. Frost: cloudy: threatening change. 22. Frost: no change: clear. 23. Frost: beautiful winter day. 24. Frost, keen: clear and fine. 25. Frost: threatening change. 26, 27. Frost: severe weather. 28. Frost: snow inch deep. 29. Frost A.M.: rain P.M. 30. Frost: heavy snow five inches deep. 31. Frost: clear.

Mean temperature of the month .......................... 33°·8
Mean temperature of Jan. 1847 .......................... 35 ·9
Mean temperature of Jan. for twenty-five years .......... 34 ·9
Rain in Jan. for twenty years ............................ 2·60 inches.

*Sandwick Manse, Orkney.*—Jan. 1. Cloudy: clear. 2. Showers: rain. 3. Cloudy. 4. Clear: cloudy. 5. Cloudy: rain: cloudy. 6. Clear: cloudy. 7. Cloudy: rain: cloudy. 8. Showers: cloudy. 9. Bright: frost: cloudy. 10. Rain. 11. Bright: rain. 12. Damp: drizzle. 13. Drizzle. 14. Drizzle: showers. 15. Sleet-showers: clear. 16. Bright: showers. 17. Bright: frost: cloudy: frost. 18. Bright: frost: clear: frost. 19. Bright: frost: cloudy frost. 20. Clear: frost. 21. Bright: frost: cloudy: frost. 22. Cloudy. 23. Snow: clear: aurora. 24. Bright: clear: aurora. 25. Clear: aurora. 26. Bright: frost: clear: aurora. 27. Bright: clear. 28. Cloudy: frost: snow-drift: aurora. 29. Clear: frost: thaw. 30. Bright: frost: clear: aurora. 31. Bright: frost: clear: frost.

#  THE LONDON, EDINBURGH AND DUBLIN PHILOSOPHICAL MAGAZINE AND JOURNAL OF SCIENCE.

[THIRD SERIES.]

*APRIL* 1848.

XXXVI. *An Account of the Speculations of* Thomas Wright *of Durham.* By Prof. DE MORGAN*.

M. ARAGO, in his account of William Herschel, published in the Paris *Annuaire* for 1842, recalled the attention of astronomers to the fact that some speculative researches into the constitution of the stellar universe had preceded those of his illustrious subject. He instances Wright, Kant and Lambert, from the second of whom he draws all his information as to the first. Professor Struve, in his recently published *Etudes d'Astronomie Stellaire*, St. Petersburg, 1847, 8vo, again mentions Wright from Kant, and gives the titles of his works from Lalande. But neither Kant, Arago, nor Struve, had seen the work of Wright in question. I propose to give an account of it, as of a speculation which must take a high rank among those daring and yet sober attempts at prediction of future results, which are, and ought to be, repaid upon success for the contempt with which they are always received on appearance. The author did not, as speculators sometimes do, attempt to discount his fame, and to procure an endorsement of good names for a bill of long date upon posterity. He published his work in a quiet way, and left time to show what it was worth.

The work† in question is entitled *Theory of the Universe,*

* Communicated by the Author.
† 'An Original Theory or New Hypothesis of the Universe, Founded upon the Laws of Nature, and solving by Mathematical Principles the General Phænomena of the Visible Creation; and particularly the Via Lactea. Compris'd in Nine Familiar Letters from the Author to his Friend. And Illustrated with upwards of Thirty Graven and Mezzotinto Plates, By the Best Masters. By Thomas Wright, of Durham.

One *Sun by Day, by Night* ten Thousand *shine,*
*And light us deep into the* DEITY.—Dr. YOUNG.

London: Printed for the Author, and sold by H. Chapelle, in *Grosvenor Street.* MDCCL.' Quarto, pp. xii. + 84, plates 32.

and was published in 1750. Kant, as appears by Professor Struve's statement, took his knowledge of it from the *Hamburgische Freie Urtheile* of 1751, and wrote on the same subject in his *Allgemeine Naturgeschichte und Theorie des Himmels*, Leipzig, 1755, 8vo. As far as I can see from Professor Struve's description of Kant's views, there is not in them any extension of Wright's, except in two points, which I shall notice in the proper place.

Wright's work consists of nine letters to a friend, and in its speculations is both astronomical and theological; the latter term including not merely expression of devotional feeling, but much actual conjecture on what astronomy may teach in relation to the future state of mankind. Omitting this, I shall proceed to register the purely astronomical doctrines of the treatise, so far as they seem peculiar to Wright.

I make one long extract from the seventh letter, which might have been shortened, and the English of it made more clear and more correct, with no loss to Wright's memory. But as this passage is very important as evidence, and is unquestionably, out of the whole book, that which most nearly contains the pith and marrow of the system, I have thought it best to extract the whole of it.

In the preface it is stated that the chief design is "an Attempt towards solving the Phænomena of the *Via Lactea*, and in consequence of that Solution, the framing of a regular and rational Theory of the known Universe, before unattempted by any." It is ".... entirely upon a new Plan, and the Beginning, as it were, of a new Science, before unattempted in any Language, the Author having dug all his Ideas from the Mines of Nature. ...." And further, "How the Author has succeeded in this Point, is a Question of no great Consequence; he has certainly done his best; another, no Doubt, will do better, and a third perhaps, by some more rational Hypothesis, may perfect this Theory, and reduce the Whole to infallible Demonstration : . . . ."

The claim which Wright makes to originality will easily be admitted; and his priority must remain uncontested until it can be impugned upon evidence. At present, neither Arago nor Struve have met with anything of the same kind anterior to Wright.

In the first letter Wright gives the opinions of preceding authors. He states that his own system was first planned in 1734. I need not describe his very imperfect enumeration of his predecessors. In 1732, *Robert* Wright, whom I ought to mention to prevent his being confounded with the subject of this notice, published his Newtonian lunar tables for the navy.

The second letter is on probability and certainty, and, though ingenious and sound, has nothing to the present purpose. It concludes with an account of celestial systems anterior to that of Copernicus.

The third letter is on the planetary motions and structures. It contains nothing peculiar to Wright, except a declaration that he is strongly of opinion that the orbits of comets have all their areas equal. This is not a happy conjecture. He draws the notion from observing that the comets of 1680 and 1682, the most and least excentric of those whose orbits had been calculated, have areas not very unequal, and such as a supposition of moderate errors of observation might make equal. The following sentence is of a better kind, be the latter part worth what it may. "....the Clouds are to us in effect no other than as so many Moons, whereby we have our artificial Day prolonged to us several Hours after the Sun is set, and likewise produced as much sooner before he rises; and were they to ascend by still stronger Power of Exhalation to an Elevation, all round the Atmosphere, so as to form a Sphere equal to four Times the Globe of the Earth, there would then be no such Thing as real nocturnal Darkness to any Part of the World."

The fourth letter continues his remarks on the nature of the heavenly bodies. That the sun is a vast body of blazing matter, he thinks will hardly admit of question: though he afterwards supposes it possible that the igneous matter may be only an envelope. Aberration is spoken of with caution. "Mr. *Bradley*, Astronomer-Royal, has, in a great measure, proved that the Aberration of the Stars hitherto mistaken for a Parallax, may arise from, and indeed seems to be no other than the progressive Motion of Light, and Change of Place to the Eye, arising from the Earth's annual Motion and Direction." His friend is recommended to procure an idea of the appearance of the sun to more distant planets than our own, by means of concave glasses fitted to reduce the apparent diameter duly. The homogeneity of the stars with our sun, both as to constitution and attendant bodies, is strongly insisted on from analogy.

The fifth letter first mentions the milky way, which he says "....still continues to be unaccounted for, and even in an Age vain enough to boast Astronomy in its utmost Perfection. What will you say, if I tell you, it is my belief we are so far from the real Summit of the Science, that we scarce yet know the Rudiments of what may be expected from it? This luminous Circle has often engrossed my Thoughts, and of late has taken up all my idle Hours; and I am now in great Hopes I have not only at last found out the real Cause of it, but also by the same Hypothesis, which solves this Appearance, shall be able to demonstrate a much more rational Theory of the Creation than hitherto has been any where advanced, and at the same Time give you an entire new Idea of the Universe, or infinite System of Things." The milky way is then described, and the opinions of the ancients upon it. A plate is given of a portion near the foot of Antinous, as observed by Wright himself with what he calls a very good reflector: the plan was formed "by a Combination of Triangles." He afterwards mentions his observing with a "one Foot reflecting Telescope." Proceeding on the opinion of Democritus and others among the ancients, and on his own partial resolution of the galactic light, he pronounces the phænomenon to arise from a congeries of small stars. He does not seem to be acquainted with the partial resolution made by Galileo: and in general, his reading in astronomy anterior to his own day seems to lie rather in classical or mediæval authors, or their translators and compilers, than in those of the seventeenth century.

Making the assumption that the stars shine by their own light, he proceeds thus: "Here it will not be amiss to observe, that it has been conjectured, and is strongly suspected, that a proper Number of Rays, meeting from different Directions, become Flame; and that hence it may prove not the Sun's real Body which we daily see, but only his inflamed Atmosphere. I begin to be of Opinion, and I think not without Reason, that the true Magnitude of the Sun is not near what the modern Astronomers have made it; and that it may not possibly be much above two Thirds of what it appears to us; ..... This, tho' I presume to call it at present only meer Hypothesis, will in a great measure account for the excessive Changes in the Constitution of our Air and Atmosphere, which we often find very unnatural to the Season; .... But all this will very naturally be accounted for by the Levity, or expanding Quality of the Sun's circumambient Flame, or Atmosphere; and hence, according to its various State, being more condensed, or rare, we may have Heat or Cold in the greatest Extream, and alternately so, in a perpetual Vicissitude."

Wright then proceeds to estimate the number of stars in the milky way, and to discuss the question of the distance of stars from our sun. Making the distance of one star from another at least about three thousand times that of the furthest planet from our sun, he argues that ".... as no sensible Disorder can be observed amongst the solar Planets, what Reason have we to suppose any can be occasioned amongst the Stars, or that a general Motion of these primary Luminaries round a common Center, should be any way irrational, or unnatural?".

The sixth letter is headed 'Of General Motion amongst the Stars, the Plurality of Systems, and Innumerability of Worlds.' That the stars are not promiscuously dispersed, he argues from the phænomenon of the milky way, supposed to be resolvable into stars. He then proceeds to say, "If any regular Order of the Stars then can be demonstrated that will naturally prove this Phænomenon to be no other than a certain Effect arising from the Observer's Situation, I think you must of course grant such a Solution at least rational, if not the Truth; and this is what I propose by my new Theory." Afterwards he adds, ".... we may reasonably expect, that the *Via Lactea*, which is a manifest Circle amongst the Stars, conspicuous to every Eye, will prove at last the Whole [creation] to be together a vast and glorious regular Production of Beings, .... and that all its Irregularities are only such as naturally arise from our excentric View: To demonstrate which absolutely and incontestibly, we shall only want this one *Postulata* to be granted, viz. *that all the Stars are, or may be in Motion.*" From thence, presuming the stars to have each its attendant system, and arguing that the motion of each primary itself is no more extraordinary than the motion about its axis (which the sun has), he proceeds to discuss the evidence, as it then existed, for apparent proper motion, and considers such a phænomenon established by various instances, and particularly by Arcturus, from comparison with old observations, after allowance for the varying obliquity of the ecliptic. He then recommends close observation of the distances between each two stars in a cluster, for detection of the proper motions, and ends this letter with an engraving of the Pleiades, laid down from his own observations.

The seventh letter gives the explanation of the phænomenon of the milky way, as now generally received. The following are the first words in which this explanation was ever offered, as it turns out. "But of this I have said enough, and think it is now more than Time to attempt the remaining Part of my Theory.

"When we reflect upon the various Aspects, and perpetual Changes of the Planets, both with regard to their[*] heliocentric and geocentric Motion, we may readily imagine, that nothing but a like excentric Position of the Stars could any way produce such an apparently promiscuous Difference in

[*] "Not to mention their several Conjunctions and Apulces to fixed Stars, &c. see the State of the Heavens in 1602, *December* the first, when all the known Planets were in one Sign of the Zodiac, *viz. Sagittarius*."

such otherwise regular Bodies. And that in like manner, as the Planets would, if viewed from the Sun, there may be one Place in the Universe to which their Order and primary Motions must appear most regular and most beautiful. Such a Point, I may presume, is not unnatural to be supposed, although hitherto we have not been able to produce any absolute Proof of it. See *Plate* XXV. This is the great Order of Nature, which I shall now endeavour to prove, and thereby solve the Phænomena of the *Via Lactea*; and in order thereto, I want nothing to be granted but what may easily be allowed, namely, that the *Milky Way* is formed of an infinite Number of small Stars.

"Let us imagine a vast infinite Gulph, or Medium, every Way extended like a Plane, and inclosed between two Surfaces, nearly even on both Sides, but of such a Depth or Thickness as to occupy a Space equal to the double Radius, or Diameter of the visible Creation, that is to take in one of the smallest Stars each Way, from the middle Station, perpendicular to the Plane's Direction, and, as near as possible, according to our Idea of their true Distance.

"But to bring this Image a little lower, and as near as possible level to every Capacity, I mean such as cannot conceive this kind of continued Zodiac, let us suppose the whole Frame of Nature in the Form of an artificial Horizon of a Globe, I don't mean to affirm that it really is so in Fact, but only state the Question thus, to help your Imagination to conceive more aptly what I would explain. *Plate* XXIII. will then represent a just Section of it. Now in this Space let us imagine all the Stars scattered promiscuously, but at such an adjusted Distance from one another, as to fill up the whole Medium with a kind of regular Irregularity of Objects. And next let us consider what the Consequence would be to an Eye situated near the Center Point, or any where about the middle Plane, as at the point A. Is it not, think you, very evident, that the Stars would there appear promiscuously dispersed on each Side, and more and more inclining to Disorder, as the Ob-

```
          B                 F
   D      A      H
      E   C              G
```

server would advance his Station towards either Surface, and nearer to B or C, but in the Direction of the general Plane towards H or D, by the continual Approximation of the visual Rays, crowding together as at H, betwixt the Limits D and

G, they must infallibly terminate in the utmost Confusion? If your Opticks fails you before you arrive at these external Regions, only imagine how infinitely greater the Number of Stars would be in those remote Parts, arising thus from their continual crowding behind one another, as all other objects do towards the Horizon Point of their Perspective, which ends but with Infinity: Thus, all their Rays at last so near uniting, must meeting in the Eye appear, as almost, in Contact, and form a perfect Zone of Light; this I take to be the real Case, and the true Nature of our *Milky Way*, and all the Irregularity we observe in it at the Earth, I judge to be intirely owing to our Sun's Position in this great Firmament, and may easily be solved by his Excentricity, and the Diversity of Motion that may naturally be conceived amongst the stars themselves, which may here and there, in different Parts of the Heavens, occasion a cloudy Knot of Stars, as perhaps at E.

" But now to apply this Hypothesis to our present Purpose, and reconcile it to our Ideas of a circular Creation, and the known Laws of orbicular Motion, so as to make the Beauty and Harmony of the Whole consistent with the visible Order of its Parts, our Reason must now have recourse to the Analogy of Things. It being once agreed, that the Stars are in Motion, which, as I have endeavoured in my last Letter to shew is not far from an undeniable Truth, we must next consider in what Manner they move. First then, to suppose them to move in right Lines, you know is contrary to all the Laws and Principles we at present know of; and since there are but two Ways that they can possibly move in any natural Order, that is either in right Lines, or in Curves, this being one, it must of course be the other, *i. e.* in an Orbit; and consequently, were we able to view them from their middle Position, as from the Eye seated in the Center of *Plate* XXV. we might expect to find them separately moving in all manner of Directions round a general Center, such as is there represented. It only now remains to show how a Number of Stars, so disposed in a circular Manner round any given Center, may solve the Phænomena before us. There are but two Ways possible to be proposed by which it can be done, and one of which I think is highly probable; but which of the two will meet your Approbation, I shall not venture to determine, only here inclosed I intend to send you both. The first is in the Manner I have above described, *i. e.* all moving the same Way, and not much deviating from the same Plane, as the Planets in their heliocentric Motion do round the solar Body. In this Case the primary, secondary, and tertiary constituent Orbits, &c. framing the Hypotheses, are represented in *Plate* XXII, and the Consequence of such a Theory arising from such a universal Law of Motion in *Plate* XXIII. where B, D denotes the local Motion of the Sun in the true *Orbis Magnus*, and E, C that of the Earth in her proper secondary Orbit, which of course is supposed, as is shown in the Figure to change its sidereal Positions, in the same Manner as the Moon does round the Earth, and consequently will occasion a kind of Procession, or annual Variation in the Place of the Sun, not unlike that of the Equinoxes, or Motion of all the Stars together, from West to East round the Ecliptic Poles, and probably may in some Degree be the Occasion of it. This Angle is represented, but much magnified, by the lines F, C, G, and the Unnaturalness, or Absurdity of a right Line Motion of the Sun by the Line I, H.

"The second Method of solving this Phænomena, is by a spherical Order of the Stars, all moving with different Direction round one common Center, as the Planets and Comets together do round the Sun, but in a kind of Shell, or concave Orb. The former is easily conceived, from what has been already said, and the latter is as easy to be understood, if you have any Idea of the Segment of a Globe, which the adjacent Figures, will, I hope, assist you to. The Doctrine of these Motions will perhaps be made very obvious to you, by inspecting the following Plates. Plate XXIV. Is a Representation of the Convexity, if I may call it so, of the intire Creation, as a universal Coalition of all the Stars consphered round one general Center, and as all governed by one and the same Law. Plate XXV. Is a centeral Section of the same, with the Eye of Providence seated in the Center, as in the virtual Agent of Creation. Plate XXVI. Represents a Creation of a double Construction, where a superior Order of Bodies C, may be imagined to be circumscribed by the former one A, as possessing a more eminent Seat, and nearer the supream Presence, and consequently of a more perfect Nature. Lastly, Plate XXVII. Represents such a Section, and Segments of the same, as I hope will give you a perfect Idea of what I mean by such a Theory. *Fig.* 1. is a corresponding Section of the Part at A, in *Fig.* 2. whose versed Sine is equal to half the Thickness of the starry Vortice AC, or BA. Now I say, by supposing the Thickness of this Shell, 1. you may imagine the middle Semi-Chord AD, or AE, to be nearly 6; and consequently, thus in a like regular Distribution of the Stars, there must of course be at least three Times as many to be seen in this Direction of the Sine, or Semi-chord AE, itself, than in that of the semi-versed Sine AC, or where near the Direction of the Radius of the space G. Q.E.D.

"But we are not confined by this Theory to this Form only, there may be various Systems of Stars, as well as Planets, and differing probably as much in their Order and Distribution as the Zones of *Jupiter* do from the Rings of *Saturn*, it is not at all necessary, that every collective Body of Stars should move in the same Direction, or after the same Model of Motion, but may as reasonably be supposed as much to vary, as we find our Planets and Comets do.

"Hence we may imagine some Creations of Stars may move in the Direction of perfect Spheres, all variously inclined, direct and retrograde; others again, as the primary Planets do, in a general Zone or Zodiac, or more properly in the manner of *Saturn's* Rings, nay, perhaps Ring within Ring, to a third or fourth Order, as shown in *Plate* XXVIII. nothing being more evident, than that if all the Stars we see moved in one vast Ring, like those of *Saturn*, round any central Body, or Point, the general Phænomena of our Stars would be solved by it; see *Plate* XXIX. *Fig.* 1. and 2. the one representing a full Plane of these Motions, the other a Profile of them, and a visible Creation at B and C, the central Body A, being supposed as *incognitum*, without the finite View; not only the Phænomena of the *Milky Way* may be thus accounted for, but also all the cloudy Spots, and irregular Distribution of them; and I cannot help being of Opinion, that could we view *Saturn* thro' a Telescope capable of it, we should find his Rings no other than an infinite Number of lesser Planets, inferior to those we call his Satellites: What inclines me to believe it, is this, this Ring, or Collection of small Bodies, appears to be sometimes very excentric, that is, more distant from *Saturn's* Body on one Side than on the other, and as visibly leaving a larger Space between the Body and the Ring; which would hardly be the Case, if the Ring, or Rings, were connected, or solid, since we have good Reason to suppose, it would be equally attracted on all Sides by the Body of *Saturn*, and by that means preserve everywhere an equal Distance from him; but if they are really little Planets, it is clearly demonstrable from our own in like Cases, that there may be frequently more of them on one Side, than on the other, and but very rarely, if ever, an equal Distribution of them all round the *Saturnian* Globe.

"How much a Confirmation of this is to be wished, your own Curiosity may make you judge, and here I leave it for the Opticians to determine. I shall content myself with observing that Nature never leaves us without a sufficient Guide to conduct us through all the necessary Paths of Knowledge; and it is far from absurd to suppose Providence may have every where throughout the whole Universe, interspersed Modules of every Creation, as our Divines tell us, Man is the Image of God himself.

"Thus, Sir, you have had my full Opinion, without the least Reserve, concerning the visible Creation, considered as Part of the finite Universe; how far I have succeeded in my designed Solution of the *Via Lactea*, upon which the Theory of the Whole is formed, is a Thing will hardly be known in the present Century, as in all probability it may require some Ages of Observation to discover the Truth of it."

The eighth and ninth letters, which are on the modes of conceiving space and time, and contain general reflections on the whole scheme, contain nothing which need be quoted. Wright seems to have been the first who started the idea of representing the solar system by selected objects on the earth. Representing the sun by the dome of St. Pauls, a sphere of eighteen inches diameter at Marylebone will be the earth, and so on. There is internal evidence that these letters were written in London.

I should sum up by saying that Wright appears to have been a man of great ingenuity, and of moderate learning, of a strong turn for the invention of hypothesis, and great power of appreciating its probability. He had a firm persuasion that astronomical discovery was then very imperfect, both in quantity and quality, a persuasion which regulated even his ordinary expressions. It is not often, in his day, that we find, as in his works, the planets described as the *known planets*, implying an assumption that there might be more. He gave the theory of the milky way which is now considered as established, contended for what is now called the central sun, inclining strongly to the belief of an actual central body, though he sometimes qualifies it by stating the alternative of a central body or a central point. He contends for the probability of different creations of the kind of which the milky way is one; but he does not seem to have known of more than half a dozen nebulæ, and he does not push his views so far as to conjecture that these "cloudy spots" are themselves other such creations: he rather refers them to condensations occurring in the mass of stars to which our sun belongs. His prediction of the ultimate resolution of Saturn's rings into congeries of small satellites remains to be verified; but it is thought by some to be most probable that such is the truth. It is hardly necessary to say that Wright supposes mutual gravitation to be the connecting agent between star and star, as well as between stars and their planets.

Kant adds to what he probably learnt from the review of

Wright, the distinct supposition that the nebulæ are other specimens of constellative systems, and that these systems, with our own, may be but parts of a larger one, and so on. He also declares for Sirius as the central body of our system. Wright considers Sirius merely as our nearest neighbour.

There is an account of Thomas Wright (with a good portrait) in the Gentleman's Magazine for 1793, vol. lxiii. pp. 9, 126, 213. He was born at Byer's Green, about six miles from the city of Durham, September 22, 1711, the son of a carpenter, a small landholder. He was apprenticed to a clock-maker, then went to sea, and afterwards struggled for many years as a maker of almanacs, a lecturer, and a teacher of mathematics. During this time he published some works. At last he seems to have risen into note as a teacher of the sciences in noble families; and we find him in affluence towards the end of his life, but how it came is not stated. He built himself a handsome house at Byer's Green in 1756-62, and died there February 25, 1786. By various communications made by him to the Gentleman's Magazine from 1744 upwards, it appears that he was an observer, particularly of comets, a calculator of their elements, &c. In his younger days he was employed by Heath and Sisson as a maker of mathematical instruments; and he wrote on navigation and taught it with a reputation which procured him, in 1742, an offer of the professorship of navigation in the Imperial Academy of St Petersburg. He was moreover an engraver, and even executed the plates for some of his own works; and as the one which I have described has so many quarto plates, effectively done in mezzotinto, and without the name of any engraver attached, I conclude, in spite of "by the best masters" in the title-page, they are of Wright's own workmanship. He had some acquired scholarship, but not of a very profound cast.

I learn from Professor Chevallier, of the University of Durham, to whom I am indebted for the references to the Gentleman's Magazine, that when the library of Mr. Allan of Darlington, the author of the memoir cited, was sold by auction in London in 1822, it contained, as the memoir states, the original copper of several of Wright's plates. And further, that Wright appears to have been consulted on matters of taste: for that in the chapter library of Durham there is a design by him for some alterations in the Cathedral, including an ornamented battlement with finials upon the western towers; which design was carried into execution, as is to be seen.

The works by Wright which are mentioned in the memoir, are some calculations of eclipses (single leaves, I suppose, descriptive of the phases, after the manner of the time); the *Pannauticon*, a work on navigation, published in 1734; *Louthiana*, a work on the antiquities of Ireland, of which one volume only was published in 1748; the treatise described in this article; and others which I do not note, as according to a common fashion of biographical memoirs, there is a confusion between works "completed" and works printed and published. Lalande mentions The Use of the Globes, London, 1740, 8vo; *Clavis Cœlestis*, being the explication of a diagram entitled A Synopsis of the Universe.... London, 1742, 4to; and the work above described.

It seems to me that Wright is entitled to have his speculations considered, not as the accident of a mind which must give the rein to imagination, and sometimes get into a right path, but as the justifiable research and successful conclusion of thought founded on both knowledge and observation. And I submit that his name ought to be enrolled in the list of discoverers.

University College,
March 7, 1848.

---

XXXVII. *On the supposed Influence of Magnetism on Chemical Action.* By ROBERT HUNT, *Esq.*

*To Richard Phillips, Esq.*

DEAR SIR,

THE question whether magnetism exerts any influence on chemical phænomena, has for a very considerable period agitated the world of science. On the one hand, we find Von Arnim, J. W. Ritter, Ludicke, Maschmann, Hansteen, Schweigger, Döbereiner, Muller, Kastner, Fresnel, Murray, Rendu, Zantedeschi, and Ampère expressing opinions, derived from their observations, that some influence is exerted, in many cases retarding, and in others accelerating chemical action; while one or two of these observers assert that magnetism has even the power of setting up chemical change. On the other hand, Steinhäuser, Erman, Dulk, Wetzlar, Otto-Linné Erdman, Berzelius, Ridolfi, Nobili and Wartmann[*], state that they have not been enabled to detect any such influence, although they have employed magnets of great power in their experiments.

It is evident, from this array of names, that the question is surrounded with considerable difficulties; and it becomes

[*] Third Memoir on Induction by Prof. Elie Wartmann, Phil. Mag. for April, 1847, p. 264.

therefore the more important to settle it with certainty, either one way or the other, if possible.

It is only honest that I should state, that the results of all my earlier experiments led me to believe that magnetism exerted a retarding influence upon chemical action; and under this impression, having made some hundreds of experiments, I submitted a communication to the Royal Society, which I afterwards withdrew, from the circumstance that under some new modifications of these experiments I obtained many exceedingly contradictory results.

It may be imagined that careless manipulation, or the interference of other influences which should have been guarded against, must have been the cause of this want of uniformity. I am unwilling to admit this; and although I feel confident that I have established clearly, in some recent experiments, the fact that *magnetism exerts no influence on the chemical action set up*, I can only explain the very decided results which crowd the pages of my note-book, and which deceived such men as Hansteen, Fresnel and Ampère, on the supposition that there exists some molecular forces with which we are not yet acquainted, but which are most sensibly affected by several of the elementary forces, and consequently determine the intensity of chemical excitement. In no other way will the phænomena admit of explanation, which I have again and again witnessed, when iron wires were placed in solutions of litmus, of sulphate of copper, of sulphuric acid, &c., and arranged in different orders in reference to the magnetic equator, or disposed in various relations as regards powerful permanent magnets and electro-magnets.

I do not deem it advisable to occupy the pages of the Philosophical Magazine with any description of these experiments at the present time, particularly, as I intend to pursue the investigation in the hope of elucidating its involved phænomena. I desire only to call attention to a form of experiment, which appears to me to be most unobjectionable, and which I think we may regard as an *experimentum crucis*.

The conditions which I thought essential to the accurate solution of this question were the following:—

1. A correct measure of the amount of chemical action.

2. Means of determining if the action was constant and unvarying.

3. The power of bringing the whole under magnetic influence without in any way disturbing the arrangement, or bringing any other forces besides magnetism into action.

This was effected in the following manner:—A soft iron wire (*a*), which previously to the experiment was ascertained not to possess polarity, was placed in a glass tube, around which was wound four or six coils of copper wire carefully

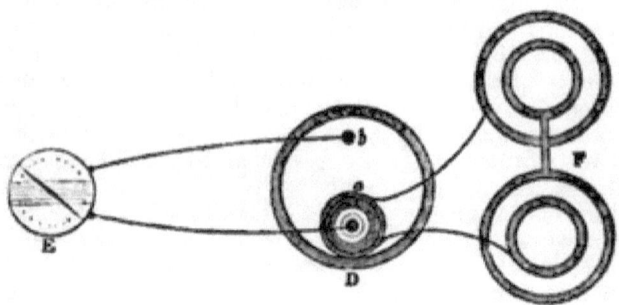

covered with sealing-wax. Thus arranged, it was placed in a vessel holding diluted sulphuric acid (D), and another wire, sometimes of copper and sometimes of iron ($b$), being placed in the same solution, both were connected by long copper wires with a galvanometer (E), placed at such a distance as to be entirely removed from the influence of magnetic attraction. One wire from the helix was connected with a pole of a galvanic battery (F), consisting of one or more pairs of plates, the other wire being so placed that the circuit could be readily made or broken. This arrangement being completed, everything was so secured that the wires in the electrolyte should not suffer the slightest disturbance when connection was made or broken between the helix and the battery.

It is evident by this means, a very delicate galvanometer being used, that I secured a most accurate measurer of the chemical action excited by the acid and the iron wire; that I had the power of rendering the iron magnetic at pleasure, and of using any amount of force I thought proper.

An iron and a copper wire being immersed in the electrolyte, the astatic needles of the galvanometer were allowed to come to absolute rest, and the permanent deflection observed. The circuit with the battery through the helix was now completed, and consequently, by induction, the iron rendered powerfully magnetic. In every instance, upon either making or breaking connection, the needle of the galvanometer vibrated from $3°$ to $5°$, but steadily returned to its permanent deflection, as previously noted.

This transient disturbance of the needle arose from the passage of an induced current through the electrolyte, and by the wires to the galvanometer, and was evidently not at all due to any magnetic influence. It was a case precisely similar to the following one, mentioned by Dr. Faraday in his Experimental Researches, 1st series, par. 20.

"When a small voltaic arrangement was introduced into the circuit between the galvanometer and its helix or wire so as to cause a permanent deflection of 30° or 40°, and then the battery of one hundred pairs of plates connected with the inducing wire, there was an instantaneous action as before; but the galvanometer-needle immediately resumed and retained its place unaltered, notwithstanding the continued contact of the inducing wire with the trough: such was the case in whichever way the contacts were made."

The direction of the current through the helix was altered, so that sometimes the north pole was in the solution and sometimes the south pole; but no difference was observed upon the galvanometer-needle.

Bunsen's battery was the one employed, and from one to six pairs were used; but the increased power did not make the slightest difference. In every experiment the iron wire was changed; for it was found that it became, when magnetized thus, being at the same time under the influence of chemical excitement, more permanently polar than electro-magnets do ordinarily.

When two iron wires were employed, one of them was almost invariably found to be positive to the other when they were first plunged into the dilute acid; but after some short time they were more equally influenced: and although the deflection may at first have been 20° or 30°, yet the galvanometer-needle slowly returned to zero, or at most indicated only a deflection of 2° or 3°. It certainly was expected that magnetism would render one wire positive to the other in a much more decided manner; but no such effect could be detected in any one of a great number of experiments; the transient tremor being the only influence observed upon the needle when the helix was connected with the battery or disconnected from it.

It was thought possible, and indeed some previous experiments with permanent magnets led me to the conclusion, that two magnets of equal power being placed in the solution, one with its north pole and the other with its south pole immersed, would give some indication of a current, arising from a difference in the chemical action upon them. With this view two helices were prepared, and arranged in the vessel D so that both of the iron wires $a$ $b$ could be rendered magnetic at the same time. Not any indication could be obtained with the galvanometer, nor could any deflection be observed even when the electro-magnetic influence was considerably different upon the two wires.

With the view of ascertaining if any diamagnetic conditions could be induced which would in any way influence chemical change, wires of copper and of zinc were substituted for those of iron; but in no case was any deflection produced upon the needle of the galvanometer which could be at all attributable to magnetic influence.

From these experiments, which of course have no bearing upon the disposition of crystals, or the direction of bodies free to move near the poles of magnets, I am compelled, notwithstanding my former impressions, to conclude that MAGNETISM *has no direct influence upon this form of* CHEMICAL ACTION *either as an accelerating or a retarding agent.*

I am, dear Sir,
Yours truly,
ROBERT HUNT.

6 Craig's Court,
March 12, 1848.

XXXVIII. *On the Solution of a particular Differential Equation.* By the Rev. BRICE BRONWIN*.

IN the seventh Number, new series, of the Cambridge Mathematical Journal, Mr. Boole gave a solution of a particular differential equation, having for its coefficients certain integral functions of $x$. The object of this paper is to show that it admits of an infinite number of solutions; or rather, that an infinite number of equations may be solved by it, and those equations not necessarily having integer coefficients. The symbols $\pi_m$ and $\pi_n$ containing symbols both of operation and quantity, the equation in question is

$$\pi_m \pi_n u + p\lambda u = X, \quad \ldots \quad (1.)$$

where $p$ is constant, $\lambda$ a function of $x$, as is also $X$, which I have added to make the equation more general. There are also the two equations of condition,

$$\pi_m \pi_n = \pi_n \pi_m + f(m)\lambda, \quad \pi_n \lambda = \lambda \pi_{m+1}. \quad \ldots \quad (2.)$$

These are here separated from their subject $u$, on which they operate. To solve (1.), make $u = \pi_{m+1} u_1$; it becomes

$$\pi_m \pi_n \pi_{m+1} u_1 + p\lambda \pi_{m+1} u_1 = X;$$

or by the second of (2.),

$$\pi_m \pi_n \pi_{m+1} u_1 + p\pi_m \lambda u_1 = X,$$

and

$$\pi_n \pi_{m+1} u_1 + p\lambda u_1 = \pi_m^{-1} X.$$

This by the first of (2.) becomes

$$\pi_{m+1} \pi_n u_1 + p_1 \lambda u_1 = \pi_m^{-1} X,$$

* Communicated by the Author.

where $p_1 = p - f(m+1)$. After $i$ transformations, this becomes

$$\pi_{m+i}\pi_n u_i + p_i \lambda u_i = \pi_{m+i-1}^{-1}\pi_{m+i-2}^{-1} \ldots \pi_m^{-1} X,$$

$$p_i = p - f(m+1) - f(m+2) \ldots - f(m+i).$$

If $p_i = 0$, we find, making $f(m) = a(n-m)$,

$$p = ia\left(n - m - \frac{i+1}{2}\right).$$

If $p$ has this value, we have

$$u_i = \pi_n^{-1}\pi_{m+i}^{-1}\pi_{m+i-1}^{-1} \ldots \pi_m^{-1} X,$$

and

$$u = \pi_{m+1}\pi_{m+2} \ldots \pi_{m+i}\pi_n^{-1}\pi_{m+i}^{-1}\pi_{m+i-1}^{-1} \ldots \pi_m^{-1} X.$$

Before I make any observations on this, I will proceed to what Mr. Boole calls the conjugate solution.

Make $u = \pi_m^{-1} u_1$, and (1.) becomes

$$\pi_m \pi_n \pi_m^{-1} u_1 + p\lambda \pi_m^{-1} u_1 = X;$$

or

$$(\pi_n \pi_m + f(m)\lambda)\pi_m^{-1} u_1 + p\lambda \pi_m^{-1} u_1 = X,$$

and

$$\pi_n u_1 + p_1 \lambda \pi_m^{-1} u_1 = X, \quad p_1 = p + f(m),$$

which, by operating with $\pi_{m-1}$ on all the terms, becomes

$$\pi_{m-1}\pi_n u_1 + p_1 \pi_{m-1} \lambda \pi_m^{-1} u_1 = \pi_{m-1} X,$$

or

$$\pi_{m-1}\pi_n u_1 + p_1 \lambda u_1 = \pi_{m-1} X.$$

Therefore, by repeating the operations,

$$\pi_{m-i}\pi_n u_i + p_i \lambda u_i = \pi_{m-i}\pi_{m-i+1} \ldots \pi_{m-1} X,$$

$$p_i = p + f(m) + f(m-1) \ldots + f(m-i+1).$$

If $p_i = 0$, and $f(m)$ as before, we have

$$p = ia\left(m - n - \frac{i-1}{2}\right).$$

$$u_i = \pi_n^{-1}\pi_{m-i+1}\pi_{m-i+2} \ldots \pi_{m-1} X$$

$$u = \pi_m^{-1}\pi_{m-1}^{-1} \ldots \pi_{m-i+1}^{-1}\pi_n^{-1}\pi_{m-i+1}\pi_{m-i+2} \ldots \pi_{m-1} X.$$

By the nature of these operations, the integer $i$ is necessarily positive. The two solutions obtained are solutions of two different equations, the quantity $p$ being different in the two cases. In the latter of them, when $X = 0$, the factors $\pi_{m-i+1}\pi_{m-i+2} \ldots \pi_{m-1}$ may be omitted; but in the former, the factors $\pi_{m+i-1}^{-1}\pi_{m+i-2}^{-1} \ldots \pi_m^{-1}$ must not be omitted. Mr. Boole

has fallen into an error in doing this. If, for example, we have
$$(1-x^2)\frac{d^2y}{dx^2}+p(p-1)y=0,$$
and we make
$$y_1=\frac{dy}{dx},\quad y_2=\frac{dy_1}{dx},\ \&c.,$$
and differentiate successively until we arrive at
$$(1-x^2)\frac{d^2y_p}{dx^2}-2px\frac{dy_p}{dx}=0,$$
$p$ being an integer; let $\frac{dy_p}{dx}=\mathrm{A}\mathrm{X}$ be the first integral, and we shall have
$$y=\mathrm{A}\mathrm{X}_1+a+a_1x+a_2x^2\ldots+a_px^p.$$
We must by substitution in the proposed determine $a$, $a_1$, &c., and we shall have only a particular integral. The supernumerary arbitraries are always to be thus determined. The two solutions we have found will only give particular integrals, as we shall presently see.

Change $f(m)$ into $f(n)=a(n-m)$, and make $u=\pi_n^{-1}u_1$. With this value (1.) becomes
$$\pi_m u_1+p\lambda\pi_n^{-1}u_1=\mathrm{X},$$
and
$$\pi_{n-1}\pi_m u_1+p\pi_{n-1}\lambda\pi_n^{-1}u_1=\pi_{n-1}\mathrm{X},$$
or
$$\pi_{n-1}\pi_m u_1+p\lambda u_1=\pi_{n-1}\mathrm{X};$$
and by the first of (2.),
$$\pi_m\pi_{n-1}u_1+p_1\lambda u_1=\pi_{n-1}\mathrm{X},\quad p_1=p-f(n-1).$$
By $i$ repetitions of this process, we arrive at a solution, if
$$p=f(n-1)+f(n-2)\ldots+f(n-i)=ai\left(n-m-\frac{i+1}{2}\right).$$

Again, make $u=\pi_{n+1}u_1$, and we have
$$\pi_m\pi_n\pi_{n+1}u_1+p\lambda\pi_{n+1}u_1=\mathrm{X},$$
$$(\pi_n\pi_m+f(n)\lambda)\pi_{n+1}u_1+p\lambda\pi_{n+1}u_1=\mathrm{X}.$$
Or if $p_1=p+f(n)$,
$$\pi_n\pi_m\pi_{n+1}u_1+p_1\pi_n\lambda u_1=\mathrm{X},$$
and
$$\pi_m\pi_{n+1}u_1+p_1\lambda u_1=\pi_n^{-1}\mathrm{X},$$
which leads to a solution if
$$p=-f(n)-f(n+1)\ldots-f(n+i-1),$$

or
$$p = ai\left(m - n - \frac{i-1}{2}\right).$$

As the two values of $p$ now found are the same as those found in the two first solutions, the two equations solved are the same; and the two sets of solutions are only particular solutions, for the solutions themselves are evidently different.

We now proceed to solve the equations (2.). Putting D for $\frac{d}{dx}$, and supposing $\varphi$, $\theta$, and $\lambda$ functions of $x$, we make
$$\tau_m = \varphi_m D + \theta_m, \quad \tau_n = \varphi_n D + \theta_n;$$
then, if we use the accent for different coefficient,
$$\tau_m \tau_n = \varphi_m \varphi_n D^2 + (\varphi_m \varphi'_n + \varphi_m \theta_n + \varphi_n \theta_m) D + \varphi_m \theta'_n + \theta_m \theta_n$$
$$\tau_n \tau_m = \varphi_n \varphi_m D^2 + (\varphi_n \varphi'_m + \varphi_n \theta_m + \varphi_m \theta_n) D + \varphi_n \theta'_m + \theta_n \theta_m.$$
Make
$$\tau_m \tau_n = \tau_n \tau_m + f(m)\lambda,$$
and we find, by substituting the above values,
$$\varphi_m \varphi'_n - \varphi_n \varphi'_m = 0, \quad f(m)\lambda = \varphi_n \theta'_n - \varphi_n \theta'_m.$$
Integrating the first of these, we have $\varphi_m = \varphi_n$, for an arbitrary constant would not add to the generality. The second thus becomes
$$f(m)\lambda = \varphi_m(\theta'_n - \theta'_m).$$

From $\tau_m \lambda = \lambda \tau_{m+1}$ by substitution we find
$$\varphi_{m+1} - \varphi_m = 0, \quad \varphi_m \lambda' + (\theta_m - \theta_{m+1})\lambda = 0;$$
or
$$\Delta \varphi_m = 0, \quad \Delta \theta_m = \varphi_m \frac{\lambda'}{\lambda}.$$

Suppose that $\lambda$ does not contain $m$ or $n$, and by integrating these we have $\varphi_m = \varphi_n =$ a constant, or rather a function of $x$, without $m$ or $n$, which we shall denote by $\varphi$; and
$$\theta_m = m\varphi \frac{\lambda'}{\lambda} + f(x),$$
where $f(x)$ is any function of $x$ whatever, provided it does not contain $m$ or $n$. And $f(m)\lambda = \varphi(\theta'_n - \theta'_m)$ gives
$$f(m)\lambda = (n-m)\varphi D\left(\varphi \frac{\lambda'}{\lambda}\right);$$
or
$$a\lambda = \varphi D\left(\varphi \frac{\lambda'}{\lambda}\right). \quad \ldots \quad (3.)$$

Make $\varphi = \lambda$, and we have $a = \lambda''$; and integrating

$$\lambda = \frac{1}{2}ax^2 + bx + c,$$

and therefore

$$\pi_m = \left(\frac{1}{2}ax^2 + bx + c\right)D + m(ax+b) + f(x).$$

This will give an infinite number of equations, to which the solutions found will apply. But in (3.) make $\varphi = \beta\lambda$; then

$$a = \beta D(\beta\lambda') = \lambda'\beta\frac{d\beta}{dx} + \beta^2\lambda''.$$

Whence by assuming either $\lambda$ or $\beta$ at pleasure, the other may be found by integrating a linear equation of the first order; and thus we shall have an infinite number of integrable equations, the coefficients being, or not being, integer functions of $x$.

Now, instead of (2.), let the conditions be

$$\pi_m\pi_n = \pi_n\pi_m + f(m)\lambda, \quad \pi_m\lambda = \lambda\pi_{m-1}. \quad . \quad . \quad (4.)$$

The first of these by substitution gives as before, and the second $\varphi_m - \varphi_{m-1} = 0$; or $\varphi_m = \varphi_n = \varphi$, a function of $x$, without $m$ or $n$. Also

$$\varphi\lambda' + \lambda(\theta_m - \theta_{m-1}) = 0, \quad \Delta\theta_{m-1} = -\varphi\frac{\lambda'}{\lambda},$$

$$\theta_{m-1} = -(m-1)\varphi\frac{\lambda'}{\lambda} + f(x), \quad \theta_m = -m\varphi\frac{\lambda'}{\lambda} + f(x).$$

Make $f(m) = a(m-n)$, and we have

$$a\lambda = \varphi D\left(\varphi\frac{\lambda'}{\lambda}\right)$$

as before.

To apply (4.) to the solution of (1.), make $u = \pi_{m-1}u_1$, and we have successively

$$\pi_m\pi_n\pi_{m-1}u_1 + p\lambda\pi_{m-1}u_1 = X, \quad \pi_m\pi_n\pi_{m-1}u_1 + p\pi_m\lambda u_1 = X,$$

$$\pi_n\pi_{m-1}u_1 + p\lambda u_1\pi_m^{-1}X, \quad \pi_{m-1}\pi_nu_1 + p_1\lambda u_1 = \pi_m^{-1}X,$$

$$p_1 = p - f(m-1).$$

And therefore

$$\pi_{m-i}\pi_nu_i = \pi_{m-i+1}^{-1}\pi_{m-i+2}^{-1}\ldots\pi_m^{-1}X,$$

if $p_i = 0$, or

$$p = f(m-1) + f(m-2) \ldots + f(m-i) = ai\left(m - n - \frac{i+1}{2}\right),$$

$$u = \pi_{m-1}\pi_{m-2}\ldots\pi_{m-i}\pi_n^{-1}\pi_{m-i}^{-1}\ldots\pi_m^{-1}X.$$

*particular Differential Equation.*

Again, make $u = \pi_m^{-1} u_1$; then

$$\pi_m \pi_n \pi_m^{-1} u_1 + p\lambda \pi_m^{-1} u_1 = X, \quad (\pi_n \pi_m + f(m)\lambda)\pi_m^{-1} u_1 + p\lambda \pi_m^{-1} u_1 = X,$$

$$\pi_n u_1 + p_1 \lambda \pi_m^{-1} u_1 = X, \quad p_1 = p + f(m),$$

$$\pi_{m+1} \pi_n u_1 + p_1 \pi_{m+1} \lambda \pi_m^{-1} u_1 = \pi_{m+1} X, \quad \pi_{m+1} \pi_n u_1 + p_1 \lambda u_1 = \pi_{m+1} X.$$

And therefore if $p_i = 0$, we have

$$\pi_{m+i} \pi_n u_1 = \pi_{m+i} \pi_{m+i-1} \ldots \pi_{m+1} X$$

$$u = \pi_m^{-1} \pi_{m+1}^{-1} \ldots \pi_{m+i}^{-1} \pi_n^{-1} \pi_{m+i-1} \ldots \pi_{m+1} X,$$

$$p = -f(m) - f(m+1) \ldots -f(m+i-1) = ai\left(n - m - \frac{i-1}{2}\right).$$

As the two last values of $p$ are different from the former, the two solutions now obtained relate to different equations.

Now change $f(m)$ into $f(n)$, and make $u = \pi_n^{-1} u_1$; then

$$\pi_n u_1 + p\lambda \pi_n^{-1} u_1 = X, \quad \pi_{n+1} \pi_n u_1 + p\pi_{n+1} \lambda \pi_n^{-1} u_1 = \pi_{n+1} X,$$

$$\pi_{n+1} \pi_n u_1 + p\lambda u_1 = \pi_{n+1} X, \text{ and } \pi_m \pi_{n+1} u_1 + p_1 \lambda u_1 = \pi_{n+1} X,$$

$$p_1 = p - f(n+1).$$

Also $p_i = 0$ gives

$$p = f(n+1) \ldots + f(n+i) = ai\left(m - n - \frac{i+1}{2}\right).$$

Make $u = \pi_{n-1} u_1$, we have

$$\pi_m \pi_n \pi_{n-1} u_1 + p\lambda \pi_{n-1} u_1 = X,$$

$$(\pi_n \pi_m + f(n)\lambda)\pi_{n-1} u_1 + p\lambda \pi_{n-1} u_1 = X,$$

$$\pi_n \pi_m \pi_{n-1} u_1 + p_1 \pi_n \lambda u_1 = X, \quad p_1 = p + f(n),$$

and

$$\pi_m \pi_{n-1} u_1 + p_1 \lambda u_1 = \pi_n^{-1} X.$$

If by $i$ operations $p_i = 0$, we have

$$p = -f(n) - f(n-1) \ldots -f(n-i+1) = ai\left(n - m - \frac{i-1}{2}\right)$$

As the two last values of $p$ are the same with the two former, we have again two sets of particular solutions to the same two equations, unless the complete solutions may be expressed in two different ways.

Instead of the second condition of (2.) and (4.), we might make

$$\pi_m \lambda = \lambda \pi_{m+r} \quad \pi_m \lambda = \lambda \pi_{m-r}$$

But then we should have to integrate

$$\varphi_{m+r} - \varphi_m = 0, \quad \theta_{m+r} - \theta_m = \varphi_m \frac{\lambda'}{\lambda}, \&c.,$$

making the arbitraries functions of $x$. This would lead to very complicated results, and therefore I shall not pursue the subject further, but shall content myself with having added another case to that treated by Mr. Boole.

Gunthwaite Hall, near Barnsley, Yorkshire,
February 17, 1848.

## XXXIX. *Researches on the Radiations of Incandescent Bodies, and on the Elementary Colours of the Solar Spectrum.* By M. MELLONI[*].

AMONG the more recent scientific publications will be found a memoir by the American Professor, J. W. Draper, On the Production of Light by Heat[†], which appears to me to merit the attentive consideration of those who interest themselves in the progress of the natural sciences. The author treats, in a very ingenious manner, some questions allied to my own researches on light and radiant heat. In reading this interesting work several ideas have presented themselves to me, which I have submitted to the test of experiment. I believe that an analysis of the memoir of Mr. Draper, accompanied with a brief account of what I have done, will not be without interest to the readers of this journal.

Every one knows that heat, when it accumulates in bodies, at last renders them *incandescent*; that is to say, more or less luminous and visible in the dark. Is the temperature necessary to produce this state of incandescence always the same, or does it vary with the nature of the body? In either case what is its degree? and what is the succession of coloured lights emitted by a given substance, when brought to temperatures more and more elevated? Finally, what is the relation that subsists at different periods of incandescence between the temperature and the quantity of light and of heat emitted by a body?

To solve these different questions, of which some have been already studied by other philosophers, Professor Draper has made use of an instrument composed of a strip of platina ignited by the action of a voltaic current. The strip was vertical, its length one inch and one-third, its width the twentieth of an inch, and its upper extremity being fastened to a firm support, it was kept stretched by a little weight furnished with a copper wire, that dipped into some mercury placed in a cup

[*] Read at the Royal Academy of Sciences at Naples, July 6, 1847, and translated for Silliman's American Journal from the *Bibliothèque Universelle* of Geneva for August 1847.
[†] Phil. Mag., May 1847, vol. xx. p. 345.

below. The electric circuit was established by placing the mercury and the upper extremity of the platina strip in communication with the poles of a Grove's battery, of which the force, properly moderated by a Whentstone's rheostat, could be kept constant for about an hour. By means of this arrangement, the strip of platina, more or less ignited by the action of the voltaic current, preserved its rectilinear direction; the copper wire which was fastened to the weight merely dipping more or less deeply into the mercury. To determine the dilatations of the strip, there was attached to its free extremity a long and very slender horizontal lever, arranged in such a manner that the point of attachment was very near one of the extremities of the lever which worked upon a pivot, and the other end traversed over a divided scale, taking a position more or less oblique to the horizon as the weight and wire descended by the dilatation of the strip, and indicating on the graduated arc the quantities sought.

The temperatures were then calculated on the hypothesis that they were proportional to the dilatation of the platinum, employing for this purpose the coefficient of Dulong and Petit. It will be understood that these calculations are easily made when we know the length of the strip and of the lever, and also the position of their point of attachment. In the instrument employed by Draper, each degree on the graduated arc corresponded to an elevation of $115°$ F. above the temperature of the air.

Suppose, now, we commence by using a feeble current, the force of which is gradually increased by means of the rheostat. The heat correspondingly augments in the strip, and finally makes it visibly red-hot in the dark room in which the experiment is to be conducted. The degree that the index marks is then to be observed. This experiment was repeated several times, and with the aid of different persons (who ought to remain for some time in the dark for their eyes to acquire a due sensibility), and from the mean of all the observations the temperature at which the platina began to be red-hot was calculated. From the experiments of our author this temperature is $977°$ F.

To determine whether all substances become red-hot at the same degree of heat, Professor Draper took a gun-barrel, the touch-hole of which was closed, and placed in it successively platina, copper, gas carbon, lead, earthenware, and other substances; then, making the barrel red-hot in the fire, he observed attentively the moment when the incandescence commenced to manifest itself in the barrel, and the substance which it contained. He could discover no difference of time between the two phænomena; for the gun-barrel and the substance under trial became simultaneously luminous as the temperature was rising, and also simultaneously lost this property when, after being removed from the fire and carried into a dark place, the temperature fell by radiation.

It is important to observe, that in some cases, for example with lead, the matter contained in the tube became incandescent some time after it had melted: this shows that the temperature necessary for the first manifestation of the luminous condition does not depend on the *solid* state of the body submitted to the experiment, and that it takes place in all substances which maintain themselves in the liquid condition without boiling at 977° F. Professor Draper excepts from this law the fluoride of calcium and carbonate of lime, which become luminous much sooner. These cases do not in reality belong to the phænomena we are now considering, but to those of *phosphorescence*, which require a lower degree of heat, according to the nature of the substance. I may add that, regarding the question in a general point of view, we should also except those cases in which the development of light arises in chemical combinations.

But these two exceptions are easily recognized by the quality of the first colours that appear. Thus the carbonate of lime emits, the moment it becomes visible, a white light, and the fluoride of calcium a blue light. Sulphur appears yellow when it combines chemically with copper, and blue when it unites with oxygen. Some philosophers of the highest eminence, among others M. Biot, suppose that the first light disengaged by incandescent bodies is of the latter colour; and they have accounted for this on the principles of a theory which is now almost universally abandoned[*]. We shall presently see what is the probable origin of the various tints that arise from phosphorescent bodies and chemical combinations: we shall merely observe here, that the colour mentioned by Biot occurs in flames; and that these cases of combustion, belonging to the class of chemical combinations, ought to be carefully distinguished from incandescence, properly speaking, which arises directly and solely, as we have already said, from an elevation of temperature in the body, and which always commences with a red light.

As to the exact degree of this temperature, the objections which might be raised against the mode employed by our author are of very little importance; if we compare the results at which he arrives with those that have been obtained by Wedgewood and Daniell, the difference is only 30° in excess for the first case, and 5° too little in the second. The differences are much greater when compared with the deductions

[*] Biot, *Traité de Physique*, vol. iv. p. 617.

of Davy and Newton, which give 812° and 635°; but those numbers, and especially the latter, were obtained by methods too imperfect to be trustworthy; consequently the number 977° F. given by our author, must approach very closely the degree of heat which produces the first incandescence of bodies.

After having studied this first question, already examined by other philosophers, Professor Draper enters on an entirely new field of research, investigating the nature of the colours which are developed by an ignited body as its temperature is increased.

For this purpose he employed a prism of fine flint glass, setting it vertically at a certain distance from the strip of platina; but previously having placed in the position the platina was to occupy, a vertical slit of the same size in a piece of metal, through which a beam of the daylight passed. The spectrum resulting from the transmission of this beam through the prism was received on a small telescope furnished with micrometric wires, and carefully examined in its different parts, for the purpose of determining exactly the position of Fraunhofer's dark lines. The strip of platina was then set in the same place, and he proceeded to make observations on the spectra produced by it at different periods of incandescence. From these it results, that the first spectrum visible in complete darkness corresponds to a temperature of 1210° F., and extends from the fixed line B to the line F; the second spectrum produced by a temperature of 1325°, commences very nearly at the same line B, and terminates at the line $d$; the third at a temperature of 1440°, appears to begin a little nearer the line A, and goes to some distance beyond G; lastly, the fourth, corresponding to a temperature of 2130°, approaches much nearer to A, and extends as far as the line $l$. In other words, the spectrum of the strip of platina which corresponds to the red extremity of the prismatic spectrum, is at first very short, and contains only the less refrangible colours; but as the temperature rises, the spectrum of incandescence extends towards the violet extremity, obtaining the more refrangible tints, and at last acquiring all the colours and all the extent of the solar spectrum, except the terminal rays at the two extremities, which escape the observer evidently on account of their extreme feebleness. The same cause (insensibility due to a want of luminous energy) makes the first spectrum appear, at the red end, a little shorter than the last; because the less refrangible rays of that colour are, as is well known, so feeble, even in the solar spectrum, that we are unable to perceive them unless they are isolated in a place that is totally dark: much more therefore ought they to remain invisible to the observer, when the spectrum arises from luminous agencies so little energetic as are those of the first periods of incandescence.

To a perfectly sensitive eye, the variations of length would evidently have taken place in the direction of the more refrangible rays only, and all the spectra would have commenced at the extreme limit of the red rays.

It results from all these observations, that when the incandescence of a body becomes more and more vivid and brilliant by the elevation of its temperature, there is not only an augmentation in the intensity of the resulting light, but also in the variety of elementary colours which compose it; there is, too, an addition of rays so much the more refrangible as the temperature of the incandescent body is higher. In this there is therefore established an intimate analogy between the progressive development of light and that of heat. Indeed, as soon as I had convinced myself of the immediate transmission of every variety of radiant heat through rock salt, I availed myself of that valuable property to study the refraction of heat from different sources; and I discovered that radiations coming from those of a high temperature contain elements more refrangible than those which are derived from sources that are not so hot.

After having pointed out how very important for the theory of the identity of calorific and luminous radiations, is the analogy or rather absolute equality which exists between his experiments and mine on the successive appearance of the elementary rays, Professor Draper passes forward to investigate the law of the increase of the luminous and calorific radiations, according as the temperature of the source of heat is elevated.

Bouguer has shown that a difference of one-sixtieth in the quantity of light which acts on the eye is insensible, and that thus this fraction constitutes the limit of perceptible variations. From this it arises, that we easily perceive differences in the intensity of light when they exceed even to the smallest extent the sixtieth part of the entire quantity. Let there be placed, for example, an opake cylinder between the red-hot platina, or other source of light, and a sheet of white paper arranged at such a distance that its surface may be illuminated all over by the light of the shining body, except on those parts where the shadow of the cylinder is thrown. Then let there be a lamp furnished with a metallic tube in which there is a small opening; let the rays of the lamp which go out through the aperture fall on the paper enlightened by the luminous source of which we wish to measure the intensity; let the lamp be gradually approached until the shadow of the cylinder is no longer sensible; let this experiment be repeated in each of the different cases we wish to compare with one another, measuring each time the distance from the lamp to the paper. It is then evident that the values sought will be in the inverse ratio of the numbers found.

This method, invented by Bouguer to determine the relative intensities of different luminous sources, and employed by Draper to measure the quantities of light emitted by a strip of platina brought to different degrees of incandescence, is the only one by which we could hope for a successful result. The method of the equality of shadows, well-known under the name of Rumford's method, would have furnished in the researches of the learned American uncertain data, on account of the difficulty of establishing an exact comparison between the *accidental green tint* introduced into the shadow enlightened by the yellow rays of the lamp, and the red light emitted by the ignited metal.

As to the measures of the radiant heat, they were determined by the aid of the thermo-multiplier; that admirable instrument which has revealed to science so many new properties of calorific radiations, and which still is rendering eminent services in the hands of able chemists far beyond the Alps. Professor Draper had only to arrange at a certain distance from his strip of platina a thermo-electric pile, and to observe for each phase of incandescence the deviation of the index of the galvanometer to determine the quantities sought. In this manner he obtained the numbers contained in the following table, divided into three columns. The first of these columns indicates the temperature for each degree of the scale of dilatation, commencing with the point of incandescence: the difference between each of the successive terms of this series is thus constant, and equal to 115°. The second and third columns give the corresponding quantities of light and heat. It is almost superfluous to add, that the unity for light is entirely independent of that for heat, and that the similar independent unities are not referable to the same point of the scale.

| Temperature of the platinum. | Intensity of light. | Intensity of heat. |
|---|---|---|
| 980  |       | ·87   |
| 1095 |       | 1·10  |
| 1210 |       | 1·50  |
| 1325 |       | 1·80  |
| 1440 |       | 2·20  |
| 1555 |       | 2·80  |
| 1670 |       | 3·70  |
| 1785 |       | 5·00  |
| 1900 | 0·34  | 6·80  |
| 2015 | 0·62  | 8·60  |
| 2130 | 1·73  | 10·00 |
| 2245 | 2·92  | 12·50 |
| 2360 | 4·40  | 15·50 |
| 2475 | 7·24  |       |
| 2590 | 12·34 |       |

The numbers of the two latter columns show evidently that the augmentations of both these agents, though feeble at first, become very rapid at last; from which it results that the radiations both of light and heat follow in the *progression of quantity* the same analogy that we have just observed in the *progression of quality*.

This parallel march of the two agents seems to have entirely changed the opinion of the author as to the nature of the rays of light and heat, and the different chemical and physiological effects due to the sun and terrestrial luminous and calorific sources. The preamble of his memoir contains the following passage relative to this point:—

"As the experiments now to be described lead to some striking and perhaps unexpected analogies between light and heat, they commend themselves to our attention, as having a bearing on the question of the identity of those imponderable principles. It is known that heretofore I have been led to believe in the existence of cardinal distinctions, not only between these but also other imponderable agents; and I may therefore state, that when this investigation was first undertaken, it was in the expectation that it would lead to results very different from those that have actually arisen."

The author adds, immediately after the experiments relative to the luminous and calorific radiations, which are simultaneously developed in the strip of platina at different phases of incandescence, "I cannot here express myself with too much emphasis on the remarkable analogy between light and heat which these experiments reveal. The march of the phænomena, in all their leading points, is the same in both cases. The rapid increase of effect as the temperature rises is common to both. And it is not to be forgotten, that, in the case of light, we necessarily measure its effects by an apparatus which possesses special peculiarities. The eye is insensible to rays which are not comprehended within certain limits of refrangibility. In these experiments, it is requisite to raise the temperature of the platinum almost to 1000° before we can discover the first traces of light. Measures obtained under such circumstances are dependent on the physiological action of the visual organ itself, and hence their analogy with those obtained by the thermometer becomes more striking, because we should scarcely have anticipated that it could be so complete."

After the second series of experiments, relative to the quality of the rays emitted as the temperature of the metal rises, Professor Draper criticises some of the facts upon which Sir D. Brewster founds his opinion on the existence of the red, yellow, and blue colours in every part of the Newtonian spectrum. These criticisms acquire more importance since the illustrious mathematician, Airy, the Astronomer Royal of England, has denied the deductions of Sir D. Brewster, and refers to several of his experimental researches in support of the view, that a particular colour corresponds to each element of the spectrum*.

"As (in the experiment in which a metal is ignited)," adds Professor Draper, "the luminous effects are undoubtedly owing to a vibratory movement executed by the molecules of the platinum, it seems from the foregoing considerations to follow, that the frequency of those vibrations increases with the temperature†. In this observation I am led by the principle, that 'to a particular colour there ever belongs a particular wave-length, and to a particular wave-length there ever belongs a particular colour;' but in the analysis of the spectrum made by Sir D. Brewster by the aid of absorptive media, this principle is indirectly controverted; that eminent philosopher showing that red, yellow, blue, and consequently white light, exist in every part of the spectrum. This must necessarily take place when a prism which has a refracting face of considerable magnitude is used; for it is obvious that a ray falling near the edge, and one falling near the back, after dispersion, will paint these several spectra on the screen; the colours of the one not coinciding with, but overlapping the colours of the other. In such a spectrum there must undoubtedly be a general commixture of the rays; but may we not fairly inquire whether, if an elementary prism were used, the same facts would hold good; or, if the anterior face of the prism were covered by a screen, so as to expose a narrow fissure parallel to the axis of the instrument, would there be found in the spectrum it gave every colour in every part, as in Sir D. Brewster's original experiment? M. Melloni has shown how this very consideration complicates the phænomena of radiant heat; and it would seem a very plausible suggestion that the effect here pointed out must occur in an analogous manner for the phænomena of light‡."

* Phil. Mag., No. 199, Feb. 1847. Sir D. Brewster's refutation of the criticisms of Mr. Airy will be found in our Number for March 1847.—Ed. Phil. Mag.

† This expression ought not to be taken in an absolute sense, but rather as relative to the new rays which at a given temperature are added to those already existing in the spectrum.—(Note of M. Melloni.)

‡ Sir David Brewster has replied to Professor Draper as follows:—"As my experiments were not made upon spectra formed upon screens by prisms with large refracting surfaces, they are not liable to this criticism, even if it were otherwise well-founded. The spectra which I use are so pure, and free from all commixture, that Fraunhofer's black lines are distinctly visible;

I shall here observe frankly, that the optical complication (alluded to in this criticism) does take place, as may be clearly proved; it is this very circumstance which led me to detect the errors which had been committed in the determination of the maximum of temperature in spectra arising from different substances. That there may remain no doubt on this point, I will transcribe from my memoir, communicated to the Royal Academy on November 24, 1843, the part that relates to this subject.

"Let one of the three surfaces of an ordinary glass prism be covered with a layer of India ink; let it dry, and then divide it into three equal portions at right angles to its axis. Remove with a penknife the ink from the middle portion, and also a band four or five millimetres wide on the sides of the two lateral compartments, so that these two bands from which the ink has been removed, may be on opposite sides, and form by their junction with the central force a kind of Z. It will be understood, that a solar beam issuing from a prism thus arranged will produce three coloured images side by side; the middle one is very luminous,—it arises from the part of the prism from which all the ink is removed; the two others, which are much paler, arise from the lateral bands. It will also be perceived, that the middle image or spectrum has each of its extremities on the boundary of one of the extremities of the lateral spectra; and that when, for example, its red extremity is in the same line with the red extremity of the left spectrum, its violet extremity will be upon the same line as the violet extremity of the right spectrum, and *vice versâ*. As to the other two extremities of the lateral spectra, they will not be found corresponding to the extremities of the central spectrum, but to some one of the interior colours, and they will evidently be more distant as the width of the uncovered bands is less in proportion to the width of the prism. In one of my experiments made with an equilateral prism of crown glass, the width of which was twenty-four millimetres, and that of the lateral bands five, I found, at a distance of two metres, that the red extremity of the left spectrum was upon the same line as the upper part of the yellow belonging to the central image, and the violet extremity of the right spectrum was and the results are precisely the same when the refracting face of the prism is reduced to the smallest possible dimensions."

"My analysis of the spectrum by absorption does not therefore *indirectly controvert* the principle, that 'to a particular colour there ever belongs a particular wave-length, and to a particular wave-length there ever belongs a particular colour,' as Dr. Draper states, in theoretical language, the well-known proposition of Sir Isaac Newton; but it *directly controverts it*, and *absolutely overturns it*."—Phil. Mag., June 1847, p. 402. (Note of M. de la R.)

upon the blue of the same image. A prism of water, prepared in like manner, of which the refracting angle was 79°, gave analogous results. In one, as in the other case, the red extremity of the left spectrum was on a level with the green of the central image, when the observations were made at the distance of a metre from the prism.

"Let us imagine the central unpainted part of our prism to be divided into a series of longitudinal elements, the width of each being equal to that of the lateral bands. It is clear that each of these elements will produce a refracted image similar to the two pale spectra arising from the lateral bands; and that the two last images of the series will be as it were continuations of those spectra. Therefore, the red and the violet which we see by the side of the yellow and blue of the central coloured spectrum, equally exist in that central spectrum, and enter into the composition of those tints. This argument is unanswerable; it establishes that, instead of being absolutely pure, or even nearly so, the gradations of the image formed by the central compartment contain different colours.*"

I had already proved, in 1843, that the colours obtained by ordinary prisms at a distance less than two metres, are composed of a mixture of colours belonging to the spectra of the different elementary bands of the prism; and that the red, the violet, and consequently all the other prismatic colours of the two extreme elements, are so much the nearer to the centre as the observation is made nearer to the prism. Now, in the experiment of Sir D. Brewster the prism is very close to the eye,—the spectrum obtained in this experiment must necessarily be formed of very impure tints; and the colour which appears in a given zone which has lost by absorption the dominant tint, does not belong to a ray of the same refrangibility as the tint absorbed, but rather to colours of the elementary spectra of the superior or inferior parts of the prism.

To prove this directly, I have repeated the fundamental experiment of Sir D. Brewster. It consists, as is well known, in interposing between the eye and the spectrum, produced by the refracted image of a luminous object seen through the prism, a slip of glass deeply coloured blue by the oxide of cobalt. The spectrum was formed from the light of a circular aperture, ten millimetres in diameter, made in a metallic plate placed in the shutter of a dark chamber. The prism was of flint glass, equilateral, twenty-five millimetres wide, and suf-

* *Museo di Scienze, Lettere ed Arti*, vol. i. fasc. 1, Napoli di 1843. *Bibliothèque Universelle*, 1844, vol. xlix. p. 141.

ficiently pure to produce distinctly the black lines of Fraunhofer. It was attached to its support by one end, placed fifteen feet from the window, and fixed horizontally in the position of minimum deviation. Its anterior face was covered for one-third of its extent with India ink. From the middle of this there was removed a longitudinal space, which ran from end to end of the blackened band, leaving free and uncovered a horizontal line little more than a millimetre in width. The slip of blue glass covered only two-thirds of the prism counting from the painted extremity.

Things being thus arranged, I observed the image of the aperture successively through the uncovered part of the prism, and then through the two portions on which the blue glass was placed. The first operation gave me the normal spectrum; the second, made after the method of Brewster, furnished a complex spectrum; the third, a spectrum arising from a little portion which may be regarded as the mean longitudinal element of the prism. Now, on comparing the first image with the second, I observed the phænomena of luminous and obscure zones so well described by Herschel. On comparing then the third image with the second, I perceived that the luminous zones belonging to the *elementary spectrum* were much more sharp, although less intense, *much narrower*, and traversed by obscure zones, much deeper, larger, and with contours more striking than those of the spectrum which came from the unpainted part of the prism. It was easy thus to convince myself, by the comparative inspection of the three images, that the differences of tint between the second and third spectrum corresponded to the colours which Sir D. Brewster imagines to have the same refrangibility as the tints absorbed. In his spectrum, for instance, the normal orange colour is replaced by an obscure zone invaded on one side by the red, and on the other by the yellow, from which he infers the presence of these two colours in the orange. Now these invasions of the yellow and red do not exist in my elementary spectrum, *in which all the space corresponding to the orange is occupied by a dark zone; the red and the yellow which limit this zone, in the spectrum produced by all the middle part of the prism covered by the blue glass, are therefore independent of this spectrum, and belong to spectra of elementary layers superior and inferior to the intermediate line.*

This last conclusion is nevertheless not exempt from objections. For in a dark room the observer must necessarily have his pupil much dilated, and his sight be more or less confused; consequently, on looking at one time through the uncovered prism, and at another through a limited space of the prism narrower than the pupil of the eye, it may happen that the greater extent of the tints transmitted by the blue glass in the first observation may arise from an indistinct vision, and not from a real overlapping of the colours from the superior and inferior parts of the prism. This conjecture seems the more plausible, since all the rays refracted by the prismatic elements are not perceived by the observer, but only those that pass through the aperture of the pupil.

To determine whether this was in reality the cause of the phænomenon, I placed four small bands of tin around the circular hole in the shutter, and arranged them so that they formed by crossing one another a perfectly square aperture, the sides of which were horizontal and vertical. Then placing before the prism a slip of glass of a deeper blue than the preceding, I saw on looking successively through the central part of the prism and the part from which the paint was partially removed, that the two spectra modified by the interposition of the coloured medium were composed of a red rectangle, almost square, followed by a broad dark zone, and then by a very brilliant yellow rectangle, of which the longer sides were directed vertically and parallel to the length of the spectrum. There came then a deep indistinct colour, then the blue, to the modifications of which it is unnecessary here to attend, but only to the changes of colour and darkness of the space already mentioned which precedes the yellow.

On observing attentively the rectangular form of the space occupied by the yellow rays in each of these spectra, it will be distinctly perceived to be less elongated in the *elementary spectrum* than in the *compound spectrum*. Now distinct vision may diminish the magnitude of the image formed upon the retina, and render the contours more decided and sharp, but it cannot vary the relations of its dimensions. The shorter length of the yellow rectangle in the elementary spectrum must then arise from an effect different from that which is produced on vision by the smallness of the aperture through which the prismatic image is observed. We cannot therefore suppose, the vertical sides of the rectangle being a little sharper and more vivid than the horizontal ones, that this difference of illumination can give origin to the phænomenon in question; for any alteration arising in that way would be in the opposite direction to that actually observed. For, in reality, the most luminous images being those which undergo the greater reduction of size in passing from confused to distinct vision, the yellow rectangle of the spectrum observed in the elementary prism ought to be shorter in the horizontal than in the vertical direction; nevertheless the difference is manifested in just the opposite manner. Therefore the elongation of the yellow rectangle in the central spectrum arises beyond all doubt, altogether or in part, from a partial overlapping of the yellow rays belonging to the spectra of the entire series of elementary prisms, the rays from which traverse the dilated pupil of the observer. This overlapping takes place perpendicularly to the axis of the spectrum, and consequently in a vertical direction in the arrangement adopted in my experiment.

The method proposed by Sir D. Brewster to determine the composition of the solar spectrum does not therefore appear to me adapted to the end in view: and until it shall have been proved that the colours of a spectrum, *perfectly pure*, change by the interposition of a medium placed near the prism, the change persisting at every other distance, *the existence of different colours in the same transverse element of the spectrum ought to be regarded as entirely hypothetical*.

I can therefore no longer admit the existence of different colours in the same part of the spectrum: I hold it as proved, that every particular tint arises from a single ray possessing a particular frequency of vibration, and a particular wave-length. I think altogether with Newton, that colour is a characteristic sign, distinctive of the different elements contained in the beams of the sun and of luminous bodies; elements which are separated only and solely under the action of the prism in virtue of their different degrees of refrangibility.

In thus rejecting a means of analysis, which has enjoyed until now much favour among philosophers, we ought to recollect that Sir David Brewster is the author of very many beautiful and important discoveries confirmed by experiment; works, from the merit of which the conclusion here arrived at can never detract, any more than the errors committed by Newton *on diffraction* and *the dispersion* of luminous rays by diaphanous bodies of different kinds, can ever lessen the glory which must belong to his optical researches, and his discovery of the system of the universe.

To return to the researches of Professor Draper. I say that they conduct, as do others heretofore known on light and radiant heat, to a perfect analogy between the general laws which govern these two great agents of nature. I will add, that I regard the theory of their identity as the only one admissible by the rules of philosophy; and that I consider myself obliged to adopt it, until it shall have been proved to me that there is a necessity of having recourse to two different principles for the explanation of a series of phænomena which at present appear to me to belong to a solitary agent.

I conclude, that the molecules of bodies, slightly heated, vibrate slowly, and produce long and invisible waves in the œthereal medium which surrounds them. As the temperature rises the molecular vibrations chiefly augment in extent, preserving the same isochronism; but some among them increase in frequency also. This increase, nevertheless, does not become very distinct until near the point of incandescence. Then a portion of the ponderable particles begin to vibrate more swiftly than the rest, and produce in the æther shorter undulations, which are consequently more refrangible; and of which some become visible; all contributing to increase the energy and variety of the radiation, until at last a great number of elements of luminous and obscure heat are found united in the radiant flux from sources of high temperature*.

There are, however, certain bodies whose state of molecular equilibrium is such that their particles possess a great facility of vibration; these particles acquiring long before the period of incandescence, altogether or partly, that rapidity of oscillation from which arises visible heat. These bodies constitute the class of phosphorescent substances.

When one body combines chemically with another, its molecules acquire in an instant a very violent vibratory motion, and then may subsequently assume vibrations that are slower. This is what appears to take place in flames, which originate in the combustion of bodies; they commence almost always by a blue or violet light, and then become white or yellow.

But to return to the case in which light and heat are developed by elevation of temperature only; we discover that œthereal undulations incapable of acting on the organ of vision are not alone found in radiations coming from hot and dark bodies, but also in those that arise from luminous sources. These invisible rays are not homogeneous: they are of different kinds; and their specific properties are altogether ana-

* These views, being the direct consequences of the undulatory theory, are not only established in the memoir of Professor Draper here reviewed by M. Melloni, but also in an earlier paper inserted in the Philosophical Magazine, Feb. 1847; of which a translation is given in the *Bibliothèque Universelle*, June 1847, respecting which M. De la Rive remarks in an introductory note, " Il nous semble, en effet, d'une importance assez grande par l'étude bienfaite et l'explication remarquable qu'il contient des phénomènes si singuliers de l'antagonism des rayons de lumière dans les effets chimiques." It also appears from that paper, that he has held them ever since 1842, and used them for the purpose of explaining those remarkable cases of chemical interference which Sir J. Herschel describes, on the hypothesis that the ætherenl waves cause the particles of surfaces on which they impinge to execute vibratory motions.—(Note of the Translator.)

logous to those of colour. Such is the origin of the curious phænomena of chemical and calorific transmission and diffusion which I had the honour to submit, many years ago, to the Academy*.

In conclusion, I cannot but express my admiration how the discovery of a series of facts, which seemed contrary to the theory of the identity of light and heat, has become now the fundamental basis of that theory. Who would not have thought at first sight, that the radiations of heat were of a nature altogether different from light, on seeing them transmitted in such different proportions through substances endued with the greatest transparency; traversing other bodies, strongly coloured, in an immediate and instantaneous manner, and this in greater abundance than through some media perfectly limpid; and going in a single rectilinear path through a plate of completely opake glass? Yet, nevertheless, these singular properties are the necessary consequences of the transparency and coloration of bodies for heat combined with different periods of the æthereal undulations. No one could have ever maintained the identity of light and heat until there had first been proved *coloration* of the one and the other of these agents, and the quality that every ray of dark heat possesses of propagating itself and being refracted in a solid body.

---

XL. *Theoretical Determination of the Velocity of Sound.* By the Rev. J. CHALLIS, *M.A., F.R.A.S., Plumian Professor of Astronomy and Experimental Philosophy in the University of Cambridge*†.

THE following mathematical investigation of the velocity of sound differs from any hitherto adopted, and conducts to a new result.

Let $a^2(1+s)$ be the pressure at any point $xyz$ of the air, at any time $t$, $s$ being a small numerical quantity, the powers of which above the first are neglected; and let $u$, $v$, $w$ be the resolved parts of the velocity at the same point and at the same time, in the directions of the axes of co-ordinates. Then retaining only the first powers of $u$, $v$, $w$, we have, as is known,

$$a^2 \cdot \frac{ds}{dx} + \frac{du}{dt} = 0, \quad a^2 \cdot \frac{ds}{dy} + \frac{dv}{dt} = 0, \quad a^2 \cdot \frac{ds}{dz} + \frac{dw}{dt} = 0,$$

and

$$\frac{ds}{dt} + \frac{du}{dx} + \frac{dv}{dy} + \frac{dw}{dz} = 0. \quad \ldots \ldots \quad (1.)$$

---

\* Sitting of Nov. 16, 1841, and Feb. 1, 1843.
† Communicated by the Author.

*the Velocity of Sound.* 277

The last of these equations gives, by means of the other three,

$$\frac{d^2s}{dt^2} - a^2 \cdot \left(\frac{d^2s}{dx^2} + \frac{d^2s}{dy^2} + \frac{d^2s}{dz^2}\right) = 0. \quad . \quad . \quad . \quad (2.)$$

Suppose, for the moment, that $s$ has been obtained from this equation by integration. Then for the velocities we have,

$$u = C - a^2 \int \frac{ds}{dx} dt = C - a^2 \cdot \frac{d \cdot \int s dt}{dx},$$

$$v = C' - a^2 \int \frac{ds}{dy} dt = C' - a^2 \cdot \frac{d \cdot \int s dt}{dy},$$

$$w = C'' - a^2 \int \frac{ds}{dz} dt = C'' - a^2 \cdot \frac{d \cdot \int s dt}{dz},$$

where C, C', and C'' are functions of co-ordinates only. It is to be observed that these values of $u$, $v$, $w$ are perfectly general, being obtained prior to any consideration of the way in which the fluid is put in motion, and consequently apply to all points of the fluid in every instance of motion in which powers of the velocity and condensation above the first may be neglected. Now the motions we are about to consider are vibratory, or at least, not such that any part of the velocity remains permanently the same at the same point of space for any length of time. Consequently $C = 0$, $C' = 0$, and $C'' = 0$. Hence if $\psi = -a^2 \int s dt$,

$$u = \frac{d\psi}{dx}, \quad v = \frac{d\psi}{dy}, \quad w = \frac{d\psi}{dz},$$

and

$$u dx + v dy + w dz = (d\psi),$$

an exact differential.

It is thus shown that the condition that $u dx + v dy + w dz$ be an exact differential, must be satisfied in a manner that shall equally apply whatever be the original disturbance of the fluid. The supposition that $\psi$ is the product of two functions $\varphi$ and $f$, such that $\varphi$ does not contain $x$ and $y$, and $f$ does not contain $z$ and $t$, will be shown in the sequel to fulfil this requisite. On this supposition,

$$u = \varphi \frac{df}{dx}, \quad v = \varphi \frac{df}{dy}, \quad w = f \frac{d\varphi}{dz},$$

and

$$u dx + v dy + w dz = \varphi \left(\frac{df}{dx} dx + \frac{df}{dy} dy\right) + f \frac{d\varphi}{dz} dz,$$

which is an exact differential of $sf$. The further consequences of this supposition, which are remarkable, I proceed to develope.

The above values of $u, v, w$, give

$$\frac{du}{dx}=f\frac{d^2f}{dx^2}, \quad \frac{dv}{dy}=f\frac{d^2f}{dy^2}, \quad \frac{dw}{dz}=f\frac{d^2\phi}{dz^2}.$$

And since $\psi=-a^2\int s\,dt$, it follows that

$$\frac{d\psi}{dt}=f\frac{d\phi}{dt}=-a^2 s,$$

and

$$\frac{ds}{dt}=-\frac{f}{a^2}\cdot\frac{d^2\phi}{dt^2}.$$

Hence, substituting in equation (1.),

$$\frac{d^2\phi}{dt^2}=a^2\frac{d^2\phi}{dz^2}+\frac{a^2}{f}\cdot\left(\frac{d^2f}{dx^2}+\frac{d^2f}{dy^2}\right)\phi.$$

Now the nature of the question under consideration requires that this, like the general equation (2.), should be *linear* with constant coefficients. Let therefore the coefficient of $\phi$ be equal to a constant $-b^2$. The above equation accordingly resolves itself into the two following:

$$\frac{d^2\phi}{dt^2}-a^2\frac{d^2\phi}{dz^2}+b^2\phi=0, \quad \ldots \quad (3.)$$

$$\frac{d^2f}{dx^2}+\frac{d^2f}{dy^2}+\frac{b^2}{a^2}f=0, \quad \ldots \quad (4.)$$

which accord precisely with the suppositions already made, that $\phi$ is a function of $z$ and $t$ only, and $f$ is a function of $x$ and $y$ only.

The equation (3.) is transformable into the following,

$$\frac{d^2\phi}{du\,dv}-\frac{b^2}{4a^2}\phi=0, \quad \ldots \quad (5.)$$

in which $u=z+at$, and $v=z-at$. (See Peacock's Examples, p. 466.) Putting for convenience sake $c$ for $\frac{b^2}{4a^2}$, and regarding $c$ as a small quantity, the integral of (5.) may be obtained by successive approximations in a series as follows:

$$\phi = F(u) + G(v) + c\{vF_1(u) + uG_1(v)\} + \frac{c^2}{1.2} \times \left\{v^2 F_2(u) + u^2 G_2(v)\right\} + \&c.,$$

where

$$F_1(u) = \int F(u)du, \quad F_2(u) = \int F_1(u)du, \quad G_1(v) = \int G(v)dv, \text{ \&c.}$$

Each of the functions F and G satisfies equation (3.). Suppose, therefore, that $F=0$; then

$$\varphi = G(v) + euG_1(v) + \frac{e^2u^2}{1.2} \cdot G_2(v) + \frac{e^3u^3}{1.2.3} \cdot G_3(v) + \text{ \&c.}$$

No inference respecting the propagation of the motion can be drawn from this result unless $\varphi$ be expressible in exact terms. The nature of the series at once suggests a form of G, which gives to $\varphi$ an exact expression, and, as we shall see, applies to the present inquiry, viz. the form $Ae^{vr}$. Since $\varphi$ must not increase indefinitely with the time, G is clearly a circular function. Let therefore $G(v) = A e^{nv\sqrt{-1}} + B e^{-nv\sqrt{-1}}$; or, what is equivalent, let $G(v) = m\cos(nv+c)$. Then,

$$G_1(v) = \frac{m}{n}\sin(nv+c) = -\frac{m}{n^2} \cdot \frac{d.\cos(nv+c)}{dv}$$

$$G_2(v) = -\frac{m}{n^2}\cos(nv+c) = \frac{m}{n^4} \cdot \frac{d^2.\cos(nv+c)}{dv^2}$$

$$G_3(v) = -\frac{m}{n^3}\sin(nv+c) = -\frac{m}{n^6} \cdot \frac{d^3.\cos(nv+c)}{dv^3}$$

&c. = &c.

Consequently,

$$\varphi = m\cos(nv+c) - \frac{d.\cos(nv+c)}{dv}\frac{meu}{n^2} + \frac{d^2.\cos(nv+c)}{dv^2}\frac{me^2u^2}{1.2} - \text{\&c.}$$

$$= m\cos\left\{n\left(v - \frac{eu}{n^2}\right) + c\right\}$$

$$= m\cos\left\{n(z-at) - \frac{e}{n}(z+at) + c\right\}$$

$$= m\cos\left\{\left(n - \frac{e}{n}\right)z - \left(n + \frac{e}{n}\right)at + c\right\}.$$

Let, now,

$$n - \frac{e}{n} = \frac{2\pi}{\lambda}.$$

Then

$$n + \frac{e}{n} = \sqrt{\frac{4\pi^2}{\lambda^2} + 4e}.$$

Hence, finally,

$$\varphi = m\cos\frac{2\pi}{\lambda}\left(z - at\sqrt{1 + \frac{e\lambda^2}{\pi^2}} + c'\right).$$

The velocity in the direction of $z$ is $f\frac{d\phi}{dz}$. Hence

$$w = \mu f \sin\frac{2\pi}{\lambda}\left(z - at\sqrt{1 + \frac{e\lambda^2}{\pi^2}} + c'\right);$$

also

$$as = -\frac{f}{a}\cdot\frac{d\phi}{dt} = \mu f\sqrt{1 + \frac{e\lambda^2}{\pi^2}}\sin\frac{2\pi}{\lambda}\left(z - at\sqrt{1 + \frac{e\lambda^2}{\pi^2}} + c'\right).$$

It hence appears that the velocity of propagation of the wave whose breadth is $\lambda$, is

$$a\sqrt{1 + \frac{e\lambda^2}{\pi^2}}.$$

The value of $e$ depends on equation (4.).

Since equation (1.) is linear with constant coefficients, it will be satisfied by the sum of any number of such solutions as that just obtained, $f$, $e$, $\mu$, $\lambda$, and $c$ being different in general for each. Hence we have generally,

$$W = \Sigma\left\{\mu f \sin\frac{2\pi}{\lambda}\left(z - at\sqrt{1 + \frac{e\lambda^2}{\pi^2}} + c'\right)\right\}$$

$$aS = \Sigma\left\{\mu f \sqrt{1 + \frac{e\lambda^2}{\pi^2}}\sin\frac{2\pi}{\lambda}\left(z - at\sqrt{1 + \frac{e\lambda^2}{\pi^2}} + c'\right)\right\},$$

where $W = \Sigma(w)$ and $S = \Sigma(s)$.

It follows, since in each of the terms under the sign $\Sigma$ the quantities which are independent of $z$ and $t$ are at our disposal, that we may satisfy by this integral any state of the fluid in the direction of $z$, subject to the limitation that the condensation and velocity are at all times small. The course of the reasoning shows that the particular form of the function G, which has conducted to the above results, has not been arbitrarily adopted, but is really the only form that determines the velocity of propagation, and gives a definite solution of the problem. Also as the particular supposition by which $udx + vdy + wdz$ was made an exact differential, has conducted to the above values of W and S, which are of general application, no want of generality has been introduced by that supposition, so far at least as the motion in the direction of $z$ is concerned. I proceed now to the consideration of equation (4.), by which the motion transverse to the axis of $z$ is defined.

As this equation does not contain $t$, there is no propagation of motion in any direction parallel to the plane of $xy$; or the propagation in the direction of $z$ takes place without lateral spreading. A value of $f$ expressed in finite terms is not therefore required, as in the case of the integration of equation (3.), for deducing velocity of propagation. It may however be argued, that as a particular value of $\varphi$ was found, by which the vibrations in the direction of $z$ were defined, prior to any consideration of the manner in which the fluid was put in motion, so a particular value of $f$ exists (whether expressible in finite terms or not), by which the condensation and velocity in directions transverse to the axis of $z$ are defined, and which is equally independent of the arbitrary disturbance. Now the form of equation (4.) clearly points to a supposition of a general nature, by which that equation is converted into another containing two variables, and consequently giving a particular expression for $f$, viz. the supposition that $f$ is a function of $r$ the distance from the axis of $z$; according to which the condensation and transverse velocity are the same at the same distance from the axis in all transverse directions. Thus *direction* of propagation is determined *ab initio*, in a manner not depending on the particular disturbance, but which is common to all disturbances; for plainly the initial direction of propagation is the axis about which the condensation is symmetrically disposed. The above supposition respecting $f$ converts equation (4.) into the following,

$$\frac{d^2f}{dr^2} + \frac{df}{r\,dr} + 4ef = 0, \quad \ldots \quad (6.)$$

the integral of which in a series is,

$$f = 1 - er^2 + \frac{e^2 r^4}{1^2 . 2^2} - \frac{e^3 r^6}{1^2 . 2^2 . 3^2} + \&c., \quad \ldots \quad (7.)$$

assuming that $f = 1$, and $\frac{df}{dr} = 0$, when $r = 0$. It is easily shown from this result, that there are an unlimited number of possible values of $r$ for which $f$ vanishes. But we have no right to conclude that equation (7.) gives the expression for $f$ that we are seeking for, unless at some distance from the axis $f$ and $\frac{df}{dr}$ vanish together; that is, unless at some distance there be neither condensation nor variation of condensation, for otherwise there will be transverse propagation. Now equation (7.) does *not* satisfy this condition, as would appear by tracing the curve which it represents. To meet this difficulty, recourse must be had to the exact equation corresponding to the approximate equation (4.). That equation I have obtained in my paper on Luminous Rays (Cambridge Philosophical Transactions, vol. viii. part 3, p. 368), to which, as the reasoning is long, I must here refer for the demonstration. The equation alluded to is

$$\frac{d^2 \cdot \frac{1}{f}}{dx^2} + \frac{d^2 \cdot \frac{1}{f}}{dy^2} - 4e\frac{1}{f} = 0, \quad \ldots \quad (8.)$$

from which, by assuming $f$ to be a function of $r$, we obtain

$$f \cdot \frac{d^2 f}{dr^2} - 2\frac{df^2}{dr^2} + \frac{f}{r} \cdot \frac{df}{dr} + 4ef^2 = 0, \quad \ldots \quad (9.)$$

whence it is clear that if $f = 0$, $\frac{df}{dr}$ also vanishes.

The integral of (9.) is derived from (7.) by putting $\frac{1}{f}$ for $f$, and $-e$ for $e$. Hence

$$\frac{1}{f} = 1 + er^2 + \frac{e^2 r^4}{1^2 \cdot 2^2} + \frac{e^3 r^6}{1^2 \cdot 2^2 \cdot 3^2} + \&c.,$$

and

$$f = 1 - er^2 + \frac{3e^2 r^4}{4} - \frac{19 e^3 r^6}{36} + \&c.$$

The *least* value of $r$ corresponding to $f = 0$, as given by this last equation, is the radius of a cylindrical surface within which the motion of the fluid *filament* under consideration is contained. It may be remarked, that the second term of equation (9.) must be very small compared to the others (excepting where $f$ approaches to zero), in order that that equation may be equivalent to a linear equation with constant coefficients. By the omission of the second term, equation (9.) becomes identical with (6.). Hence the least value of $r$ corresponding to $f = 0$ is very nearly the same as derived from either equation. Let $l = $ this least value. Then the value of $l$ is obtained by finding the least root of the equation,

$$0 = 1 - el^2 + \frac{e^2 l^4}{1^2 \cdot 2^2} - \frac{e^3 l^6}{1^2 \cdot 2^2 \cdot 3^2} + \&c.$$

Hence $el^2$ is a numerical quantity which may be calculated. Let $el^2 = q$. Then

$$\frac{e\lambda^2}{\pi^2} = \frac{q\lambda^2}{\pi^2 l^2} = k \text{ suppose.}$$

Hence $k$ is constant for all vibrations if the ratio $\frac{\lambda}{l}$ be constant.

Now it may be thus argued that $\lambda$ and $l$ have to each other a constant ratio. These quantities must be related in some way, otherwise the motion is not defined. Let $F(\lambda, l, \sigma) = 0$ express this relation, $\sigma$ being the maximum condensation corresponding to $f=1$. As there are no other quantities concerned in this relation, and as $\lambda$ and $l$ are the only linear quantities, this equation is equivalent to $\frac{\lambda}{l} = \chi(\sigma)$. And we have above

$$\frac{\lambda}{l} = \pi \sqrt{\frac{k}{q}}.$$

Hence

$$\pi \sqrt{\frac{k}{q}} = \chi(\sigma).$$

But it has already been shown that $k$ is independent of $\sigma$. Hence $\chi(\sigma)$ is a constant, and $k$ is the same for all vibrations.

We have thus been led, by reasoning exclusively on hydrodynamical principles, to the following conclusion. The velocity of transmission of a vibration in a medium, for which the relation between the pressure and the density is given by the equation $p = a^2 \rho$, is not simply $a$, but a greater quantity $a\sqrt{1+k}$, which is the same for vibrations of different magnitudes.

To ascertain the numerical value of $k$, it would be necessary in a particular instance to obtain by experiment the ratio $\frac{\lambda}{l}$.

The application of the foregoing result is not confined to particular cases of disturbance. For according to the mathematical theory above given, the state of the fluid, whatever it may be, is, at every instant, and therefore at the instant of disturbance, composed of vibrations in fluid filaments unlimited in number, and unlimited as to the directions of their propagation. In all these filaments the velocity of propagation is the same.

I cannot avoid adverting here to a difficulty which has long presented itself to me, with respect to the explanation usually given of the excess of the velocity of sound above the value $a$. Admitting that a sudden condensation by developing heat produces a higher degree of temperature, and therefore of elastic force, than would exist in the same state of density without such development, does it not thence follow, that a sudden rarefaction, by absorbing heat, produces a lower temperature and a less elastic force than would exist in the same state of density without such absorption? But the observed increase of velocity of propagation requires an *increase* of elastic force, as well where the fluid is rarefied as where it is condensed. May it not be that the developed heat (whether positive or negative) is carried off too quickly by radiation to affect the temperature of the fluid? And does not the mathematical investigation contained in this communication sufficiently account for the observed velocity of sound on purely hydrodynamical principles?

Cambridge Observatory,
March 17, 1848.

---

XLI. *On the Development of Functions of the form* $F(z+x)$. *By* SAMUEL ROBERTS, *B.A. Manchester New College*\*.

IT is the object of the present paper to derive Laplace's development of $\psi u$, where $u = F(z + a\varphi u)$, by a simple combination of differential and integral processes; and likewise Lagrange's and Taylor's theorems, which are particular cases of that form, but may be immediately arrived at by a similar method.

Let $F(z+x)$ be any function of $(z+x)$, $z$ and $x$ being variable; without inquiring whether $z$ and $x$ are dependent or independent, we have

$$F(z+x) - Fz = \int_0^x \frac{d}{dt} \cdot F(z+t) dt,$$

regarding $t$ as the variable concerned in the differentiation and integration.

From the manner in which $z$, $x$ enter into the function,

$$\frac{dF(z+t)}{dt} = \frac{dF(z+t)}{dz}.$$

Hence

$$F(z+x) - Fz = \int_0^x \frac{d}{dz} F(z+t) dt.$$

Similarly,

$$F(z+t) - Fz = \int_0^t \frac{d}{dz} F(z+t') dt'$$

is true for any value of $t$, and so on.

By successive substitution we obtain

$$F(z+x) - Fz = \int_0^x \frac{d}{dz} Fz \cdot dt + \int_0^x \frac{d}{dz} \int_0^t \frac{d}{dz} Fz \cdot dt\, dt'$$

$$+ \int_0^x \frac{d}{dz} \int_0^t \frac{d}{dz} \int_0^{t'} \frac{d}{dz} Fz\, dt\, dt'\, dt''$$

$$+ \&c.,$$

---

\* Communicated by the Author.

the $n$th term being represented by

$$\{n \text{ alternations of } \int \text{ and } \frac{d}{dz}\} Fz.dt.dt'.dt''. \&c.$$

But since all the limits are determined by the outermost limits 0 and $x$, we may take away the accents from $t'$, $t''$, &c., and the notation of the limits from all the signs of integration but the first, and write the development thus:

$$F(z+x) - Fz = \int_0^x \frac{d}{dz} . Fz . dt + \int_0^x \frac{d}{dz} . \int_0^x \frac{d}{dz} Fz . (dt)^2 + \&c.$$

Since we have not determined whether $x$ shall or shall not be a function of $z$, we do not know whether or not we may invert the order of differentiation and integration. In the first term, however, the function under the sign of differentiation does not contain $t$ explicitly, and therefore it becomes

$$\frac{d}{dz} Fz \int_0^x dt \text{ or } \frac{d}{dz} Fz.x.$$

Now Laplace's theorem is a case in which $x$ is a function of $z$, such that we *may* change the order of integrations and differentiations in all but the *first* term. For let

$$\frac{dt}{dz} = -1,$$

then if $n$ be a whole number but not cipher,

$$\int_0^x \frac{d}{dz} \psi z . t^n . dt = \int_0^x \left( \psi' z . t^n + \psi z . n t^{n-1} \frac{dt}{dz} \right) dt$$

$$= \psi' z \frac{x^{n+1}}{n+1} + n \psi z . \int_0^x \frac{dt}{dz} t^{n-1} dt$$

$$= \psi' z \frac{x^{n+1}}{n+1} - \psi z . x^n ;$$

and

$$\frac{d}{dz} \int_0^x \psi z t^n . dt = \frac{d}{dz} . \psi z . \frac{x^{n+1}}{n+1}$$

$$= \psi' z . \frac{x^{n+1}}{n+1} + \psi z . x^n \frac{dx}{dz}$$

$$= \psi' z \frac{x^{n+1}}{n+1} - \psi z x^n ;$$

and generally

$$\frac{d^n}{dz^n} \int_0^x \psi z . t^n dt \text{ also } = \int_0^x \frac{d^n}{dz^n} \psi z . t^n dt ;$$

286  On the Development of Functions of the Form $F(z+x)$.

for

$$\frac{d^m}{dz^m}\psi z t^n \text{ and } \frac{d^m}{dz^m}\psi z \frac{t^{n+1}}{n+1}$$

are of the following forms respectively:

$$\frac{d^m}{dz^m}\psi z . t^n = \psi^m z . t^n - m . n . \psi^{m-1} z . t^{n-1} + \frac{m(m-1)}{1.2} n(n-1)$$

$$\psi^{m-2} z . t^{n-2} - \&c.,$$

since

$$\frac{dt}{dz} = -1,$$

and

$$\frac{d^m}{dz^m}\psi z . \frac{x^{n+1}}{n+1} = \frac{1}{n+1}\left\{\psi^m z . x^{n+1} - m . (n+1) . \psi^{m-1} z . x^n \right.$$

$$\left. + \frac{m(m-1)}{1.2}(n+1)n . \psi z^{m-2} . x^{n-1} - \&c.;\right.$$

and it is clear that the former, integrated between the limits relative to $t$, is equivalent to the latter.

Applying this property successively to the terms of the development, we have

$$F(z+x) - Fz = F'z . x + \frac{d}{dz}(F'z . x^2)\frac{1}{2} + \frac{d^2}{dz^2}(F'z . x^3)\frac{1}{1.2.3} + \&c.$$

Now we have assumed $\frac{dx}{dz} = -1,$

$$\therefore x = -z + C.$$

Hitherto we have not performed any operation relative to any variables but $x$ and $z$. If therefore $x$ be assumed a function $(a\varphi u)$ of $u$, the truth of the development is not affected. C in this case must be a function of $u$, let it be $(fu)$. Then

$$fu = z + x = z + a\varphi u,$$

or

$$u = F_1(z + a\varphi u);$$

and by the above theorem,

$$Fu = FF_1 z + \frac{d}{dz}(FF_1 z)\varphi u . a + \frac{d}{dz}\left(\frac{d}{dz}FF_1 z . (\varphi u)^2\right)\frac{a^2}{1.2} + \&c.,$$

which is Laplace's theorem.

Lagrange's theorem is obtained by supposing $C = u$, in which case

$$x = a(\varphi u) = -z + u, \text{ or } u = z + a(\varphi u);$$

and applying the theorem, we get

$$Fu = Fz + F'z\varphi u . a + \frac{d}{dz}(F'z(\varphi u)^2)\frac{a^2}{1.2} + \&c.$$

To obtain Taylor's theorem, $x$ must be regarded as entirely independent of $z$ or $\frac{dx}{dz}=0$. In this case the differentiations will not be affected by entirely separating them from the integrations, so that the fundamental development becomes

$$F(z+x) - Fz = F'z.x + F''z.\frac{x^2}{1.2} + \&c.,$$
$$+ F^n z . \frac{x^n}{1.2.\&\, n} + \int_0^x \frac{d}{dz} \int \frac{d}{dz} \&c.\ F(x+t)(dt)^{n+1}.$$

## XLII. *Notices respecting New Books.*

*An Account of the Measurement of the Lough Foyle Base in Ireland, with its verification and extension by Triangulation; together with the various methods of Computation followed on the Ordnance Survey, and the requisite Tables.* By Captain WILLIAM YOLLOND, *of the Royal Engineers, F.R.A.S. Published by Order of the Honourable Board of Ordnance.*

IN our Number for January 1843, we announced the publication, under the authority of the Board of Ordnance, of a volume containing the observations of stars made with Ramsden's zenith sector, at ten different stations on, or connected with, the arc of meridian which extends from Dunnose in the Isle of Wight to Balta, in Shetland. It was announced in that volume, that the triangulation was then in so forward a state that the printing of the geodetical observations would shortly be commenced. Though five years have elapsed since that announcement, the triangulation, it appears, is not yet completed; and in the mean time we are favoured with the present volume, giving an account of the measurement of the Lough Foyle Base, preparatory to the survey of Ireland, with the detail of numerous experiments on the expansion of metals and comparisons of various standards of measure; a description of the methods followed at the Ordnance Map Office in the computation of the triangulation, and of the altitudes, longitudes, latitudes, and bearings of the stations; together with sundry tables for facilitating the calculations. This base, it is to be observed, was measured in 1827 and 1828, that is to say, twenty years ago. Why the account of the measurement was not given sooner, or why it is given at this particular juncture without the triangulation, does not very clearly appear; but the delay which has taken place cannot but be regarded as unfortunate. Of the officers who were concerned in the operation, the two who took the most active and prominent part (Captain Drummond and Lieutenant Murphy) have died; others have retired from the service; and the consequence is, that the description, both of the apparatus and the details of proceeding, does not come from one who was personally engaged in the operation, and who could supply deficiencies of record by his own knowledge or recollections, but has been compiled, in part at least, from loose notes and memoranda, not always full, and in some cases discrepant. Captain Yolland, on whom the duty of drawing up the account devolved, has executed the task with great ability; and it must be confessed that his intimate acquaintance with the methods followed in the survey department, and the great interest he manifestly takes in the subject, tend in no small degree to counteract the disadvantage under which he has been placed in consequence of his non-participation in the actual measurement. But while we willingly concede all praise to the editor of the work, we cannot forbear remarking on the circumstance, that the account of so essential and important a part of a great and costly national undertaking is given to the country without the name of the officer who was officially charged with its superintendence.

The portion of this volume to which the greatest interest attaches, or rather would have attached, had it appeared at an earlier period, is the description of the measuring apparatus, of which no detailed account had been published, and little more was generally known than that it had been invented or suggested by Major-General Colby, and was constructed on the principle of eliminating the effects of variations of temperature by compensation or self-adjustment. But information on this subject has now also been supplied by the publication of Colonel Everest's late work on the measurement of two arcs of meridian in India, in which a similar apparatus used for the measurement of the bases connected with those operations is minutely described. Captain Yolland gives the following as the reasons which led to the adoption of the method in question:—

"All the methods of measuring base lines which had been in use previously to the commencement of the present survey, were more or less dependent for their accuracy on the knowledge of the temperature of bars or chains when applied in measuring. But as the temperature of the air is seldom equable for any considerable portion of the day, and the time which substances occupy in heating or cooling varies according to their nature, their masses, and their surfaces, *it did not appear that a thermometer had been or could be devised which would give the knowledge of the temperature of a bar or chain throughout its whole length at the moment it was used as a measure.* This led to the principle of compensation; a principle which had long been in use in pendulums, and which had been applied to them in many ingenious ways."—P. 7.

We demur to the opinion stated in the sentence we have printed in italics. The apparatus used by Delambre in the measurement of the bases for the French arc of meridian, indicated the relative lengths of a bar of copper and a bar of platina, and thence gave the absolute expansion of the platina or measuring bar "throughout its whole length at the moment it was used as a measure." Bessel's apparatus (on the same principle, though differently constructed) also showed the expansion of the measuring bar at the time it was in use. In both cases the apparatus formed of itself a *metallic thermometer*; and we conceive that the expansion (for which alone a knowledge of the temperature is necessary) was indicated by both methods with a precision equal to that with which the absolute lengths of the bars can be determined. In the case, indeed, of the long steel chains formerly used in the Ordnance Survey, the uncertainty respecting the temperature of the different parts of the measuring chain forms a serious objection; but with respect to simple bars of a moderate length, the practical difficulty of determining the expansion at the moment of the measure does not seem insuperable.

The following is the description of the measuring bars, omitting the references to the plates:—

"The compensation bar consists of two bars, of brass and iron, 10 feet 1·5 inch long, 0·5 inch broad, placed 1·125 inch apart, supported on brass rollers at one-fourth and three-fourths of their length, and firmly fixed together at their centres by transverse steel cylinders 1·5 inch in diameter, and being free to expand from, or contract towards, their centres independently of each other. At the extremity of, and at right angles to, each of these bars is a flat steel tongue 6·2 inches long, 1·1 inch broad, and 0·25 inch thick; projecting 3·25 inches on the side of the iron bar, and moving freely on conical brass pivots, riveted into the brass and iron bars, each axis being perpendicular to the surface of the tongue, allowing it to be inclined at slightly different angles to these bars according to their expansion from, or contraction to, their centres. The centres of the two axes are at 0·5 inch and 2·3 inches from the end of the tongue next the brass bar. On the tongue, and flush with its upper surface near the (projecting) extremity, is inserted a silver pin, with a dot marked on it, as the compensation point."—P. 10.

The number of such bars used in the measurement was six.

Besides the compensation of the expansion of the measuring bars, and the consequent avoidance of all reductions to the normal temperature, another object, which was considered of importance, was aimed at in the new apparatus. "To avoid the possibility of accidental displacements incident to the ordinary mode of measuring base lines by the contacts of the ends of rods, or by the adjustments of the coincidences of lines, it was deemed advisable that the several parts of the apparatus should be combined by visual contacts." Accordingly an interval of about six inches was left between the measuring bars, when placed in the line of the base, for the accurate measurement of which a microscopic apparatus, also on the principle of compensation, was contrived. It is described as follows:—

"The compensation microscope consists of three microscopes, placed 3 inches from centre to centre, connected by two bars of brass and iron, 7 inches long, 0·6 inch broad, and 0·375 inch thick, 2·5 inches apart, firmly secured together by means of a brass collar and cylinder, forming part of the tube of the centre or telescopic microscope; the two bars carrying with them the outer microscopes, of two inches focal distance, being free to expand from, and contract towards the central microscope, independently of each other, and thereby forming with it small angles of inclination similar to the steel tongues of the compensation bars. The compensated point of each is so adjusted as to be in the outer focus of its object-glass. The microscopes revolve on the axis of the telescopic microscope in a tube fastened to a horizontal plate attached to a tripod-stand with levelling-screws, and furnished with longitudinal and lateral adjusting screws. On one side, secured to the brass bar, is the spirit-level for levelling the microscopes; and on the other, firmly attached to the centres of the bars by a brass plate, is a telescope embraced by a brass collar with a small cylinder projecting from one side, which turns in a socket attached to the plate: thus affording it a vertical motion, allowing objects to be seen in opposite directions..... The compensation microscopes are seven in number; the weight of each microscope is 5 lbs."—P. 11.

The mode of using the apparatus will be readily apprehended from the above description. When the several sets of bars and microscopes are properly adjusted in the line of the base, the microscopes stand vertically over the tongues at the adjacent ends of each two sets of bars, and the dots on the tongues are respectively bisected by the wires of the two outer microscopes, so that the distance between the dots is the same as that between the foci of the microscopes.

The first question which arises in respect to the new apparatus is this: Has the attempt to effect a perfect compensation been practically successful? The answer, we apprehend, will scarcely be satisfactory. It was seen from the first that a disturbing cause exists in the unequal facilities with which different metals receive and part with heat, in consequence of which the two bars, at the time they were used in the measurement, would probably have different temperatures; in which case the distance between the compensation points would necessarily be altered, and the error arising from such alteration might even exceed the whole amount of the expansion of a simple bar for a corresponding variation of temperature. To remedy this inconvenience, the idea was suggested of covering the bars with coats of varnish, so as to produce at least a similarity of surface. A great number of experiments were made with a view to test the adequacy of this remedy; and as the results were considered to be satisfactory, the measuring bars, as well as the connecting bars of the microscopic apparatus, were varnished accordingly. In the present measurement it seems to be assumed that the disturbing cause was by this means completely removed. Colonel Everest, on the contrary, found that this was not by any means the case; and he explicitly states that he considered the advantages of the varnish to be more imaginary than real. But it is manifest that if the compensation is only partially effected, the method loses at once all its theoretical advantages; and is even attended with this disadvantage, that inasmuch as the effect of a varying temperature on the compound bars is unknown, no allowance can be made for it as in the case of a simple bar whose rate of expansion is determined, and follows a known law.

As the distance between the compensation points of a set of bars cannot by any effort of art be made equal to 10 feet *exactly*, and as the distance in respect of any two sets will not be *exactly* the same, each of the six sets used in the measurement, after the compensation points had been fixed, was carefully compared with a standard iron bar of 10 feet, and the difference ascertained at the temperature of 62° Fahrenheit's thermometer. The unit of the measure, therefore, so far at least as it depends on the measuring bars, was this 10-foot iron bar. For the same reason it was necessary to determine the exact distance between the outer foci of the microscopes, in each of the seven sets of microscopic apparatus, in terms of a certain standard. The standard used for this purpose was a brass scale, on which the fine dots were marked at a distance of 6 inches. In this proceeding we find another objection to the method. The part of the base to which the bars were applied, that is to say $\frac{10}{11}$ of the whole, is referred to a standard iron bar of 10 feet, and the remaining $\frac{1}{11}$ to a brass standard scale of 6 inches. In order, therefore, to obtain the length in terms of a single standard, it becomes necessary to determine the exact relation of the 6-inch scale to the 10-foot bar, for at least the whole range of temperature within which the measuring apparatus was compared with the respective standards. Hence it is necessary to determine, not only the exact relation of two scales of very unequal lengths at a given temperature, but also their rates of expansion. The circumstance of the two standards being constructed of different metals seems an unnecessary complication.

The site selected for the measurement was on the eastern border of Lough Foyle, in the county of Londonderry. It was proposed to commence the measurement from the strand, near Mount Sandy, at the entrance of the Lough, but the rugged and broken nature of the ground, composed of low sand-hills, made it necessary to begin about two miles to the south of the intended limit. From the point which was selected the measurement was carried southward to a small rising ground called Sheep Hill, about a quarter of a mile south-east of the church of Ballykelly. The distance between the north end and Mount Sandy was afterwards determined by triangulation. The mean height of the ground above the sea at high-water was about 18 feet.

The whole length of the base, to which the measuring apparatus was applied, is 41640·8873 feet, or nearly $7\frac{18}{19}$ miles. The extension from the north end to a station near Mount Sandy is 11559·8270 feet, or nearly $2\frac{1}{4}$ miles. This last number is the mean of the results of the triangulation computed in eight different ways. It is probably just as accurate as that which expresses the measured part of the base; but admitting it to be so, we confess our inability to perceive what particular advantage was proposed to be gained by the prolongation. It gives no additional security whatever for the accuracy of the computed distances, which depend solely and absolutely on the portion actually measured. If triangulation is to be admitted, the side of any triangle, determined with equal precision, may just as well be assumed as the base of the survey.

For the purpose of verification the base was divided into seven sections, and after two of them had been measured by the apparatus, the length of the second section was computed from the first by a triangulation. All the other parts were verified in a similar manner. The differences between the computed and measured lengths were found to be exceedingly minute, excepting in one case, where the proportionate error amounted to a foot in 9·8 miles. It is not likely, however, that the probable error of the whole length exceeds 3 or 4 inches.

Unusual precautions were taken for the purpose of preserving the base points, so that they may be available, if required, at any future time. And this was done not only at the two points where the measurement commenced and terminated, but also at an intermediate station (Minearney), and at Mount Sandy, to which the base was prolonged by triangulation. At each of those four points a circular piece of ground, to the extent of 30 feet in diameter, was purchased by the Ordnance and enclosed. The foundations of the stations were laid in solid masonry. "When the exact position of the points had been determined, jumper-holes, $1\frac{1}{4}$ inch in diameter and 6 inches deep, were bored in the upper blocks, and pieces of platina wire, $\frac{1}{16}$ of an inch in diameter, were inserted in the jumper-holes, and retained in a vertical position by fine wire twisted round each, with ends projecting to the sides. The holes were then run in with lead to within about one inch of the surface of the stone. This last inch was filled up with a mixture of cement and sand that the jumper-holes might resemble the rest of the stones, and the platina wires were cut off level with the surface. The dots on the wires were made with the point of a needle.......... The points at these four stations are now being further secured from injury by surrounding them with small dwarf walls, and covering each of them with a tumulus of earth; another dwarf wall, with an iron railing, will encircle the space at each station purchased by the Board of Ordnance."—P. 152.

The above precautions were no doubt justified by the importance of the object, for it would seem that this Lough Foyle base, upon which the triangulation of Ireland depends, is to be assumed also as the unit of the measure of the whole British arc of meridian from Dunnose to Balta. Considering the great precision now attained in such operations, we are not prepared to say that a verificatory base is indispensable, even for an arc of $10°$; yet, we should be sorry to see it dispensed with in the present case. The bases measured by Roy and Mudge in the early stages of the survey will not, we suppose, be considered as sufficiently accurate for this purpose, and if so, it would seem to be very desirable that another base should still be measured somewhere in the south of England, and nearer to the line of the meridian.

All the details connected with the measurement, both with the bars and by triangulation, are very fully given; and we have also the results of a great number of experiments, made in different years since 1827, for ascertaining the relation of the different sets of compensation bars to the standard 10-foot iron bar; of this bar to another similar bar, and to various standards of length which have acquired authority or reputation from the comparisons to which they have been subjected; of the microscopic apparatus to the standard 6-inch brass scale; and of this scale to various other scales as well as to the 10-foot standard bar. As there is at present no legal standard of British measures, the results are provisionally expressed in terms of the 10-foot iron bar. In these details we see abundant reasons to justify our regret that an account of the measurement was not given by the persons by whom the operation was actually performed, and our desire to have another base measured in England, now that the experience which has been gained would lead us to expect still greater precision. It appears that while the measurement was proceeding two records of observations were kept; these are found in many cases to differ from each other, particularly in the readings of the thermometer, and no means now exist of determining with certainty which of the two is the correct one. All the comparisons for ascertaining the relation of the 6-inch scale to the 10-foot bar made prior to 1844 have been discarded as unsatisfactory in some respects, and it would seem that we have only very recently, if we have yet, become acquainted with the proper manner of making experiments of such extreme delicacy, and with some of the properties of matter on which the results depend. Captain Yolland informs us, that "during the present year (1847) it has been ascertained, that if a steel bar be raised to a red heat and then cooled, either gradually or by immersion in water or oil, it does not return precisely to the same condition as existed prior to its being heated; it remains, in fact, enlarged."

It would be interesting to know how nearly the lengths of the sides of the triangles deduced from the Lough Foyle base agree with the same distances computed from the bases formerly measured in England with the chain; but on this point we have not yet any direct information. It appears, however, from comparisons made at Southampton of the Ordnance new standard bar with a 20-foot iron bar, from which the lengths of the chains were laid off by Ramsden, that Ramsden's bar exceeded two lengths of the Ordnance standard bar by 192·795 divisions of the micrometer, or by ·0091877 parts of an inch. This amounts to rather more than a foot in five miles—an error too great to be tolerated at the present time. But as other errors would arise in transferring the length of the bar to the chain, and that of the chain to the base, the discordance of the computed distances may be less or greater than in the proportion just stated.

The methods of computing the distances, and the longitudes, latitudes, azimuths and heights of the stations, which are appended to the volume, would form an appropriate introduction to the details of the triangulation; for their appearance here the following reason is assigned:—"The principal reason why the calculations for latitudes, longitudes, &c. are now entered on, is, that the formulæ and tables may be available for those who may require them, as they are believed to be more accurate than any hitherto published." It is satisfactory to be put in possession of formulæ and tables more accurate than any which previously existed; but who the parties may be who are likely to require those in question, or to what purpose they can be applied until the observations are given, we are at a loss to imagine. Connected with this subject the following piece of information strikes us as curious. For some time the latitudes, longitudes and reciprocal bearings are stated to have been calculated from formulæ furnished by the Astronomer Royal. These formulæ, which of course are only approximative, were found not to be sufficiently exact when applied to some of the large triangles which occur in the Ordnance Survey, and on the occasion of the recent chronometrical measurement of the arc of parallel between Greenwich and Valentia, the Astronomer Royal furnished a new set of formulæ in order that the geodetic longitude of the latter place might be more rigorously computed. The new formulæ, along with others, were subjected to the most rigid tests that tables of logarithms to ten places rendered possible, and the following result is announced:—

"On trial it was found that none of the approximate processes given by the various writers on geodesy were sufficiently exact to reproduce the original assumed latitude, longitude and bearing, on carrying the calculations to the point at which they commenced; and even the formulæ given by the Astronomer Royal failed to do so, until it was found that the normal, or radius of curvature perpendicular to the meridian for the latitude of the given station, must be used in the determination of that of the second station, and the normal for the latitude of the second in the determination of that of the third, and so on, instead of using any *approximate radius*. This was ascertained by the non-commissioned officer in charge of the calculations, after repeated attempts had been made, without success, to alter or modify the various approximate processes which had been tried, so as to cause them to reproduce the assumed data, on continuing the calculations to the original point," &c.

Far be it from us to disparage a discovery so made; but we would beg leave to suggest, that if the substitution of the successive normals for the approximate radius be really an improvement on the method, there must be a reason why it is so; which reason should be given, in order that it may not appear to be the practice in the Ordnance Survey to follow empirical modes of calculation, found by groping to answer in some particular cases.

With respect to the future progress of the survey Captain Yolland observes, "the present, or at all events the succeeding season will serve for the completion of the observations at all the stations required for giving a connected general triangulation of the United Kingdom, including the Western, Orkney and Shetland Islands, with the necessary data for the comparisons between the astronomical and geodetical determinations; these will be the more valuable, as the result of the late operations at the Cape of Good Hope, for the measurement of an arc of meridian depending on a base measured with the compensation apparatus described in this work, and *reducible to the same unit of measure*, may ere long be expected to be published."— p. vii. No doubt the result of the Cape measurement will be very interesting, but in what respect it will render the British are more valuable is not apparent, unless for the general reason that every new datum for the figure of the earth may be said to increase the value of all the foregoing. Captain Yolland says because it will be *reducible to the same unit of measure*. Are we to infer from this that the meridional arcs measured in France, Germany, Russia, and other countries are not reducible to the same unit with those measured by the compensation apparatus? If so, both the British arc and the Cape are will be of comparatively little value; for assuredly the figure of the earth will be determined with greater certainty from all the continental measurements taken together than from those two alone, whatever advantage may be attributed to the use of the compensation bars. But surely there can be no greater difficulty in determining the relation of the French *toise*, or *mètre*, to the standard of the Irish base than in determining the ratio of the 6-inch scale to the 10-foot bar. All the arcs whose standards have been preserved must be susceptible of reduction to the same unit of measure; and we trust Captain Yolland will not think it necessary (if the matter depend on him) to defer the publication of the triangles connected with the meridian until the results of the Cape measurement are known, on the ground that there are no other arcs with which our own is directly comparable. We would remind him that the Indian arcs measured by Colonel Everest (of which, by the way, he makes no mention) are not less important than the Cape arc will be for the determination of the figure of the earth. They depend on bases which have been measured with similar apparatus, and Captain Yolland has himself already compared their standards with those of the Ordnance Survey.

But although the observations may possibly be completed in the course of the present season, it does not follow that they will be speedily communicated. "Major-General Colby's retirement from the superintendence of the Ordnance Survey at the end of the present month (March 1847), leaves me unable to state the arrangements which are likely to be made for publishing the mass of Trigonometrical Observations made by the Survey Department during the last thirty-six years."

To those who have been looking forward to the termination and publication of the results of this great national undertaking, the announcement we have just quoted is not calculated to afford much satisfaction. The last account we have of the trigonometrical observations was published in 1811. Since that year the survey has been in progress; it is said that upwards of a million and a half has been expended on it; and arrangements are still to be made for the publication of the observations which have been accumulated in the long interval\*. That the work will be found to have been executed

---

\* The subject acquires an immediate interest, from the project which has been entered upon of an Ordnance Survey of the metropolis for the alleged but unexplained purposes of the Sanitary Commission. From the discussion of this project in the House of Commons, March 24, on the Ordnance Estimates it would appear that no one could tell what it was to cost, how it was to be paid for, or what purpose it was to answer.

in a highly satisfactory manner, the details given in the present volume leave no room to doubt; yet however assured we may be in this respect, we cannot help thinking that, so far at least as regards the meridional arc, it is important that the final results should be given under the highest scientific authority. It appears to us, therefore, to be desirable, that, on the completion of the triangulation (in the present year, or whenever it may happen), the observations should be transferred to the Astronomer Royal, to whose department in fact the determination of the meridian may be considered as properly belonging in order that the length of the arc may be deduced under his direction and superintendence. The mapping of country could not possibly be better executed than it has been under the present arrangements.

*A Description of Active and Extinct Volcanos, of Earthquakes, and of Thermal Springs, with remarks on the causes of these phænomena, the character of their respective products, and their influence on the past and present condition of the Globe.* By CHARLES DAUBENY, M.D., F.R.S. (*Second Notice.*)

The subject of thermal springs has attracted a large share of Dr. Daubeny's attention. From their chiefly occurring in the vicinity of volcanos, or along lines of geological disturbance, as well as from the peculiar chemical products which they contain, he shows that in the majority of cases they must be intimately connected with volcanic operations. Nevertheless, we are disposed to qualify this generalization in the case of thermal springs no less than of earthquakes. Whatever opinion may be held as to the fluidity of the earth's nucleus, there is no denying that the interior of the earth (as far as we know it) is hotter than the surface. A thermal spring therefore, when it occurs at a distance from the direct heat of an active volcano, merely means a spring which rises from a great depth, of which we have a notable instance in the *artificial* hot-spring of Grenelle, obtained by boring in the middle of the Paris basin, at a great distance from volcanic operations or disturbed strata. A *natural* hot-spring of course implies the existence of a deeply extending fissure, up which it finds a vent; and if we admit that other causes besides volcanos have had a share in breaking up the crust of the earth, these causes would also contribute to bring thermal

---

Mr. Wyld, to whom we should give credit for practical knowledge, was of opinion "that the survey undertaken for the Sanitary Commission was entirely unnecessary, a waste of public money, and would not answer the purpose contemplated." Colonel Anson stated that six persons were employed and that the expense already incurred would "probably be under 1000*l*., and that he believed matters were on a very excellent footing." Lord Morpeth spoke of a "moderate sum." His predecessor, Lord Lincoln, stated that the estimates had risen from 25,000*l*. to 100,000*l*. According to Mr. Wyld, a similar survey of Dublin had cost 200,000*l*. Mr. Wyld stated that "there had been sufficient surveys provided for London under the Parochial Assessment's Act, for which the inhabitants had already paid 300,000*l*."

waters to the surface. And although, as Dr. Daubeny shows, we find in springs remote from volcanos similar gaseous products to those emitted by volcanos themselves, yet it is possible that the production of these gases may be a general occurrence in the subterranean regions, and in that case they would escape wherever they can find an exit, either by the thermal spring or the volcanic chimney.

Concluding his summary of the facts of volcanic geology, Dr. Daubeny proceeds in part 3 to draw conclusions from them as to the causes of volcanos, the circumstances that influence the character of their products, and the uses they fulfil in the œconomy of Nature.

The two principal theories now maintained, as to the causes of volcanic action, are the mechanical one and the chemical; the former of which supposes that the earth's crust floats on a nucleus of melted matter, the heat of which produces the expansive and explosive forces of the volcano; while the latter maintains that volcanic heat is the direct effect of local chemical operations going on beneath the district where the phænomena are displayed. As we can never hope to obtain any positive knowledge of the regions where volcanos originate, and can only speculate as to their causes by studying a multitude of very complicated effects, it is probable (and the reflection is consolatory) that these rival theories may continue to enliven the meetings of the Geological Society in future ages, long after every region of the world has been mapped, every section measured and every fossil described.

Dr. Daubeny has for many years been an advocate of the chemical theory, and supposes volcanic heat to arise from the access of oxygen to the metallic bases of the alkalies and earths. All who have witnessed the combustion of potassium or of sodium by the contact of water must admit that this is a possible hypothesis, and the question therefore is merely whether that or the mechanical theory is the more probable. In proof of his opinion, Dr. Daubeny adduces the vicinity of volcanos to the sea, the aqueous vapours which they emit, and the hydrogen, nitrogen and other gases which indicate the decomposition of air and of water, and the absorption of oxygen. He has argued this question with great ability on chemical grounds, and has certainly made out a very good case, though we are not prepared as yet to enlist ourselves under either banner. Both theories may easily be true. Central heat and central fluidity may still exist as a relic of the chaotic epoch, and would even be auxiliary to the chemical operations which may take place in the more superficial regions of the earth's interior.

Dr. Daubeny adopts to a great extent the views of Von Buch regarding "craters of elevation," that is, cavities formed by the upheaving and consequent separation of the superficial strata, as distinguished from "craters of eruption," caused by the accumulation of ejected matter round the orifice of a volcano. Like all doctrines which assume a controversial form, the elevation theory has been pushed too far by one party and unreasonably cried down by another. Whenever beds of sedimentary origin possess an anticlinal or quaquaversal dip, at a higher angle than water could have deposited them, they may be said, in a general sense, to form a "crater of elevation." This crater may be either circular or elliptical; or the ellipse may be so long as to appear linear; it may arise from the direct outbreak of a volcano, or from those other causes of elevation which probably exist; it may have a symmetrical cavity in its centre, or it may be filled up by the elevated matter, and have no cavity at all;—yet the mechanical elements of an elevation-crater remain unaltered. We have plenty of such craters in our own land; the Weald of Kent (allowing for subsequent denudation) is an elevation-crater; so are the more symmetrical domes of limestone near Dudley (one of which has a crateriform depression on its summit); and so are the beautiful valleys of Woolhope in Herefordshire and of Ashover near Matlock. Wherever the inclined beds are of *aqueous deposition* (whether their *ingredients* are volcanic or not is immaterial), there is no difficulty in attributing their present arrangement to elevatory forces. But when a crateriform cavity is surrounded by inclined masses of lava, scoriæ, or other purely igneous matter, the problem is far more difficult, and becomes a fair question for controversy. Whether the materials which form a volcanic cone are elevated or erupted, they equally assume a quaquaversal inclination, and it is often impossible to determine whether they have originally formed a continuous stratum or have been outpoured at successive epochs. Nor does the difficulty appear to us to be diminished by the presence in a crater of a trachytic nucleus, which Dr. Daubeny considers to be conclusive evidence of elevation; for if the trachyte has once been fluid, why may it not have been ejected up the funnel of the volcano in a semi-liquid form? In some countries, Asia Minor for instance, there are regular *coulées* of trachyte which have flowed down the existing valleys, and we do not therefore see why trachyte in a less perfect state of fluidity may not have blocked up the mouths of volcanos, or even, when in an almost solid state, have formed conical masses, like the Puy de Dome, on the surface of the earth.

It is nevertheless highly probable that nearly every volcanic cone has a nucleus of *elevated* rocks. Before a volcano can *commence* at a new point a vent must be made for it, either by pushing the incumbent strata laterally, or, which is far easier, by bursting them upwards. But in the majority of cases these rocks so elevated would soon be buried far from human ken by the accumulations of erupted matter.

The author next treats of the subject of basaltic or trap rocks, which he considers to be caused by volcanic eruptions taking place under submarine pressure, instead of exploding into the atmosphere like ordinary volcanos. It was hardly necessary at this time of day to go into much detail to prove the connection between trap and volcanic rocks; we should rather go a step further, and assert the actual *identity* of the operations which produce them. It appears to us that *pressure of any kind* is sufficient to account for the difference between ordinary volcanic products and those commonly called trap. This pressure is no doubt often due to the presence of a deep sea over the point of eruption, but the hydrostatic pressure of an ascending column of lava is a still more powerful agent. The lava in a volcanic chimney may be compared to the scum and slag in an iron furnace, while trappean rocks represent the heavy and fluid metal which lies beneath it. The pressure of a column of fluid lava 10 or 20,000 feet high would inject the denser matter below into every accessible crevice, horizontally as well as vertically, and when exposed in after ages by denudation, it would exhibit those dykes and tabular masses of basaltic rocks which Dr. Daubeny refers more exclusively to submarine eruption.

Our author attributes the columnar and jointed structure of basalt to its aggregation, in the act of cooling, into spheroidal masses, which by their mutual pressure acquire a subhexagonal form. It appears to us, however, that *contraction*, and not *pressure*, is the "appropriate idea" to be applied to the prismatic structure of basalt. Dr. Daubeny, indeed, maintains that the columns often approximate so closely that no contraction can have taken place. But the fact of the rock separating into columns proves that a certain interval exists between them, and the smallness of this interval merely shows that the contraction was small in amount. From the moment that the basalt begins to solidify, the cooling process *must* be accompanied by contraction, and although the rock may then have a tendency to assume a spheroidal or concretionary structure, we do not see how such concretions can exert a mutual *pressure* at the same time that they are separating from each other by *contraction*. Moreover, the spheroidal structure is often absent, and the basaltic prisms then present a homogeneous texture through their whole length. The subhexagonal structure would therefore appear to be the first or normal condition which a tabular mass of basalt tends to assume, and the spheroidal arrangement to be the offspring and not the parent of that structure.

This volume is appropriately concluded by a chapter on the final causes of volcanos, in which those who have exclusively regarded these igneous operations in the light of destructive agents, will be gratified by some sound and philosophical views as to the benefits which they confer on the organic creation. We will quote the following as an example:—

"Potass, soda, certain earthy phosphates, lime, magnesia, must be present wherever a healthy vegetation proceeds. Now some of these bodies are naturally insoluble in water, whilst others are dissolved with such readiness, that any conceivable supply of them, in their isolated condition, would be speedily carried off and find its way into the ocean. The first, therefore, must be rendered more soluble, the latter less so, than they are by themselves. Now the manner in which nature has availed herself of the instrumentality of volcanos to effect both these opposite purposes is equally beautiful and simple.

"She has in the first place brought to the surface, in the form of lava and trachyte, vast masses of matter containing the alkalies, lime and magnesia, in what I have termed a *dormant* condition, that is, so united by the force of cohesion and of chemical affinity as not to be readily disengaged and carried off by water. * * * *

"Now nature has provided, in the carbonic acid which is so copiously evolved from volcanos, and which consequently impregnates the springs in those very countries, more particularly where volcanic products are found, an agent capable, as completely as muriatic acid, though more slowly, of acting upon these descriptions of rock, of separating the alkali and alkaline earths, and of presenting them to the vessels of plants in a condition in which they can be assimilated.

"Thus every volcanic as well as every granitic rock contains a storehouse of alkali for the future exigences of the vegetable world, whilst the former is also charged with those principles which are often wanting in granite, but which are no less essential to many plants—I mean lime and magnesia.

"Had the alkalies been present in the ground in beds or isolated masses, they would have been speedily washed away, and the vegetables that require them would by this time have been restricted to the immediate vicinity of the ocean."—P. 701.

## XLIII. *Proceedings of Learned Societies.*

### ROYAL SOCIETY.

[Continued from p. 231.]

Feb. 10, 1848. "EXAMINATION of the Proximate Principles of the Lichens." By John Stenhouse, Esq., Ph.D.

The author, after adverting to the labours of Robiquet, Heeren, Dumas, and Kane in the investigation of the proximate principles of the lichens, especially of those which yield red colouring matter with ammonia, and also of the more recent inquirers on this subject, such as Schunck, Rochleder, Heldt and Knop, who have greatly extended our knowledge of this interesting but difficult department of organic research, proceeds to state that nearly two years ago his attention was directed by Dr. Pereira to a kind of Orcella weed, which had been recently imported into London from the Cape of Good Hope, but which had been rejected by the London archil manufacturers as being unfit for their use, from the small quantity of colouring matter it yields when subjected to the usual process. With a view to ascertain whether or not the red dyes obtained from the various lichens result from the action of ammonia on a certain crystalline principle, described by Schunck under the name of *lecanorine*, the author procured quantities of the several lichens usually employed by the archil makers, and subjected them to investigation; the minute details of which, together with the results, are given at length in the present paper.

The specimens examined are the following:—

I. *South American variety of* Roccella tinctoria.

The lichen was cut into small pieces and macerated with a large quantity of water for some hours, then quick-lime was added. A yellow solution was obtained, from which muriatic acid precipitated the colouring matter, as a bulky gelatinous mass; this was washed, dried on a plate of gypsum, and dissolved in hot spirits of wine (not boiling). The solution on cooling deposited the colouring principle in small white prismatic needles arranged in stars. This is—

1. *Alpha-Orsellic acid* (hydrated) .......... $C_{22}H_{13}O_{13}+HO$
and its salt of baryta—
*Alpha-Orselliate of baryta* .............. $C_{22}H_{13}O_{13}+BaO$

2. *Alpha-Orsellesic acid* was obtained by mixing crude gelatinous orsellic acid with a little water, neutralizing with lime or baryta, and precipitating with muriatic acid. A gelatinous hydrate is obtained, which may be purified by solution in dilute alcohol and crystallization. The composition of this acid and its baryta salt is as follows:—

*Alpha-Orsellesic acid* ...... $C_{16}H_{8}O_{7}+HO$
*Alpha-Orsellesiate of baryta* $C_{16}H_{8}O_{7}+BaO$

This acid gives a fugitive bluish-red or violet tint with hypochlorite of lime. Orsellic acid gives a deep blood-red tint, quickly changing to yellow.

3. *Orsellesic ether*, $C_{16}H_{8}O_{7}+C_{4}H_{5}O$, is obtained from alpha-orsellic acid by boiling in strong alcohol, evaporating to dryness, and dissolving in boiling water. It crystallizes on cooling in long flat needles, having a yellowish colour from adhering resin.

II. Roccella tinctoria *from the Cape of Good Hope.*

By processes similar to those just mentioned, this lichen yielded—

1. *Beta-Orsellic acid.*.......... $C_{34}H_{17}O_{14}+HO$
*Beta-Orselliate of baryta* .... $C_{34}H_{17}O_{14}+BaO$

2. *Beta-Orsellesic acid* (formula to be given hereafter).

3. An ether compound, which is probably orsellesic ether. By three experiments its composition was found to be—

|   | I. | II. | III. |
|---|---|---|---|
| C | 60·82 | 60·75 | 60·83 |
| H | 6·27 | 6·15 | 6·27 |
| O | 32·91 | 33·10 | 33·00 |
|   | 100·00 | 100·00 | 100·00 |

4. *Roccellinine.*—Obtained by drying the gelatinous mass which is precipitated from the lime solution by muriatic acid, and boiling in strong spirit. The ether compound dissolves, and roccellinine remains behind. It is purified by repeated crystallization from strong spirit, aided by animal charcoal, and presents itself in soft hair-like crystals about an inch long, arranged in stars. It is a very indifferent substance, appearing however to be a feeble acid.

Its empirical formula is $C_{23}H_{17}O_{15}$.

III. *Roccella Montagnei.*

By similar treatment yielded—

    1. *Erythric acid*........ $C_{20}H_{10}O_9 + HO$.

This acid gives a blood-red colour with hypochlorite of lime.

    2. *Erythric ether* ...... $C_{20}H_{10}O_9 + C_4H_5O$.
    3. *Erythric methylic ether* $C_{20}H_{10}O_9 + C_2H_3O$.

This ether crystallizes in longer and narrower prisms than erythric ether.

    4. *Erythrelesic acid* is analogous to alpha- and beta-orsellesic acids.

    5. *Picro-erythrine.*—By neutralizing crythric acid with lime or baryta, and throwing down erythrelesic acid with muriatic acid, a mother-liquid is obtained containing picro-erythrine, from which that substance may be separated in the form of yellowish crystals; and these may be purified and decolorized by repeated crystallization from hot water aided by the use of animal charcoal. Picro-erythrine gives a blood-red colour with hypochlorite of lime.

Its empirical formula is $C_{34}H_{24}O_{20}$.

    6. *Pseudo-orcine*, of which the empirical formula is $C_{10}H_{13}O_{10}$. It is obtained by boiling the lime solution of *R. Montagnei* till it is reduced to one-fourth of its bulk, passing carbonic acid in excess through the liquid, and evaporating the filtered liquid to the consistence of a syrup; this is introduced into a flask and digested with a large quantity of ether, which dissolves orcine and leaves pseudo-orcine. On being crystallized two or three times from strong spirit, it is obtained in large shining colourless crystals. Still larger crystals may be obtained from an aqueous solution. Hypochlorite of lime has no action upon it.

The author then gives a mode of extracting the colouring principles of the lichens, so as to make them portable for commercial purposes. The extraction might be performed in the country where the lichens grow, by cutting them up into small pieces, macerating in milk of lime, neutralizing with muriatic or acetic acid, collecting the gelatinous precipitate on cloths, and drying it at a gentle heat.

He also suggests two modes of estimating the quantity of colouring matter in the lichens.

    1. By macerating a known quantity of the lichen in milk of lime, and adding bleaching powder of known strength from an alkalimeter till all colour disappears from the liquid, and noting the quantity of solution required. It is thus found that—

| | | |
|---|---|---|
| Angola lichen requires............ | 200 measures | 1·00 |
| American lichen requires.......... | 120 .. | 0·60 |
| Cape lichen requires............. | 35 .. | 0·17 |
| *Lecanora Tartarea* (from Germany, near Giessen) requires........ | 25 .. | 0·12 |

    2. By extracting the lichen with milk of lime, precipitating with acetic acid, collecting the precipitate on a weighed filter, drying and weighing it.

### IV. *Evernia Prunastri.*

1. *Evernic acid* is obtained by extracting the lichen with milk of lime, precipitating with muriatic acid, drying the precipitate, and digesting in weak spirit till nearly two-thirds are dissolved. The solution yields crystals of *evernic acid*. The insoluble part is usnic acid. Evernic acid yields only a slight yellow colour with hypochlorite of lime.

Formula of hydrated *evernic* acid .. $C_{34} H_{18} O_{13} + HO$
Formula of everniate of potash .... $C_{34} H_{18} O_{13} + KO$
Formula of everniate of baryta .... $C_{34} H_{15} O_{13} + BaO + Aq.$

2. *Evernesic acid* is obtained by dissolving evernic acid in a slight excess of caustic potash, passing carbonic acid gas through the solution to saturation, and concentrating the solution: evernesiate of potash crystallizes out. From this the acid may be separated by means of muriatic acid. It gives a yellow colour with hypochlorite of lime.

Formula of hydrated acid......... $C_{18} H_{3} O_{7} + HO$
Formula of evernesiate of baryta.. $C_{18} H_{9} O_{7} + BaO + Aq.$
Formula of evernesiate of silver .. $C_{18} H_{9} O_{7} + AgO.$

### Orcine.

This substance is always obtained when any of the colouring principles of the lichens which yield red dyes with ammonia are subjected to particular processes. The best way of obtaining it pure is to boil the alpha-, or beta-orsellesic acid, or the erythrelesic acid in water for about an hour. Carbonic acid is given off, and crystals of colourless orcine are deposited. It gives a dark purple red colour with hypochlorite of lime, quickly changing into deep yellow.

Empirical formula......... $C_{16} H_{11} O_{7}.$

Brom-orceide, $C_{16} H_{31} Br O_{13}$ (empirical), is obtained by pouring bromine into a concentrated aqueous solution of orcine; when pure it forms long white adhering needles; it has no taste or smell.

Chlor-orceide, a similar compound, is obtained by passing chlorine gas through a solution of orcine.

### Usnic Acid.

This principle is found in *Usnea florida, U. hirta, U. plicata, U. barbata, Ramalinea calicaris, R. Frasinia, Evernia Prunastri,* and *Cladonia Rangeferina.* It is best obtained from *Cladonia Rangeferina* and *Usnea florida,* by the use of lime and muriatic acid.

Its empirical formula is $C_{28} H_{17} O_{14}.$

Feb. 17,—"On a Formula for the Elastic Force of Vapour at different Temperatures." By Captain Shortrede. Communicated by Lieut.-Col. Sykes, F.R.S.

The author adopts as the basis of his formula the first series of experiments at high temperatures made by the French Academy, and those of Magnus at low temperatures. For the Academy's experiments, he adopts the indications of the smaller thermometer in the steam in preference to those of the larger thermometer in the water. Of Dr. Young's sort of formulæ, he notices that of the Academy and several others with exponents varying from 5 to 7. From the elasticity at freezing, as given by Magnus, compared with four of the Academy's experiments, he shows that for the range of observation the number 6 is preferable to 5 as an exponent; but, as he states, no formula of this sort with a constant index can be found to agree with the observations throughout.

The formula of Magnus he finds to agree with these observations better than any of the others; but being adapted to the air-thermometer, and therefore not convenient for ordinary use, he gives his own formula adapted to the mercurial thermometer,

$$t = \frac{500 + 225 \log A}{5 - \log A},$$

$t$ being the temp. Cent., and $A$ the elasticity in atmospheres of $0^m \cdot 76$ at zero, or 30 inches at $58°$ Fahr.; ∴ the temperature being given, the formula becomes

$$\log A = 5 - \frac{1625}{225 + t}.$$

The author compares with the experiments the formula of the Academy and those of Southern, Coriolis, Tredgold, and one deduced as above; also that given by August, and the same modified so as to give at freezing the elasticity found by Magnus; also that of Magnus, and the same reduced to the mercurial thermometer by the data of Dulong and Petit; and lastly, his own formula. Then assuming that the experiments of Magnus are represented by his formula, he compares the other formula with it at every $10°$ from $-10°$ to $100°$ Cent. He shows that for the range of their experiments the Academy's formula is better than the others of Dr. Young's sort; but at low temperatures it is very erroneous. Southern's formula at low temperatures is better than that of Coriolis, but at high temperatures not so good. Tredgold and the other like it are better at low temperatures than that of Coriolis, but worse at high temperatures. August's formula is very erroneous; and in its modified form it is still worse, the errors increasing to about $10°$ or more, showing that the theoretic considerations by which it is deduced are not founded in truth. With the Academy's experiments, the errors of Magnus's formula are $-$, but when reduced to the mercurial thermometer they are all $+$, the mean of the whole being $0° \cdot 33$. With the new formula the errors are nearly balanced, the sums on the thirty experiments being $-1° \cdot 78$ and $+3° \cdot 55$, in only two cases amounting to half a degree. On the twelve experiments, at or near the maximum, the errors are $-1° \cdot 12$ and $+0° \cdot 43$.

From zero to $100°$ the differences between the new formula and that of Magnus are all of one kind; and when reduced to temperature are less than $0° \cdot 4$, which the author thinks to be within the probable difference between the air and mercurial thermometers, and within the errors of observation.

He then gives a table of temperature corresponding to elasticity of vapour in atmospheres. Also modifying his formula,

$$\log f \, 6{\cdot}47712125 - \frac{2925}{373+t},$$

to give $f =$ the elasticity in inches of mercury for temp. Fahr., he gives a table of $f$ for every degree from $-40°$ to $+360°$, by the help of which he compares with his formula, the experiments of Robison, Southern, Dalton, Taylor, Arsberger, Ure, and those of the American Committee, and shows that they differ more widely from each other than from the formula.

Considering the care bestowed to ensure the elasticities being correctly measured, the author is disposed to attribute a great part, but not the whole, of the discordance on the several results to errors in the measures of temperature arising from smallness of scale or incorrectness of division.

Feb. 24.—"On the Moist-Bulb Problem." By Captain Shortrede. Communicated by Lieut.-Colonel W. H. Sykes, F.R.S.

The author adopts the notation of Professor Apjohn, and by a similar method deduces the fundamental equation, which is then translated into numbers, taking $1175°$ F. as the sum of the latent and sensible heats, $0{\cdot}267$ as the specific heat of dry air, the weight of aqueous vapour as five-eighths of that of air, and its specific heat $=0{\cdot}867$, that of water being unity.

The coefficient for barometric pressure is resolved into a simple change on the temperature of the air, and consequently also on the depression of the moist bulb; and the equation is put into a shape convenient for use, and shown to be free from objection. The author uses the table of the force of vapour, given in the accompanying preceding paper, and then gives a table of maximum depressions for every degree of the moist bulb from $-40°$ to $212°$, and another table interpolated from it for every degree of temperature of the air from $0°$ to $212°$.

Gay-Lussac's depressions are then compared with those of the new formula; and the errors are shown to be almost insensible near the freezing-point, but increasing gradually, till at 25 Cent. it is about 10 per cent. The author attributes these errors to the gradual deterioration of the chloride of lime during the experiments.

The author then compares Prinsep's maximum depressions collected and given in vol. v. of the Journal of the Asiatic Society of Bengal. The observed depressions are generally below those given by the new formula, like those of Gay-Lussac. The errors on those where the air was heated by a steam-pipe, are not greater than on those at natural temperatures; and that with air passing through a porcelain tube at an orange heat, falls within the limits assigned by Prinsep in estimating the temperature of the air.

Apjohn's maximum depressions are then compared with the new formula. And here the errors are of an opposite character to those preceding, which the author attributes to the lowering of temperature occasioned by expansion on escaping from the compression used to force the air in a rapid current through the apparatus. Apjohn's dew-point observations are then compared, and the errors are found to be similar to the preceding, and apparently from the same cause.

To make the formula generally useful, the author gives a table of the depression of dew-point below temperature for every degree of depression of the moist bulb, at every 5° of temperature from 0° to 100°, and for every 10° from 100° to 140°, which he protracts on a chart, so as to give the dew-point in every case with little more trouble than is required for reading a common thermometer, and also at the same time the elasticity of vapour in the atmosphere.

"Experiments on the influence of Magnetism on Polarized Light." By Professor Carlo Matteucci. Communicated by Sir John F. W. Herschel, Bart., V.P.R.S. &c.

The object of this notice is to communicate some recent experiments on diamagnetism, and particularly on the influence of magnetism on polarized light. The following extracts are in the words of the author:—

"The apparatus I employed in these experiments was an electromagnetic apparatus invented by M. Rumkorf, and described by M. Biot at a meeting of the Academy of Sciences of Paris, and consisting of a powerful electro-magnet, of which the soft iron cylinder is traversed by a hole in the direction of the length of the axis, through which hole the ray of polarized light is made to pass; and the voltaic current which I employed on this occasion was that of seven pair of Grove's construction. I made my first experiment with a piece of *heavy glass*, which I received from Faraday himself. In order to assure myself of the exact amount of rotation induced by magnetic action, I caused the ray of light, before it reached the heavy glass, to pass through the system invented by M. Soleil, consisting of two equal plates of perpendicular quartz, placed side by side; the one turning to the right, the other to the left. I ascertained, first of all, the rotation produced by making the current pass sometimes in one direction, and sometimes in the other; the two rotations, one to the right, the other to the left, thus produced, were exactly the same. Then I compressed slightly the middle part of the piece of heavy glass, in the same manner as one compresses pieces of glass. I was then obliged to turn the eyepiece in a certain direction in order to restore the image to its first condition; in my experiments I always had to turn it, after compression, towards the right. I next made the current pass, first in one direction, then in the other. The general facts which I have observed constantly and without exception are the following:—*The rotation produced by the magnet on the compressed piece of heavy glass is not the same to the right as it is to the left: the rotation produced by the magnet is considerably greater in the direction of the rotation produced by compression than it is in the contrary direction: the rotation produced by the magnet on the compressed heavy glass, and in the direction of the rotation produced by the compression, is greater than that produced by the same magnet on glass which has not been compressed, and the rotation in the contrary direction is less.* The following are the numerical results.

"In one experiment I obtained on a piece of heavy glass not compressed, 3° of rotation to the right or to the left, according to the direction of the current: on slightly compressing the glass, I had to turn to the right the eyepiece to 4°, 5°, and even to 8° in order to restore the image to its first condition. In closing the circuit, the rotation produced in the same direction as that due to compression was $3\frac{1}{2}$° or 4°, while the rotation produced in the contrary direction was from 2° to $1\frac{1}{2}$°. On ceasing to compress the glass, I obtained the same phænomena as I had observed before the compression.

"I have made in the same manner experiments with a piece of flint-glass, which produced a rotation of 2° under the influence of the magnet. When I applied the same magnet to pieces of compressed flint-glass, I could not discover the slightest sensible rotation in whatever direction I might make the current pass. Plates of quartz cut perpendicularly or parallel to the axis, and compressed in various directions, did not acquire any rotatory power under the influence of the magnet. I think that the peculiarity exhibited by compressed heavy glass is of some interest, in as far as it appears likely to lead to a more satisfactory explanation of the want of rotatory power communicated by magnetism in crystalline bodies.

"I shall conclude by communicating the negative results of some experiments I attempted with a view to discover the action of diamagnetic bodies on each other, and of magnetism on gaseous bodies. I suspended small needles of bismuth between the poles of a very powerful electro-magnet, and with a good chronometer I counted the number of their oscillations, either alone or in the vicinity of pieces of bismuth of various shapes and sizes. I repeated these experiments with all possible care, avoiding the slightest current of air, reckoning the smallest oscillations, and those of the same extent in the different cases. I never obtained any differences beyond half a second, which existed equally whether the pieces of bismuth were near or not. The experiment therefore does not serve to show the action of diamagnetic bodies on each other; an action which naturally ought to exist, but which perhaps is overpowered by the stronger action of the magnet.

"I afterwards counted the oscillations of a small needle of bismuth, which I succeeded in suspending by a silk fibre (*fil de cocon*) inside of a glass ball blown at the top of a barometer-tube. The ball was placed between the poles of my electro-magnet. In this experiment the bismuth needle was held sometimes in a nearly perfect vacuum, at others in atmospheric air. The number of oscillations in both cases was exactly the same.

"We must therefore give up the idea of explaining diamagnetic phænomena by a magnetic action, which would be stronger upon the air than upon bismuth."

XLIV. *Intelligence and Miscellaneous Articles.*

ON A LATE SOLAR SPOT.

*To the Editors of the Philosophical Magazine and Journal.*

GENTLEMEN,

HAVING received on the 9th instant a letter from Sir J. W. Lubbock, informing me that he had observed a spot on the sun on the 19th of November last year, very similar to that which I took the liberty to notify in the Philosophical Magazine of last month, I beg to be allowed to make the observations, which he places at my disposal, public through the medium of your pages; as well to furnish another satisfactory proof of what appears not to have been sufficiently noted or credited, in general, as to acknowledge the priority of his observation of the fact in question. Comparing the appearances of the two spots, Sir J. W. Lubbock says,—

"Like yours it was seen as one with the naked eye by my children and by my labouring people, with whom I happened to be, and who called my attention to it. Like yours it was seen as two spots in a telescope, with a number of smaller ones under it. I enclose a copy of a drawing I made at the time. Like yours it was seen through a fog, the sun's disc being of a blood-red colour. It would seem that there must have been about sixty-seven days intervening between your observation and mine; and as the sun revolves about its axis in 25·4 days, I presume either the spot must have changed its place, or it was not the same."

Though the sketch referred to has certainly some general resemblance to the spot of the 25th of January, the central nuclei of the latter were much more oblong, or rather stripe-shaped; and the aggregation of spots and shallows on one side of these formed the aspect of a crescent, or segment of a circle, not unlike an eyebrow, relative to the others when viewed through a telescope. Still such transmutations might be expected to have occurred between November and January in the same spot. Had the position been nearly the same, and the period of revolution completely accorded, the spots might have been considered identical.

I had some difficulty in recognizing the spot of the 25th of January after its reappearing, which I first noticed on the 14th of February. As it advanced, however, I think I found sufficient similarity of features to identify it, the time also agreeing with the period of apparent rotation. The whole seemed contracted, and the various umbræ had become conjoined more or less, the arched cluster also forming a junction with the central penumbra. Some of the smaller spots had run into one, and the two long central spots had also united. A detached spot west of these had probably broken out since the disappearance. Such was its aspect on the 22nd of February; unfavourable weather and other circumstances prevented my inspecting it oftener. From a conversation I had lately with my friend Mr. J. Adie, optician, who had also seen the spot with the naked eye, I am inclined to think I had over-estimated its dimensions. Probably a fifteenth part of the solar diameter would be nearer the truth. The obscuration was however so large as to attract the notice of the most unobservant. People in Prince's Street, I understand, were gazing at it as they lounged along. Having no pretension myself to astronomical acquirements, I can claim only to be considered as a simple eye-witness to a fact, and shall be glad if chance has led me to corroborate the observations of Sir J. W. Lubbock or others. The latter gentleman, in his Note on Shooting Stars, also mentions having recently seen other solar spots with the naked eye, which disappeared altogether in a day or two. This I had read before receiving his obliging communication. The natural inference from similar repeated observations I imagine must be, that the great forces in operation on the solar surface are gradually increasing and extending their energies; so that we may possibly have, in process of time, half of the sun's body obscured, as Abulferagius relates occurred in the seventeenth year of the emperor Heraclius during the space of nine months! The solution of this mighty solar problem is yet to be achieved; and perhaps it would be a step to our knowledge of the physical constitution of the sun, if by calculating the perturbations of some comet, as suggested by Sir J. W. Lubbock, its origin could be traced back to the solar mass, from which it had been projected by the tremendous forces there in obvious operation.

I am, Gentlemen,
Your very obedient Servant,
Edinburgh, March 11, 1848.
W. PRINGLE.

## ON A NEW METHOD OF DISTINGUISHING THE PROTOXIDE OF IRON FROM THE PEROXIDE BY THE BLOWPIPE. BY E. J. CHAPMAN, ESQ.

The presence of iron in any compound may be detected, it is well known, and with great certainty, by the blowpipe; but no method has hitherto been given by which the protoxide of iron can be distinguished from the peroxide by means of that instrument. After several trials to accomplish this, I discovered the following method, which is both decisive and simple, requiring moreover for its performance but the ordinary reagents of the blowpipe-case.

A very minute quantity of oxide of copper is to be dissolved in a bead of borax on the platinum wire until the glass be faintly coloured; and the substance under examination being added to it, the whole is to be subjected, but for an instant only, to a reducing flame; when, if protoxide of iron were originally present in the assay-matter, the CuO will be reduced to $Cu^2 O$, forming small red spots or streaks, which become visible as the glass cools. The FeO is converted into $Fe^2 O^3$ at the expense of the oxygen of the copper.

In the above experiment, if the glass were exposed for too long a time, the oxide of copper might become reduced, even if the substance under examination contained only the peroxide of iron, as this would be converted by the flame into protoxide, and thus act, as before stated, on the oxide of copper; and if, furthermore, this latter substance were contained in too large a quantity in the borax glass, it might become reduced by the sole action of the yellow flame, and thus give rise to an erroneous result. To obviate, therefore, all doubt as to the presence or absence of FeO in any compound, I find it advisable to conduct the operation in a different manner, by which not the slightest uncertainty can be experienced.

The borax bead must be coloured by a sufficient quantity of oxide of copper to render it of a fine blue tint, but transparent, when cold. To this the substance under examination in powder must be added, and the bead exposed for a moment, or until the iron compound begins to dissolve, to an oxidating flame. If peroxide of iron alone be present, the glass will remain transparent, and of a green or bluish-green colour; but, on the contrary, if the added substance contained protoxide of iron, the glass on cooling will be marked with opake red patches, due to the reduction of the CuO to $Cu^2O$, as before explained. Care must be taken not to continue the blast too long, otherwise the suboxide of copper might be again oxidized, and the whole of the protoxide of iron converted into peroxide. After one or two trials, however, no error can possibly arise.

This reaction is not prevented by the presence of silica or other acids. Amongst the silicates, the *hedenbergite* (a variety of *augite*) $3CaO, 2SiO^3 + 3FeO, 2SiO^3$, the dark-coloured *hornblendes* $\genfrac{\}{\}{0pt}{}{CaO}{MgO}\} SiO^3 + 3FeO, 2SiO^3$, *lievrite* $3(\genfrac{}{}{0pt}{}{CaO}{FeO} SiO^3) + 2(Fe^2O^3, SiO^3)$, and other minerals, give very positive results.

Finally, it will be perceived that in certain cases the protoxide of iron, either alone or in combination as a salt, may serve to replace tin in the detection of oxide of copper by the blowpipe. For instance, when testing for minute portions of copper with borax on the platinum wire, the glass must be removed to a piece of charcoal if we wish to render evident the red suboxide by means of tin; for otherwise the end of the wire would be destroyed, the tin forming with it a fusible alloy. By employing, however, a small fragment of sulphate of iron to ensure this reduction, the bead may still be retained on the platinum wire; and we shall thus effect a saving of time and trouble, and preserve our charcoal for other experiments, an advantage of no little consequence when travelling, or in situations where good charcoal is not easily procurable. Nevertheless, it must be confessed, that, under other circumstances, tin is, for this purpose, the better reagent of the two.—*From the Chemical Gazette for March* 1, 1848.

### ON THE EXISTENCE OF SEVERAL METALS IN THE HUMAN BLOOD, AND THE FIXED SALTS IT CONTAINS.

M. Millon states, that when blood flowing from a vein is received into about three times its bulk of water, and after this dilution is introduced into a bottle of chlorine gas, it coagulates, becomes of a brown colour, and forms a gray amorphous mass, in which the organization of the red particles entirely disappears. When it is thrown upon a cloth and pressed, a liquid flows from it which filters rapidly and remains limpid.

If this reaction be minutely examined, it is found that a peculiar development of the elements of the blood has occurred. The organized portions are found almost entirely in the coagulated portion; while, on the contrary, all the saline principles are collected in the liquid.

This separation is so perfect, that when the coagulum is first washed and afterwards burnt, it is destroyed without leaving any residue. On the other hand, the liquid evaporated to dryness and burnt in the organic analysis tube, yields so little carbonic acid, that it cannot be estimated at more than 1 per cent. of the organic matter of the blood, which chlorine does not coagulate.

It is easy to determine that the coagulum furnished by the organic principles does not contain the fixed salts of the blood, and does not condense them, but contains such a quantity only as is proportional to the quantity of the water with which it is impregnated; so that if the water in which the blood is received be weighed, and it be again weighed afterwards, a known weight of the filtered liquid may be acted upon as a determinate quantity of the blood

This liquid is so proper for all analytical researches, whether qualitative or quantitative, that the fixed salts of the blood are immediately discovered and their quantity ascertained. To give some idea of this rapidity, two or three minutes are sufficient to obtain from the blood even the iron which it contains, in the state of a limpid solution, in which all the reactions of this metal are discoverable.

The other fixed salts are also recognized, and their quantity determined, without incurring the tediousness and well-known difficulties attendant upon the calcination of organic matters.

This method is, in fact, an analysis of the fixed salts of the blood in the humid way: it cannot fail to be advantageously applied to other tissues, and to other liquids of the animal œconomy; added to which, the most repulsive organic matters are by the action of the chlorine converted into common saline solutions.

The facility of isolating the saline portion of the blood leads to other results well-worthy of notice. Human blood is known always to contain silica, manganese, lead and copper. The proportion of silica and of the metals is sufficient to prevent the necessity of any peculiar modification in the analysis. After having evaporated to dryness the liquor left after the action of the chlorine, the residue is to be calcined for a short time, to get rid of the small quantity of organic matter which the chlorine has not rendered insoluble. The insoluble portion of the ashes is then to be treated like a mineral, in which the quantities of silica, lead, copper, and manganese are to be determined. It is found that 100 parts of the insoluble residue of ashes of the blood yield—

| | | |
|---|---|---|
| Silica from | 1 | to 3 parts |
| Lead | 1 | to 5 .. |
| Copper | 0·5 | to 2·5 .. |
| Manganese | 10 | to 24 .. |

After this determination, so easily effected, it became a curious subject of inquiry, whether the copper and the lead are disseminated throughout the whole mass of the blood, or if, as happens with the iron, they are confined to the red particles.

Experience has left no doubt on this subject. One kilogramme of the clot, carefully separated from the serum of many bleedings, yielded 0·083 gr. of lead and copper; one kilogramme of serum separated from the preceding clot yielded only 0·003 gr. of these two metals. These three milligrammes of lead and copper contained in the serum, ought undoubtedly to be attributed to the red globules dissolved or suspended in the lymph.

It appears, then, that the copper and the lead are not diffused throughout the blood, but are fixed with the iron in the globules; and everything leads to the conclusion that they contribute, as it does, to organization and to life. Do they exert a decided influence on the health? Does chlorosis exist on account of deficiency of copper, lead and manganese? or is their excess the secret cause of any obscure and disordered affection? Therapeutics ought to answer these questions, and enlighten us in its turn. Legal medicine, on its part, will perhaps draw up useful hints as to the permanent presence of these metallic poisons, and with respect to their enormous variations, even in the midst of life.—*Comptes Rendus*, Janvier 10, 1848.

## ON THE ARTIFICIAL FORMATION OF CRYSTALLIZED MINERALS.
### BY M. EBELMEN.

The author observes, that hitherto only two methods have been employed to obtain crystallized and definite combinations in the dry way. One consists in submitting to igneous fusion bodies, either simple or compound, alone or mixed with each other in certain proportions proper to constitute definite compounds. It often happens, in this case, that crystals are formed and are isolated throughout the fused mass during its cooling. It is in this way that various compounds which have been isolated, have been found in the products of glass-houses, and in the scoriæ of metallurgic processes, which M. Mitscherlich has found perfectly to resemble the products of the mineral kingdom. It is by the same method that M. Berthier has prepared a certain number of crystallized borates and silicates. It has as yet been applied only to compounds which are fusible at the temperature of the furnaces to which the mixture of substances is exposed.

The second method can only be employed with compounds which are distillable or volatile. It has long been known to chemists by the name of sublimation.

The process which M. Ebelmen has employed is perfectly new,

and quite different from the two preceding. The object was to discover a substance which possesses, at a high temperature, the property of water at common temperatures, or a little higher, with respect to the substances which it holds in solution. It is well-known that the evaporation of the water admits of the formation of many crystallized bodies.

It is well-known that there are some substances which are volatilized at very high temperatures, and which are nevertheless powerful solvents, when in fusion, of the greater number of metallic oxides; among these there may be cited boracic acid, borate of soda, phosphoric acid, and the alkaline phosphates. It seemed reasonable to suppose that, by employing some one of these substances with calculated proportions of certain oxides, and exposing the mixture to a high temperature in open vessels, crystallized combinations might be obtained by the evaporation of the solvent. Experiment perfectly confirmed this conjecture.

The author commences with the production of various minerals, which may be considered as formed of a compound of one equivalent of oxides constituted of two atoms of metal and three atoms of oxygen, with one equivalent of an oxide constituted of one atom of oxygen and one of metal.

The greater number of these minerals are very hard, and belong to the class of precious stones; and they constitute a natural family, comprehending a great number of species, as the spinelles, cymophane, chromate of iron, oxidulated iron, &c. All these minerals, except cymophane, are isomorphous, and generally crystallize in regular octahedrons. The author attempted to produce some of these minerals by the method just described.

*Spinelle.*—This, as is well-known, is an aluminate of magnesia, the formula of which is $Al^2 O^3 MgO$. Nature presents it to us possessing different colours. The red spinelle is that most valued by lapidaries, and it owes its colour to about $\frac{1}{180}$th of oxide of chromium. When the magnesia is partly replaced by protoxide of iron, the varieties are more or less coloured and opake; all crystallize in regular octahedrons, slightly or not at all modified, with the exception of the variety known by the name of pleonaste, which crystallizes in rhombic dodecahedrons.

The hardness of the natural spinelle is 8; it scratches quartz readily; its density varies from 3·523 to 3·585.

All varieties are infusible by the blowpipe. The red varieties become black and opake; on cooling they assume, by transmitted light, a greenish tint, and then their original colour is restored.

M. Ebelmen then proceeds to state, that having weighed each of the fixed matters separately which were to enter into the compound, and the fused boracic acid reduced to powder, the whole was heated on a sheet of platina in the mode which the author details. Various precious stones were formed, as spinelle of various colours and colourless, and cymophane, and several other crystalline compounds. To give an example of the method adopted, and the success attending it, we will quote the formation of the rose-coloured spinelle.

This was several times prepared, and the proportions followed in the greater number of experiments were—

| | |
|---|---|
| Alumina | 6·00 grs. |
| Magnesia | 3·00 |
| Fused boracic acid | 6·00 |
| Green oxide of chromium | 0·10 to 0·15 gr. |

By heating this mixture, well-defined and brilliant crystals of a rose-red colour were obtained, the form of which was easily distinguished by a glass. They were regular octahedrons, truncated on the twelve edges, constituting the *octaèdre émarginé* of Haüy. Quartz was readily scratched by the mass; by treating this with hydrochloric acid repeatedly, the crystals were left unacted upon and separate; their density was 3·548, while that of the natural spinelle varies from 3·523 to 3·585.

By analysis the author found these crystals to yield—

| | |
|---|---|
| Alumina | 71·9 |
| Magnesia | 27·3 |
| Oxide of chromium | 1·2 |
| | 100·4 |

the formula being $Al^2O^3 MgO$, which agrees with the statement already made as to the composition of the rose spinelle. Various other crystals of this substance when submitted to analysis showed their agreement in composition with the natural minerals.—*Ann. de Ch. et de Phys.*, Fevrier 1848.

### ON THE CRYSTALLINE FORM OF METALLIC ZINC.

M. J. Nicklès observes, that the crystalline form of pure zinc has already been described by M. Noeggerath (*Poggendorff's Annalen*, vol. xxxix. p. 324), who found this metal in prisms with hexagonal bases. Zinc, antimony and arsenic, are then the only crystalline metals, the form of which does not belong to the regular system. The metals of the magnesian series do however crystallize in this system; and if zinc has hitherto formed an exception, it may be hoped that dimorphism will eventually connect this metal with the group of metals to which it belongs by its chemical properties; and the author mentions that he is enabled to state this fact already with respect to some crystals of pure zinc prepared by M. Favre according to the process of M. Jacquelain.

These crystals are very distinct pentagonal dodecahedrons, very similar to the form of iron pyrites and gray cobalt.

This example of dimorphism is not unique among metals. Prof. Miller, who has examined the crystalline form of tin, has shown that it crystallizes in the system of the prism with a square base. M. Frankenheim has observed the same metal crystallized in cubes; and very lately M. G. Rose (*Poggendorff's Annalen*, vol. lv. p. 329) has announced that platina and iridium are isodimorphous. Both crystallize in the rhombohedric and cubic system.

According to these statements, it will not be surprising to observe antimony and arsenic subject to the common law, and belong to the regular system, which appears really to be that of all the metals.—*Ann. de Ch. et de Phys.*, Janvier 1848.

### ON THE CRYSTALLIZED MONOHYDRATE OF ZINC.
#### BY M. J. NICKLÈS.

The author states that a mineral exists, and is known by the name of cupreous hydrate of zinc, which contains the hydrates of zinc and copper, and has the cleavages of a right rhombic prism; and wishing to know the relation it might bear to the artificial monohydrate of zinc, he prepared some of it to examine its crystalline form.

Runge was the first who observed the formation of crystallized hydrate of zinc on a pile, the elements of which, iron and zinc, were immersed in ammonia, potash or soda. Schindler found it to consist of—

| | |
|---|---|
| Oxide of zinc .......... | 81·62 |
| Water .............. | 18·36 |

These numbers agree with calculation, which requires 81·71 of oxide and 18·29 water. Two experiments gave M. Nicklès the same number.

The process recommended by M. Runge is very simple. It is sufficient to introduce iron and zinc into a bottle containing either potash or ammonia; after some time, small crystals of the monohydrate are deposited on the sides of the bottle; very pure hydrogen gas is given out during the action.

This hydrate has the form of very limpid right rhombic prisms. When prepared from the zinc of commerce, these crystals frequently contain a black nucleus derived from the impurity of the zinc. This nucleus diminishes their limpidity, but renders the faces more reflective. The crystals are generally modified in the same manner. The summit is terminated by a bevil parallel to the great horizontal axis, and the lateral edges are generally truncated by a terminal face. It will be observed that these crystals belong to the same system as the hydrate of zinc and copper of mineralogists.

The author states that some observations were made by him during the preparation of the crystals, which he transcribes: the laminated zinc of commerce is more readily attacked than the fused metal: some of the latter was introduced into ammonia, with another portion of the same zinc laminated; the laminated zinc was dissolved in a short time, but the fused metal was hardly acted upon. When it is recollected that laminated zinc is denser than fused, the difference of solubility appears singular; but it is readily explained by considering the texture of both. In fact, when fused and cooled, zinc has a crystalline structure, which it loses completely by laminating; and it is well-known, that in general crystallized substances do not so readily dissolve as amorphous bodies.

The state of the iron employed also influences the energy of the reaction; but in this case it is the less dense metal which acts the best. Iron turnings favour the reaction, but laminated or forged iron retards it. In the first case the metal has not lost its crystalline structure; in the second all crystallization is destroyed. Moreover, the homogeneity of the surface must also diminish the influence of laminated iron.

It will be observed, that this opposition of effects is subordinate to the part which the metal ought to play in the reaction; for the zinc only dissolves, the iron serves merely as a negative pole.

The briskness of the action is measured by the hydrogen disengaged. This is abundant with ammonia, potash or soda, when laminated zinc and iron turnings are employed; but, on the contrary, it is more or less slow, according as the conditions are varied: 1 part of iron turnings, 3 parts of laminated zinc, and 300 cubic centimetres of solution of ammonia, yielded crystals in ten days; the iron did not dissolve, its action was constant, and it was requisite merely to replace the zinc from time to time as it disappeared.

The crystals are deposited wherever there are inequalities. They are very small if the action is rapid; but when it is moderately slow, they are very well-formed. They are always very brilliant when obtained with ammonia; when with potash or soda, they are entirely opake: this happens because the greater part of the hydrate of zinc is decomposed in these solutions, and a magma is deposited which contains but few crystals.

An experiment in which iron was replaced by lead, gave in four months rather large crystals, considering the quantity of ammonia employed.

In another experiment commenced the same day, there were employed ammonia, copper turnings and laminated zinc; after four months there were deposited large prisms upon the inequalities of the copper. It is to be observed, that during the whole of this time the ammonia did not become blue, and yet it was left exposed to the air. The author ascertained that in general the ammonia under these circumstances is not rendered blue in the air, if the two metals are completely immersed.

This fact is so simple, that it is astonishing that it has not been long known. Finally, it belongs to the series of observations which Davy has made on the influence of saline solutions on copper. This metal, in fact, cannot be attacked by oxygen, when in the presence of a metal which is more electro-negative than it, in the medium under consideration.

This is so true, that if instead of zinc we make use of iron or tin, or of metals in fact which are negative in ammonia with relation to copper, the ammoniacal liquor becomes as blue in the air, at least as rapidly as if copper alone were employed.

The same does not occur if copper be immersed in a solution of zincate of ammonia in contact with the air, but without metallic zinc. The liquor, it is true, does not become coloured for some hours; but in twenty-four hours small crystals of hydrate of zinc are formed*.

* If the arrangement be so made as not to immerse the whole of the copper in order to favour the absorption of oxygen, the precipitation is much more rapid and abundant; the monohydrate is deposited as a granular powder, mixed with a few crystals.

The zinc has then been replaced by copper. If this ammoniacal solution of copper be agitated with zinc, this metal, conformably to its greater affinity for oxygen, will in its turn displace the copper, and it is precipitated upon the zinc in a very fine powder, and in a short time the liquor ceases to be blackened by sulphuretted hydrogen.

This, then, furnishes an example of reciprocal affinity which is worthy of attention, and from which chemical analysis may derive utility.—*Ann. de Ch. et de Phys.*, Janvier 1848.

## ON THE HYDRATE OF CADMIUM. BY M. J. NICKLÈS.

This hydrate may be obtained, like that of zinc, by means of ammonia, iron and cadmium, or by causing copper to act upon an ammoniacal solution of oxide of cadmium.

It is but slightly permanent, and is partially decomposed in the liquid in which it is formed. It would seem that this ready decomposition is owing to the energy of the reaction; at any rate the author has obtained it perfectly homogeneous, operating slowly by putting a strip of cadmium in communication with a bar of hardened iron, and immersing the whole in a U-shaped tube full of ammonia.

By allowing the ammoniacal mother-waters to stand, a fresh quantity of hydrate is deposited. If the surface of evaporation is great, it is deposited in flocculi; if, on the contrary, the evaporation takes place in an imperfectly corked bottle, it is formed in mammillated masses, with traces of crystallization; and this is the form in which the author has usually obtained it.

M. Nicklès had only a small portion of this substance for analysis. It yielded—

|  |  |
|---|---|
| Oxide of cadmium.... | 89·74 |
| Water ............ | 10·26 |
|  | 100·00 |

Calculation requires 87·63 of oxide and 12·37 of water; the substance had therefore evidently undergone some change previous to analysis.—*Ibid.*

## ACTION OF ACIDS AND ALKALIES ON ASPARAGIN AND ASPARTIC ACID. BY M. PIRIA.

The author observes, that all chemists who have examined asparagin have observed the great tendency which it possesses to be decomposed by acids and alkalies, yielding ammonia and aspartic acid. M. Liebig states, even aspartic acid, when boiled in strong hydrochloric acid or fused with potash, is converted into ammonia and a new acid. M. Piria has arrived at a very different conclusion; he finding that neither hydrochloric nor sulphuric acid sensibly acts on aspartic acid, nor is any effect produced by nitric acid when free from nitrous vapour. Asparagin, on the other hand, is decomposed by various acids at a boiling heat, yielding ammonia, which combines with the acid employed, and free aspartic acid.

M. Piria found that crystallized asparagin, boiled for about an hour in concentrated hydrochloric acid, gave a solution which yielded no crystals on cooling.

The liquid being evaporated to a syrupy consistence yielded crystalline laminæ, which were very soluble in water, and deliquesced by exposure to the air. M. Piria at first thought he had obtained the new acid mentioned by Liebig; but he found it was aspartic acid, and that the liquid contained sal-ammoniac. Aspartic acid treated in the same way yielded crystalline laminæ of the acid unchanged, but the solution contained no sal-ammoniac.

It appears, therefore, that concentrated hydrochloric acid when heated converts asparagin into aspartic acid and ammonia, and by combining with the latter forms sal-ammoniac; the hydrochloric acid renders the aspartic acid soluble, without it the acid is scarcely soluble in cold water.

Aspartic acid retains hydrochloric acid even after evaporation to dryness and heated to 212°; this dissolved in water abundantly precipitates nitrate of silver. The substance which M. Liebig supposed to be a new acid is a concentrated solution of aspartic and hydrochloric acids. With nitric acid, aspartic acid and nitrate of ammonia were obtained; when pure nitric acid is employed, no nitrous or other gases are evolved.

Aspartic acid obtained by means of nitric acid gave—

|  | Experiment. | Calculation. |
|---|---|---|
| Carbon | 35·99 | 36·09 |
| Hydrogen | 5·47 | 5·26 |
| Nitrogen | 10·78 | 10·53 |
| Oxygen | 47·76 | 48·12 |
|  | 100·00 | 100·00 |

The formula is $C^8 H^7 N O^5$, as already determined.

From these and various other experiments M. Piria has arrived at the following conclusions:—

1st. Asparagin, discovered by Vauquelin and Robiquet in asparagus, and since in many other vegetables, exists in great abundance in vetches.

2nd. Asparagin does not pre-exist in the seed, but is developed during germination and vegetation, either in the light or in the dark, and disappears at flowering time.

3rd. Asparagin, hitherto regarded as a neutral body, possesses an acid reaction, and displaces acetic acid from its combination with oxide of copper; the compound of which with asparagin has for its formula $CuO, C^8 H^7 N^2 O^5$, and proves that asparagin, heated to 212° F., that is, till it ceases to lose weight, still contains one equivalent of water separable by bases.

4th. Asparagin dissolved in water with the presence of the juice of vetches, undergoes a kind of fermentation, by which it is converted into succinate of ammonia, appropriating four equivalents of hydrogen and two equivalents of oxygen.

5th. Asparagin, boiled in pure hydrochloric acid, or in nitric acid free from nitrous acid, is converted into ammonia, which remains combined with the acid, and into aspartic acid. When fused with potash it disengages ammonia and afterwards hydrogen, and is changed into acetic and oxalic acids.

6th. Asparagin and aspartic acid, treated with hyponitric acid, are converted, like the amides, into water, nitrogen, and into malic acid, which remains in the liquor. This result leads to the adoption of the opinion that these two bodies are amides of malic acid, corresponding to oxamide and oxamic acid.—*Ann. de Ch. et de Phys.*, Fevrier 1848.

### METEOROLOGICAL OBSERVATIONS FOR FEB. 1848.

*Chiswick.*—February 1, 2. Clear and fine. 3. Cloudy. 4. Overcast: rain. 5. Densely overcast: heavy rain at night. 6. Overcast and mild. 7. Densely overcast: rain. 8. Cloudy and fine. 9. Cloudy: boisterous: clear. 10. Very fine: heavy rain at night. 11, 12. Very fine. 13. Overcast. 14. Rain. 15. Densely overcast: rain. 16. Frosty: clear and fine. 17. Clear: cloudy and fine. 18. Fine. 19. Rain: hazy and damp. 20. Foggy: cloudy: clear. 21. Overcast: rain. 22. Rain. 23. Heavy clouds: fine. 24. Densely overcast: rain. 25. Rain: showery. 26. Barometer most remarkably low: boisterous, with heavy rain. 27. Heavy rain: clear and boisterous at night. 28. Fine: clear. 29. Very clear: boisterous, with rain at night.

| | |
|---|---|
| Mean temperature of the month | 39°·62 |
| Mean temperature of Feb. 1847 | 34 ·79 |
| Mean temperature of Feb. for the last twenty years | 39 ·32 |
| Average amount of rain in Feb. | 1·95 inch. |

*Boston.*—Feb. 1, 2. Fine. 3. Cloudy. 4. Rain. 5. Cloudy: rain P.M. 6. Rain. 7. Cloudy. 8. Cloudy: rain P.M. 9. Cloudy: rain early A.M.: rain A.M. 10—13. Fine. 14. Rain: rain P.M. 15. Cloudy: rain early A.M. 16—18. Fine. 19. Cloudy: snow early A.M. 20. Rain. 21. Fine: rain P.M. 22. Cloudy: rain P.M. 23. Fine: rain P.M. 24. Cloudy: rain P.M. 25. Fine. 26. Fine: rain early A.M. 27. Cloudy: rain early A.M.: rain A.M. 28. Cloudy. 29. Fine.

*Applegarth Manse, Dumfries-shire.*—Feb. 1. Hard frost A.M.: thaw and rain P.M. 2. Thaw: threatening frost again. 3. Thaw: rain: high wind. 4. Heavy rain: snow gone. 5. Heavy rain: floods. 6. Moist A.M.: showery P.M. 7. Thick fog ending in rain. 8. Heavy rain all day. 9. Rain A.M.: cleared: rain P.M. 10. Slight showers. 11. Very fine spring day. 12. Dull morning: wet P.M. 13. Heavy rain and high winds. 14. Fair, but threatening change. 15. Rain all day. 16. Frost: a shower of snow. 17. Hard frost: hills white: snow. 18. Hard frost: rain P.M. 19. Showery. 20. Beautiful day: slight frost A.M. 21. Raw frost A.M.: moist. 22. Storm of rain and wind: flood. 23. Stormy day: violent showers. 24. Snow for two hours: heavy rain. 25. Fair and milder. 26. Fair A.M.: drizzle P.M. 27. Heavy rain all day. 28. Heavy rain: thunder. 29. Showers: hail.

| | |
|---|---|
| Mean temperature of the month | 40°·1 |
| Mean temperature of Feb. 1847 | 36 ·2 |
| Mean temperature of Feb. for twenty-five years | 37 ·3 |
| Rain | 5·53 inches. |
| Mean rain in Feb. for twenty years | 2·04 ,, |

*Sandwick Manse, Orkney.*—Feb. 1. Snow showers: cloudy. 2. Frost: clear. 3. Cloudy: showers. 4. Rain: damp. 5. Snow-drift: snow. 6. Snow: cloudy. 7. Rain. 8. Bright: showers. 9. Cloudy: damp. 10. Rain: cloudy. 11. Bright: cloudy. 12. Rain: showers. 13. Showers. 14. Showers: clear. 15. Damp: rain. 16, 17. Bright: frost. 18. Sleet: rain. 19. Sleet-showers: showers. 20. Bright: snow-showers. 21. Snow: red aurora. 22, 23. Cloudy: rain: aurora. 24. Bright: frost: fine: aurora. 25. Showers. 26. Cloudy: showers. 27. Showers: rain. 28. Damp: rain. 29. Clear: cloudy.

The following are the averages for Dec. 1847, with which we have been favoured by our correspondent the Rev. Ch. Clouston of Sandwick Manse, whose usual report miscarried owing to the stormy weather which then prevailed:—

| Barometer. | | Thermometer. | | Rain |
|---|---|---|---|---|
| A.M. | P.M. | A.M. | P.M. | in inches. |
| 29·597 | 29·595 | 39·93 | 40·66 | 5·24 |

*Meteorological Observations made by* Mr. Thompson *at the Garden of the Horticultural Society at* Chiswick, *near London; by* Mr. Veall, *at* Boston; *by the* Rev. W. Dunbar, *at Applegarth Manse,* Dumfries-shire; *and by the* Rev. C. Clouston, *at Sandwick Manse,* Orkney.

| Days of Month. | Barometer. | | | | | | | Thermometer. | | | | | | | Wind. | | | | Rain. | | | |
|---|---|---|---|---|---|---|---|---|---|---|---|---|---|---|---|---|---|---|---|---|---|---|
| | Chiswick. | | Boston. 8½ a.m. | Dumfries-shire. | | Orkney, Sandwick. | | Chiswick. | | Boston. 8½ a.m. | Dumfries-shire. | | Orkney, Sandwick. | | Chiswick. 1 p.m. | Boston. | Dumfries-shire. | Orkney, Sandwick. | Chiswick. | Boston. | Dumfries-shire. | Orkney, Sandwick. |
| 1848. Feb. | Max. | Min. | | 9 a.m. | 9 p.m. | 9¼ a.m. | 8½ p.m. | Max. | Min. | | Max. | Min. | 9¼ a.m. | 8½ p.m. | | | | | | | | |
| 1. | 30·071 | 29·763 | 29·45 | 29·60 | 29·70 | 29·53 | 29·70 | 37 | 26 | 29·5 | 36½ | 09½ | 31 | 31 | nw. | nw. | ne.sw. | n. | ...... | ...... | ...... | ...... |
| 2. | 30·315 | 30·153 | 29·76 | 29·88 | 29·97 | 29·90 | 29·67 | 46 | 29 | 38 | 41½ | 34½ | 29 | 41½ | w. | n. | ene. | sw. | ...... | ...... | ...... | ·28 |
| 3. | 30·363 | 30·241 | 29·94 | 29·90 | 29·75 | 29·55 | 29·39 | 46 | 33 | 37 | 43 | 35½ | 43 | 48 | sw. | wsw. | s. | sw. | ·01 | ...... | ...... | ·05 |
| 4. | 30·167 | 30·111 | 29·73 | 29·66 | 29·63 | 29·36 | 29·69 | 51 | 39 | 40 | 47 | 42 | 47 | 40 | sw. | sw. | sw. | n. | ·03 | ...... | ...... | ·65 |
| ● 5. | 30·100 | 30·059 | 29·65 | 29·69 | 29·70 | 29·92 | 30·06 | 53 | 48 | 53 | 52 | 45 | 32 | 32½ | sw. | calm | sw. | e. | ·23 | ·04 | ...... | ·08 |
| 6. | 30·139 | 30·075 | 29·63 | 29·94 | 29·94 | 30·20 | 30·13 | 55 | 46 | 51·5 | 49½ | 37½ | 35 | 35 | w. | calm | ene. | ese. | ·01 | ·18 | ...... | ...... |
| 7. | 29·997 | 29·818 | 29·54 | 29·70 | 29·61 | 29·75 | 29·60 | 52 | 40 | 46 | 46 | 38 | 36½ | 44 | sw. | ssw. | ssw. | wsw. | ·25 | ·06 | ...... | ·40 |
| 8. | 29·859 | 29·694 | 29·44 | 29·59 | 29·20 | 29·53 | 29·12 | 52 | 44 | 43 | 47 | 36 | 41½ | 41 | sw. | calm | s. | se. | ·26 | ...... | 1·50 | ·26 |
| 9. | 29·096 | 29·027 | 28·62 | 28·64 | 28·56 | 28·88 | 28·77 | 51 | 36 | 49 | 48 | 43½ | 41 | 40 | sw. | calm | sw. | ne. | ·01 | ·64 | ...... | ·06 |
| 10. | 28·986 | 28·840 | 28·57 | 28·55 | 28·59 | 28·48 | 28·67 | 49 | 37 | 40 | 43½ | 38½ | 40½ | 38 | sw. | calm | sw. | n. | ·52 | ·03 | ...... | ·18 |
| ☽ 11. | 29·548 | 28·984 | 28·72 | 28·96 | 29·38 | 29·01 | 29·32 | 47 | 30 | 32 | 48 | 34½ | 43 | 35½ | nw. | calm | w. | wnw. | ...... | ...... | ...... | ...... |
| 12. | 29·946 | 29·892 | 29·50 | 29·51 | 29·50 | 29·17 | 29·00 | 48 | 36 | 36 | 47 | 34½ | 40 | 43 | w. | calm | sw. | w. | ...... | ...... | ...... | ·15 |
| 13. | 30·051 | 29·936 | 29·56 | 29·51 | 29·35 | 29·12 | 29·07 | 51 | 47 | 47·5 | 51 | 38½ | 42 | 43 | sw. | calm | sw. | sw. | ...... | ...... | ...... | ·27 |
| 14. | 29·863 | 29·658 | 29·40 | 29·44 | 29·44 | 29·12 | 29·46 | 53 | 48 | 52 | 50½ | 43 | 42½ | 36½ | sw. | w. | sw. | e. | ·04 | ...... | ...... | ·18 |
| 15. | 29·544 | 29·174 | 29·10 | 29·33 | 29·30 | 29·43 | 29·45 | 49 | 26 | 45 | 43 | 39½ | 40 | 38½ | s. | calm | sw. | ne. | ·03 | ·52 | ...... | ·11 |
| 16. | 29·956 | 29·713 | 29·40 | 29·59 | 29·95 | 29·80 | 30·11 | 44 | 25 | 35 | 40½ | 32 | 40½ | 35 | n. | calm | wnw. | n. | ...... | ...... | 0·65 | ·42 |
| 17. | 30·456 | 30·244 | 29·91 | 30·24 | 30·31 | 30·31 | 30·26 | 45 | 29 | 35 | 41 | 28½ | 35 | 34½ | ne. | calm | se. | s. | ...... | ...... | ...... | ...... |
| 18. | 30·420 | 30·182 | 30·08 | 30·15 | 29·64 | 29·84 | 29·34 | 42 | 25 | 32·5 | 40½ | 26 | 39 | 42 | s. | calm | e.-sw. | ssw. | ·16 | ...... | ...... | ...... |
| ○ 19. | 29·778 | 29·553 | 29·45 | 29·46 | 29·28 | 29·20 | 29·27 | 49 | 32 | 37 | 46½ | 38½ | 42½ | 37 | w. | sw. | wsw. | w. | ·02 | ...... | ...... | ·25 |
| 20. | 29·744 | 29·364 | 29·05 | 29·30 | 29·56 | 29·50 | 29·42 | 48 | 25 | 40 | 46 | 33½ | 35 | 37 | nw. | calm | w. | w. | ·02 | ...... | ...... | ·24 |
| 21. | 29·790 | 29·595 | 29·38 | 29·49 | 29·42 | 29·43 | 29·51 | 46 | 39 | 36 | 42 | 33 | 30 | 29½ | sw. | w. | w. | calm | ·11 | ·43 | ...... | ·19 |
| 22. | 29·478 | 29·142 | 29·10 | 29·02 | 28·64 | 28·87 | 28·47 | 51 | 39 | 41 | 48½ | 33½ | 37 | 36½ | sw. | w. | sw. | sse. | ·08 | ·09 | ...... | ...... |
| 23. | 29·341 | 29·002 | 28·58 | 28·58 | 28·96 | 28·46 | 28·74 | 55 | 41 | 45 | 47 | 38 | 40½ | 34½ | sw. | w. | w. | w. | ...... | ·17 | 1·67 | ·75 |
| 24. | 29·323 | 29·172 | 28·90 | 29·97 | 28·74 | 29·03 | 29·03 | 53 | 44 | 45 | 40½ | 35½ | 37½ | 35 | sw. | calm | e. | e. | ·14 | ·05 | ...... | ·17 |
| 25. | 30·050 | 30·031 | 28·64 | 28·60 | 28·73 | 28·79 | 28·92 | 54 | 43 | 48 | 49½ | 35½ | 37½ | 36 | sw. | w. | nw. | e. | ·16 | ·09 | ...... | ·15 |
| 26. | 29·209 | 28·452 | 28·35 | 28·62 | 28·97 | 28·96 | 29·07 | 51 | 39 | 46·5 | 47½ | 39 | 40 | 38 | w. | calm | ne. | e. | ·48 | ·17 | ...... | ·03 |
| ☾ 27. | 29·103 | 28·795 | 28·54 | 28·59 | 28·34 | 28·82 | 28·51 | 55 | 42 | 46 | 46 | 35½ | 40½ | 39 | sw. | s. | e.-sw | e. | ·22 | ·10 | ...... | ·12 |
| 28. | 29·419 | 29·244 | 28·82 | 28·80 | 28·94 | 28·60 | 28·72 | 56 | 35 | 47 | 49 | 35 | 42 | 43 | sw. | w. | wsw. | wsw. | ·01 | ·08 | ...... | ·32 |
| 29. | 29·462 | 28·839 | 29·00 | 28·92 | 28·79 | 28·90 | 28·75 | 49 | 37 | 42 | 46 | 37½ | 42 | 40 | s. | w. | w.-sw. | w. | ·23 | ...... | 1·73 | ·26 |
| Mean. | 29·777 | 29·550 | 29·23 | 29·352 | 29·341 | 29·291 | 29·283 | 42·69 | 36·55 | 41·9 | 45·6 | 35·5 | 38·72 | 38·08 | | | | | 3·02 | 2·65 | 5·53 | 5·57 |

#  THE LONDON, EDINBURGH AND DUBLIN PHILOSOPHICAL MAGAZINE AND JOURNAL OF SCIENCE.

[THIRD SERIES.]

*MAY* 1848.

XLV. *On the Heat disengaged during the Combination of Bodies with Oxygen and Chlorine.* By THOMAS ANDREWS, *M.D., M.R.I.A., Vice-President of Queen's College, Belfast*[*].

[With a Plate.]

§ I. *Combination of Oxygen with the permanent Gases.*

THE determination of the quantity of heat evolved during the combination of oxygen with hydrogen has occupied at different periods some of the most distinguished cultivators of chemical science, among whom we may cite the names of Crawford, Lavoisier, Dalton, Davy, and in more recent times, of Despretz and Dulong. The heat produced in other cases of gaseous combination has been made the subject of investigation by Dalton, Davy and Dulong; but the methods employed by the two former were so defective as to render their results of comparatively little value.

The experiments of Lavoisier were performed with his calorimeter, an instrument capable of yielding accurate results in certain cases, and when all due precautions are taken, but for obvious reasons now rarely, if ever, employed in investigations of this kind. Of the method employed by Despretz no detailed description, so far as I am aware, has been published. From the brief notice given by M. Cabart, we are made acquainted with the general form of apparatus employed by Dulong. It is evident from this description that Dulong's mode of operating must have been entirely different from that adopted in the present investigation. This circumstance should be kept in mind in comparing the results.

In the following experiments, the mixtures of the gases, prepared in the same manner as for a common eudiometric

[*] Extracted from a memoir communicated to the Academy of Sciences of Paris in March 1845.

experiment, were introduced into a copper vessel (Plate III. figs. 3 and 4), whose capacity was about 380 cubic centimetres. A vessel made of thin sheet copper will resist the force of the explosion of this quantity of even a mixture of olefiant gas and oxygen. It was closed by a screw, as shown in the figure, the head of which is perforated with a conical aperture (the apex towards the outside) to admit a very tightly-fitting cork. Through this cork a silver wire $a\,a$ passes, and another $b$ is soldered to the side of the screw; these wires, as shown in the figure, are connected by a very fine platina wire. When the vessel is closed (fig. 3), the first silver wire is brought into contact with a narrow band of copper $c\,c$, which surrounds the upper edge of the vessel, but is at the same time insulated from it.

The vessel containing the mixed gases, and adjusted in the manner described, was introduced into another of larger capacity, which was then filled with water at the proper temperature. The latter was suspended in a cylinder having a moveable cover at both ends, and the whole was finally introduced into an outer vessel, also of a cylindrical shape, and which was capable of being rapidly rotated round its shorter axis. The whole arrangement will be understood by inspecting fig. 5, in which the several parts of the apparatus are represented.

Before observing the initial temperature, the apparatus was rotated for sometime in order to establish a complete uniformity of temperature through all its parts. The apparatus being fixed in the position shown in fig. 5, the thermometer was next introduced through the apertures shown in the lids, and the temperature observed. On the removal of the thermometer, the exterior of the apparatus was brought into contact with one pole of a voltaic battery, while the other pole was passed through the water till it came into contact either with the central silver wire, or with the copper band ($c\,c$, fig. 3). The position of the wires at this period of the experiment is shown in fig. 5. By this arrangement the circuit was completed through the fine platina wire, which, becoming instantly ignited, caused the mixture to explode. The orifice of the calorimeter was then quickly closed with a good cork, the lid of the outer vessel shut down, and the whole rotated for thirty-five seconds, in which short space of time the heat produced by the combination was found to be uniformly distributed through the apparatus. This rapid distribution of the heat was greatly facilitated by the presence of a small quantity of water in the inner vessel. The thermometer, previously brought as nearly as possible to the expected temperature of the liquid, was again introduced, and the increment of heat observed.

The duration of the experiment was so short, that scarcely any correction for the cooling and heating influence of the air was required. The temperature of the air was in general a little above the mean between the initial and final temperatures of the apparatus: the heat, however, was given out so rapidly, that the latter must have been nearly at the final temperature during the greater part of the time. After each experiment, the apparatus was again rotated for a period of thirty-five seconds, and the loss of heat from cooling observed. I have assumed one-half of this loss to be the required correction, except in the case of olefiant gas, when the initial temperature was a little lower than usual. The correction so applied, it will be seen, never exceeded $0°·005$ C.

The thermal values of the different parts of the apparatus in terms of water were as follows:—

| | | | |
|---|---|---|---|
| Copper 170 grms. | × 0·095 | . . | 16·15 |
| Brass 111 ... | × 0·094 | . . | 10·43 |
| Solder 15 ... | × 0·043 | . . | 0·64 |
| Leather, cork, &c. | . . . . | . . | 0·48 |
| Thermal value | . . . . | . . | 27·70 |

The amount of water was always determined by weighing the apparatus with its contents after each experiment, and deducting the weight of the same when dry.

### Hydrogen and Oxygen.

The hydrogen gas was purified, according to the method of M. Dumas, by passing it through a series of tubes in which it was successively exposed to solutions of the acetate of lead, sulphate of silver, and hydrate of potash. It was afterwards collected over water in a graduated vessel. In this way it became contaminated with a small quantity of atmospheric air, the amount of which it was necessary to ascertain with precision. This was effected by an independent experiment, in which the gas was collected in exactly the same manner. In the case of other gases, the true volume was inferred from the diminution which occurred after the explosion. The difficulty of obtaining accurate results in experiments upon gases collected over water (which for obvious reasons could not be avoided in this inquiry) is so well-known to chemists, that I deem it unnecessary to dwell upon this point. I have endeavoured in every case to determine by experiment, and to apply the necessary corrections for absorption, &c., but at the same time I have always given the results immediately obtained by observation.

In the following table, H represents the volume of the hydrogen gas in cubic centimetres as obtained by observation; Hc, the same corrected for admixture of air, absorption by water, &c.; B, the height of the barometer in English inches reduced to $0°$ C; T, the temperature of the hydrogen gas in centigrade degrees; E, the excess of the final temperature of the water in the calorimeter above the air; I, the increment of temperature found; Ic, the same corrected; W, the weight of the water in the calorimeter expressed in grammes; and V the thermal value of the vessels.

|    | 1.          | 2.          | 3.          | 4.          |
|----|-------------|-------------|-------------|-------------|
| H  | 229·3 c.c.  | 229·2 c.c.  | 229·1 c.c.  | 229·5 c.c.  |
| Hc | 226·8 c.c.  | 226·7 c.c.  | 226·6 c.c.  | 227·0 c.c.  |
| B  | 30·17 in.   | 30·16 in.   | 30·04 in.   | 29·97 in.   |
| T  | $19°·7$     | $19°·8$     | $19°·3$     | $20°·0$     |
| E  | $0°·9$      | $0°·9$      | $0°·8$      | $0°·9$      |
| I  | $2°·074$    | $2°·063$    | $2°·071$    | $2°·074$    |
| Ic | $2°·079$    | $2°·068$    | $2°·075$    | $2°·079$    |
| W  | 275·7 grms. | 278·7 grms. | 277·9 grms. | 273·4 grms. |
| V  | 27·7 grms.  | 27·7 grms.  | 27·7 grms.  | 27·7 grms.  |

Hence we have for the heat evolved during the combination of one litre of dry hydrogen gas measured at $0°$ C., and under a pressure of 29·92 in. (0·76 m.) with oxygen,—

| 1.   | 2.   | 3.   | 4.   |
|------|------|------|------|
| 3025 | 3043 | 3052 | 3023 |

Taking the mean of these numbers, we deduce for the heat produced during the combination of—

| One litre hydrogen with oxygen   | 3036  |
|----------------------------------|-------|
| One litre oxygen with hydrogen   | 6072  |
| One gramme oxygen with hydrogen  | 4226  |
| One gramme hydrogen with oxygen  | 33808 |

The unit to which these numbers are referred is the same as that adopted by Dulong, viz. the amount of heat required to raise, through one degree centigrade, one gramme of water taken at the temperature at which the experiment is performed.

The above results fully confirm the accuracy of Dulong's experiments, the mean of which gives 3107 units for the heat produced by the combustion of one litre of hydrogen gas.

The heat obtained in the union of oxygen and hydrogen arises from two distinct causes; one the chemical combination, the other the condensation of the vapour formed by the combination. The latter is an accidental complication, which would not have interfered with the result if the experiment had been performed at a temperature superior to 100° C. If we assume the latent heat of steam at 20° to be 611 units, the heat evolved by the condensation of 1·125 grm. steam will be 687, which, taken from 4226, leaves 3539 for the true heat due to the chemical combination of 1 grm. oxygen with hydrogen; and a similar correction may be applied to the other numbers.

### Carbonic Oxide and Oxygen.

The carbonic oxide was prepared by the action of sulphuric acid on oxalic acid, the carbonic acid formed during the process being absorbed by a solution of caustic potash. To ensure complete combustion, an excess of oxygen was always employed. The residual gas, after being deprived of its carbonic acid, was measured, and the original volume of carbonic oxide was deduced from the reduction of volume of the mixture after combustion. As before, I have endeavoured to correct the volumes actually found for the errors inevitable to eudiometric experiments performed over water. A small allowance was also made for the air extracted from the water (about 20 grms.), which was always left in the inner vessel.

In the subsequent tables, M designates in cubic centimetres the volume of the gaseous mixture before combustion; Mc, the same corrected for absorption by water during the transference from one vessel into another, &c.; R, the volume of the residue (consisting chiefly of the excess of oxygen) after combustion and removal of the carbonic acid; Rc, the same corrected. The other letters have the significations already explained.

|     | 1.          | 2.          | 3.          | 4.          |
|-----|-------------|-------------|-------------|-------------|
| M   | 362·2 c.c.  | 362·5 c.c.  | 362·0 c.c.  | 361·8 c.c.  |
| Mc  | 361·3 c.c.  | 361·6 c.c.  | 361·1 c.c.  | 360·9 c.c.  |
| R   | 24·2 c.c.   | 24·2 c.c.   | 23·3 c.c.   | 23·9 c.c.   |
| Rc  | 24·3 c.c.   | 24·3 c.c.   | 23·4 c.c.   | 24·0 c.c.   |
| B   | 30·09 in.   | 30·09 in.   | 30·08 in.   | 30·04 in.   |
| T   | $15°·7$     | $15°·8$     | $15°·5$     | $15°·7$     |
| E   | $1°·0$      | $0°·9$      | $0°·9$      | $1°·0$      |
| I   | $2°·148$    | $2°·132$    | $2°·151$    | $2°·167$    |
| Ic  | $2°·153$    | $2°·137$    | $2°·156$    | $2°·172$    |
| W   | 270·7 grms. | 272·0 grms. | 271·0 grms. | 266·6 grms. |
| V   | 27·9 grms.  | 27·9 grms.  | 27·7 grms.  | 27·7 grms.  |

The heat evolved during the combustion of one litre of dry carbonic oxide gas, measured at 0° and under a pressure of 29·92 inches, is therefore—

| 1.   | 2.   | 3.   | 4.   |
|------|------|------|------|
| 3063 | 3053 | 3060 | 3051 |

Hence we have for the heat evolved during the combination of—

|  |  |
|---|---|
| One litre carbonic oxide with oxygen | 3057 |
| One litre oxygen with carbonic oxide | 6114 |
| One gramme oxygen with carbonic oxide | 4255 |
| One gramme carbonic oxide with oxygen | 2431 |

The mean of Dulong's experiments is 3130 for the combustion of one litre of carbonic oxide.

### Marsh Gas and Oxygen.

The marsh gas was obtained from a stagnant pool. It contained an unusually large proportion of nitrogen. A large excess of oxygen was employed to burn it.

| | | | |
|---|---|---|---|
| M  | 360·2 c.c.   | 359·0 c.c.   | 360·0 c.c. |
| Mc | 359·3 c.c.   | 358·1 c.c.   | 359·1 c.c. |
| R  | 105·0 c.c.   | 108·5 c.c.   | 125·2 c.c. |
| Rc | 105·8 c.c.   | 109·4 c.c.   | 126·1 c.c. |
| B  | 30·10 in.    | 30·10 in.    | 30·10 in. |
| T  | $15°·8$      | $15°·7$      | $14°·1$ |
| E  | $1°·0$       | $1°·0$       | $1°·0$ |
| I  | $2°·504$     | $2°·457$     | $2°·317$ |
| Ic | $2°·509$     | $2°·462$     | $2°·322$ |
| W  | 268·1 grms.  | 268·7 grms.  | 268·7 grms. |
| V  | 28·1 grms.   | 28·1 grms.   | 28·1 grms. |
|    | 1.           | 2.           | 3. |
|    | 9413         | 9431         | 9420 |

We have, therefore, for the heat evolved during the combination of—

|  |  |
|---|---|
| One litre marsh gas with oxygen | 9420 |
| One litre oxygen with marsh gas | 4716 |
| One gramme oxygen with marsh gas | 3277 |
| One gramme marsh gas with oxygen | 13108 |

A single experiment with the gas prepared artificially from the acetate of potash, gave 9171 units for the heat produced by the combustion of one litre. The gas however was not free from empyreumatic odour.

If we apply a similar correction for the heat produced by the condensation of the vapour of water to that employed before in the case of the combustion of hydrogen, we shall obtain for the true heat due to the combination of one gramme of oxygen with marsh gas 2931 units.

### Olefiant Gas and Oxygen.

The olefiant gas, prepared and purified by the usual processes, was still found to contain 6·4 vols. of carbonic oxide in every 100 vols., in accordance with the observation first made by Dr. J. Davy. It is necessary, in reducing the results, to take into account the heat produced by the combustion of this portion of carbonic oxide. In order to ensure the complete combustion of the gas, and at the same time to diminish the force of the explosion, nearly four and a half volumes of oxygen were taken for every volume of olefiant gas.

| | | | |
|---|---|---|---|
| M  | 364·8 c.c.    | 364·0 c.c.    | 364·2 c.c. |
| Mc | 363·9 c.c.    | 363·1 c.c.    | 363·9 c.c. |
| R  | 110·3 c.c.    | 106·4 c.c.    | 110·4 c.c. |
| Rc | 111·2 c.c.    | 107·3 c.c.    | 111·3 c.c. |
| B  | 30·15 in.     | 30·23 in.     | 30·23 in. |
| T  | 13°·6         | 13°·3         | 13°·7 |
| E  | 0°·8          | 1°·0          | 1°·0 |
| I  | 3°·015        | 3°·163        | 3°·033 |
| Ic | 3°·017        | 3°·166        | 3°·036 |
| W  | 265·3 grms.   | 255·7 grms.   | 264·2 grms. |
| V  | 28·1 grms.    | 28·1 grms.    | 28·1 grms. |
|    | 1.            | 2.            | 3. |
|    | 15056         | 14979         | 15012 |

Hence we obtain for the heat evolved during the combination of—

| | |
|---|---|
| One litre olefiant gas with oxygen      . | 15016 |
| One litre oxygen with olefiant gas .    . | 5005 |
| One gramme oxygen with olefiant gas      | 3483 |
| One gramme olefiant gas with oxygen      | 11942 |

The experiments of Dulong vary from 15051 to 15576 for one litre of olefiant gas.

Corrected for the heat produced by the condensation of the vapour of water, the number 3483 given above becomes reduced to 3252, and the other numbers in the same proportion.

§ II. *Combination of Oxygen with Solid and Fluid Bodies.*

A considerable modification of the apparatus was required for the determination of the heat produced during the combination of solid and liquid substances with oxygen. The slowness of the combustion in most cases made it necessary to operate upon a larger scale; and as the apparatus could no longer be inverted, it was also necessary to distribute the heat by a different method.

Fig. 1 exhibits the general form of the apparatus. The combination took place in a copper vessel of about four litres capacity. The combustible was placed in a platina cup, shown in fig. 2, which is suspended from the lid of the copper vessel by means of platina wires. A fourth wire, also of platina, but insulated by being surrounded by a glass tube, descends through an opening in the lid, and is connected below with the platina cup through the medium of a very fine platina wire, and above with a circular disc of copper, which is seen detached in fig. 2, and in its proper position in fig. 1. Before the commencement of an experiment, this disc was firmly fixed to the lid of the copper vessel, but it was also carefully insulated from it. Thus, by bringing the disc and any other part of the copper vessel into contact with the opposite poles of a voltaic battery, the fine platina wire could be instantly ignited.

In performing an experiment, the copper vessel was first filled with pure oxygen gas, the lid carrying the platina cup, &c. then introduced into its place, the copper disc attached to the lid, and its metallic connexion with the insulated wire $c$ carefully secured. The whole was next placed in the calorimeter, which contained the proper quantity of water previously cooled to the required temperature, and weighed. The inner vessel was secured in its place by the vertical rod $a\,a$. The calorimeter was covered with a lid containing apertures for the vertical rod and the thermometer, and the whole was surrounded by an outer vessel of tin plate to prevent the effects of radiation. The details of the arrangement will be obvious from an inspection of fig. 1. By means of the horizontal arm $c\,c$, the inner vessel could be agitated through the water in the calorimeter. A pin shown at $b$ restrained the motion of the vertical rod within such limits that the inner vessel was never permitted to rise during the agitation above the surface of the water in the calorimeter. Upon the sides and bottom of the inner vessel small hollow knobs were placed, which maintained at all times a certain distance between the two vessels.

Previous to the commencement of an experiment, the inner vessel was gently moved up and down till every part of the apparatus had acquired the same temperature. The ignition was effected by a similar method to that already described in the previous section, by bringing the vertical rod and the copper disc respectively into contact with the terminal wires of a galvanic arrangement. The same aperture in the lid served for the introduction of the thermometer and afterwards of the galvanic wire. After the combination had begun, the inner vessel was gently moved up and down within the calorimeter for a sufficient period of time to allow, not only the combustion to be completed, but the heat thereby produced to be uniformly distributed through the whole of the apparatus. In every experiment, after the observation of the final temperature, the agitation was again repeated during two minutes, in order to ascertain positively that the whole of the heat had been obtained.

The longer period of time occupied in these experiments rendered the corrections for the cooling and heating influence of the air of more importance than in the former observations. To determine with absolute accuracy the value of these corrections, under the varying circumstances of each experiment, would have been extremely difficult. It has therefore been my endeavour so to arrange the experiments, that the amount of correction to be applied in each case may be very small; so small, indeed, that the application of an imperfect approximation may be practically sufficient. From the effects of friction, the proximity of the person of the observer and other causes, the rate of heating was always greater than the rate of cooling for equal differences between the temperature of the air and of the apparatus; and for the same reasons, the latter was found to maintain a stationary temperature only when the thermometer in it indicated a temperature about $0°·3$ C. higher than that of the surrounding air. If we represent by $a$ the difference between the temperature of the air and of the apparatus, the correction V for the gain or loss of heat sustained by the apparatus during $m$ minutes will be expressed by the formula,

$$V = \mp m(a \pm 0°·3) \, 0°·0025.$$

The values of V given by this expression agree within the ranges of temperature which occurred in these experiments, very closely with the direct results of observation.

The usual time which elapsed between the observation of the initial and final temperatures was sixteen minutes; and in such cases it was assumed that the apparatus was at the minimum temperature during one and a half minute, at the maximum during eight minutes, and during the intermediate period at the temperature of the air. In other cases, where the combination took place more quickly, the corrections were made on the assumption that the apparatus was at the minimum point during one minute, and at the maximum during one-half of the whole time occupied by the experiment.

### Carbon and Oxygen.

The carbon was employed in the form of wood-charcoal. It was purified by the method of M. Dumas from all oxidable matters; first by ebullition in strong nitro-muriatic acid, and afterwards by exposure for several hours at a strong red heat to the action of dry chlorine gas. To expel all volatile compounds, it was finally exposed to a strong white heat under a layer of charcoal. The earthy impurities, together with a certain portion of carbon (which, notwithstanding the great excess of oxygen, always escaped combustion), remained in the platina dish after each experiment. By deducting the weight of this residue from that of the carbon originally taken, the weight of the carbon consumed was immediately obtained. To obtain with accuracy the weight of the charcoal, it was introduced in the state of fine powder into the platina cup already referred to; and after being heated nearly to ignition, the latter was enclosed in a copper box, which, when covered by its lid, communicated with the external air only by a very small aperture. The whole was then allowed to cool *in vacuo* over sulphuric acid; and when cold, a stream of dry air was admitted into the receiver. The aperture in the lid being now closed, the weight of the entire was determined.

To obtain complete combustion, a very large excess of oxygen was employed; but even with this precaution, carbonic oxide was discovered in the residual gas in several of the following experiments.

In the subsequent tables, M designates the weight of the substance burned; T, the temperature of the air, and the other letters the same quantities as before.

|    | 1.         | 2.         | 3.         | 4.         |
|----|------------|------------|------------|------------|
| M  | 1·088 grm. | 1·177 grm. | 0·980 grm. | 0·957 grm. |
| T  | 10°·6      | 10°·4      | 9°·6       | 10°·3      |
| E  | 0°·3       | 0°·5       | 0°·7       | 0°·5       |
| I  | 2°·473     | 2°·648     | 2°·238     | 2°·194     |
| Ic | 2°·464     | 2°·644     | 2°·239     | 2°·191     |
| W  | 3183 grms. | 3214 grms. | 3176 grms. | 3193 grms. |
| V  | 180 grms.  | 180 grms.  | 180 grms.  | 180 grms.  |

|    | 5.         | 6.         | 7.         | 8.         |
|----|------------|------------|------------|------------|
| M  | 0·974 grm. | 0·550 grm. | 0·510 grm. | 0·626 grm. |
| T  | 10°·0      | 9°·8       | 9°·0       | 9°·0       |
| E  | 0°·5       | 0°·9       | 0°·3       | 0°·8       |
| I  | 2°·153     | 1°·438     | 1°·430     | 1°·627     |
| Ic | 2°·150     | 1°·447     | 1°·425     | 1°·633     |
| W  | 3229 grms. | 2768 grms. | 2728 grms. | 2723 grms. |
| V  | 180 grms.  | 174 grms.  | 174 grms.  | 174 grms.  |

| 1.   | 2.   | 3.   | 4.   | 5.   | 6.   | 7.   | 8.   |
|------|------|------|------|------|------|------|------|
| 7616 | 7624 | 7667 | 7722 | 7825 | 7760 | 7658 | 7557 |

We have, therefore, for the heat evolved during the combination of—

      One gramme carbon with oxygen  .   7678
      One gramme oxygen with carbon  .   2879
      One litre oxygen with carbon . , .   4137

These numbers cannot be considered perfectly accurate, but are probably a little below the truth, in consequence of the formation of the small quantity of carbonic oxide to which reference has already been made. The results of M. Dulong differ from one another still more than the preceding; no doubt from the operation of the same cause, namely the formation of variable quantities of carbonic oxide. His numbers for one litre of oxygen consumed vary from 3770 to 4004 units, the mean result indicating 7288 units for the heat produced during the combustion of one gramme of carbon. The number given by Despretz for the same is 7912 units. The ancient experiments of Lavoisier present a remarkable coincidence with the results now obtained; and considering the form of apparatus employed, and the infant state of the science at the time they were performed, are deserving of special reference, as furnishing a singular example of the accuracy and ability by which so many of the works of that eminent philosopher are distinguished. He found that 1 lb. of carbon in burning melted 96·5 lbs. of ice, which corresponds to 7624 units. In deducing the latter number, the latent heat of water has been taken to be 79°, in accordance with the experiments of Provostaye and Desains. The results of Crawford and Dalton on the heat evolved during the combustion of charcoal are altogether erroneous*.

* Since the above was written, the results of an extended inquiry into the same subject have been communicated to the French Academy by MM. Fabre and Silbermann. (*Comptes Rendus*, xx. 1565, and xxi. 944.) They find that the development of heat is considerably affected by the physical state in which the carbon exists before combustion. Thus the mean quantity of heat disengaged, according to their experiments, by the diamond, amounts to 7824 units, by natural graphite to 7796, by artificial graphite to 7760, and by wood-charcoal to 8080 units. In these experiments, the quantity of carbonic oxide formed during each combustion was determined, and the result obtained by direct experiment was corrected accordingly. Considering the great importance of the subject, I have long intended to resume the inquiry, and have indeed already obtained some new results, but they are still in a very imperfect state. From a rude estimate of the quantity of carbonic oxide which was formed in the experiments described in the text, I inferred at the time that the true quantity of heat disengaged during the conversion of carbon into carbonic acid amounts to about 7900 units, or nearly the number already obtained by Despretz. On repeating these experiments, I found that if the charcoal be suspended in a cage formed of fine platina wire instead of being placed in a cup, the combustion proceeds with such vivacity that not more than $\frac{1}{350}$th part of the carbon is converted into carbonic oxide. In a single experiment performed in this way with wood-charcoal (not however perfectly purified), I obtained 7860 units of heat, which, corrected for the carbonic oxide formed, would correspond to 7881 units, as expressing the entire heat produced by the conversion of carbon into carbonic acid. This nearly agrees with the experiments of Fabre and Silbermann on the combustion of the diamond and

### Sulphur and Oxygen.

The sulphur was employed in the state of flowers of sulphur deprived of the acid with which they are always contaminated by washing. A small quantity of earthy residuum remained, the weight of which was determined at the end of each experiment, and deducted from the original weight of the sulphur. During the combustion, a small quantity of sulphuric acid (corresponding to about 3 per cent. of the sulphur) was formed, for which reason the experimental results must indicate a little more than the true quantity of heat due to the conversion of sulphur into sulphurous acid. The heat in these experiments was given out in the course of eight minutes.

|    | 1.         | 2.         | 3.         | 4.         |
|----|------------|------------|------------|------------|
| M  | 3·087 grms.| 3·089 grms.| 3·240 grms.| 3·114 grms.|
| T  | 10°·4      | 12°·8      | 8°·0       | 8°·7       |
| E  | 1°·0       | 1°·0       | 1°·5       | 0°·9       |
| I  | 2°·510     | 2°·436     | 2°·467     | 2°·461     |
| Ic | 2°·512     | 2°·438     | 2°·476     | 2°·462     |
| W  | 2699 grms. | 2739 grms. | 2818 grms. | 2737 grms. |
| V  | 175 grms.  | 175 grms.  | 175 grms.  | 175 grms.  |

|   1.  |   2.  |   3.  |   4.  |
|-------|-------|-------|-------|
| 2338  | 2300  | 2287  | 2302  |

We have, therefore, for the heat evolved during the combination of—

    One gramme sulphur with oxygen . 2307
    One gramme oxygen with sulphur . 2307
    One litre oxygen with sulphur . . 3315

Dulong's experiments indicate from 2452 to 2719 units of heat for each gramme of sulphur burned.

graphite, but differs from their experiments with wood-charcoal itself. Further researches are required to settle this difficult question. At present I will only venture to direct attention to the apparently anomalous circumstance in Fabre and Silbermann's results, that while wood-charcoal extricates so much more heat in combining with oxygen than graphite or the diamond, the two latter yield very nearly the same quantity of heat. The analogy of the specific heats of these three forms of carbon is at variance with such a result, as will immediately appear from the following comparison:—

|                | Specific heat (Regnault). | Heat of combination (Fabre and Silbermann). |
|----------------|---------------------------|---------------------------------------------|
| Diamond        | 0·147                     | 7824                                        |
| Graphite       | 0·201                     | 7778                                        |
| Wood-charcoal  | 0·242                     | 8080                                        |

Thus, while wood-charcoal has both a higher specific heat, and gives more heat of combination than graphite, the latter, with a higher specific heat, produces less heat of combination than the diamond.

### Alcohol and Oxygen.

The alcohol employed was perfectly pure. Its density at 15° was 0·7959, and it was always redistilled from a large excess of pure lime immediately before being used. The principal difficulty in examining the heat produced by the combustion of this substance, was to complete all the preliminary arrangements after its introduction into the oxygen gas so as to ignite it before any appreciable quantity had evaporated. The shortest time in which I was able to accomplish this was seven minutes; but there can be little doubt that any portion of alcohol which might rise into the state of vapour during this time would become ignited along with the rest. The duration of each experiment was five minutes.

|    | 1.         | 2.         | 3.         | 4.         |
|----|------------|------------|------------|------------|
| M  | 1·063 grm. | 0·890 grm. | 0·943 grm. | 0·962 grm. |
| T  | 9°·4       | 10°·1      | 9°·8       | 9°·5       |
| E  | 1°·4       | 0°·7       | 1°·2       | 1°·0       |
| I  | 2°·555     | 2°·040     | 2°·204     | 2°·288     |
| Ic | 2°·558     | 2°·039     | 2°·206     | 2°·289     |
| W  | 2686 grms. | 2773 grms. | 2742 grms. | 2745 grms. |
| V  | 174 grms.  | 174 grms.  | 174 grms.  | 174 grms.  |

|   1.   |   2.   |   3.   |   4.   |
|--------|--------|--------|--------|
| 6883   | 6752   | 6821   | 6946   |

We have, therefore, for the heat evolved during the combination of—

| One gramme alcohol with oxygen  | . | 6850 |
| One gramme oxygen with alcohol  | . | 3282 |
| One litre oxygen with alcohol   | . . | 4716 |

In two experiments, Dulong found the heat produced during the combination of one litre of the vapour of alcohol with oxygen to be 14310 and 14441 units. The corresponding number deduced from the preceding experiments is 14156.

### Phosphorus and Oxygen.

The inner vessel was filled with dry oxygen gas by displacement. A shallow dish of thin Dresden porcelain was substituted for the platina cup, as platina enters into combination with phosphorus at the elevated temperature at which the latter burns in oxygen gas. The experiment occupied ten minutes, from the slowness with which the porcelain dish gave out its heat.

|   |            |            |            |
|---|------------|------------|------------|
| M | 0·764 grm. | 0·773 grm. | 0·729 grm. |
| T | 4°·5       | 4°·8       | 4°·1       |
| E | 1°·2       | 1°·4       | 1°·7       |
| I | 2°·504     | 2°·498     | 2°·321     |
| Ic| 2°·511     | 2°·509     | 2°·336     |
| W | 1644 grms. | 1659 grms. | 1658 grms. |
| V | 117 grms.  | 117 grms.  | 117 grms.  |
|   | 1.         | 2.         | 3.         |
|   | 5788       | 5764       | 5688       |

Hence we have for the heat evolved during the combination of—

One gramme phosphorus with oxygen . 5747
One gramme oxygen with phosphorus . 4509
One litre oxygen with phosphorus . . . 6479

### Zinc and Oxygen.

The zinc employed in the following experiments was carefully distilled from the purest varieties of the metal in commerce. It was scarcely attacked in the cold by dilute sulphuric acid. It still however contained 0·0005 lead; but this trace of impurity could exercise no influence on such experiments as the present.

To prevent the agglutination of the fine parts of the zinc during the combustion, it was mixed in the state of very fine filings with one-half its weight of pulverized quartz. The ignition of the zinc was effected by the assistance of a small portion of phosphorus (about 0·008 grm. in each experiment), which was inflamed in the usual way by the voltaic battery. In calculating the results, the heat produced by the combustion of the phosphorus was estimated and deducted.

In the case of this metal, it would have been manifestly impossible to collect the oxide formed by the combustion; nor was it practicable to ascertain the weight of metallic zinc which had escaped oxidation, as an alloy was formed in every experiment between the zinc and platina. To protect the platina cup from being rapidly destroyed by the latter action, it was even found necessary to place a thin sheet of platina below the zinc, and this required to be renewed after every experiment. For these reasons, no alternative remained but to measure the oxygen consumed in each experiment. This was effected by ascertaining, after the increment of temperature had been observed, the volume of gas which had disappeared. There was some difficulty in making this determination with accuracy, but every possible precaution was taken to avoid error. In the next two tables, M is the volume of oxygen consumed. It was measured in a moist state.

| M  | 715 c.c.    | 793 c.c.    | 697 c.c.    |
|----|-------------|-------------|-------------|
| B  | 30·16 in.   | 30·14 in.   | 30·10 in.   |
| T  | 6°·7        | 6°·9        | 7°·4        |
| E  | 1°·7        | 2°·3        | 1°·3        |
| I  | 3°·077      | 3°·436      | 3°·027      |
| Ic | 3°·099      | 3°·471      | 3°·041      |
| W  | 1617 grms.  | 1599 grms.  | 1611 grms.  |
| V  | 117 grms.   | 117 grms.   | 117 grms.   |
|    | 1.          | 2.          | 3.          |
|    | 7717        | 7728        | 7684        |

From these data we obtain for the heat evolved during the combination of—

    One gramme zinc with oxygen  .  1301
    One gramme oxygen with zinc  .  5366
    One litre oxygen with zinc . . . 7710

Dulong found from 7378 to 7753 for the heat given out during the combination of one litre of oxygen gas with zinc.

### Iron and Oxygen.

The experiments with this metal were performed in the same manner as the preceding, with this difference, that no quartz was added to the finely divided metal. The ignition was effected by means of 0·001 grm. phosphorus.

| M  | 957 c.c.    | 982 c.c.    | 859 c.c.    |
|----|-------------|-------------|-------------|
| B  | 30·21 in.   | 30·06 in.   | 30·01 in.   |
| T  | 7°·9        | 7°·4        | 8°·6        |
| E  | 1°·4        | 1°·2        | 0°·8        |
| I  | 3°·180      | 3°·272      | 2°·821      |
| Ic | 3°·193      | 3°·281      | 2°·822      |
| W  | 1610 grms.  | 1611 grms.  | 1615 grms.  |
| V  | 117 grms.   | 117 grms.   | 117 grms.   |
|    | 1.          | 2           | 3.          |
|    | 5935        | 5970        | 5914        |

We have, therefore, for the heat evolved during the combination of—

    One gramme oxygen with iron  .  4134
    One litre oxygen with iron . . . 5940

### Tin and Oxygen.

In the experiments with this and the remaining metals, the amount of oxygen was ascertained by determining the increase of weight of the metal after the combustion was finished. The tin was mixed with half its weight of pulverized and recently ignited quartz, and the weight of the mixture carefully determined both before and after the experiment. To produce ignition, only 0·001 grm. phosphorus was required. The heat evolved by the combustion of this weight of phosphorus is nearly six units; but as a part entered into combination with the tin and thus escaped combustion, I have taken only four units from the final results as a correction. The same small quantity of phosphorus was found to be sufficient in all the subsequent experiments with oxygen. In some instances, indeed, its presence might have been wholly dispensed with; but as it rendered the success of the experiment in all cases very certain, and at the same time introduced a very trifling correction, I always employed it. In the tables which follow, M designates the weight of oxygen absorbed by the metals or oxides.

|     | 1. | 2. | 3. |
|-----|-----|-----|-----|
| M   | 1·574 grm.  | 1·256 grm. | 1·072 grm. |
| T   | 9°·1        | 10°·3      | 7°·6       |
| E   | 2°·4        | 1°·2       | 0°·9       |
| I   | 3°·815      | 3°·060     | 2°·611     |
| Ic  | 3°·850      | 3°·072     | 2°·615     |
| W   | 1616 grms.  | 1620 grms. | 1611 grms. |
| V   | 117 grms.   | 117 grms.  | 117 grms.  |

|  1.  |  2.  |  3.  |
|------|------|------|
| 4235 | 4244 | 4210 |

We have, therefore, for the heat evolved during the combination of—

    One gramme oxygen with tin . . 4230
    One litre oxygen with tin . . . 6078

### Protoxide of Tin and Oxygen.

The protoxide of tin was prepared, according to the directions of Frémy, by boiling the hydrated oxide in a dilute solution of hydrate of potash. It was afterwards dried at a low red heat in a current of dry carbonic acid gas. The experiment was performed in the same manner as the last. The whole of the heat was given out in sixteen minutes.

|     | 1. | 2. | 3. |
|-----|-----|-----|-----|
| M   | 1·716 grm.  | 1·213 grm. | 1·085 grm. |
| T   | 8°·0        | 9°·3       | 11°·3      |
| E   | 2°·8        | 1°·5       | 1°·6       |
| I   | 4°·286      | 3°·013     | 2°·723     |
| Ic  | 4°·329      | 3°·029     | 2°·744     |
| W   | 1611 grms.  | 1618 grms. | 1610 grms. |
| V   | 117 grms.   | 117 grms.  | 117 grms.  |

|  1.  |  2.  |  3.  |
|------|------|------|
| 4353 | 4328 | 4364 |

We have, therefore, for the heat evolved during the combination of—

One gramme oxygen with protoxide of tin . 4349
One gramme protoxide of tin with oxygen . 521
One litre oxygen with protoxide of tin . . 6249

### Copper and Oxygen.

The copper employed was obtained by reducing the pure oxide by means of hydrogen gas. The experiment was in all respects similar to the two last.

|    | 1.          | 2.          | 3.          |
|----|-------------|-------------|-------------|
| M  | 1·629 grm.  | 2·040 grms. | 2·387 grms. |
| T  | 8°·9        | 9°·2        | 9°·6        |
| E  | 0°·3        | 0°·4        | 1°·4        |
| I  | 2°·310      | 2°·834      | 3°·258      |
| Ic | 2°·302      | 2°·826      | 3°·272      |
| W  | 1603 grms.  | 1613 grms.  | 1609 grms.  |
| V  | 117 grms.   | 117 grms.   | 117 grms.   |
|    | 1.          | 2.          | 3.          |
|    | 2427        | 2393        | 2362        |

We have, therefore, for the heat evolved during the combination of—

One gramme oxygen with copper . 2394
One litre oxygen with copper . . . 3440

### Protoxide of Copper and Oxygen.

The protoxide of copper was obtained by the action of glucose at the boiling temperature upon a solution of sulphate of copper to which caustic potash had been added. The oxide thus obtained was dried, first in the air at a temperature not exceeding 100°, and afterwards at a low red heat in a current of dry carbonic acid gas. It was burned in the usual manner; but the results in different trials did not agree well with one another, and the combustion proceeded so slowly that nearly half an hour was occupied in each experiment. It was assumed in correcting for the cooling influence of the air, that the apparatus was at the maximum temperature during twenty-two minutes.

|    | 1.          | 2.          | 3.          |
|----|-------------|-------------|-------------|
| M  | 1·289 grm.  | 1·785 grm.  | 1·814 grm.  |
| T  | 9°·2        | 10°·3       | 11°·0       |
| E  | 0°·9        | 0°·9        | 0°·9        |
| I  | 1°·662      | 2°·338      | 2°·437      |
| Ic | 1°·690      | 2°·365      | 2°·464      |
| W  | 1597 grms.  | 1603 grms.  | 1614 grms.  |
| V  | 117 grms.   | 117 grms.   | 117 grms.   |

|     1.    |    2.   |   3.   |
|-----------|---------|--------|
|   2243    |   2275  |  2347  |

We obtain, therefore, for the heat evolved during the combination of—

| One gramme oxygen with protoxide of copper | 2288 |
|---|---|
| One gramme protoxide of copper with oxygen | 256 |
| One litre oxygen with protoxide of copper | 3288 |

The last four sets of experiments are favourable to the view proposed, I believe, by Dulong, that the quantities of heat produced by the combination of a metal and of its oxide with oxygen are the same for equal quantities of oxygen absorbed. Thus in the case of tin and its protoxide, we have for one gramme of combining oxygen the numbers—

4230
4319;

and for copper and its protoxide—

2394
2288.

The experiments of Dulong on tin and its protoxide agree with this conclusion. I may remark, however, that the results now obtained with the protoxide of copper can only be considered to be approximations; and that further researches will be necessary to discover whether the above differences will disappear when the true numbers are exactly ascertained, or be increased. The principle will in any case only apply to metals, such as tin and copper, which are capable of forming oxides inferior to those produced by their combustion in oxygen gas.

Among the gaseous combinations, the heat evolved by the combustion of equal volumes of hydrogen and carbonic oxide is nearly the same, viz. 3036 for one litre of the former, and 3057 for the same volume of the latter; but this agreement is more apparent than real, and would entirely disappear if the experiments were made under strictly identical circumstances, that is, in such a way as to obtain the resulting compounds in both cases in the aëriform state. In fact, if we correct the number expressing the heat due to the combustion of hydrogen for the latent heat of the vapour of water, it will become reduced to 2540, a number which is far from identical with 3057.

It has been inferred from the experiments of Dulong, that the heat evolved in the combustion of a compound gas is the same as that evolved in the combustion of its constituents. This principle would lead to the very improbable conclusion, that the separation of the elements of the compound gas is not attended with any thermal change. But whether this be the case or not, the principle itself certainly does not follow as a legitimate consequence, either from the experiments of Dulong, or from those contained in this paper. If, on this hypothesis, we attempt to deduce the heat evolved in the combustion of one litre of the vapour of carbon from the results obtained with marsh gas and olefiant gas, we are led in the two cases to very different numbers. Thus,

|  | Dulong. | Author. |
|---|---|---|
| One litre marsh gas gives | 9588 | 9420 |
| Two litres hydrogen give | 6212 | 6072 |
| One litre vapour of carbon should give | 3376 | 3348 |
| One litre olefiant gas gives | 15338 | 15014 |
| Two litres hydrogen give | 6212 | 6072 |
| One litre vapour of carbon should give | 4563 | 4471 |

The experimental results when interpreted in this way lead therefore to two very different numbers to express the heat due to the conversion of the vapour of carbon into carbonic acid.

[To be continued.]

XLVI. *The* ASTRONOMER ROYAL'S *Remarks on* Professor Challis's *Theoretical Determination of the Velocity of Sound.*

*To the Editors of the Philosophical Magazine and Journal.*

GENTLEMEN,

THE publication of an essay in your Magazine is commonly understood to be a challenge to discussion. With this understanding, I beg leave to transmit to you a few remarks on a paper by my friend Professor Challis printed in the last Number of the Philosophical Magazine.

The conclusions at which Professor Challis arrives are very startling,—that soniferous vibrations may be communicated along a limited cylinder or "filament" of air without affecting the air which surrounds it; and that the theoretical velocity of sound is not that in which all mathematicians, who have hitherto investigated the subject, have agreed. I need not say that such conclusions cannot be admitted without the most distinct evidence; and I think that I shall be able to show that this evidence is not to be found in Professor Challis's paper.

I see no ground to question any important step (except one of interpretation near the bottom of page 280) as far as page 281 line 5 from the bottom; and I will briefly call your attention to the state in which the problem is there left by the mathematical investigation. On page 278 a constant $-b^2$ {whose sign is fixed without any ostensible reason, but for which I shall hereafter give a reason} has been introduced; it is indeterminate; there is no *à priori* reason for thinking that it has any assignable value, or that it is needed at all: but as it is possible that such a constant may be admissible, it is quite proper that it should be introduced for trial in the subsequent parts of the investigation. It is accordingly introduced and tried, and we immediately perceive that, if it has a value different from zero, the result of non-diffusion of vibrations, which Professor Challis considers tacitly as the first object to be secured, (see p. 281, line 10 from the bottom,) cannot be obtained. Most reasoners would conclude, either that such a result is not legitimately to be expected, or that a last trial should be made by supposing $b^2 = 0$. Instead of this, Professor Challis has recourse to *another* equation, extracted from *another* memoir, and not demonstrated here, which he considers more accurate than his equation (4.); and he then uses this *new* equation in conjunction with equation (3.), and thus obtains the startling results to which I have alluded.

I must request you to record my protest against the introduction of this new equation. The equations (3.) and (4.) have been fairly and honestly obtained together, and they ought to be fairly and honestly retained together. One cannot be obtained without the other, and one ought not to be changed without reinvestigating the other and changing it if necessary.

I must also object to the application of the word "approximate" to the equation (4.). The equation is perfectly accurate as far as the first order of disturbances of particles, which is the limit of the investigations in this paper.

As the remainder of the paper, except the last paragraph, is entirely founded upon the introduction of the new equation, I conceive that it offers no evidence whatever for Professor Challis's conclusions.

I will now point out what I conceive to be the legitimate conclusions from equations (3.) and (4.).

($\alpha$.) We may suppose $e = 0$ or $b = 0$. The equation (6.) is then reduced to

$$\frac{d^2f}{dr^2} + \frac{1}{r} \cdot \frac{df}{dr} = 0,$$

and the equation (4.) is reduced to

$$\frac{d^2f}{dx^2} + \frac{d^2f}{dy^2} = 0.$$

The general solution of the former of these equations contains logarithms, and the general solution of the latter contains exponentials and multiples of $x$ and $y$; all of which, as they may be infinite, are unsuited for our purposes. We can only adopt the value $f =$ constant; and the definition of the air-disturbance will be given by equation (3.) reduced to the form

$$\frac{d^2\varphi}{dt^2} - a^2 \frac{d^2\varphi}{dz^2} = 0,$$

from which the usually received consequences follow.

($\beta$.) We may suppose $b^2$ to have a value; and this value must have the sign which Professor Challis has given it, as otherwise the solution of equation (4.) would contain exponentials. The most general solution of the equation which I can then give, free from exponentials, is

$$f = \Sigma . A \cos(px + qy + B),$$

where

$$p^2 + q^2 = \frac{b^2}{a^2} = 4e.$$

Multiplying this expression by Professor Challis's expression for $\varphi$, namely,

$$m . \cos\left\{\left(n - \frac{e}{n}\right)z - \left(n + \frac{e}{n}\right)at + C\right\},$$

and expanding the product of the cosines, we find that the value of $f$ will be expressed by the two series of terms

$$\Sigma . \frac{mA}{2} . \cos\left\{\left(n - \frac{e}{n}\right)z + px + qy - \left(n + \frac{e}{n}\right)at + C'\right\}$$

$$+ \Sigma . \frac{mA}{2} . \cos\left\{\left(n - \frac{e}{n}\right)z - px - qy - \left(n + \frac{e}{n}\right)at + C''\right\}.$$

Each of these represents a series of plane waves of indefinite extent, the position of the plane at any instant being defined by the equation

$$\left(n - \frac{e}{n}\right)z + px + qy = \text{a given quantity},$$

or

$$\left(n - \frac{e}{n}\right)z - px - qy = \text{a given quantity}.$$

If we put R for the normal drawn from the origin of co-ordinates upon the former plane, it is easily found that

$$R = \frac{\left(n - \frac{e}{n}\right)z + px + qy}{\sqrt{\left\{\left(n - \frac{e}{n}\right)^2 + p^2 + q^2\right\}}} = \frac{\left(n - \frac{e}{n}\right)z + px + qy}{n + \frac{e}{n}},$$

and therefore
$$\left(n - \frac{c}{n}\right)z + px + qy = \left(n + \frac{c}{n}\right)R,$$
and the expression for $fz$ or $\psi$ is
$$\Sigma \cdot \frac{mA}{2} \cdot \cos\left\{\left(n - \frac{c}{n}\right)R - \left(n + \frac{c}{n}\right)at + C\right\}.$$

The velocity of the wave in the direction perpendicular to the wave-plane is clearly $a$, as found by ordinary investigations.

It appears from the form of this result, that though the equation $\psi$ does not contain $t$, yet there is propagation of motion in a direction inclined to $z$, with lateral spreading to an indefinite extent; and thus the inference by Professor Challis on page 280 line 4 from the bottom is not supported.

7. As we may combine as many of these plane waves as we please, it follows that we may take an indefinitely great number of plane waves, so arranged, that their normals shall all be in a conical surface of which $z$ is the axis, and shall make with each other equal small angles. The former condition, it is easily seen, is obtained by making
$$p = \frac{b}{a} \cdot \cos \vartheta, \quad q = \frac{b}{a} \cdot \sin \vartheta;$$
and the latter, by supposing the small increments of $\vartheta$, in passing from the normal of one wave to that of another, to be equal. Also let $\varpi$ be the angle which the plane passing through the point $xyz$ and the axis of $z$ makes with the axis of $x$, so that $x = r \cos \varpi$, $y = r \sin \varpi$. Then the expression for $f$ becomes
$$\Sigma \cdot A \cdot \cos\left\{\frac{br}{a} \cos(\vartheta - \varpi) + B\right\},$$
or, as our summation is now supposed to apply only to a series of waves for which $\vartheta$ varies by very small equal quantities,
$$f = \int_{\vartheta} A \cdot \cos\left\{\frac{br}{a} \cos(\vartheta - \varpi) + B\right\}.$$
The value of this integral in series, from $\vartheta = 0$ to $\vartheta = 2\pi$, is given by me in the Philosophical Magazine, vol. xviii. p. 6; with the proper change of notation it is
$$2\pi A \times \left\{1 - \frac{b^2 r^2}{a^2(2)^2} + \frac{b^4 r^4}{a^4(2.4)^2} - \frac{b^6 r^6}{a^6(2.4.6)^2} + \&c.\right\},$$
or, as $\frac{b^2}{a^2} = 4c$, the integral is
$$2\pi A \times \left\{1 - \frac{c r^2}{1} + \frac{c^2 r^4}{(1.2)^2} - \frac{c^3 r^6}{(1.2.3)^2} + \&c.\right\}.$$

This series is precisely that which Professor Challis has found on page 281. And thus it appears that the solution in which that series is concerned does in reality express the interference of an indefinite number of plane waves, all travelling with the velocity assigned by the ordinary theory, and all indefinitely extended in the direction of their planes. These waves cannot all originate from one source, and therefore this solution does not relate to the problem of sound, in its ordinary acceptation.

I will only further allude to the difficulty to which Professor Challis adverts in his last paragraph. The difficulty must arise, in some way, from misunderstanding on words. The most trifling examination of the process in the investigation of the velocity of sound serves to show that the velocity does not depend on the absolute pressure of the air in its normal state of density, but upon the proportion of the change of pressure to the change of density. This is increased by the suddenness of condensation in one part, which when the elastic force is great makes it still greater, and by the suddenness of rarefaction in another part, which when the elastic force is small makes it still smaller; thus in both ways increasing the change of pressure.

I am, Gentlemen,
Your obedient Servant,
G. B. AIRY.

Royal Observatory, Greenwich,
April 10, 1848.

XLVII. *On the Constitution of the Luminiferous Æther.* By G. G. STOKES, *M.A., Fellow of Pembroke College, Cambridge*\*.

THE phænomenon of aberration may be reconciled with the undulatory theory of light, as I have already shown (Phil. Mag., vol. xxvii. p. 9), without making the violent supposition that the æther passes freely through the earth in its motion round the sun, but supposing, on the contrary, that the æther close to the surface of the earth is at rest relatively to the earth. This explanation requires us to suppose the motion of the æther to be such, that the expression usually denoted by $udx + vdy + wdz$ is an exact differential. It becomes an interesting question to inquire on what physical properties of the æther this sort of motion can be explained. Is it sufficient to consider the æther as an ordinary fluid, or must we have recourse to some property which does not exist in ordinary fluids, or, to speak more correctly, the existence of which

* Communicated by the Author.

has not been made manifest in such fluids by any phænomenon hitherto observed? I have already attempted to offer an explanation on the latter supposition (Phil. Mag., vol xxix. p. 6). Professor Challis, in his last communication, has considered the æther as an ordinary fluid.

In my paper last referred to, I have expressed my belief that the motion for which $udx + \&c.$ is an exact differential, which would take place if the æther were like an ordinary fluid, would be unstable; I now propose to prove the same mathematically, though by an indirect method.

Even if we supposed light to arise from vibrations of the æther accompanied by condensations and rarefactions, analogous to the vibrations of the air in the case of sound, since such vibrations would be propagated with about 10,000 times the velocity of the earth, we might without sensible error neglect the condensation of the æther in the motion which we are considering. As far as the case in hand is concerned, Professor Challis might have regarded $\rho$ as constant, and treated $p$ as he has treated $s$. Suppose, then, a sphere to be moving uniformly in a homogeneous incompressible fluid, the motion being such that the square of the velocity may be neglected. There are many obvious phænomena which clearly point out the existence of a tangential force in fluids in motion, analogous in many respects to friction in the case of solids. When this force is taken into account, the equations of motion become (Cambridge Philosophical Transactions, vol. viii. p. 297)

$$\frac{dp}{dx} = -\rho \frac{du}{dt} + \mu \left( \frac{d^2u}{dx^2} + \frac{d^2u}{dy^2} + \frac{d^2u}{dz^2} \right), \quad \ldots \quad (1.)$$

with similar equations for $y$ and $z$. In these equations the square of the velocity is omitted, according to the supposition made above, $\rho$ is considered constant, and the fluid is supposed not to be acted on by external forces. We have also the equation of continuity

$$\frac{du}{dx} + \frac{dv}{dy} + \frac{dw}{dz} = 0, \quad \ldots \quad \ldots \quad (2.)$$

and the conditions, (1) that the fluid at the surface of the sphere shall be at rest relatively to the surface, (2) that the velocity shall vanish at an infinite distance.

For my present purpose it is not requisite that the equations such as (1.) should be known to be true experimentally; if they were even known to be false they would be sufficient, for they may be conceived to be true without mathematical absurdity. My argument is this. If the motion for which $udx + \ldots$ is an exact differential, which would be obtained from the common equations, were stable, the motion which would be obtained from equations (1.) would approach indefinitely, as $\mu$ vanished, to one for which $udx+\ldots$ was an exact differential, and therefore, for anything proved to the contrary, the latter motion might be stable; but if, on the contrary, the motion obtained from (1.) should turn out totally different from one for which $udx+\ldots$ is an exact differential, the latter kind of motion must necessarily be unstable.

Conceive a velocity equal and opposite to that of the sphere impressed both on the sphere and on the fluid. It is easy to prove that $udx+\ldots$ will or will not be an exact differential after the velocity is impressed, according as it was or was not such before. The sphere is thus reduced to rest, and the problem becomes one of steady motion. The solution which I am about to give is extracted from some researches in which I am engaged, but which are not at present published. It would occupy far too much room in this Magazine to enter into the mode of obtaining the solution: but this is not necessary; for it will probably be allowed that there is but one solution of the equations in the case proposed, as indeed readily follows from physical considerations, so that it will be sufficient to give the result, which may be verified by differentiation.

Let the centre of the sphere be taken for origin; let the direction of the real motion of the sphere make with the axes angles whose cosines are $l$, $m$, $n$, and let $v$ be the real velocity of the sphere; so that when the problem is reduced to one of steady motion, the fluid at a distance from the sphere is moving in the opposite direction with a velocity $v$. Let $a$ be the sphere's radius: then we have to satisfy the general equations (1.) and (2.) with the particular conditions

$$u=0,\ v=0,\ w=0,\text{ when } r=a; \quad\quad (3.)$$
$$u=-lv,\ v=-mv,\ w=-nv, \text{ when } r=\infty, \quad (4.)$$

$r$ being the distance of the point considered from the centre of the sphere. It will be found that all the equations are satisfied by the following values,

$$p = \Pi + \frac{3}{2}\mu v \frac{a}{r^3}(lx+my+nz),$$
$$u = \frac{3}{4}v\left(\frac{a}{r^3}-\frac{a^3}{r^5}\right)x(lx+my+nz) + lv\left(\frac{1}{4}\frac{a^3}{r^3}+\frac{3a}{4r}-1\right),$$

with symmetrical expressions for $v$ and $w$. $\Pi$ is here an arbitrary constant, which evidently expresses the value of $p$ at an infinite distance. Now the motion defined by the above expressions does not tend, as $\mu$ vanishes, to become one for which $udx + \ldots$ is an exact differential, and therefore the motion which would be obtained by supposing $udx + \ldots$ an exact differential, and applying to the æther the common equations of hydrodynamics, would be unstable. The proof supposes the motion in question to be steady; but such it may be proved to be, if the velocity of the earth be regarded as uniform, and an equal and opposite velocity be conceived impressed both on the earth and on the æther. Hence the stars would appear to be displaced in a manner different from that expressed by the well-known law of aberration.

When, however, we take account of a tangential force in the æther, depending, not on relative velocities, or at least not on relative velocities only, but on relative displacements, it then becomes possible, as I have shown (Phil. Mag., vol. xxix. p. 6), to explain not only the perfect regularity of the motion, but also the circumstance that $udx + \ldots$ is an exact differential, at least for the æther which occupies free space; for as regards the motion of the æther which penetrates the air, whether about the limits of the atmosphere or elsewhere, I do not think it prudent, in the present state of our knowledge, to enter into speculation; I prefer resting in the supposition that $udx + \ldots$ is an exact differential. According to this explanation, any nascent irregularity of motion, any nascent deviation from the motion for which $udx + \ldots$ is an exact differential, is carried off into space, with the velocity of light, by transversal vibrations, which as such are identical in their physical nature with light, but which do not necessarily produce the sensation of light, either because they are too feeble, as they probably would be, or because their lengths of wave, if the vibrations take place in regular series, fall beyond the limits of the visible spectrum, or because they are discontinuous, and the sensation of light may require the succession of a number of similar vibrations. It is certainly curious that the astronomical phænomenon of the aberration of light should afford an argument in support of the theory of transversal vibrations.

Undoubtedly it does violence to the ideas that we should have been likely to form *à priori* of the nature of the æther, to assert that it must be regarded as an elastic solid in treating of the vibrations of light. When, however, we consider the wonderful simplicity of the explanations of the phænomena of polarization when we adopt the theory of transversal vibrations, and the difficulty, which to me at least appears quite insurmountable, of explaining these phænomena by any vibrations due to the condensation and rarefaction of an elastic fluid such as air, it seems reasonable to suspend our judgement, and be content to learn from phænomena the existence of forces which we should not beforehand have expected. The explanations which I had in view are those which belong to the geometrical part of the theory; but the deduction, from dynamical calculations, of the laws which in the geometrical theory take the place of observed facts must not be overlooked, although here the evidence is of a much more complicated character.

The following illustration is advanced, not so much as explaining the real nature of the æther, as for the sake of offering a plausible mode of conceiving how the apparently opposite properties of solidity and fluidity which we must attribute to the æther may be reconciled.

Suppose a small quantity of glue dissolved in a little water, so as to form a stiff jelly. This jelly forms in fact an elastic solid: it may be constrained, and it will resist constraint, and return to its original form when the constraining force is removed, by virtue of its elasticity; but if we constrain it too far it will break. Suppose now the quantity of water in which the glue is dissolved to be doubled, trebled, and so on, till at last we have a pint or a quart of glue water. The jelly will thus become thinner and thinner, and the amount of constraining force which it can bear without being dislocated will become less and less. At last it will become so far fluid as to mend itself again as soon as it is dislocated. Yet there seems hardly sufficient reason for supposing that at a certain stage of the dilution the tangential force whereby it resists constraint ceases all of a sudden. In order that the medium should not be dislocated, and therefore should have to be treated as an elastic solid, it is only necessary that the amount of constraint should be very small. The medium would however be what we should call a fluid, as regards the motion of solid bodies through it. The velocity of propagation of normal vibrations in our medium would be nearly the same as that of sound in water; the velocity of propagation of transversal vibrations, depending as it does on the tangential elasticity, would become very small. Conceive now a medium having similar properties, but incomparably rarer than air, and we have a medium such as we may conceive the æther to be, a fluid as regards the motion of the earth and planets through it, an elastic solid as regards the small vibrations which constitute light. Perhaps we should get nearer to the true nature of the æther by conceiving a medium bearing the same relation to air that thin jelly or glue water bears to pure water. The sluggish transversal vibrations of our thin jelly are, in the case of the æther, replaced by vibrations propagated with a velocity of nearly

200,000 miles in a second: we should expect, *à priori*, the velocity of propagation of normal vibrations to be incomparably greater. This is just the conclusion to which we are led quite independently, from dynamical principles of the greatest generality, combined with the observed phænomena of optics*.

I take this opportunity of making a few remarks on my explanation of aberration (Phil. Mag., vol. xxvii. p. 9), more especially as Professor Challis's words at page 168 of the present volume would naturally lead to the idea, which, however, I believe was not intended, that I had only explained the change in the direction of the normal to a wave of light, so that something was wanting to complete, on the suppositions adopted, the explanation of aberration. To prevent misapprehension, I would observe, that in the explanation of aberration I here include the explanation of the rectilinear propagation of light, if the explanation of aberration be divided into two parts; the first, the explanation of rectilinear propagation; the second, the explanation of aberration on the assumption of rectilinear propagation. To my own mind, the undulatory theory cannot be said to explain aberration unless it explains, either rectilinear propagation, or what is equivalent to it; for had the stars never been observed, I should have thought it excessively improbable that the path of a ray was rectilinear in the neighbourhood of the earth. As to the necessity for an explanation of aberration on any theory of light, I quite agree with Professor Challis, as he has stated. Indeed, if I ever appeared to differ from him on this point, it was not because I held a different opinion, but because I failed to catch his meaning.

In my first paper on aberration, it is true that I did not investigate the nature of the path of a ray of light in space; but this was only because the method I employed did not require any such investigation. I showed that, on the suppositions adopted, the path of a ray, not in space but relatively to the earth, was in the immediate neighbourhood of the observer directed to the apparent place of the heavenly body from which it came, that is, its place as affected by the observed aberration; and that was sufficient for my purpose. My explanation was not even deficient in consequence of not taking account of the light coming from the wire to which the star was referred; for according to my method, everything was reduced to the case in which the earth and the æther in its immediate neighbourhood are supposed to be at rest; so

---

* See the introduction to an admirable memoir by Green, On the Reflexion and Refraction of Light.—*Cambridge Philosophical Transactions*, vol. vii. p. 1.

that there was no more occasion to notice *explicitly* the light coming from the wires, than there would have been if the earth had really been at rest. While, however, I would vindicate my explanation from any flaw or deficiency of reasoning (unless the not noticing formally and explicitly the light coming from the wires be regarded as such), I allow that, without investigation, I fancied the path of a ray in space to be curvilinear. It was first virtually proved by Professor Challis, though not explicitly stated, that the path was rectilinear throughout. Consequently the angle *peq* (Phil. Mag., vol. xxvii. p. 14), which I argued was insensible, is in fact zero. The method which consists in considering the rectilinear propagation of light as resulting from the supposition that $udx + \ldots$ is an exact differential, and then the law of aberration as resulting from the rectilinear propagation, instead of considering the whole at once, has the advantage of showing that we are at liberty to suppose the velocity of the æther at the surface of the earth to be of any amount relatively to the surface. I had not contemplated this case; for it was the precise object of my investigation to get rid of the apparent necessity of supposing the æther to be rushing through the air and through the earth itself as the earth moves round the sun.

XLVIII. *On Shooting Stars.* By J. P. JOULE, *Corresponding Member of the Royal Academy of Sciences, Turin, Secretary to the Literary and Philosophical Society, Manchester*[*].

I HAVE read with much interest the valuable papers on shooting stars inserted by Sir J. W. Lubbock in the Numbers of the Philosophical Magazine for February and March. This philosopher seems to have placed the subject in a fair way for satisfactory solution. He has advanced three hypotheses to account for the sudden disappearance of these bodies, the last of which he has enabled us to prove or disprove by actual observation.

I have for a long time entertained an hypothesis with respect to shooting stars, similar to that advocated by Chladni to account for meteoric stones, and have reckoned the *ignition* of these miniature planetary bodies by their violent collision with our atmosphere, to be a remarkable illustration of the doctrine of the equivalency of heat to mechanical power or *vis viva*. In a popular lecture delivered in Manchester on the 28th of April 1847, I said, "You have, no doubt, frequently observed what are called *shooting stars*, as they appear to emerge from the

[*] Communicated by the Author.

dark sky of night, pursue a short and rapid course, burst, and are dissipated in shining fragments. From the velocity with which these bodies travel, there can be little doubt that they are small planets which, in the course of their revolution round the sun, are attracted and drawn to the earth. Reflect for a moment on the consequences which would ensue, if a hard meteoric stone were to strike the room in which we are assembled with a velocity sixty times as great as that of a cannon-ball. The dire effects of such a collision are effectually prevented by the atmosphere surrounding our globe, by which the velocity of the meteoric stone is checked, and its living force converted into heat, which at last becomes so intense as to melt the body and dissipate it in fragments too small probably to be noticed in their fall to the ground. Hence it is, that although multitudes of shooting stars appear every night, few meteoric stones have been found, those few corroborating the truth of our hypothesis by the marks of intense heat which they bear on their surfaces*."

The likelihood of the above hypothesis will be rendered evident, if we suppose a meteoric stone, of the size of a six-inch cube, to enter our atmosphere at the rate of eighteen miles per second of time, the atmosphere being $\frac{1}{800}$dth of its density at the earth's surface. The resistance offered to the motion of the stone will in this case be at least 51,600 lbs.; and if the stone traverse twenty miles with this amount of resistance, sufficient heat will thereby be developed to give 1° Fahrenheit to 6,967,980 lbs. of water. Of course by far the largest portion of this heat will be given to the displaced air, every particle of which will sustain the shock, whilst only the surface of the stone will be in violent collision with the atmosphere. Hence the stone may be considered as placed in a blast of intensely heated air, the heat being communicated from the surface to the centre by conduction. Only a small portion of the heat evolved will therefore be received by the stone; but if we estimate it at only $\frac{1}{100}$dth, it will still be equal to 1° Fahrenheit per 69,679 lbs. of water, a quantity quite equal to the melting and dissipation of any materials of which it may be composed.

The dissolution of the stone will also be accelerated in most cases by its breaking into pieces, in consequence of the unequal resistance experienced by different parts of its surface, especially after its cohesion has been partially overcome by heat.

It appears to me that the varied phænomena of meteoric stones and shooting stars may all be explained in the above

* Manchester Courier newspaper, May 12, 1847.

manner; and that the different velocities of the meteorolites, varying from four to forty miles per second according to the direction of their motions with respect to the earth, along with their various sizes, will suffice to show why some of these bodies are destroyed the instant they arrive in our atmosphere, and why others, with diminished velocity, arrive at the earth's surface.

I cannot but be filled with admiration and gratitude for the wonderful provision thus made by the Author of nature for the protection of his creatures. Were it not for the atmosphere which covers us with a shield, impenetrable in proportion to the violence which it is called upon to resist, we should be continually exposed to a bombardment of the most fatal and irresistible character. To say nothing of the larger stones, no ordinary buildings could afford shelter from very small particles striking at the velocity of eighteen miles per second. Even dust flying at such a velocity would kill any animal exposed to it.

XLIX. *Analysis of the Theory of Equations, with a few Remarks on recent English Works on the subject.* By JAMES COCKLE, *Esq., M.A., Barrister-at-Law. In a Letter to* T. S. DAVIES, *Esq., F.R.S., &c.: with Notes on some of the Topics, by* Mr. DAVIES*.

*To the Editors of the Philosophical Magazine and Journal.*

GENTLEMEN,

THE inclosed letter appears to me to contain a very perspicuous statement of the character, present state, and ulterior modes of proceeding of the algebraic theory of equations; and I think it contains many important suggestions for those analysts who may hereafter give their attention to the subject. I have ventured to add a few notes, chiefly relative to numerical equations,—a subject to which particular but well-known circumstances have caused me to give much attention. These notes, I hope, will not be without their use.

I am, &c.,

Royal Military Academy, March 9, 1848.

T. S. DAVIES.

MY DEAR SIR,

2 Church yard Court, Temple, February 19, 1848.

IN our conversation of yesterday, I mentioned to you an idea that has for some little time occupied my thoughts.

* Communicated by Mr. Davies. For distinction, Mr. Davies's notes are printed in smaller type.

You will not be surprised to find that I now proceed to throw that idea into form, and to execute my project of mapping out the theory of equations, and pointing out what parts of the field have been occupied by writers on the subject, but more especially by the authors of recent English treatises.

Algebra, arithmetical and symbolical, is capable of division into three parts. The subject of *identity* might be made to constitute the first of these divisions; that of *equality* the second; and that of incongruity or *absurdity* the third. These divisions are of a purely theoretical character; practically speaking, the subjects of them are treated indiscriminately as occasion requires (a).

(a). Of these three cases (which are perfectly distinct) it may be remarked, that the identity can only arise from the values of the functions on both sides of the equation being *essentially equivalent* for all values of the terms that enter into the composition of the equation. It can never, therefore, arise in the equations which express the conditions of a *problem*. On the other hand, the second is the result of expressing a problem algebraically; and it can never appear as the result of an alleged *theorem*; whilst the third may make its appearance either from the expression of a theorem which is not true, or from that of a problem, the conditions of which are incompatible with each other. My views on this latter subject have been briefly explained in an article (for temporary private reasons given anonymously) which appeared awhile ago in the Phil. Mag. vol. xxix. p. 171.

It has been usual in treatises on algebra to speak of $\sqrt{-1}$ (or of $a \pm \beta \sqrt{-1}$) as though it were in some peculiar manner, the *one* symbol of incongruity. It is, undoubtedly, the first form in which contradictory conditions are usually encountered in algebra; and, possibly, with sufficient labour and ingenuity, all other forms or indications of incongruity may be reduced to this type. Yet it is altogether unnecessary to reduce, for instance, $\log(-1)$ as an expression, or $\sin \theta = 2$ as an equation to such a form; and it would manifestly, be a still greater waste of time to reduce more complex functions to such a form when they already involve a perceptible contradiction. As well might Euclid have imposed upon himself the condition of reducing all his *ex absurdo* demonstrations to a contradiction of the 10th axiom, because his first demonstration of a proposition by the method (prop. iv. book i.) happened to be so effected.

The assertion that *one is equal to one*, is an identity; that $x$ *is equal to one*, an equation; that *two is equal to one*, an absurdity or *contradiction*. Whether they indicate identity, equality or contradiction, these three species of proposition are all exhibited in algebra under the form of equations: thus,

$$1=1; \quad x=1; \quad 2=1;$$

but it is often a very difficult matter to determine whether what purports to be an *equation* in the strict sense of the term be really so, or whether it be not an identity or a contradiction.

In one point of view, then, the whole of algebraic science may be said to be contained in the theory of equations. Even when the latter term is used in its restricted meaning, the theory is intimately connected with every part of the science, and we find ourselves face to face with it at a very early period of our progress into the domain of algebra.

The vast and illimitable field comprehended under the phrase theory of equations must undergo a minute subdivision before we shall be in a condition, either to examine it with anything like ease, or to arrive at a just appreciation of those whose labours have advanced it to its present state, or to form a proper estimate of what may be expected from future researches.

Corresponding to each of the following topics there is a distinct department of the theory of equations, and this distinctness we must keep steadily before us. The topics in question are as follows:—

I. The finite and rigorous solution of a given equation or system of equations. II. The transformation of a given equation into another of a different form. III. The number of solutions of a given equation or system of equations. IV. The relations between the coefficients and roots of equations. V. The nature of the roots. VI. The limits within which they lie. VII. Their numerical values.

We may also regard the theory of equations as consisting of two great parts: the theory of *algebraic* equations, and the theory of *numerical* equations. In the former part, accurate results are *exclusively* aimed at; and the algebraic theory may be defined as that which treats of the rigorous solution and transformation of equations, and the number and properties of their roots symbolically considered; and we may here include the theory of symmetric functions.

The aim of the numerical theory is to ascertain the nature and limits of the roots of equations, and to arrive at values which shall enable us to satisfy equations, either accurately or to any required degree of approximation. The subject of transformation plays an important part in this as well as in the algebraic theory.

A literal equation may be treated either as an algebraic or a numerical one. In the latter case the letters stand for generalized numbers, and the processes applied to them are but universal types or examples of those which are to be employed when concrete are substituted for abstract numbers. It is only in their possible application to particular numerical instances that such processes are of any value whatever.

On the other hand, a numerical equation (as we may call an equation with numerical coefficients) may be treated as an algebraical one, that is to say, by the algebraical theory. We may obtain rigorous expressions for its roots, ascertain their number, discuss their relations to the coefficients, or transform the equation itself by rigorous processes and under exact forms, as well when the coefficients are numbers as when they are symbols.

The different branches of the subject will thus be distinguished by bearing in mind their end and object, and not by the circumstance of the equation under discussion being numerical or not in its form (*b*).

(*b*). This distinction is very important, and has been too much overlooked by analysts. It does not, however, appear to be very probable that the solution of numerical equations is ever likely to receive much improvement from the most extended researches into the algebraical theory. Even could we find "rigorous expressions for the roots of an equation in terms of its coefficients," it is proved by the algebraical theory, and justified also by analogy, that these "rigorous expressions" will contain *radicals* of a degree as high as the index of the equation itself. The roots to be extracted would thus become immensely numerous in equations of only a moderately elevated degree. Now it is a remarkable fact, that by Horner's process the gradual evolution of the figures of the root involves no more labour than the similar evolution in a binomial equation of the same degree. It hence follows that any system of solution which should aim to present us with the radical expressions for the root, would for all *numerical* purposes be utterly useless, since it would add the most intolerable complication and labour to the *practical* part of the process. This, too, would be the case, even were we to bring into play the most powerful engines for extraction we possess, viz. the methods of Horner and Weddle for the evolution of the figures. The method proposed would be strikingly retrograde; and those who have given the closest attention to the question under this aspect are, I believe, fully satisfied that this stage (evolution of the figures) has attained its final simplification. It is the only one, however, of which this can be said.

If by the *order* of an equation we denote the number of unknown quantities which enter into it, an equation will be completely defined when its degree and order are given. Now equations of the first order present features so peculiar to themselves, that it might almost be thought that the best course would be to treat the theory of equations of that order in the first instance and separately, and afterwards to engraft on it such extensions as may be necessary for the purpose of adapting it to the higher orders. This course I shall adopt in pointing out the paths which discovery has taken; but it is not perhaps the most strictly correct one; for in solving a cubic by the method handed to us by Cardan, we have to satisfy two simultaneous equations of the second order. Equations of this order (and with them the process of elimination) are, in fact, in the ordinary course of study, brought under our notice before we come to the subject of cubics of the first order; and perhaps the first example that we see of the *transformation* of an equation is presented in the solution of two quadratic equations of the second order each of which has on one side a number and on the other a homogeneous function of the two unknowns.

Engaged, then, on a subject matter that seems to set precise classification at defiance, unless we take a view other than the historical one of the solution of the cubic, I shall for the present confine myself to the subject of equations which involve only one unknown quantity: and, first, to their solutions.

1. The solution of linear and quadratic equations was understood by the Hindoo algebraists, and the processes employed did not differ in any essential respect from those now in use (c). But something more than reduction and evolution

(c). But the Hindû method of "completing the square" is certainly more convenient *in practice* than the Italian one which is in common use. It is surprising, indeed, that the Hindû process is not more generally insisted on in our elementary books, than we find it to be. Even where it is noticed at all, it is never so much spoken of in respect to its utility as it is under the character of an exotic curiosity, the chief merit of which arises from its being "old" and being "Indian."

was required for the purpose of solving a cubic. The principle employed by Tartalea (and Ferrei?) was that of rendering the equation *indeterminate* by introducing two unknowns instead of one. The introduction of *two* unknowns suffices not only for the solution of a cubic, but also for that of a biquadratic, as has been shown by Pilntte (*Annales de Mathématiques*, tome ii. pp. 152-154). But Euler had previously solved the biquadratic by substituting for $x$ the sum of *three* unknowns.

The solution of Ferrari, the first in order of time, was effected, not by substituting for $x$, but by giving the biquadratic a new form by means of a subsidiary quantity introduced for that purpose into the equation. I have shown (Phil. Mag. S. 3. vol. xxii. pp. 502-503) that a cubic can be solved by the same means.

All these solutions are *direct*: they do not depend upon any assumption as to the number of roots of the given equation. The solution of a biquadratic by Descartes is also a direct one; and the same remark applies to the solutions of a cubic given by Tschirnhausen at pp. 206, 207 of the *Acta Eruditorum* (Leipsig) for 1683.

Euler's solution of a biquadratic, just alluded to, will be found in a paper by him, at pp. 216-231 of the sixth volume of the Petersburgh *Commentarii*. His solution of a cubic there given does not differ in any material respect from that of Cardan; but Euler has exhibited both these solutions as consequences of one method. In fact, if we omit the radical signs which Euler attaches to the indeterminate quantities, his method may in the case of cubics be said to be identical with Cardan's, and in that of biquadratics to be a legitimate extension of it. Euler's solution of a biquadratic is often exhibited without the radical signs attached to the indeterminate quantities.

The earlier processes given by Bezout for the solution of a cubic (*Mém. de l'Acad.* for 1762, pp. 23-25), and of a biquadratic (Ibid. p. 52), are direct. But his subsequent ones (*Mém. de l'Acad.* for 1765, pp. 533-552), and those given by Euler in the ninth volume of the *Novi Commentarii* (pp. 70-98), are *indirect*. The fundamental assumption depends upon our knowledge of the number of roots of a binomial equation of the same degree as that under discussion.

It must not be supposed that there is any inferiority in the indirect methods; on the contrary, there is perhaps a greater degree of uniformity and coherence in them than in the direct processes. The method of Lagrange is an indirect one, and depends essentially upon our knowledge of the number of roots of a given equation, and of the theory of their symmetric functions. To the indirect class must be added the method of Spence, and that given by Murphy in the Philosophical Transactions for 1837 (pp. 161-178), and commented on by Sir W. R. Hamilton at pp. 256-259 of the eighteenth volume of the Transactions of the Royal Irish Academy.

I shall not stop to discuss particular cases in which equations admit of solution,—Demoivre's form of the equation of the fifth degree for instance. Abel has however given very general discussions of such cases, of which Dr. Peacock has given an account at pp. 318-320 of the Sixth Report of the British Association.

Curious illustrations of the manner in which the different departments of the theory of equations are, practically speaking, blended one with the other, are afforded by the facts, that before we can apply Cardan's rule to a cubic, we must deprive the equation of its second term, and so have recourse to a *transformation*, and that many important particulars respecting equations depend upon a knowledge of the number of their roots. How a knowledge of equations of the second order is necessary in Cardan's solution of a cubic, I have already remarked; but it remains to be observed, that in the transition from equations involving one to those involving two unknowns, we have the subject of *elimination*, which is incidental to that transition, forced upon us. The present, then, would seem to be the proper place to discuss the subject. But such discussion is not now my object, except to the extent of remarking that, when the unknown quantities are sufficiently numerous, the obstacles to the solution of a number of simultaneous equations involving those quantities do not arise from elevation of degree incurred by elimination. That such elevation of degree may be avoided, has been shown by Mr. Jerrard in his Mathematical Researches: as may be expected, the number of unknowns must, in order to the application of his processes, considerably exceed in number the given simultaneous equations. The methods of Mr. Jerrard are in fact indeterminate, and he has thrown open the gates that lead to the higher parts of this species of analysis.

Results similar to those of Mr. Jerrard may be obtained by means of the method of vanishing groups. The latter method will enable us to satisfy *three* homogeneous and simultaneous quadratics between *six* undetermined quantities without making those quantities equal to zero *or decomposing them*, and without having to solve other equations than a biquadratic, two quadratics, and two linear equations. And for this system of homogeneous quadratics we may of course substitute three ordinary quadratics between *five* unknowns, and arrive at the same results by the same means.

The present appears to be a proper place for noticing the subject of equations that have *no* root. An instance of such an equation is given by Garnier at p. 335 of his *Analyse* (Par. 1814). The subject of "congeneric surd equations" was however first, I believe, discussed in anything like detail by Horner in a letter to yourself, published in the year 1836 (Phil. Mag. vol. viii. pp. 43-50). In the last edition of Wood's Algebra, doubts have been expressed as to the fact of the non-existence of roots of a surd equation; and it is suggested that possibly the method of solution is at fault. But it may easily be shown that no quantity other than a root of the rational product of the surd congeners can satisfy any of those congeners. Hence, when a congener is not satisfied by a root of such product, it has no solution whatever; and I have shown in the Mechanics' Magazine (current and last volumes), that the symbolical impossibility or contradiction expressed by such an equation is convertible into an arithmetical one (*d*).

(*d*). Previous to my first noticing an equation of this class (in Hind's Algebra) I had looked upon all attempts to prove that every equation had *at least one root*, as a superfluous labour; and I know that not a few algebraists still take the same view of it. The letter of Mr. Horner's, referred to by Mr. Cockle, was in reply to one which I addressed to Mr. Horner a few days before, when the subject was new to me, respecting the particular equation referred to; and I think the question of *fact*, as to there being innumerable equations which have no root, is set at rest by the discussion in that letter. Not only the fact, however, is there established, but also the true *principle* which runs through such equations: and whilst I have no reason to think that Mr. Horner was acquainted with Garnier's solution, I need not urge upon any one who compares what Garnier and Horner have done, the utter impossibility of the solution of the former having furnished any suggestion for the discussion of the latter. Mr. Cockle's supplementary discussion, referred to above, appears to me to complete the inquiry.

As regards the doubt thrown out by the editor of Wood's Algebra, whether the fault be not in the method of searching for the root, it may be remarked that such conjectures are scarcely allowable in pure science except some method of bringing the question to a decisive test be at least suggested. It may further be remarked, that if we admit the proposed hypothesis, it would follow that, when the equation and its congener were reduced to a single equation free from radicals, this new equation would have a greater number of roots than it had units of dimension; viz. those alleged to belong to the surd equation, and those which are admitted to belong to its congener. This consequence is contradictory to one of the simplest and best established of all our propositions respecting the composition of equations; and it never could have occurred to the able editor of that valuable work when he proposed the hypothesis in question.

2. The transformation by which the second term is taken away from an equation has been long known. In the case of a perfect cubic, it was absolutely necessary in order to the application of the rule of Cardan. This transformation is effected *linearly*, that is to say, the equation connecting the roots of the original and of the transformed equation only contains the first power of those roots, together with an arbitrary quantity, which is determined so as to satisfy the required condition. This it may be made to do by solving a linear equation. In the same manner, by determining the arbitrary quantity so as to satisfy a certain quadratic, cubic or biquadratic, the third, fourth, or fifth terms of the transformed equation might be made to vanish. But the linear

transformation is inadequate to the removal of more than one term at a time.

To Tschirnhausen is due the introduction of quadratic and the suggestion of higher transformations. Without this improvement all progress in the theory of transformation would have been stopped. The two different quadratic transformations which he gives for the annihilation of the middle terms of a cubic are well-worthy of attention. In the first of them (*Acta* for 1683, p. 206), the equation which connects the roots of the original and transformed equations involves first and second powers of the former roots, and first powers only of the latter; but in the second transformation of a cubic (Ibid. p. 207) the case is reversed, and the original roots only enter to one dimension, while the roots of the transformed equation enter to two. To Tschirnhausen must be given a very exalted position among the cultivators of the theory of equations.

Elevation of degree from elimination would seem to impose insuperable obstacles to any material extension of Tschirnhausen's views. However, by a combination of the indeterminate method with that of Tschirnhausen, Mr. Jerrard has overcome this difficulty; and as one of his earliest results, I may mention his *transformation of the general equation of the fifth degree to a trinomial form*. Mr. Jerrard has shown how to annihilate any three of its four middle terms. It is true that in the transformations of Tschirnhausen the transformed equations are indeterminate; but then no more indeterminate quantities are introduced than there are conditions to satisfy. The transformed equations of Mr. Jerrard are indeterminate in another sense; they involve more disposable quantities than the number of conditions to be satisfied by the coefficients of the transformed equation. The difference between Tschirnhausen's and the modern method of determining the roots of the original cubic, when those of the transformed are known, will be seen on comparing the course pursued at p. 206 of the *Acta* (1683) with that given at pp. 27-29 of Mr. Jerrard's Researches, and subsequently extended (Ibid. pp. 36-39). As to the eliminations requisite for the formation of the transformed equation, they may either be performed directly, or may be made to depend upon the theory of symmetric functions; and in the latter case, a knowledge of the number of the roots of a given equation is taken for granted. In effecting the transformation above alluded to of the equation of the fifth degree, the principal difficulty consists in forming the new equation; that once done, the difficulty of giving the required form to its coefficients is not great. In its application to this transformation, my method (of vanishing groups) only requires us to assume an expression consisting of *four* terms for the purpose of representing the root of the transformed equation. Every diminution of the number of the terms of this expression very greatly facilitates the formation of the transformed equation.

A purely indirect method of transformation is that which I sent through you to the Philosophical Magazine, and which will be found at pp. 383–384 of the twenty-sixth volume of that work. It proceeds by modifying the roots at once.

3. On our knowledge of the number of the roots of a given equation is founded much of the theory of algebraic equations; so that it becomes absolutely necessary that a demonstration that the number of its roots equals the number of its dimensions should be found in every work treating of the subject. So far as the *algebraic* theory is concerned, the demonstration of Cauchy, of the existence of a root of an equation, is perhaps the preferable one.

4. The number of the roots of an equation once known to be in general the same as the index of its dimensions, the combination of the theory of *symmetric functions* with that of equations at once ensues. By means of this combination, the elimination requisite in the transformation of algebraic equations is greatly facilitated. An instance of this occurs in the improvements effected by Sir J. W. Lubbock in the processes of Bezout, and in Mr. Jerrard's eliminations. The latter mathematician has made an important advance in this branch of science, by preserving the notation unaltered in the case where different terms of a symmetric function become identical.

We thus see that indirect methods of elimination may be preferable to direct ones; and the same theory of symmetric functions which enables us to employ them with effect, is equally essential to the efficiency of the (indirect) general method of solving equations given by Lagrange. It is not my intention to enter into the subject of the finite solution of equations of the fifth degree; but, on the development of Lagrange's method in such a case, there is much information to be obtained from a paper by Sir W. R. Hamilton ('Transactions of the Royal Irish Academy, vol. xix. pp. 329–376) on the Formulæ of Professor Badano.

5. The rule of Descartes (or more properly perhaps of Harriot) enables us to ascertain the greatest number of positive or of negative (real) roots that can possibly enter into a given equation. The number of unreal roots is capable of being infallibly ascertained by the criterion of Sturm; but the labour which its application requires is a serious objection (*e*).

(*e*). This objection was, I believe, first made in the Phil. Mag.

vol. viii. pp. 408–409. Analysts were so enraptured with the theoretical beauty of Sturm's criterion, that some time elapsed before they thought of testing its *practical value*—the only special value, indeed, to which the author made the least pretension. So far is it deficient in this respect, that it has not in the hands of any one whose pursuits lead him to resolve numerical equations, been able to supersede the method of Budan, indirect and sometimes unsatisfactory as this is admitted on all hands to be. Seldom, however, has so small a degree of scientific service been so brilliantly rewarded; for the French Academy elected him one of their own august body; and the Royal Society awarded him a Royal Medal. Sturm, however, has earned for himself a name of more enduring honour by his other researches, than future times will accord to him for this once-eulogised criterion.

The same remark applies to that of Fourier and Lagrange. I fully agree with the view that you have taken of this subject in the last edition of Hutton's *Course*, and with your amendment of the criterion of De Gua, which forms a very pretty corollary to the rule of signs. The criterion of Budan is well worthy of attention (*f*).

(*f*). The criterion of Budan in the form in which he himself presented it, is entirely useless; and I am bold to say that it would not have attracted the least notice but for the form in which Mr. Horner arranged the algorithm and explained the principle of it. However (to use the language of Mr. Horner with respect to the criterion of De Gua), the employment of the method is more effective than might at first sight appear. For instance, under one aspect, an application of the Hornerian transformation to the reciprocal equation is often effective, as is shown by Mr. Christie, Phil. Mag. vol. xxi. p. 96: and other methods might be suggested but for the space they would occupy. I believe that those mathematicians who employ themselves on numerical solutions in this country, invariably employ Budan's criterion (either immediately or modified)—availing themselves, however, where possible from the occurrence of zero-coefficients in the *transformées*, of De Gua's as an auxiliary.

The drawback upon Sturm's method arises from the uncouth, inartificial and laborious process of finding the common measure of two integer functions of $x$. The mere œconomy of space and of writing by a different arrangement of the work and by the use of detached coefficients, which I first gave in the "Solutions of the Questions in Hutton's Course" (1839), is altogether insufficient to render the process a practicable one, except in very special cases. The same may be said of Professor De Morgan's mode of working, which is a little different from mine (Penny Cycl. art. INVOLUTION). Professor Young, in his "Dissertations" and in his "Theory of Equations," has given a method of taking two steps of the process at once, which is a material improvement. It is, however, only by the employment of some totally new consideration (I ought, perhaps, to say some *new principle*) as to the formation of those functions which occur in Sturm's process, that we can look with any degree of hope to obtaining the means of rendering Sturm's criterion of practical usefulness.

Some very interesting discussions connected with this subject may be consulted with advantage in Professor Young's "Researches on the Imaginary Roots of Numerical Equations" (1844). Those founded on taking away the terms of the direct and reciprocal equations by transformation are peculiarly elegant; and the entire treatise bears witness to the justice with which the author's high scientific character is accorded to him by mathematicians in general. Perhaps I ought to add that a very faithful translation of Sturm's *Mémoire* was published by Mr. W. H. Spiller, in 4to, 1837.

6. On the subject of the limits within which the roots of equations lie I shall make a few comments further on.

7. Among those who have devised processes for determining the numerical values of the roots of equations, the first place must be given entirely and without reservation to Horner. The extension of the approximative principle involved in the extraction of the square root to the general solution of equations was, it is true, arrived at by Vieta; but it is only by combining that principle with an easy process that we can derive much practical benefit from it. Practically speaking, the whole method of approximation is due to Horner, for his process alone renders it a working instrument. One splendid result of his labours in this field was his invention of synthetic division, which constitutes a radical, material, and important improvement of one of the elementary processes of algebra, and presents the curious spectacle of a simplification of such a kind overlooked for centuries. For appropriate and simple investigations of synthetic division science is indebted to you, as she is for your zealous and unintermitting enforcement of the views and rights of its illustrious inventor (*g*).

(*g*). I am by no means sure that my mode of investigating the synthetic division is more simple than Mr. Horner's, in any other sense than that it is more elementary, and on that account better adapted to the purposes of instruction. Of the two modes which I have given, that first offered (Hutton's Course by Dr. Gregory, 11th ed. 1835) is found by experience to be the more easily comprehended by young students; whilst as an investigation, in the stricter sense of the term, that printed in the Mathematician (vol. i. p. 74) seems to me the preferable one. A different method (but which led to nearly the same praxis in reference to the single purpose of transforming equations, though it was inapplicable to many other important purposes which the synthetic division can be employed to effect) was proposed a little after the synthetic division was made known by Mr. Peter Nicholson. This method has been repeatedly given in Nicholson and Rowbottom's Algebra, which has gone through eight or perhaps nine editions; and it has been recently reproduced by Mr. Christie in his Algebra for the use of the Royal Military Academy, 1844.

Mr. Horner first arrived at the method by considerations founded on the doctrine of recurring series; and he was so well satisfied with the investigation as he first gave it in a paper sent to the Royal Society in 1823, that he never attempted any change. It is easy to see, however, that a common principle runs through his investigation and mine; though there may be very little in either method to *suggest* the other. My own, indeed, occurred to me almost momentarily, in the midst of my professional duties, at a time when they included that subject.

I feel it necessary once for all to say, that as far as regards the subject of numerical equations, I have never had any object in view further than to facilitate the operations of resolution and mainly to render the remarkable methods of my deceased friend more generally accessible and more facile in practice. As the possessor of Mr. Horner's papers, I feel it to be due alike to my own honour and to Mr. Horner's memory, never to publish anything of my own on the subject.

Another method of approximation is that by *recurring series*, a subject treated by Euler and other able mathematicians, and to which Fourier has contributed considerable extensions. This method is of great importance in the solution of equations with unreal roots.

It is not my intention to discuss at any length the different methods that have been proposed for the numerical solution of equations; but that of Mr. Weddle appears to be deserving of mention, as one of those which is likely to be generally and permanently adopted in those cases for which it is more peculiarly adapted.

The series by which Murphy expresses a root (Theory of Equations, art. 64, pp. 83–84) of an equation is most remarkable, not only in itself and for the process by which it is derived, but also for its principle of derivation, which is capable of application in a variety of other cases.

The principal treatises on the theory of equations in the English language are those of Murphy, Hymers, Young, and Stevenson.

That of Murphy abounds in traces of the great genius of that lamented analyst. I have just alluded to an interesting feature of his work: amongst the many others I shall content myself with citing his discussion of the theorems of Fourier respecting the solution of equations by recurring series. Admitting the originality of the view taken by the latter philosopher, Murphy shows that he is incorrect in his details, and supplies the necessary corrections.

If we put the subject of actual and practical numerical solution out of the question, the work of Dr. Hymers is a most useful and excellent one. It devotes some space to the question of the *limits of the roots*,—an inquiry of importance, inasmuch as it assists us in obtaining a first approximation. I observe that you prefer the method of trying the factors of the absolute term as an initial experiment (Hutton, p. 234) (*h*). Would it not be as well if the concluding chapter of Dr. Hymers' work were removed to the end of that which treats of algebraic (rigorous) solution, and the connexion between the ordinary methods and that of Lagrange explicitly exhibited?

(*h*). This is not quite the way in which I wished to be understood: for I was then speaking of any proposed equation, that *might contain* integer roots, from which it is always desirable in the outset to clear it. When this is done, the method of superior and inferior limits will sometimes effect our purpose readily; though it is often so wide of the mark as to become practically inconvenient, if not absolutely useless. I know of no infallible rule that can be applied: and when I was a good deal accustomed to such computations, I found it to be most convenient to try the effect of diminishing the roots by unit-transformations for a step or two; and if this did not much alter the coefficients, to employ a similar process with tens or hundreds, as the case may seem to require. If the changes of the coefficients with a unit-transformation were great, the use of ·1 or ·01 as the quantities by which the roots were diminished, always led with tolerable facility to the desired information.

When, however, the coefficients are large, especially "the absolute term," the employment of the reciprocal equation for this purpose will be convenient: and in all cases, attention to punctuation (after the manner that numbers are "pointed off" for the extraction of the square and cube roots) will greatly facilitate this initial inquiry. It is, however, unnecessary to say more upon such a question, where, after all, our mode of proceeding is essentially *a tentative one.*

So far as the question of numerical solution is concerned, the work of our friend Professor Young is without a rival. In it the method of Horner is fully developed, and lucid and laboriously calculated examples serve to exhibit it in all its real utility (*i*). In the subject of *algebraic* equations, Mr. Young

(*i*). It should have been added, that the Very Reverend the Dean of Ely has also given Horner's process in his elaborate and most valuable treatise on algebra; and that Dr. James Thompson of Glasgow has also done the same in an elementary work on the same subject. An improvement in the process of synthetic division has also been given by the latter gentleman: and one very analogous to it, but a little different in form, had been previously given by Professor Christie in his Algebra, already mentioned. That promising and able young analyst, Mr. Weddle, has also published a method of solving numerical equations, as far as the evolution of the figures of the root is concerned, which, like Horner's, is a thing *per se*. It has, moreover, no one principle or idea in common with Horner's method; and, of course, there can be nothing in common as to the modes of investigation. Horner's consecutive corrections are *addends* to the root already evolved: Weddle's are *factors* of it. Horner uses as many columns as there are units in the dimension of the equation: Weddle only employs the columns that have coefficients in the given equation different from zero. Horner's is the briefer and more manageable where the terms of the equation are numerous and the figures of the root required to be many; Weddle's when the terms are few and the figures of the root not required to be numerous. Weddle's may be benefited as to applicability by such processes as Mr. Jerrard's for diminishing the number of terms of the equation (if, indeed, the actual labour of doing this would not more than counterbalance the opposite advantage): but such transformations would not subserve Horner's process in the slightest degree.

Of the valuable contributions of Professor De Morgan to the illustration of Horner's process, and of his earnest enforcement of its merits on all occasions, I ought to express the very high estimate that I form. It would however only be "to gild refined gold" to attempt that expression; and I need only refer to his articles in the Penny Cyclopædia and its Supplement, and to his paper in the Companion to the Almanac and the recent edition of his Elements of Arithmetic.

has given a *quadratic* transformation, of which, if I recollect right, there is no example in the treatises of Dr. Hymers or Mr. Stevenson, and to which I think there is but one approach in that of Murphy—I mean in his remarks on Sir J. W. Lubbock's improvements in Bezout's processes. I think that it was Professor Young who first introduced Sturm's theorem into this country; he has introduced considerable improvements into its *praxis*. Upon this subject I concur with the note at p. v. of the preface to your Hutton.

The treatise of Mr. Stevenson is a very elegant one. Its author has given what I conceive to be a very proper and prominent position to Cauchy's demonstration of the existence of a root of an algebraic equation, from which the existence of n roots may be arrived at without much difficulty (*j*).

(*j*). Of the works enumerated by Mr. Cockle I am not disposed to offer any general opinion: but I may remark, that Mr. Young's is the only one amongst them which even professes to aim at giving the *actual practice of solution*. Whatever other merits the several works may have (and each has its merits), they are of an algebraical rather than of a numerical character: whilst in Young's, the algebraical theory itself is more fully developed than in any of the others—and with quite as much skill and elegance.

If I may be permitted to offer a few suggestions in connection with future inquiries on equations, they would be of the following kind:—

1. That the algebraic investigation should be as little cramped as possible by reference to the object of solving the numerical equations. The general properties of equations are of high interest and furnish exercise for transcendent skill, independently of all collateral practical applications of the results obtained. Any attempt to keep in view simultaneously two distinct purposes is calculated to frustrate the accomplishment of each. From the cornucopia (to adopt a happy metaphor of Sir John Herschel on another subject) of results obtained by the algebraical investigation, some property may fall out, that would effect all that is required in the numerical investigation. Numerical aims, however, only clog the wings of the general algebraic investigator; and if numerical solution shall be benefited by such means, it will be only accidentally so—like Girard's spherical excess in the geodetical problem.

2. That the attention of those who aim at the numerical solution should be directed to obtaining more simple means (I mean *less laborious*) of accomplishing the following purposes:—

($\alpha$). Finding the equal roots.

($\beta$). Finding the limits between which the several roots lie without transforming the equation and without the substitution of particular numbers in any equation, either the original or any one derived from it by any process whatever.

($\gamma$). An infallible criterion whether the roots lying within a given interval be real or imaginary—however closely the real ones may approach to each other, and however small the value of $\beta$ may be in the expression $\alpha \pm \beta \sqrt{-1}$ when they are imaginary.

($\delta$). The relations between the limiting values of an imaginary pair, and the real and imaginary parts of that pair. "The real part may lie in the positive region and yet the pair be indicated in the negative region."—Young, Researches, p. 54.

($\epsilon$). Supposing the roots of the given equation to be represented by $\alpha_n \pm \beta_n$, and when the equation is of an odd degree $(2n+1)$ we introduce the new root $\alpha_o - \alpha_o$, and denote the corresponding odd one by $\alpha_o + \alpha_o$, we shall have the equation converted into one perhaps better adapted to examination. If we can form two subsidiary equations, one involving all the $\alpha$s and the other all the $\beta$s; and if we can moreover discover any criterion by which the proper assortment of $\alpha$s and $\beta$s can be effected, the *complete numerical solution* will be within our reach. It must be remarked that the $\beta$s only appear of even powers in the substitution, and hence we should get at once a knowledge whether they involved the symbol $\sqrt{-1}$.

The method of Lagrange involves both the $\alpha$s and the $\beta$s in one expression, and possibly the proposal ($\epsilon$) may be supposed to be mixed up in the method of that distinguished analyst: but to be really effective, some method of separating the two parts of each root is essential. If we can effect this, we shall not only be able to tell which roots are imaginary, but also to assign their values, if such a term may be allowed in speaking of imaginaries.

A very interesting discussion of the analogy between the methods of Lagrange and Sturm, by Mr. R. Leslie Ellis, will be found in the Cambridge Mathematical Journal, vol. ii. pp. 256–258.

To the *depression* of equations and one or two other topics, I do not think it desirable that these remarks should extend. Apologizing to you for my prolixity,

I remain, my dear Sir,

Yours most truly,

JAMES COCKLE.

To T. S. *Davies, Esq., F.R.S. L. & E.,*
&c. &c. &c., *Woolwich.*

---

XLIX. *On Quaternions; or on a New System of Imaginaries in Algebra.* By Sir WILLIAM ROWAN HAMILTON, *LL.D., V.P.R.I.A., F.R.A.S., Corresponding Member of the Institute of France, &c., Andrews' Professor of Astronomy in the University of Dublin, and Royal Astronomer of Ireland.*

[Continued from vol. xxxi. p. 519.]

56. IF we denote by $b$ the length of the common radius of the two diametral and circular sections, or the mean semiaxis of the ellipsoid, which is also the radius of that concentric sphere of which the equation (24.) was assigned in art. 44, we shall have, by the formula (26.) of that article, the following expression for this radius, or semiaxis:

$$b = \frac{x^2 - \iota^2}{T(\iota - x)}. \quad \ldots \quad (81.)$$

And hence, on account of the general formula,

$$\iota\rho + \rho x = (\iota - x)\left(\rho + \frac{x\rho + \rho x}{\iota - x}\right), \quad \ldots \quad (82.)$$

which holds good for *any* three vectors, $\iota$, $x$, $\rho$, the quaternion equation of the ellipsoid may be changed from a form already assigned, namely

$$T(\iota\rho + \rho x) = x^2 - \iota^2, \; (9.), \text{ art. 38,}$$

to the following equivalent form:

$$T\left(\rho + \frac{x\rho + \rho x}{\iota - x}\right) = b. \quad \ldots \quad (83.)$$

If then we introduce a new vector-symbol $\lambda$, denoting a line of variable length, but one drawn in the fixed direction of ι−κ, or in the exactly opposite direction of κ−ι, and determined by the condition

$$\lambda(\kappa-\iota)=\kappa\rho+\rho\kappa, \quad \ldots \ldots \quad (84.)$$

we shall have also

$$T(\rho-\lambda)=b; \quad \ldots \ldots \quad (85.)$$

and thus the equation (83.) of the ellipsoid may be regarded as the result of the elimination of the auxiliary vector-symbol $\lambda$ between the two last equations (84.) and (85.). But if we suppose that this symbol $\lambda$ receives any *given* and constant value, of the form

$$\lambda=h(\iota-\kappa), \quad \ldots \ldots \quad (86.)$$

where $h$ is a scalar coefficient, which we here suppose to be constant and given, and if we still conceive the symbol $\rho$ to denote a variable vector, drawn from the centre of the ellipsoid as an origin, the equation (84.) will then express that this vector $\rho$ terminates in a point which is contained on a *given plane* parallel to that one of the two cyclic planes of the ellipsoid which has for its equation

$$\kappa\rho+\rho\kappa=0, \; (23.), \text{art.} 44;$$

while the equation (85.) will express that the same vector $\rho$ terminates also on a given spheric surface, of which the vector of the centre (drawn from the same centre of the ellipsoid) is $\lambda$, and of which the radius is $=b$. The *system of the two equations*, (84.) and (85.), expresses therefore that, for any given value of the auxiliary vector $\lambda$, or for any given value of the scalar coefficient $h$ in the formula (86.), the termination of the vector $\rho$ is contained on the circumference of a *given circle*, which is the mutual intersection of the plane (84.) and of the sphere (85.). And the equation (83.) of the ellipsoid, as being derived, or at least derivable, by elimination of $\lambda$, from that system of equations (84.) and (85.), is thus seen to express the known theorem, that the surface of an ellipsoid may be regarded as the locus of a certain *system of circular circumferences*, of which the planes are parallel to a fixed plane of diametral and circular section.

57. *One set* of the known circular sections of the ellipsoid, in planes parallel to *one* of the two cyclic planes, may therefore be assigned in this manner, as the result of a very simple calculation; and the *other set* of such known circular sections, parallel to the *other* cyclic plane, may be symbolically determined, with equal facility, as the result of an entirely similar process of calculation with quaternions. For if, instead of

(82.), we employ this other general formula, which likewise holds good for any three vectors,

$$\iota\rho + \rho\kappa = \left(\rho + \frac{\iota\rho + \rho\iota}{\kappa - \iota}\right)(\kappa - \iota), \quad \ldots \quad (87.)$$

we shall thereby transform the lately cited equation (9.) of the ellipsoid into this other form,

$$T\left(\rho + \frac{\iota\rho + \rho\iota}{\kappa - \iota}\right) = b; \quad \ldots \ldots \quad (88.)$$

which is analogous to the form (83.), and from which similar inferences may be drawn. Thus, we may treat this equation (88.) as the result of elimination of a new auxiliary vector symbol $\mu$ between the two equations,

$$\mu(\iota - \kappa) = \iota\rho + \rho\iota; \quad \ldots \ldots \quad (89.)$$
$$T(\rho - \mu) = b; \quad \ldots \ldots \quad (90.)$$

of which the former, namely the equation (89.), is, relatively to $\rho$, the equation of a *new plane*, parallel to that other cyclic plane of the ellipsoid for which we have seen that

$$\iota\rho + \rho\iota = 0, \ (25.), \text{ art. 44};$$

while the latter equation, namely (90.), is that of a *new sphere*, with the same radius $b$ as before, but with $\mu$ for the vector of its centre: which sphere (90.) determines, by its intersection with the plane (89.), a *new circle* as the locus of the termination of $\rho$, when $\mu$ receives any given value of the form

$$\mu = h'(\kappa - \iota), \quad \ldots \ldots \quad (91.)$$

where $h'$ is a new scalar coefficient. The ellipsoid (9.) is therefore the locus of all the circles of this second system also, answering to the equations (89.), (90.), as it was seen to be the locus of all those of the first system, represented by the equations (84.), (85.); which agrees with the known properties of the surface.

58. For any three vectors $\iota$, $\kappa$, $\rho$, we have (because $\rho^2$, $\kappa^2$, and $\kappa\rho + \rho\kappa$ are scalars) the general transformations,

$$\left.\begin{aligned}(\iota\rho + \rho\iota)(\kappa\rho + \rho\kappa) &= \iota(\kappa\rho + \rho\kappa)\rho + \rho(\kappa\rho + \rho\kappa)\iota \\ &= (\iota\kappa + \kappa\iota)\rho^2 + \iota\rho\kappa\rho + \rho\kappa\rho\iota \\ &= -(\iota - \kappa)^2\rho^2 + (\iota\rho + \rho\kappa)(\rho\iota + \kappa\rho);\end{aligned}\right\} \quad (92.)$$

and therefore, with the recent significations of the symbols $b$, $\lambda$, $\mu$, expressed by the formulæ (81.), (84.), (89.), the equation of the ellipsoid assigned in a foregoing article, namely

$$(\iota\rho + \rho\kappa)(\rho\iota + \kappa\rho) = (\kappa^2 - \iota^2)^2, \ (21.), \text{ art. 44},$$

takes easily this shorter form,
$$\rho^2 + b^2 = \lambda\mu. \quad \ldots \quad (93.)$$
If now we cut this surface by the system of two planes, parallel respectively to the two cyclic planes (23.) and (25.), and included in the joint equation
$$\{\lambda - h(\iota - \varkappa)\}\{\mu - h'(\varkappa - \iota)\} = 0, \quad \ldots \quad (94.)$$
which is derived by multiplication from the equations (86.) and (91.), we are conducted to this other equation,
$$\rho^2 + b^2 = h(\iota\rho + \rho\iota) + h'(\varkappa\rho + \rho\varkappa) + hh'(\iota - \varkappa)^2; \quad (95.)$$
which may be put under the form
$$-b^2 = (\rho - h\iota - h'\varkappa)^2 - (h + h')(h\iota^2 + h'\varkappa^2); \quad \ldots \quad (96.)$$
or under this other form,
$$T(\rho - \xi) = r, \quad \ldots \quad (97.)$$
if we write, for abridgement,
$$\xi = h\iota + h'\varkappa, \quad \ldots \quad (98.)$$
and
$$r = \sqrt{\{b^2 - (h + h')(h\iota^2 + h'\varkappa^2)\}}. \quad \ldots \quad (99.)$$

Any two circular sections of the ellipsoid, parallel to two different cyclic planes, or belonging to two *different* systems, are therefore contained upon one *common* sphere (97.), of which the radius $r$, and the vector of the centre $\xi$, are assigned by these last formulæ: which again agrees with the known properties of surfaces of the second order. And the equation of the *mean sphere* which contains the two *diametral* and circular sections, is seen to reduce itself, in this system of algebraical geometry, to the very simple form*
$$\rho^2 + b^2 = 0. \quad \ldots \quad (100.)$$

59. The expressions (86.), (91.), (98.), for $\lambda$, $\mu$, $\xi$, give
$$\frac{\xi - \lambda}{\varkappa} = \frac{\xi - \mu}{\iota} = \frac{\lambda - \mu}{\iota - \varkappa} = h + h'; \quad \ldots \quad (101.)$$
if then we regard $\lambda$, $\mu$, $\xi$ as the vectors of the three corners L, M, N of a plane triangle, and observe that $0$, $\iota - \varkappa$, and $-\varkappa$ were seen to be the vectors of the three corners A, B, C of the *generating triangle* described in our construction of the ellipsoid, we see that the new triangle LMN is similar to that generating triangle ABC, and similarly situated in one common plane therewith, namely in the plane of the greatest and least axes of the ellipsoid; the sides LM, MN, NL of the one triangle being parallel and proportional to the sides AB, BC, CA of the

---

* Compare article 21, in the Phil. Mag. for July 1846.

other, while the points L and M are situated on the same indefinite straight line as A, B; that is, on the axis of that circumscribed cylinder of revolution which has been considered in former articles. The vectors of the points D, E, in the same construction of the ellipsoid, (if drawn from its centre as their origin,) having been seen to be respectively $\sigma-\varkappa$ and $\rho$, (compare article 40,) the equation

$$\sigma\rho+\rho\varkappa=0 \text{ (16.), art. 41,}$$

combined with (84.) and (86.), gives for their product the expressions:

$$(\sigma-\varkappa)\rho=\lambda(\iota-\varkappa)=h(\iota-\varkappa)^2; \quad . \quad . \quad . \quad (102.)$$

and in general if two pairs of co-initial vectors, as here $\sigma-\varkappa$, $\rho$, and $\lambda$, $\iota-\varkappa$, give, when respectively multiplied, one common scalar product, they terminate on four concircular points: the four points D, E, L, B are therefore contained on the circumference of one common circle: and consequently the point L may be found by an elementary construction, derived from this simple calculation with quaternions, namely as the second point of intersection of the circle BDE with the straight line AB (which is situated in the plane of that circle). Again, the equations (85.) and (90.) give

$$T(\rho-\lambda)=T(\rho-\mu); \quad . \quad . \quad . \quad . \quad (103.)$$

therefore the point E of the ellipsoid is the vertex of an isosceles triangle, constructed on LM as base; and the point M may thus be found as the intersection of the same straight line AB or AL, with a circle described round the point E as centre, and having its radius $=\overline{\mathrm{EL}}=b=$ the mean semiaxis of the ellipsoid. When the two points L and M have thus been found, the third point N can then be deduced from them, in an equally simple geometrical manner, by drawing parallels LN, MN to the sides AC, BC of the generating triangle ABC, from which the ellipsoid itself has been constructed; these sides LN, MN, of the new and variable triangle LMN, will thus be parallel to the two cyclic normals of the ellipsoid; and the foregoing analysis shows that they will be portions of the axes of the two circles, which are contained upon the surface of that ellipsoid, and pass through the point E on that surface: while the point N, of intersection of those two axes, is the centre of that common sphere (97.), which contains both those two circular sections. It is evident that this common sphere must *touch* the ellipsoid at E, since it is itself touched at that point by the two distinct tangents to the two circular sections of the surface; and hence we might infer that the semidiameter NE or $\xi-\rho$ of the sphere, of which the length $r$ has been assigned in the formula (99.), and which is terminated at the point x by the plane of the generating triangle, must coincide in direction with the *normal* to the ellipsoid; of which latter normal the direction may thus be found by a simple geometrical construction, and an expression for it be obtained without the employment of differentials. But to show that this geometrical result agrees with the symbolical expression already found for ν, by means of differentials and quaternions, we have only to substitute, on the one hand, in the expression 9x. for ξ, the following values for $h$ and $h'$, derived from 84.), 86., and from 89.., 91.):

$$h = \frac{x\rho + \rho x}{-(1-x)^2}; \quad h' = \frac{\iota\rho - \rho\iota}{-(1-x)^2}; \quad . \quad . \quad (104.)$$

and to observe, on the other hand, that the equation (91.), which has served to determine the normal vector of proximity ν, may be thus written:

$$(x^2 - \iota^2)^2\nu = (1-x)^2\rho + \iota(x\rho + \rho x) - x(\iota\rho + \rho\iota); \quad . \quad (105.)$$

for thus we are conducted, by means of 81., to the formula:

$$\xi - \rho = b^2\nu; \quad . \quad . \quad . \quad . \quad (106.)$$

which expresses the agreement of the recent construction with the results that had been previously obtained.

60. If we introduce two new constant vectors $\iota'$ and $x'$, connected with the two former constant vectors $\iota$, $x$, by the equations

$$\iota\iota' = \iota'x = T.\iota x, \quad . \quad . \quad . \quad . \quad (107.)$$

which give

$$\iota'^2 = \iota^2, \quad x'^2 = x^2, \quad \iota x' = x\iota, \quad . \quad . \quad . \quad (108.)$$

then one of the lately cited forms of the equation of the ellipsoid, namely the equation

$$T(\iota\rho + \rho x) = x^2 - \iota^2 \quad (9.), \text{ art. } 38,$$

takes easily, by the rules of this calculus, the new but analogous form:

$$T(\iota'\rho + \rho x') = x'^2 - \iota'^2. \quad . \quad . \quad . \quad . \quad (109.)$$

The perfect similarity of these two forms, (9.) and (109.), renders it evident that all the conclusions which have been deduced from the one form can, with suitable and easy modifications, be deduced from the other also. Thus if we still regard the centre A as the origin of vectors, and treat $\iota' - x'$ and $-x'$ as the vectors of two new fixed points B' and C', we may consider AB'C' as a *new generating triangle*, and may derive from it the *same ellipsoid* as before, by a geometrical process of generation or construction, which is similar in all respects to the process already assigned. (See the Numbers of

\* Philosophical Magazine for June, September, and October,

1847; or the Proceedings of the Royal Irish Academy for July, 1846.) Hence the two new sides B'C' and C'A, which indeed are parallel by (107.) to the two old sides AC and CB, or to κ and ι, must have the directions of the two cyclic normals; and the third new side, AB', or ι'−x', must be the axis of a *second cylinder of revolution*, circumscribed round the same ellipsoid. If we determine on this new axis two new points, L' and M', as the extremities of two new vectors λ' and μ', analogous to the recently considered vectors λ and μ, and assigned by equations similar to (84.) and (89.), namely

$$\lambda'(x'-\iota') = x'\rho + \rho x', \quad \mu'(\iota'-x') = \iota'\rho + \rho\iota', \quad . \quad . \quad (110.)$$

we shall have results analogous to (85.) and (90.), namely

$$T(\rho-\lambda') = b; \quad T(\rho-\mu') = b; \quad . \quad . \quad . \quad (111.)$$

with others similar to (101.), namely

$$\frac{\xi-\lambda'}{x'} = \frac{\xi-\mu'}{\iota'} = \frac{\lambda'-\mu'}{\iota'-x'}; \quad . \quad . \quad . \quad (112.)$$

the common value of these three quotients being a new scalar, but ξ being still the same vector as before, namely that vector which terminates in the point N, where the normal to the surface at E meets the common plane of the new and old generating triangles, or the plane of the greatest and least axes of the ellipsoid. It is easy hence to infer that the new variable triangle L'M'N is similar to the new generating triangle AB'C', and similarly situated in the same fixed plane therewith; and that the sides L'N, M'N, having respectively the same directions as AC', B'C', have likewise the same directions as BC, AC, and therefore also as MN, LN, or else directions opposite to these; in such a manner that the two straight lines, L'M, M'L, must cross each other in the point N. But these two lines may be regarded as the diagonals of a certain quadrilateral inscribed in a circle, namely the plane quadrilateral L'M'ML; of which the four corners are, by (85.), (90.), and (111.), at one common and constant distance $= b$, from the variable point E of the ellipsoid. If then we assume it as known that the vector $b^2\gamma$, which is in direction opposite and is in length reciprocal to the perpendicular let fall from the centre A on the tangent plane at E, must terminate in a point F on the surface of *another ellipsoid, reciprocal* (in a well-known sense) to that former ellipsoid which contains the point E itself, or the termination of the vector ρ; we may combine the recent results, so as to obtain the following geometrical construction[*], which serves *to gene-*

[*] This is the construction referred to in a note to article 54. It was communicated by the author to the Royal Irish Academy, at the meeting of November 30, 1847. See the Proceedings of that date.

*rate a system of two reciprocal ellipsoids, by means of a moving sphere.*

61. Let then a sphere of constant magnitude, with centre E, move so that it always intersects two fixed and mutually intersecting straight lines, AB, AB′, in four points L, M, L′, M′, of which L and M are on AB, while L′ and M′ are on AB′; and let one diagonal LM′, of the inscribed quadrilateral LMM′L′, be constantly parallel to a third fixed line AC, which will oblige the other diagonal ML′ of the same quadrilateral to move parallel to a fourth fixed line AC′. Let N be the point in which the diagonals intersect, and draw AF equal and parallel to EN; so that AENF is a parallelogram: then *the locus of the centre E of the moving sphere is one ellipsoid, and the locus of the opposite corner F of the parallelogram is another ellipsoid reciprocal thereto.* These two ellipsoids have a common centre A, and a common mean axis, which is equal to the diameter of the moving sphere, and is a mean proportional between the greatest axis of either ellipsoid and the least axis of the other, of which two last-mentioned axes the directions coincide. Two sides AE, AF, of the parallelogram AENF, are thus two semidiameters which may be regarded as mutually *reciprocal*, one of the one ellipsoid, and the other of the other: but because they fall at *opposite* sides of the *principal plane* (containing the four fixed lines and the greatest and least axes of the ellipsoids), it may be proper to call them, more fully, *opposite reciprocal semidiameters*; and to call the points E and F, in which they terminate, *opposite reciprocal points.* The two other sides EN, FN, of the same variable parallelogram, are the *normals* to the two ellipsoids, meeting each other in the point N, upon the same principal plane. In that plane, the two former fixed lines, AB, AB′, are the *axes of two cylinders of revolution*, circumscribed about the first ellipsoid; and the two latter fixed lines, AC, AC′, are the *two cyclic normals* of the same first ellipsoid: while the diagonals, LM′, ML′, of the inscribed quadrilateral in the construction, are the *axes of the two circles* on the surface of that first ellipsoid, which circles pass through the point E, that is through the centre of the moving sphere; and the intersection N of those two diagonals is the centre of another sphere, which cuts the first ellipsoid in the system of those two circles: all which is easily adapted, by suitable interchanges, to the other or reciprocal ellipsoid, and flows with facility from the quaternion equations above given.

[To be continued.]

L. *On an easy method of measuring the distance and height of an elevated point, accessible or inaccessible, fixed or moveable, by means of a single instrument, and by taking the observation from only one station.* By M. ELIE WARTMANN, *Professor of Physics in the Academy of Geneva*[*].

GEODESICAL and astronomical operations very frequently require the knowledge of the distance of a remote object. If the object be fixed, the ordinary processes of trigonometry readily lead to the desired result. It is only necessary to determine a base, and to measure, from each of its extremities, the angle between the other extremity and the object; we thus obtain the value of two angles and of the adjacent side, from which the triangle is easily resolved.

But for the case in which the distant object is in motion,—a case of great importance, and which occurs in several strategical and cosmological problems, the operation is by no means so simple. It would be necessary first to measure a straight line, more or less extended, and to station at its extremities two observers, who at the same instant should direct the telescopes of their theodolites to the same point of the object. When the point is simultaneously visible from the two stations, and the chronometers compared, and when above all the object preserves exactly its form, or only changes it imperceptibly, it is conceivable that this method may succeed; and the result will be more exact as the readings are repeated at shorter intervals, in order to lessen the probable errors by means. But when these different circumstances do not exist, when there is only a single observer, or the object varies in appearance, or is not visible at the same time from both extremities of the base, then the execution of the process becomes impossible.

Such are the objections which may be made to the method proposed by M. Pouillet[†] for estimating the *height of the clouds*, a problem which has already attracted the attention of several eminent philosophers, such as James Bernoulli[‡], Brice[§], Lambert[||], and more recently M. Arago[¶]. The following is the method which I propose for its solution.

---

[*] Bulletin of the Sittings of the Vaudois Society of Natural Sciences, tome i. p. 21. (Sitting of February 2, 1842.) See also Pogg. *Ann.*, tom. lvi. p. 635; and Gehler's *Physikalisches Wörterbuch*, tom. xi. p. 700.

[†] Note on the Height, Velocity, and Direction of the Clouds; *Comptes Rendus* of the Academy of Sciences of Paris, tom. xi. p. 717 (Nov. 9, 1840).

[‡] *Acta Eruditorum*, 1688. [§] Philosophical Transactions, 1766.

[||] Memoirs of the Academy of Berlin, 1773.

[¶] *Comptes Rendus*, tom. xi. p. 323 (August 24, 1840). Annual of the Bureau of Longitudes, 1840, p. 316.

Let us select in a motionless cloud, or in one which does not move with too great velocity, any point N, fig. 1, distinguishable

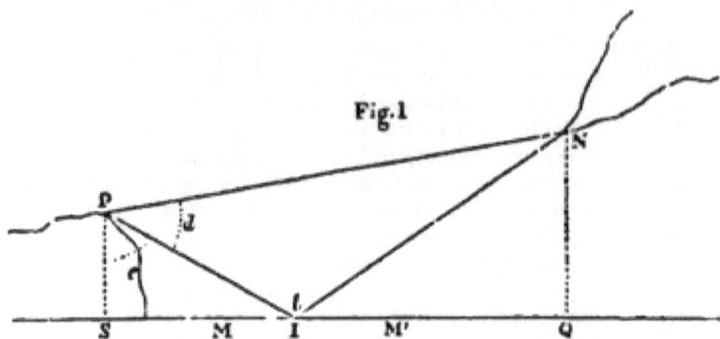

Fig. 1

by its colour or peculiar form. Let us place ourselves on an elevated point P, on the summit of a hill or a tower, or even at the window of the upper story of a house. Let us have under us a reflecting plane MM', such as a tranquil surface of water or mercury, or a large horizontal glass. The angle of incidence of a luminous ray which strikes a mirror being equal to the angle of reflexion, it will suffice to determine the angle $d$ formed by the ray which reaches the eye directly from the point N, with the ray PI which reaches it by reflexion in I, and to estimate the length PI, in order to solve the problem.

In fact, calling $e$ the angle formed by the reflected ray PI with the vertical PS, which passes through the centre of the instrument with which the angle is taken, it is evident that the angle $l$ contained by the incident and reflected rays $= 2e$. The two angles $d$ and $l$ being known, it only remains to measure PI. As it might be difficult to determine precisely the point I of the reflecting surface, we may turn the telescope round the vertical, keeping the angle $e$ constant, and seek the length PL or PE of the line joining the point P with the object L or E situated on its margin (fig. 2). If the observer is on the top of a vertical wall, or on a tower or house, he will only have to measure its height above the reflecting plane $PS = h$ to deduce

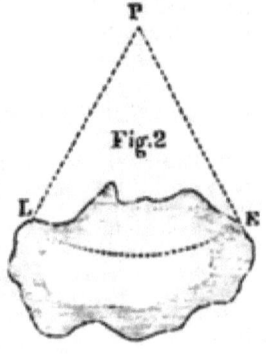

Fig. 2

$$PI = \frac{PS}{\cos e} = \frac{h}{\cos e}.$$

This value being known, we deduce from it
$$h = \text{PI} \cos e.$$
In like manner since the incident ray
$$\text{IN} = \text{PI} \cdot \frac{\sin d}{\sin(d+l)},$$
therefore the vertical height $\text{NQ} = \text{H}$ of the cloud above the mirror is
$$\text{H} = \text{IN} \cdot \cos e = h \frac{\sin d}{\sin(d+l)},$$
and its height $\Delta = \text{H} - h$ above the observer
$$\Delta = h \left\{ \frac{\sin d}{\sin(d+l)} - 1 \right\}.$$

It is sufficient in practice to employ a circle placed vertically and furnished with a tube without lenses. A metallic plate, blackened and pierced at its centre with a small hole, serves instead of an eye-glass. The tube, the interior of which is likewise black, is furnished with cross wires, and a sufficient length is given it to admit only the useful rays, and not those which are reflected by objects surrounding the point which is observed. The reflecting surface may be a pond, a lake, a large sheet of water or mercury, &c.

Beside its simplicity, the process which I have described, and which evidently applies in the same cases as the other methods which have been proposed, appears to me to offer some advantages over them. It is absolutely independent of the presence of the sun above the horizon. The larger the base to be measured PI, the greater will be the approximation. If the point N is only slowly moved, we may employ Borda's method for the repetition of the angles, and thus limit more nearly their exact value: we may, moreover, observe at short intervals of time, and determine the velocity of translation of the object,—a circumstance which it is often useful to ascertain. We remark, lastly, that there is no longer any possibility for a single observer to confound the point of vision with other surrounding points. Now this confusion frequently occurs in the case of a fleeting cloud, and which requires less time to lose its form than is required, in M. Pouillet's method, for two observers to regain their post and observe after having met to make their arrangements.

If the wind or any other cause prevents the employment of a liquid as the mirror, a very smooth silvered glass might be substituted, of as large dimensions as possible, and be placed horizontally by means of levels or screws, or thin wedges.

Professor Whewell has very recently proposed* to ascertain the height of the clouds or of a mountain by means of the formula

$$H = h \cdot \frac{\sin(\alpha+\beta)}{\sin(\alpha-\beta)},$$

in which

H is the height of the cloud above a horizontal mirror,
$h$ the vertical height of the observer above this mirror,
$\alpha$ the angle of depression of the image of any point of the cloud below the horizontal plane passing by the eye of the observer,
$\beta$ the angle of elevation of the same point above this plane.

It is evident that this formula is identical with that† which I published four years ago, and which has been reproduced in the scientific journals of Germany. The learned Master of Trinity forgot that at the time when he made his communication to the Section of Physics of the British Association at Southampton, I informed him that what he proposed as new was already in print.

## LI. *Notices respecting New Books.*

*Results of Astronomical Observations made during the years* 1834, 1835, 1836, 1837, 1838, *at the Cape of Good Hope; being the Completion of a Telescopic Survey of the whole Surface of the visible Heavens, commenced in* 1825. *By* Sir John F. W. Herschel, *Bart., K.H., &c. &c.* London: Smith, Elder and Co. 1847.

AS many of our readers may not have had an opportunity of perusing the exceedingly important and interesting volume recently published under the above title, we propose to make a few extracts from it for the purpose of giving them an idea of its principal contents. Where it may appear desirable (having regard to our narrow limits) to condense or abridge, we shall make it a rule to adhere as closely as may be to the language of the author.

In his Introduction, the author states that the present work completes a review of the sidereal heavens which he commenced in 1825, with the object of re-examining the nebulæ and clusters of stars discovered by Sir William Herschel in his Sweeps of the Heavens, and described in three catalogues published in the Philosophical Transactions for 1786, 1789 and 1802. The result of the re-examination was given in a paper printed in the Phil. Trans. for 1833, in the form of a catalogue arranged in the order of right ascension, and

---

* Reports of the British Association for 1846; Transactions of the Sections, p. 15.
† Ibid.

containing 2306 nebulæ and clusters, of which 1781 are identical with objects occurring in Sir W. Herschel's catalogues or in other works, and the remaining 525 are new. Besides nebulæ and clusters, which were the special objects of attention, there were observed in the course of the review between 3000 and 4000 double stars, of all classes and orders, the positions of which, accompanied with a great number of highly interesting remarks descriptive of their appearance or peculiarities, were given in six catalogues which have been published in the Memoirs of the Royal Astronomical Society. Having completed this review, and having acquired during the eight years' practice sufficient mastery of the instrument (a reflecting telescope of $18\frac{1}{4}$ inches clear aperture, and 20 feet in focal length), and of the delicate process of polishing the specula, and being moreover strongly incited by the peculiar interest of the subject, he resolved to attempt a completion of the survey by extending it to the whole surface of the heavens. For this purpose it was necessary to transport the instruments into the other hemisphere; and the Cape of Good Hope was selected as the most convenient and eligible station.

Sir John, accompanied by his family, and carrying with him the 20-foot reflector above alluded to, an achromatic telescope of seven feet in focal length mounted as an equatorial, and other astronomical apparatus, sailed from Portsmouth for the Cape in the East India Company's ship, the Mount Stewart Elphinstone, on the 13th of November 1833, and arrived in Table Bay on the 15th of January 1834. Having disembarked his apparatus (which was found not to have sustained the slightest injury), his first care was to seek out a residence in a suitable locality. This he fortunately succeeded in speedily finding at the mansion of a Dutch proprietor, at a distance of about six miles from Cape Town. The place, which bears the name of Feldhuysen or Feldhausen, is charmingly situated on the last slope at the base of the Table Mountain, and was well-sheltered from dust, and also from the winds which at some seasons prevail there with great violence. All his preparations were made and the telescope set up by the end of February, and on the night of the 5th of March he commenced a regular course of sweeping\*. Shortly after a building was begun for the reception of the equatorial, for which he had carried out with him a moveable roof constructed in England, and on the 2nd of May the instrument was brought into approximate adjustment, and a series of micrometrical measures of southern double stars was commenced. The great reflector stood of course in the open air; and his whole establishment was within an enclosure surrounded by trees, but commanding a tolerably near approach to the horizon on all sides, excepting the western, where the nearer vicinity of the trees shut out a part of the sky.

The exact geographical position of Feldhausen (which, like Rhodes or Huen, is destined to be an object of interest to the astronomers of all future ages) is in latitude $33° 58' 56''\cdot55$ S., and longitude $22^h 46^m$

---

\* This term is used by the author to designate the system of observation in zones of 3° breadth in polar distance in search of new objects.

9″·11 from Greenwich, as determined by a triangulation connecting it with the Royal Observatory at the Cape. The altitude was found, by barometric measurement, to be about 142 feet above the mean sea level at Table Bay.

For the purpose of working the sweeping and other mechanical movements of the reflector and executing necessary repairs, Sir John engaged the services of an attendant, who, besides possessing the qualifications of a ready mechanic, had acquired considerable experience in the management of the instrument during the review of the northern heavens. With the exception of this indispensable aid, "the whole of the observations, as well as the entire work of reducing, arranging, and preparing them for the press," were executed by the author himself. We risk little in asserting that the annals of astronomy afford no more remarkable example of the patience of the observer and computer united with the highest order of genius than that which is furnished by the present volume.

Sir John left the Cape about the end of January 1838, having passed four years and a few days in the colony. Making every allowance for the energy, skill and experience of the observer, so great a multitude of difficult observations (not merely for ascertaining the places of the various objects which came under review, but their peculiarities of aspect and physical structure for which attentive and repeated examination was frequently necessary) could not possibly have been accumulated in so short a period of time excepting under tolerably favourable conditions. The climate of the Cape, he observes, must be regarded as on the whole favourable for astronomical observations, though there are some drawbacks. In the hot season, from October to March, the nights are for the most part superb; but in the vicinity of the mountains the south wind frequently brings with it a belt of clouds, extending many miles from the hills, and cutting off the view of the sky. Very often too, the excessive heat and dryness of the plains gives rise to a disturbance of the optical tranquillity of the air, and greatly impairs distinct vision; the images of the stars being in some cases violently dilated, and converted into ill-defined nebulous balls or puffs of 10″ or 15″ in diameter; in others forming round pellets of 3″ or 4″ in diameter, unlike spurious discs, and rather resembling planetary nebulæ; while on a few occasions the appearances have been very perplexing, and such as there is difficulty in accounting for on any optical principle whatever. In the cooler months, from May to October inclusive, and particularly in June and July, the finest opportunities occur; the state of the atmosphere is in these months habitually good, and imperfect vision is rather the exception than the rule. The best nights occur after the heavy rains, which fall at this season, have ceased for a day or two. On these occasions hardly any limit is set to magnifying power except what the aberrations of the specula necessitate. Among the phænomena incidental to the climate he makes mention of a "nebulous haze," which comes and disappears very suddenly, and of which the effect is to convert every star of the 9th magnitude and upwards into a "nebulous star," *i. e.* a well-defined star surrounded by a nebulous photosphere of greater or less extent, according to its brightness. He also notices, as a peculiarity of the climate which gave occasion to frequent remark, the great opacity of cloud as compared with that which prevails in this country.

The climate was found to have a much more prejudicial effect on the metallic specula than had been anticipated. He had provided himself with three mirrors (each of 18¼ inches in clear diameter of polished surface), but fortunately he had taken the precaution also to carry out with him the polishing apparatus, and he soon found that the operation was very much more frequently required than in England. At first some slight imperfections of surface, induced by exposure, were tolerated from an apprehension that in a climate so much warmer difficulties would arise in hitting the proper temperature of the polishing material; but confidence in this respect being once restored, and practice constantly improving, he soon became fastidious, "and on detection of the slightest dimness on any part of the surface the metal was at once remanded to the polisher." It is scarcely necessary to add that the polisher was Sir John himself. To no other hands than his own could that delicate operation have been entrusted.

The "Introduction," from which the preceding details are taken, concludes with the following statement:—

"It remains to say something as to the mode of introducing this work into the world. To the munificent destination of His Grace, the late Duke of Northumberland, of a large sum in aid of its publication, it owes its appearance as a single and separate work, instead of a series of unconnected memoirs scattered over the volumes of academical bodies. The lamented decease of that illustrious nobleman prevented his witnessing its final completion. His liberal intentions however have been fully carried out by the worthy successor to his titles and his spirit; whose kind and gracious interest in it, I should be wanting in all proper feeling, were I to omit this opportunity of acknowledging."

The contents of the volume are arranged under seven chapters, which are headed as follows:—

I. Of the Nebulæ of the Southern Hemisphere.

II. Of the Double Stars in the Southern Hemisphere.

III. Of Astrometry, or the Numerical Expression of the Apparent Magnitude of the Stars.

IV. Of the Distribution of Stars, and of the Constitution of the Galaxy in the Southern Hemisphere.

V. Observations of Halley's Comet, with Remarks on its Physical Condition, and that of Comets in general.

VI. Observations of the Satellites of Saturn.

VII. Observations of the Solar Spots.

There are besides four short appendices, and the work is illustrated by seventeen beautiful plates, giving representations of the more remarkable objects from drawings made by the author himself, who thus appears to include among his other accomplishments the skill of a first-rate artist. These delineations, it may be proper to observe, have an object beyond the ordinary purposes of illustration. They are executed with extreme care and accuracy, and with the view of enabling future astronomers, by comparing the present representations with the actual appearances of the objects some ages hence, to determine whether they remain permanently the same, or are gradually undergoing changes in their physical condition.

Chap. I. *Of the Nebulæ of the Southern Hemisphere.*—The subject of this chapter is a catalogue of the nebulæ and clusters of stars, containing the reduced results of all the observations of each object which occurred in the regular course of sweeping, in which either the place of the object was taken, or any particular in its appearance or physical character noted, *without any selection of good, or suppression of discordant observations whatever*. In its arrangement and construction it is similar in every particular to the catalogue of Northern Nebulæ and Clusters printed in the Philosophical Transactions for 1833, and is reduced to the same epoch, namely the beginning of 1830. The Introduction contains general observations respecting the mode of observing and registering the observations, the explanation of the abbreviations, &c. The whole number of nebulæ and clusters is 1708. Of these 89 are identical with objects formerly observed by Sir John himself at Slough; 135 are contained in Sir William Herschel's catalogues; 9 are Messier's, and 206 have been identified (though with considerable doubt in many cases) with objects observed by Mr. Dunlop. The remaining 1269 are a new acquisition to astronomy.

In the "Remarks on the Catalogue," Sir John first considers the degree of precision which may be ascribed to the place of an object determined by a single observation; a great number of them having been observed only once. As it is found that the cases are comparatively rare in which two observations of the same object differ by a whole minute in NPD, or by a quantity in RA, which when converted into space would give the same amount of discordance in the direction of the parallel, he infers that, with the exception of large clusters having no centrally situated remarkable star, and large ill-defined or irregularly shaped nebulæ, the error of a single observation (taking the error at half the discordance) is in general within half a minute of a degree. As to errors of reading and reduction, it is presumed, from the care that was taken and the re-examinations made, that they are very unfrequent. The reductions were carefully re-examined whenever there appeared the smallest ground for suspicion.

He then proceeds to explain the figures and drawings to which reference is made in the catalogue, and to give detailed descriptions of some of the more remarkable objects; discussing, incidentally, the presumptions of a change of state afforded by comparison of their present appearances with former descriptions and drawings. He also describes the method he followed in laying down the monographs, and determining the positions of the stars visible in the nebulæ. The usual process was as follows. The differences of RA and NPD of the principal stars were taken with the equatorial micrometer. Adopting these as a basis of projection, the more conspicuous of the remaining ones were determined from them by triangulation;—the angles being measured with the position micrometer of the twenty-foot reflector, and projected on the chart by means of a protractor. From the stars thus laid down by triangulation, others depending on eye-drafts were then inserted in the chart; and, finally, the differences in RA and NPD were read off from the chart by means of diagonal scales, and the whole entered in a catalogue. The nebulæ were then worked in upon the chart according to the united evidence of all the drawings and diagrams. An idea will be given of the immense labour bestowed on these drawings by stating, for a few cases, the number of small stars within their boundaries whose places were approximately determined. In the monograph of the nebula marked λ. 2941, the number of stars laid down is 105; in λ. 3722, the number is 186; in the cluster λ. 3435, 110; in the nebula about θ Orionis, 150; and so on.

We have no room to enter into details respecting the objects figured in the six plates which belong to this chapter, and compression or abridgement is scarcely possible. We shall therefore content ourselves with a brief allusion to the two principal ones:—the great nebula in the sword-handle of Orion, and that about the star η Argûs. The former of these objects was described by Sir John in 1824 (Mem. R. Astron. Society, vol. ii.), and subsequently by Dr. Lamont of Munich, as also by Rondoni, a Roman artist, and by the astronomer De Vico. He observes,—

"It may be supposed that in a situation so favourable for viewing this magnificent object as the Cape, where it passes the meridian at an altitude of 60°, with the additional advantage of a sky of perfect purity, and of mirrors in a constant course of repolishing, I should eagerly seize the opportunity to re-examine my earlier delineation of it, with a view to the detection of change, the correction of error, and the observation of further particulars as to its form, extent and structure which had escaped previous observation." The first glance at the object, under these favourable circumstances, showed a multitude of nebulous branches, convolutions, and other details of which he had not before had the least suspicion. Great pains were accordingly taken in the delineation of the figure here given. He observes that although a comparison of it with the former representations might convey an impression of great and rapid changes in the nebula, he is far from participating in such an impression, and is disposed to think that the disagreements in his own two drawings, though confessedly great, are not more so than may be attributed to inexperience in the case of the earlier one, the greater care bestowed on the latter,—and above all to the advantage of local situation, and the very great superiority in respect both of light and of defining power in the telescope at the latter period. There is only one particular on which he is at all inclined to insist as evidence of change—and this refers to the situation and form of one of the branches of the nebula.

The other nebula to which we have adverted—that about the star η Argûs—is a far more extensive object. The space which it occupies in the figure extends in right ascension from $-3^m 45^s$ to $+3^m 0^s$

from the principal star, and in polar distance from −24′ to +44′, comprising in the whole an area of almost exactly a square degree. "It would be impossible by verbal description to give any just idea of the capricious forms and irregular gradations of light affected by the different branches and appendages of this nebula. Nor is it easy for language to convey a full impression of the beauty and sublimity of the spectacle it affords when viewed in a sweep, ushered in as it is by so glorious and innumerable a procession of stars, to which it forms a sort of climax, justifying expressions, which, though I find them written in my Journal in the excitement of the moment, would be thought extravagant if transferred to these pages. In fact, it is impossible for any one, with the least spark of astronomical enthusiasm about him, to pass soberly in review, with a powerful telescope and in a fine night, that portion of the southern sky which is comprised between $6^h$ and $13^h$ of RA and from $146°$ to $149°$ NPD, such are the variety and interest of the objects he will encounter, and such the dazzling richness of the starry ground on which they are represented to his gaze."—P. 38.

The star η Argûs, which is surrounded by this magnificent nebula, is itself an object of no ordinary interest, on account of the singular changes in lustre it appears to have undergone. In Halley's catalogue (1677) it is set down as a star of the 4th magnitude; in the catalogues of Lacaille, Brisbane, Johnson, Fallows, and Taylor, as of the 2nd. Sir John had himself been accustomed to regard it as of the 2nd, or at most as a small star of the 1st. On the 16th of December 1837, he was astonished by seeing it appear as one of the very brightest of the 1st magnitude. "It exceeded α Orionis, and the only star (Sirius and Canopus excepted) which could at all be compared with it was Rigel, which it somewhat surpassed." On the 28th of December it far surpassed Rigel, and equalled α Centauri; after the beginning of January it began to fall off. From subsequent observations made by Mr. Maclear at the Cape, it appears that in March 1843 it was superior to Canopus. About the 19th of that month it began again to decrease. On the 3rd of January 1845 it is described by Mr. Maclear as being again much larger than Canopus. Sir John asks—"What origin can we ascribe to these sudden flashes and relapses? What conclusions are we to draw as to the comfort or habitability of a system depending for its light and heat on so uncertain a source?"

A general catalogue is given of the stars known to exist within the limits of RA and PD which bound the monograph chart of this singular object. They amount to no fewer than 1216.

After this follows the "Reduced Observations of Nebulæ and Clusters of Stars." The catalogue occupies 78 pages, and gives the following particulars:—1st, the author's number; 2nd, the synonym; 3rd, the RA for 1830; 4th, NPD for 1830; 5th, description, remarks, &c.; and 6th, the number of the sweep. By means of the abbreviations we have already alluded to, the descriptions are generally given in a very small space, frequently in a single line. Many of the objects described are extremely remarkable.

The catalogue is followed by a chapter on the law of Distribution of Nebulæ and Clusters over the surface of the Heavens. After giving a table showing the number of these objects observed in each hour of RA in the northern catalogue, the author observes, " It is evident from this that the great mass of the nebulæ visible in our latitudes is accumulated upon the 6 hours of RA between $9^h$ and $15^h$; on both sides of which the falling off is rapid, and after $15^h$ very sudden; while within the 6 hours in question the condensation increases to a very marked maximum between the hours 12 and 13." (Between $12^h$ and $13^h$ the number in the catalogue is 441; between $15^h$ and $16^h$ it is only 42.) In order however to obtain a better view of the mode in which they are grouped, and a measure of their condensation, he projects them on a chart, adopting a mode of projection by which equal areas on the sphere are represented by equal areas on the chart. On this principle he constructed charts representing the northern and southern hemispheres divided into zones of $3°$ in breadth or polar distance, and into hours of RA (subdivided into quarters), on which he laid down the nebulæ from the contents of both catalogues, so as to obtain a *coup-d'œil* of their distribution over the whole heavens. The principal conclusions arrived at by this laborious mode of proceeding are the following:—

" 1st. The distribution of the nebulæ is not, like that of the Milky Way, in a zone or band encircling the heavens, or if such a band can be at all traced out, it is with so many interruptions, and so faintly marked out through by far the greater part of its circumference, that its existence as such can be hardly more than suspected.

" 2ndly. One-third of the whole nebulous contents of the heavens are congregated in a broad irregular patch, occupying about one-eighth of the whole surface of the sphere; chiefly (indeed almost entirely) situated in the northern hemisphere, and occupying the constellations Leo, Leo Minor, the body, tail, and hind legs of Ursa Major, the nose of the Camelopard, and the point of the tail of Draco, Canes Venatici, Coma, the preceding leg of Bootes, and the head, wings, and shoulder of Virgo.

" 3rdly. Within this area there are several local centres of accumulation where the nebulæ are exceedingly crowded, viz. 1st, from $59°$ to $62°$ of NPD in the 13th hour of RA between the northern part of Coma and the fore legs of Chara, as also (in the same hour) from $72°$ to $78°$ NPD between the palm branch and the northern wing of Virgo; and again, in the same hour, from $80°$ to $87°$ NPD in the northern wing and breast of Virgo. Northward the nebulous area terminates almost abruptly with a very rich patch between the nose of the Camelopard and the tail of Draco. The line of greatest condensation connecting these most condensed patches is irregular and wavy, without appearance of reference to any one particular centre, and the shading off, though patchy, is on the whole gradual."—P. 135.

After some further remarks on the distribution of the nebulæ in the northern hemisphere, he thus proceeds:—

" In the southern a much greater uniformity of distribution prevails. If we except the two Nubeculæ (which are full of nebulæ, and the greater part of which is even richer in objects of that class than the densest portion of the northern group), the general character of this hemisphere is that of alternating patches of nebulæ and vacuities of greater or lesser extent, some of the latter however being very extensive. In one of these vacuities, in which comparatively few nebulæ occur, the south pole is situated, having one nebula, however, within half a degree of it (as the north pole has also one within five or six minutes). This barren region extends nearly 15° on all sides of the pole, and immediately on its borders occurs the smaller nubecula.

"One of the most remarkable features in the southern nebulous system is the extraordinary display of finely resolved and resolvable globular clusters which occurs between $16^h 45^m$ and $19^h$ in RA in the region occupied by Corona Australis, the body and head of Sagittarius, the tail of Scorpio, with part of Telescopium and Ara. Here, in a circular space of 18° in radius, we find collected no less than thirty of these beautiful and exquisite objects. This is certainly something beyond a mere accidental coincidence. Are we to suppose that in this direction the visual ray encounters some branch of the general nebulous system nearer to us than the rest? Or are we to connect it with the very peculiar structure of the Milky Way in this particular part of its course, which is here unlike in its constitution to any other portion of that zone, and which passes diametrically across the circular area in question? It can hardly be doubted that some at least of these objects belong to and form a part of the Milky Way.

"The general conclusion which may be drawn from this survey, however, is, that the nebulous system is distinct from the sidereal, though involving, and perhaps, to a certain extent, intermixed with the latter. The great nebulous constellation in the northern hemisphere, which I have called the region of Virgo, being regarded as the main body of this system, and subtending at our point of view an angle of 80° or 90°, it is evident that, supposing its form to approach to the spherical, our distance from its centre must be considerably less than its own diameter, so that our system may very well be regarded as placed somewhat beyond the borders of its denser portion, yet involved among its outlying members, or forming an element of some one of its protuberances or branches of which the individuals are the sporadic nebulæ confusedly scattered over the general surface of the heavens, and of which the prolongation in a direction towards the constellation Pisces may give rise to the apparently denser grouping of the nebulæ in that region."—P. 136.

The author next treats of the "Classification of Nebulæ." He observes that "the distinction between nebulæ and clusters of stars must depend on two very different considerations:—1st, on the power of our instrument to distinguish the very minute individuals of which a resolvable cluster, or one entirely composed of stars, may consist; and 2ndly, on the idea we attach to the word 'nebulous,' that is to say, on the distinction which we conceive to exist between objects physically nebulous and objects only optically so. An object really composed of discrete stars may appear nebulous either because it consists of stars so small as to be separately indiscernible by the light of the telescope, or of stars so close as to be incapable of being separated by its defining and magnifying powers, and under different degrees of instrumental imperfection such an object may offer any variety of appearance." Hence the distinction between nebulæ properly so called, and those which we are to consider as certainly or very probably clusters of stars, can never become a permanent ground of classification. Their degree of resolvability, however, connected as it is with the absolute brightness of their constituent stars, and their distance from us, must always form an important character in their description. He further observes that when sensible objects possess no qualities but such as are common to them all, and differ only in the greater or less degree in which those qualities are present in them, the only classification they admit is a *classificatio per gradus*. From these considerations he considers it sufficient to divide the whole nebulous system into three great classes:—I. Regular Nebulæ; II. Irregular Nebulæ; III. Irregular Clusters. Those of the first class are described under five different characters, and in each character he recognises five degrees,—two extreme and three medial. The characters and degrees forming the system of sub-classification, are arranged in a particular order as follows:—

| Subclass in respect of | Magnitude. | Brightness. | Roundness. | Condensation. | Resolvability. |
|---|---|---|---|---|---|
| 1. | Great. | Lucid. | Circular. | Stellate. | Discrete. |
| 2. | Large. | Bright. | Round. | Nebular. | Resolvable. |
| 3. | Middle-sized. | Faint. | Oval. | Concentrate. | Granulate. |
| 4. | Small. | Dim. | Elongate. | Graduating. | Mottled. |
| 5. | Minute. | Obscure. | Linear. | Discoid. | Milky. |

By giving to the first five numerical digits an absolute value denoting the degree, and a value depending on position denoting the character, the description of the nebula is rendered very compendious. Thus the combination I. 32155 expresses "A Regular Nebula, Middle-sized, Bright, Circular, Discoid, Milky." The utility of this system, he remarks, "in affording in a very small compass a good deal of information respecting the physical (or optical) characters of a nebula, in thus rendering possible a general descriptive catalogue of convenient magnitude for reference, will, I am disposed to think, be found considerable." The sub-classification, it will be observed, is founded entirely on the optical aspect of the nebulæ, without reference to any notions we may entertain of their intimate nature.

This first chapter concludes with a description of the Magellanic clouds—the Nubeculæ Major and Minor. The general appearance of the two objects to the naked eye, on a clear night, and in the absence of the light of the moon, is described to be "that of pretty conspicuous nebulous patches of about the same intensity with some of the brighter portions of the Milky Way." In a paper published in the Philosophical Transactions for 1828, representations, which are there stated to be from very correct drawings, are given of their appearance; but it would seem very unsuccessfully, for Sir John observes that if the drawings in question were telescopic representations, he is unable to reconcile them with his own observations as regards the greater part of the details; and if they were eye-drafts, "they certainly tend to convey such a conception of their appearance as must inevitably create a sentiment of disappointment in the mind of any one who, having his imagination excited by representations so striking and extraordinary, is presented for the first time with a view of the real objects."

The Nubecula Minor is situated between the parallels of 162° and 165° NPD, and between the meridians of $0^h\ 28^m$ and $1^h\ 13^m$ RA. It is of a generally round form to the unaided eye; in the telescope the most conspicuous and resolvable region appears to be somewhat to the south of its middle. It is situated in one of the most barren regions of the heavens, and the access to it on all sides is described as being "through a desert." Neither with the naked eye nor with the telescope is any connection to be traced either with the greater Nubecula or with the Milky Way. An idea of its general character and appearance is conveyed in the following note:—"Re-examined by the side motion the whole *cloud* in detail and in general. The main body *is* resolved, but barely. I see the stars with the left eye. It is not like the *stippled* ground of the sky. The borders fade away quite insensibly, and are less or not at all resolved. The body of the cloud does not congregate *much* into knots; and altogether it is in no way a striking object apart from the nebulæ and clusters."—P. 145.

The Nubecula Major is situated between the parallels of 156° and 162° NPD, and the meridians of 4° 40' and 6° 0' in RA. "Like the Minor it consists partly of large tracts and ill-defined patches of irresolvable nebulæ, and of nebulosity in every stage of resolution up to perfectly resolved stars like the Milky Way, as also of regular and irregular nebulæ properly so called, of globular clusters in every stage of resolvability, and of clustering groups sufficiently insulated and condensed to come under the designation of clusters of stars. In the number and variety of these objects, and in general complexity of structure, it far surpasses the lesser Nubecula." The concentration of the objects is such as to very far exceed anything to be met with in any other region of the heavens. "Even the most crowded parts of the stratum of Virgo in the wing of that constellation, or in Coma Berenices, offer nothing approaching to it. It is evident from this, and from the mixture of stars and unresolved nebulosity which probably might be resolved with a higher optical power, that the Nubeculæ are to be regarded as systems *sui generis*, and which have no analogues in our hemisphere."

"The immediate neighbourhood of the Nubecula Major is somewhat less barren of stars than the Minor, but it is by no means rich, nor does any part of the Milky Way whatever form any certain and conspicuous junction with, or include it..... I have encountered nothing that I could set down as *diffused nebulosity* anywhere in the neighbourhood of either Nubecula."—P. 147.

The excessive complexity of detail in this singular object baffled every attempt to delineate the whole or any large portion of it by the aid of the telescope. He was desirous of giving a correct and magnified drawing of both Nubeculæ; and to this end he took the place, with the equatorial, of every star visible in that instrument down to the 10th magnitude, in both objects, with a view to the formation of detailed charts to serve as the groundwork of the drawings. This very laborious operation was satisfactorily executed, but the execution of the drawings proved to be beyond his unassisted power, and he was obliged, though with regret, to rest content with having prepared the way for the more successful operations of some other astronomer, to whom he recommends the completion of a work at once so interesting in its performance and instructive in its result.

Catalogues of the objects (stars, nebulæ and clusters), observed in both Nubeculæ, including those observed with the 20-foot reflector as well as the equatorial, are given. In the Nubecula Minor the number is 244; in the Major 919. They are reduced by clock and index errors obtained from stars occurring in the zones, and, as in the other catalogue, the epoch is 1830. Numerous as are the objects whose places are thus for the first time determined and recorded, the author does not regard his work as more than a commencement, and he calls it, simply, a "First approximation towards a Catalogue of Objects in the Magellanic Clouds .. preparatory to the Construction of Charts of the Nubeculæ, and to the future execution of Drawings of them in detail."

We propose to give, in a future Number, an abstract of the second chapter of the work, which treats of the Double Stars of the Southern Hemisphere.

## LII. *Proceedings of Learned Societies.*

### ROYAL SOCIETY.

[Continued from p. 307.]

Nov. 25, 1847. POSTSCRIPT to Mr. W. H. Barlow's paper on Alternating Diurnal Currents of Electricity at the Terrestrial Surface.

The author states that since his paper was read to the Society, he had made further experiments to determine with greater accuracy the direction in which the daily electrical currents travel, and also how far the motions of the horizontal magnetic needle correspond with that of the telegraph. With regard to the latter, he finds that although they agree as to the general character of their deflexions, there is no decided simultaneous coincidence in their movements.

"Magnetical experiments on board H.M. Iron Steam Vessel 'Bloodhound.'" By Captain Edward Johnson, R.N., F.R.S. Communicated to the President by the Lords Commissioners of the Admiralty, and communicated to the Society by the President.

These experiments were undertaken with the view of ascertaining whether the action of steam upon the hull of an iron vessel affects a compass, properly placed, in any degree that may be of practical importance in its navigation; and also whether the keeling of the vessel produces any alteration in the deviations, or disturbs a compass so placed to any considerable extent. The former question is, from the results of these experiments, resolved in the negative; but with respect to the second, it appears that the deviations produced by keeling are very marked, and could not be safely disregarded. These observations completely confirm those already made by Mr. Walker and Commander Shaugh on board H.M. Iron Brig 'Recruit,' Commander A. Slade, and they prove the necessity that exists for ascertaining the deviations of the compass in all ships, not only at the beginning and end of their voyage, but likewise at intermediate stations; as also constant observation of the course which the ship may be steering.

Jan. 6, 1848.—"On Terrestrial Magnetism." By William A. Norton, A.M., M.A.P.S., Professor of Mathematics and Natural Philosophy in Delaware College, United States of America. Communicated by Lieut.-Colonel Edward Sabine, R.A., For. Sec. R.S.

The object of the author in the present memoir is to show that, by adopting certain fundamental conceptions with respect to the terrestrial magnetic forces, the magnetic may be deduced from the thermal elements of the earth. The following are the propositions which he considers he has established by his inquiries.

1. All the magnetic elements of any place on the earth may be deduced from the thermal elements of that place; and all the great features of the distribution of the earth's magnetism may be theoretically derived from certain prominent features in the distribution of its heat.

2. Of the magnetic elements, the horizontal intensity is nearly proportional to the mean temperature, as measured by Fahrenheit's thermometer; the vertical intensity is nearly proportional to the difference between the mean temperatures, at two points situated at equal distances north and south of the place, in a direction perpendicular to the isothermal line; and, in general, the direction of the needle is nearly at right angles to the isothermal line, while the precise courses of the inflected line, to which it is perpendicular, may be deduced from Sir David Brewster's formula for the temperature, by differentiating and putting the differential equal to zero.

3. As a consequence, the laws of the terrestrial distribution of the physical principles of magnetism and heat must be nearly the same; and these principles themselves must have towards one another the most intimate physical relations.

4. The principle of terrestrial magnetism, in as far as the phenomena of the magnetic needle are concerned, must be confined to the earth's surface, or to a comparatively thin stratum of the mass of the earth.

5. The mathematical theory of terrestrial magnetism which has been under discussion must be true in all its essential features.

6. We may derive the magnetic elements by very simple formulæ,

and with an accuracy equal to that of Gauss's formulæ, from a very small number of magnetic data determined by observation, and the mean annual temperature of the place.

Jan. 13.—"On the Disruptive Discharge of accumulated Electricity, and the Proximate Cause of Lightning." By Isham Baggs, Esq. Communicated by S. Hunter Christie, Esq., Sec. R.S.

The author proposes to inquire into the principal causes of the violent and disruptive union of opposite electricities which constitutes the electric discharge; and to apply the knowledge thus gained to the explanation of natural phenomena, and the further proof of the identity of frictional and voltaic electricities. He describes two instruments which he employed for the purpose of regulating the discharges of a Leyden jar, or battery, by adjusting with precision the distances between two brass balls, forming a communication between the inner and outer coatings; allowing of their being charged only to a limited degree of intensity, by carrying off all the electricity beyond that extent; and thus guarding the glass from the dangers of fracture from an excess of charge. He is led to the conclusion, that with a given dialectric, such as glass, the limit to the intensity of the charge it can receive varies directly as the cube of its thickness, being in the compound ratio of the resistance it presents to the discharge, which is simply as the thickness, and of the square of the distance of the two charged surfaces, such being the law of electric action.

When a number of insulated Leyden jars, arranged in a consecutive series by connecting the outer coating of each with the inner coating of the next, is charged by means of an electrical machine, the tension of the charge diminishes in each jar as they follow in the series, that of the terminal jar being exceedingly small. On the other hand, when each jar has been charged separately in the same manner and to an equal extent, and then quickly arranged in a series, the jars not touching one another, but the knobs connected with the inner coating of each jar, after the first, being placed at a certain distance from the outer coating of the preceding jar, which in such an arrangement is charged with an electricity of an opposite kind to that of the knob adjacent to it, the author found that the tension of the electricities was greatly augmented, giving rise to violent explosions whenever a discharge occurred. He considers a battery thus constituted as bearing the same relation to a single Leyden jar as the voltaic pile does to a single galvanic circle; and as affording in like manner the means of exalting, to any assignable degree, the electric tension. Adopting the views of Mr. Crosse as to the constitution of a thunder-cloud, namely, that it is formed of a number of concentric zones of electricity, alternately positive and negative, the central one having the highest intensity, and the tension diminishing in the successive zones surrounding the innermost, till it became inappreciable in the one most remote; the author considers this condition of the cloud to be analogous to that of the battery above described, and the phenomena of the former to receive complete illustration from the experimental results obtained with the latter.

Jan. 20.—"On the Heat disengaged during Metallic Substitutions." By Thomas Andrews, M.D., M.R.I.A., Vice-President of Queen's College, Belfast, &c. Communicated by Michael Faraday, Esq., D.C.L., F.R.S. &c.

In a paper which was published in the Philosophical Transactions for 1844, the author deduced from the experimental inquiry there recorded the general law, that when one base displaces another from any of its neutral combinations with an acid, the heat evolved or abstracted is always the same, whatever that acid element may be, provided the bases are the same. Extending a similar inquiry to salts with metallic bases, he establishes, as the result of the investigation of which an account is given in the present paper, the general principle that when an equivalent of one and the same metal replaces another in a solution of any of its salts of the same order, the heat developed is, with the same metals, constantly the same, the expression "of a solution of the same order" being understood to mean a solution in which the same precipitate is produced by the addition of an alkali, or, on one view of the composition of such salts, in which the metal exists in the same state of oxidation. The metallic salts, in the precipitation of which by other metals the evolved heat was ascertained, were those of copper precipitated by zinc, iron or lead ; of silver, precipitated by zinc or copper ; and of lead, mercury, and platinum precipitated by zinc : and the acid elements were either the sulphuric, hydrochloric, acetic or formic acids. From the last series of experiments the author deduces, that if three metals A, B, and C, be so related that A is capable of displacing B and C from their combinations, and also B capable of displacing C, then the heat developed in the substitution of A for C will be equal to that developed in the substitution of A for B added to that developed in the substitution of B for C ; and a similar rule may be applied to any number of metals similarly related.

## LIII. *Intelligence and Miscellaneous Articles.*

ACTION OF NITRIC ACID ON BRUCIA. BY M. AUG. LAURENT.

IT is well known to chemists that brucia, when treated with nitric acid, becomes of a very intense red colour. Some time since, M. Gerhardt, on examining this phænomenon attentively, observed that there was disengaged at common temperatures, a gaseous body slightly soluble in water, which had a very decided smell of apples, and burnt with a yellowish flame, accompanied with nitrous vapours. For want of material M. Gerhardt did not continue his observations ; nevertheless he concluded from them that the gas disengaged from brucia is nitrous æther.

M. Liebig has repeated this experiment, and expresses himself as follows in the miserable diatribe which he has aimed at us :—" The production of nitrous æther by a body which contains neither alcohol nor æther appears to me as remarkable as it is important in the history of æthereal combinations, on which account I undertook to repeat the experiments of M. Gerhardt. I condensed a portion of the gas which is disengaged from the brucia, and obtained a liquid which was immiscible with water, was more dense than dilute nitric acid, and boiled at from 158° to 167° F."

Not being able to conceive how a gaseous body at common temperatures could yield a liquid which boils only at 158° to 167° F., I resolved in my turn to repeat the experiment of M. Gerhardt.

I operated on 15 to 20 grammes of brucia. After having passed the gas over lime, I condensed it in a U-shaped tube, having at its curvature a small tube terminated by a bulb; by the help of a mixture of ice and salt I obtained about 1 gramme of a very fluid liquid, which was lighter than water, and had a strong smell of apples. I slowly distilled this liquid, almost to the last drop, at a temperature approaching 50° F., and without making it boil; I then submitted it to analysis; 0·550 gr. of the substance yielded 0·553 of carbonic acid and 0·290 of water. Nitrous æther contains—

|   |   | Calculation. | Experiment. |
|---|---|---|---|
| $C^4$ | 24 | 32·0 | 29·0 |
| $H^5$ | 5 | 6·6 | 6·1 |
| $N$ | 14 | .. |   |
| $O^2$ | 32 | .. |   |
|   | 75 | 100 |   |

The hydrogen and carbon are precisely in the same proportions as in nitrous æther. As to the loss, it is easily understood, when the smallness of the quantity of the liquid which I possessed, and the difficulties attendant upon the analysis of so volatile a substance, are considered.

Nitrogen was disengaged during the whole of the operations. Though the relations which exist between the composition, the atomic weight and boiling-points have been but slightly considered, it will be readily seen to be impossible that a substance which does not contain more than 29 to 30 per cent. of carbon and 6 of hydrogen, should contain more than 1 atom of nitrogen; for if we double the formula by putting either $C^4 H^{10}$ or $H^5$, or $H^4$; $N^2 O^4$ or $O^3$, a similar combination would have a boiling-point much higher than 50° or 60° F.

This experiment has also been repeated by M. Fournet, who also obtained a liquid possessing all the properties of nitrous æther.—*Ann. de Ch. et de Phys.*, Avril 1848.

---

ON CACOTHELIN. BY M. AUG. LAURENT.

When nitric acid has ceased to act upon brucia at common temperatures, it deposits a crystalline substance of a fine orange-yellow colour, which the author has named cacothelin. It is insoluble in water and slightly soluble in alcohol. When kept in a stopped bottle, and exposed to diffused light, it quickly becomes brown on the surface. By analysis it gave results which indicated the annexed formula:—

|  | Calculation. | Experiment. | |
|---|---|---|---|
|  |  | I. | II. |
| $C^{21}$ ....... 252 | 51·4 | 51·3 | 51·5 |
| $H^{22}$ ....... 22 | 4·5 | 4·6 | 4·4 |
| $N^4$ ....... 56 | 11·4 | 11·2 | 11·2 |
| $O^{10}$ ....... 160 | 32·7 | 32·9 | 32·9 |
|  490 | 100· | 100· | 100· |

1 equivalent of brucia ........ $C^{23}\ H^{26}\ N^2\ O^4$
3   ..    nitric acid ....  $H^5\ N^3\ O^9$
                            $\overline{C^{23}\ H^{31}\ N^5\ O^{13}}$

Deducting
1 equivalent of nitrous æther .... $C^2\ H^5\ N\ O^3$
1      ,,         water ......  $H^2\ O$
   There remains 1 equivalent ....  $\overline{C^{21}\ H^{22}\ N^4\ O^{10}}$ of cacothelin.

The colour of this substance and the action of heat upon it prove that it contains nitrous acid, and that the formula is probably $C^{21}\ H^{24}\ X^2\ N^2\ O^6$. Treated with ammonia it immediately dissolves in it, and gives a yellow liquid, which by ebullition becomes first green and afterwards brown, and is a new base insoluble in water or alcohol, but still contains nitrous acid. It dissolves immediately in hydrochloric acid, and this solution forms a yellow gelatinous precipitate; with ammonia and bichloride of platina it gives an orange-red precipitate, the colour of which is heightened considerably by drying; when it is perfectly dry the colour is so deep as to appear perfectly black, with golden-green reflexion. If it be moistened with a drop of alcohol, its orange-red colour is restored.

If it be very strongly dried in a porcelain capsule, it assumes a rich rose tint mixed with blue; a drop of alcohol restores its orange-red colour. This platina salt dissolves in hot sulphuric acid, and gives it a fine rose colour, which at a higher temperature becomes lilac-blue. When calcined it decomposes, giving sparks, and leaving about 23 per cent. of platina.

The action of nitric acid upon brucia has been recently again examined in the laboratory of Giessen. There has been found at length a very volatile liquid, containing as much carbon as nitrous æther, but more hydrogen. Nevertheless, observes M. Laurent, they will not give way, which, he adds, is readily conceivable.—*Ann. de Ch. et de Phys.*, Avril 1848.

---

ON A NEW METHOD OF ESTIMATING ARSENIC, ANTIMONY AND TIN. BY PROF. H. ROSE.

Chloride of ammonium can be usefully employed in analytical investigations, from its property of decomposing several oxides at a high temperature and forming with the metals highly volatile chlorides. The experiments frequently give far more accurate results, in the shortest time and with the least trouble, than have hitherto been obtained by the usual methods of analysis.

It is well known what difficulties accompany the separation of the acids of arsenic and of antimony, as likewise that of the peroxide of tin, from bases. In general these metallic acids are separated from the solutions of most of their salts in hydrochloric acid, or to which hydrochloric acid has been added, by sulphuretted hydrogen, as sulphurets, and the base in the filtered liquid determined in the state of chloride. If the latter happens to be one which is easily decomposed at an elevated temperature, and not volatile or only so at a very high temperature, the liquid, which is frequently very considerable in quantity, has to be evaporated to dryness, and the residue ignited more or less strongly. Every one accustomed to analytical investigations must be sufficiently well acquainted with the inconveniences which accompany the evaporation of large quantities of liquids containing small amounts of alkaline salts, which have to be determined quantitatively.

The difficulties attending such an investigation become greater when the salt of the metallic acid is not at all, or very sparingly, soluble in water and in hydrochloric acid, or one which is easily decomposed. Now this is frequently the case with a salt of this class when it has been heated to redness, which is requisite in determining the amount of water directly.

All these difficulties may in many cases be avoided by the use of chloride of ammonium. Suppose we have a salt of one of these metallic acids with an alkaline base to examine, it is only requisite to mix it, after having ignited and weighed it in the finely-pulverized state, with from five to eight times the quantity of pure powdered chloride of ammonium, and to heat the mixture in a small porcelain crucible which may be covered with a concave platinum lid, over an Argand lamp until the whole of the chloride of ammonium is volatilized. The alkali is left behind in the state of chloride, the quantity of which may be very accurately determined. So long as chloride of ammonium is volatilized, the temperature is so low that none of the alkaline chloride can escape. As soon as the ammoniacal salt is driven off, the temperature is moderated, so that the residue in the porcelain crucible does not fuse. After weighing, it is mixed with a fresh quantity of chloride of ammonium and again heated, in order to see whether the weight of the residue remains constant or is diminished, in which latter case the treatment with chloride of ammonium must be repeated. Sometimes, owing to the access of air, the platinum lid is coated with a film of the metallic acid, especially with peroxide of tin when stannates are examined. In this case, the lid, in the subsequent ignition, is covered with a little of the ammoniacal salt.

I will here describe some experiments which have been made by M. Weber:—0·609 grm. of ignited *arseniate of soda*, $2NaO + AsO^5$, afforded, after being once treated with five times the amount of chloride of ammonium, 0·455 grm. chloride of sodium. The weight remained the same after repeating the treatment with chloride of ammonium. The quantity of chloride of sodium corresponds to 35·46 per cent. soda in the salt; the theoretical quantity is 35·18.

1·018 grm. *antimoniate of soda* ($NaO\ SbO^5 + 7HO$), the amount of soda in which, according to Fremy's analysis, is 11·9 per cent., afforded, after five ignitions with chloride of ammonium, a constant weight of 0·429 grm. chloride of sodium, which corresponds to 12·58 per cent. of soda; the salt had been dried for a length of time at 212°, and it is possible that it had lost some of its water of crystallization.

*Stannate of Potash.*—This salt had been precipitated by alcohol from the solution of the peroxide of tin in hydrate of potash, washed with alcohol, then dissolved in water and evaporated. It formed, after drying under the air-pump over sulphuric acid, a gummy mass, which again easily dissolved in water; it contained the *b*-modification of the oxide of tin. According to an examination after the usual method, the salt dried at 212° consisted, in 100 parts, of—

| | | |
|---|---|---|
| 87·34 peroxide of tin | 18·67 oxygen. | |
| 8·02 potash | 1·35 | ... |
| 4·64 water | 4·11 | ... |

According to this the composition of the salt is $KO + 7SnO^2 + 9HO$. The acid metastannate of potash is, according to Fremy, $KO + 6SnO^2 + 5HO$. It is possible therefore that the salt prepared by me contained a quantity of a still more acid salt mixed with it.

Of the salt used for the above analysis, 1·013 grm. was mixed with 5 times the amount of chloride of ammonium and heated to redness; this was repeated twice with smaller quantities of chloride of ammonium, when the weight of the residue no longer varied; 0·131 grm. chloride of potassium was obtained, corresponding to 8·09 per cent. of potash. All the chlorides obtained dissolved entirely in water, and when tested did not exhibit the least trace of the metallic acids. The use, however, of chloride of ammonium in analytical chemistry is not restricted to the compounds above mentioned; it is capable of considerable extension, as I intend to point out in a subsequent paper.—*From the Chemical Gazette for April* 15, 1848.

### ON A REAGENT FOR STRYCHNIA.

In 1843 M. Marchand described the remarkable and perfectly characteristic property possessed by strychnia of giving a magnificent blue colour, passing quickly to violet, and lastly to yellow, when triturated with peroxide of lead, and a few drops of concentrated sulphuric acid, containing $\frac{1}{100}$dth of its weight of nitric acid. Since the period above-mentioned several chemists have examined this reaction, and M. Herzog has proposed to omit the nitric acid as useless; another chemist proposes to substitute peroxide of manganese for peroxide of lead, and M. Otto prefers bichromate of potash to these oxides, which, according to him, gives rise to a much finer violet colour, and to a certain extent this is certainly the case.

M. Marchand proposes certain objections to these omissions and substitutions, and demonstrates that the reagents which he has proposed are the best suited to the purpose.

First, the nitric acid added in the proportion of $\frac{1}{100}$dth to the sulphuric acid is not useless, as stated by M. Herzog; for by its influence the series of colours is produced much more readily and sensibly than when it is omitted. M. Marchand states that he was aware that strychnia yielded a fine blue colour by the action of pure sulphuric acid and peroxide of lead only; but that it is almost impossible to perceive the red and yellow colours, which are readily perceptible in the conditions described by him: and the author adds that he never said or believed, as supposed by M. Herzog, that strychnia, when placed in the circumstances described, might serve as a reagent for nitric acid.

As to the substitution of peroxide of manganese for that of lead, the author has only one objection to make, which is that the salts of manganese sometimes possessing a red colour, there can be no certainty that the series of colours obtained belongs properly to the substance supposed to be strychnia, since one of the reagents employed may itself give rise to one of the colours indicated.

The same is the case with the bichromate of potash recommended by M. Otto. This salt produces by its solution in sulphuric acid a yellow or green colour, and it follows that the series of colours indicated by M. Marchand is diminished by at least one colour, and sometimes by two, the yellow and the red, and consequently the reaction is far from being complete.

The method of employing M. Marchand's process is that of triturating the strychnia with peroxide of lead and concentrated sulphuric acid containing 1 per cent. of nitric acid; by this process the colours obtained are blue, becoming rapidly violet, then gradually red, and lastly, after some hours, it assumes a delicate yellow colour.—*Journ. de Ch. Méd.*, Avril 1848.

### ON THE PRESENCE OF SELENIUM IN THE IODIDE OF POTASSIUM.

M. de Trez, when acting upon a solution of protiodide of mercury and iodide of potassium by acids, perceived a smell of sulphuretted hydrogen during the operation; he subsequently discovered that the smell arose from hydroselenic acid, the odour of which strongly resembles that of hydrosulphuric acid.

The selenium exists in the iodide of potassium in the state of seleniate of potash. To determine the presence of this substance M. de Trez advises an acid to be added to the solution of the iodide, and to receive the gas disengaged in a solution of acetate of lead. The grayish-black precipitate which is formed in this case being collected, washed and dried, is to be introduced into a glass tube, the bent extremity of which is to be immersed in a bottle containing distilled water; through the other end of the tube a current of chlorine gas is to be passed; as soon as the tube is heated by charcoal, a liquid of a deep yellow colour flows into the receiver; this is followed by whitish vapours, which condense in the cool part of the tube, and when this is heated the vapours pass into the receiver, and are dissolved in the water; the liquor then contains selenious acid and hydrochloric acid resulting from the decomposition of the proto- and deuto-chloride of selenium in water.

On the addition of hydrochloric acid, and then sulphite of ammonia, this salt is decomposed by the hydrochloric acid, and the sulphurous acid which is set free precipitates the selenium in the state of a grayish powder, which afterwards becomes yellowish-white.

M. Trez thinks that the seleniate of potash may either have been fraudulently added, or that it was extracted with the iodine.—*Journ. de Ch. Méd.*, Avril 1848.

---

ON TRANSPARENT AND OPAKE ARSENIOUS ACID. BY M. BUSSY.

It is well known that arsenious acid exists in the different states above-mentioned, and also that the transparent variety becomes opake; it has been stated that the former is less soluble in water than the latter. By performing experiments to determine this point, M. Bussy has arrived at the following conclusions:—

1st. That the transparent acid, far from being less soluble than the opake, as stated by several chemists, is, on the contrary, much more so; the difference is nearly as 3 to 1, at the temperature of about $55°$ F.; thus a litre of water which dissolves 40 grammes of the transparent acid dissolves only 12 to 13 grammes of the opake.

2nd. That the transparent acid dissolves much more rapidly than the opake.

3rd. That neither of these acids possesses a perfectly constant degree of solubility.

4th. That the opake acid is converted into the transparent by long-continued boiling in water, that is to say, it acquires the same degree of solubility as the transparent acid, which is such that 100 grammes of acid dissolve in a litre of water at $212°$.

5th. That under the influence of water and a low temperature the transparent is converted into the opake acid.

6th. That the mixture of the two varieties of acid in the same solution explains the anomalies observed in the solubility of arsenious acid.

7th. That division which facilitates the solution of the opake arsenious acid without increasing its solubility, considerably diminishes that of the transparent acid, and to such an extent, that the latter, reduced to fine powder and levigated, is not sensibly more soluble in the cold than the opake acid; this effect undoubtedly results from a transformation which it undergoes, either at the moment of pulverizing, or of its contact with water.

8th. That the acid which has become opake by the slow transformation of the transparent, by the action of ammonia, and the acid crystallized in water, are similarly acted upon by water, and appear to belong to the same variety.

9th. That under the influence of dilute hydrochloric acid, the opake acid dissolves more slowly than the transparent; this circumstance, which modifies the nature of the products formed during solution, explains why the phænomena observed by M. Henri Rose during the crystallization of the transparent acid, are not in general so intense in the solution of the opake acid.

10th. That the difference which has been observed in the action of the two arsenious acids on the tincture of litmus is merely apparent.—*Journ. de Chim. Méd.*, Fevrier 1848.

---

## METEOROLOGICAL OBSERVATIONS FOR MARCH 1848.

*Chiswick.*—March 1. Constant rain: barometer very low. 2. Cloudy and damp. 3. Very fine. 4. Hoar-frost: slight haze. 5. Rain. 6. Cloudy: fine: overcast. 7. Foggy: slight haze: clear. 8. Frosty and foggy: overcast: slight rain. 9. Overcast and mild. 10. Rain: fine: cloudy. 11. Boisterous, with heavy showers. 12. Showery. 13. Cloudy and cold: heavy rain at night. 14. Fine: clear and frosty. 15. Overcast. 16, 17. Rain. 18. Foggy: fine. 19. Foggy: fine: showery. 20. Heavy rain. 21. Hazy and damp: cloudy: showery: clear: frosty at night. 22. Cloudless: boisterous, with rain at night. 23, 24. Cloudy and fine. 25. Uniform haze: cloudy and fine. 26. Overcast: slight rain. 27. Foggy: drizzly. 28. Very fine: rain at night. 29. Hazy and damp: fine. 30. Foggy: slight rain: clear. 31. Hazy: very fine: clear at night.

  Mean temperature of the month ............................... 42°·5
  Mean temperature of March 1847................................ 40·11
  Mean temperature of March for the last twenty years......... 42·8
  Average amount of rain in March .................................. 1·36 inch.

*Boston.*—March 1. Cloudy: rain last night. 2. Cloudy: rain P.M. 3. Fine: rain P.M. 4. Fine. 5. Rain. 6—9. Cloudy. 10, 11. Cloudy: rain A.M. 12. Cloudy: rain A.M. and P.M. 13. Fine: rain P.M. 14, 15. Fine. 16. Rain: rain A.M. and P.M. 17. Cloudy: rain A.M. and P.M. 18. Cloudy. 19. Cloudy: rain P.M. 20. Fine. 21. Rain: rain A.M. and P.M. 22. Fine: rain P.M. 23—25. Cloudy. 26. Cloudy: rain P.M. 27. Cloudy: rain A.M. and P.M. 28. Rain: rain A.M. 29. Cloudy: rain A.M. 30. Fine: rain P.M. 31. Rain.

*Applegarth Manse, Dumfries-shire.*—March 1. Fair, but cloudy and raw. 2, 3. Fair and clear: raw frost A.M. 4. Fair and clear: hard frost A.M.: rain P.M. 5—7. Cloudy, but fair. 8. Fine: wet A.M.: cleared. 9. Rain in the night: cleared P.M. 10. Showers: hail. 11. Frequent showers: hills covered with snow. 12. Clear cold day. 13. Clear cold day: frost A.M.: fine. 14. Frost A.M.: cloudy: rain P.M. 15. Frequent showers. 16. Fair, but chilly. 17. Rain during night: drizzling A.M. 18. Rain early A.M.: fine. 19. Rain and hail: snow P.M. 20. Frost: hail: thaw P.M. 21. Frost: snow on hills: hail. 22. Frost A.M.: heavy rain P.M. 23. Frequent showers. 24. Very fine: warm. 25. Very fine. 26. Rain nearly all day. 27. Very fine. 28. Wet till noon: cleared. 29. Fine: clear: cold. 30. Fine all day: light clouds. 31. Very fine: clear and warm.

  Mean temperature of the month ............................... 41°·2
  Mean temperature of March 1847................................ 42·5
  Mean temperature of March for twenty-five years ...... 39·1
  Mean rain in March for twenty years ..................... 2·35 inches.
  Rain in March 1847 ............................................ 1·27 „

*Sandwick Manse, Orkney.*—March 1. Clear. 2. Clear: cloudy. 3. Clear. 4. Damp. 5. Damp: drops. 6. Damp: cloudy. 7. Cloudy. 8. Showers: clear: aurora. 9. Bright: showers. 10. Clear: hoar-frost. 11. Cloudy: showers. 12. Bright: clear. 13. Clear: hoar-frost. 14. Cloudy: rain. 15. Bright: clear: aurora. 16. Showers. 17. Cloudy: showers. 18. Bright: cloudy. 19. Bright: clear: aurora. 20. Snow: clear: aurora. 21. Clear: frost: cloudy. 22. Clear: cloudy. 23. Rain: drops. 24. Clear: cloudy. 25. Bright: cloudy. 26. Rain. 27. Clear: fog. 28. Fog: rain. 29, 30. Bright: cloudy. 31. Clear: cloudy.

*Meteorological Observations made by* Mr. Thompson *at the Garden of the Horticultural Society at* Chiswick, *near London; by* Mr. Veall, *at* Boston; *by the* Rev. W. Dunbar, *at Applegarth Manse,* Dumfries-shire; *and by the* Rev. C. Clouston, *at Sandwick Manse,* Orkney.

| Days of Month. | Barometer. | | | | | | | Thermometer. | | | | | | | Wind. | | | | Rain. | | | |
|---|---|---|---|---|---|---|---|---|---|---|---|---|---|---|---|---|---|---|---|---|---|---|
| | Chiswick. | | Boston. 8½ a.m. | Dumfries-shire. | | Orkney, Sandwick. | | Chiswick. | | Boston. 8½ a.m. | Dumfries-shire. | | Orkney, Sandwick. | | Chiswick. 1 p.m. | Boston. | Dumfries-shire. | Orkney, Sandwick. | Chiswick. | Boston. | Dumfries-shire. | Orkney, Sandwick. |
| 1848. March. | Max. | Min. | | 9 a.m. | 9 p.m. | 9¼ a.m. | 8½ p.m. | Max. | Min. | | Max. | Min. | 9¼ a.m. | 8½ p.m. | | | | | | | | |
| 1. | 28·907 | 28·637 | 28·39 | 28·68 | 28·83 | 28·82 | 29·14 | 46 | 30 | 40·5 | 44 | 36 | 40 | 40 | sw. | calm | nnw. | e. | ·11 | ·15 | | ·07 |
| 2. | 29·540 | 29·106 | 28·80 | 29·13 | 29·58 | 29·45 | 30·22 | 46 | 36 | 41 | 47 | 34½ | 41 | 40½ | nw. | nw. | n. | n. | ·11 | | | ·35 |
| 3. | 30·064 | 29·870 | 29·54 | 29·88 | 29·93 | 30·43 | 30·34 | 49 | 23 | 40 | 47 | 34½ | 42 | 33 | n. | nw. | n. | e. | ·03 | ·16 | | |
| 4. | 30·122 | 30·000 | 29·77 | 29·94 | 29·73 | 29·85 | 29·69 | 48 | 32 | 36 | 47 | 29½ | 42 | 40½ | s. | calm | sw. | se. | ·04 | | | |
| ● 5. | 29·808 | 29·742 | 29·49 | 29·55 | 29·70 | 29·60 | 29·77 | 42 | 36 | 40 | 47 | 37½ | 41½ | 42 | s. | e. | sw. | s. | ·40 | ·09 | | ·23 |
| 6. | 29·859 | 29·787 | 29·52 | 29·73 | 29·60 | 29·83 | 29·72 | 46 | 28 | 39 | 45½ | 35 | 43 | 39 | nw. | wnw. | sw. | se. | | ·20 | | ·03 |
| 7. | 30·177 | 29·797 | 29·53 | 29·74 | 29·98 | 29·78 | 29·91 | 46 | 22 | 39 | 46 | 35½ | 41 | 40½ | e. | e. | ne. | sw. | | | | |
| 8. | 30·262 | 30·058 | 29·88 | 29·90 | 29·86 | 29·75 | 29·81 | 50 | 41 | 36 | 50 | 38½ | 44½ | 41 | sw. | s. | w. | sw. | ·02 | | 0·50 | ·07 |
| 9. | 29·960 | 29·654 | 29·55 | 29·64 | 29·23 | 29·50 | 29·13 | 53 | 36 | 49 | 51 | 42 | 46 | 42 | w. | wsw. | sw. | sw. | ·01 | | | |
| 10. | 29·449 | 29·391 | 29·00 | 29·10 | 29·10 | 29·21 | 29·07 | 49 | 38 | 41 | 45½ | 36 | 40 | 36 | sw. | s. | wnw. | se. | ·29 | | | ·07 |
| 11. | 28·942 | 28·745 | 28·50 | 28·59 | 28·50 | 28·62 | 28·83 | 47 | 35 | 44 | 45 | 35 | 40½ | 37 | sw. | w. | w. | e. | ·20 | ·22 | | |
| ☽ 12. | 28·909 | 28·697 | 28·34 | 28·10 | 29·04 | 29·03 | 29·25 | 44 | 34 | 42 | 44½ | 36½ | 40 | 38 | nw. | nw. | nnw. | n. | ·07 | ·08 | | ·09 |
| 13. | 29·471 | 29·204 | 28·85 | 29·25 | 29·50 | 29·45 | 29·62 | 44 | 36 | 38 | 47½ | 33½ | 41½ | 34 | nw. | nnw. | nw. | | ·18 | ·10 | | ·07 |
| 14. | 29·874 | 29·758 | 29·44 | 29·69 | 29·60 | 29·61 | 29·44 | 49 | 24 | 41 | 46 | 28½ | 40½ | 39½ | ne. | n. | nw. | w. | | ·04 | | |
| 15. | 29·770 | 29·389 | 29·36 | 29·50 | 29·33 | 29·36 | 29·61 | 52 | 30 | 45 | 46½ | 36½ | 43 | 38 | sw. | s. | wsw. | e. | ·06 | | | ·14 |
| 16. | 29·484 | 29·467 | 29·20 | 29·59 | 29·59 | 29·91 | 29·91 | 44 | 36 | 42 | 47½ | 34½ | 44 | 41 | ne. | n. | ne. | n. | ·26 | ·07 | 1·10 | ·04 |
| 17. | 29·401 | 29·324 | 29·06 | 29·45 | 29·50 | 29·86 | 29·81 | 42 | 36 | 40 | 43½ | 39 | 39½ | 41 | s. | e. | nne. | nne. | ·15 | ·31 | | ·03 |
| 18. | 29·404 | 29·245 | 29·15 | 29·44 | 29·20 | 29·62 | 29·24 | 54 | 27 | 44 | 49 | 38 | 40 | 38 | se. | e. | ne. | se. | | ·08 | | ·08 |
| ○ 19. | 29·174 | 29·035 | 28·82 | 28·91 | 28·74 | 28·93 | 28·81 | 53 | 29 | 40 | 44 | 34 | 42 | 40 | sw. | s. | s. | se. | ·15 | | | |
| 20. | 29·005 | 28·910 | 28·66 | 28·74 | 28·74 | 28·69 | 28·85 | 53 | 30 | 40 | 43 | 29½ | 40 | 37 | sw. | s. | s. | sse. | ·36 | ·02 | | ·62 |
| 21. | 29·448 | 28·726 | 28·50 | 28·88 | 29·15 | 29·07 | 29·22 | 50 | 25 | 43 | 45 | 31½ | 41 | 39½ | w. | se. | ne.,nw | ese. | ·08 | ·36 | | |
| 22. | 29·638 | 29·574 | 29·26 | 29·37 | 29·16 | 29·42 | 29·39 | 56 | 47 | 40 | 46 | 27½ | 41½ | 40 | sw. | w. | ne. | ese. | ·02 | ·06 | | |
| 23. | 29·860 | 29·670 | 29·16 | 29·18 | 29·50 | 29·33 | 29·68 | 58 | 44 | 50 | 50 | 42 | 41½ | 40½ | sw. | sw. | sw. | ne. | | ·09 | 1·70 | ·09 |
| 24. | 30·105 | 29·994 | 29·53 | 29·84 | 30·00 | 30·02 | 30·17 | 55 | 30 | 47·5 | 55½ | 44 | 45½ | 43½ | nw. | w. | ne. | e. | | | | |
| 25. | 30·130 | 30·015 | 29·71 | 30·03 | 29·85 | 30·09 | 29·88 | 55 | 35 | 42·5 | 54 | 35 | 43½ | 42½ | nw. | nw. | se. | sse. | | | | |
| 26. | 29·858 | 29·714 | 29·44 | 29·61 | 29·57 | 29·75 | 29·66 | 54 | 39 | 45 | 49 | 45 | 43 | 42 | sw. | s. | w.-sw. | se. | ·05 | | | ·19 |
| 27. | 29·669 | 29·655 | 29·33 | 29·55 | 29·55 | 29·70 | 29·80 | 57 | 40 | 47 | 47 | 40 | 44 | 39 | sw. | s. | s. | se. | ·24 | ·07 | | ·40 |
| ☾ 28. | 29·813 | 29·731 | 29·33 | 29·50 | ...... | 29·78 | 29·64 | 59 | 41 | 45 | ... | 41 | 45 | 43 | sw. | sw. | se. | ese. | ·21 | ·20 | | ·07 |
| 29. | 29·899 | 29·824 | 29·46 | ...... | 29·60 | 29·69 | 29·54 | 61 | 32 | 46 | 45 | ... | 46½ | 44 | sw. | nw. | s. | s. | | ·30 | | ·10 |
| 30. | 29·831 | 29·760 | 29·40 | 29·60 | 29·65 | 29·56 | 29·72 | 62 | 39 | 50·5 | 56 | 33 | 46 | 44 | s. | sse. | s. | w. | ·01 | | 0·80 | |
| 31. | 29·998 | 29·899 | 29·50 | 29·81 | 29·89 | 29·92 | 29·90 | 71 | 35 | 52 | 63 | 38 | 45 | 42½ | s. | s. | sw. | sse. | | | | ·05 |
| Mean. | 29·672 | 29·492 | 29·21 | 29·410 | 29·440 | 29·536 | 29·573 | 51·45 | 33·74 | 42·8 | 47·9 | 35·9 | 42·40 | 39·95 | | | | | 3·05 | 2·60 | 4·10 | 2·79 |

#  THE LONDON, EDINBURGH AND DUBLIN PHILOSOPHICAL MAGAZINE AND JOURNAL OF SCIENCE.

[THIRD SERIES.]

*JUNE* 1848.

LIV. *On the Decomposition and Dispersion of Light within Solid and Fluid Bodies.* By Sir DAVID BREWSTER, *K.H., D.C.L., F.R.S., and V.P.R.S. Edin.*[*]

[With a Plate.]

HAUY[†], and other mineralogists, observed the two colours which are visible in several varieties of fluor-spar. He regarded the two tints as complementary, and explained them, as he did every other analogous phænomenon, by a reference to the colours of thin plates. In describing a species of dichroism noticed by Dr. Prout[‡] in the purpurates of ammonia and potash, Sir John Herschel ascribes the green reflected light[§] " to some peculiar conformation of the green surfaces producing what may be best termed a *superficial colour,* or one analogous to the colour of thin plates, and striated or dotted surfaces." And he adds—" A remarkable example of such superficial colour, differing from the transmitted tints, is met with in the green fluor of Alston Moor, which, on its surfaces, whether natural or artificial, exhibits in certain lights a *deep blue* tint, not to be removed by any polishing."

Having, many years ago, found the same property in the Derbyshire fluor-spars, I was led to study it with particular attention; and in 1838 I communicated the results of my observations to the British Association at Newcastle[||]. In every specimen in which the colour in question exists, I found it to arise from *internal,* and not from *superficial* reflexion. In an extensive series of experiments on the absorption of light by the aqueous and alcoholic solutions of the colouring matter of plants, I found this property of internal dispersion in thirty or forty of these solutions. The most remarkable of these

[*] From the Edinburgh Transactions, vol. xvi. part 2. Read Feb. 2, 1846.
[†] *Traité de Minéralogie,* tom. i. p. 512, 521.
[‡] Philosophical Transactions, 1818, p. 424.
[§] Treatise on Light, art. 1076.
[||] See Report of the Eighth Meeting, and Trans. of Sections, p. 10–12.

was the alcoholic solution of the colouring matter of the leaves of the common laurel. At first its colour is a bright green, afterwards changing into a fine olive colour; but in all its stages it disperses light of a *brilliant blood-red colour*, which forms a striking contrast with the transmitted tint. After a long exposure to light, the transmitted tint almost wholly disappears, while the dispersed light retains its red colour*. Another very remarkable example of internal dispersion, pointed out to me by Mr. Schunck, is exhibited in an alkaline or in an alcoholic solution of a resinous powder produced from *orcine* by contact with the oxygen of the air. Its colour by transmitted light is reddish brown, and the light which it disperses is of an exceedingly rich *green* colour.

Since these experiments were made, my attention has been called to two interesting papers by Sir John Herschel in the last part of the Philosophical Transactions; the one *on a case of superficial colour presented by a homogeneous liquid internally colourless*, and the other *on the epipolic (or superficial) dispersion of light*; and as these papers contain results incompatible with those which I had previously published, I found it necessary to resume the investigation of the subject.

The two papers now referred to are chiefly occupied with a description of the phænomena of coloured dispersion, as exhibited in a diluted solution of *sulphate of quinine* in weak sulphuric acid. Owing to the solution being nearly colourless by transmitted light, the general phænomenon is very beautiful. The line of bright blue light dispersed by the stratum of fluid immediately beneath the surface of incidence, and about the fiftieth of an inch thick, *appears* to be confined to that stratum; and it is in this respect only that the phænomenon differs from that which is exhibited by fluor-spar and the vegetable solutions which I have mentioned.

### 1. *On the Internal Dispersion of Fluor-Spar.*

There are many varieties of fluor-spar in which no dispersion of the intromitted light takes place. It does not exist in

---

* I showed this experiment in 1836, at Lacock Abbey, to Mr. Fox Talbot, and several members of the British Association. At the meeting of the British Association at Manchester, in 1842, a friend handed to me, in the sectional meeting, a "solution of stramonium in æther," which dispersed a *bright green light*. I described the phænomenon to the meeting, and it is noticed in the Transactions of the Sections, p. 14. Upon making the solution myself, I cannot obtain the same tints, either from the stalk or the dried leaves of the plant. The solution of the leaves disperses a brilliant red tint, like that mentioned in the text. The solution put into my hands must therefore have been one of the seeds of stramonium, or of some other substance possessing internal dispersion in a high degree.

the *yellow*, *red*, and bright *blue* varieties which I have examined. It occurs chiefly in the *green* fluor from Alston Moor, and in several *pink* and *bluish-yellow* varieties from Derbyshire. In order to observe the phænomena of dispersion most distinctly, I transmit a condensed beam of the sun's light through the specimen when partially covered with black wax or black velvet. In some specimens, the intromitted beam is partially dispersed in a fine blue tint from every part of the solid which it traverses; but in other specimens, which are composed of strata of different colours, parallel to the faces of the cube, a very different and a very instructive phænomenon is displayed. The intromitted beam ABC, fig. 1, Plate V., is crossed with bands of dispersed light of different colours and of different intensities. In one case, a *pink* light was dispersed from the stratum close to the surface of incidence; from the next stratum there was *no dispersion* at all; this was followed by a narrow stratum, which dispersed a *bright whitish light*; then succeeded a stratum of non-dispersing fluor, and alternately dispersing and non-dispersing strata, scattering the fine blue light which has already been mentioned.

These results, which I have shown to different persons, are incompatible with those obtained by Sir John Herschel with the very same variety of *fluor-spar*. He regards the blue dispersed light as *strictly* an *epipolic* or *superficial* tint,—so superficial, indeed, "that it might be referred to a peculiar texture of the surface, the result of crystallization, were it not that it appears equally on a surface artificially cut and polished*." Were I to hazard a conjecture respecting the cause of this difference in our results, I would ascribe it to the different degrees of light in which the observations were made. While I used a condensed beam of the sun's light, Sir John Herschel seems to have employed chiefly the ordinary light of day. In studying the phænomena in the solution of quinine, he "exposed it to strong daylight or sunshine;" and in another experiment, which pre-eminently required a powerful illumination, he "directed a sunbeam downwards on the surface, by total reflexion from the base of a prism," which was in reality inferior to the ordinary sun's light. In the case of fluor-spar, however, he states that the epipolic colour is seen in perfection when "exposed to daylight at a window." In such a feeble light I could not have seen the phænomena I have described; and it is owing chiefly to the intensity of the light which I employed, that I have been enabled to place it beyond a doubt that the blue light dispersed by fluor-spar is reflected from every part of the interior of the crystal, and is

* Philosophical Transactions, 1845, p. 143.

not produced by any action either strictly or partially superficial, or solely by any stratum near the surface.

Sir John Herschel mentions that the green fluor-spar of Alston Moor is the only solid in which he has observed an epipolic tint. It is the only mineral in which I have found an internal dispersion, excepting, of course, the minerals which exhibit the analogous phænomena of opalescence and chatoyance; but I have found several glasses which possess it, one in particular of a *yellow* colour, which disperses a *brilliant green* light, and another of a *bright pink* colour, which also disperses a *green* light, and a third of an *orange* colour, which disperses rays of a *whitish-green* colour. In these cases, the glass has a decided colour of its own; but I have found many specimens, both of colourless plate and colourless flint-glass, which disperse a beautiful green light.

### 2. *On the Internal Dispersion of the Solution of Sulphate of Quinine.*

Sir John Herschel describes the epipolic dispersion of this solution as "occupying a very narrow parallelogram, having a breadth of about a fiftieth of an inch, of a vivid and nearly uniform blue colour over its whole breadth*;" but upon "directing a sunbeam downwards on the surface, by total reflexion from the base of a prism, a feeble blue gleam was observed to extend downwards below this vivid line to nearly half an inch from the surface, thus leaving it doubtful whether some small amount of dispersion may not be effected in the interior of the medium at appreciable depths." By using condensed solar light, this doubt is immediately removed, and the phænomenon ranks itself as one of internal dispersion, differing only in the law of its intensity from those which I have already described. In the one the dispersible rays are thrown *gradually*, in the other *quickly*, from the intromitted beam,—a phænomenon to a great extent identical with what takes place in the analogous phænomena of absorption.

If the dispersing action of the solution were rigorously confined to a stratum the fiftieth of an inch thick, it would have followed of necessity, that "*an epipolized beam of light* (meaning thereby a beam which has been once transmitted through a quiniferous solution, and undergone its dispersing action) *is*

---

* The best method of seeing this experiment, is to take the solution into the open air, where the whole light of a blue sky can fall upon its surface. I have in this way seen the blue line perfectly luminous at that stage of a December twilight when there was not light enough to read by. I consider, therefore, the light of the sky as peculiarly susceptible of this species of dispersion.

*incapable of further undergoing epipolic dispersion;*" but as the dispersing action is not thus limited, that conclusion must be incorrect. Sir John Herschel, indeed, has deduced this result from direct experiment with a plate of glass immersed vertically in a quiniferous solution. In this case he could perceive no trace of colour, either at the ingress or egress of the epipolized beam which was incident upon the plate. Sir John does not mention the distance of the plate from the epipolizing stratum. If the distance was small, we are confident, from direct experiment, that the blue tint would have been seen; but if the distance was considerable, then the beam, incident upon the glass, must have been previously shorn of all its dispersible rays.

In examining the blue rays themselves, Sir John found that they consisted of a " small per-centage of rays, extending over a great range of refrangibility." They formed, however, a continuous spectrum deprived of the less refrangible red, nearly of the whole orange, and all the yellow; a rich and broad band of fine green light, slightly fringed with red, passed into a copious indigo and violet without the intermediate blue.

The comparatively feeble light of the dispersed blue rays renders it difficult to ascertain their susceptibility of being a second time dispersed. Sir John Herschel could not obtain any indication of this susceptibility; but we have no doubt that, with condensed light, their second dispersion will be discovered: and we are led to this opinion by the fact, that Sir John believed that the epipolic dispersion takes place in all directions, and therefore expected to discover a second dispersion under circumstances in which, according to my experiments, it could not be found.

Sir John has clearly shown, that the light is dispersed outwards as well as laterally; but as he was conversant only with the phænomena of a narrow blue line, and had not seen the blue cone of rays dispersed from the cone of condensed light, he could not be aware of the changes which take place in its colour while the eye passes from the azimuth of 90° to that of 100°.

These changes are very decided, and will be understood from fig. 2, in which MNOP is a horizontal section of the vessel containing the solution; RR' a beam of solar light incident upon an achromatic lens LL, and condensed into the luminous cone ACB. Now, the blue colour produced by the first stratum, next to the side AB, is exceedingly strong, and that which occupies the rest of the cone ACB comparatively faint. When we view the bright blue stratum in the direction NM, or in the azimuth of 90°, the tint is very brilliant, because the eye receives all the blue rays dispersed by the whole length AB of the stratum; whereas, when we view it in the direction R'C, in the azimuth of 0°, we only see the tint corresponding to the thickness of the stratum. The tint, however, is, in reality, a maximum in the azimuth of 0°, and gradually diminishes till it ceases in the azimuth of 180°, or in the direction CR'.

If we now immerse in the fluid a plate of colourless glass, whose section is DE, so as to receive the beam ABED, we shall find that there is no peculiar dispersion, as Sir John Herschel observed, either at its surface of incidence or emergence. Hence he concluded that the epipolized beam ABED "is incapable of undergoing further epipolic dispersion;" and that having thus "lost a property which it originally possessed, it could not therefore be considered *qualitatively* as the same light."

Now, in using a condensed beam of light, as we have done, we find that the whole cone ABC, even when *two* inches long, and with a December sun, disperses the blue light, and the stratum behind the glass plate DE nearly as much as the stratum before it. In fluor-spar and in the other fluids I have mentioned, this is still more strikingly the case\*, and hence neither of the conclusions drawn by Sir John Herschel are admissible.

The following appear to me to be the deductions which the experiments actually authorize:—

1. A beam of light which has suffered dispersion by the action of a solid or fluid body (that is, an *epipolized* beam), is capable of further undergoing epipolic dispersion, provided the thickness of the medium is not so great as to have dispersed all the dispersible rays.

2. When such a medium is thus rendered incapable of dispersing more light, it is not because it has lost a property which it originally possessed, but because it is deprived of all the dispersible rays which it contained.

It is no doubt an interesting fact, that a small number of differently coloured rays, constituting blue light by their mixture, should possess this property of being dispersed, while

---

\* In one of these experiments, a piece of green fluor from Alston Moor, when immersed in the quiniferous solution, dispersed a fine *violet blue* light, at the distance of *three-fourths* of an inch from its surface. In another experiment, a beam of light that had been dispersed in the solution of quinine, again suffered dispersion at *two inches* distance from the surface of a piece of Derbyshire fluor.

A beam of light that has passed through the esculine solution disperses blue light, but not copiously, when transmitted through the quinine solution; but the beam that has passed through quinine is copiously dispersed when transmitted through esculine.

other rays of the same refrangibility are either less dispersible, or apparently indispersible, by the same medium; but the fact will appear less surprising and anomalous when we advert to certain phænomena of absorption in which the same property is displayed.

The difference between the *absorption* and the *internal dispersion* of light is simply this. In the one case the portion of light withdrawn from the intromitted beam is *extinguished* and *invisible*, and in the other *dispersed* and *visible*; and we may compare the two classes of phænomena, by *supposing* that the light extinguished by absorption is rendered visible as if by dispersion. Now it is a remarkable fact, that almost the whole of the blue light absorbed by the mineral called *native orpiment* is extinguished during the passage of the light through the first stratum, whose thickness is less than the fiftieth of an inch; and hence it is that the thinnest slice of this substance has nearly as deep a yellow colour as the thickest. Were the absorbed blue rays to become visible by dispersion, we should actually see a more striking example of epipolism, or dispersion confined to the first stratum, than in the quiniferous solution. Even the condensation of the beam would not in this case give us a blue cone of light.

The analysis of the blue line, indeed, would indicate a difference between the two phænomena. It would show that the blue light was derived chiefly from the *violet, indigo*, and *blue* spaces, and but partially from the *green, yellow, orange* and *red*, having appropriated the whole of the more refrangible rays, and but a very small portion of the less refrangible ones; whereas the blue light from the quiniferous solution is derived almost in equal proportions from all the coloured spaces excepting the least refrangible, red. The limitation of the rays capable of absorption, like the limitation of the dispersible rays in the quiniferous solution, is shown in the action of various bodies on the spectrum. Such bodies change the colour of certain spaces in the spectrum, without continuing to absorb the residual rays; that is, when the absorbable rays are removed by a certain thickness of the body, an additional thickness operates very feebly, as in the quiniferous solution, in altering the colour of the residual beam.

I have pointed out these analogies between the phænomena of absorption and dispersion to meet the case of the bright blue line in the quiniferous solutions. The dispersion of fluor-spar, and of the glasses and vegetable solutions already described, is of a different character. In fluor-spar the dispersion effected by the first stratum is by no means very abundant; and the intromitted beam, even after passing through one or more undispersing strata, is dispersed nearly as copiously as before. In the glasses and in the vegetable solutions there are no peculiarities which require explanation, excepting those which arise from the absorption of the dispersed beam in passing through the coloured medium.

When the phænomena of internal dispersion are exhibited in coloured fluids and solids, the influence of absorption upon the dispersed light is very interesting. Previous to its dispersion, the light has the same colour as the transmitted light; were it to emerge at that point of its path, and when viewed at an azimuth above $90°$, a portion of the dispersed light has that colour. The quantity of light possessing this colour increases between the azimuth of $90°$ and $180°$. In order to see this effect disembarrassed from another influence, we must make the intromitted beam parallel to the surface of the fluid or solid, so as just to graze it. In this way the dispersed light is not changed in its passage to the eye after dispersion. When the beam passes through the coloured medium without this precaution, it again suffers absorption proportional to the thickness of the coloured substance through which it has passed, and sometimes disappears altogether. This effect is finely seen in the darker solutions, which disperse a brilliant *red*, or a brilliant *green* light; the colour of the former becoming *yellowish-green* and *whitish*, while that of the latter becomes *whitish-yellow*.

### 3. *On the Polarization of Dispersed Light.*

As the dispersed light is turned from its path by reflexion, and is reflected at angles proper for polarizing it, its partial polarization at least might have been anticipated. Sir John Herschel viewed it through a tourmaline, and states that no signs of polarization were perceived in it; but his method of obtaining the blue line from light diverging from a large area of the sky, and therefore reflected at various angles far above and far below the polarizing angle, rendered it impracticable to detect its state of polarization. The method which I adopted, of using a narrow cylindrical beam of strong light, affording a bright dispersed beam more than an inch in length, enabled me to discover its polarization, and to investigate its peculiarities.

Upon examining the blue beam in the quiniferous solution with an analysing rhomb of calcareous spar, I found that a considerable part of it, consisting chiefly of the less refrangible portion of its rays, was polarized in the plane of reflexion; while the more refrangible of its rays, constituting an intensely blue beam, had a different state of polarization.

This insulation of the bluer rays greatly increased the beauty of the phænomenon, and promised to throw some light upon its cause. I was therefore anxious to ascertain their state of polarization, which was not indicated by the analysing rhomb.

With this view I transmitted through the solution a strong beam of polarized light, and was surprised to find that the blue beam, which it yielded by dispersion, retained the same intensity in every position of the analysing prism, and therefore possesses a *quaquaversus* polarization, such as that which light receives when transmitted through a congeries of minute doubly refracting crystals, having their axes in all possible directions.

In making the same experiment with other dispersing fluids and solids, I found some in which the whole beam was completely polarized in the plane of reflexion, and others in which it exhibited solely a *quaquaversus* polarization; but as these experiments indicate new processes in the decomposition and polarization of light, which require a more extended analysis, I shall resume the subject in a separate communication, contenting myself at present with a general account of the more important facts, and the results to which they lead.

Having transmitted a condensed beam of light through an alcoholic solution of the leaves of the common laurel, or of tea, either green or black, I found that the *bright red beam* which it dispersed, possessed, like the *blue* one in the quiniferous solution, a *quaquaversus* polarization, a small portion of the light being polarized in the plane of reflexion. The *green* beam dispersed by the preparation of *orcine* has the same properties, the white portion of it disappearing and reappearing during the revolution of the analysing rhomb. In the aqueous solution of *esculine*\*, the dispersed pencil consists of two finely-contrasted pencils; the one *whitish* and polarized in the plane of reflexion, and the other a *very deep blue*, having *quaquaversus* polarization. The *white* pencil is more intense than the *blue* one, which is the very reverse of what takes place in the solution of quinine. The alcoholic solution of the seeds of the *Colchicum autumnale* gives a bright and copious *green* beam of dispersed light, which consists of two pencils, one whitish and polarized in the plane of reflexion, and the other bright green, with a *quaquaversus* polarization. The same property is possessed by a solution of *guaiacum* in alcohol, which disperses, by the stratum chiefly near its surface, a beautiful *violet* light; and also by an alcoholic solution of *sulphate of strychnine*, which disperses a green light, *after it has*

\* In the alcoholic solution of esculine, the *faint-blue* approaches to *violet*. The polarization is like that in quinine.

stood for some days. The same property is possessed by almost all the oils, in some of which the dispersed light is exceedingly beautiful, varying from a pale green to a blue tint.

The polarization of the dispersed beam in one plane, namely in the plane of reflexion, is exhibited in several fluids and solids. It is very marked in the bile of the ox, which disperses an olive-green light; in a solution of gum-myrrh in alcohol diluted with water, which disperses a bright white beam; and in an orange-coloured glass, which disperses a pale greenish beam.

In many fluid solutions, the beam with a *quaquaversus* polarization is very intense, when compared with the faint pencil which is polarized in the plane of reflexion; but in a specimen of *yellow Bohemian glass*, which gives a copious and brilliant *green* beam by dispersion, the whole of the beam possesses a *quaquaversus* polarization.

When we view the dispersed beam in different azimuths, some very interesting phænomena present themselves to our notice. In general, the colour of the dispersed light suffers a considerable change, passing, between the azimuths of 90° and 180°, from the colour of the dispersed beam to the colour of the transmitted beam. This effect is finely seen in the alcoholic solution of tea, where the brilliant *red* light passes into an *olive* tint; but it is still more remarkable in a mixture of *prussian blue* and water. The dispersed beam is polarized in the plane of reflexion. It is *bluish* in the azimuth of 90°; *pinkish* about the azimuth of 100°; *greenish* in that of 120°; *bluish* in azimuth 150°; and again *pinkish* in azimuth 170°. These three last tints may be all seen at the same time.

Such are the general phænomena of internal dispersion, a subject which promises to throw some light on the constitution of those solid and fluid bodies by which it is produced. The *apparently superficial dispersion* in the quinine solution, to which Sir John Herschel has given the name of *epipolism*, is obviously a single case of the general phænomenon, in which the ordinates of the curve of dispersion diminish rapidly after the light has entered the stratum nearest the surface; while the *real epipolism*, which he ascribes to fluor-spar, so far from being an action of the surface, is much less so than that of the quiniferous solution, and entirely similar in its character to that which is produced by the fluids and solids which I have examined.

The phænomenon of internal dispersion, when considered merely as a case of reflexion and polarization, possesses much novelty and interest. If the exciting beam, as we may call it, is cylindrical, we have before us an experiment, in which the phænomena of *cylindrical reflexion* and *cylindrical polariza-*

*tion* are at once exhibited to us. The innumerable reflecting surfaces, receiving the intromitted beam at all possible angles, reflect the incident light in all possible directions, so that the eye, wherever it is placed, sees the beam as if it were self-luminous; and while the eye is made to revolve in a circle round the cylindrical beam, it receives a pencil of polarized light—polarized in a plane passing through the eye and the axis of the cylinder; or, what is the same thing, a thousand spectators viewing this beam in the same azimuth, but in directions differently inclined to the horizon, would all see exactly the same phænomena of reflexion and polarization!

4. *On the Causes of the Internal Decomposition and Dispersion of Light.*

In imperfectly crystallized minerals, such as particular specimens of *adularia, chrysoberyl, opal* and *sapphire*, the white and coloured opalescence, and the asterial radiations, have been shown to arise from minute vacuities, or from open spaces with crystallized sides, or from narrow pipes, or linear spaces parallel to the edges of the primitive or secondary forms of the mineral. In tabasheer, where the vacuities contain air, which we can expel and send back at pleasure, a fine blue light is dispersed, depending no doubt on the size of the vacuities. In a very remarkable specimen of calcareous spar, crowded with hemitrope veins, I have observed a copious internal dispersion produced by the reflexion of light at the different surfaces, which, though in optical contact, have different degrees of extraordinary refraction.

All these phænomena, however, are essentially different from those which form the subject of this paper, with the exception of the phænomena of fluor-spar, in so far at least as they are the result of imperfect crystallization. The *epipolism* which Sir John Herschel ascribes to this mineral, or its *internal dispersion*, according to my experiments, does not belong to the species, but only to particular varieties, and not even to the variety, but merely to particular parts of it; it is therefore the result of unequal or imperfect crystallization. The nucleus is perfect, a coating supervenes, having a different tint by transmitted light, and dispersing a fine blue light, and so on through a succession of strata, dispersing differently coloured lights, and separated by non-dispersing spaces. An extraneous element, therefore, depending on the state of the solution, has been successively introduced into the crystal; and if it had the same refractive and dispersive power as the fluor-spar, it could not reflect any portion of the intromitted beam. But if there is any difference in the mean refraction, or in the dispersive power, or if the difference consists merely in the unequal length of certain portions of the two spectra, then in all these cases light will be dispersed by the extraneous element. If, for example, we place a film of oil of cassia between two prisms of flint glass, the light reflected from the film will be *blue*. The index of refraction for certain of the *red* rays is the same in the glass and in the oil, and consequently none of these rays enter into the reflected pencil, which must therefore be *blue*, whatever be the inclination of the incident rays. If we now suppose this film of oil to be solidified, and disseminated in infinitely small atoms through flint glass, or a fluid that has the same action as the glass upon light, we should have the phænomenon of a blue dispersion*.

A beam of blue light thus produced should be polarized at the polarizing angle, and partially polarized at other angles; and if this is not its character, we must look for some cause by which it has been counteracted. We have already seen that, in the Bohemian yellow glass, none of the light is polarized by reflexion; and that in the quiniferous solution only a part of it is so polarized, the whole pencil in the one case, and the residual pencil in the other, having a *quaquaversus* polarization. This effect cannot be the result of an opposite polarization by the refraction of the dispersed light at the surfaces of the reflecting particles, because such an action would only reduce the amount of polarization by reflexion; and I have found by direct experiment, namely, by making the blue light pass through different thicknesses of the fluid, that such an effect is not produced. Unless, therefore, we suppose that this *quaquaversus* polarization is a new property of light, produced by a peculiar action of certain solid and fluid bodies, we are driven to the conclusion, no less remarkable, that it is produced by an infinite number of doubly refracting crystals, having their axes of double refraction lying in every possible direction, and therefore reflecting from their posterior surfaces a pencil of light with *quaquaversus* polarization.

St. Leonard's College, St. Andrews,
January 30, 1846.

* In the experiment with *prussian blue*, which is a very splendid one, the particles are mechanically suspended in the water; so that we have here an ocular demonstration that the particles are the cause of the dispersion and the *quaquaversus* polarization.

LV. *Remarks on a Paper by the* Rev. Brice Bronwin, *On the Solution of a particular Differential Equation.* By GEORGE BOOLE, *Esq.*

*To the Editors of the Philosophical Magazine and Journal.*

GENTLEMEN,

THE current Number (April) of the Philosophical Magazine contains a paper by the Rev. Brice Bronwin, On the Solution of a particular Differential Equation, upon which I beg leave to offer a few remarks. Mr. Bronwin is pleased to consider his researches as supplementary to an investigation of my own, which was published in the Cambridge Mathematical Journal, New Series, Jan. 1847, and he is led by them to dispute the accuracy of certain conclusions at which I had arrived. My immediate design in the present communication, is to show that these conclusions are, on the contrary, perfectly lawful; but in doing this, I must ask permission to make such accompanying observations as may render it unnecessary for me to trouble you, under any circumstances, with another letter on the subject.

It will not be irrelevant to premise, that the original design of my investigation was to integrate the equation of Laplace's functions in such a form as would permit the calculation of their actual values. This object I had previously attempted by a method which I have given in the Philosophical Transactions for 1844, part 2, On a General Method in Analysis. That method is founded on the proposition, that every linear differential equation and every linear equation in finite differences, whose coefficients are rational functions of $x$, can be reduced to the form

$$f_0\pi(x)u + f_1(x)\rho u + f_2(x)\rho^2 u \ldots = X, \quad \ldots \quad (1.)$$

$\pi$ and $\rho$ being operative functions, which satisfy the conditions

$$\pi\rho u = \rho(\pi+1)u, \quad f(\pi)\rho^m = f(m)\rho^m.$$

It may be mentioned, that the integrable forms of a differential equation of this description can be determined in various cases, and especially in this, viz. when the equation has but two terms in its first member. Now the equation of Laplace's functions, treated according to the above method, was found to have three terms in its first member; nor was it included in those other forms of the same kind, the integrability of which I had at that time ascertained.

It occurred to me, therefore, to devise an analogous form of the differential equation, in which the operating symbol $\pi$ should be replaced by two symbols $\pi_m$, $\pi_n$, and I was led to consider the equation

$$\pi_m \pi_n u + q\rho u = 0, \quad \ldots \ldots \quad (2.)$$

in which $\pi_m$, $\pi_n$, and $\rho$ satisfy the conditions

$$\pi_m \rho u = \rho \pi_{m+1} u, \quad \pi_n \rho u = \rho \pi_{n+1} u$$
$$\pi_m \pi_n u = \pi_n \pi_m u + a(n-m)\rho u$$

(Mr. Bronwin has changed $\rho$ into $\lambda$ and $q$ into $p$). Of the above equation I assigned two complete forms of solution, and I showed that Laplace's equation might be treated as a very particular example of the more general problem thus introduced. But at this stage of the inquiry, a transformation suggested itself to me by which Laplace's equation was made to satisfy the condition to which I had previously failed to subject it. This led to a resumption of the prior method, and to the complete accomplishment of all that I at first contemplated (Cambridge Mathematical Journal, New Series, vol. i. p. 10). It led also to the abandonment of any further researches on the equation (2.). What had been accomplished was, however, published in the same journal, Jan. 1847. It is this unfinished episode in the investigation, if I may be allowed the expression, which Mr. Bronwin has undertaken to complete; and it is to the correction of some misapprehensions which I venture to think that he has formed as to the principles upon which such investigations are to be conducted, that I am here desirous of contributing.

Mr. Bronwin rightly apprehends that the solution of the general equation

$$\pi_m \pi_n u + q\rho u = X$$

would be

$$u = \pi_{m+1} \pi_{m+2} \cdots \pi_{m+r} \pi_n^{-1} \pi_{m+r}^{-1} \pi_{m+r-1}^{-1} \cdots \pi_m^{-1} X; \quad . \quad (3.)$$

but he conceives that I have erred in rejecting the inverse factors

$$\pi_{m+r-1}^{-1} \pi_{m+r-2}^{-1} \cdots \pi_m^{-1}$$

in the particular case of $X=0$. He asserts that it is always necessary to retain such inverse factors, and to determine the values of the arbitrary constants by final substitution in the original equation; and he adduces, by way of illustration, the equation

$$(1-x^2)\frac{d^2u}{dx} + p(p-1)u = 0.$$

There are here involved, if I am not deceived, both a false analogy and an erroneous principle. First, the equation adduced is not analogous to the one which was under consideration, and it is not solved by an analogous process. The relative position of the direct and the inverse factors of operation in the one case, is the reverse of what it is in the other.

Secondly, it is quite within the province of theory to determine how the superfluous constants of the solution of a differential equation shall be disposed of,—to decide which of the operating factors *must* be retained, and which of them *may* be rejected. It was upon a theoretical consideration that I decided upon placing certain elements of the solution at which I arrived, in the latter class; but instead of enforcing that consideration here, I prefer to prove the correctness of the conclusion to which it led me, by exhibiting the result in a purely quantitative form. It will be interesting to show how, in a case of more than ordinary difficulty, the conclusions of theory may be practically verified. For the laws which govern the application of the inverse factors, in connexion with the more general method already adverted to, I must refer, in illustration of the above remarks, to the original memoir in the Philosophical Transactions, p. 249.

Let us then first consider the solution

$$u = \pi_{m+1} \pi_{m+2} \cdots \pi_{m+r} \pi_n^{-1} \pi_{m+r}^{-1} \cdots \pi_m^{-1} 0, \quad \quad (4.)$$

in which all the factors are retained.

Since $\pi_0 \rho = \rho \pi_1$, we have $\pi_1 = \rho^{-1} \pi_0 \rho$, and by induction, $\pi_m = \rho^{-m} \pi_0 \rho^m$, from which we readily obtain

$$\pi_{m+1} \pi_{m+2} \cdots \pi_{m+r} = \rho^{-m} \rho^{-1} \pi_0 \rho^{-1} \pi_0 \cdots \rho^{m+r} = \rho^{-m} (\rho^{-1} \pi_0)^r \rho^{m+r}.$$

Again, since $\pi_a = \rho^{-a} \pi_0 \rho^a$, we have on inversion

$$\pi_n^{-1} = \rho^{-n} \pi_0^{-1} \rho^n.$$

Lastly, reducing in this way the remaining inverse factors, we have

$$\pi_{m+r}^{-1}, \pi_{m+r-1}^{-1} \cdots \pi_m^{-1} = \rho^{-(m+r)} (\pi_0^{-1} \rho)^{r+1} \rho^{m-1};$$

and substituting these forms in the general solution, there results

$$u = \rho^{-m} (\rho^{-1} \pi_0)^r \rho^{m+r-n} \pi_0^{-1} \rho^{-(m+r-n)} (\pi_0^{-1} \rho)^{r+1} \rho^{m-1}. \quad (5.)$$

Now the forms of $\pi_0$ and $\rho$ employed in my paper were

$$\pi_0 = \phi(t) \frac{d}{dt}, \quad \rho = \phi(t),$$

in which

$$\phi(t) = \frac{at^2}{2} + bt + c.$$

Hence we have

$$\rho^{-1} \pi_0 = \frac{d}{dt}, \quad \pi_0^{-1} \rho = \left(\frac{d}{dt}\right)^{-1},$$

and substituting

$$u = \{\phi(t)\}^{-m}\left(\frac{d}{dt}\right)^r \{\phi(t)\}^{m-r-n}\left(\frac{d}{dt}\right)^{-1}\phi'(t)^{-m+r-n-1}\frac{d}{dt}^{-r+1}0$$

$$= \phi(t)^{-m}\left(\frac{d}{dt}\right)^r \{\phi(t)\}^{m-r-n}\left(\frac{d}{dt}\right)^{-1}\phi'(t)^{-m+r-n-1}\Sigma c_\lambda t^\lambda, \quad (6.)$$

$c_0, c_1$, &c. being arbitrary constants, and the summation denoted by $\Sigma$ extending from $\lambda = 0$ to $\lambda = r$. And a little attention to the above result will show that it may be written thus,

$$u = \{\phi'(t)\}^{-m}\left(\frac{d}{dt}\right)^r x,$$

when $x$ is the complete integral of the differential equation

$$\phi'(t)\frac{d}{dt}w - (m+r-n)\phi''(t)w = \Sigma c_\lambda t^\lambda.$$

In this equation let us replace $\phi'(t)$ by its value $\dfrac{at^2}{2} + bt + c$, and integrate the result in a series. We shall thus find

$$w = A_0 + A_1 t + A_2 t^2 + A_3 t^3 + \&c., \quad \ldots \quad (7.)$$

$A_0$ being a new arbitrary constant, and the remaining coefficients determined by a law whose expression is

$$A_p = \frac{c_{p-1} - b(p-m-r+n-1)A_{p-1} - a\left(\dfrac{p}{2} - m - r + n - 1\right)A_{p-2}}{cp} \quad (8.)$$

Now since the values of $c_{p-1}$ range from $c_0$ to $c_r$, i. e. from $p=1$ to $p=r+1$, after which they vanish, it follows from the above that the values of $A_p$ will be arbitrary up to $A_{r+1}$, after which they will be formed from the preceding coefficients by a law whose expression is

$$A_p = -\frac{b(p-m-r+n-1)A_{p-1} + a\left(\dfrac{p}{2} - m - r + n - 1\right)A_{p-2}}{cp} \quad (9.)$$

Now

$$u = \left(\frac{at^2}{2} + bt + c\right)^{-m}\left(\frac{d}{dt}\right)^r w.$$

When, moreover, the operation $\left(\dfrac{d}{dt}\right)^r$ is performed upon the successive terms of $w$, the first $r$ terms will vanish, and we shall have

$$u = \left(\frac{at^2}{2} + bt + c\right)^{-m}\left\{A_r \frac{\Gamma(r+1)}{\Gamma(1)} + A_{r+1}\frac{\Gamma(r+2)t}{\Gamma(2)} + A_{r+2}\frac{\Gamma(r+3)t^2}{\Gamma(3)}\ldots\right\} \quad (10.)$$

the two first coefficients of the bracketed series being arbitrary and independent, and the remaining coefficients formed from these according to a general law of successive derivation. It is thus seen that the performance of the direct operations $\pi_{m+1}\pi_{m+2}\ldots\pi_{m+r}$ has caused the virtual disappearance of the superfluous arbitrary constants introduced by the performance of the operations which are inverse.

Let us now consider the solution given in the Mathematical Journal, viz.
$$u = \pi_{m+1}\pi_{m+2}\ldots\pi_{m+r}\pi_n^{-1}\pi_{m+r}^{-1}\,0.$$
Effecting, as before, the requisite reductions, we successively get
$$u = \rho^{-m}(\rho^{-1}\pi_0)^r \rho^{m+r-n}\pi_0^{-1}\rho^{-(m+r-n)}\pi_0^{-1}\rho^{m+r}0$$
$$= \{\varphi(t)\}^{-m}\left(\frac{d}{dt}\right)^r \varphi(t)^{m+r-n}\left(\frac{d}{dt}\right)^{-1}\{\varphi(t)\}^{-(m+r-n)-1}\left(\frac{d}{dt}\right)^{-1}0$$
$$= \{\varphi(t)\}^{-m}\left(\frac{d}{dt}\right)^r w,$$
where $w$ is the complete integral of the differential equation
$$\left(\frac{at^2}{2} + bt + c\right)\frac{dw}{dt} - (m+r-n)(at+b)w = c_0.$$
Integrating this equation in a series, we have
$$w = A_0 + A_1 t + A_2 t^2 + \&c., \quad \ldots \quad (11.)$$
where $A_0$ is a new arbitrary constant, and the remaining coefficients are determined by the law (8.), provided that we regard $c_{p-1}$ as vanishing for every value of $p$ except $p=1$. Here, then, the coefficients $A_0\,A_1$ must be considered arbitrary, and the remaining coefficients as formed from these in subjection to the law (9.). Hence
$$\begin{aligned}u &= \left(\frac{a}{2}t^2 + bt + c\right)^{-m}\left(\frac{d}{dt}\right)^r w \\ &= \left(\frac{a}{2}t^2 + bt + c\right)^{-m}\left\{A_r\frac{\Gamma(r+1)}{\Gamma(1)} + A_{r+1}\frac{\Gamma(r+2)t}{\Gamma(2)}\right. \\ &\quad \left. + A_{r+2}\frac{\Gamma(r+3)t^2}{\Gamma(3)}\ldots\right\}\end{aligned} \quad (12.)$$

The two first coefficients of the bracketed series being distinct functions of the arbitrary and independent constants $A_0\,A_1$, are themselves arbitrary and independent, and the remaining coefficients are derived from these according to the same continuous law as are the coefficients of the former solution. The two solutions therefore agree; and the rejection of the inverse factors $\pi_{m+r-1}^{-1}\pi_{m+r-2}^{-1}\ldots\pi_m^{-1}$ in the symbolical solution (4.) does not at all affect the final issue.

After this it is scarcely necessary to observe, that the solution (3.) is also general and not particular; and that while the arbitrary constants introduced by the inverse factors $\pi_n^{-1}\pi_{m+r}^{-1}$

*must* be retained, those which are introduced by the other inverse factors may indifferently be retained or rejected. There are two or perhaps three distinct fallacies in Mr. Bronwin's reasonings on these points; but the remarks already offered,—offered, I trust, in no captious spirit,—may be deemed sufficient.

It is indeed with sincere pleasure that I quit a topic, upon which, had my reputation alone been concerned, I would willingly have been spared the necessity of writing, and acknowledge that upon some other points Mr. Bronwin has added to the completeness of the investigation. To each of the two cases already determined, he has added another form of solution; and the value which he has assigned to $\pi_m$, though not *quite* the most general*, is much more general than the one which I had contented myself with employing.

It is further but just to Mr. Bronwin to remark, that in questions like that which he has undertaken to examine, far more than the ordinary caution which the mathematician is bound to exercise appears to be demanded. A settled conviction that there is no anomaly which may not be explained, no exception but which may and which ought to be referred to some governing principle, with the corresponding habit of patient research and cautious inference, is essential to the success of this class of speculations. Dismissing, however, the more immediate subject of these comments, I cannot but observe upon the fact as somewhat remarkable, that in pure mathematics, controversy and misunderstanding should be so rife, as for some years they appear to have been. It would, I conceive, be interesting to inquire into the causes of a state of things which, judging *à priori*, we should so little expect. One reason is undoubtedly to be found in the unmeasured capabilities of the modern analysis for the expression of general theorems, and in the practically frequent employment of analogy and induction, especially as suggestive aids, in contradistinction to the purely deductive processes and more limited conclusions of the ancient geometry. But it may be doubted whether this is a sufficient explanation of the fact in question. A far more influential cause is, I believe, to be found in the almost entire absence of any direct study of the laws of correct reasoning in connexion with the practical discipline of modern science. But this is a topic which I do not venture upon the present occasion more fully to discuss.

I remain, Gentlemen,
Your obedient faithful Servant,

Lincoln, April 8, 1848.
GEORGE BOOLE.

* Even *of the kind*; there also exists, as I discovered shortly after publishing the original paper, another value of a quite distinct kind.

LVI. *Geometry and Geometers.* Collected by T. S. DAVIES, Esq., F.R.S. and F.S.A.

No. I.

THERE are many interesting scraps of minor information respecting Mathematics and its cultivators, contained in letters and stray papers, which it is desirable to preserve; either as affecting the characters of the men or explaining the circumstances attending their discoveries and publication. A few such have fallen in my way at different times; and if you think them adapted to the pages of your Magazine, I shall now and then send a few, as you can find room for them.

I shall in all cases state the sources of my information, and where the documents are deposited; so that the extracts may be hereafter verified by any one who shall feel desirous of doing so. Possibly some of your readers who may take an interest in the minutiæ of scientific history, may be induced also to contribute anything of a similar kind that may fall in their way.

My first set of extracts will be made from a series of letters addressed by different mathematicians to the celebrated publisher, John Nourse of the Strand, which were placed in my hands by Mr. Maynard (of Earl's Court, Leicester Square), and which, when fully examined, will be returned to him. Meanwhile, he has allowed me to make this or any other use of them that I may think proper.

These letters place Nourse in a very estimable light as a liberal patron of mathematical authors; and they prove that he was well-versed in the science in which he principally dealt—not " the mere merchant of other men's brains."

Amongst the letters are twenty-seven from Dr. Robert Simson, commencing in 1751 and terminating in 1768, the year before the Doctor's death. They mainly relate to the *Euclide* and the *Loci Plani*. From these I shall send a few extracts for your next number; for as this introductory notice will take up some space, there would scarcely be room in the present one. On this account, I shall now give a copy of a letter from the son of the great MacLaurin to Nourse, respecting one of those vulgar attempts to render eminent men ridiculous (even where there was not the least ground for the story) which were so common in the last century. Even within the last few months this story has been repeated in one at least (probably in more) of our periodicals. Most likely the story was originally a hoax upon Goldsmith.

" Edinburgh, 23rd December, 1775.

" SIR,—As I see from the title-page of Goldsmith's History

of the Earth that you are the publisher of that work, and as the author is dead, to you I must complain of a most injurious though not scandalous misrepresentation of my deceased father, which is to be found in it, vol. ii. p. 91. There t'other day happening accidentally to take up the book, I to my astonishment read the following passage:—'For one person to yawn is sufficient to set all the rest of the company a yawning. A ridiculous instance of this was *commonly* practised upon the famous MacLaurin, one of the Professors at Edinburgh. He was very subject to have his jaw dislocated, so that when he opened his mouth wider than ordinary, or when he yawned, he could not shut it again. In the midst of his harangues, therefore, if any of his pupils began to be tired of his lecture, he had only to gape or yawn and the Professor instantly caught the sympathetic affection, so that he thus continued to stand speechless, with his mouth wide open, till his servant from the next room was called in to set his jaw again.'

"Nothing, Sir, can be more ridiculous and more contemptuous than this description, at the same time nothing can be more false, as hundreds of the most respectable persons in England can attest. Mr. MacLaurin had no such defect, nor indeed any defect at all in his person, being (what scarce any other philosopher hitherto has been) a man of a handsome person, elegant manners, and graceful delivery. It is very hard therefore that he should be thus held forth as an object of laughter and contempt in a book which, from the nature of the subject and supposed merit of the author, will probably reach posterity, and be dispersed thro' the World in different translations.

"I think I would be wanting in duty to my father were I to pass over this insult to his memory without animadversion. In what manner I shall contradict and resent it I have not yet determined, but I thought it my duty to inform you as soon as I knew of it. You, Sir, are a stranger to me, but as you are, I understand, a gentleman of eminence and character in your profession, I cannot doubt that you will immediately give the necessary orders for checking the further propagation of this falsehood, and repairing as far as is possible the injury that has been already done. The love of truth and respect for the deceased will, I am persuaded, prompt you to do so. I shall expect to hear from you, and am, Sir,

"Your most obedient Humble Servant,
"Jo. MacLaurin.

"Direct for me to Mr. John MacLaurin, Advocate, Edinburgh."

The letter itself appears (from the folding) to have been placed in a cover, and there is no superscription or direction. Though, therefore, I have supposed that it was addressed to Nourse, I have no other ground for such an opinion than that it was found amongst a mass of letters which were so addressed. My own impression is that Andrew Millar was the early publisher of Goldsmith's work, though I have no means of consulting a copy of a date antecedent to this letter. There are, at all events, no other letters to Millar amongst these: and the chief difficulty is to conjecture how a letter addressed to one publisher should get amongst those of his neighbour; especially as no very friendly feeling existed between the publishers, nor much of sympathy between the scientific and literary classes of that period.

Royal Military Academy,
   February 15, 1849.

---

LVII. *On certain Researches of* Murphy. *By* JAMES COCKLE, *Esq., M.A. of Trinity College, Cambridge, and Barrister-at-Law of the Middle Temple* [*].

AT page 129 of a memoir referred to below[†], Murphy has given a rule by means of which we may express in the form of a series a root of any equation containing only positive and integer powers of the unknown quantity. In this memoir there is no allusion to any prior discovery of the rule; and Murphy subsequently[‡] refers to the process without mention of any other writer in connexion with it, and appears to regard himself as its originator. The rule seems to have been hitherto attributed to him[§], and I have fallen into the same error at page 363 of the present volume of this Journal[‖]. It

---

[*] Communicated by the Author.
[†] On the Resolution of Algebraic Equations. Published at pp. 126-153 of vol. iv. of the Transactions of the Cambridge Philosophical Society. See more particularly section 1, pp. 129-133.
[‡] Camb. Phil. Trans., vol. iv. p. 355. See also Murphy's Theory of Equations, p. 77, commencement of article (62.). It is to this article (pp. 77-82) of Murphy's work that I ought to have made reference *supra*, page 363.
[§] See Dr. Peacock's Report on Analysis (to the British Association, Meeting of 1833), p. 350.
[‖] Among the defects of my paper here referred to, are the having omitted to make mention of the name of Vandermonde, the great rival of Lagrange in the department of science there discussed, and also of Simpson's (subsidiary) and Professor J. R. Young's (indirect) solution of a biquadratic. And Mr. Davies has requested me to say, that from the haste with which his notes on my paper were written, he omitted to refer to a very neat and elegant

will however be found that Lagrange had long before arrived at the same result. In his memoir cited below*, the last-mentioned illustrious analyst expresses the root of such an equation as that above alluded to by means of the same (logarithmic) process as that employed in the derivation of the rule of Murphy. Although the results of Lagrange and Murphy are identical, yet the great fame of the latter philosopher is fixed upon too sure a basis to be in the slightest degree shaken, even when we shall have restored this discovery to him to whom it is justly due. This is not the place to dwell on the relative lengths to which those two analysts have pushed their researches in this direction. I may observe, that my attention was attracted to the memoir of Lagrange by seeing it referred to by Garnier at page 355 of his *Analyse* (Paris, 1814), but my leaving town on circuit and other circumstances prevented me from noticing it till now.

2 Church-Yard Court, Temple,
May 13, 1848.

---

LVIII. *Abstract of Meteorological Observations made during the year 1847 at Gongo Soco, in the interior of Brazil.* By WILLIAM JORY HENWOOD, *F.R.S., F.G.S., Member of the Geological Society of France, Chief Commissioner of the Gold Mines of Gongo Soco and Bananal, &c. &c.*†

THE instruments, their situations, and the hours of observation have been the same as in former years‡; and I have again to thank Captains Blaney, Pengilly, Luke and Guy, for the results obtained at midnight and at 3 A.M.

exposition of Horner's method by Mr. Peter Gray, printed in the Mechanics' Magazine for March 1844. Mr. Davies also requests me to state, that a paper sent to the Royal Society in 1823 by Mr. Horner himself, has been printed in the Mathematician, vols. i. and ii.; a paper to which Mr. Davies considers it important to direct the attention of every one who takes interest in the problem of the numerical solution of algebraic equations.

\* *Nouvelle Méthode pour résoudre les équations littérales par le moyen des séries.* Par Mr. de la Grange. Published in the Berlin Memoirs for 1768, pp. 251–326. See the seventh article, pp. 261–263.
† Communicated by the Author.
‡ Phil. Mag. 1846, xxviii. pp. 364, 366.

## Table I.

### Hourly extreme and mean temperatures for every month.

| | 3 A.M. | | | 6 A.M. | | | 9 A.M. | | | Noon. | | | 4 P.M. | | | 6 P.M. | | | 8 P.M.* | | | 9 P.M. | | | Midnight. | | |
|---|---|---|---|---|---|---|---|---|---|---|---|---|---|---|---|---|---|---|---|---|---|---|---|---|---|---|---|
| | Max. | Min. | Mean. | Max. | Min. | Mean. | Max. | Min. | Mean. | Max. | Min. | Mean. | Max. | Min. | Mean. | Max. | Min. | Mean. | Max. | Min. | Mean. | Max. | Min. | Mean. | Max. | Min. | Mean. |
| Jan. | 68·8 | 60·8 | 65·3 | 69·5 | 63·2 | 66·2 | 72·8 | 63· | 68·6 | 80·2 | 65· | 73·9 | 80·8 | 62· | 74·9 | 77·3 | 64·8 | 72·7 | 74·2 | 63·5 | 70· | 73· | 63· | 69·1 | 70·8 | 62·8 | 66·4 |
| Feb. | 70·8 | 61·8 | 67·9 | 70· | 64· | 68· | 77· | 65· | 71· | 83· | 67· | 76·8 | 83·5 | 66· | 77·2 | 78·2 | 65·1 | 74·6 | 74· | 65· | 71· | 73·6 | 61·7 | 70·2 | 71·8 | 61·8 | 68·4 |
| Mar. | 69·8 | 60·8 | 65· | 69·8 | 61·8 | 66·1 | 72· | 66· | 69·4 | 79· | 66· | 74·6 | 79·8 | 66·8 | 75·3 | 77·2 | 66· | 72·8 | 73·3 | 65· | 69·7 | 72·3 | 64· | 69· | 70·8 | 61·8 | 66·1 |
| Apr. | 66·8 | 53·8 | 62· | 67· | 57· | 63·1 | 63·6 | 62· | 63·9 | 71· | 64· | 71·1 | 74·9 | 66· | 73·3 | 74·2 | 65· | 68·9 | 66·5 | 62· | 66·2 | 69·6 | 61·2 | 63·6 | 66·8 | 56·8 | 62·9 |
| May | 63·8 | 48·8 | 56· | 61· | 47·3 | 55·6 | 71· | 56· | 62·4 | 75· | 64·8 | 68·6 | 74· | 65· | 69·1 | 74·2 | 63· | 70· | 66·5 | 55· | 60·8 | 65·8 | 53·7 | 59·7 | 61·8 | 50·8 | 57·8 |
| June | 62·6 | 47·8 | 55·2 | 61·5 | 46·8 | 54·4 | 64· | 53·8 | 59·6 | 68·5 | 62·8 | 65·9 | 73· | 63·5 | 67·5 | 66·7 | 56· | 62·7 | 64·5 | 52·8 | 58·7 | 64· | 51·4 | 57·0 | 62·8 | 49·8 | 56·6 |
| July | 61·8 | 47·8 | 55·1 | 62· | 41·6 | 53·8 | 66· | 51·8 | 59·1 | 73· | 61· | 65·6 | 73·9 | 62· | 67·1 | 69·5 | 57· | 62·1 | 64·5 | 52·3 | 58· | 63·2 | 51·1 | 57·2 | 62·8 | 48·8 | 56·1 |
| Aug. | 61·6 | 44·8 | 55·8 | 62·5 | 42·8 | 53·9 | 71· | 52·2 | 61· | 75· | 58· | 68· | 76· | 57· | 68·9 | 70·3 | 56· | 64·8 | 68· | 55· | 59·6 | 67·8 | 55· | 58·6 | 63· | 47·8 | 56·8 |
| Sep. | 68·8 | 55·8 | 61· | 67·2 | 51· | 60· | 72· | 62· | 66·2 | 80· | 67·5 | 73·9 | 80·3 | 69· | 75·7 | 76·4 | 67·6 | 71·7 | 73· | 61· | 66·6 | 71·4 | 60· | 65·3 | 68·8 | 56·8 | 61·8 |
| Oct. | 66·8 | 50·8 | 60·1 | 67· | 51·2 | 61·1 | 71· | 61·8 | 66·5 | 84· | 67· | 74·5 | 84·5 | 68· | 75·9 | 77·8 | 67· | 72·5 | 73·2 | 58· | 66·8 | 72·2 | 57·4 | 63·5 | 67·8 | 52·8 | 62·1 |
| Nov. | 68·8 | 56·8 | 62·8 | 69· | 58·4 | 64·6 | 72· | 63· | 68·2 | 81·8 | 66· | 73·7 | 81·8 | 67·8 | 74·4 | 79· | 66· | 72·1 | 74·6 | 64· | 68·6 | 73·8 | 63·6 | 67·8 | 68·8 | 58·8 | 63·8 |
| Dec. | 70·8 | 58·8 | 65·8 | 71· | 61· | 67· | 77· | 62·1 | 70·5 | 81· | 63·1 | 75· | 85·8 | 65· | 75·6 | 83· | 64· | 73·3 | 76· | 62·8 | 70·4 | 74·8 | 63·7 | 69·7 | 70·8 | 60·8 | 66·7 |

## Table II.

### Mean temperature of each month.

| | | | | |
|---|---|---|---|---|
| January | 69·64 | May | 61·67 | September | 66·99 |
| February | 71·76 | June | 59·97 | October | 67·27 |
| March | 69·82 | July | 59·51 | November | 68·42 |
| April | 66·42 | August | 61·22 | December | 70·45 |

* The observations at 8 P.M. are not employed in calculating the monthly and annual means.

Table III.—Mean temperature of each of nine hours.

| | | | | |
|---|---|---|---|---|
| 3 A.M. | 61° | 4 P.M. | | 72·79 |
| 6 ... | 61·31 | 6 ... | | 69·36 |
| 9 ... | 65·7 | 8 ... | | 65·53* |
| Noon | 71·8 | 9 ... | | 64·66 |
| | | Midnight | | 62·15 |

These observations give 66°·095 as the mean temperature of the year 1847†; and 9459 observations give 66°·411 as the average of the years 1845, 1846 and 1847.

Table IV.—Comparative temperature in shade and in open sunshine.

| Date. | Shade. | Sunshine. | Remarks. |
|---|---|---|---|
| April 19, 2 P.M. | 74° | 92·4 | Light breeze N.W. |
| ... 28, 4 ... | 73·7 | 85· | Light breeze E. |
| May 11, ... | 66·8 | 76·5 | Brisk breeze E. |
| ... 22, ... | 73·4 | 94· | Brisk breeze E. |
| ... 23, ... | 71·3 | 91·6 | Brisk breeze E. |
| June 11, ... | 67· | 79· | Light breeze E. |
| ... 12, ... | 65· | 77· | Light breeze E. |
| ... 13, Noon. | 66·5 | 87· | Brisk breeze N.W. |
| ... ... 4 P.M. | 69·8 | 87·5 | Brisk breeze N.W. |
| ... 19, Noon. | 68·8 | 80·8 | Brisk breeze W. |
| ... 26, 4 P.M. | 67·2 | 80·8 | Light breeze E. |
| July 10, ... | 64·5 | 73·5 | Brisk breeze S.E. |
| ... 17, ... | 70·5 | 91· | Light breeze W. |
| ... 21, Noon. | 68·2 | 87· | Light breeze W. |
| Aug. 15, ... | 71· | 93·8 | Light breeze S.W. |
| ... 22, ... | 62·6 | 95·5 | Brisk breeze E. |
| Sept. 12, 4 P.M. | 76·4 | 103·8 | Light breeze S.W. |
| ... 19, Noon. | 75·3 | 98·5 | Brisk breeze E. |
| ... 26, ... | 75·3 | 100· | Brisk breeze N. |
| Oct. 17, ... | 77·4 | 103·8 | Brisk breeze N. |
| ... 24, ... | 72·4 | 100·5 | Gale N. |
| ... 25, 4 P.M. | 78·2 | 92·5 | Brisk breeze E. |
| ... 26, 9 A.M. | 67· | 97·8 | Very light breeze E. |
| ... ... 4 P.M. | 81·7 | 95·3 | Light breeze E. |
| Nov. 23, 9 A.M. | 71·5 | 104·8 | Light breeze S.W. |
| ... ... 4 P.M. | 84·8 | 106·7 | Brisk breeze S.W. |

* The observations at 8 P.M. are not employed in calculating the monthly and annual means.

† In my observations for 1845 (Phil. Mag., xxviii. p. 366), I have made a correction of 2°·3, and deduced a mean temperature of 65°·14 for the year 1845. The reduction should have been 1°·3, and the mean of the year 66°·14.

The coldest day was the 4th of August, when the mean of the twenty-four hours was 55°·95; the hottest was the 31st of December, which averaged 71°·09.

The last fire-fly was seen on the 10th of May, when the twenty-four hours' average temperature was 60°·87, and the minimum was 50°·8. The first fire-fly appeared on the 25th of July, of which the lowest temperature was 52°·1, and the mean 61°·1.

The large South-American swallow (*Andorinha*) was first seen on the 15th of September, when the mean temperature was 65°·56, and the lowest 56°·8.

The American robin (*Sabea*) commenced its song on the 12th of August, when the average temperature was 61°·1, and the minimum 55°·8. About the same time also the humming-bird ceased its low monotonous chant, which during the cold season might have been heard from every low-sheltered bush on the open grounds (*Campos*) between Gongo and Cattas Altas.

Table V.—Quantity of rain.

|  | No. of rainy days. | Rain. |
|---|---|---|
| January | 27 | 35·82 inches. |
| February | 22 | 17·86 |
| March | 22 | 17·44 |
| April | 20 | 8·36 |
| May | 4 | 1·22 |
| June | 4 | 0·82 |
| July | 6 | 0·87 |
| August | 10 | 1·04 |
| September | 3 | 0·40 |
| October | 9 | 3·41 |
| November | 22 | 16·78 |
| December | 28 | 27·72 |
| Total in 1847 |  | 131·77 |

The heaviest showers during the year were
January 1, when 7·5 inches of rain fell in 10 hours.
... 1 & 2, ... 10·   ...   ...   36 ...
...   18, ...  6·68 ...   ...   24 ...
October 1, ...  2·24 ...   ...   1¼ ...

We have had neither hoar-frost nor hail for the year, the cold season having been very mild, and the rainy period remarkably cool.

I shortly remove to another residence; this communication therefore records my last year's observations in Gongo.

Gongo Soco Gold Mines,       W. J. HENWOOD.
 January 15, 1848.

LIX. *On the Heat disengaged during the Combination of Bodies with Oxygen and Chlorine.* By THOMAS ANDREWS, *M.D., M.R.I.A., Vice-President of Queen's College, Belfast.*

[Continued from p. 339.]

§ III. *Combinations of Chlorine.*

MOST of the experiments to be described in this section were performed with dry chlorine gas. The combining substance, included in a hermetically sealed and very fragile glass ball, was first introduced into the glass vessel destined to contain the gas. The latter was then filled by displacement with pure and dry chlorine, and was afterwards closed by a dry cork, which was traversed by a small glass tube terminating externally in a capillary point. After the chlorine had attained the temperature of the external air, the capillary orifice was hermetically sealed. During this period the surface of the cork was attacked by the chlorine; but careful experiments proved that the amount of gas afterwards absorbed by the cork was quite insignificant, at least during the length of time occupied by the experiment.

The glass vessel thus prepared was introduced into another of copper, which served as a calorimeter, and was similar to that employed in the experiments on the combination of the gases, but of smaller size. The calorimeter was suspended, as before, in a cylindrical vessel of tin plate. The temperature of the water in the calorimeter was taken before introducing the apparatus into the rotating cylinder. The whole apparatus was then quickly shaken in order to rupture the glass ball, and immediately placed in the rotating cylinder, in which it was agitated for five minutes and a half. After the final temperature had been observed, the agitation was repeated for one minute more, and the experiment was not considered accurate unless the thermometer afterwards indicated a slight loss of heat. Finally, the glass vessel was inverted under water, the capillary point of the tube broken, and the weight of the water that rushed in (the levels having been duly adjusted) ascertained. The residual air did not, in general, amount to more than one or two per cent. of the whole, and was in all cases free from the slightest odour of chlorine.

The determination of the heat evolved during the combination of potassium with chlorine involved experimental difficulties, which for some time appeared likely to prove insuperable, but were finally overcome by the employment of a somewhat novel form of apparatus. The chief source of difficulty arose from the intensity of the heat produced by the combination, which was such that no glass vessel could resist it without breaking. Having formerly observed that chlorine gas, if perfectly dry, has not the slightest action in the cold on copper or zinc, it occurred to me that the experiment might perhaps succeed, if a brass vessel were substituted for the glass one to contain the chlorine. On making the trial with the requisite precautions, it succeeded perfectly. The chlorine must, however, be dried with the greatest care, and the lid of the brass vessel closed by ground metallic surfaces without the interposition of leather. The apparatus is represented in Plate III. fig. 6. The lid $b$ has attached to it two copper tubes, by means of which the vessel is filled with chlorine. It is fixed in its place by means of the coupling screw $c$. As soon as the air has been swept away by the current of chlorine, the ends of the copper tubes are closed by small pins of the same metal, which are secured in their places by caoutchouc covers. While filling the brass vessel with gas, two similar glass vessels were connected with it, one on each side, so as to be filled by the same stream of gas; and the purity of the chlorine contained in the intermediate brass vessel was ascertained by analysing the gas in the other two vessels.

The combining substance was in all cases employed in considerable excess; and from the constant agitation, the whole of the chlorine entered into combination in the course of a very short time.

The formula deduced from direct observation to express the correction required in this apparatus for the heating and cooling influence of the air, during $m$ minutes ($a$, as before, being the difference between the temperature of the apparatus and of the air), was the following:

$$V = \mp m(a \pm 0°\cdot 5).0°\cdot 01.$$

In applying this formula, it was assumed that the apparatus was at the initial temperature during one minute, and at the final temperature during three minutes.

### Potassium and Chlorine.

In the following tables, M designates the volume of chlorine (dry) in cubic centimetres.

| | | | | |
|---|---|---|---|---|
| M | 80·3 c.c. | 80·4 c.c. | 80·6 c.c. | 80·4 c.c. |
| B | 30·00 in. | 29·63 in. | 29·48 in. | 29·12 in. |
| T | 8°·6 | 12°·4 | 12°·8 | 10°·8 |
| E | 1°·5 | 1°·5 | 1°·9 | 1°·6 |
| I | 3°·00 | 2°·95 | 2°·92 | 2°·86 |
| Ic | 3°·01 | 2°·96 | 2°·95 | 2°·88 |
| W | 215·4 grms. | 218·3 grms. | 218·4 grms. | 220·4 grms. |
| V | 23·8 grms. | 23·8 grms. | 23·8 grms. | 23°·8 grms. |

| 1. | 2. | 3. | 4. |
|---|---|---|---|
| 9218 | 9374 | 9380 | 9344 |

We have, therefore, for the heat evolved during the combination of—

    One litre chlorine with potassium . . 9329
    One gramme chlorine with potassium . 2943
    One gramme potassium with chlorine . 2655
    One equivalent chlorine with potassium 13008

The assumed equivalent of chlorine is its atomic weight, that of oxygen being $=1$.

### Tin and Chlorine.

|    | 1. | 2. | 3. | 4. |
|---|---|---|---|---|
| M  | 132·2 c.c.   | 143·1 c.c.   | 135·1 c.c.   | 140·4 c.c.   |
| B  | 30·03 in.    | 30·03 in.    | 30·03 in.    | 29·90 in.    |
| T  | 10°·6        | 10°·8        | 12°·2        | 13°·2        |
| E  | 0°·9         | 1°·3         | 1°·3         | 1°·3         |
| I  | 2°·21        | 2°·47        | 2°·34        | 2°·28        |
| Ic | 2°·20        | 2°·48        | 2°·35        | 2°·29        |
| W  | 144·4 grms.  | 136·0 grms.  | 132·9 grms.  | 144·4 grms.  |
| V  | 22·5 grms.   | 22·5 grms.   | 22·5 grms.   | 22·5 grms.   |

| 1. | 2. | 3. | 4. |
|---|---|---|---|
| 2874 | 2843 | 2803 | 2857 |

Hence we obtain for the heat evolved during the combination of—

    One litre chlorine with tin . . 2844
    One gramme chlorine with tin . 897
    One gramme tin with chlorine . 1079
    One equivalent chlorine with tin 3966

The compound formed in this reaction was the bichloride $SnCl_2$.

### Antimony and Chlorine.

|    | 1. | 2. | 3. | 4. |
|---|---|---|---|---|
| M  | 126·3 c.c.   | 149·6 c.c.   | 137·6 c.c.   | 131·5 c.c.   |
| B  | 29·09 in.    | 30·28 in.    | 30·06 in.    | 30·08 in.    |
| T  | 4°·5         | 6°·7         | 9°·1         | 8°·1         |
| E  | 1°·1         | 1°·9         | 1°·4         | 1°·4         |
| I  | 2°·21        | 2°·74        | 2°·40        | 2°·32        |
| Ic | 2°·21        | 2°·77        | 2°·41        | 2°·33        |
| W  | 128·6 grms.  | 124·8 grms.  | 127·6 grms.  | 131·6 grms.  |
| V  | 21·8 grms.   | 21·9 grms.   | 21·1 grms.   | 19·5 grms.   |

| 1. | 2. | 3. | 4. |
|---|---|---|---|
| 2739 | 2748 | 2680 | 2743 |

The compound formed in these experiments was a crystalline, easily fusible solid. On the addition of water, a white insoluble precipitate was formed; but when a solution of tar-

taric acid was substituted for the water, the precipitate which at first appeared was completely redissolved. It was therefore the terchloride of antimony $SbCl_3$. The perchloride ($SbCl_5$) described by M. Rose was not produced in any appreciable quantity.

We obtain, therefore, for the heat evolved during the combination of—

| | |
|---|---|
| One litre chlorine with antimony . . | 2726 |
| One gramme chlorine with antimony | 860 |
| One gramme antimony with chlorine | 707 |
| One equivalent chlorine with antimony | 3804 |

### Arsenic and Chlorine.

| | 1. | 2. | 3. | 4. |
|---|---|---|---|---|
| M | 138·7 c.c. | 145·1 c.c. | 150·0 c.c. | 134·1 c.c. |
| B | 29·40 in. | 29·45 in. | 29·92 in. | 30·08 in. |
| T | 6°·9 | 7°·0 | 6°·3 | 10°·6 |
| E | 1°·7 | 1°·7 | 1°·4 | 0°·8 |
| I | 1°·90 | 1°·93 | 2°·06 | 1°·78 |
| Ic | 1°·93 | 1°·96 | 2°·07 | 1°·77 |
| W | 132·6 grms. | 140·2 grms. | 134·9 grms. | 141·8 grms. |
| V | 21·1 grms. | 21·1 grms. | 21·1 grms. | 22·5 grms. |
| | 1. | 2. | 3. | 4. |
| | 2230 | 2271 | 2202 | 2227 |

The compound formed was fluid, and when added to water, was converted into the hydrochloric and arsenious acids, without the formation of a trace of arsenic acid. It was, therefore, the terchloride of arsenic $AsCl_3$.

We have, therefore, for the heat evolved during the combination of—

| | |
|---|---|
| One litre chlorine with arsenic . . | 2232 |
| One gramme chlorine with arsenic . | 704 |
| One gramme arsenic with chlorine . | 994 |
| One equivalent chlorine with arsenic | 3114 |

### Mercury and Chlorine.

This metal combines more slowly with chlorine than any of the preceding. Ten minutes of agitation were required to obtain the whole of the heat extricated during the combination.

| | 1. | 2. | 3. |
|---|---|---|---|
| M | 119·2 c.c. | 120·1 c.c. | 139·5 c.c. |
| B | 29·64 in. | 29·64 in. | 29·25 in. |
| T | 11°·6 | 11°·7 | 11°·5 |
| E | 0°·9 | 0°·9 | 1°·1 |
| I | 1°·81 | 1°·88 | 2°·01 |
| Ic | 1°·83 | 1°·90 | 2°·04 |
| W | 139·1 grms. | 137·0 grms. | 140·8 grms. |
| V | 22·6 grms. | 22·6 grms. | 22·6 grms. |

|   | 1. | 2. | 3. |
|---|----|----|----|
|   | 2611 | 2658 | 2547 |

The primary compound formed in this reaction is probably the chloride $HgCl$; but by the action of the excess of mercury, a portion of it is afterwards converted into the subchloride $Hg_2Cl$. We have, therefore, for the heat evolved during the combination of—

| | |
|---|---|
| One litre chlorine with mercury | 2605 |
| One gramme chlorine with mercury | 822 |
| One equivalent chlorine with mercury | 3633 |

### Phosphorus and Chlorine.

|   | 1. | 2. |
|---|----|----|
| M | 145·4 c.c. | 144·6 c.c. |
| B | 29·85 in. | 29·85 in. |
| T | 11°·5 | 11°·3 |
| E | 0°·6 | 1°·3 |
| I | 1°·62 | 1°·62 |
| Ic | 1°·61 | 1°·63 |
| W | 143·2 grms. | 140·5 grms. |
| V | 23·2 grms. | 23·2 grms. |

|   | 1. | 2. |
|---|----|----|
|   | 1924 | 1926 |

The compound formed was the solid perchloride, $PCl_5$, accompanied by a small quantity of the terchloride, $PCl_3$. These experiments with phosphorus and chlorine can only be considered to be imperfect approximations.

We obtain, therefore, for the heat evolved during the combination of—

| | |
|---|---|
| One litre chlorine with phosphorus | 1925 |
| One gramme chlorine with phosphorus | 607 |
| One gramme phosphorus with chlorine | 3422? |
| One equivalent chlorine with phosphorus | 2683 |

### Zinc and Chlorine.

As dry chlorine gas has no action upon zinc at ordinary temperatures, it was necessary to introduce a little water into the vessel in which the reaction took place. In the experiment, however, when thus arranged, two distinct sources of heat existed; one, the combination of the zinc and chlorine, the other, the solution of the compound formed. To determine the amount of the latter, an independent experiment was made; and by subtracting it from the whole quantity of heat at first obtained, there remained the increment of temperature due to the chemical combination. A small quantity of subchloride of zinc was always formed by the action of the excess of zinc upon the solution. This would tend to render the results a little too high; but its precise effect I had no means of ascertaining. The quantity of chlorine which entered into combination in each experiment, was determined by precipitating the solution (previously acidulated with nitric acid to dissolve the subchloride) by nitrate of silver and weighing the chloride of silver. The apparatus was considerably larger than that employed in the foregoing experiments. In the next table, M designates the weight of the chloride of silver.

|   | 1. | 2. | 3. |
|---|---|---|---|
| M | 2·911 grms. | 3·140 grms. | 2·793 grms. |
| T | 16°·1 | 15°·0 | 14°·2 |
| E | 1°·0 | 1°·7 | 1°·3 |
| I | 2°·79 | 3°·10 | 2°·60 |
| Ic | 2°·78 | 3°·12 | 2°·60 |
| W | 380·0 grms. | 365·3 grms. | 399·7 grms. |
| V | 27·5 grms. | 27·5 grms. | 27·5 grms. |
|   | 1. | 2. | 3. |
|   | 1577 | 1580 | 1610 |

In two experiments, the number 162 was obtained for the heat arising from the solution of the chloride of zinc, which being deducted from the mean number 1589, there remains 1427 for the heat of combination.

We have, therefore, for the heat evolved during the combination of—

| One litre chlorine with zinc | . . | 4524 |
| One gramme chlorine with zinc | . | 1427 |
| One gramme zinc with chlorine | . | 1529 |
| One equivalent zinc with chlorine | | 6309* |

*Copper and Chlorine†.*

The experiments with copper were in all respects similar to those with zinc, except that the chlorine was estimated by volume and not by weight.

|   | 1. | 2. | 3. | 4. |
|---|---|---|---|---|
| M | 246·0 c.c. | 241·5 c.c. | 233·5 c.c. | 246·4 c.c. |
| B | 29·53 in. | 29·73 in. | 29·56 in. | 29·56 in. |
| T | 17°·8 | 18°·9 | 18°·4 | 19°·3 |
| E | 0°·6 | 0°·6 | 0°·7 | 0°·7 |
| I | 1°·71 | 1°·62 | 1°·63 | 1°·67 |
| Ic | 1°·71 | 1°·62 | 1°·63 | 1°·67 |
| W | 371·3 grms. | 382·1 grms. | 382·8 grms. | 382·7 grms. |
| V | 27·3 grms. | 27·3 grms. | 27·3 grms. | 27·3 grms. |

* These results are almost identical with those which I obtained formerly by a process differing slightly from that now described (Transactions of the Royal Irish Academy, xix. p. 406).

† These experiments were not in the original paper.

|   1.  |   2.  |   3.  |   4.  |
|-------|-------|-------|-------|
| 3037  | 2927  | 3061  | 2950  |

The heat due to the solution of the compound, referred to one litre of chlorine as unit, was found to be 260 units.

We have, therefore, for the heat evolved during the combination of—

| | |
|---|---|
| One litre chlorine with copper | 2734 |
| One gramme chlorine with copper | 859 |
| One gramme copper with chlorine | 961 |
| One equivalent chlorine with copper | 3805 |

The results of the foregoing experiments are contained in the following table. I have adopted the number 7900, for the reasons given in the note, to express the heat produced during the combustion of carbon; and have also added, from a former publication, the numbers which correspond to the heat evolved during the combination of chlorine and iron.

*Combinations of Oxygen.*

|  | Of oxygen. | | Of substance. |
|---|---|---|---|
|  | 1 litre. | 1 grm. or equiv. | 1 grm. |
| Hydrogen | 6072 | 4226 | 33808 |
| Carbonic oxide | 6114 | 4255 | 2431 |
| Marsh gas | 4716 | 3278 | 13108 |
| Olefiant gas | 5005 | 3483 | 11942 |
| Alcohol | 4716 | 3282 | 6850 |
| Carbon | 4256 | 2962 | 7900 |
| Sulphur | 3315 | 2307 | 2307 |
| Phosphorus | 6479 | 4509 | 5747 |
| Zinc | 7710 | 5366 | 1301 |
| Iron | 5940 | 4134 |  |
| Tin | 6078 | 4230 |  |
| Protoxide of tin | 6249 | 4349 | 521 |
| Copper | 3410 | 2394 |  |
| Protoxide of copper | 3288 | 2288 | 256 |

*Combinations of Chlorine.*

|  | Of chlorine. | | | Of substance. |
|---|---|---|---|---|
|  | 1 litre. | 1 grm. | 1 equiv. | 1 grm. |
| Potassium | 9329 | 2943 | 13008 | 2655 |
| Tin | 2844 | 897 | 3966 | 1079 |
| Antimony | 2726 | 860 | 3804 | 707 |
| Arsenic | 2232 | 704 | 3114 | 994 |
| Mercury | 2605 | 822 | 3633 |  |
| Phosphorus | 1925 | 607 | 2683 | 3422 (?) |
| Zinc | 4524 | 1427 | 6309 | 1529 |
| Copper | 2734 | 859 | 3805 | 961 |
| Iron | 2920 | 921 | 4072 | 1745 |

From a cursory inspection of the above numbers, it will be evident that the quantities of heat evolved during the combination of different metals with chlorine or oxygen are very different, varying, in the case of the compounds of chlorine, from 13008 to 3114 units for each equivalent of chlorine. On the other hand, there is a general resemblance between the amounts of heat obtained when the same metal combines with oxygen and chlorine. Thus iron yields 4134 units with oxygen, 4072 with chlorine; antimony, 3817 with oxygen (Dulong), 3804 with chlorine; tin, 4230 with oxygen, 3966 with chlorine. In the case of zinc there is less agreement, and in that of copper, the results differ considerably; but this may perhaps arise from the compounds of chlorine with those metals being obtained after each experiment in the state of aqueous solutions. The determination of the heat evolved during the combustion of potassium in oxygen gas would throw much light on this question. The only non-metallic element examined is phosphorus, and it gave nearly twice as much heat in combining with oxygen as with chlorine.

It may be interesting to inquire whether the thermal effects described in the foregoing extract can be connected with those obtained when compounds formed of the same bodies react upon one another by the moist way. Such a comparison is difficult and liable to much uncertainty, from the many intermediate reactions that occur during the formation of these compounds. But there are two cases that admit to some extent of this comparison, and it may be interesting briefly to refer to them.

I have elsewhere shown, that when one and the same base displaces another from any of its neutral combinations, the same development of heat occurs[*]; and in a paper lately read before the Royal Society, I have endeavoured to extend a similar principle to the substitutions of metals for one another, and have also measured the quantities of heat evolved in many reactions of this kind. For my present object, it is only necessary to refer to two of these results, viz. the heat due to the substitution of an equivalent of oxide of zinc for oxide of copper (953 units), and that due to a like substitution of metallic zinc for metallic copper (3435 units). Now on the common view of the constitution of salts and of their solutions, the heat evolved during the precipitation of metallic copper by zinc should be equal to the difference of the quantities of heat disengaged during the combination of zinc and copper respectively with oxygen, added to the heat due to the substitution of oxide of zinc for oxide of copper. This assumes the truth of the principle (which I have in other inquiries endeavoured

[*] Philosophical Transactions for 1844, p. 21.

to illustrate, and is indeed almost self-evident), that when, in the course of any chemical reaction, the constituents of a compound are separated from one another, there is a quantity of heat thereby absorbed, equal to that which would have been evolved if the same substances had entered into combination. Applying the numerical quantities, we have—

$$\begin{aligned}
&\text{Zn} + \text{O} \ \ldots \ldots \ldots \ldots \ldots \ldots \ 5366\\
&\text{Cu} + \text{O} \ \ldots \ldots \ldots \ldots \ldots \ldots \ \underline{2394}\\
&(\text{Zn} + \text{O}) - (\text{Cu} + \text{O}) \ \ldots \ldots \ \ 2972\\
&\text{Substitution of ZnO for CuO in salts of latter} \ \ \underline{353}\\
&\hspace{8cm} 3325
\end{aligned}$$

This number 3325 should, therefore, represent the heat due to the substitution of metallic zinc for copper. The result actually obtained by direct experiment was 3435, an excellent approximation when all the varying circumstances of the particular experiments are taken into consideration.

On the other hand, in the combination of chlorine with zinc and copper, we have—

|  | Compound dry. | Compound in solution. |
|---|---|---|
| Zn + Cl | 6309 | 7025 |
| Zn + Cu | 3805 | 4167 |
|  | 2504 | 2858 |

Neither of these numbers agrees with that first given for the heat produced by the substitution of zinc for copper. The thermal effects are therefore not favourable to the hypothesis that the metallic chlorides exist, as such, in solution.

In making these observations, I do not wish to attach to them more importance than they deserve. I am fully aware of the uncertainty of conclusions derived from a new and difficult inquiry. But as the heat developed in chemical reactions may be taken as a measure of the forces brought into play, I deemed it proper to refer to the foregoing cases, if only for the purpose of directing attention to the intimate relations which inquiries of this kind have with some of the most interesting questions of molecular chemistry.

---

LX. *Description of some Parhelia seen at Portsea on the 29th of March* 1848; *with some Remarks on these Phænomena generally.* By EDWARD LACY GARBETT[*].

[With a Plate.]

I. *Description.*

THE accompanying drawings represent two exhibitions of parhelia which were seen at Buckland, a village about the centre of the isle of Portsea, on the 29th of March last.

[*] Communicated by Professor Miller of King's College, London.

seen at Portsea on the 29th of March 1848.     435

The first exhibition was seen in great perfection at half-past 10 A.M., when it was first pointed out to me; and as it was then declining in brilliancy, and continued to do so till its disappearance soon after 11, it is probable that it might have appeared much earlier, and attained its greatest distinctness before I saw it. The most conspicuous and beautiful part of this phænomenon was a well-defined narrow white band, passing horizontally through the sun's disc, and continued entirely round the sky, but apparently preserving everywhere the same altitude as the sun, or about 40°. In the annexed figure this band is represented by the large outer circle, and in

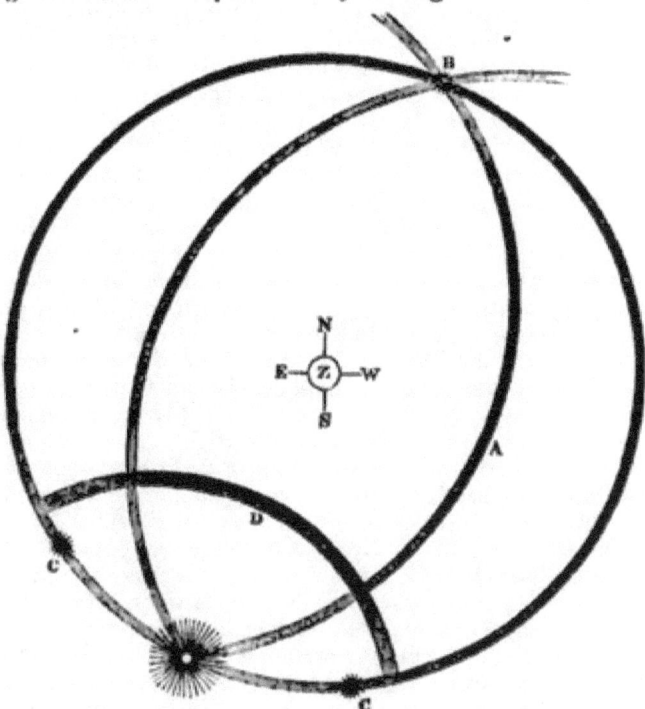

Fig. 1. View of the morning parhelia looking upwards, the lights and shades reversed.

fig. 2 (Plate IV.) by the large colourless ellipse; in which figure, to render the position of the different parts more intelligible, I have taken the same licence that is always taken in the common diagrams to illustrate the theory of the rainbow, viz. that of representing the bows as if they were tangible bodies, and could be seen in perspective by a person at a distance from

2 F 2

the scene of the phænomenon; but it will of course be understood that each spectator saw only his own halos and parhelia, as each one sees only his own rainbow.

Having no means of angular measurement, I cannot be certain that the pole of this large circle was exactly in the zenith, but it appeared to be so; and in that case, as it always passed through the sun, its diameter would necessarily vary with his altitude, and would be about 102° when I first saw it, and 98° when it vanished. The width of this band seemed no greater than the sun's diameter, or half a degree, its upper and lower edges being well-defined, though there was a faint light diffused beyond them, as if the intensity throughout the whole width of the band varied something like the ordinates of such a curve as A (fig. 4), where it is plain that, at the two points of contrary flexure, the rapid change of intensity would give the effect of sharply defined edges, though the light continued to diminish beyond them, making the whole breadth of the band perhaps $1\frac{1}{2}°$ or 2°; but the width of the conspicuous central part was only equal to the sun's diameter.

There was no trace of colour in this band, and its absolute brightness might possibly have been equal throughout its whole circuit; but this could not be estimated; for owing to the varying contrast afforded by the background of sky, the band necessarily *appeared* to grow more and more distinct as it receded from the glare of the sun, till, on the opposite or N.N.W. side, it stood out in bold relief from the bluest part of the sky, and it was difficult not to refer this to a gradation in the intensity of the luminous band itself.

The two curves of largest radius in fig. 1 represent two other luminous bands which were much fainter, and accordingly disappeared much sooner than any other part of the phænomenon. These bands diverged from the sun, passed overhead as in Plate IV. fig. 2, and met again at the opposite point of the large white circle, where, by their intersection with it, they formed a knot of nebulous light, rather brighter perhaps than would have resulted from the mere crossing of the three luminous bands, but hardly bright or definite enough to deserve the name of a mock-sun. The two arcs last mentioned were most distinct where they approached the zenith; and here their distance apart seemed to the naked eye about three-fifths of the diameter of the large circle, or about 60°. From these points they diminished in brightness each way, quickly as they approached the sun, but more slowly as they approached their other intersection, below which they could still be traced for a few degrees, while, on the other hand, they could not be traced below the sun. These bands seemed rather wider than the large circle; and their edges, instead of being sharp and colourless, were slightly fringed on the outer or convex side with *red*, and on the inner side with *violet*; and these coloured margins, which were not visible near the sun, became more decided the further they receded from him, as if the bands were formed by the overlapping of innumerable spectra having their red ends directed exactly from the sun; so that by their combination they would render each band white where it had the same direction as the spectra, but more and more coloured as it became more oblique to them; its central line however being white throughout its length. The knot at the triple intersection was also colourless.

A fourth luminous arc was formed immediately over the sun, but not concentric with him, like the common halo. The distance of its vertex from him was indeed the same as the radius of an ordinary halo, or about 23°; but this curve was described with a longer radius, its centre being, as shown in the figures, some degrees *below* the sun, if indeed it was not, as I sometimes thought, a portion of an ellipse with its long axis horizontal; and I had afterwards an opportunity of convincing myself that this eccentricity was not a mere perspective deception. This arc was brighter and lasted longer than the large horizontal circle, though it was not so much noticed by most spectators from its inconvenient nearness to the sun. It consisted of all the prismatic colours arranged with the red underneath or next the sun. The colours were much more decided than those of the common halo, though not quite so positive as those of the primary rainbow, but much brighter than either, especially at the summit of the arch, from whence its intensity rapidly declined each way, so that it could not be traced quite down to its intersections with the large circle. There was no particular appearance where it crossed the other arcs.

The only remaining feature of this first exhibition consisted of two detached single spectra or mock-suns, placed at equal distances to the right and left of the real sun, and on the white horizontal circle; but what I thought very strange, they were not at its intersections with the coloured eccentric arch, but rather nearer the sun. I thought at first that they might be at the places where an ordinary halo would have crossed the horizontal circle; but neither was this the case; for in the afternoon, when such a halo appeared, these spectra were left outside its circumference, and independent alike of the common and the eccentric halo. These spectra had their red sides next the sun, and their colours were as positive, though not so bright, as those of the eccentric arch.

Below these phænomena and near the horizon were faint traces of two other coloured arcs, which, however, were so much more distinct in the second display, that they might be regarded as belonging to it exclusively.

All these appearances gradually faded, till soon after 11 A.M. they had completely vanished. A little before 1 P.M. however, I was surprised to find the large horizontal circle reappearing; and though it never regained its former distinctness, there were some other appearances different from those of the morning, but equally complex. These are represented in fig. 3, projected in the same manner as fig. 2, so as to admit of a comparison with it. The two faint arcs of large radius passing near the zenith, were never seen in this second display, nor yet the white parhelion at their intersection; but the two coloured parhelia next the sun were much brighter than in the morning, and the coloured arch over the sun became so bright toward its vertex as to be painful to the naked eye. This increased brilliancy seemed to arise from the coalescence of this arch with another, which was concentric with the sun, like a common halo, and surrounded him at apparently the usual distance of $23°$. Its appearance therefore corrected two errors into which I might otherwise have fallen. It showed that the eccentricity of the other coloured arch was real, and not an effect of perspective, and also that the two prismatic mock-suns were independent, and not formed by an intersection of halos.

It will be observed that this circular halo, though complete, was by no means regular, but strongest at the upper and lower parts, from whence it declined in brilliancy till it was hardly perceptible at the sides, where it crossed the horizontal circle. Its summit exactly coincided with that of the eccentric arch, so that their overlapping produced a dazzling brilliancy at that part; and as the colours of both arcs were arranged in the same order (the red inwards), they were not altered by their combination.

The inner edge of both these halos was, as usual, the only one sharply defined; the outer limits of both died away gradually; and at their common vertex, the light often appeared to graduate upwards with the curious *rayed* or *hairy* appearance shown in the figure, reminding one of the representation of an auroral arch, in miniature. A similar appearance, but inverted, was also seen below the foot of the circular halo, where it seemed to touch the summit of another very luminous but ill-defined arch, or rather nebulous mass of light, the upper limit of which was arched, but which graduated downwards with the bearded appearance shown in the figure. This imperfect arc was colourless, but the brightest part of the whole exhibition, except the common summit of the two coloured arches.

At equal distances to the right and left of these phænomena, and much nearer the horizon, were the two fragments of coloured arcs faintly seen in the morning, but which now became as distinct as common secondary rainbows, which they greatly resembled in breadth and colour, except that the order of their colours was like that of the primary rainbow, the red being on the convex side, which was next the sun, as shown in the figure. These arcs, though very faint, lasted as long as any of the others.

The large white circle was in the afternoon very irregular in its intensity, owing to many light cirrous clouds crossing it, some of which had the effect of extinguishing it, while others, on the contrary, rendered it more luminous, but always less distinct, causing it often to spread upwards and downwards with a bearded appearance like that already described; and wherever this appearance was seen, the rays or hairs were exactly *vertical*.

There was however always an increase in the light of this horizontal band where it approached the outer sides of the two prismatic mock-suns, so as to give the idea of white tails proceeding from them on the side furthest from the sun. There was also, as long as the phænomenon lasted, a very definite concentration of light much brighter than the rest of the circle, at a spot which seemed about 120° of azimuth to the left of the sun, so that another such focus corresponding to it on the opposite side would nearly have divided the circle into three equal parts; but of this last mock-sun I could never catch a glimpse, though the other continued distinct enough for more than half an hour.

It may be observed, that these phænomena occurred precisely at the time of a most remarkable change in the weather, especially in the temperature, which for the previous few days had been such as is usually felt at this season; but the 29th of March was the first of a series of five days which excited general surprise, as being some of the warmest ever known for the season. On this day the sun was unusually powerful, but the sky a very pale blue. The wind was, at Portsea, S. by E., in which direction there were no clouds, but light cirri overhead, and a very regular wall of cumuli about 5° high round the northern horizon. The barometer was at 29·8 and rising. Though the parhelia gradually vanished, the common circular halo seemed rather to increase. The following morning was wet; but at 11, when it became very clear, at Brighton there was a common halo, by far the finest I ever saw, but no traces of any other arcs. On the afternoon in London there was still a faint halo, but on the next day nothing remarkable.

## II. *Remarks.*

The extreme variety and complexity of phænomena of this kind render it difficult to determine the peculiar *structure* requisite in the atmosphere to produce them. If the common halo can only be satisfactorily accounted for by the supposition of innumerable crystals of ice turned in all possible directions, the present phænomenon requires us to suppose all these crystals turned in *one* direction, or at least having all their *axes* parallel. This is plain from the fixed relation which all the appearances bore to the horizon and zenith, as well as to the sun.

Let us take, for instance, the case of the most conspicuous feature, which happens also to be that which admits of the simplest explanation, viz. the white horizontal circle. All the rays by which this was seen had the same inclination to the horizon as the direct solar rays (or *some* of them, viz. those coming from *some* part of the sun's disc). Moreover, the absence of colour showed that these rays had either suffered no refraction, or equal and opposite amounts of refraction, so that their change of direction could be due only to *reflexion*. Now in order that a reflected ray may retain the same inclination to the horizon that it had before reflexion, it is plain that the reflecting surface must be *vertical*, though it may be turned towards any azimuth. The appearance of this circle therefore requires us to suppose innumerable reflecting surfaces turned to all possible azimuths, but all of them truly vertical. This would be the case if the air contained innumerable prisms of ice, having all their axes vertical, but their sides turned in all directions. All the light reflected from these sides, without entering the prisms, would contribute to form the white circle above described. And this would also be the case with that light which entered the prism and suffered an internal reflexion from the opposite side, provided it passed out again through a vertical face; for though the two refractions might not always compensate each other *horizontally*, so as to produce no change of *azimuth* in the ray, yet they would always compensate each other *vertically*, so that the ray would suffer no change of *inclination*, and consequently no dispersion into colours in a vertical plane: and its dispersion horizontally would not impair the achromatism of the appearance; for if the circle were composed of innumerable horizontal spectra overlapping each other, it would still be colourless.

If we further trace the light that passes through two vertical sides of these prisms without suffering reflexion, we shall see that it emerges with no change of *inclination*, but with a change of *azimuth* depending chiefly on the inclination of the two refracting faces to each other. Now prisms of ice are either three- or six-sided. In either case, the two faces through which the light passes can only be either parallel or inclined $60°$ to each other: when parallel they will produce no refraction, and when inclined $60°$, a refraction never less than $23°$, but sometimes a few degrees greater. Hence the common halo of $46°$ in internal diameter, produced when these prisms are turned in all directions, so as to refract in all possible planes that pass through the sun. But when the prisms are all parallel, as we have supposed, they can refract in only two directions, so that all the light which would otherwise form the halo will be collected at two opposite points of its circumference; and if all the axes of the prisms be vertical, the only portions of the halo that will be visible will be those to the right and left of the sun, and on the horizontal circle passing through his disc: hence the two single spectra or mock-suns, which formed so striking a part of this display. Nor is there any difficulty in understanding why these spectra were *not* exactly on the circumference of the common halo (see fig. 4), but rather further from the sun. This was a necessary consequence of the plane of refraction being *inclined* to the axes of the prisms, the effect of which was to render their refracting angle *virtually* greater than $60°$, and the refraction therefore greater than $23°$. In the formation of the common halo, this cause must also operate in a great number of the prisms; for if they lie in all directions, the refraction cannot always take place in a plane perpendicular to the prism's axis. This is generally overlooked in popular explanations of the theory of the halo, and hence arises a discrepancy that has often puzzled the writer, between that theory and the appearance itself; for whoever regards a common halo, will see that it is not, as theoretically described, a luminous ring or band of definite breadth like the rainbow, but only the boundary between a less luminous and a more luminous space. The whole sky outside this boundary is brighter than within it, though this brightness rapidly diminishes from the circle outwards. If we regard it as a luminous ring, therefore, only its inner edge is defined, and only on this edge is there any appearance of colour, viz. red, orange, yellow, and then *white*, with perhaps a very faint tinge of green; but beyond the yellow, or the point of maximum brilliancy, there is no other decided colour, and the colourless light dies away so gradually that it is impossible to assign its outer limit. This is by no means then a complete spectrum, like the rainbow.

Now if we consider that the prisms producing the halo may, owing to their various positions, produce various amounts of refraction, but in no case *less* than a certain amount, this limit being about $23°$, but different for the different colours; if we further remember, that the nearer a prism may be to this limiting position which gives the *least* refraction, the more *slowly* will the amount of refraction change with the change of position; and further, that (for more causes than one) the *more* refraction any prism may produce, the *less* light will it transmit;—we shall see that if a halo were formed by homogeneous light coming from a source of no appreciable size, such as a star, the circle of maximum brilliancy would be *at its inner edge*, from whence the light would diminish outwards as the ordinates of some curve *very concave*, something like B, fig. 4, which curve being cut out and placed on the blackened rim of a wheel, with its broader end towards the axis, would, on

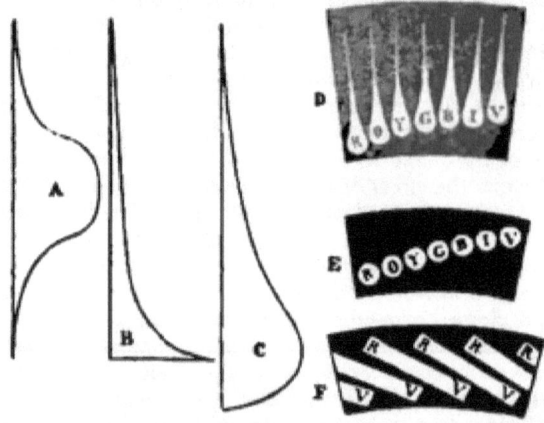

Fig. 4.

being rapidly revolved, give the appearance of such a halo[*]. But if the light came from a source whose diameter was about $30'$, such as the sun, the inner diameter of the halo would be diminished by about $30'$, and the circle of greatest brilliancy,

[*] Light figures placed on a dark wheel and made to revolve in this manner afford a good means of illustrating a large number of optical facts besides the composition of colours. To make the results obvious, the figures should be repeated as many times as the circumference of the wheel will contain them.

remaining where it was, would be 15′ from the inner edge; which edge, however, would still be very sharply defined, for the light would diminish towards it like the ordinates of some such curve as C (fig. 4), so that the halo would resemble that formed by placing C on a black wheel, and making it revolve instead of B. Finally, when the light is not homogeneous but *white*, and comes from a source of 30′ diameter, innumerable halos are formed, each resembling that last described, but all having different radii, the red least and the violet greatest. To imitate this effect, therefore, take several such figures as C (say seven, painted with the seven principal colours), and place them on the black wheel at different distances from its axle, as in fig. D. This arrangement, when revolving, would give nearly the appearance of the common halo; though to give it exactly, would require an infinite number of such figures, at distances and with colours, intermediate between R and O, between O and Y, &c.

In this way the difference between the colours of the halo and those of the rainbow may be well shown. For it is plain that if a rainbow were formed by homogeneous light coming from a star, or a physical *point*, the bow would be a mere physical *line*. Let the light come from a source of 30′ diameter, and the homogeneous bow will be 30′ broad, and its intensity will vary from side to side according to the ordinates of a *circle*. Such a bow may be seen by turning a black wheel, on which are one or more equal circular discs of colour, at equal distances from the axle. *Both* the edges of such a bow will be well-defined. Now to imitate the bow formed by *white* light, the discs must have various colours, and be placed at unequal distances from the axle, as at E (fig. 4), the imitation being more exact, the larger the number of discs having different tints and distances, provided they be all confined to a ring no wider than about three and a half times their own diameter (for the primary, or six times for the secondary bow).

In the same way, a figure or repetition of figures like A, placed at *equal* distances from the axle of the wheel, will on revolving give the appearance of the large horizontal band in the phænomena above described; and a number of complete spectra arranged as at F, will produce the effect of one of the bands of large radius near the zenith in figs. 1 and 2.

As all the effects above stated, in the case of a halo, must take place equally in that of the lateral mock-suns, which are in fact merely detached portions of a very intense halo, this explains why they appear to have colourless *tails* directed from the sun, and fading gradually as they recede from him. These tails correspond to the outer and colourless portion of a halo.

If all the icy prisms contained in the air have their axes truly parallel, it is plain that these phænomena will be unaccompanied by any ordinary halo; as in the first of the displays above described: but if a portion of the crystals be dispersed by the wind, or a cessation of the cause (electrical induction, or whatever it might be) that kept them in their polar state, the portion so scattered would, by refracting in all directions, produce a circular halo in addition to the former appearances; as actually happened in the afternoon display: but as long as this scattering was not complete, so as to turn the prisms in all directions *equally*, the halo would not be equally luminous throughout, but as shown in fig. 3. On the following day, however, all vestiges of a polar arrangement had disappeared, and the refraction being performed *equally* in all directions, produced a *regular* halo of greatly increased splendour, but without any of the other appearances.

We have as yet spoken only of the light reflected and refracted by the *sides* of the icy prisms; but it is plain that their *ends*, whether flat, or terminated by pyramids or any other forms, must produce effects of a similar kind, but more complicated; and to their action we must refer the various other arcs and parhelia described and figured above, and *differently* in every different account of such phænomena. If we consider in how many different ways a prismatic crystal may be terminated, from a flat face to the most complex pyramids, or the *tables* and still more complex forms observed in snow and rime, we shall indeed find no difficulty in believing, that hardly any two displays of parhelia agree in the form and arrangement of their circles and arcs, *except* so far as regards the white horizontal circle and the two spectra with tails, on the right and left of the sun, which seem to be common to all accounts of these phænomena; as they must be if due, as we have suggested, to the action of the invariable *sides* of the prisms, independently of their *ends*.

It would doubtless be possible, from the description of one of these exhibitions, to determine the precise form of both the upper and lower ends of the icy crystals which produced it; or, conversely, to determine what appearances would be produced in an atmosphere charged with crystals of a given form. Both these problems, however, would be very laborious; but there is a way of solving the second of them by *experiment*, which I think will serve to show very clearly the *rationale* of these appearances.

Suppose that in a dark room we have a large white hemispherical surface, placed like a basin, with its edge horizontal, and in the centre of its concavity we suspend from above a small prismatic crystal of any kind, with its axis vertical. This crystal should be of *ice*, to imitate truly the effects observed in nature; but for merely showing the *principle* of these effects, any crystal of nearly similar shape, one of quartz for instance, will answer the purpose, though from its higher refractive power it will produce different curves from those produced by an ice crystal of the same shape.

Now if we admit into this arrangement a very small sunbeam, barely large enough to illuminate the whole of the crystal and nothing else, a portion of this beam, either passing by the edges of the crystal or through two parallel faces of it, will continue its course unaltered, and fall on the same spot of the basin as if no crystal had intervened. We will call this spot the *direct image*. Now the faces of the crystal will, by reflexion and refraction (even omitting the consideration of its double refraction), divide the remainder of the light into several beams of various intensities, according as they have, or have not, suffered one or more partial reflexions. These beams proceeding to various parts of the basin, will there paint various spots, some white and others coloured, according as they have been formed by reflexion or by refraction, or both. Now to see *all* the positions of these spots, arising from all possible positions of the crystal (with its axis vertical), we have only to turn it round on its axis, and if we then mark with a pencil the path of each moving spot, we shall obtain curves similar to the various bands and halos seen in these phænomena, and having the same positions with regard to the *direct image* and the *edge of the basin*, that the actual appearances have with regard to the sun and the *horizon*. Some of the spots will remain *stationary* or nearly so, and these will correspond with the places of the *mock-suns*. The whole appearance however might be exhibited to the eye far more correctly, by making the crystal revolve round its vertical axis *rapidly*, so that the spots being seen in all parts of their track at once, will appear as curves, and the whole hemispherical surface will then form an inverted representation of the sky during these phænomena, the various parhelia and bands being seen in their true colours, and with their true gradations of intensity. If the crystal have three or six vertical sides, it will on revolving always produce the white horizontal circle passing through the sun, and the two coloured mock-suns with tails. The rest of the appearances will vary with the form of the upper and lower terminations of the crystal.

The common halo cannot be imitated in this way, for this would require the crystal to revolve in every direction at once; but if we substitute for the crystal a small globe of water, then (provided the sun's altitude be below $42°$) the primary and secondary rainbows will be formed; inverted, of course, but in their true positions with regard to the direct solar image, and the horizon or edge of the basin, and in this case no rotation is necessary.

In these experiments, a single globule or crystal turns the various coloured rays into certain definite directions, which are obviously exactly opposite to those directions in which such rays will arrive *from* an innumerable assemblage of such drops or crystals (illuminated by *parallel* sunbeams) *towards* any single point, such as the spectator's eye. The experiments therefore produce an exact inversion of all those figures that would be seen by an eye placed in or near such an assemblage, and explain most clearly the production of the *rainbow* by an atmosphere loaded with watery globules;—of the *halo* when it is charged with icy prisms turned in all directions;—and of the various kinds of *parhelion* when all the prisms have their axes in one direction.

LXI. *On the Additions made to the Second Edition of the* Commercium Epistolicum. *By* Prof. DE MORGAN[*].

THE *Commercium Epistolicum* is the work which contains the final elaboration of the charge made by Newton's friends in England against Leibnitz, in which the latter is accused in many places of taking his *differential Calculus* from the *Fluxions* of the former. It is an *ex-parte*[†] statement to which no answer was returned, and which was said by its partizans, and by Newton himself, to be unanswerable. The first edition, then, the one which Leibnitz had the option of seeing and answering, is a document in the case which no editor could possess a right to alter, whether by addition or diminution. That any variations, inserted in a reprint, whether for explanation or reinforcement, ought to have been separated and distinctly described as new, is too obvious to need proof. As the laws of literary honour are now understood, any alteration made to pass as part of the original publication, would be looked upon as fraudulent if it served a purpose, and as most

[*] Communicated by the Author.
[†] It bears so much the form of the report of a judicial investigation and finding, that most subsequent writers have considered it as such. I believe I have sufficiently shown that it was never intended for anything but an *ex-parte* statement. See the Philosophical Transactions for 1846, p. 107, and the life of Newton in Knight's British Worthies. The Committee, had it been a jury, would now be considered as having been packed: but as composed of agents and counsel, it was a very different thing. Nevertheless there was some unfairness in the judicial form of the report with which the publication ends.

## Second Edition of the Commercium Epistolicum. 447

improper even if it were not material. Those however who are acquainted with the bibliographical habits of the beginning of the last century, will not hastily impute wilful unfairness even to such additions and suppressions as some of those I shall have to describe.

Various circumstances not necessary to recount, and knowledge of those bibliographical habits among them, made me think it desirable to compare the second edition of the *Commercium Epistolicum* with the first. The latter is extremely scarce, the copy which belonged to Cavendish being, I believe, the only one brought to the hammer for many years: the former is comparatively common. Having borrowed a copy of the first edition from the library of the Royal Society, I made a close collation of the two editions, and found, as I thought likely, that several additions, upwards of twenty in number, had been made, some of them important. I drew up an account of these, and transmitted it to the Royal Society, by which I was informed, after the usual interval, that it was not intended to print the communication. One of my reasons for sending it to the Royal Society was the obvious one, namely, that the memory of Leibnitz has a peculiar claim upon that body for reparation of many wrongs. One of them, as I now make known, I believe for the first time, was the falsification of a record in a matter affecting his character, done under the name of the Society. I hold that the Royal Society of this day is the same scientific corporation which existed more than a century ago, deriving honour from the recollections of its former history, and therefore morally liable to make amends for former errors. Within about eighteen months of each other I presented two papers; the first intended to protect the memory of *Newton* against an imputation which, from oversight of historians, *might* have been cast, but *was not*, and incidentally to clear the Royal Society itself from the charge of packing a jury: the second intended to point out and repair a small portion of the wrong which *actually was done under the name of the Society to Leibnitz*. The first was printed, the second was archived. It is then the duty and pleasure of the Society to guard the fame of Newton, not only from what has been, but what might be, said against it; but it is affirmed to be either not its duty or not its pleasure to repair the effect of falsifications made in a publication issued under its name, when the sufferer, if any, must be Leibnitz.

Having presented that second paper (which, after the first, I could not but do, seeing that to have offered it elsewhere would have looked like an assumption that the Society would act as it has done), I cannot omit notice of the fact; nor, noting the fact, can I do less than enter a protest. I must notice the fact, because, with reference to the paper decently interred at Somerset House, but exhumable at pleasure of any Fellow of the Society, it is necessary that I should announce that the present communication is altogether rewritten, without my even* seeing the former one.

It is obvious that, from the moment when the fact of interpolation is known, the second edition can be no longer cited. But as the scarcity of the first (of which only a few copies were printed, and those all distributed as presents,—it was very scarce even in 1715) makes the citation of it almost impossible, the remedy is to publish a full account of all the variations. This I do, excepting of course alterations of reference, and excepting also trifling changes of idiom, to mend the Latin, such as altering an indicative into a subjunctive, and the like.

The first edition† was published in 1712. Leibnitz died in 1716. The second edition exists with two‡ title pages, one of 1722, the other of 1725, but both from the same type. Something which cannot now be explained occurred in the printing. Sheet K ends with page 144, but L begins with a second page 129; and this wrong paging is continued to the end of M, after which N begins with 177, as it would have done if there had been no interruption. In the *Ad Lectorem*, page 169 is referred to, which does not exist: that which should have been 169 is the second 153, and there the matter is found to which reference was made.

---

* I am quite aware that the Society would have allowed me to copy it, if I had been so inclined.

† Its title is "Commercium Epistolicum D. Johannis Collins, et aliorum de Analysi promota: jussu Societatis Regiæ In lucem editum. Londini: typis Pearsonianis, Anno M DCC XII." Quarto (folio signatures), pp. iv + 122.

‡ The first has after the word *editum*, "Et jam Una cum ejusdem Recensione præmissa, et Judicio primarii, ut ferebatur, Mathematici subjuncto, iterum impressum. Londini: Ex Officinâ et impensis J. Tonson, et J. Watts, prostant venales apud Jacobum Mack-Euen, Bibliopolam Edinburgensem. M DCC XXII." Octavo, pp. vi + 250 + 1 (errata).

The second is "Commercium Epistolicum de Varia Re Mathematica, Inter Celeberrimos præsentis seculi Mathematicos. Viz. Isaacum Newtonum Equitem Auratum. Dnum Isaacum Barrow. Dnum Jacobum Gregorium. Dnum Johannem Wallisium. Dnum J. Keillium. Dnum J. Collinium. Dnum Gulielmum Leibnitium. Dnum Henricum Oldenbourgum. Dnum Franciscum Slusium. Et alios. Jussu Societatis Regiæ in lucem editum. Et jam Una cum Recensione præmissa insignis Controversiæ inter Leibnitium et Keillium de primo Inventore Methodi Fluxionum; et Judicio primarii, ut ferebatur, Mathematici subjuncto, iterum impressum. Londini: Impensis J. Tonson et J. Watts, Prostant venales apud J. Mac Euen ad Insigne Georgii Buchannani e regione templi Sancti Clementis in vico vulgo dicto the Strand. 1725." Octavo, &c., as before.

With the new *Ad Lectorem*, the *Recensio* taken from the Philosophical Transactions, the reprint of John Bernoulli's letter and the comments on it, I have nothing to do; this is all avowedly new matter. The *reprint* commences with the old title-page, the words *typis Pearsonianis* being omitted. The variations are as follows: the first paging being that of the first edition, the second of the second.

I. (12, 80). The following note is added: "* N.B. eodem sensu quo *Newtonus* utitur symbolo $\boxed{\dfrac{aa}{64x}}$ *Leibnitius* utitur Symbolo S $\dfrac{aa}{64x}$." Interpreting this note in the sense of all the rest, it implies of course that Leibnitz took Newton's meaning and adapted it to a new symbol. This is not correct in any particular; for Newton's symbol merely means "area to the ordinate $aa : 64x$," while Leibnitz's symbol means the sum of differentials or integral. And moreover Leibnitz does not use the symbol $Sy$ but $Sydx$, involving a very different idea. Neither is it pretended that Leibnitz, before publication of his system, ever saw the letter on which this note is written, or any other which contains the symbol above given.

II. (18, 90). All the words in the note from "Eadem explicatur" to "Anno 1669" are new. The new editors undertake to assert that *a* method, which Newton only alludes to, must have been *the* method in the fifth proposition of the book on Quadratures. That is to say, those who in their new *Ad Lectorem*, construe Leibnitz's silence as an admission of everything, make him admit one proposition more. This remark of course may be made throughout.

III. (19, 91). This note is new: "*Leibnitius* scribit $dx$ pro $o$ vel $ox1$, $dz$ pro $ov$ vel $oy$." Another unfairness of the same sort as in (I.). It is not pretended that Leibnitz ever saw this letter, or any other in which $x+o$ is written for $x$; but under the assertion that Leibnitz saw *certain letters*, the new editors exaggerate the prevailing fallacy of the old ones, namely, the assumption of the right to bring *any letters* forward as proving that what Leibnitz had in common *with* them must have been taken *from* them. Those who remember the rational protest which the English made against the editors of the Leipsic Acts (January 1705), for using words implying substitution instead of independent adoption, when describing what Newton had done, and the lame answer which was made to that protest, will recognise a parallel in the conduct of both sets of editors, new and old, of the *Commercium Epistolicum*.

IV. (22, 96). The note is new. Gregory states that he had derived a method of tangents from that of Barrow; on which the new editors say, " Hinc innotuit Methodum Tangentium *Gregorii* et *Slusii* ex methodo *Barrovii* consequi." Here *consequi*, as to Gregory, means by his statement, that his *knowledge* of his own method came from his *knowledge* of Barrow's; and there is every appearance of the word being intended to apply in the same manner to Slusius.

V. (29, 103). The note is new. It is immaterial, and merely amounts to reminding the reader that *several* is at least *two*.

VI. (30, 105). The following note is new. " * Sc. in tractatu quem *Newtonus* scripsit Anno 1671. Missum autem fuit Apographum hujus Epistolæ ad *Tscurnhausium* mense Maio 1675, et ad Leibnitium mense Junio 1676." The assertion about Leibnitz will presently occur more definitely. How the fact was known with reference to Tschirnhausen is not stated.

VII. (37, 113). The first sentence of the note, consisting of the three words " Imo observata fuit," is new. Slight as the matter is, the general tendency of the additions to bring out the unfairness of the original, and to convert hints into assertions, is curiously exemplified. The reader will see that the meaning of the addition is as follows:—Leibnitz says it is wonderful that Pascal did not notice, that when the binomial coefficients are set down in rows, the columns are the triangular, pyramidal, &c. (or what were also called *figurate*) numbers. The note of the old editors says in effect, " He did not *exactly* notice this, but still you are not *much* in advance of Pascal, for the latter *did* note a very remarkable property of these columns, which is known to belong to the figurate numbers." But the words added by the new editors turn the note into " He *did* notice it, and you are *not at all* in advance of Pascal, for, &c." Leibnitz was quite right, and the more so from Pascal's knowledge of the property. Both the original and the augmented notes are unmerited comments on the modest remark by which Leibnitz accompanies his natural expression of wonder, " Sed est profecto casus quidam in inveniendo, qui non semper maximis ingeniis maxima, sed sæpe etiam mediocribus nonnulla offert."

VIII. (37, 114 and 115). One of the connecting comments runs thus in the two editions.

| *First Edition.* | *Second Edition.* |
|---|---|
| Quinetiam duæ aliæ D. Leibnitii ad Oldenburgum Epistolæ, altera Anno 1674 Julii 15, altera Octob. 26 sequente, Parisiis datæ, le- | Hactenus D. Leibnitius in Arithmetica versabatur, jam ad Geometriam se convertit, et Anno proximo ad Oldenburgium scribit Epistolas duas |

| | |
|---|---|
| guntur in Lib. Epist. Regiæ Societatis Nº. 7. pag. 93 et 110, eædemque reperiuntur impressæ in Tomo tertio Operum Mathematicorum D. J. Wallis. | Parisiis Jul. 15 et Oct. 36[sic] datas, quæ leguntur in Lib. Epist. Regiæ Societatis Nº 7. pag. 93 et 110, eædemque reperiuntur impressæ in Tomo tertio Operum Mathematicorum D. J. Wallis, et in scriniis Reg. Societatis asservantur earum Autographa. |

It is particularly to be noted, that the additions make it appear that new access had been obtained to the stores of the Royal Society; and this shows, on the one hand, that the new edition* came from the Society, and on the other, that there is *pro tanto* evidence for the facts stated. The new editors have prefixed to the extract from the letter of July 15 the first words of the letter, " Diu est quod nullas a me habuisti literas."

With regard to the assertion about Leibnitz, first made after his death, that up to 1673 he had concerned himself with arithmetic only, and from that time applied himself to geometry, it is founded upon his having first corresponded on arithmetic and afterwards on geometry. It was intended to prejudice his cause, by producing the impression that at the time of his announcement of the differential Calculus he was but a new student of the higher analysis. With the statement, however, I have nothing to do here, except to note the unfairness of printing it as if he had been challenged to deny it during his life, and had not done so. Remembering how nearly the life of Leibnitz was absorbed in jurisprudence, politics, history and metaphysics, and how little of it remained for mathematics,— remembering also the uniform manner in which Leibnitz's later declarations of this press of occupation were treated as evasion,—it would have been fairer if one of the earlier declarations, made before any question arose, had been inserted by the original editors from the first of these two letters, " Incumbunt enim mihi labores quidem inter se plane diversi; quos partim Principes a me exigunt, partim Amici. Unde parum temporis restat quod inquisitioni Naturæ, et contemplationibus Mathematicis impendere possim."

* This, I believe, was never doubted, though the names of the editors have never been published that I know of. Another fact is, that the diagrams of the second edition are from the same wood-blocks as those of the first, which certainly were the property of the Society. Biot attributes the publication to Newton himself, of which there is no proof. Newton may have suggested or approved a second edition; but that he should take any part in its preparation, at the age of eighty-two, is very unlikely.

IX. (43, 123). The note "N.B. In hoc .... impressæ" is new. It is not material.

X. (45, 125). The first sentence of the extract, "Dearum tibi literarum debitor, rogo ne sequius interpreteris silentium meum, soleo enim interrumpi nonnunquam, et hæc studia per intervalla tractare," is the insertion of the new editors, who may have been desirous to clear the old ones of the suppression to which I alluded above.

XI. (46, 127). In "Hoc anno cum D. Gregorius anno superiore ad finem vergente emortuus esset," the five words *anno .... vergente* are new.

XII. (47, 128). In the following comment the bracketed parts are new:—

"In hac Collectione habetur [Epistola superius impressa Gregorii ad Collins 5 Sept. 1670. Habetur et] Epistola superius impressa, quo (sic; qua in original) Gregorius Quadraturam prædictam Arithmeticam initio Anni 1671 cum D. Collins communicavit: Habetur et Epistola D. Newtoni ad D. Collins, 10 Decemb. 1672 data, et superius impressa, in qua Newtonus se Methodum generalem habere dicit ducendi Tangentes, quadrandi Curvilineas, et similia peragendi; et Methodum Exemplo ducendi Tangentes exponit: quam Methodum D. Leibnitius *differentialem* postea vocavit. [Hæc Collectio ad D. Leibnitium missa fuit 26 Junii 1676]."

With this must be joined the addition presently marked XVIII., announcing the date at which Collins died. The second addition above is the most unjustifiable of all, as being the most important. In fact, this one addition makes the second edition of the *Commercium Epistolicum* a very different thing from the first, as I shall proceed to show.

Look at the final report of the Committee, and it will appear that two distinct points are enunciated and declared to be sustained by the evidence printed before that report: first, that Newton had his method at an early date; secondly, that Newton's method had been communicated to Leibnitz. With the first I have here nothing to do. The second point is summed up by saying, that Leibnitz had no other differential method except that of Mouton "before his letter of [the] 21st of June 1677, which was a year after a copy of Mr. Newton's letter, of [the] 10th of December 1672 had been sent to Paris to be communicated to him; and above four years after Mr. Collins began to communicate that letter to his correspondents; in which letter the method of Fluxions was sufficiently describ'd to any intelligent person." The bracketed words are additions.

Look back at the evidence which is meant to support this

assertion, and it will appear that a parcel is said to exist in the handwriting of Collins with this title, "Excerpta ex D. Gregorii Epistolis cum D. Leibnitio communicanda, tibique postquam perlegerit ille reddenda." The party addressed is Oldenburg. Not one word is said of any date at which the parcel was sent; and this defect the new editors supply in the second addition to the paragraph above. Suppose Collins never to have fulfilled his intention of sending this parcel, and all presumption raised in the report against the originality of Leibnitz disappears. The importance and the unfairness of the addition will now be clearly seen.

Where did the new editors get this date? Had it existed in the handwriting of Collins or Oldenburg, they would have gladly certified it, according to their usual practice. I suspect they saw that the next communication from Oldenburg to Leibnitz was marked (49, 131) as having been forwarded to Leibnitz* on the 26th of June; and jumped (might I not almost say sneaked) to a conclusion, that the parcel was forwarded at the same time, and announced the conclusion without grounds. Observe that the letter of advice, which was part of this parcel, written to Oldenburg by Collins, *is given without date* by the original editors, and no date is supplied by the new ones. They always give dates in other cases.

I have looked carefully through the original edition, and I find that every letter is fully dated except four: and that of the four exceptions, one is dated by year and month (the day being omitted); one is Collins's copy of one of his own letters, and the editors seem to be inclined to take Collins's full date as that of the copy (I should take it of course to be that of the letter); one is Keill's letter to Leibnitz, written by order of the Society, which is only dated as to when it was read to the Society, Keill being left to put the date of transmission afterwards. One remains wholly undated, and without any account of the reason why; and that one is the letter on which the whole turns. Everything depends on Collins sending a certain letter to Oldenburg, with other letters which the first directs him to send on to Leibnitz; and that first letter is the only one in the whole book of the date of which nothing is said.

Collins was an accomptant, a writer on book-keeping, an immense correspondent, one of that class who are usually rather pedantic than otherwise about dates, dockets, and directions. We are left to believe, first, that he did not date this

* Leibnitz, in his answer, acknowledges letters of the 26th of *July*: but between *Junii* and *Julii* the difference is so slight, that we may suspect a printer's or writer's error. It is not of much consequence.

letter; secondly, that having marked the parcel as containing letters from *Gregory*, he inserted one of *Newton* without any notice, either on the parcel or in the letter of advice.

I have called this *collectio* a parcel, presuming it to have consisted of detached papers. Had it been otherwise, the Committee would certainly have noted the unity of the material; they would have seen that it established Newton's letter as a constituent part of the communication, in spite of the title only mentioning Gregory. They must have seen that their evidence on this point was singularly uncircumstantial: they must have known that their report on the date of transmission was wholly unsupported, even by assertion. It is impossible to suppose that they did not look for and mention all attainable facts tending to authenticate their final conclusion. Moreover, the old editors mention two species of papers as written by Collins; *collectio* and *schediasma*. Had they used the first word only, it might have been judged possible that they would apply it to a number of extracts, all on one paper. But, seeing that they use both words, and both for collections of copies or extracts, surely the first must have meant a parcel of papers, and the second a parcel of extracts on one paper.

Connected with this parcel, is their suppression of the material fact of the time at which Collins died, which was supplied by the new editors (see XVIII.). He died in 1682, and his papers were examined in 1712. Where they had been during these thirty years the Committee do not state, nor how and when they came into the possession of the Royal Society. If, as I think sufficiently established, we are to call the *Collectio* a parcel of detached papers, then we are called upon to believe, as a matter of course, that Collins's executors tied up the voluminous papers which they examined in the same parcels as were untied, and that the same luck attended this one parcel at least, during thirty years. This is but poor foundation for a charge of plagiarism.

Further, we are to suppose that Newton, in his celebrated *epistola posterior*, written to be sent to Leibnitz, wrapped up his method of fluxions in a cipher, though he knew that Collins had been for four years communicating on all sides, and to Leibnitz himself, a letter in which that method "was sufficiently described to any intelligent person."

XIII. (71, 149 of the wrong paging). The words in the note "Et Newtonus .... p. 105" are new.

XIV. (72, 150 of the wrong paging). The words in the note "et per Epistolam .... 84" are new.

XV. (74, 153 of the wrong paging). The note is new.

XVI. (86, 189). The note " ‡ Surdos indices D. Leibnitius

in Epistola sequente mutavit in fluentes, et inde natus est calculus exponentialis" is new. The insinuation is of a piece with the rest.

XVII. (95, 202). Leibnitz announces a theorem to which the old editors append the following note: " † Rogatur D. Leibnitius ut hoc Theorema lucem tandem videat." The new editors suppress this note, apparently as thinking it useless to make the request of Leibnitz after he was dead. This is something in their favour, as to motive: it shows that their incorrect notions of a reprint acted both ways. So far as not answering the challenge would leave Leibnitz under the imputation of having boasted of what he could not do, and thereby diminish the probability of his having been original in what he said he did do, so far they abandoned an advantage.

XVIII. (97, 205). In the summary of events the bracketed words are new: " Brevi postea, Autumno scilicet anni 1677, mors Oldenburgi huic literarum Commercio finem imposuit. Deinde anno 1682 [Collins mortuus est, et] Acta eruditorum Lipsiæ primum edita sunt," &c.

I have before pointed out (see XII.) the effect of this insertion. The occurrence of the death of Oldenburg, followed by the very date of that of Collins, must have suggested the mention of the death of the latter. I am afraid the omission must be considered as an advised suppression by the original editors.

XIX. (100, 210). The last sentence of the note, " Et *Pellius* cui hæ series ignotæ non erant, cum *Leibnitio* de seriebus verba habuit." The new editors did not like to lose a chance.

XX. (101, 211). The words in the note " Alteras *Newtoni* olim acceperat ab *Oldenburgo*" are new.

XXI. (108, 222). In the third note the word *Corollarium* is altered in the second edition into *Scholium*.

I shall now mention a matter in which the two editions closely agree, but which, I think, has escaped notice. The report of the Committee is English, with a Latin translation in the form of foot notes for the use of foreigners. Two decided mistranslations occur, of which I should pass over the first, if it were not that the Committee have a right to such presumption as it will afford that the second was carelessness or oversight. The first is as follows:—" and compar'd those of Mr. Gregory with one another, and with Copies of some of them taken in the Hand of Mr. Collins," is rendered by " Literas autem quæ Gregorium præ se ferebant auctorem, ipsius esse cognovimus fide Collinii, qui nonnullas earum Gregorio assignatas manu sua exscripserat." The second is as follows:—" In which Letter the Method of Fluxions was sufficiently describ'd to any intelligent Person," is rendered by "In hac autem Epistola Methodus Fluxionum idoneo harum rerum cognitori evidenter satis describitur." If not from carelessness, this version arises from an intention, that no foreigner might see the assertion that Newton had written on Fluxions to the comprehension of any intelligent person, mathematician or not. Perhaps some may think that the word *intelligent* had not then obtained its modern signification of general power of understanding. Perhaps it had not, quite: but that the thing was monstrous, even at the time, is made evident by a contemporary writer, who certainly did not strain at gnats, finding this rendering rather too much of a camel. Raphson it was who, in his history of Fluxions (printed both in English and Latin), showed his power of going all lengths by declaring his belief that Leibnitz had discovered Newton's *cipher* (which we all know was not a cipher, being only the letters of a sentence placed in alphabetic order), and thereby discovered fluxions. But rather than print the assertion about an intelligent person, he adopted the Latin as the original, and printed an English translation of his own, in which, instead of "to any intelligent person," we read "to any proper judge of these matters."

The more the whole matter is looked into from its beginning to its end, the more will the evidences of reckless injustice thicken about the inquirer. The Newtonian partizan may find a poor consolation in balancing the sins of a like character committed by the opposite party against those of his own. But all who do not allow a set-off to be pleaded in matters of right and wrong will, I think, if they look for themselves, find it necessary to disavow the cause and the conduct, and to regret the consequences.

---

LXII. *The Law of the Nutrition of Animals pointed out by Dr. R. D. Thomson, illustrated by* F. KNAPP, *Ph.D., Professor of Technology and Chemistry in the University of Giessen*\*.

ON the farm of Boussingault at Bechelbronn, in order to ascertain the quantity of milk produced, seven cows were subjected to an accurate series of experiments extending over a whole year. They received daily 30 pounds of hay, or of those roots similar in composition, and yielded together

\* Translated from Knapp's *Lehrbuch der Chemischen Technologie*, band ii. by Mr. John Brown.

An English translation of the first volume of this work by Messrs. Ronalds and Richardson has just appeared.

8788 maass (3837 quarts). The time during which they supplied milk was 302½ days. This gives as a mean 4·1 maass (1·8 qt.) daily for each cow. But the quantity of milk varies very much; for in the months of July and August they yielded above 6 maass (2·64 qts.), while in February and March they gave only about 2½ maass (1·1 qt.). From observations of a similar nature, made however upon only one cow, the average daily quantity of milk yielded was 3·7 maass (1·63 qt.). If we take 2½ maass (1·097 qt.) as the lowest quantity, and 7 maass (3·073 qts.) as the highest, we get daily, for one cow, from 10·3 lbs. to 29 lbs. of milk, which contain—

|  |  |
|---|---|
| 4·69 oz. troy to | 13·04 oz. butter. |
| 7·08 ... ... | 20·02 oz. sugar of milk and sol. salts. |
| 7·88 ... ... | 22·18 oz. caseine and insol. salts. |
| Total 19·65 ... ... | 55·24 oz. solid matter. |

In reference to the influence which the food has upon the quantity of milk, all farmers know that cows give most milk with green food and less with hay, &c. In other respects the influence of the food is not so great as might be expected.

Boussingault and Le Bel agree upon this point, at least so far as concerns the quantity of milk[*]. Dr. R. D. Thomson, on the contrary, draws from similar and equally extensive experiments the conclusion, that the quantity of milk and butter increases in proportion to the quantity of nitrogen (contained in the plastic matter) of the food. He has drawn this conclusion from experiments upon two cows during periods of five days. His results are shown in the following table, in which grass is the only exception[†].

| Kind of food. | Pounds of milk. | Pounds of butter. | Nitrogen in the food in 5 days, in lbs. |
|---|---|---|---|
| Grass | 114 | 3·50 | 2·32 |
| Barley and hay | 107 | 3·43 | 3·89 |
| Malt and hay | 102 | 3·20 | 3·34 |
| Barley, molasses and hay | 107[‡] | 3·44 | 3·82 |
| Barley, linseed and hay | 108 | 3·48 | 4·14 |
| Beans and hay | 108 | 3·72 | 5·27 |

[*] Boussingault has recently found that hay is equally efficacious with grass in producing milk and muscle; a result which is certainly not applicable to hay made in usual seasons in this country.—Tr.

[†] Dr. Thomson attributes the superiority of grass to the proper balance of the proximate principles, which in hay and grain is much altered by the drying process.—Tr.

[‡] In Dr. Knapp's work the number taken from the original is 106. The present number has been recalculated from the original data.—Tr.

Another table gives the average quantity of solid constituents of the milk for periods of five days.

| Kind of food. | Grass. | Barley entire. | Malt entire. | Barley crushed. | Malt crushed. | Barley and Molasses. | Barley and Linseed. | Beans. |
|---|---|---|---|---|---|---|---|---|
| | lbs. | lbs. | lbs. | lbs. | lbs. | lbs. | lbs. | lbs. |
| Milk | 29·64 | 25·57 | 24·82 | 28·12 | 26·61 | 26·96* | 27·48 | 27·0 |
| Butter | 5·96 | 5·56 | 6·56 | 6·87 | 6·43 | 7·00 | 7·00 | 7·5 |

The milk consists of—water, 87·19; butter, 3·70; sugar, 4·35; caseine, 4·16; sol. salts, 0·15; insol. salts, 0·44. The constituents of the butter are oil, 86·3; caseine, 0·9; water, 12·8.

The fact that not merely the quantity of milk but also that of the butter increases with the amount of nitrogenous matter in the food (that is, with the proportion of plastic nourishment), is worthy of notice; for from the absence of nitrogen in the butter, we should be apt to expect the contrary. Playfair, in his experiments, has certainly inferred this; for according to him, those substances which do not contain nitrogen (potatoes, &c.), yield milk rich in butter, and rest (stall-feeding) acts in the same way; while if the animal be allowed to feed on poor pasture, where it must move about a good deal, it yields milk rich in caseine. But his experiments are continued for such short periods, that important conclusions cannot be deduced from them. From Dr. Thomson's observations, we find that if a cow always receives the same kind of food, the quantity of milk gradually decreases; but if its diet be changed, it rapidly increases. A frequent change of diet is therefore advantageous. He has also established the rule, that the quantity of milk obtained from a cow is greater in the morning than in the evening.

When fed on barley and hay, they yielded—

|  | Aug. 1. | Aug. 2. | Aug. 3. | Aug. 4. |
|---|---|---|---|---|
| Morning | 11¼ lbs. | 11⅛ lbs. | 10⅒ lbs. | 10¾ lbs. |
| Evening | 10½ | 9¼ | 9¼ | 9¼ |

[The following observations of Dr. Knapp are founded on a table given by Dr. Thomson, deduced from his own experiments, in which the relation between the nutritive and calorifiant matter is stated for different kinds of food.

---

* This number is 25·69 in the original German, but has been recalculated from the English data.—Tr.

|  | Relation of nutritive to calorifiant matter. |
|---|---|
| Cow's milk—food for a growing animal | 1 to 2 |
| Human milk ... ... ... | 1 ... 6 |
| Beans ... ... ... | 1 ... 2½ |
| Oatmeal ... ... ... | 1 ... 5 |
| Semolina } Barley ... ... ... | 1 ... 7 |
| English wheat flour—food for an animal at rest. | 1 ... 8 |
| Potatoes ... ... ... | 1 ... 9 |
| Rice ... ... ... | 1 ... 10 |
| Turnips ... ... ... | 1 ... 11 |
| Arrow-root } Tapioca Sago ... ... ... | 1 ... 26 |
| Starch ... ... ... | 1 ... 40 |

(Thomson on the Food of Animals, p. 167.)

From this table it appears, that an animal taking exercise should be supplied with food formed upon the same principles as the first-mentioned six; and that in proportion to the exertion, the closer should be the relation between the ingredients.—Tr.]

In order to judge of the values of different kinds of food for practical purposes, it must first be ascertained in what relation the blood-forming or nutritive constituents stand to the calorifiant. The kind of food must also vary with age, kind of employment, way of living, climate, &c. With the highest probability we may predicate, that a man in an employment demanding great mental activity will require, in addition to a greater proportional amount of bodily rest, that the calorifiant and blood-forming constituents should be in a different proportion in the food, to that of the man whose employment requires great bodily activity.

Thomson has traced out a very simple and ingenious method of supplying this defect in our knowledge. He ascertains the weight and composition of the food given in a certain time, as also that of the excrement thrown out. From both factors he is enabled to calculate the quantity of food assimilated, as also the relation of the calorifiant to the blood-forming constituents. He found that a cow, stall-fed, assimilated daily 15·28 lbs. of rye-grass, which contained 1·56 lbs. of blood-forming and 13·00 lbs. of calorifiant matter. They thus stand in the relation of 1 to 8⅓, a proportion which, it is highly probable, is much more nearly related in man, as the relation in the various kinds of farinaceous food is about 1 to 5 or 1 to 6. We know with certainty that in the infant the relation, as in milk, must be 1 to $2\frac{1}{4}$.

A company of soldiers were fed on flesh, bread, vegetables, legumes, beer, brandy, fat, &c.; and from the experiments made on these by Liebig, the relation of the blood-forming to the calorifiant matter in the food may be accurately determined. By ascertaining the amount of food taken and the excrement thrown out, the quantity of food assimilated may be determined, as also the above-mentioned relation. In this manner the following results were obtained:—

|  | Water. | Solid matter. | Relation of the blood-forming to the calorifiant matter with solids. |
|---|---|---|---|
| Pounds of food consumed | 4001 | 1655 | 2346 | 298 : 1357 |
| Pounds of excrement . . | 294 | $220\frac{1}{2}$ | $73\frac{1}{2}$ | 13 : 51 |

Relation of the blood-forming to the calorifiant matter in the food assimilated } 285 : 1306 = 1 : 4·7.

As this number 4·7 is calculated from experiments made on persons who undergo considerable bodily exercise, it will increase\* in those whose employment is sedentary. Although these numbers are not absolutely correct, some important conclusions may be drawn from them.

It is evident that the relation 1 to 4·7 is almost exactly that which exists naturally in the various kinds of grain. Those barbarous nations which live entirely on flesh, receive a large excess of blood-forming matter, which may be counterbalanced either by the addition of calorifiant matter, or by increased bodily exercise. On the contrary, the poorer classes amongst us are obliged to live on the cheapest food they can obtain, such as potatoes, &c.†, which are one half poorer in blood-forming or nutritive matter than the different kinds of grain. In the first case nature has only to get rid of an excess; but in the latter she has to supply a deficiency, which must be done by bread, milk, &c. It must be evident to every one that this way of living is unnatural in the extreme. A person living

---

\* The word in the original is "vermindern;" but in the present case it is obvious that the author means the reverse of diminution.

† "The previous views," says Dr. Thomson (on Food, p. 173), "sufficiently explain the experiments which have been made upon cows, in which the result was unfavourable when they were fed on potatoes and beetroot in considerable quantities, as both of these substances contain an excess of calorifiant matter. It is well-known to feeders of cattle, that an animal fed on large quantities of potatoes is liable to such complaints as affections of the skin, and also to loss of weight. These consequently, it may be readily inferred, arise from the want of the proper balance between the elements of the food."—Tr.

entirely on potatoes may be said to be on the brink of a precipice without a single inch of ground before him, where the only safety lies in retreat. Its disadvantages may be shown in three different ways:—1st. It leads to imperfect bodily strength and unsoundness of health. 2nd. To increased mortality and shortness of life. 3rd. To loss of energy and to a kind of stupidity, and want of interest in everything but what concerns the merest animal interests. A country in this state is always ripe for rebellion, and ready to join in every insurrection.

From the above remarks, it would appear that the manufacture of brandy from potatoes is a separation of the excess of calorifiant matter, whilst the residue contains all the blood-forming constituents. It is mixed with the gluten of the malt, and thus forms a half-soluble food. In order however that it may suit the nature of ruminating animals, straw or some such food should be added to it. As potatoes contain about one part of albumen for ten of starch, the half of the starch may be converted into spirit, while the remainder will consist of a mixture having the nutritive and calorifiant constituents in the same proportion as in grain (1 : 5).

LXIII. *Objections to the Theories severally of* Franklin, Dufay *and* Ampère, *with an Attempt to explain Electrical Phænomena by Statical or Undulatory Polarization*\*. *By* ROBERT HARE, M.D., *Emeritus Professor of Chemistry in the University of Pennsylvania*†.

1. IT appears, from the experiments of Wheatstone, that the discharge of a Leyden jar, by means of a copper wire, takes place within a time so small, that were the transfer of a

\* Agreeably to Faraday's researches and general experience, we have reason to believe that all particles of matter are endowed with one or the other of two species of polarity. This word polarity conveys the idea that two terminations in each particle are respectively endowed with forces which are analogous, but contrary in their nature; so that of any two homogeneous particles, the similar poles repel each other, while the dissimilar attract; likewise when freely suspended they take a certain position relatively to each other, and on due proximity, the opposite polar forces, counteracting each other, appear to be extinct. When deranged from this natural state of reciprocal neutralization, their liberated poles react with the particles of adjacent bodies, or those in the surrounding medium. Under these circumstances, any body which may be constituted of the particles thus reacting, is said to be polarized, or in a state of polarization.

Statical implies stationary; undulatory, wave-like.

† Read before the Academy of Natural Sciences, and communicated, with corrections and additions, by the Author.

fluid from the positive to the negative surface requisite for its accomplishment, a current having a velocity exceeding two hundred thousand miles in a second would be necessary.

2. The only causes for the velocity of an electric current, according to Franklin, are the repulsion between the particles of the electric fluid of which it has been assumed to consist, and the attraction between those particles and other matter. These forces are alleged to concur in distributing the supposed fluid throughout space, whether otherwise void, or partially occupied by conducting solids or fluids. Hence, when between two or more spaces, surfaces, or conducting masses, there is an unequal distribution of the electric fluid, the equilibrium is restored whenever a communication is opened by means of a sufficiently conducting medium. Agreeably to this view of the subject, there seems to be a resemblance between the supposed effort of the electrical fluid to attain a state of equable diffusion, and that which would exist in the case of a gas confined in adjoining receivers, so as to be more dense within one than within the other; for, however the subtilty of the supposed electric fluid may exceed that of any gas, there seems to be an analogy as respects the processes of diffusion which must prevail. But on opening a communication between cavities in which any aëriform fluid exists in different degrees of condensation, the density must lessen in one cavity and augment in the other, with a rapidity which must diminish gradually, and become evanescent with the difference of pressure by which it is induced. Far from taking place in an analogous manner, electrical discharges are effected with an extreme suddenness, the whole of the redundancy being discharged at once, in a mode more like the flight of a bullet projected with infinite velocity, than that of a jet gradually varying in celerity from a maximum to a minimum.

3. So far, in fact, is an electrical discharge from displaying the features which belong to the reaction of a condensed elastic fluid, that, agreeably to the observations of our distinguished countryman Henry, the result is more like the vibrations of a spring, which, in striving to regain its normal position, goes beyond it. The first discharge between the surfaces of a Leyden jar is not productive of a perfect equilibrium. The transfer of different polarities goes beyond the point of reciprocal neutralization, producing a state, to a small extent, the opposite of that at first existing; and hence a refluent discharge ensues, opposite in direction to the primary one. But even this does not produce an equilibrium, so that a third effort is made. These alternate discharges were detected

by means of the magnetism imparted to needles exposed in coils of copper wire*.

4. Supposing one or more rows of electrical particles, forming such a filament of electricity as must occupy the space within a wire of great length, to be made the medium of discharge to a Leyden jar; agreeably to the hypothesis of one fluid, the electrical filament must be attracted at one end of the wire, and propelled at the other, as soon as its terminations are brought into due communication with the coatings of the jar. Yet the influence of the oppositely charged surfaces of the jar cannot be conceived to extend to those portions of the electricity which are remote from the points of contact, until they be reached by a succession of vibrations. Hence it is inconceivable that every particle in the filament of electric matter can be made at the same time to move, so as to constitute a current having the necessary velocity and volume to transfer, instantaneously, the electricity requisite to constitute a charge. Even the transmission of the impulses, in such an infinitesimal of time, seems to be inconceivable.

5. In reply to these objections, it has been urged by the Franklinians, that a conductor being replete with electricity, as soon as this fluid should be moved at one end, it ought to move at the other. This might be true of a fluid if incompressible, but could not hold good were it elastic. A bell wire moves at both ends when pulled only at one; but this would not ensue were a cord of gum elastic substituted for the wire.

6. But if the flow of one fluid with the enormous velocity inferred be difficult to conceive, still more must it be incomprehensible that two fluids can rush with similar celerity from each surface of the jar, in opposite directions, through the narrow channel afforded by a wire, especially as they are alleged to exercise an intense affinity; so that it is only by a series of decompositions and recompositions that they can pass each other. That, agreeably to the theory of Dufay, equivalent portions of the resinous and vitreous fluids must exchange places during an electrical discharge, will appear evident from the following considerations:—

7. One surface being redundant with vitreous and deficient commensurately of resinous electricity, and the other redundant with the resinous and deficient of the vitreous fluid, it is inevitable that to restore the equilibrium, there must be a simultaneous transfer of each redundancy to the surface wherein there is a deficiency of it to be supplied. If, after decomposing a large portion of the neutral compound pre-

* Communicated to the American Philosophical Society.

viously existing on the surfaces of the jar, and transferring the ingredients severally in opposite directions so as to cause each to exist in excess upon the surface assigned to it, it were necessary that the redundancies thus originated should be neutralized by meeting in the discharging rod, neither surface could recover its quota of the electrical ingredient of which it must have been deprived agreeably to the premises.

8. This calls to mind the fact, that no evidence has been adduced of the existence of any tertium quid, arising from the union of the supposed electricities, founded on any property displayed by their resulting combination in the neutral state. It must, if it exist, constitute an anomalous matter, destitute of all properties, and of the existence of which we have no evidence, besides that founded on the appearance and disappearance of its alleged ingredients.

9. But however plausibly the discharges consequent to making a conducting communication from one electrified mass or surface to another mass or surface in an opposite state, may be ascribed to accumulations either of one or of two fluids; neither, according to one theory nor the other, is it possible to account satisfactorily for the stationary magnetism with which steel may be endowed, nor the transitory magnetism or dynamic power of induction acquired by wires transmitting galvanic discharges.

10. For the most plausible effort which has been made for the purpose of reconciling the phænomena of electro-magnetism with the theory of two fluids, or with that of one fluid, so far as these theories are convertible, we are indebted to Ampère.

11. According to the hypothesis advanced by this eminent philosopher, the difference between a magnetized and an electrified body is not attributable to any diversity in the imponderable matter to which their properties are respectively due, but to a difference in the actual state or distribution of that matter. Statical polarity is the consequence of the unequal distribution of the two electric fluids whose existence he assumes; while magnetical polarity is the consequence merely of the motion of those fluids, which in magnets are supposed to gyrate in opposite directions about each particle of the mass. These gyrations are conceived to take place only in planes at right angles to the axis of the magnet; so that in a straight magnet the planes of the orbits must be parallel to each other[*].

12. The aggregate effect of all the minute vortices of the electrical fluids, in any one plane, bounded by the lateral

[*] The words gyration, vortex and whirl, are considered as synonymous, and used indifferently to avoid monotony.

surfaces of the magnet, is equivalent externally to one vortex, since in either case every electric particle on that surface will so move as to describe tangents to a circle drawn about the axis of the magnet. When the electrical vortices of the pole of one magnet conflict in their direction with those of another, as when similar magnetic poles are approximated, repulsion ensues; but if the vortices are coincident in direction, as when dissimilar poles are near, attraction takes place. When a current through a galvanized wire* concurs in direction with the magnetic vortices, as above described, attraction ensues; repulsion resulting when it does not so concur. Hence the magnet, if moveable, will strive to assume a position in which its electrical currents will not conflict with those of the wire on one side more than on the other: also the wire, if moveable, will tend so to arrange itself as to produce the same result, which can arrive only when the needle is at right angles to the wire, and its sides consequently equidistant therefrom.

13. Electric currents will produce magnetic vortices, and, reciprocally, magnetic vortices will produce electric currents. Hence the magnetism imparted to iron by galvanized spirals, and the Faradian currents produced by magnetized iron within spirals not galvanized.

14. Ampère's theory has, in a high degree, the usual fault of substituting one mystery for another; but, on the other hand, it has, in an equally high extent, the only merit to which any theory can make an indisputable claim: I mean, that of associating facts so as to make them more easy to comprehend and to remember, enabling us by analogy to foresee results, and thus affording a clue in our investigations. Evidently, the author of this theory was guided by it, in his highly interesting and instructive contrivances; and Professor Henry ascribes his success in improving the electro-magnet, to the theoretic clue which he had received from Ampère.

15. Nevertheless, the postulates on which this Amperian hypothesis is founded, appear to me unreasonable. They require us to concede that about every atom of a permanent magnet a process is going on, analogous to that generally admitted to exist in a galvanic circuit, where two fluids pass each other in a common channel by a series of decompositions and recompositions (7). In the galvanic circuit this process is sustained by chemical reaction; but without any co-enduring cause, how is it to be sustained permanently in a magnet? Is it reasonable to assume that the heterogeneous constituents

* I consider a wire as galvanized when it is made the medium of the discharge from a galvanic battery.

of an imaginary *tertium quid* are perpetually separating only to reunite? (S.)

16. In cases of complex affinity, where four particles, A B C D, are united into two compounds A B, C D, it is easy to conceive that, in obedience to a stronger affinity, A shall combine with C, and B with D: but, without any extraneous agency, wherefore, in any one compound, should a particle A quit one particle B, in order to unite with another particle of the same kind; or wherefore should any one, B, quit one A, in order to combine with another A?

17. That such a process should take place in consequence of the inductive agency of a similar process already established in a magnet or galvanized wire were difficult to believe; but it would seem utterly incredible that the most *transient* influence of such induction should be productive of such permanent electrolytic gyration as has been above specified. Moreover, it is inconceivable that the particles of any matter should, as required by this hypothesis, *merely by being put into motion*, acquire a power of reciprocal repulsion or attraction of which it were otherwise destitute.

18. The vortices being assumed to take place about each atom, cannot severally occupy an area of greater diameter than can exist between the centres of any two atoms. Of course, the gyratory force exercised about the surface of a magnet by the aggregate movements of the vortices, cannot extend beyond the surface more than half the diameter of one of the minute areas of gyration alluded to. Wherefore, then, do these gyrations, when similar in direction, from their concurrence approach each other; when dissimilar in direction from contrariety, move away, even when situated comparatively at a great distance?

19. I should consider Ampère's theory as more reasonable, were it founded upon the existence of one fluid; since, in that case, vortices might be imagined without the necessity of supposing an endless and unaccountable separation and reunion of two sets of particles; not only devoid of any property capable of sustaining their alleged opposite gyrations, but actually endowed with an intense reciprocal attraction which must render such gyrations impossible. But even if grounded on the idea of one fluid, this celebrated hypothesis does not seem to me to account for the phænomena which it was intended to explain. If distinct portions of any fluid do not attract or repel each other when at rest, wherefore should they either attract or repel each other when in motion? Evidently mere motion can generate neither attraction nor repulsion. Bodies projected horizontally gravitate with the

same intensity, and consequently, in any given time, fall to the earth through the same perpendicular distance, whether moving with the celerity of a cannon-ball, or undergoing no impulse excepting those arising from their own unresisted weights.

20. The objections which are thus shown to be applicable in the case of liquids, of which the neighbouring particles are destitute of the reaction requisite to produce the phænomena requiring explanation, must operate with still greater force where œthereal fluids are in question, of which the properties are positively irreconcileable with the phænomena. According both to Franklin and Dufay, bodies, when similarly electrified, should repel each other; yet in point of fact, collateral wires, when subjected to similar voltaic discharges, and of course similarly electrified, become reciprocally attractive, while such wires, when dissimilarly electrified by currents which are not analogous, become reciprocally repulsive.

21. Agreeably to Ampère, an iron bar, situated within a coil of wire subjected to a galvanic current, is magnetized, because the current in the wire is productive of an electrical whirlpool about every particle of the metal. When the iron is soft, the magnetism, and of course the gyrations of which its magnetism consists by the premises, cease for the most part as soon as the circuit through the coil is broken; but when the iron is in the more rigid state of hardened steel, the gyrations continue for any length of time after the exciting cause has ceased.

22. This theory does not explain wherefore the hardening of the steel should cause the gyration to be more difficult to induce yet more lasting when its induction is effected. Evidently the metallic particles must take some part in the process; since it is dependent for its existence and endurance upon their nature and their state. Yet no function is assigned to these particles. In fact, it is inconceivable, either that they can participate in, or contribute to, the supposed gyration.

23. The electrical fluid in an iron bar cannot form a vortex about each particle, all the vortices turning in one direction, without a conflict between those which are contiguous. In order not to conflict with each other, the alternate vortices would have to turn in different directions, like interlocking cog-wheels in machinery. But in that case, if magnetism be due to currents, the magneto-inductive influence of one set would neutralize that of the other. Again, how can a current, excited by a battery in one circuitous conductor, cause, by dynamic induction, a current in the *opposite direction*, through another conductor parallel to the first, but insulated there-

from? How can a current of quantity in a ribbon coil* give rise to one of intensity in a coil of fine wire, rushing of course with a velocity commensurate with the intensity thus imparted?

24. From the preceding considerations, and others which will be stated, it follows, that it has been erroneously inferred that the only difference between galvanic and frictional electricity is dependent on quantity and intensity. It must be evident that there is a diversity in the nature of these affections of matter, sufficient to create a line of demarcation between them.

25. Having stated my objections to the electrical theories heretofore advanced, it may be proper that I should suggest any hypothetical views which may appear to me of a character to amend or to supersede those to which I have objected. But however I may have been emboldened to point out defects which have appeared to me to be inherent in the theories heretofore accredited, I am far from presuming to devise any substitute which will be unobjectionable. I am fully aware that there is an obscurity as respects the nature and mutual influence of chemical affinity, heat, light, electricity, magnetism and vitality, which science can only to a minute extent dispel.

26. The hypothesis which I now deem preferable is so much indebted to the researches and suggestions of Faraday and others, that, were it true, I could claim for myself but a small share of the merit of its origination. That sagacious electrician employs the following language:—"*In the long-continued course of experimental inquiry in which I have been engaged, this general result has pressed upon me constantly, namely, the necessity of admitting two forces or directions of force combined with the impossibility of separating these two forces or electricities from each other.*"—*Experimental Researches*, 1169.

27. Subsequently (1244), after citing another proof of the inseparability of the two electric forces, he alleges *it to be* "*another argument in favour of the view that induction and its concomitant phænomena depend upon* a polarity of the particles of matter!"

### Supposed grounds for a Theory.

28. The grounds upon which I venture to advance a theory, are as follows:—

The existence of two heterogeneous polar forces acting in opposite directions, and necessarily connate and co-existent, yet capable of reciprocal neutralization, agreeably to the

* See Silliman's Journal, vol. xxxviii. p. 215. 1840.

authority of Faraday and others; the polarity of matter in general, as displayed during the crystallization and vegetation of salts; also as made evident by Faraday's late researches, and the experiments and observations of Hunt; the very small proportion of the space in solids, as in the instance of potassium and other metals, which can be occupied by the ponderable atoms; while, agreeably to the researches and speculations of Faraday (rightly interpreted), the residual space must be replete with imponderable matter. The experiments and inferences of Davy and others, tending to sanction the idea that an imponderable æthereal fluid must pervade the creation; the perfect identity of the polarizing effects, transiently created in a wire by subjection to a galvanic discharge, with those produced by the permanent polarizing power of a steel magnet; the utter heterogeneousness of the powers of galvanic and frictional electricity, as respects ability to produce sparks before contact, and likewise of the polarities which they respectively produce; the superficiality of electricity proper during discharge as well as when existing upon insulated surfaces, as demonstrated by atmospheric electricity when conveyed by telegraphic wires, agreeably to Henry; the sounds observed severally by Page, Henry and Marrian, as being consequent to making and breaking a galvanic circuit through a conductor, or magnetizing or demagnetizing by means of surrounding galvanized coils.

*Proofs of the existence of an enormous quantity of Imponderable Matter in Metals.*

29. It has been most sagaciously pointed out by Faraday, that 430 atoms which form a cube of potassium in the metallic state, must occupy nearly six times as much space as the same number of similar atoms fill when existing in a cube of hydrated oxide of potassium of the same size; which, besides 700 metallic atoms, must hold 700 atoms of hydrogen and 1400 of oxygen, in all 2800 atoms; whence it follows that, in the metallic cube, there must be *room* for six times as many atoms as it actually holds.

30. With all due deference, I am of opinion that this distinguished philosopher has not been consistent in assuming that, agreeably to the Newtonian idea of ponderable atoms, the space in potassium not replete with metal must be vacant; since, according to facts established by his researches, or resulting therefrom, an enormous quantity, both of the causes of heat and of electricity, exists in metals. Moreover, agreeably to his recent speculations, those causes must consist of

material, independent, imponderable matter, occupying the whole of the space in which their efficacy is perceptible. To the evolution of the imponderable matter thus associated, the incandescence of a globule of potassium on contact with water may be ascribed, since it is the consequence of the displacement of such matter by the elements of water which, in replacing it, converts the metal into the hydrated oxide called caustic potash.

31. The existence both of the causes of electricity and heat in metals, is likewise confirmed by the fact, that the inductive influence of a magnet is sufficient to cause all the phænomena of heat, electrolysis and magnetism, as exemplified by the magneto-electric machine. The existence of the cause of heat in metals is also evident from the ignition of an iron rod when hammered, or the deflagration of wire by the discharge of a Leyden battery.

32. The superiority of metals as electrical conductors, may be the consequence of the pre-eminent abundance of imponderable matter entering into their composition, as above alluded to in the case of potassium.

33. Graham, in his Elements, treating of electricity, alleges that the "great discoveries of Faraday have completely altered the aspect of this department of science, and suggests that all electrical phænomena whatever involve the presence of matter." Unless the distinguished author from whom this quotation is made intended to restrict the meaning of the word *matter* to ponderable matter, there was no novelty in the idea that electrical phænomena involve the presence of matter, since the hypotheses of Franklin and Dufay assume the existence of one or more imponderable material fluids. But, on the other hand, if the meaning of the word *matter* is only to comprise that which is ponderable, the allegation is inconsistent with the authority cited. According to the researches of Faraday, there is an enormous electrical power in metals, and according to his speculations, such powers must be considered as imponderable material principles, pervading the space within which they prevail, independently of any ponderable atom acting as a basis for material properties, the existence of such atoms being represented as questionable.

*Electrical Phænomena attributed to Stationary or Undulatory Polarization.*

34. It having been shown that in electrical discharges there cannot reasonably be any transfer of matter, so as to justify the idea of their being effected either by one current or by two currents, the only alternative seems to be that the phænomena

are due to a progressive affection of the conducting medium, analogous in its mode of propagation to waves, as in the case of liquids, or the aërial or æthereal undulations to which sound and light are ascribed (1, 2, 3, &c. &c.).

35. The idea intended to be conveyed by the word wave, as applied in common to the undulatory affections above-mentioned, and that which is conceived to be the cause of the phænomena usually ascribed to one or more electrical currents, requires only that there should be a state of matter, which, while it may be utterly different from either of those which constitute the waves of water, light or sound, may, nevertheless, like either, pass successively from one portion of a mass to another.

36. The affection thus designated may be reasonably distinguished from other waves as a *wave of polarization*, since the wire acts, so long as subjected to the reiterated discharges of a voltaic series, as if it were converted into innumerable small magnets, situated like tangents to radii proceeding from its axis.

37. But if a polarizable medium be requisite to electrical discharges, since they pass through a space when devoid of *ponderable* matter, there must be some *imponderable* medium through which they can be effected. Hence we have reason to infer that there is an imponderable matter existing throughout all space, as well as within conductors, which is more or less the medium of the opposite waves essential to electric discharges. Quoting his own language, Davy's experiments led him to consider "that space (meaning void space), where there is not an appreciable quantity of this matter (meaning ponderable matter), is capable of exhibiting electrical phænomena:" also that such phænomena "are produced by a highly subtile fluid or fluids." Moreover, that "it may be assumed, as in the hypothesis of Hooke, Euler, and Huygens, that an æthereal matter susceptible of electrical affections fills all space."

38. Agreeably to the suggestions above made, all ponderable matter which is liable to be electrified *internally* by electrical discharges, may be considered as consisting of atoms composed of imponderable æthereo-electric particles in a state of combination with ponderable particles, analogous to that which has been supposed to exist between such particles and caloric when causing expansion, liquidity or the aëriform state. Atoms so constituted of æthereal and ponderable particles, may be designated as æthereo-ponderable atoms[*].

[*] Pouillet suggests that when the passage of a ray of light through glass is influenced by a powerful magnet, agreeably to the experiments of Faraday,

39. A quiescent charge of frictional electricity only affecting the superficies of any ponderable mass with which it may be associated, and having no influence upon the component æthereo-ponderable atoms severally, is not to be ascribed to redundancies or deficiencies of the æthereal matter, but to different states of polarization produced in different sets of the particles of such matter existing about the electrifiable bodies*. During the action of an electrical machine, these particles are polarized by the opposite polarities transiently induced in the surfaces subjected to friction; one set of particles going with the electric, the other remaining with the rubber.

40. The particles thus oppositely polarized, severally divide their appropriate polarities with other æthereal matter surrounding the conductors, and this, when insulated, is retained until a further polarization results from the same process. Thus are the æthereo-electric atmospheres respectively surrounding the positive and negative conductors oppositely polarized, and consequently charged to the degree which the machine is competent to induce. Under these circumstances, if a conducting rod be made to form between them a communication, by touching each conductor with one of its ends, the polarities of the æthereo-electric atmospheres by which they are severally surrounded, propagate themselves, by a wave-like process, over and more or less through the rod, according to its nature and dimensions, so as to meet intermediately, and thus produce reciprocal neutralization.

---

" consistently with the undulatory theory of light, it is the æther of the body submitted to the experiment which would be modified by the magnetism, and that it would be very difficult to recognize whether it is modified without any participation of the ponderable matter with which it is so intimately connected." Thus the existence of matter, composed of æthereal as well as ponderable particles, is sustained by all the evidence which has been brought to uphold the undulatory theory of light.—L. & E. Phil. Mag. &c. for 1846, vol. xxviii. page 335.

* The word statical has been used to designate phænomena which are the effects of electricity when at rest, as when accumulated upon conductors or the surfaces of panes or jars. Phænomena which are supposed to arise from electricity in motion (forming a current), are designated as dynamic. Thus when charging one side of a pane produces the opposite state in the other, the effect upon the latter is ascribed to *statical* induction; but when a discharge of electricity through one wire causes a current in another, forming an adjacent circuit, the result is ascribed to *dynamic* induction. This method of designation is employed whether the alleged current be owing to electricity generated by friction, as in the case of a machine, or generated by chemical reaction, as in the case of a galvanic battery. A good word is wanting to distinguish electricity, when produced by friction, from electricity produced by galvano-chemical reaction: for want of a better, I will resort to that employed by Noad (*frictional*), which has the advantage of being self-explanatory.

41. When the oppositely polarizing waves, generated by friction as above described, are by means of a conducting communication transmitted to the surfaces of a coated pane, the two different portions of the electro-æther there existing are severally polarized in opposite ways, one being endowed with the properties usually called vitreous or positive, the other with those usually called resinous or negative. In fact, the two polarized atmospheres thus created may be conveniently designated as the "*two electricities*," and alluded to in the language heretofore employed in treating of phænomena, agreeably to the hypothesis which assumes the existence of heterogeneous fluids, instead of heterogeneous polarities.

42. Of course it will follow that the oppositely polarized æthereal atmospheres thus produced, one on each surface of the electric which keeps them apart, must exercise towards each other an attraction perfectly analogous to that which has been supposed to be exercised by the imaginary heterogeneous electric fluids of Dufay. The electro-æther\* being elastic, a condensation over each of the charged surfaces proportionable to the attractive force must ensue; while over the surface of an electrified conductor, the similarly polarized atoms not being attracted by those in an oppositely polarized atmosphere beneath the surface, tend, by their reciprocally repulsive reagency, to exist further apart than in a neutral state. Hence the electro-æther, as it exists over the surface of an insulated conductor, is rendered rarer, while, as existing over the surfaces of charged panes or Leyden jars, it must be in a state of condensation†. And consequently, while the space perceptibly electrified by the charge of a conductor, for equal areas and charging power, is much more extensive than the space in which the charge of a coated pane is perceptible, the striking distance being likewise much greater; yet upon any body successively subjected to a discharge from each, the effect will be more potent when produced by means of the pane.

*Ignition, Electrolysis and Magnetism, Secondary Effects of Frictional Discharges; or, in other words, of Polarizing Electro-æthereal Waves.*

43. In proportion as a wire is small in comparison with the charge which it may be made the means of neutralizing, the conducting power seems to be more dependent on the

---

\* As the word æther is used in various senses, the syllables "*electro*" being prefixed, serve to designate that which is intended.

† See my communication on "*Free Electricity*" in Silliman's American Journal of Science, vol. iii., New Series, Number for May 1847.

sectional area*, and less upon the extent of surface. The reciprocal repulsion of the similarly polarized æthereal particles must tend always to make them seek the surface, but at the same time their attraction for the æthereo-ponderable particles composing the wire has the opposite effect, and tends to derange these from their normal polar state of quiescence. Commensurate with the extent in which this state is subverted, is the resulting heat, electrolytic power, and electro-magnetic influence. The phænomena last mentioned are, however, secondary effects consequent to the participation of the æthereo-ponderable matter in the undulations resulting from the statical discharge.

44. Such effects, making allowance for the extreme minuteness of the time occupied by the process, are probably in all cases proportional to the degree in which the ponderable matter is affected, up to the point at which it is dissipated by deflagration; but the duration of a statical discharge being almost infinitely minute for any length of coil which can conveniently be subjected thereto, the electro-magnetic and other effects of a statical discharge are not commensurate with the intensity of the affection of the wire.

45. There is, in fact, this additional reason for the diversity between the electro-magnetic power of a statical discharge, as compared with that of the voltaic series: any wire which is of sufficient length and tenuity to display the maximum power of deflagration by the former, cannot serve for the same purpose in the case of the latter. Moreover, the form of a helix closely wound, so that the coatings may touch, which is that most favourable for the reiteration of the magnetic influence of the circuit upon an iron rod, cannot be adopted in the case of statical discharges of high intensity, since the proximity of the circumvolutions would enable the æthereal waves, notwithstanding the interposition of cotton or silk, to cross superficially from one to the other, parallel to the axis of the included iron, instead of pursuing the circuitous channel afforded by the helix with the intensity requisite to the polarization of the ponderable atoms.

*The extreme diversity, as respects striking distance, between the direct effects of Frictional Electricity and those directly arising from Galvanic Reaction.*

46. The intensity of the excitement produced by different electrical machines, is estimated to be as the relative lengths of the sparks which proceed from their prime conductors

---

* The sectional area of a conductor is the area of the superficies which would be exposed by cutting it through at right angles to its axis.

respectively. Admitting that the relative intensity were merely as the length of the spark, not as the square of that length, still there would be an infinite difference between the intensity of a voltaic series and that of electrical machines, if measured by this test. Large electrical machines, like that at the Polytechnic Institution, London, give sparks at twenty inches and more; while, agreeably to Gassiot's experiments, a Grove's battery of 320 pairs in full power, would not before contact give a spark at *any distance, however minute*. It follows, that, as respects the species of intensity which is indicated by length of sparks, or striking distance, the difference between the electricity of the most powerful voltaic series and electrical machines is not to be represented by any degree of *disparity*; it proves that galvanism proper and electricity proper are heterogeneous.

47. It should be recollected that the intensity of galvanic action, in a series of 320 pairs, excepting the loss from conduction, would be to that of one pair as 320 to 1\*. Of course, the striking distance of a battery of one pair would be 320 times less than nothing : 320 below zero.

48. We may infer that the undulatory polarization of æthereo-ponderable matter is the primary, direct, and characteristic effect of galvanic excitement, in its more energetic modifications; yet, that by peculiar care in securing insulation, as in the water batteries of Cross and Gassiot, æthereal undulations may be produced, with the consequent accumulation of æthereal polarity requisite to give sparks before contact, agreeably to the experiments of those ingenious philosophers.

49. Hence it may be presumed, that during intense æthereo-ponderable polarization, superficial æthereal waves may always be a secondary effect, although the conducting power of the reagents requisite to the constitution of powerful galvanic

---

\* According to Coulomb's experiments, electrical attraction and repulsion are inversely as the squares of the distances, and the inductive power of statical charges which is produced by those forces, and which precedes and determines the length of the resulting spark, must, of course, obey the same law.

If this calculation be correct, the intensity must be as the squares of the striking distances, as indicated by sparks.

It may be urged, that the striking distances, as measured by the length of the sparks, is in the compound ratio of the quantity and intensity. As to the quantity, however, galvanic sources have always been treated as pre-eminent in efficacy, so that on that side there could be no disparity. Moreover, I have found that in galvanic apparatus of only one, or even of two pairs, as in the calorimotors, the intensity lessened as the surfaces were enlarged. By a pair of fifty square feet of zinc surface, a white heat could not be produced in a wire of any size, however small. The calorific power of such apparatus can only be made evident by the production of a comparatively very low temperature, in a comparatively very large mass.

batteries, is inconsistent with that accumulation of æthereal polarity which constitutes a statical spark-giving charge.

50. As all the members forming a voltaic series have to be discharged in one circuit, the energy of the effort to discharge, and the velocity of the consequent undulations must be, *ceteris paribus*, as the number of members which co-operate to produce the discharge. Of course the more active the æthereoponderable waves, the greater must be their efficacy in producing æthereal waves of polarization as a secondary effect, agreeably to the suggestions above made (49, 36).

51. Hence in a battery consisting of one galvanic pair excited by reagents of great chemical energy and conducting power, the electro-magnetic effects are pre-eminent; while De Luc's electric columns consisting of several thousands of minute pairs, feeble as to their chemical and conducting efficacy, are pre-eminent for statical spark-giving power (48). This seems to be quite consistent, since on the one hand, the waves of polarization must be larger and slower, as the pairs are bigger and fewer; and on the other hand smaller and more active, as the pairs are more minute and more numerous.

*On the perfect similitude between the Polarity communicated to Iron Filings by a Magnetized Steel Bar, and a Galvanized Wire.*

52. If by a sieve, or any other means, iron filings be duly strewed over a paper resting on a bar magnet, they will all become magnets, so as to arrange themselves in rows like the links of a chain. Each of the little magnets thus created, will, at its outermost end, have a polarity similar to that of the pole (of the magnet) with which it may be affiliated. Of course the resulting ferruginous rows formed severally by the two different poles of the bar, will have polarities as opposite as those of the said poles.

53. In an analogous mode, *if* two wires be made the media of a galvanic discharge, iron filings, under their influence, will receive a magnetic polarity, arranging themselves about each wire like so many tangents to as many radii proceeding from its axis; those magnetized by one wire reacting with such as are magnetized by the other.

54. The affections of the ferruginous particles during the continuance of the current so called, are precisely like those of the same particles when under the influence of the bar magnet. The great discordancy is in the fact, that the influence of the magnet *is* permanent, while that of the wire *is* indebted for existence to a series of oppositely polarizing but transient impulses which proceed towards the middle of the

circuit from each side, so as to produce reciprocal neutralization by meeting midway.

55. The effect upon the filings, as originally pointed out by Œrsted, is precisely such as would arise were the ponderable matter of the wire resolved by each impulse into innumerable little magnets, situated so as to form tangents to as many radii proceeding from the axis of the wire.

56. Independently of the filings, the wires react with each other as if their constitution, during subjection to the discharge, were such as above supposed. When the discharges through them concur in direction, they attract, because the left side of one is next the right side of the other, bringing the opposite poles of their little magnets into proximity; but when the discharge is made in opposite directions, the two right or the two left sides will be in proximity, and will, by the consequent approximation of the similar poles of the little magnets, be productive of repulsion.

57. From these last-mentioned facts and considerations, it must be evident that, assuming that there is in a galvanized wire a derangement of the poles of the constituent æthereo-ponderable particles analogous to that permanently existing in magnetized steel, involves no contradiction, no absurdity, nor any thing but what is consistent with the researches and inferences of Davy, Faraday, and other eminent investigators of the phænomena of nature.

*Process by which the Æthereo-ponderable Atoms within a Galvanic Circuit are polarized by the Chemical Reaction.*

58. In order that an æthereo-ponderable particle of oxygen in any aqueous solution shall unite with an æthereo-ponderable particle of zinc in a galvanic pair, there must be a partial revolution of the whole row of æthereo-ponderable zinc atoms, with which the atom assailed is catenated by the attractions between dissimilar poles. Moreover, at the same time that the metallic atoms are thus affected, the atoms of water between the metallic surfaces must undergo a similar movement, by an analogous reaction with poles of an opposite character, and this movement must extend through the negative plate to the conductor, by which it communicates with the zinc or electropositive plate. When the circuit is open, the power of combination exercised by the zinc and oxygen is inadequate to produce this movement in the whole chain of atoms, liquid and metallic; but as it is indifferent whether any two atoms are united with each other, or with any other atoms of the same kind, the chemical force easily causes them to exchange

partners, as it were, when the whole are made to form a circuitous row in due contiguity.

59. As we know that during their union with oxygen metals give out an enormous quantity of heat and electricity, it is reasonable to suppose that whenever an atom of oxygen and an atom of zinc jump into union with each other, a wave is induced in the æthereo-ponderable matter, and that this wave is sustained by the decompositions and recompositions by means of which an atom of hydrogen is evolved at the negative plate and probably enabled to assume the aëriform state. There must at the same time be a communication of wave polarity by contact of the negative plate with the connecting wire, by which the positive wave in the wire is induced. Although the inherent polarities of the metals are not, agreeably to this view, the moving power in galvanism, yet they facilitate, and in some cases induce the exercise of that power, by enabling it to act at a distance, when otherwise it might remain inert.

60. This, I conceive, is shown in the effect of platina sponge upon a mixture of the gaseous elements of water; also in Grove's *gas* battery, by means of which hydrogen and oxygen gas severally react with water in syphons, so as to cause each other to condense, without any communication besides that through the platina, and an electrolytic decomposition and recomposition extending from one of the aqueous surfaces in contact with one of the gases, to the other surface in contact with the other gas.

### *Difference between Electro-æthereal and Æthereo-ponderable Polarization.*

61. There are two species of electro-polarity which come under the head of statical electricity. One of these Faraday illustrates by supposing three bodies, A, B and C, in proximity, but not in contact, when A, being electrified, electrifies B, and B electrifies C by induction. This Faraday calls an *action* of the particles of the bodies concerned, whereas, by his own premises, it appears to me to be merely a superficial affection of the masses or of a circumambient æthereal matter. This species of polarization, to which the insulating power of air is necessary, affects the superficies of a body only, being displayed as well by a gilt globe of glass, as a solid globe of metal. No sensible change appears to be produced in the ponderable conducting superficies by this inductive superficial electrification of masses; and of course no magnetism.

62. When a small image, of which the scalp has been abundantly furnished with long hair, is electrified, the hairy

filaments extend themselves and move apart, as if actuated by a repulsive power: also when iron filings are so managed as to obey the influence of the poles of a powerful magnet (51), they arrange themselves in a manner resembling that of the electrified hair. There is, moreover, this additional analogy, that there is an attraction between two portions of hair differently electrified, like that which arises between filings differently magnetized; yet the properties of the electrified hair and magnetized filings are, in some respects, utterly dissimilar. A conducting communication between differently electrified portions of hair would entirely neutralize the respective electrical states; so that all the electrical phænomena displayed by them would cease. Yet such a communication made between the poles, exciting the filings, by any non-magnetic conductor, does not in the slightest degree lessen their polar affections and consequent power of reciprocal influence. Upon the electrified hair, the proximity or the contact of a steel magnet has no more effect than would result under like circumstances from any other metallic mass similarly employed; but by the approximation, and still more, the contact, of such a magnet, the affection of the filings may be enhanced, lessened, or nullified, according to the mode of its employment. In the case of the hair, the affection is superficial, and the requisite charging power must be in proportion to the extent of surface. In the case of the magnetized ferruginous particles, it is the mass which is affected, and, *cæteris paribus*, the more metal, the greater the capacity for magnetic power. In the instance of the electrified hair, as in every other of frictional excitement, the electrical power resides in imponderable æthereo-electric atmospheres which adhere superficially to the masses, being liable to be unequally distributed upon them in opposite states of polarity, consequent to a superficial polarization of the exciting or excited ponderable masses; but in the instance of bodies permanently magnetic, or those rendered transiently magnetic by galvanic influence, the æthereo-electric matter and the ponderable atoms are inferred to be in a state of combination, forming æthereo-ponderable atoms; so that both may become parties to the movements and affections of which the positive and negative waves consist.

63. Thus an explanation is afforded of the hitherto mysterious diversity of the powers of a gold leaf electroscope and galvanoscopes, although both are to a miraculous degree sensitive; the latter to the most feeble galvanic discharge, the former to the slightest statical excitement; yet neither is in the most minute degree affected by the polarization which affects the other.

64. The charge which may exist in a coated pane affords another exemplification of statical or electro-œthereal polarity. In this case, according to Faraday, the particles of glass are thrown into a state of electro-polarity, and are, in fact, partially affected as if they belonged to a conductor; so that insulators and conductors differ only in the possession in a high degree by the one, of a susceptibility of which the other is possessed to an extent barely perceptible. The facts seem to me only to show, that either an insulator or conductor may be both affected by the same polarizing force, the transmission of which the one facilitates, the other prevents. I am under the impression that it is only by the disruptive process that electricity passes through glass; of course involving a fracture. It gets through a pane or jar, not by aid of the vitreous particles, but in despite of their opposing coherence. The glass in such cases is not liable to be fused, deflagrated, or dissipated, as conductors are. It is forced out of the way of the electrical waves, being incapable of becoming a party to them. Discharges will take place through a vacuity, rather than through the thinnest leaf of mica. But if, as Faraday has alleged, from within a glass flask hermetically sealed, an electrical charge has been found to escape after a long time, it proves only that glass is not a perfect insulator, *not that perfect insulation and perfect conduction are different extremes of the same property.* On the contrary, the one is founded upon a constitution competent to the propagation within it of the electro-polarizing waves, with miraculous facility, while the other is founded either on an absolute incapacity, or comparatively an infinitely small ability to be the medium of their conveyance. The one extremely retards, the other excessively expedites its passage through a space otherwise void*.

*Competency of a Wire to convey a Galvanic Discharge is as its sectional area, while statical discharges of frictional electricity preferring the surface are promoted by its extension. Yet in proportion as such discharges are heavy, the ability of a wire to convey them and its magnetic energy become more dependent on its sectional area and less upon extent of surface.*

65. Reference has been made to two modes of electrical conduction, in one of which the efficacy is as the surface; in the other, as the area of a section of the conductor. Although glass be substantially a non-conductor, the power of the surface of glass when moistened, or gilt, to discharge statical

* By a void, I mean a Torricillian vacuum. The omnipresence of the electro-œther must render the existence of a perfect void impossible.

electricity, is enormous. It has been generally considered, that as a protection against lightning, the same weight of metal employed as a pipe, would be more efficacious than in the usual solid form of a lightning rod; yet this law does not hold good with respect to galvanic discharges, which are not expedited by a mere extension of conducting surface. Independently of the augmentation of conducting power, consequent to radiation and contact with the air, the cooling influence of which, according to Davy, promotes galvano-electric conduction, a metallic ribbon does not convey a galvanic discharge better than a wire of similar weight and length*.

66. Agreeably to the considerations above stated, the sectional area of a conductor remaining the same, in proportion as any *statical* accumulation which it may discharge is greater, the effects are less superficial; and the æthereo-ponderable atoms are affected more analogously to those exposed to galvanic discharges. It is in this way that the discharge of a Leyden jar imparts magnetic polarization. Thus, on the one hand, the electro-æthereal matter being polarized and greatly condensed, combines with and communicates polarization, and consequently magnetism, to æthereo-ponderable bodies; while, on the other hand, these, when polarized by galvanic reaction, and thus rendered magnetic, communicate polarity to the electro-æther. Hence statical electricity, when produced by galvanism, and magnetism, when produced by statical electricity, are secondary effects.

67. Where a wire is of such dimensions, in proportion to the charge, as to be heated, ignited, or dispersed by statical electricity, there seems to be a transitory concentration of the electric power, which transforms the nature of the reaction, and an internal wave of electro-ponderable polarization, similar to those of galvano-electricity, is the consequence.

68. As above observed (31), the current produced by the magneto-electric machine has all the attributes of the galvano-electric current; yet this is altogether a secondary effect of the changes of polarity in a keeper, acting upon a wire solely

---

* It is well known that Wollaston effected the decomposition of water by the aid of a powerful electrical machine. Having enclosed platina wires within glass tubes, these were fused so as to cover the ends. The glass was afterwards so far removed, by grinding, as to expose minute metallic points to the liquid. Under these circumstances, the electricity conveyed by the wires, being prevented from proceeding over them superficially, was obliged to make its way through the æthereo-ponderable matter of which metals consist (38). Instead of proving the identity of galvanism with frictional electricity (note 39), this experiment shows that in one characteristic at least there is a discordancy. At the same time it may indicate that æthereal may give rise to æthereo-ponderable undulations.

by dynamic induction. But if, by mere external influence, the machine above mentioned can produce within a circuit a current such as above described, is it unreasonable to suppose that the common machine, when it acts upon a circuit, may put into activity the matter existing therein, so as to produce waves of polarization, having the power of those usually ascribed to a galvano-electrical current?

69. It has been shown that both reason, and the researches and suggestions of Faraday, warrant the inference that ponderable atoms in solids and liquids may be considered as swimming in an enormous quantity of condensed imponderable matter, in which all the particles, whether ponderable or imponderable, are, in their natural state, held in a certain relative position due to the reciprocal attraction of their dissimilar poles. A galvano-electrified body differs from one in its ordinary state, in having the relative position of the poles of its æthereo-ponderable atoms so changed, that their inherent opposite polarities not being productive of reciprocal neutralization, a reaction with external bodies ensues.

70. In statical excitement the affection is superficial as respects the ponderable bodies concerned, while in dynamic excitement the polarities of the whole mass are deranged oppositely at opposite ends of the electrified mass; so that the oppositely disturbing impulses, proceeding from the poles of the disturbing apparatus, neutralize each other intermediately. Supposing the ponderable as well as the imponderable matter in a perfect conductor to be susceptible of the polar derangement, of which an electrified state is thus represented to consist, non-conductors to be insusceptible of such polar derangement, imperfect conductors may have a constitution intermediate between metals and electrics. When an electrical discharge is made through any space devoid of air or other matter, it must then find its way solely by the polarization of the rare imponderable matter existing therein; and consequently its coruscations should be proportionably more diffuse, which is actually found to be true; but when gaseous æthereo-ponderable atoms intervene, they enable competent waves to exist within a narrower channel, and to attain a greater intensity. I consider all bodies as insulators which cause discharges through them to be more difficult than through a vacuum, and which, by their interposition within a circuit, can prevent that propagation of the oppositely polarizing undulations which would otherwise ensue. This furnishes a good mean of discrimination between insulators and conductors, the criterion being, that a discharge ensues more readily as there is more of the one and less of the other in the way; that the

one leads the waves where they would not go, the other impedes their going where they would proceed. Both in the case of disruptive discharge through air, producing a spark, or of a deflagrating discharge through wire, causing its explosion, there is a dispersion of intervening ponderable particles; and yet there is this manifest discordancy, that in one case the undulatory process of transfer is assisted, in the other resisted. The waves follow the metallic filament with intense attraction, while they strive to get out of the way of those formed by the aëriform matter, as if repelled. Hence the term disruptive, from *dirumpo*, to break through, was happily employed by Faraday to designate spark discharges. The zigzag form of the disruptive spark shows that there is a tendency in the aëriform particles to turn the waves out of that straight course, which, if unresisted or facilitated, they would naturally pursue. On the one hand the aërial filaments being unsuitable for the conveyance of the electric waves, these are forced by them out of the normal path, first in one direction, then in another; while on the other hand, the finest metallic filament furnishes a channel for the electric waves, so favourable that this channel is pursued, although the consequent polarization of the conducting particles be so intense as to make them fly asunder with explosive violence. Even when a bell wire has been dissipated by lightning, it has been found to facilitate and determine the path of the discharge.

71. The various forms of the electric spark resulting from varying the gas through which it may be made to pass, agreeably to the researches of Faraday, is explained by the supposition that the peculiarities of the spark is partially the consequence of the polarizability of the gaseous atoms through which the discharge is made, and varies accordingly in its appearance.

*Difference between Frictional Electricity and Galvanic does not depend on the one being superior as to quantity, the other as to intensity, but on the different degrees in which the æthereo-ponderable atoms of the bodies affected are deranged from their natural state of Neutralized Polarity.*

72. I infer that all magneto-polar charges are attended by an affection of ponderable particles; and that the reason why the most intense statical charge does not affect a galvanometer, is, that it is only when oppositely excited bodies are neutralized by the interposition of a conductor, as during a discharge, that æthereo-ponderable particles are sufficiently polarized to enable them to act upon others in their vicinity, so as to produce a polar affection the opposite of their own. In this way dy-

namic induction is consistently explained, by supposing that the waves of polarization, in passing along one conductor, produce, *pari passu*, the opposite polarization in the proximate part of any neighbouring conductor suitably constituted, situated and arranged to allow it to form a part of a circuit.

73. It is only during the state of the incessant generation and destruction of what has been called the two electricities, that the circuit, which is the channel for the passage of the polarizing waves, is endowed with electro-magnetic powers. It was, no doubt, in obedience to a perception of this fact, that Œrsted ascribed the magnetism of a galvanized wire to a conflict of the electricities. Undoubtedly that state of a conductor in which, by being a part of an electrical circuit, it becomes enabled to display electro-magnetic powers, is so far a conflict of the two electricities, as the affections of matter, which are denominated electrical, consist of two opposite polar forces, proceeding, agreeably to the language of Faraday, in opposite directions from each side of the source, and conflicting with each other so as to be productive of reciprocal annihilation.

74. That a corpuscular change in conductors is concomitant with their subjection to, or emancipation from, a galvanic current, is proved by an experiment of Henry's, which he afforded me an opportunity, on one occasion, of witnessing. I allude to the fact that sound is produced whenever the circuit is suddenly made or suddenly ruptured. By I. P. Marrian it has been observed, that a similar result takes place during the magnetization or demagnetization of iron rods, by the alternate establishment or arrestation of galvanic discharges through wires coiled about them so as to convert each into an electro-magnet. Mr. Marrian represents the sound as resembling that produced by striking a rod upon one of its ends*. Sounds from this source were observed by Dr. Page in 1838. See Silliman's Journal for that year, vol. xxxiii.

75. Thus it appears that there is an analogy between the state of matter which involves permanent magnetism, and that which constitutes a galvanic current, so far as this; that either by one or the other, during either its access or cessation, an affection of the ponderable particles concerned ensues, sufficient to produce sound.

76. Simultaneously with the production of sounds as above stated, by the opening or closing of the galvanic circuit through

* Agreeably to recent experiments of Faraday, the particles of a glass prism may be so influenced by an electro-magnet as to affect the passage of polarized light. See Phil. Mag. and Journ., vol. xlv. p. 383, 1844.

a metallic rod or the coils of an electro-magnet, secondary waves are induced, called secondary currents. It seems reasonable to ascribe these waves to the same shifting of the poles which produces the sonorific undulations*.

* These phænomena excite more interest in consequence of the employment, for medical purposes, of an apparatus originally contrived by Callan, but since ingeniously modified by our countryman, Dr. Page, into a form which has been designated as the electrotome. A coil of coarse copper wire, covered with cotton, like bonnet wire, is wound about a wooden cylinder. Around the coil thus formed, a coil of fine copper wire similarly covered is wound, leaving the extremities accessible. One end of the coarse coil communicating constantly with one pole of a galvanic battery, the other end is left free; so that by scraping with it the teeth of a rasp attached to the other pole, a rapid closing and opening of the circuit may be effected. Under these circumstances, an observer, holding the ends of the fine coil, receives shocks more or less severe, according to the construction of the battery, the energy of the agents employed to excite it, or the total weight and relative dimensions of the coils, as to length and sectional area. Agreeably to the received doctrine, the shocks thus produced are owing to secondary currents caused by dynamic induction. Agreeably to the hypothesis which I have advanced, the atoms of the coarse wire, polarized by waves proceeding from the poles of the battery, induce a corresponding polarization of the atoms of the fine wire; the aggregate polarity imparted being as the number of atoms in the former to the number of atoms in the latter; or (to use an equivalent ratio) as the weight of the coarse to the weight of the fine wire. But as on breaking the circuit, through the coarse wire, the æthereo-ponderable atoms in both wires resume their neutral positions, while this requires each circuit to be run through within the same minute interval, the velocities of their respective waves will be inversely as their sectional areas and directly as their lengths; in other words, the velocity of the fine wire will be as much greater as the channel which it affords is narrower and longer. The cylinder, included within the coils as above stated, being removed, a cylindrical space is vacated. If into the cavity thus made, iron rods, like knitting needles, be introduced, one after the other, while the apparatus is in operation, the shocks increase in severity as the number augments; so that from being supportable they may be rendered intolerable. The shock takes place without the presence of iron, but is much increased by its assistance[1].

These facts appear to me to justify a surmise, that the æthereo-ponderable atoms of iron, in becoming magnetized and demagnetized, co-operate with the æthereo-ponderable atoms of the copper coils in the induction of secondary undulations. It is conceived that these may be owing to the intestinal change, attended by sound, as above stated (73); this being caused by a sudden approximation of the poles of the atoms, previously moved apart by the influence of the galvanized coil. But if this sudden coming together of the previously separated poles of atoms within a magnetized cylinder of iron can contribute to the energy of secondary waves, it is consistent to infer that these waves owe their origin to an analogous approximation of the separated poles of the cupreous atoms, forming the finer coil,

[1] Agreeably to the usual construction, the cylinder about which the inner coarse wire coil is wound is originally of iron, so that there is as much of this metal contained as it can hold. Various contrivances are resorted to for the closing and opening of the circuit, which are more ingenious and convenient than scraping a rasp, as above described.

77. Within the bodies of animals and vegetables, the electro-æther may be supposed to exist as an atmosphere surrounding the æthereo-ponderable atoms of which their organs are constituted, so as to occupy all the space which is not replete with such atoms. Hence a discharge of frictional electricity may indirectly polarize the whole animal frame, by producing æthereo-ponderable polarization in the constituent atoms of the fibres of the nerves and muscles. Probably this polarization is produced more immediately in the ponderable solids, by a discharge from a voltaic series, or a wire subjected to electro- or magneto-dynamic induction. In the latter instances the shock is reiterated so rapidly as to appear more enduring, while in the former it is more startling and producible at an infinitely greater distance.

78. Agreeably to Faraday's researches (1485 to 1543), there is reason to suppose that in frictional spark discharges, the consequent shock, light, and other peculiarities, are in part owing to waves of æthereo-ponderable polarization indirectly produced in the intervening gaseous matter (71).

### Of Æthereo-ponderable Deflagration.

79. It is well known, that between two pieces of charcoal severally attached, one to the negative, the other to the positive pole of a numerous and well-excited voltaic series, an arch of flame may be produced by moving them apart after contact. This phænomenon evidently depends upon the volatilization of the ponderable matter concerned; since it cannot be produced before the carbon has been volatilized by contact, nor by any body besides charcoal, this being the only conductor which is sufficiently infusible, and yet duly volatilizable. Metals similarly treated fuse at the point of contact and cohere. On separation, after touching, a single spark ensues;

in which the secondary undulations may be created, without the presence of iron. Of course this reasoning will apply to all cases in which the phænomena hitherto attributed to Faradian currents are the result of dynamic induction.

Thus it appears that the polarization of magnets, and that created and sustained when a galvanized coil or helix acts upon another in proximity, have the same relation to galvanic discharges that the charges upon insulated surfaces have to their appropriate discharges. The permanent magnetism of steel seems to have some analogy with the charge upon a coated pane, while we may consider as analogous with the charges upon insulated conductors, already adverted to (61, 62), that state of the æthereo-ponderable particles (38) of a wire helix, which *state*, resulting from the influence of an included magnet, or neighbouring galvanized coil, and being discharged on a change of relative position, or breach of the galvanizing circuit, is productive of spark, shock, ignition, or electrolysis, as exemplified by Callan's coil, Page's electrotome, or the magneto-electric machine.

which, without repetition of contact, cannot be reproduced. Hence it may be inferred that the carbonaceous vapour is indispensable to this process, as a medium for the æthereo-ponderable polarizing waves, being soon consumed by the surrounding atmospheric oxygen. The excrescence upon the negative charcoal, observed by Silliman, together with the opposite appearance on the positive charcoal, may be owing to the lesser affinity for oxygen on the negative side*.

80. There may be some resemblance imagined between this luminous discharge between the poles, and that which has already been designated as disruptive (69); but this flaming arch discharge does not break through the air, it only usurps its place gradually, and then sustains this usurpation. It differs from the other as to its cause, so far as galvanic reaction differs from friction: moreover, it requires a volatilizable, as well as a polarizable ponderable conducting substance to enable its appropriate undulations to meet at a mean distance from the solid polar terminations, whence they respectively proceed.

81. The most appropriate designation of the phænomenon under consideration, is that of ætherco-ponderable undulatory deflagration. Under this head, we may not only place the flaming arch, but likewise the active ignition and dissipation of fine wire or leaf metal, when attached to one pole, and made barely to touch the other.

82. In one of Faraday's experiments, a circuit was completed by subjecting platina points, severally proceeding from the poles of a voltaic series, while very near to each other, to the flame of a spirit-lamp. This was ascribed by him to the rarefaction of the air, but ought, as I think, to be attributed to the polarizable æthereo-ponderable matter of the flame, performing the same office as the volatilized carbon in the flaming arch between charcoal points, to which reference has been made.

*Summary.*

From the facts and reasoning which have been above stated, it is presumed that the following deductions may be considered as highly probable, if not altogether susceptible of demonstration.

The theories of Franklin, Dufay and Ampère, are irreconcilable with the premises on which they are founded, and with facts on all sides admitted.

A charge of frictional electricity, or that species of electric excitement which is produced by friction, is not due to any

* American Journal of Science, vol. x. p. 121. 1826.

accumulation, nor to any deficiency either of one or of two fluids, but to the opposite polarities induced in imponderable æthereal matter existing throughout space however otherwise void, and likewise condensed more or less within ponderable bodies, so as to enter into combination with their particles, forming atoms which may be designated as æthereo-ponderable.

Frictional charges of electricity seek the surfaces of bodies to which they may be imparted, without sensibly affecting the æthereo-ponderable matter of which they consist.

When surfaces thus oppositely charged, or, in other words, having about them oppositely polarized æthereal atmospheres, are made to communicate, no current takes place, nor any transfer of the polarized matter: yet any conductor touching both atmospheres, furnishes a channel through which the opposite polarities are reciprocally neutralized by being communicated wave-like to an intermediate point.

Galvano-electric discharges are likewise effected by waves of opposite polarization, without any flow of matter meriting to be called a current.

But such waves are not propagated superficially through the purely æthereal medium; they occur in masses formed both of the æthereal and ponderable matter. If the generation of frictional electricity, sufficient to influence the gold leaf electrometer, indicate that there are some purely æthereal waves caused by the galvano-electric reaction, such waves arise from the inductive influence of those created in the æthereo-ponderable matter.

When the intensity of a frictional discharge is increased beyond a certain point, the wire remaining the same, its powers become enfeebled or destroyed by ignition, and ultimately deflagration: if the diameter of the wire be increased, the surface, proportionally augmented, enables more of the æthereal waves to pass superficially, producing proportionally less æthereo-ponderable undulation.

Magnetism, when stationary, as in magnetic needles and other permanent magnets, appears to be owing to an enduring polarization of the æthereo-ponderable atoms, like that transiently produced by a galvanic discharge. (Note page 461 and paragraph 68.)

The magnetism transiently exhibited by a galvanized wire is due to oppositely polarizing impulses, severally proceeding wave-like to an intermediate part of the circuit where reciprocal neutralization ensues.

When magnetism is produced by a frictional discharge operating upon a conducting wire, it must be deemed a secondary effect, arising from the polarizing influence of the æthereal waves upon the æthereo-ponderable atoms of the wire.

Such waves pass superficially in preference; but when the wire is comparatively small, the reaction between the waves and æthereo-ponderable atoms becomes sufficiently powerful to polarize them, and thus render them competent, for an extremely minute period of time, to produce all the affections of a galvano-electric current, whether of ignition, of electrolysis, or magnetization. Thus, as the æthereo-ponderable waves produce such as are purely æthereal, so purely æthereal waves may produce such as are æthereo-ponderable.

The polarization of hair upon electrified scalps is supposed to be due to a superficial association with the surrounding polarized æthereal atoms, while that of iron filings, by a magnet or galvanized wire, is conceived to arise from the influence of polarized æthereo-ponderable atoms, consisting of æthereal and ponderable matter in a state of combination.

Faradian discharges are as truly the effects of æthereo-ponderable polarization, as those from an electrified conductor, or coated surfaces of glass are due to static æthereal polarization (39, 40, 41); last paragraph, note, page 485.

It is well known that if a rod of iron be included in a coil of coated copper wire on making the coil the medium of a voltaic discharge, the wire is magnetized. Agreeably to a communication from Joule, in the Phil. Mag. and Journ. for Feb. 1847, the bar is at the same time lengthened without any augmentation of bulk; so that its other dimensions must be lessened in proportion to the elongation.

All these facts tend to prove that a change in the relative position of the constituent æthereo-ponderable atoms of iron accompanies its magnetization, either as an immediate cause, or as a collateral effect.

---

LXIV. *Observations on the Elementary Colours of the Spectrum, in reply to* M. Melloni. *By* Sir DAVID BREWSTER, *K.H., D.C.L., F.R.S., and V.P.R.S. Edin.**

IT is with considerable reluctance that I have been induced to notice the criticisms of M. Melloni, on my Analysis of the Spectrum, which occupy so large a portion of his paper published in the Phil. Mag. for April last. Had these criticisms emanated from any inferior person, I should have regarded them as sufficiently refuted by the few remarks which I made on the analogous observations of Dr. Draper. The high and well-merited reputation, however, of M. Melloni, and the singular confidence which he seems to place in his own results, render it necessary that I should do more than

* Communicated by the Author.

merely pronounce them to be incorrect, and to have no real bearing, even if correct, upon the views which they are brought forward to overturn.

M. Melloni asserts that he has repeated my *fundamental experiment*, which, he says, "consists, as is well-known, in interposing between the eye and the spectrum a slip of glass, deeply coloured by the oxide of cobalt," &c. &c.; and he goes on to describe the phænomena exhibited by a spectrum formed from the light of a *circular aperture, ten millimetres or four-tenths* of an inch in diameter, and by means of an equilateral prism in the position of minimum deviation. *I never made such an experiment, and never would have thought of employing a spectrum thus produced.* The spectrum described by Fraunhofer was obtained from an aperture *one-fiftieth of an inch wide*; Dr. Wollaston used an aperture *one-twentieth* of an inch, while M. Melloni uses one *twenty-fiftieths*,—twenty times wider than Fraunhofer's aperture, and *eight* times wider than Dr. Wollaston's! In such a spectrum, therefore, the separation of the colours must have been much less complete than in those studied by Fraunhofer, Wollaston and myself; and the *yellow* and the *red* rays must have invaded the *orange*, as observed by Melloni. As this commixture of rays did not appear when a narrow stripe* of the prism was used, that is, in his *elementary spectrum*, as he calls it, he concludes that my results were owing to the use of a prism with a wide surface, and that I had therefore used a *complex spectrum*. I should have been ashamed of my inexperience had I used such an aperture and such a spectrum as that which Melloni employed; and I can assure him that he has formed a very low estimate of the time and labour which I have devoted to these researches, and of the manner in which they were conducted.

Dreading, as he justly does, that his own results might be

---

* This narrow stripe, a "little more than a millimetre in width," was formed in a layer of Indian ink on a face of the prism. As the light was incident very obliquely on the prism, a millimetre, or the twenty-fifth of an inch, would be reduced to nearly the fortieth of an inch when multiplied by the cosine of the angle of incidence. Divergent light passing through so narrow an aperture, would produce diffraction-fringes injurious to the distinctness and purity of Melloni's elementary spectrum. I have repeated my experiments with spectra much more distinct and pure than any that can be produced by the contrivance of our author, and I have obtained precisely the results contained in my original memoir. These spectra were formed by the finest glass prisms, both single and compound, and by prisms of rock salt, so perfectly homogeneous and colourless, that in looking into the prism the substance of the salt is invisible. I have used prisms with refracting angles of all magnitudes, and some of them so great that the blue and violet rays did not emerge from the second surface, and in all the spectra thus produced I have obtained the very same results.

affected by the dilatation of the pupil, and the consequent confusion of vision, M. Melloni repeats the experiment which he calls mine, but which I disavow, with a *square aperture* in place of a *circular one*. What would Fraunhofer, Wollaston, and Young think of a spectrum produced from a *square* aperture inscribed in a circle *four-tenths* of an inch in diameter*! But waiving this objection, let us examine the experiment itself. He goes on to say, that he sees "a *red* rectangle *almost square*†, followed by a broad dark zone, and then by a very *brilliant yellow* rectangle, of which the longer sides were directed vertically and parallel to the length of the spectrum‡; there came then a deep *indistinct colour*, then the *blue*." This *yellow* rectangle was found to be more elongated horizontally in the *elementary spectrum*, or that produced by a narrow prism, than in the spectrum produced by a wider prism; and hence Melloni concludes that the increased elongation arises from the overlapping of the rays produced by the wide prism, and not from *confused vision*§, because there is no increase in a vertical direction. He *takes it for granted* that I have used a wide prism, and consequently infers that I studied a spectrum in which the colours were overlapped. I deny the assumption as well as the inference.

Viewing the experiments of Melloni by themselves, and admitting the longitudinal expansion of the luminous rectangles to be a fact, I ascribe it principally to the width of his aperture, and in a secondary degree to irradiation; or it may arise from an indistinctness of vision, or from an unusual quantity of filaments floating in the vitreous humour of his eye.

In describing the colours of his spectrum as altered by absorption, he mentions a *red* rectangle, a *dark* space, a *yellow* rectangle, then a DEEP INDISTINCT COLOUR, then the *blue*. Now we ask him what he means by a deep *indistinct colour?* Is it *yellow*, or *green*, or *yellowish-green* ? It must be one of these. If it is *yellowish-green* or *greenish-yellow*, then certain

* "If," says Dr. Young, "the breadth of the aperture viewed through a prism be *somewhat* increased, each portion encroaches on the neighbouring colours and is mixed with them," &c.—Lect. on Nat. Phil., vol. i. p. 439. M. Melloni increased the aperture of Fraunhofer from one-fiftieth to twenty-fiftieths, and hence he used a *mixed spectrum*.

† The word *almost* is not known in geometry. The prismatic image of a *square* aperture could only be a *square* when every ray of light passing through that aperture had the same index of refraction.

‡ This is to us quite unintelligible; but we presume the author means that the yellow rectangle was longer in the direction of the length of the spectrum than in a vertical direction.

§ M. Melloni does not seem to be aware that the apparent magnitudes of luminous spaces depend upon irradiation, or an expansion of the image on the retina, which varies with the degree of illumination.

*yellow* and *green* rays which compose it must have the same refrangibility as I maintain they have. If it is *yellow* or *green*, why not say so? This *deep indistinct colour* is, doubtless, neither *yellow* nor *green*. We believe, or rather we conjecture (for we cannot speak with certainty as we do not know precisely what glass he used), that it is a *gray*, that is, a *dirty white*, consisting of *red*, *blue* and *yellow* light, not in such proportions as to make *white* light.

We shall admit, however, for the sake of argument, that our author's experiments are perfectly correct, and that there has been an overlapping of rays in the spectrum which I employed. The admission would not in the slightest degree affect my analysis of the spectrum. M. Melloni and Dr. Draper cannot surely have read my original memoir in the Edinburgh Transactions. Do they know that I have insulated a *wide* beam of *white light* in the most luminous part of the spectrum? Do they know that I have done this in spectra divided by interference into dark and luminous portions where there are no lateral rays to invade the portion subjected to absorption? Do they know that I have found green light near the line C of Fraunhofer, and considerably within the red space? Have they repeated these experiments, or do they possess an apparatus fitted for their repetition? I believe they have not; and I am persuaded that the experiments described in the memoir referred to have not been repeated by any living philosopher.

Although I feel no disposition to adduce any new arguments in support of opinions which I consider as beyond the reach of challenge, I am, nevertheless, desirous of stating some facts, as observed by others, which may influence the views of those who are not qualified, or who may not have the desire, to investigate the subject experimentally.

Dr. Wollaston, in his elegant examination of the spectrum produced from the light of the sky with an aperture of one-twentieth of an inch, found only four colours, *red, yellowish-green, blue* and *violet*. He saw no *yellow*. Dr. Thomas Young informs us that "he repeated Dr. Wollaston's very interesting experiments with perfect success." He calls Dr. Wollaston's description of the spectrum the "correction of the description of the spectrum;" and he modifies his own theoretical views by substituting *red* and *green* in place of *red, orange* and *yellow*, when treating of the colours which compose the less refrangible portion of the spectrum[*]. In

---

[*] Philosophical Transactions, 1802; or Lect. on Nat. Phil., vol. ii. pp. 637, 638.

elsewhere speaking of Dr. Wollaston's observations, Dr. Young observes, "Dr. Wollaston has determined the division of the spectrum *in a much more accurate manner than had been done before.* \* \* \* The spectrum formed in this manner consists of *four colours only, red, green, blue* and *violet.* \* \* \* The colours differ scarcely at all in *quality* within their respective limits; but they vary in brightness, the greatest intensity of light being in that part of the *green* which is nearest to the *red*\*."

Such is the composition of the *daylight*, or the *blue sky*, spectrum, as we may call it. It has no *yellow* space†. But in the solar spectrum there is a distinct *yellow space* of considerable breadth lying between the *red* and *green* spaces, as clearly defined in the beautiful drawing of Fraunhofer. What then has become of this *yellow space* in the *daylight* spectrum? Something has been absorbed by reflexion from the sky or the clouds which has reduced the *yellow* light to *green*. This *something* is a portion of *red* light; because it is *demonstrable*, and it has been maintained by Wollaston and Young, that *red* and *green* make *yellow*. Now this *yellow* space in the solar *spectrum*, made *yellowish-green* in the daylight spectrum, may in its *green* state be again made *yellow*‡, and also *yellowish-white* and *white* by different absorbents. Hence it follows from Fraunhofer's, and Wollaston's and Young's observations taken by themselves, *that the quality of the colours of the brightest* part of the spectrum is changed from *yellow* to *yellowish-green*, or *green* according to Dr. Young. And it follows from my observations, combined with theirs or when standing alone, that in the same part of the spectrum there exist *red, yellow*, and *blue* rays of the very same refrangibility.

As M. Melloni does not seem to have read my reply to the Astronomer Royal§, I shall merely refer him to it for a notice of the experiments made by Sir John Herschel, which confirm my analysis of the spectrum. That the *quality* of the colour of the *red* and *orange* spaces is altered by absorption, is clearly proved by a casual experiment of Sir William Herschel's ‖. He found that "clear turned *brass* made the *red rays appear like orange*, and made the *orange* colour different from what it ought to be."

Supported by the experiments and observations of such

\* Philosophical Transactions, vol. i. p. 348.
† I take no notice of the exceedingly narrow line of yellow light which Dr. Young speaks of as *generally* seen at the limit of the *red* and *green*, and to the mixture of which it is ascribed, because its existence or non-existence does not affect my argument.
‡ Edinburgh Transactions, vol. ix. p. 442.
§ Phil. Mag., March 1847, p. 153.
‖ Phil. Trans., 1800, vol. xc. p. 255.

distinguished philosophers as Wollaston, Young, and Sir William and Sir John Herschel, I feel assured that my Analysis of the Spectrum will be confirmed by future observers who may repeat my experiments with the same care with which they were made, and without any prejudice in favour of their own speculations.

St. Leonard's College, St. Andrews,
May 3, 1848.

LXV. *On the Velocity of Sound, in Reply to the Remarks of the* Astronomer Royal. *By the* Rev. J. CHALLIS, *M.A., F.R.A.S., Plumian Professor of Astronomy in the University of Cambridge*[*].

THE mathematical investigation of the velocity of sound which I gave in the Philosophical Magazine for last April, has elicited Remarks from the Astronomer Royal, on which I must make a few observations, before I proceed to defend the principles of my investigation against the arguments which the Astronomer Royal has brought forward.

The not giving a reason for attaching a negative sign to $b^2$, was an omission on my part, which Mr. Airy has supplied exactly according to my views.

After allowing that the constant $b^2$ is admissible and may be introduced for trial, Mr. Airy adds, "It is accordingly introduced and tried, and we immediately perceive that if it has a value different from zero, the result of non-divergence of vibrations cannot be obtained. Most reasoners would conclude, either that such a result is not legitimately to be expected, or that a last trial should be made by supposing $b^2 = 0$." The result of non-divergence of vibrations is obtained by that part of my reasoning which terminates at line 8 of page 280, in which Mr. Airy "sees no ground for questioning any important step." I am not, therefore, chargeable with acting differently from "most reasoners" in not coming to the conclusion that such a result is not to be expected. Respecting the case in which $b^2 = 0$, which is that of plane-waves, I propose to speak shortly.

In the next sentence Mr. Airy goes on to say, "Instead of this, Professor Challis has recourse to *another* equation extracted from *another* memoir, and not demonstrated here, which he considers more accurate than his equation (4.), and he then uses this new equation in conjunction with equation (3.), and thus obtains the startling results to which I have alluded."

[*] Communicated by the Author.

The results alluded to, viz. the non-divergence of the vibrations, and a greater velocity of propagation than the value $a$, are obtained by the part of the reasoning terminating, as already specified, in page 280, *before* the introduction of the new equation, which is first mentioned towards the bottom of page 281. This equation in no way applies, unless the reasoning be carried beyond the first order of approximation.

I admit that there is inconvenience in referring to a separate investigation, contained in another work, and undertaken for a different purpose; and for this reason, as well as for another which I shall mention hereafter, I will omit all consideration of the equation against the introduction of which Mr. Airy protests. If, however, the results derived from the approximate equations (3.) and (4.) be liable to objection because those equations are approximate, it will be proper to investigate and to use the corresponding exact equations, which I am prepared to do in the pages of this Journal. The course of the argument will thus be clear, and equations (3.) and (4.) will be employed together as "fairly and honestly" as Mr. Airy can desire.

I now maintain that I have proved, supposing $b^2$, or $e$, to have a value different from zero, that the waves are non-divergent, and that the velocity of propagation is greater than $a$. At the bottom of page 279 of my paper, the following equation is obtained by reasoning which has not been objected to,

$$\varphi = m \cos \frac{2\pi}{\lambda} \left( z - at \sqrt{1 + \frac{e\lambda^2}{\pi^2}} + c' \right);$$

from which, since

$$u = \varphi \frac{df}{dx}, \quad v = \varphi \frac{df}{dy}, \quad w = f \frac{d\varphi}{dz}, \text{ and } as = -\frac{f}{a} \cdot \frac{d\varphi}{dt},$$

it follows that

$$u = m \frac{df}{dx} \cos \frac{2\pi}{\lambda} \left( z - at \sqrt{1 + \frac{e\lambda^2}{\pi^2}} + c' \right)$$

$$v = m \frac{df}{dy} \cos \frac{2\pi}{\lambda} \left( z - at \sqrt{1 + \frac{e\lambda^2}{\pi^2}} + c' \right)$$

$$w = -\frac{2\pi m f}{\lambda} \sin \frac{2\pi}{\lambda} \left( z - at \sqrt{1 + \frac{e\lambda^2}{\pi^2}} + c' \right)$$

$$as = -\frac{2\pi m f}{\lambda} \sqrt{1 + \frac{e\lambda^2}{\pi^2}} \sin \frac{2\pi}{\lambda} \left( z - at \sqrt{1 + \frac{e\lambda^2}{\pi^2}} + c' \right).$$

As $f$ is a function of $x$ and $y$ only, these equations show that the velocity and density at all points of any *plane* perpendicular to the axis of $z$, are propagated unaltered in a direction parallel to that axis with the uniform velocity $a\sqrt{1+\dfrac{e\lambda^2}{\pi^2}}$; in other words, the waves are non-divergent, and the velocity of propagation is greater than $a$.

I shall next maintain that $e$ must have a value different from zero.

In p. 277 I have come to a conclusion which has not been disputed, and which is expressed in these words: "It is thus shown that the condition that $udx + vdy + wdz$ be an exact differential, must be satisfied in a manner which shall equally apply whatever be the original disturbance of the fluid." The supposition that $u$, $v$, and $w$ are functions of the distance from a fixed plane, is one of a general nature, by which $udx + vdy + wdz$ becomes an exact differential, and which, consequently, is as much entitled to consideration as that which I have adopted. This is, in fact, the case of plane-waves, and coincides with the supposition that $b^4 = 0$. If the motion be parallel to the axis of $z$, $w = \dfrac{d\varphi}{dz}$, and the exact equation applicable to plane-waves is

$$\frac{d^2\varphi}{dt^2} - \left(a^2 - \frac{d\varphi^2}{dz^2}\right)\frac{d^2\varphi}{dz^2} + 2\frac{d\varphi}{dz}\cdot\frac{d^2\varphi}{dz\,dt} = 0, \quad . \quad . \quad (A.)$$

which, as is known, is satisfied by the equation

$$w = f(z - (a + w)t).$$

The function $f$ being quite arbitrary, we may give it a particular form. Let, therefore,

$$w = m \sin \frac{2\pi}{\lambda}(z - (a + w)t).$$

This equation shows that at any time $t_1$ we shall have $w = 0$ at points on the axis of $z$, for which

$$z - (a + w)t_1 = \frac{n\lambda}{2},$$

or

$$z = at_1 + \frac{n\lambda}{2}.$$

At the same time $w$ will have the value $\pm m$ at points of the axis for which

$$z - (a + m)t_1 = \left(\frac{n}{2} - \frac{1}{4}\right)\lambda,$$

or

$$z = at_1 + \frac{n\lambda}{2} + mt_1 - \frac{\lambda}{4}.$$

Here it is observable that no relation exists between the points of no velocity and the points of maximum velocity. As $m$, $t_1$, and $\lambda$ are arbitrary constants, we may even have

$$mt_1 - \frac{\lambda}{4} = 0,$$

in which case the points of no velocity are also points of maximum velocity. This is a manifest absurdity. No step, however, of the reasoning by which this result has been obtained can be controverted. What then is the meaning of it? Clearly the analysis rejects the supposition of plane-waves, by giving an integral which admits of no physical interpretation. Plane-waves are thus shown to be physically impossible.

Another way in which $udx + vdy + wdz$ becomes an exact differential, is to suppose the velocity to be a function of the distance from a fixed centre, that is, to suppose the waves to be spherical. In this case an exact integral is not obtainable. But it may be shown by an integral of the known approximate equation

$$\frac{d^2 \cdot r\phi}{dt^2} = a^2 \cdot \frac{d^2 \cdot r\phi}{dr^2},$$

that the analysis rejects this supposition also. The equation is satisfied if $r\phi = f(r - at)$; whence

$$as = -\frac{d\phi}{adt} = \frac{f'(r-at)}{r}.$$

We may therefore have

$$as = \frac{m}{r} \sin \frac{2\pi}{\lambda} (r - at);$$

and putting $r - at = c$, it follows that a given phase of the wave is carried with the uniform velocity $a$, the condensation ($s$) varying inversely as the distance $r$. This conclusion is generally adopted: but a very simple application of the principle of constancy of mass will prove that it is false. For if $\sigma_1$, $\sigma_2$ be the condensations in spherical shells of indefinitely small thickness $\alpha$, at corresponding parts of the same wave when at different distances $r_1$, $r_2$, the above-named principle requires that $2\pi r^2_1 \sigma_1 \alpha$ should be equal to $2\pi r^2_2 \sigma_2 \alpha$, so that $r^2_1 \sigma_1 = r^2_2 \sigma_2$, and the condensation varies inversely as the *square* of the distance. The inevitable conclusion from this reasoning is, that the analysis rejects the supposition of spherical waves.

There remains the supposition which I have adopted to satisfy the condition that $udx + vdy + wdz$ be an exact differential ($d\psi$), viz. that $\psi$ is the product of a function of $x$ and $y$, and a function of $z$ and $t$; according to which, if $b^2$ have a value different from zero, the waves are neither plane nor spherical. No incompatibility here presents itself, at least, as far as to the first order of approximation. We may even explain, on this hypothesis, the contradictions met with in the other two. For supposing non-divergence to be the normal condition of waves, a plane-wave, or a spherical wave, is possible only when it is compounded of an unlimited number of non-diverging waves: and in the case of a spherical wave so compounded, the variation of condensation is inversely as the *square* of the distance from the centre, as we have shown that it ought to be.

The argument respecting this third supposition is evidently incomplete, unless it be proved that no incompatibility is met with when the reasoning is conducted by exact equations. I propose in another communication to consider this part of the subject, which requires a mode of treatment different from that in my paper on Luminous Rays (Camb. Phil. Trans., vol. viii. part 3, p. 865). I have there made use of equation (A.), not being at the time aware of what is the true interpretation of its integral. Consequently the equation which Mr. Airy has objected to, though not upon a consideration of its merits, and which I have avoided introducing into this communication, is as yet unsupported.

What I have said above will suffice for an answer to Mr. Airy's arguments in paragraphs ($\beta$.) and ($\gamma$.). In the former, the motion results from two systems of plane-waves propagated in directions making an angle whose cosine is $\dfrac{n - \frac{c}{n}}{n + \frac{c}{n}}$ with the axis of $z$ on opposite sides, and therefore diverging from that axis. In the latter, the motion results from systems of plane-waves also. I have nothing to urge against the mathematical reasoning: my sole answer is, that plane-waves are physically impossible.

The difficulty respecting the augmentation of the velocity of sound by the development of heat, cannot be so summarily disposed of as Mr. Airy appears to imagine. I shall perhaps succeed better in conveying my meaning by using symbols. If $\theta$ be the temperature where the pressure is $p$ and density $\rho$, and $\theta_1$ the temperature in the quiescent state of the fluid, we have, by a known equation,

$$p = a^2 \rho (1 + \alpha(\theta - \theta_1)).$$

Hence

$$\frac{d^2z}{dt^2} = -\frac{dp}{\rho dz} = -\frac{a^2 d\rho}{\rho dz} \cdot a^2 \alpha(\theta - \theta_1)\frac{d\rho}{\rho dz} - a^2\alpha\frac{d\theta}{dz}.$$

The usual theory explains how the third term of the right-hand side of this equation may be in a given ratio to the first; but my difficulty is to conceive how the same can be the case also with the *second* term, since it changes sign with the change of sign of $\theta - \theta_1$.

Cambridge Observatory,
May 19, 1848.

---

LXVI. *On some New Lines in the Solar Spectrum.* By Professor ELIE WARTMANN[*].

THE study of the spectrum has long occupied the attention of philosophers. As early as 1802 Wollaston made known the existence of some obscure rays perpendicular to its length. Twelve years later Fraunhofer again discovered them, and gave an analysis of them, which is a masterpiece of patience and skill. We know that he used these lines as extremely valuable marks for the construction of achromatic refractive systems. Having been sought for in spectra produced with different sources of illumination, and with prisms and absorbing media of various kind, they have likewise become of considerable interest, as affording geometricians an opportunity of discussing the comparative merits of the theories of light.

In 1840 I made a series of experiments on the spectrum with an excellent prism of flint-glass, the last cut by the illustrious Bavarian optician. These experiments led me to several results, which I communicated to my pupils and showed to some amateurs; but I desired to increase their number before publishing them in a connected form. At present, not having the apparatus which I employed any longer at my disposal, it is useless to make further delay. Notwithstanding their imperfection, I may be allowed to make known some details that I believe to be new. I extract them briefly from the note-book of my laboratory, dated April and May 1841.

"The lecture-room of the Academy of Lausanne having been darkened, a beam of solar light, thrown by a tinned or blackened mirror, was made to pass through a vertical slit of $0^{mm}\cdot 8$ in width. This beam is refracted in Fraunhofer's prism fixed in a vertical position at the distance of eight metres. Directly behind this instrument is placed an achromatic theodolite of $0^{m}\cdot 04$ aperture, made at Aarau, or a comet seeker

[*] Communicated by the Author.

by Cauchoix, magnifying seven times, with a focal distance of $0^{m}.66$, and an objective the diameter of which measures $0^{m}.069$. The prism, the refracting angle of which is $45°\ 4'\ 20''$, is arranged in the position of minimum deviation.

"I thus discovered in the luminous field of the spectrum projected horizontally, a great number of *longitudinal* straight lines, some thicker than others, parallel to each other and to the length of the spectrum. They are therefore perpendicular to the transverse rays already known. They are perceptible before the telescope is drawn out sufficiently for the latter to be seen distinctly. I rarely succeeded in obtaining a view of the two systems at once. These longitudinal lines do not arise from an impurity in the prism or in the glasses of the telescope, for they appear the same with other refractive apparatus. Neither can they be attributed to inequalities in the rectilinear margins of the opening, nor to an imperfect state of the surface of the mirror. But their general aspect depends upon the size of the aperture, on the distance and the position of the prism, on the state of the atmosphere, on the height of the sun above the horizon, and on the hour of observation. It often appeared to me that several of them became displaced and extinguished, as if the transparency of the air had suddenly changed. By varying the distance of the eye-glass from the objective, they are partially, if not all, changed from black into luminous lines, and *vice versâ*. These appearances, not having the fixity and the distinctive characters of the lines figured by Fraunhofer, must be assigned to a different cause.

"The longitudinal stripes, examined by the help of a very excellent equilateral prism by Soleil, generally appear so much the more visible as the aperture is larger. Whether it be of a circular or rectangular form is of no consequence. By removing the exterior mirror and employing direct light, the lines are seen to vary in number and position, according as the naked eye, placed immediately against the prism, moves parallel to its vertical edges\*. These appearances are owing to the interference of the central rays with those which are reflected against the edges of the opening. They disappear when all reflexion is rendered impossible in this as in the prism, and when the axis of the eye or of the glass is suitably directed. They do not change when the light of a lamp is

---

\* The prism is of such pure flint, that with direct light, in misty weather, it is possible to see with *the naked eye* at least sixty of Fraunhofer's lines. The two marked B and C in the red are perceived very distinctly; but the bundle H, and especially that which follows it in the violet, are not clear. The experiment constantly succeeded at six metres, with an aperture of $1^{m}.4$.

substituted for that of the clouds or of the sun, nor when coloured media are interposed in the passage of the rays before or after their dispersion. In short, they may be produced *at will* by placing one or two plain mirrors near the extremities of the aperture made in the shutter, and by giving them a horizontal inclination of variable extent, such that the brilliant image which they receive produces a spectrum which is partly superposed upon that of the direct rays. This well deserves to be made a class experiment, as a variety of that of the two mirrors of Fresnel. It is much easier, does not require any delicate or costly apparatus, and extends simultaneously to all the monochromatic zones of the spectrum.

"As the band of light which is admitted into the prism proceeds from different parts of the sky, it is easy to account for the changes in the appearance of the longitudinal lines according to the degree of transparency of the atmosphere. The modifications which this system undergoes with the changes of exterior illumination are explained by the unequal distribution of diurnal light, which, during a state of greater or less complete serenity of the air, varies with the distance of the sun from the meridian.

"These lines of interference have not been mentioned by any author, at least as far as I can learn."

In 1844, M. Ad. Erman seems to have had a glimpse of the phænomenon which I had discovered, but attributed it to the *accidental defects of the vessels* which he employed, and did not pay any attention to it[*]. It is but somewhat recently that the horizontal bands have become the subject of investigation by two experimenters, well-located for optical researches, M. Zantedeschi at Venice, and M. Ragona-Scinà in Sicily.

M. Zantedeschi has published the results of his experiments in a separate volume, which has not yet been reviewed in France. Only a hundred copies of this work having been printed[†], it will not be out of place here to give its conclusions, which confirm mine on almost every point.

"The appearance of the lines of the solar spectrum is in a necessary relation with the smallness of the aperture, and with the interval which separates the prism from it. At a constant distance the transversal lines appear with

---

[*] On the Law of Absorption of Light by the Vapours of Iodine and Bromine.—*Comptes Rendus*, t. xix. p. 832.

[†] *Ricerche fisico-chimico-fisiologiche sulla Luce*; in 4to. Venice, 1846. In this the author treats of the influence of solar light on the germination of seeds, on the changes of colour produced in organic and mineral substances by the action of light alone, on a new analysis of the solar spectrum; in short, on the conversion (*passage*) of ponderable matter to the radiant state (?)

the widest aperture, the longitudinal with the smallest, and the two systems with the mean one. With a constant aperture the vertical lines appear at the greatest distance, the horizontal at the smallest, and the double system at the mean distance. The angle of incidence for the transversal lines alone, is a little larger than that which gives a distinct vision of the longitudinal alone. The arrangement of the longitudinal lines varies with the distance of the prism from the aperture. The first transversal as well as longitudinal lines which begin to appear in the field of the solar spectrum, are those which, in the entire system, are the most intense and the widest. In each system the focus of the lines varies with the size of the aperture. The intensity of the luminous lines in each of the three systems is greater than that of the remainder of the field of the solar spectrum: this is what Fraunhofer discovered for the transversal lines. The state of the atmosphere modifies the focal distance of the longitudinal as well as of the transversal lines. This state also influences the position, number, size and force of the longitudinal and transversal lines. To each system of lines corresponds an aperture, which is best suited for its being projected most distinctly.

"Fraunhofer refers the cause of the black lines to the nature of the light. With him, the spectrum was a means of verifying the identity or diversity of the light emanating from different sources. Herschel ascribes the origin of it to the positive absence of luminous rays, whether in the act of their development, or by absorption in the media which they have to pass through. This opinion is very nearly the same as that entertained by Brewster and Erman. The former considers that the rays which are defective are absorbed by the gases produced in the combustion which engenders the light, or by the media through which they must pass. The latter is of opinion that the medium traversed by the luminous ray separates it into two or into several parts, each of which is retarded in a different manner; on this account he distinguishes simple and double interference.

"All these opinions appear to me to be defective, although they all seem to have a true side. Fraunhofer refers the entire phænomenon to the nature of the luminous ray alone; Herschel, Brewster, and Erman to the simple influence of the different media interposed. But in these phænomena, the apparatus itself which is used for the experiment plays an important part. It is now a well-proved fact, that the appearances of the spectrum vary with the size of the aperture and the interval which separates it from the prism, the nature and dimensions of this and its distance from the screen. The whole of these circumstances necessarily leads me to admit, that these appearances of the luminous spectrum are produced by the different distribution of the rays, caused by the different media which they have to pass through. The monochromatic light of the lateral spectra, the production of such different lines by the simple variation of the distance of projection, the transformation of the systems of lines into forms so varied by the alteration of size of the aperture through which the light is admitted, the increase of tints in the obscure lines, and the strengthening of the luminous ones, are, in my opinion, so many clear proofs of variations in the reflexion, refraction, and dispersion of light. I do not thereby wish to deny that any ray is extinguished by absorption or by interference, but only to show that these two acts, such as they are considered in the undulatory system, are not causes really sufficient to produce the phænomena of the luminous spectrum. It cannot be absorption; for if the black lines are really produced by absorbed rays, and not by rays differently distributed, it is impossible that the increase or decrease of the black tints should always be accompanied by an analogous variation in the intensity of the luminous lines, and the thickening or attenuation of the black lines always by the enlargement or diminution of the luminous lines. The large systems of obscure lines produced by nitrous gas and by the vapours of iodine, are traversed in their centre by a zone of very bright light three or four millimetres wide. The systems of uniform and excessively fine lines present a tranquil light, which is spread equally throughout the height of the spectrum, so as not to be remarked by an eye not accustomed to similar researches. It cannot be interference; for in the space or in the line itself, where rays which should go on increasing the intensity of light should meet, this still shows itself diminished or extinguished: the lines are sometimes luminous, white, sometimes coloured, sometimes of a more or less perfect black. I have verified this phænomenon *some hundreds of times.* It entirely upsets and destroys the doctrine of interference, as I shall show in a future communication, in which I intend to make known the rest of my observations.

" I said that the solar spectrum is the most exquisite photoscope known. The following are some of the experiments in support of this assertion. Before the aperture, which was two millimetres wide, I placed a bottle of the purest white crystal with parallel sides. No line appeared in the solar spectrum on the screen placed at 2·39 metres from the prism. The bottle was at $0^{m}\cdot 1$ from that, and the projection of the spectrum was $0^m \cdot 16$ in length and $0^m \cdot 055$ in height. I ought also to notice that the flat sides of the bottle were five millim. thick, and at $0^m \cdot 043$ distant from each other. I introduced into it some crystals of iodine, which I caused to pass slowly into the state of vapour. The bottle was placed on some sand, and it was heated by means of some incandescent charcoal placed on the sheet of iron, which sustained it as well as the sand. As soon as the vaporization of the iodine had begun, some excessively thin and ill-defined lines appeared in the field of the spectrum. By increasing the quantity of vapour, this spectrum appeared covered with thousands of longitudinal, exceedingly fine black lines; by degrees they united in a system of large and small, accompanied by some which were luminous, and at last they divided into two excessively black systems, one superior, the other inferior, separated by a zone of intense light five millim. in width. After the fire had been removed, the vapour of iodine returned by degrees to the solid state, and the two black systems were subdivided as well as the luminous band. I have observed perfectly similar phænomena with nitrous gas. It is wonderful to see some thousands of longitudinal lines in constant motion, owing to variations of temperature*.... I have thus convinced myself of the existence of the two following facts:—1, the internal motion of the vapours, as well as that of the translation of the vessel, produce an indescribable variety in the distribution of the black and luminous lines; 2, rarefaction of the gases causes a subdivision of the black lines, condensation unites or increases these lines. All this is in perfect harmony with the variations produced by the atmosphere. When a subtle veil of vapour suspended in the upper regions merely softens the intensity of the azure of our sky, the spectrum presents some excessively fine longitudinal lines in its field, so fine that the eye, not aware of their existence, is unable to perceive them. The lines marked $q$ in my figure have several times presented the phænomenon of their separation and reunion, accompanied by the successive appearance or disappearance of an interposed luminous line. These variations were observed for more than ten days, during which the state of the atmosphere constantly varied; and I have also always detected changes in the focal distance†."

\* The author does not appear to have paid any attention to the movements of the heated air around his prism.

† Those who may consult the work from which we have translated the preceding lines, will perhaps not consider as out of place some critical notes on the chapter which now occupies us. In the first place, the simplified method employed by the author in order to project his lines upon a screen, is due to M. de Haldat, who described it as early as 1838 in the *Mémoires*

M. Zantedeschi's publication has induced Prof. Ragona-Scinà of Palermo to extend this new field of inquiries. The following are some of the principal results which he has made known[*]. The horizontal and vertical lines may be perceived by placing a small Galilean telescope against a prism lighted by an aperture of 0$^{mm}$·33. The principal of them may even be seen by the naked eye. They likewise exist in the ordinary and extraordinary spectra which a doubly refracting body produces. The horizontal lines may be obtained without the help of a prism, by examining obliquely across a biconcave lens the interval which had remained bright between the two shutters of a window closed to within a decimetre[†]. Lastly, the system of horizontal lines is submitted to an hourly periodical return, whilst that of Fraunhofer's lines is perfectly fixed. This assertion is contrary to that of M. Zantedeschi.

M. Ragona endeavours to explain the lines of Fraunhofer by attributing them to the encroachment of the four simple colours, red, yellow, blue and green. M. Zantedeschi speedily acknowledged himself of this opinion, and also explained, *by the reciprocal influence* of the luminous rays, *his* longitudinal lines [‡]. This is proved, according to him, by their appearing so much the more distinct the narrower and longer the spectrum is; whilst the contrary conditions favour the visibility of

de l'Académie Royale des Sciences de Nancy. We know that Cooper had announced the existence of a visible brightness beyond the red rays (Proceedings of the Royal Society of London, vol. iv. p. 146). The Venetian Professor has not only verified the fact, but he also thinks that he has found an analogous appendage at the opposite extremity. Moreover, the discovery of an extension in the solar spectrum, beyond the violet, is due to Sir John Herschel. He made it as early as 1819, whilst repeating some experiments on the polarized rings with Biot's apparatus; but he did not describe it till 1840, in his beautiful memoir On the Chemical Action of the Rays of the Solar Spectrum on preparations of Silver and other Substances, in the Philosophical Transactions. In the § 56, entitled "Extension of the Visible Prismatic Spectrum, a new Prismatic Colour," he says expressly that there exists, beyond the violet, some luminous rays of a different colour from that of the different bands of the spectrum, and which is of a lavender-gray. M. Zantedeschi owes to the sky of Venice, which is much more propitious than that of Collingwood, the possibility of studying this extension of coloration in detail, which will no doubt be of some importance in the question of the real number of simple colours, and to which I called attention in my memoir on Daltonism (Taylor's Scientific Memoirs, vol. iv. p. 156). Lastly, the author mentions the existence of tints of bright blue, visible above and below some prismatic zones of a horizontally projected spectrum, and he proposes calling these tints *secondary spectra*. But this denomination cannot be adopted, since it has for a long time been applied to the spectra produced by a prism achromatized for the extreme rays.

[*] *Sulle righe trasversali e longitudinali dello spettro luminoso e su ta'uni fenomenti affini.*—*Raccolta Fisico-Chimica Italiana*, t. ii. p. 483.

[†] It is as well to remark, that the lens performs the part of a prism with concave surfaces, with a more or less decided curve.

[‡] *Raccolta*, t. ii. p. 507.

the transversal lines. Strange as may seem M. Ragona's theory, it deserves examination; but I confess that that of the Venetian Professor appears to me to be very obscure. To explain the encroachments of the coloured bands in the longitudinal direction, we must admit that the spectrum is double, and that its elements overlap at right angles. The too great brevity of the author, which is limited to the paragraph above quoted, does not allow us to suppose that such is his opinion. Moreover, these lines, far from constituting a fact opposed to the theory of undulations, are, on the contrary, an interesting confirmation of its truth.

## LXVII. Remarks on the Weather during the Quarter ending March 31, 1848. By JAMES GLAISHER, Esq., of the Royal Observatory, Greenwich*.

IN the February Number of your Magazine you did me the favour to insert my remarks upon the weather during the quarter ending December 31, 1847. The weather of the past quarter has been as unusual as that of the preceding, and some account of it may probably interest your readers.

The quarterly meteorological returns for the past quarter furnished to the Registrar-General have been obtained from thirty-five different places, situated between the longitudes of $5°\ 18'$ W. and $0°\ 16'$ E.; and between the latitudes of $50°$ and $55°$. These observations have been all rigorously examined and reduced by myself, and their results are worthy the attention of meteorologists. The following are the particulars of the weather during the quarter ending March 31, 1848.

The weather during the past quarter has been remarkable in many respects. The daily temperature of the air has for the most part been above the average, yet there was a period of exceedingly cold weather between the 20th and 28th of January; the departures from the average on the 26th, 27th, and 28th, were $12°·8$, $10°·8$, and $16°$ respectively. The temperature then suddenly increased to $6°·5$ above the average on the 30th; and for the most part the daily values afterwards exceeded those of the average, or differed very little from them.

It may perhaps tend to clearness if I speak of each subject of investigation separately.

*The mean temperature of the air at Greenwich—*

For the month of January was $34°·6$, which is $1°·7$ *above* that of 1842, $4°·5$, $3°·7$, $9°·1$, and $0°·5$ *below* those in the years 1842 to 1847 respectively; or it is $3°·8$ *below* the average of these six years.

* Communicated by the Author.

For the month of February was 43°·4, which is 2°·6, 7°·4, 8°·2, 10°·7 *above* those of the years 1842 to 1845 respectively, 0°·5 *below* that in 1846, and 8°·0 *below* that of 1847; or it is 2°·6 *above* the average of these six years.

For the month of March was 43°·8, which is 1°·1 *below* that of 1842, 0°·9, 2°·3, 8°·6, 0°·5 and 2°·8 *above* those of the years 1843 to 1847 respectively; or it is 2°·3 *above* the average of these six years.

The mean value for the quarter was 40°·6; that for 1841 was 38°·4; for 1842 was 39°·5; for 1843 was 39°·6; for 1844 was 38°·5; for 1845 was 35°·4; for 1846 was 43°·6; and for 1847 was 37°·2; so that the excess for this quarter *above* the corresponding quarter in the years 1841, 1842, 1843, 1844, 1845 and 1847, were 2°·2, 1°·1, 1°·0, 2°·1, 5°·2, and 3°·4 respectively; the only year between 1841 and 1847 whose mean temperature for this period exceeded that of the present year was 1846; the excess of the period in this year exceeded that of the corresponding period of 1848 by 3°·0. The average value for this quarter from the seven preceding years was 38°·9, so that the mean temperature of the air for the past quarter exceeds that of the corresponding quarter in the seven preceding years by 1°·7. This excess is remarkable, from the circumstance of the mean temperature of the preceding quarter being in excess to the large amount of 3°·4, so that the temperature of the period between 1847, September 30, and 1847, March 31, exceeds the average by 2°·55.

*The mean temperature of the evaporation at Greenwich—*

For the month of January was 32°·6, which is 4°·7 *below* that for the preceding six years.

For the month of February was 41°·6, which is 5°·8 *above* that for the preceding six years.

For the month of March was 41°·6, which is 2°·2 *above* that for the preceding six years.

The mean value for the quarter was 38°·6, which is 1°·1 *above* that for the corresponding period of the preceding six years.

*The mean temperature of the dew-point at Greenwich—*

For the month of January was 31°·7, which is 1°·7 *above* that for 1842, 5°·6, 4°·4, 4°·2, 9°·1, and 1°·9 *below* those of the years 1843 to 1847 respectively; or it is 3°·9 *below* the average of these six years.

For the month of February was 38°·8, which is 0°·4, 5°·4, 7°·0, 10°·3 *above* those of the years 1842 to 1845, 1°·1 *below* that of 1846, and 7°·8 *above* that of the year 1847; or it is 5°·0 *above* the average for these years.

For the month of March was 38°·5, which is 2°·2 and 0°·4 *below* those of the years 1842 and 1843, 1°·9, 8°·5, 0°·2, and

$5^\circ \cdot 0$ *above* those of the years 1844 to 1847 respectively; or it is $2^\circ \cdot 2$ *above* the average value for these six years.

The mean value for the quarter was $36^\circ \cdot 3$, which is $1^\circ \cdot 1$ *above* the average for the six preceding years.

*The mean weight of water in a cubic foot of air* for the quarter was 2·7 grains, which is of the same value as that of the average for the six preceding years.

*The additional weight of water* required to saturate a cubic foot of air was 0·47 grain; the average for the six preceding years was 0·36 grain.

*The mean degree of humidity* of the atmosphere for January was 0·837, for February was 0·864, and for March was 0·839; these values being *less* than the average for the six preceding years by 0·077, 0·029, and 0·002 respectively; the value for the quarter was 0·846, which is 0·036 less than the average for these years.

*The mean elastic force of vapour* for the quarter was 0·230 inch, which is 0·006 inch *above* the average for the six preceding years.

*The mean reading of the barometer* at Greenwich for January was 29·816 inches, for February was 29·517 inches, and for March was 29·505 inches; these values are 0·057 inch *above*, 0·199 inch *below*, and 0·256 inch *below* respectively, the averages for the seven preceding years. The mean value for the quarter was 29·613 inches, which is 0·132 inch *below* the average for these years. The readings of the barometer during the greater part of the quarter were remarkable, and will be spoken of presently.

*The average weight of a cubic foot of air* under the average temperature, humidity and pressure, was 545 grains; the average for the six preceding years was 549 grains.

The rain fallen at Greenwich in January was 1·2 inch; in February was 2·6 inches; and in March was 3·1 inches; the average values for the seven preceding years were 1·9 inch, 1·6 inch, and 1·4 inch respectively. The total amount fallen in the quarter was 7·9 inches, which is 3·0 inches greater than the average for the years 1841 to 1847. I shall presently speak of this large amount of rain.

*The temperature of the Thames water* was $39^\circ \cdot 3$ by day, and $37^\circ \cdot 0$ by night. The water, on an average, was $2^\circ \cdot 4$ *warmer* than the air.

*The horizontal movement of the air* was about 168 miles daily, being somewhat more than its average value.

*The highest and lowest readings of the thermometer* in air at the height of four feet above the ground, and protected as much as possible from the effects of radiation and rain, were $71^\circ \cdot 5$ and $15^\circ \cdot 8$.

The average daily range of the readings of the thermometer in air at the height of four feet, was 11°·1, which is 0°·8 *greater* than the average range for the seven preceding years.

In January the *readings of the thermometer on grass* were at or below 32° on twenty-seven nights, and the lowest reading was 12°·5. In February it was at or below 32° on fourteen nights, and the lowest reading was 20°. In March it was at or below 32° on twenty-one nights, and the lowest reading was 18°. These low readings have generally taken place at times when the sky has suddenly become clear, and for the most part their periods of continuance have been short, as the amount of clear sky at night during the quarter has been small. The observer at Durham says, that on the night of January 19, the reading of a thermometer on grass fell below zero.

The *mean amount of cloud* for the quarter was such as to cover upon the average four-fifths of the whole sky. The amount of cloud during the period from 1847, November 30, to 1848, March 31, was larger than in any period of equal length for many years.

In the last report I spoke of the smallness of the amount of the *electricity* which had existed in the air at Greenwich during the *quarter ending* 1847, *December* 31. In consequence of this remark, Francis Ronalds, Esq., the Director of the Observatory at Kew, communicated with me, and he has kindly lent the original Electrical Observations made at that Observatory, both in that quarter and in the one just ended. By an examination of this journal, it appears that during the quarter ending December 31, 1847, the electricity of the atmosphere was *never* in a neutral state at Kew, excepting for the short period of time in its transmission from the one to the other state. The situation of the Observatory is in the Old Deer Park, at Richmond, and near the river Thames.

The electricity during the past quarter at Greenwich has been about its usual amount at this period of the year. At Kew the amount has been at all times very much larger than at Greenwich, and there does not appear to have been any period during which the instruments were unaffected.

During the quarter there were five exhibitions of the aurora borealis, which occurred on the following days, viz. February 20, 22, March 19, 20, and 31. At these times the magnets were disturbed.

The approximate mean monthly temperatures for other places besides Greenwich are shown in the tables printed in the Registrar-General's quarterly report, and they differ from those at Greenwich by small quantities only; those places situated south of Greenwich being somewhat higher, and those situated north of Greenwich being lower than at Greenwich, according to the difference of latitude and elevation.

The mean monthly temperatures of the places in Cornwall and Devonshire, in each of these three months, were *above* those of other places. At Exeter, however, the values were intermediate between those at places situated within these counties, and those situated out of them in the same latitude.

On March 29 *a remarkable solar halo* was seen from many places in England, and in the Isles of Wight, Guernsey, and Jersey. This halo, with its accompanying parhelia*, was well seen, and the descriptions of the phænomena from different localities agree better with each other than is usually the case with these optical phænomena. The following are the principal facts:—

1st. A coloured circle, whose diameter was 22°, the centre of which was occupied by the sun; seen by all the observers.

2nd. A colourless circle, whose diameter was 22°, the centre of which was situated a little to the east of the sun; seen by the observers at Guernsey and the Isle of Wight.

3rd. A coloured arc of a circle, of which the sun occupied the centre, whose diameter was 44°; seen at Oxford.

4th. A large white brilliant circle, whose centre was the zenith, passing through the sun; seen by all the observers.

5th. There were on this circle four parhelia, two of them a little beyond the first-mentioned circle, at its intersections with the large white horizontal circle; these were seen by most of the observers.

6th. There were two parhelia opposite to the sun, the one above, the other below him, at the intersections of the 1st and 2nd described circles; seen at Guernsey.

7th. The 5th and 6th parhelia were white; they were placed on the circumzenithal circle, as near as I can tell, at the points of intersections of a circle with a radius of 90°, with the sun for its centre; these were seen at Christchurch.

8th. At the culminating point of the first-mentioned circle there was a bright and coloured arc, which was concave towards the sun; this was seen at Christchurch and Oxford.

9th. The observer at Guernsey† saw four arcs of circles, one situated on either side of the two first-mentioned parhelia, one below the parhelia mentioned in No. 6, and one near the parhelia situated on the circumzenithal circle in the N.E.; these arcs were convex towards the sun.

10th. There were two coloured arcs of circles, convex

[* For a description of this halo with its accompanying parhelia, as seen at Portsea, see p. 434 of the present volume of this Journal.—ED. *Phil. Mag.*]

† The appearance of the halo, as seen at Guernsey, was engraved in the Illustrated London News of April 8, 1848.

towards the sun, and situated at the distance of 22° from the circle first mentioned, the one S.E., and the other S.W. of the sun; the latter of these was seen at Christchurch, and both were seen at the Isle of Wight.

At Stone, near Aylesbury, the observer saw some phænomena at 3ʰ P.M., different in some respects from those seen by the other observers.

1st. The upper part of the circle of 22° radius, of which the sun occupied the centre, was seen, and the colours were vivid.

2nd. There were segments of two circles, about 95° in extent, whose diameters were both 22°, and which cut each other vertically above the sun.

3rd. These segments terminated at the distance of about 14° on each side of the sun, and at these points there were two bright and luminous mock suns. The one on the W. was accompanied by a bright and long ray of light. The phænomena were visible during two hours, and an elaborate drawing was made of the appearances.

The whole of the papers and drawings are deposited in the archives of the Royal Observatory at Greenwich.

The following meteorological observations made at the Royal Observatory at about the time of the appearance of the halo, are published by permission of the Astronomer Royal.

| 1848. Day and hour. | Barometer readings corrected, and reduced to 32°. | Readings of thermometers. | | Temperature of the declared dew-point. | Dew-point temperature below air temperature. | Weight of vapour in a cubic foot of air. | Degree of humidity. | Amount of clouds. | Direction of wind. |
|---|---|---|---|---|---|---|---|---|---|
| | | Dry. | Wet. | | | | | | |
| | in. | | | | | gr. | | | |
| March 29, 6 A.M. | 29·732 | 44·8 | 44·5 | 44·1 | 0·7 | 3·4 | 0·973 | 10 | w.s.w. |
| „ 9 A.M. | 29·767 | 48·1 | 47·3 | 46·4 | 1·7 | 3·5 | 0·932 | 10 | e. by n. |
| „ Noon. | 29·783 | 55·2 | 49·5 | 44·9 | 10·3 | 3·6 | 0·707 | 4 | n.n.w. |
| „ 3 P.M. | 29·760 | 58·1 | 49·9 | 43·3 | 14·8 | 3·5 | 0·632 | 4 | s. |
| „ 6 P.M. | 29·733 | 51·5 | 46·6 | 41·7 | 9·8 | 3·2 | 0·700 | 8 | s. by e. |
| „ Midnight. | 29·709 | 41·6 | 40·3 | 38·6 | 3·0 | 2·9 | 0·901 | 10 | Calm. |
| March 30, 6 A.M. | 29·659 | 43·5 | 43·0 | 42·3 | 1·2 | 3·3 | 0·965 | 7 | s.e. |
| „ 9 A.M. | 29·662 | 51·5 | 50·1 | 48·7 | 2·8 | 4·1 | 0·903 | 10 | s.e. |
| „ Noon. | 29·663 | 53·5 | 51·2 | 48·9 | 4·6 | 4·1 | 0·848 | 10 | s. by e. |
| „ 3 P.M. | 29·669 | 60·5 | 54·5 | 50·4 | 10·1 | 4·2 | 0·708 | 10 | s. |

March 29, 6 A.M.—Overcast; a heavy rain has been falling since March 28ᵈ 10ʰ P.M.
„ 9 A.M.—Overcast; no rain falling.
„ Noon.—Cirrostratus near the horizon; the zenith clear.
„ 3 P.M.—The zenith and around it clear; banks of cumuli near the horizon; the halo visible.
„ 6 P.M.—The sky is for the most part covered by thin cirrostratus.
„ Midnight.—Overcast; cirrostratus.
March 30, 6 A.M.—Cirri, cirrostrati, and haze.
„ 9 A.M.—Overcast.
„ Noon.—Overcast.
„ 3 P.M.—Overcast.

From the circumstance of the increasing temperature during the continuance of the halo, both evaporation and the ascending current of air were increasing, and they would be at about their maxima at about $3^h$ P.M. From the numbers in the 5th column, it seems the temperature of the dew-point was becoming less as the temperature was increasing, so that the ascending current not only carried with it all the water then evaporating, but also some of that which had evaporated previously. It seems, therefore, highly probable, that at the time of the appearance of the halo the largest quantity of water was mixed with the air in its locality, and also, as at this place the temperature of the air during the day was without change, and probably below the freezing-point of water, that the degree of humidity was at the time at a maximum value.

As this halo is one of the best ever observed, and it seems to have been dependent upon the humid state of the air, it is very desirable that observations of the dry and wet bulb thermometers taken at about the time, should be collected together from different places, and I should be glad if such were forwarded to me.

The reading of the barometer during the months of February and March have been remarkable for large fluctuations. Although I have detailed them in the Registrar-General's weekly reports for these months, it is desirable to mention them here also. On February 1, at $6^h$ A.M., the reading was 29·505 inches; this increased to 30·274 inches by February 3, at $9^h$ A.M. The reading decreased day by day till the 10th, at midnight, when it was 28·598 inches; it then turned to increase, which, during the 11th, amounted to one inch nearly; and at noon, on the 13th, the reading was 29·944 inches, when it turned to decrease. On the 15th, at $3^h$ P.M., it was 29·373 inches. On the 18th, at $9^h$ A.M., it was 30·333 inches, being the highest during the month. On the 20th, at noon, it was 29·288 inches, which increased to 29·618 inches at midnight, and continued to increase slowly afterwards till the 21st at $9^h$ A.M., when the reading was 29·684 inches, after which it decreased. On the 23rd, at $6^h$ A.M., it was 28·888 inches; at midnight it was 29·229 inches; shortly after this it decreased, and continued to decrease till the 26th at $9^h$ $45^m$ A.M., when the remarkably low reading of 28·299 inches took place, a reading lower than that of the 18th by 2·034 inches; it then turned to increase, but did not pass the point 29 inches till midnight on the 27th, and reached only to 29·343 inches on the 29th at $9^h$ A.M., when it again began to decrease, and by $6^h$ P.M. again decreased below 29 inches. On March 1st, at $9^h$ A.M., the reading was 28·530 inches; it then turned to increase, which during the 2nd amounted to half an inch nearly. On the 4th, at $6^h$ A.M., the reading was 30·070 inches; on the 5th, at $6^h$ P.M., it was 29·658 inches; on the 8th, at $9^h$ A.M., it was 30·147 inches, which was the highest value reached during the month. Early in the morning of the 11th, the reading passed below 29 inches, and decreased to 28·582 inches by $11^h$ A.M. on the 12th. Between this time and the 14th, at midnight, the reading increased to 29·716 inches; it then turned to decrease, and passed the point 29 inches on the 19th at $6^h$ P.M., and to 28·630 inches by $6^h$ A.M. on the 21st; at midnight, on this day, the reading was 29·330 inches, the increase in the previous 12 hours having been as large as 0·79 inch; after this time the reading slowly increased to 30·000 inches by the 25th at $9^h$ A.M. Between this time and the end of the month, the lowest reading was 29·540 inches at midnight on the 27th.

Between February 9 and March 21, the reading of the barometer was below 29 inches on parts of sixteen days; nine of these were in February, and seven were in March. The average reading for the whole day was below 29 inches on ten of these days, viz. on February 9, 10, 25, 26, 27, March 1, 11, 12, 20 and 21.

I have examined the readings of the barometer on every day since 1800, and I find the average number of instances in one year that these readings have been below 29 inches on parts of a day, at the height of 150 feet, is seven. In the years 1829 and 1832 there was no instance of the barometer reading so low as 29 inches. In the year 1809 there were thirteen such instances, six of which were in December. In 1816 there were sixteen cases, seven of which were in January. In 1817 there were seventeen cases, six of which were in March. In 1820 there were seventeen cases, twelve of which were in October. In 1823 there were twenty. In 1824 and 1825 there were fourteen in each year; in the latter year there were eight in November. In 1836 there were thirteen instances, nine of which occurred in February and March; and in 1845 there were thirteen. Therefore there has not been any similar instance in this century of such a succession of low readings, as sixteen cases out of forty days. The year whose corresponding period most nearly resembles that of the present year in these particulars, is 1836.

The mean reading of the barometer for February and March was 29·51 inches, being less than the mean value of any consecutive two months in this century, with the solitary exception of the same two months in the year 1836, whose mean barometer reading was somewhat below that of the present year.

Usually a period of many years passes between two readings of the barometer so low as 28·3 inches. In the last quarter I spoke of the remarkably low reading of 28·383 inches as occurring on December 7 at $9^h$ A.M.; it will be seen from the preceding accounts, that on February 26, at $9^h$ $45^m$ A.M., the reading was lower than that in the preceding December, being 28·299 inches. This circumstance, in addition to the other successive low readings, render this period one of the most remarkable in a meteorological point of view; and an investigation of the several successive barometrical waves would be highly instructive. The returns I have received do not enable me to indicate the direction of motion of a single wave. The observer at Stonyhurst says, "On February 27, at $1^h$ P.M., the reading of the barometer was the lowest during the quarter, being 28·140 inches; and during the period between February 22 and March 1, the reading was always below 28·8 inches."

The observer at Latimer says, "On February 3, at $9^h$ A.M., the reading was 30·048 inches; on the 10th, at $3^h$ P.M., it was 28·556 inches; on the 18th, at $9^h$ A.M., it was 30·132 inches; on the 26th, at $9^h$ A.M., it was 28·096 inches; on the 29th, at $9^h$ A.M., it was 29·108 inches; on March 1, at $9^h$ A.M., it was 28·455 inches; on March 8, at $9^h$ A.M., it was 29·974 inches; and on March 12, at $9^h$ A.M., it was 28·442 inches."

The observer at Cardington says, "The following extremely low readings of the barometer have taken place. On February 12, at $9^h$ A.M., it was 28·63 inches; on the 26th, at noon, it was 28·63 inches; on March 1, at $9^h$ A.M., it was 28·64 inches; on the 12th, at $9^h$ A.M., it was 28·63 inches; and on the 21st, at $9^h$ A.M., it was 28·74 inches."

It appears, therefore, that the great fluctuations of the readings of the barometer have been general.

The unusual meteorological character of the period which we have just experienced, together with its influence on the public health, makes it an object of general interest to trace the cause of so remarkable a phænomenon. To enable persons who have time at their disposal for this investigation, I have detailed the principal meteorological facts for England for the period, and which may be briefly mentioned as exhibiting an excess of temperature for the six months ending 1848, March 31, of 2°·55 upon the average for the same period from the seven preceding years,—an excess remarkable both for its amount and continuance. During the past quarter, the amount of water mixed with the air has been about its average value, although in consequence of the high temperature, the humidity of the air has been less. We have had an unusual prevalence of S.W., W.S.W., and S.S.W. winds at this season, when they are usually replaced by dry and cold N. and N.E. winds. The air has been in frequent rapid motion, and during the period between January 22 and March 4, it passed over Greenwich at the rate of 220 miles daily.

The barometer readings have been remarkable for great and frequent oscillations and very low readings, exhibiting a difference in these particulars from any period since the year 1800 (records previous to this date I have not examined). The amount of rain in March was very nearly double its usual amount; and that for the quarter exceeds the average, reckoned from 1815 to the present time, by $2\frac{1}{4}$ inches. The water-sodden state of the soil, in many parts, has prevented wheat-sowing and preparing the land at the proper season. The observer at Leeds says, "The rivers in the West Riding of Yorkshire have been much swollen during February and March, and farming operations have, as far as relates to outdoor work, been completely at a stand. Horned cattle and sheep have suffered severely from disease of the lungs." The year whose corresponding period most nearly resembles that of the present, is 1836. From the preceding remarks, it will be seen that the weather during the past quarter has been as unusual as that of the preceding.

To the report of the Registrar-General are appended the monthly values at every station, from which the average values for the quarter have been determined, and which are contained in the following table.

From the numbers in the first column it seems that the volume of dry air was the same at all parts of the country. The mean of all these results is 29·512 inches, and this value may be considered as the pressure of dry air for England during the quarter ending March 31, 1848.

From the numbers in the second column, we find for the quarter ending March 31, 1848, that the mean temperature of the air for the counties of Cornwall and Devonshire was 42°·1, and for the remaining places, excepting Brighton, Liverpool and Whitehaven, was 38°·9.

The average daily range of the temperature of the air in Cornwall and Devonshire was 9°·2; at Brighton, Liverpool and Whitehaven, was 6°·7; that at Brighton was 5°·1 only, and seems to be too small; at places situated between the latitudes of 51° and 53° was 11°·0, except at London, where the range was 8°·9 only; and at all places N. of 53°, was 10°·3.

The greatest mean daily ranges took place at Hartwell,

| Names of Stations | [illegible] |
|---|---|
| Helston | [illegible] |
| Falmouth | [illegible] |
| [illegible] | [illegible] |
| [illegible] | [illegible] |
| [illegible] | [illegible] |
| Brighton | [illegible] |
| Chichester | [illegible] |
| [illegible] | [illegible] |
| Beckington | [illegible] |
| Royal Observatory, Greenwich | [illegible] |
| Whitworth | [illegible] |
| St. John's Wood, London | [illegible] |
| Latimer Rectory | [illegible] |
| Aylesbury | [illegible] |
| [illegible] Observatory | [illegible] |
| Hartwell House | [illegible] |
| Saffron Walden | [illegible] |
| Pool Cottage, Hereford | [illegible] |
| Cardington | [illegible] |
| Thwaite | [illegible] |
| Norwich | [illegible] |
| Derby | [illegible] |
| Highfield House, Notts | [illegible] |
| Liverpool Observatory | [illegible] |
| Wakefield | [illegible] |
| Stonyhurst Observatory | [illegible] |
| Leeds | [illegible] |
| York | [illegible] |
| Scarva, Ireland | [illegible] |
| Whitehaven | [illegible] |
| Durham | [illegible] |
| Newcastle | [illegible] |

Latimer, Leeds, Beckington, Aylesbury, &c., and the least occurred at Brighton, Liverpool, Scarva, Torquay, &c.

The highest reading during the quarter was at Greenwich and Lewisham, which was 71°·5, and the lowest was at Durham, which was 3°·8. The extreme range of temperature in England, during the quarter, was therefore 67°·7.

The average quarterly range of the reading of the thermometer in Cornwall and Devonshire was 35°·6; at Brighton, Liverpool and Whitehaven, was 38°·1; at those places situated between the latitudes of 51° and 52° was 51°·3; and between the latitudes of 52° and 55° was 48°·3.

The mean direction of the wind was S.W. At Exeter it was N., but this is probably wrong.

From the numbers in the ninth column, the distribution of cloud seems to have been the same in amount nearly at all parts of the country, and such as to have covered about three-fourths of the sky. The actual amount I believe to have been greater than three-fourths.

The fall of rain during the quarter has greatly exceeded the average amount for the season, and it has fallen on a greater number of days than usual. At Highfield House, it fell on 71 days; at Helston, on 67; at Leeds, on 63; at Falmouth, Truro and Saffron Walden, each 60. The places at which rain fell on the least number of days were Hereford, Durham, Thwaite, Newcastle, &c. The places at which the largest falls have taken place, are Whitehaven, Stonyhurst, Truro, Falmouth, Helston, Derby, Newcastle, &c.; and the places where the fall has been the least in amount, are Walworth, Cardington, Saffron Walden, &c.; generally the fall has been much smaller on the east coast than on the west coast. The average amount for the quarter in Cornwall and Devonshire was 12 inches, at places situated between 51° and 53° was 8·2 inches, and at places N. of 53° was 10·7 inches.

Columns 12 to 16 contain the mean hygrometrical results, and they are as nearly identical as can be expected from uncompared instruments. At Beckington the air seems to have been near saturation. At Hartwell the results cannot be correct; these instruments, however, are to be shortly compared with standards. At Leeds the results are evidently erroneous; the instruments here are to be replaced by new ones. Omitting the results from these places, we find that the mean weight of vapour in a cubic foot of air for England (excepting Cornwall and Devonshire) in the quarter ending March 31, 1848, was 2·7 grains. The mean additional weight required to saturate a cubic foot of air in the quarter ending March 31, 1848, was 0·3 grain. The mean degree of humidity in the quarter ending March 31, 1848, was 0·888. The mean amount of vapour mixed with the air would have produced water, if all had been precipitated at one time on the surface of the earth, to the depth of (in the quarter ending March 31, 1848) 3·25 inches. And these values for Cornwall and Devonshire were 2·7 grains; 0·5 grain; 0·863 grain; and 3·6 inches.

The results from the station in Ireland, depending on the temperature of the air, the direction of the wind, and the amount of clouds, agree with those in England at the same latitude; but the results which depend on the humidity of the air and the amount of rain, exhibit an excess over those in England, and the daily and monthly ranges of the readings of the thermometer are less than those in England.

May 25, 1848.

## LXVIII. *Notices respecting New Books.*

*Results of Astronomical Observations made during the years 1834, 1835, 1836, 1837, 1838, at the Cape of Good Hope; being the Completion of a Telescopic Survey of the whole Surface of the visible Heavens, commenced in 1825.* By Sir JOHN F. W. HERSCHEL, Bart., K.H., &c. &c. London: Smith, Elder and Co. 1847. (*Second notice.*)

Chap. II. *Of the Double Stars of the Southern Hemisphere.*

IN the Introduction to the Catalogue of Southern Double Stars the author observes, that as the principal object kept in view by him during the progress of his southern sweeps was the discovery of new nebulæ, or the determination of the places of those already known, the detection and measurement of double stars was regarded as of subordinate interest, and allowed to interfere as little as possible with what was looked upon as the main inquiry. When nebulæ were expected, and especially on new ground, little leisure was afforded for any minute examination of stars; but in regions which had been already examined, or where nebulæ were thinly scattered, stars down to the sixth or seventh magnitude were seldom dismissed till they had undergone the application of one or more of the diaphragms. To have executed a regular review of the southern heavens with the 20-foot reflector, for the purpose of detecting close double stars, would have required at least two additional years, probably more. When double stars occurred they were of course always taken, and a measured angle of position secured as accurate as a single rapid setting of the wires afforded; but excepting in special circumstances no close examination was made, unless some suspicion, excited under the ordinary sweeping power (180), induced an application of high magnifying powers, and in such cases it would occasionally happen that a long and pertinacious scrutiny took place.

This system of observing, he thinks, may probably account in some degree for the comparative deficiency in the catalogue of double stars of the first or closest class, *i. e.* stars of which it can be confidently asserted that the angular distance of the individuals is under 2″. But he states, that independently of such drawbacks, although he has no direct statistical facts to bear out the assertion, he cannot help putting on record " a strong *impression* that the extra-tropical part of the southern hemisphere is really poorer in very close double stars than the northern, at least in those regions of it which come to be observed on the meridian in the best seasons for definition. The almost total absence of objects of this description from the Catalogue in the last six hours of right ascension is the more striking, as these are precisely the best hours for definition, coming to be observed from June to October, when the atmosphere is in the most favourable condition." Under circumstances of the best possible definition, when the discs were reduced to mere points, and when it was hardly possible that an interval from centre to centre of moderately unequal stars exceeding three-fourths of a second, or at all events a whole second, could escape detection, remarks of the following kind stand recorded in the Journal :—" July 23, 1835. The extreme paucity, or rather total absence of close double stars in the late sweeps, in such wonderful nights and such perfect action of the instrument, is really surprising."—" July 24. I begin to think I shall never see another close double star. It is wonderful how entirely devoid of these objects are all the last sweeps, and *that* in the finest picked opportunities for detecting them. It is a remarkable feature. *Eo ipso notantur quod non videntur.*"—P. 166.

The present chapter contains two Catalogues :—I. Reduced Observations of Double Stars made with the 20-foot Reflector; and II. Micrometrical Measures of Double Stars with the 7-foot Equatorial. To the last is appended a Synopsis of the Results of the Micrometrical Measures, and a Comparison of Angles of Position taken with the two instruments; and the chapter concludes with some " Special Remarks on particular Double Stars in the foregoing Catalogues."

The first Catalogue includes 2103 stars, not found marked as double in former Catalogues, and interspersed with which are a large number which had been noted by previous observers. The new double stars are numbered (in continuation of the lists formerly given by the author) from 3347 to 5449, both inclusive. Among them are a few respecting whose double nature, owing to their extreme closeness, doubts may be entertained. "The unnumbered stars occur for the most part in Struve's Catalogue; some are noticed as double in the Brisbane Catalogue, and a considerable number are identifiable with objects described in Mr. Dunlop's Catalogue of 253 double stars, published in the third volume of the Memoirs of the Royal Astronomical Society." The Catalogue likewise includes such double stars (not previously noted by other observers) as were encountered in the course of an examination, with the equatorial, of the Brisbane Stars, as well as those which occurred in the partial and imperfect execution of a series of zone observations with that instrument, which he found it impossible to carry out. In its arrangement the Catalogue is similar to the Catalogues of double stars previously communicated by the author to the Royal Astronomical Society. It consists of nine columns, the first containing the reference-number prefixed to the new double stars; the second and third the RA and NPD, reduced to 1830; the fourth the angles of position; the fifth the estimated distances; the sixth the magnitudes; the seventh notes made at the time of the observation; the eighth references to other Catalogues with which the stars in this may have been identified, either as single or double stars; and ninth, the number of the sweep. The Catalogue occupies seventy-two pages.

With respect to the angles of position, it is remarked that "they are by no means to be regarded as of equal authority with the results of an equal number of measures taken with the equatorial, for several reasons. 1st. They are for the most part much less deliberately taken. 2nd. When taken with care, and when time has been allowed for a repetition of measures, a peculiar bias of judgement seems in some cases to have influenced them, which makes it necessary to be cautious in combining them with the equatorial measures of the same stars. This is, no doubt, partly owing to the different position of the person and head of the observer at the two instruments—in the one case looking down, in the other up. To this we must add the difference of inversions due to the optical construction of the two instruments; the achromatic operating a complete, and the reflector only a semi-inversion. Owing to this cause the situation of the line of junction of the two stars observed on the meridian will stand in a different relation to the *optical bias* of the eye habitually used for observing, and thus angles obtained with the two instruments will cease to be comparable. As a general principle, indeed, it may be borne in mind that no measured angle of position of a double star, no matter with what instrument taken, can be considered free from bias, unless their line of junction lie in the principal section of the eye, and unless the diurnal motion be either eliminated by clockwork, or by a perfectly equable movement given by hand, a condition tolerably well satisfied in my observations with the equatorial, by long practice in the use of the right ascension handle, but which the construction of the reflector rendered it almost impossible to fulfil with any degree of exactness."—P. 168.

In respect of the estimated distances of the component stars, Sir John observes, that he considers them in general too small in the closer stars; "they are also affected by the apparent size, neatness of definition, &c. of the stars, and are of course in a very high degree vague and precarious, serving for little more than general classification."

In the Introduction to the Micrometrical Measures with the 7-foot equatorial, some particulars are given respecting the instrument, the building in which it was placed, and the construction of the revolving roof. No alteration was made in the mode of mounting the instrument, excepting a change in the length of the polar axis necessary to adapt it to a different latitude; and the movement necessary for following a star in the act of measurement was communicated, as previously, not by a clock-work mechanism, but by a screw movement worked by a long handle and a Hook's joint. As respects the micrometer, its readings of position are stated to have been always unexceptionable, but in regard of the distances the case was far otherwise. "The inherent defect of the instrument (a very costly one), that of the *hitching* of the parallel spider's threads in the act of crossing, could never be fairly overcome. It was in vain that, previously to quitting England, it was placed in the maker's hands for the express purpose of remedying this annoying evil. For a while, indeed, it performed satisfactorily, but the mischief soon recurred, and grew at length so obvious a source of error, that already in October 1834, I began occasionally to substitute for the system of measures by cross zeros, with the spider lines, that of an absolute zero, with one-sided measures between the inner edges of two thick parallel wires, which have been added to the system of wires in the micrometer, and which could be brought into the centre of the field by the screws, to the exclusion of the spider-threads." But this was a less eligible mode of measurement, and gave rise to a great deal of trouble; nevertheless, as the evil with the spider-threads continued to increase, in April 1835 they were removed, and from this time till June 1836 the thick wires were alone used in the measurement of distances. The micrometer was then refitted by Mr. Maclear, with a pair of beautifully even and delicate threads of the Bermuda spider. "These went on very well for some time, but in April 1837 the hitching was again remarked, and from this time to the conclusion of the observations continued a more or less frequent source of annoyance."

The measures of distance taken with the thick wires, when compared with those observed with the spider-lines, exhibit a systematic disagreement, in consequence of which a correction must be applied before the results by the two methods can be compared. To facilitate the reduction, a table is computed, which gives the correction for each second of distance from 2″ to 110″. The tabular corrections are applied to all the measurements with the thick wires, as part of the reductions.

The results set down in the Catalogue are the means of the several measures, and *weights* are attached, depending on the number and presumed goodness of the observations. "Individual measures are in no case given, excepting under some remarkable circumstance, or if, as sometimes happens, only a single measure was procured. To have done so would have entailed an immense mass of printing, without any corresponding advantage."

"Appended to the micrometrical measures registered as the results of single nights' observations, is a synoptic view of the general mean results reduced to mean epochs."

The Catalogue of Micrometrical Measures is arranged in ten columns, giving the following particulars:—1st, the index number; 2nd, the synonyms; 3rd and 4th, the RA and NPD for 1830; 5th and 6th, the angle of position and weight or value attributed; 7th and 8th, the distance and value attributed; 9th, the magnitude; and 10th, the date of the observation. The number of stars is 1802. The Catalogue occupies sixteen pages, the accompanying notes eleven pages, and the Synoptic Table seven pages.

The author then institutes a comparison between the angles of position measured with the 7-foot equatorial and the 20-foot reflector. He states that on comparing the results given by the two instruments, "material discordances will be found in a great many instances, such as cannot be wholly accounted for either by the comparatively greater attention to precision in this respect in the equatorial measures, and the greater time and care bestowed on them, or by the greater number of measures actually taken with the latter instrument. It is true that several cases of great disagreement may be perfectly well accounted for in this way, when the closeness of the stars measured, their inequality, and even the difficulty of seeing them at all with the smaller instrument, are taken into account. But on subjecting the matter to a more particular examination, it becomes very evident that these causes alone are not sufficient to account for the discordances, and that there exists a *systematic bias*, from whatever cause arising, which has affected all the 20-foot measurements (as compared with the equatorial)—and *that differently according to the different direction of the small star with respect to the large one*. What is more singular, and indeed, so far as I see, unaccountable, is, that neither the *amount* nor *direction* of this bias is the same for all the four quadrants of position; nor is it even the same in the same direction for positions differing by 180°." From a comparison of results given by both instruments he constructs a table of reductions for every 10°, from 0° to 360°, exhibiting what may be called the bias-correction to the positions measured with the 20-foot instrument, by the application of which a much better general accordance, and an even distribution of positive and negative errors were produced. He also remarks, that on examining with care all the cases of comparison, he found no distinct ground for concluding that either the magnitude of the stars or the angular distances (when well seen and well separated) exercised any systematic influence on the angles, or on the amount of the bias-correction.

The details given on this subject are extremely interesting, from their bearing on certain phænomena of vision not yet well understood. They also show how much caution is necessary in the comparison of observations of so delicate a kind when made with different instruments, or in a different manner; and they give a lively idea of the numerous difficulties which were encountered in carrying out the undertaking to a successful issue—difficulties of a harassing and perplexing kind, which only a practical astronomer can fully appreciate.

The "Special Remarks" on the measures of particular double stars in the two Catalogues, with which the chapter concludes, relate principally to the evidence of angular movement furnished by the comparison of the observations. About twenty-two objects are remarked on, but we shall confine our extracts to the two which may be regarded as the most interesting in the present state of our knowledge, namely, γ Virginis, and α Centauri,—the former deriving its interest from the circumstance of its being a revolving double star which has recently been observed to pass through an important phase of its revolution, and from the pains that have been taken to determine its orbit; and the second from its being, with a single exception, the only star whose distance from our system has been determined with a degree of evidence which astronomers seem disposed to regard as satisfactory and conclusive.

The double star γ Virginis was one of the first which was recognized as forming a revolving system, and the orbital motion is so considerable that the greater part of a revolution has been described since the relative situation of the two component stars in respect of the fixed circles of the sphere—the angle of position as it is called—was first determined. And no sooner was the fact of the revolving motion of the companion-star established, than it became a matter of the utmost interest to determine whether the motion is performed in an elliptic orbit, because on the solution of this question depends that of another, which must be regarded as one of the most interesting within the range of theoretical astronomy, namely, whether the Newtonian law of gravitation which governs the motions of the bodies belonging to the solar system prevails also among the distant stars.

From angles of position measured by various astronomers, including one by Bradley in 1718, and another by Mayer in 1756, and assuming the Newtonian law, Sir John Herschel had computed the elements of an elliptic orbit in a paper communicated to the Royal Astronomical Society, and printed in Vol. V. of their Memoirs, which appeared in 1833; and in Volume VI. of the same series he gave the results of a second calculation of the elliptic elements, in which some more recent measures were included. According to the latter calculation the periodic time of revolution was about 629 tropical years, and the epoch of the perihelion passage the middle of the year 1834. He also predicted that the appulse of the two stars would prove so close as to cause them to appear as a single star in all but the most powerful and perfect telescopes under the most favourable circumstances. The passage did not take place till near the middle of 1836, but the other part of the prediction was fully verified, the star having been observed for some time by Sir John himself at the Cape, and by Captain Smyth at Bedford, as *completely round*. Sir John remarks, that in no part of the interval from 1835·971 to 1837·545 " was it possible to observe any certain elongation of the united discs with the 7-foot equatorial capable of being in the smallest degree relied on as a measure." During the year 1836 and part of 1837 the star was frequently observed in the 20-foot reflector, and though an elongation was sometimes fancied, the general conclusion was that the star was single, and perfectly round.

Observations made subsequently to the publication of Sir J. Herschel's paper above referred to, showed that his elements were incapable of representing the motion of the stars far beyond the limits for which they had been calculated; but the question having attracted much attention, various other orbits have been computed,—by Mädler, Encke, Henderson, and Hind, and again by Sir John himself,—all representing, with more or less accuracy, the observations made use of, but differing very considerably in some respects, particularly in the period of revolution. In the present work the periodic time is reduced from 629 to 182·12 years. Mädler's last orbit (he has calculated four) gives 148·78 years for the periodic time, and Henderson found 143·44 years. Sir John remarks, " Comparing the orbits which seem entitled to most reliance, it appears certain that the eccentricity lies between 0·855 and 0·880, the inclination between 23° and 27°, the perihelion epoch between 1836·20 and 1836·45, and the period between 140 and 190 years*."—P. 299.

Notwithstanding all the labour which has been expended on this remarkable binary star, considerable doubt still remains as to the accuracy of the computed elements, a circumstance indeed which might be expected when we take into account the uncertainty of even the apparently best measures. On projecting the positions measured by different observers, for the purpose of inter-comparison, it was apparent that those of Struve, from 1828·38 to 1834·38, could not possibly be used with the rest of the series. " A curve drawn through the points representing these observations separates itself gradually and systematically from that which expresses with the utmost consistency and regularity the general course of the movement, as deduced from all the other authorities, the amount of deviation reaching no less than 9°, after which it ceases abruptly; the subsequent results of Struve's measurements, as well as those previous to 1828, being in good accordance with all the rest, on their whole evidence, as so represented."—P. 295. Sir John further states, in a note, that he had received a series of observations from Mr. Mädler, which, when projected separately, exhibit a systematic and regularly increasing deviation from the projection of Mr. Dawes's and Captain Smyth's observations of the very same nature as was exhibited by Struve's Dorpat observations. " Facts of this kind," he observes, " go to prove that full confidence cannot yet be placed in *any* micrometrical measures, even of position angles and in the case of easy stars (as this is once more become); and they lead us to insist on the necessity of an immense accumulation of observations from a variety of observers, and unremittingly continued for a series of years, as the only ground of hope for the attainment of *accurate* elements of this or any other double star."—P. 299.

The star α Centauri is " a superb double star, beyond all question the most striking object of the kind in the heavens." The component stars are both of a high ruddy or orange colour, though that of the smaller is of a somewhat more sombre or brownish cast. Together they constitute a star which, to the naked eye, is equal or somewhat

* For further information respecting γ Virginis the reader may be referred to the second volume of Smyth's Cycle of Celestial Objects. The first volume of the same work contains a very interesting letter from the late Professor Henderson, explaining the method by which he deduced the orbit from the observations.

superior in lustre to Arcturus. All observers are agreed in regarding the principal star as of the first magnitude. Lacaille and others down to Sir John Herschel have estimated the smaller star as of the fourth. Sir John says his habitual judgement has inclined him rather to the first than the second magnitude, and he is disposed to assign to it a magnitude which may be deemed indifferently either a very low first or a very high second. And he accounts for the very different estimates given of its magnitude by former observers to the known fact (whatever the cause may be) that the apparent inequality of two stars seen at once in the same field of view diminishes as the light of the telescope is greater.

Among the circumstances which render this star remarkable, one is its very great proper motion, which, according to the determination of the late Professor Henderson, amounts to $3''\cdot 58$ in a year, in the arc of a great circle. This circumstance affords in the first place a very strong presumption that the two stars are physically connected; for the chances may be regarded as almost infinite against the agreement of the proper motions of two independent stars, both in quantity and direction; and that such agreement exists in the present case in both respects is manifest, for if the motion of translation through space were not common to the two stars, the one would, in the century which has elapsed since the observations of Lacaille, have left the other behind nearly $5'$ in arc.

But the existence of a large proper motion affords also a *primâ facie* reason for presuming the relatively greater proximity of the star to the earth, by which the apparent motion, whether referred to the star or to the translation of the solar system, would be increased. The presumption of proximity thus arising has been confirmed in the present instance by Professor Henderson, who deduced from his meridional observations made at the Cape an annual parallax amounting to about $1''$ of arc. It is this circumstance which renders α Centauri an object of so much interest to astronomers, for with the exception of 61 Cygni (also double), there is no star whose distance can be regarded as determined with the same certainty; and in the case of the latter, the parallax, as found by Bessel, scarcely exceeds one-third of a second.

The micrometrical measures of α Centauri give no decided evidence of angular motion. Sir John however observes, that there can be no doubt that the distance between the two stars has gone on steadily increasing since 1822 at least. The small amount of variation in the angle of position shows that the plane of the orbital motion (supposing such to exist) passes nearly, but not quite, through our system, while its actual tendency to increase exemplifies the general law of increase of angular velocity with diminution of distance. He finds also, from a comparison of measures, that the major axis of the orbit must materially exceed $24''$; whence, taking the coefficient of parallax at the amount given by Henderson, it will follow that the real diameter of the relative orbit of the companion-star cannot be so small as that of the orbit of Saturn, and exceeds in all probability that of the orbit of Uranus.

Having mentioned 61 Cygni as the only other star for which a sensible parallax can at the present time be regarded as established with reasonable certainty, we may transcribe the following note:—
"It is impossible not to be struck with the parallel which obtains, in a great many physical particulars, between the two double stars α Centauri and 61 Cygni. Both consist of nearly equal stars, which in both cases are of a colour strongly verging to red. Both have very unusually large proper motions. Both have measurable amounts of parallax; and both are clearly binary systems of unusually large apparent angular dimensions."—P. 302.

### POPULAR SCIENTIFIC LITERATURE.

1. *Elements of Plane Geometry, according to Euclid; with several new improvements and additions.* By A. BELL. 12mo. Edinb.: Chambers.
2. *Principles of Geometry, Mensuration, Trigonometry, Land-surveying, and Levelling.* By THOMAS TATE. 12mo. London: Longman and Co.

It is probable that few of our readers take the trouble of looking closely into the elementary works that are annually issued for popular instruction. It is not an inviting occupation; and men who read chiefly for the purpose of adding to their previous knowledge, do not expect to derive advantage from compositions of this class. Neither have we the least intention to urge such a practice; and it is with some reluctance that we have entered upon our present task of calling attention to one or two of them. As long as the public reads for mere amusement, whether the fictions that please them be literary or scientific, we should consider it beyond our province to discuss the character of the works which furnish that amusement. It appears to us pretty much the same whether a concourse of well-dressed people frequent the opera-house, the legitimate theatre, or the lecture-theatre of the Polytechnic Institution:—they are pleased, and thereby better prepared for the next day's contest with the realities of life.

With works relative to the subjects of our very early studies (viewing our studies as a portion of *real education*) we are brought into somewhat closer contact; yet still there is a limit to our functions, even under this aspect. From this limit we now depart, viz. from the commencement of *Geometry as a science*. Even in this case it is only under peculiar circumstances that we should interfere:—when, in fact, a work comes before us that appears calculated to facilitate the study by means of some real improvement in the development; or else when works are obtruded on the public of a pernicious tendency, and supported by social influences that are likely to gain for them a diffusion to which their intrinsic qualities do not entitle them.

Since "general education" has become a political stalking-horse, and the Government has laid the foundation for carrying out the principle of "centralisation" in educating the people, there have been several speculations made in the composition of works of an elementary class, under the hope of the publisher's or author's influence with the Educational Board being able to get them enforced by an "Order in Council," upon all the schools that receive aid from the Parliamentary Fund. If our general education is to be thus controlled, and class-books are to be forced upon the public, it surely becomes important that the books selected for that purpose should be such as judicious and scientific men can approve; and not such as are alone recommended by their price, or by the influence of their authors with the subordinate functionaries of the Government. We hope that it will be rendered *imperative* upon the Educational Board to appoint a commission of competent persons to decide upon the works that shall be used in these schools; if, indeed, any such books shall be forced upon the public by such authority,—a step the wisdom of which we strongly question. In sporting phrase, the two works at the head of this review are the present "favourites," and "betting upon them is nearly equal." It is not, then, for any intrinsic merit they possess that we notice them at all; for in this respect they would be classed with the thousand-and-one abortions that annually issue from the British press in this *soi-disant* "educated age," and they might therefore be allowed to sink into oblivion with the mass to which they belong.

But when it is contemplated to give to one or other of these works a peculiar patent (the patent of a *forced sale*), it becomes necessary to analyse them with some degree of care; and under the conviction that the Government would commit a grave mistake and a great wrong by such an adoption of them, we feel ourselves bound to draw the attention of our readers to the character of the works, in order to enlist their cooperation in the prevention of a design fraught with so much real injury to the fundamental principles of science in this country.

Mr. Bell tells us that his "Treatise on Geometry consists of the *usual* six elementary books," &c.; and states, further on, that their "basis is Euclid's Elements of Geometry, as given in the improved editions of Simson and Playfair." He also tells us that "there are several *improvements* in this edition of the six books;" that "many additional and *useful definitions* have been added, which tend to improve the language of geometry in respect to conciseness and precision;" that "several propositions have been inserted, as being valuable on account of their practical utility;" and that "numerous scholia have been added, explanatory of the utility or connection of some of the propositions."

Did the execution correspond to the professions of the author, this would be no ordinary book. The numberless logical blunders committed by those who, year after year, and age after age, have undertaken the "improvement" of Euclid's Elements, would operate as a warning to men of sound geometrical knowledge, not to be too rash in identifying every change with an *improvement*. We are bold to say that every change which Mr. Bell's temerity has led him to propose, is a *deterioration* of the "Elements," and a perversion of the essential principles of geometrical logic. We may indeed say of it, "whatever is good is not new, and whatever is new is not good." Even when he appropriates an idea, he mangles it in the expression; as for instance in his remarks upon "mathematical taste" (Pref. xi.), taken from Lawson, or his description of "Analysis" (p. 205), imitated from Leslie. Nor are his appropriations of particular processes of demonstration materially different in their characteristic features.

Supposing, however, that we divest this edition of all its superfluities, and view it as a bare treatise on Geometry, we do not deem it a safe one to follow; inasmuch as the author having adventured upon changes in the text, and finding in his addenda the most unquestionable evidences of his heterodoxy in respect to the *principles* of geometry, we should feel no confidence (without an entire collation and careful examination of all the steps) that some of the "improvements" which would invalidate the argument had not been made even here. The price we know is a temptation to schoolmasters; but he who adopts this edition without complete assurance of its not being vitiated, is false to the trust reposed in him. We express no decided opinion as to the extent to which Mr. Bell has carried his "improvements" of the general text, though we could quote a few instances of such that we think ought to open the eyes of even official personages. We will rather turn, then, to the parts which are professedly Mr. Bell's own contributions to Geometry; and we do it in confidence of showing that this gentleman and his employers were alike incompetent to presume upon any "improvements" upon the Elements of Euclid—at least if the most complete ignorance of the ordinary terms of geometrical science be any proof.

First, then, his *definitions*. There grew up with the renovated science of the mediæval period, a practice of *seeming to be systematic*; and this was especially evinced by an attempt to *define every term*. Thus, mathematics, geometry, algebra, mechanics, and every other branch of science was described by some circumlocutory phrases; and this was called "definition." Such definitions are vicious: they are always either defective from their involving terms that have themselves not been defined, or insignificant from their not expressing the defined subject at all. The usual definition of mechanics falls under the first head, from its involving the word "force;" and that of geometry under the second, from its conveying no descriptive idea whatever. Archimedes, we believe, attempted no definition of mechanics; and Euclid, we are sure, attempted none of geometry. Mr. Bell's "improvements," however, do not go to the exclusion of such inane practices from our books, but to the "addition of many useful definitions." Let us see how far a few of these fulfill his promise—that they "tend to improve the language of geometry in respect to *conciseness* and *precision*."

Def. 1. "*Mathematics* is that branch of science which treats of Measurable Quantity."

Now the "conciseness" of this passage consists of two counterparts:—the interpolation of the metaphorical term "branch," which is altogether superfluous, and the elision of the term that would bring *number* into the domain of mathematics. Its "precision" consists in suggesting an erroneous idea of the essential character of one-half of mathematical science, and never at all referring to the other half. The idea of "measure" is never brought under any aspect into theoretical geometry, such as that of Euclid; all idea of number (and hence of algebra) is excluded from mathematics in this definition; and it is not true that we actually measure all the quantities that become the subjects of mathematical investigation—as forces, heat, &c.

Def. 2. "*Geometry* is a branch of mathematics which treats of that species of quantity called magnitude."

Here again the "precision" depends upon the definition of *magnitude*: whilst its *conciseness* consists of the needless interpolations of the "branch" and the "species of quantity;" and of the total omission of two out of three of the essential characters of geometrical magnitude, *species* and *position*.

Def. 3. "*Magnitudes* are of one, two, or three dimensions; as lines, surfaces and solids. They have no material existence, but they may be represented by diagrams."

The first part of this is "concise" enough certainly; of its "precision" we must leave our readers to judge, keeping in mind that the term "dimension" has not been defined.

Respecting the latter part, we scarcely see how the statement of "mathematics treating of measurable quantities," and this branch of mathematics treating of things which have "no material existence," are to be considered as "tending to precision of geometrical language," or even to precision of idea. Neither do we understand the precision of the language which tells us that immaterial existences may be "represented by diagrams." It seems not altogether unlike a ghost upon canvass.

Def. 4. "That branch of geometry which refers to magnitudes described upon a plane, is called *Plane Geometry*."

Indeed! What, then, did the ancients call a "a solid problem?" In our own simplicity, we have always believed that plane geometry was the geometry which involved *only the straight line and circle*; and that every problem which involved any other curve than the circle was called a solid problem. We have never till now heard that the conic sections (to say nothing of the higher classes of curves, transcendental and all) were comprised by geometers in plane geometry. Were we to admit that Mr. Bell had any right to change the signification of a term so universally employed in one sense to suit his *penchant* for "improvement," we should still consider his representation of his own being *the usual meaning*, as a discreditable imposition upon his readers.

Mr. Bell's definition of a point is that of Professor Jardine, first published by Playfair. It has been much eulogised: but we are not disposed to discuss it here. We may, however, state that we consider the definition of Euclid to be more in keeping with Euclid's general idea of his own system than the amended one. We would only suggest that this definition harmonizes but strangely with Mr.

Bell's previous definitions of mathematics and geometry; except, indeed, he means to say that *position* is "a mensurable quantity," and yet not one of the objects of geometrical conception. Even then it would be difficult to understand how this quantity which has no *magnitude* is to be *measured*; except, again, its immateriality should aid its mensuration.

His definition of a *line* is Euclid's: but he deduces from it as a *corollary* (without showing any reason for his deduction), that "the extremities of a line are points; and the intersections [plural in the text] of one line with another are points." Yet in the next line he *defines* straight lines as those which "cannot coincide in two points without coinciding altogether." Out of this "definition" he extracts Euclid's tenth axiom; and likewise the corollary to Euclid's eleventh proposition as given in Simson. By what process he extracts them, he has not, however, condescended to inform us. It would appear that Mr. Bell's conceptions of the character of an axiom, a corollary, and a definition are all equally muddy and confused. We will try to ascertain presently: but we must first finish his *first page*.

DEFS. 4, 5, 6. "A *crooked* or *broken* line is composed of two or more straight lines.

"A line of which no part is a straight line, is called a *curved line*, a *curve line* or *curve*.

"A *convex* or *concave* line is such that it cannot be cut by a straight line in more than two points; the *concavity* of the intercepted portion is turned towards the straight line, and the *convexity* from it."

We have always understood the word "crooked" to be a vulgar term to express that a thing was *not straight*, without specifying in what way it "divaricated from rectilinearity." A "crooked stick" is generally "bowed" (scientifically speaking, according to Mr. Bell, curved); a "crooked temper" is on the contrary often very "angular," and sometimes "flies off *at* a tangent." A "shepherdess's crook" is a long staff with a graceful *bow* at the top; a "crooked spine" is a portion of an inscribed polygon of a thousand sides; and a "crooked path in life" is one composed of ten thousand "doublings," a few rectilinear but of erratic directions, and among which some are as complicated in their "doublings" as the wreath of roses which Guido Grandi presented to the Royal Society a century and a half ago. This, we suppose, is one of the "precise" contributions made by Mr. Bell to the Geometry of Euclid, and to the intellectual progress of the "rising generation" of England. We cannot, still, bring ourselves to think that this is anything more than a piece of sheer vulgarism in reference to the study of geometry.

Is Mr. Bell quite sure of the fact that a curve line cannot be cut by a straight line in more points than two? If his assertion be correct, let our geometry be reformed; and let his celebrated countryman, Maclaurin, be called to account for leading even his Scottish compatriots astray on this subject. Let Newton too be arraigned, and Des Cartes put in the pillory. Let the mathematical world no longer labour under the hallucination that a curve of the $n$th degree may be cut by a straight line in *n* points! Mr. Bell has pronounced his veto upon its being cut in more than two: and we must bow, on Governmental authority, to his decision,—that such shall, in all after times, be the mathematical creed of England.

It would also seem, that besides a curve line we are to admit another class of lines, the "convex" and the "concave" line; whilst it would appear that a curve line is neither the one nor the other. The *usual* mathematical criterion of convexity and concavity is to be laid aside (viz. the position of the centre of curvature with respect to the tangent), and the words "from" and "towards" with respect to some unspecified secant, are by some hocus-pocus system of thinking, to do the business for us which in the dark ages now closing have been only effected by means of a second differential. The millenium of science is, surely, dawning upon us at last!

We have not picked out subjects of comment, in the shape of isolated passages taken apart from their explanatory context: we have taken a single page, and that the opening one, which in a work of science is the key to the whole system. We have discussed the first specimen that offered itself of Mr. Bell's peculiar excellence in "concise and precise" didactic composition; and our readers, should they (unlike the actors in the Hampden controversy) take the trouble to read the book itself, will find that our's is no garbled version of Mr. Bell's mathematical heterodoxy. From such a foundation in science, what sort of a structure *can be* raised? We sympathise with the future youth of England who may have this book "to get up;" and we sympathize, too, with the future schoolmaster of England who may be compelled for the sake of the "government grant" to submit to

"......... rear the tender thought
And teach the young idea how to shoot."

We might close here: but still it appears necessary to exhibit his views on other matters of a still wider range than the mere definitions of terms.

His idea of a PROPOSITION (*p.* 6) is, that "it is a portion of science, and is a theorem, a problem or a lemma."

Geometers, however, class propositions differently from Mr. Bell, and substitute the "porism" for his "lemma." The office of a lemma, like that of a corollary, has been altogether perverted amongst these "improvements."

"A THEOREM is a truth which is established by a demonstration." Nothing of the kind: a theorem is a theorem *independently* of its demonstration, and would be such, had no demonstration ever been given of it. A theorem merely states that if certain conditions be fulfilled, certain relations amongst the component parts must exist. The name has reference to the *form* of the proposition only.

"A PROBLEM *either* proposes something to be effected, as the construction of a figure; *or* it is a question that requires solution."

A distinction without a difference: further than this—that the latter form is vague as to both the terms "question" and "solution."

be cut by a straight line in *n* points! Mr. Bell has pronounced his veto upon its being cut in more than two; and we must bow, on Governmental authority, to his decision,—that such shall, at al. after times, be the mathematical creed of England.

It would also seem, that besides a curve line we are to admit another class of lines, the "convex" and the "concave" line; whilst it would appear that a curve line is neither the one nor the other. The usual mathematical criterion of convexity and concavity is to be laid aside (viz. the position of the centre of curvature with respect to the tangent), and the words "from" and "towards" with respect to some unspecified secant, are by some known process system of thinking, to do the business for us which in the dark ages was always to have been only effected by means of a second differential. The melenium of science is, surely, dawning upon us at last.

We have not picked out subjects of comment, in the shape of isolated passages taken apart from their explanatory context: we have taken a single page, and that the opening one, which in a work of science is the key to the whole system. We have discussed the first specimen that offered itself of Mr. Bell's peculiar excellence in "concise and precise" didactic composition; and our readers should they (unlike the actors in the Hampden controversy) take the trouble to read the book itself, will find that ours is no garbled version of Mr. Bell's mathematical heterodoxy. Upon such a foundation to science, what sort of a structure can be raised. We sympathise with the future youth of England who may have this book "to get up;" and we sympathise too, with the future schoolmaster of England who m——— ———lled for the sake of the ——— ———

It is rarely, if ever, used in pure geometry, except by very ignorant or very careless writers.

"A LEMMA"—this requires modification to pass muster; and more especially to justify the previous classification of theorems, problems and lemmas.

"A HYPOTHESIS is a *fact assumed without proof*, either in the enunciation of a proposition, or in the course of a demonstration."

Let him who can, interpret this:—we cannot. Mr. Bell seems to have attempted to give a definition which should apply to what is called an hypothesis in mathematics and to those notions which have borne the same name in physics:—A good illustration of the old English proverb respecting "two stools."

"A COROLLARY is a consequence easily deduced from one or more propositions."

The ancients understood a corollary to be a distinct and separate enunciation of some property which was discovered, or *contained in* the demonstration of another proposition. The moderns use the word more loosely; and we will give Mr. Bell the advantage of the practice.

"A SCHOLIUM is a remark on one or more propositions, which explains their application, connection, limitation, extension, or some other important circumstance in their nature."

The ancient geometers had no scholia in this or any other sense. The "connections and limitations" were parts of the actual solution; and are known amongst geometers worthy of the name, in modern times, under the general title of "determinations." The mere statement of particular circumstances relating to the history or collateral relations of particular propositions was introduced by the commentators of the middle ages. The slovenly practice of throwing out mere hints about those determinations and limitations which are partly seen and partly guessed at, amongst modern writers deserves to be strongly condemned, whether they take the form of corollaries or of scholia. They, however, enter more largely than usual into Mr. Bell's "improvements;" but whether it be intended for "concisenees" or "precision" we do not pretend to determine.

"A DEMONSTRATION is a process of reasoning, and is either direct or indirect. A *direct* demonstration is a regular process of reasoning from the premises to the conclusion. An *indirect* demonstration establishes a proposition, by proving that any *hypothesis* contrary to it, is contradictory or absurd."

Here, unfortunately, the terms "premises," "conclusion," "proposition" and "process of reasoning" are employed pretty much as if the words had been showered out of a pepper-box, or made up of printers' pie, to take their chance of a possible meaning. The same confusion runs through the following:—

"The DATA or PREMISES of a proposition are the relations or conditions granted or given, from which new relations are to be deduced, or a construction to be effected."

The "or" in this passage has either the force of signifying that the words or phrases on each side of it are identical in signification:

or that the leading terms refer to the problem and the subsequent to the theorem :—both being propositions. The first supposition is too novel a mode of interpretation, we should suppose, even for Mr. Bell in his rage for " improvements in conciseness and precision:" and we will, for the sake of trying to make something out of it, separate the definition into its two cases.

| " The *data* of a problem are the relations granted, from which new relations are to be deduced." | " The *premises* of a theorem are the conditions given, from which a construction is to be effected." |

Was there ever such monstrous absurdity palmed upon a government, and that government call it geometry? But this is not all; though we must hasten forward.

" *Synthetic geometry*, or the ordinary didactic method, affords in the gradual exposition of geometrical truth, excellent specimens of the most clear and satisfactory reasoning; and *that branch of it called geometrical analysis, affords*, in addition, examples of the *resolution of truth into its simple elementary principles*. But *analytical geometry and the other analytical branches of the science* supply the best examples of the *resolution of complex questions*— a process which must be effected before the conditions can be comprised in *symbolical expressions*; they [who? or what?] also accustom the mind to comprehensive views, and afford excellent specimens of subtle reasoning; and exercise the mind in the *interpretations* of the final result."—*Preface*, p. 9.

Geometrical analysis a " branch " of geometrical synthesis! Why not geometrical synthesis a " branch" of geometrical analysis? Not only the ancients, but the moderns without a single exception, till Mr. Bell created one, have considered analysis and synthesis to be co-ordinate with each other. This new " northern-light " has decreed that the ancients and moderns were alike wrong: that the term synthesis shall no longer be considered to signify " composition," nor analysis "resolution." D'Alembert, indeed, introduced the general use of the term analysis to signify algebraic resolution, from the fact, that the majority of algebraic processes was analytical; and in conformity with his view, the works in which geometry was treated by means of algebra after the fashion of Des Cartes, were called treatises on analytical geometry. Then Mr. Bell, who is evidently as confined in his reading as he is confused in his thinking, comes forward with a grand discrimination between synthetic geometry and analytical geometry: which we venture to predict will by some future Montucla eternalize his memory as a splendid instance of ignorant temerity and impudent self-sufficiency. The entire paragraph is one tissue of blunders and mis-statements, that would be unpardonable in a mere boy who had received a respectable course of elementary mathematical instruction. Nor does his description of geometrical analysis in the body of the work itself at all redeem him from the charge.

"*Def. of* GEOMETRICAL ANALYSIS.—In the method of Geometrical Analysis, the process of demonstration follows an order the reverse of that observed in the ordinary Synthetic Method. The latter method proceeds from established principles, and, by a chain of reasoning deduces new principles from these; the former proceeds from the principles that are to be established considered as known, and from these, taken as premises, arrives, by reversing the chain of reasoning, at known principles. The latter method is the didactic method used in communicating instruction; the former is rather employed in the discovery of truth."—P. 205.

It may be as well to remark, once for all, that though the description of geometrical analysis given by Pappus does certainly admit (rather by implication than by direct statements) of the belief that the ancients did apply the analytical method to the discovery of the demonstration of theorems, yet its principal use was to trace the relations between the data and quæsita of problems, so as to deduce a method of constructing them. We may likewise inform Mr. Bell, and such as him (if indeed such there be), that the details of an analytical process in the two cases had so great a dissimilarity in everything but the one general idea, as to be incapable of description in the same form of expression. The analysis of a theorem indeed differs but little from Euclid's *reductio ad absurdum* :—merely, in fact, in assuming the conclusion to be true instead of false. The reasoning ended in the deduction of a known truth, instead of the contradiction of one. As, however, Mr. Pott's has very clearly explained the analysis of theorems and of problems in the Appendix to his Euclid (8vo ed.), we shall refer to that valuable tract instead of quoting it at length here.

We shall only quote two other examples of Mr. Bell's method of improving geometry. Concise enough they are : but the " perspicuity " is beyond our power of detecting.

"*Def.* PLANE LOCI.—If the position of a point is determined by certain conditions; also, if every point in some line, and no other point, fulfil these conditions, the line is said to be a locus of the point.

"As a simple illustration of a locus, consider that of a point which is always equally distant from a given point. This is obviously a circle, whose radius is equal to that distance. So the locus of a point which is always equally distant from a given straight line, is a line parallel to it, and at a distance equal to the given distance."—P. 207.

"*Def.* PORISMS.—A *porism* is a proposition of an indeterminate nature, such that an indefinite number of quantities must fulfil the same conditions. As a simple example of a porism, let it be required to find a point such, that all straight lines drawn from it to the circumference of a given circle shall be equal. This point is evidently the centre of the circle. Problems of loci and porisms are in many cases convertible. The preceding problem becomes a problem of the latter [form?] kind when the centre is given, and it is required to find the locus of all the points that are at a given distance from it."—P. 208.

Mr. Bell is not the only one who has blundered about the "porisms;" but he is, we think, the only one who has blundered quite so egregiously. His description amounts to nothing, except a complete proof that he does not understand what a porism is. But supposing that he understood the subject ever so well, can anybody but himself think that the two definitions quoted above (plane loci and porisms) are adequate to give a learner the slightest conception of the *mode*, to use Mr. Bell's expression, of "solving problems of loci and porisms?" He indeed puts down thirteen loci, either theorems or problems, as "Exercises," and three porisms; all clearly taken from Leslie's Geometrical Analysis: but not a single example of the method, or a single hint for the student's guidance, is vouchsafed. And this is Messrs. Chambers's "Geometry for the People!" This book is one of the candidates for being adopted by the Educational Committee of the Privy Council!!

We had almost forgotten the rival work, Mr. Tate's; and, fortunately, it will require much less space to give it all the notice it deserves. He makes no parade of "improving Euclid's Elements" like Mr. Bell, nor does he flourish about analysis and synthesis, or plane loci and porisms. His preface is candour itself; and there is no possibility of supposing him to be apparently aiming at one thing, and really aiming at another. He simply, with a passing compliment, consigns Euclid to oblivion, and "to persons who are already mathematicians" (Pref. p. vii.): and he supplies a substitute founded on the principles of "common sense," "graphic interest," "tracing the origin of our ideas in geometry," the use of instruments, the evidence of sight and touch, and an endless amount of that kind of jargon which old ladies call "twaddle." As to the "artificial verbiage of a technical logic," and the "tedious verbiage of a rigorous demonstration," they are left for the amusement of those who have nothing better to do than to become "mathematicians," and "who can enter into its metaphysical subtleties."

Mr. Tate seems to understand the constitution and practice of departmental boards, in respect to books, very clearly. He knows full well that the influence of a preface is wonderful upon the people who usually sit at those boards; and, indeed, that the book itself is scarcely ever looked into for the verification of the professions made in the preface. Now Mr. Tate's English composition is very far above mediocrity; and his prefaces are in general very elaborately and ably written. The present, however, is not the best of them that we have seen; but there was this difficulty in the way. He had a delicate part to play in persuading our hypothetical Board, that though Euclid's Elements possessed every other perfection that could be named, yet the all-important one of being adapted to the *requirements* of the Board was wanting in Euclid, and completely fulfilled in Tate. Euclid is enshrouded in his own clouds of greatness and vastness of conception, such that every-day people cannot read him: but Tate shines with his own bright, steady, familiar light, so that "he who runs may read," and he who reads cannot fail to understand! Mr. Tate is modesty personified—modesty denuded of all conventional investiture. However, let him speak for himself with respect to Euclid.

"However, it must be conceded, that whatever may be its excellences as a book of reference to the mathematician, its defects, as an initiatory system of geometry, are too apparent to admit of even an apology. A great book is, in many respects, a great evil; the very elements constituting its greatness,—its refinement and comprehensiveness,—tend to throw over it

...an air of mystery and dignity, which distracts and oppresses the unpractised student, in the place of giving him that encouragement and sympathy, which he certainly requires, in his first feeble efforts in the pursuit of abstract knowledge. The geometry of Euclid is a highly artificial system, which can only be read, thoroughly, by a person who is already a mathematician, and who can enter into its metaphysical subtleties, and beautiful yet operose demonstrations. The principle of motion gives a simplicity and clearness to many geometrical conceptions, but from an imagined inconsistency in the use of such a method, Euclid employs it neither for the purpose of demonstration nor illustration. The method of superposition, which in reality lies at the very basis of geometrical demonstration, and, in many cases, gives a graphic interest to an investigation, is employed in the fourth proposition of his first book, and then, as if ashamed of the low origin of geometry, he scarcely uses it afterwards. Many of his problems are solved by methods which are never used in practice; for example, when a given portion is to be cut off from a straight line, instead of supposing the given portion to be simply transferred to, or placed upon the straight line, &c., which we really do in practice, Euclid must describe circle after circle, in order to accomplish the problem. The doctrine of similar triangles is, unquestionably, one of the most important propositions in the whole range of geometry, yet the student is not permitted to understand this proposition, until he has gone through the fifth book, which, to a large class of students, must for ever remain a sealed book. It is desirable that practical men should comprehend the leading propositions in solid geometry; but Euclid's method of treating this subject is so operose and refined as to place it beyond the reach of persons whose time for study is limited, or whose mathematical talents are not of a superior order."—*Preface*, pp. vii. viii.

Now we have no hesitation in saying (and we say it to those who are able to judge whether we are right or not) that there is not one single assertion in this long extract which is not directly false, or else so gross a perversion of the truth as to be false under the ordinary meaning of the terms employed. We do not think the perversion was deliberate, but the result of total misconception: a perversion of the intellect rather than of the moral sense. He is an enthusiast in the cause of "common sense;" and he has only exercised the advocate's privilege. His own reputation is bound up in the cause; and he makes the best he can of it.

We shall close our extracts with one which developes Mr. Tate's style of teaching and mode of demonstrating geometrical truth very clearly. It is a dialogue between the teacher and pupil.

"Nearly all the geometrical knowledge contained in this work may be conveyed to the pupil in this manner.

"*Teacher.* What is the line A B called?

"*Pupil.* It is called a straight line.

"*T.* Of the two straight lines A B and D C, which is the greater?

"*P.* The line A B is the greater.

"*T.* How should you ascertain this with certainty?

"*P.* By laying the line D C upon A B.

"*T.* What sort of line is A F B (see *fig.* Art. 2.)?

"*P.* It is a crooked line.

"*T.* True; but it is also called a *curved* line. Whether is the curved line A F B or the straight line A B the shorter?

" *P.* The straight line A B.

" *T.* If you wanted to go from Battersea school to the church in what line should you walk?

" *P.* In a straight line. (Why?) Because a straight line is the shortest distance between the school and the church.

" *T.* What have you to say relative to the two straight lines A B and C D?

" *P.* They appear to be of the same length; and moreover they appear to lie even with each other.

" *T.* In other words you might say, C D = A B; and also C D is *parallel* to A B. Is C D now parallel to A B?

" *P.* No; for C D would meet A B on the left side.

" *T.* On which side would they now meet?

" *P.* On the right hand side.

" *T.* What is therefore the peculiar property or definition of parallel lines?

" *P.* That if they be carried out ever so far, on either side, they will never meet.

" 7. A surface is called a *plane*, or flat even surface, when the line between any two points upon it is straight. Thus the surface of the table is a plane if a straight-edge exactly fits it when applied in every direction. To ascertain when a surface is a plane, bring your eye on a level with it, and if you find that every point in the surface can be seen at the same time, it will show that the surface is a plane. Our figures are supposed to be drawn on planes."—Pp. 3, 4.

We now ask, and we do it emphatically and earnestly, whether our readers, as men of science, are disposed passively to allow such works as these to be quietly foisted on the youth of England, and upon English teachers, by a mere act of official patronage, and this at the public expense? Men of science have *a right* to be heard in such a case as this; and they should remember that they *can* make themselves heard. If books are to be forced upon all schools, let us at least have the benefit of the judgment of our most eminent and experienced tutors in the universities and out of them both. Let the selection be one that will not be without the weight of experience on its side; let it not be a job that would disgrace our scientific character throughout all lands.

---

LXIX. *Proceedings of Learned Societies.*

ROYAL SOCIETY.

[Continued from p. 392.]

March 4, 1848. "ON the Corrections necessary to be applied to Meteorological Observations made at particular periods, in order to deduce from them Monthly Means." By James Glaisher, Esq., of the Royal Observatory. Communicated by G. B. Airy, Esq., F.R.S., &c., Astronomer Royal.

The author, under whose immediate superintendence the whole of the magnetical and meteorological observations taken at the Royal Observatory at Greenwich have been conducted, by direction of the Astronomer-Royal, has communicated in the present paper various tabular results deduced from the meteorological observations, reserving for future notice those deduced from the magnetical series. His chief object has been to determine the corrections which are applicable to the results obtained by different observers at various times, so as to render them comparable with one another. The barometrical and thermometrical observations here recorded have been made at every hour of Gottingen mean solar time, during the whole of five years, namely, from the end of 1840 to that of 1845. The mean of each hour represents the results deduced from about 150 observations; those for each month represent about 1800 observations; and those for the year represent upwards of 21,000 observations of each element.

Tables are given representing the excess of the mean value of each element at every hour of observation, in every month, above the mean value for the month; and also the mean of the numbers so found, arranged for the different years, and likewise for the same hours in every month. The numbers were then laid down on paper, as ordinates to a curve of which the times were the abscissæ, and a curve passed through, or very near each point; and the ordinates at every Greenwich hour were measured from that curve, and their values given in a table. The accordance of the results thus obtained for the same hours in the same months of the different years is very close and satisfactory; and shows that observers may obtain very valuable approximate results, by taking a comparatively small number of observations in each day at hours by no means inconvenient in ordinary life, furnishing a close approximation to the mean and extreme values, as well as to the diurnal and annual variations of atmospherical phenomena.

March 9 and 16.—"Report of Experiments made on the Tides in the Irish Sea; on the similarity of the Tidal phenomena of the Irish and English Channels; and on the importance of extending the experiments round the Land's-End and up the English Channel." Embodied in a letter to the Hydrographer, by Captain F. W. Beechey, R.N., F.R.S. Communicated by G. B. Airy, Esq., F.R.S., Astronomer Royal.

The author commences by stating, that the set of the tides in the Irish Sea had always been misunderstood, owing to the disposition to associate the turn of the stream with the rise and fall of the water on the shore. This misapprehension, in a channel varying so much in its times of high water, could not fail to produce much mischief; and to this cause may be ascribed, in all probability, a large proportion of the wrecks in Caernarvon Bay.

The present inquiry has dispelled these errors, and has furnished science with some new and interesting facts. It has shown that, notwithstanding the variety of times of high water, the turn of the stream throughout the north and south Channels occurs at the same hour, and that this time happens to coincide with the times of high and low water at Morecombe Bay, a place remarkable as being the spot where the streams coming round the opposite extremities of Ireland finally unite. These experiments, taken in connexion with those of the Ordnance made at the suggestion of Professor Airy, show that there are two spots in the Irish Sea, in one of which the stream runs with considerable rapidity, without there being any rise or fall of the water, and in the other the water rises and falls without having any perceptible stream; that the same stream makes high and low water in different parts of the channel at the same time; and that during certain portions of the tide, the stream, opposing the wave, runs up an ascent of one foot in three miles, with a velocity of three miles an hour.

The author then enters minutely into the course of the stream; shows that the point of union of the streams from the opposite channels takes place on a line drawn from Carlingford through Peel in the Isle of Man on to Morecombe Bay; and concludes his remarks on this part of the subject, by adverting to the great benefit navigation will derive from the present inquiry.

The author then notices a chart of lines of equal range of tide, which has been compiled partly from the ranges published by the Royal Society*, and partly from observations made on the present occasion; and has annexed a table†, by the aid of which the seaman will be able to compare his soundings taken *at any time of the tide* with the depths marked upon the Admiralty charts.

Next follows the mention of a feature in the motion of the tide-wave, which Captain Beechey thinks has hitherto escaped observation; viz. that the upper portions of the water fall quicker than the lower, or in other words, that the half-tide level does not coincide with the place of the water at the half-tide interval; that this difference in the Bristol Channel amounts to as much as four feet‡, and that the law seems to be applicable to all the tides of the Irish Sea§.

We are next presented with a table (No. 5) exhibiting the various curves assumed by the tide-wave, and with the durations of the ebb and flood at each place.

Having explained these observations in the Irish Sea, the author proceeds to apply to the tides of the English Channel the law which he found to regulate the stream of the Irish Channel, availing himself of the observations of Captain M. White and others for this purpose. There was no difficulty in adapting the rule in the upper part of the Channel; but below the contraction of the strait, the apparent discordance was so great, that nothing but a reliance on the general accuracy of the observations prevented the inquiry being abandoned.

It seemed that the streams are operated upon by two great forces, acting in opposition to each other; viz. that there is a great offing stream setting along the western side of the British Isles, and flowing in opposition to the tides of the Channel above the contraction, turning the stream with greater or less effect as the site is near to, or removed from, the points of influence. By pursuing this idea, it was immediately seen that the observations in the English Channel respond to it; and then applying it to the offing of the Irish Sea, and considering that channel to comprise within its limits the Bristol

---

\* Philosophical Transactions, 1836, part 1.    † Table X.
‡ See Diagram, No. 9.    § Diagram, No. 11.

Channel, as the English Channel does the Gulf of St. Malo, it was found that the observations there also fully bear out the idea. So that there was afterwards but little difficulty in tracing the course of the water, and bringing into order what before appeared to be all confusion.

The author then traces the great similarity of tidal phenomena of the two channels, and proceeds to describe them. For this purpose he considers the Irish Channel as extending from a line connecting the Land's End with Cape Clear to the end of its tidal stream, or virtual head of the tide at Peel; and the English Channel from a line joining the Land's End and Ushant, to the end of its tidal stream off Dungeness. With these preliminary lines, he shows that both channels receive their tides from the Atlantic, and that they each flow up until met by counter-streams; that from the outer limit of the English Channel to the virtual head of its tide the distance is 262 geographical miles; and in the Irish Channel, from its entrance to the virtual head of its tide, it is 265 miles.

In both channels there is a contraction about midway; by Cape La Hague in the one, and by St. David's Head in the other, and at nearly the same distance from the entrance. In both cases this contraction is the commencement of the regular stream, the time of the movement of which is regulated by the vertical movement of the water at the virtual head of the channel; situated in both cases 145 miles above the contraction, and the actual time of this change, or Vulgar Establishment, is the same in both cases. Below the contraction of the strait, in both cases the stream varies its direction according to the preponderance of force exerted over it by the offing stream. In both cases, between the contraction and the southern horn of the channel, there is a deep estuary (the Bristol Channel and the Gulf of St. Malo) in which the times of high water are nearly the same, and where, in both, the streams, meeting in the channel, pour their waters into these gulfs, and in both raise the tide to the extraordinary elevation of forty-seven feet. From the Land's End to the meeting of these streams in one case is seventy-five miles, and in the other the same.

In one channel, at Courtown, a little way above the contraction, and at 150 miles from the entrance, there is little or no rise of the water; and in the other, about Swanage, at the same distance from the entrance, there is but a small rise of tide also (five feet at springs). In both cases these spots are the node or hinge of the tide-wave, on either side of which the times of high water are reversed. And again, near the virtual head of the tide, in both cases there is an increased elevation of the water on the south-east side of the channel of about one-third of the column; the rise at Liverpool being thirty-one feet, and at Cayeux thirty-four feet.

The author traces a further identity in the progress of the tide-wave along the sides of both channels *opposite to that of the node*. In the first part of the channel the wave in each travels at about fifty miles per hour; in the next, just above the node, this rate is brought down to about thirty miles per hour in one, and to sixteen miles in the other; it then in both becomes accelerated, and attains to about seventy-six miles per hour.

Lastly, the author observes that the node or hinge of the tide, placed by Professor Whewell (in his papers on the Tides) in the North Sea, is situated at the same distance nearly from the head of the tide off Dungeness, as the node near Swanage is on the opposite side of it; and that in the Irish Channel, at the same distance nearly as the node at Courtown is from the head of the tide off Peel, there is a similar spot of no rise recently observed by Captain Robinson.

The author concludes this paper by urging a further investigation of the tidal phenomena of the English Channel, on the ground of the great advantage navigation, as well as science in general, would derive from such an examination.

Captain Beechey's letter is illustrated by twelve charts and diagrams, showing the identity and singular phenomena of these two great channels.

## LXX. *Intelligence and Miscellaneous Articles.*

### ON THE ADVANTAGE OF ELECTROTYPING DAGUERREOTYPE PLATES.

*To the Editors of the Philosophical Magazine and Journal.*

Gentlemen,   234 Regent Street, May 23, 1848.

THE following simple experiment, demonstrating the advantages of electrotyping Daguerreotype plates, may be interesting to many of your readers, but more especially to amateurs in that beautiful art.

Purity of silver for the plates has always been much insisted on; and of the various means that have been resorted to to obtain this, the battery process offers the most simple as well as the most satisfactory means of accomplishing it.

Prepare a plate for silvering; but in the place of depositing electrotype silver over the whole face of the plate, only permit the deposit to take place over one-half, by immersing the plate only half way in the decomposition trough. [With a one quart Smee's battery, one minute will be sufficient.] Finish the plate afterwards on removing it from the battery in the usual way, as when preparing it to receive the sensitive coating; and when "cross buffed," it will be perceived, on examining the surface, how much *blacker* and more brilliant is the polish on the electrotyped silver half, the remaining half appearing by contrast quite greasy. The importance of this depth of black will at once be appreciated, when it is remembered that it is the black burnish of the silver which forms the dark portions or blacks of the Daguerreotype picture. If the plate thus prepared be now made sensitive and placed in the camera, it will be found that the electrotype half has also an advantage in sensitiveness, the " halved image " being about four seconds, or about one-third of the exposure in advance of the other side not coated in the battery. I have tried this with a great variety of solutions, and always with the same result.

I am, Gentlemen,
Your most obedient Servant,
WILLIAM E. KILBURN.

### ON THE ACIDS OF PINES. BY M. AUG. LAURENT.

Pinic and sylvic acids were first analysed by M. Rose, who gave as their formula $C^{40} H^{64} O^4$, their salts being represented by $C^{40} H^{64} O^4 + M^2 O$. More recently M. Liebig has shown that sylvic acid contains $C^{40} H^{60} O^4$, and M. Laurent states he has found that pinic acid has the same formula.

M. Laurent, on examining six or seven years since the resin which flows from the *Pinus maritima* of the heaths of Bordeaux, met with a new acid which he called *pimaric acid*, and which possesses the same composition as the preceding. When pimaric acid is distilled *in vacuo*, it is converted into pyromaric acid, without change of composition; and eventually this same acid, when crystallized and left to itself, undergoes an isomeric modification, and is converted into amorphous uncrystallizable pimaric acid.

The salts of all these acids are represented by the following formula, $C^{40} H^{70} O^4 + M^2 O$, which does not agree with opinions entertained by the author and M. Gerhardt.

These salts should contain, either $C^{40} H^{38} M^2 O^4$, or $C^{40} H^{60} M^2 O^3$; the salts examined by MM. Rose and Laurent are those of silver and lead. As it would have been difficult in a fresh analysis of these salts to determine whether they contain $H^2 O$ more or less, the author endeavoured to ascertain whether the preceding acids, on combining with anhydrous oxides, did or did not disengage water. For this purpose pulverized sylvic and pimaric acids were mixed with recently fused and pulverized litharge. The mixture, introduced into a glass drying vessel, was heated in a current of dry air; a small quantity of water, amounting to about one-third of an atom, was disengaged. Presuming that the contact of the acid and the oxide was not sufficient, a little æther was poured on the mixture, and it was heated to 284° F.

1·000 gramme of fused pimaric acid lost 0·028 of water.
1·000 gramme of fused sylvic acid lost 0·034 of water.
1·000 gramme of fused pimaric acid, heated alone to 284°F., lost 1 milligramme.
1·000 gramme of fused sylvic acid, heated alone to 284° F., lost 2 milligrammes.

According to the formula—

| | |
|---|---|
| $C^{40}$ | 3000·0 |
| $H^{38}$ | 362·5 |
| $H^2 O$ | 112·5 = 3·00 |
| $O^3$ | 300·0 |
| | 3775·0 |

the loss should have been 3·00. The salts of the preceding acids ought to be represented by $C^{40} H^{33} M^2 O^4$, or by $C^{20} H^{27} M O^2$.

It is stated in chemical works, that sylvic acid crystallizes in four-sided tables, and as pyromaric acid crystallizes in isosceles triangular tables, the author has considered it as a different acid from the preceding; but having an opportunity of seeing sylvic acid, the author found it possessing the same form as pyromaric acid, and M. Mitscherlich made the same observation.

Pimaric acid is the natural acid which flows from *Pinus maritima*. When it is heated for the purpose of separating the oil of turpentine, a resin remains which is usually a mixture of pimaric and sylvic acids. As to amorphous pimaric acid, it is possibly identical with pinic acid, if the latter be actually uncrystallizable in alcohol.

It becomes then requisite to examine the resins which flow from other species of pines, to determine whether they contain pimaric or sylvic acid, or whether the latter is not a product of the action of heat upon the former. As to pinic acid, it must also be examined whether it exists in the fresh resins of the pines, or whether it is derived from a modification of pimaric acid, by the agency of time.

It is to be remembered that crystallized pimaric acid is converted either into amorphous acid, or pinic acid by the influence of time, whereas the acid which has been fused undergoes no modification. When pimaric acid is very pure, it may partly crystallize, after having been fused; if ten grammes be operated on, it assumes a granular appearance like sugar; when a smaller quantity is employed, it remains transparent and vitreous on cooling.

The author states, that the acid which crystallizes from alcohol, dissolves in about ten times its weight of this liquid, whereas the same acid, when fused and then powdered, immediately dissolves in its own volume of alcohol, but almost directly separates from it, and becomes the crystallized modification, soluble in 10 parts of alcohol.

Pimaric acid, crystallized by fusion, acts with alcohol nearly in the same way as the acid which has been crystallized in it.

*Nitromaric Acid.*—M. Laurent formerly gave the name of azomaric acid to a product which he obtained by treating pimaric acid with boiling nitric acid for a long time; and he has repeated the experiment, continuing the ebullition for only seven or eight minutes. The product washed with water, then dissolved in alcohol and precipitated by water, gave by analysis similar results to those obtained in the first operation:—

|   | First. | Second. |
|---|---|---|
| C | 57·2 | 57·0 |
| H | 5·6 | 5·9 |
| N | 7·2 | 7·1 |
| O | 30·0 | 30·0 |
|   | 100·0 | 100·0 |

This acid is yellow, amorphous and resinous; by heat it softens, fuses and decomposes. Its ammoniacal salt, which is very soluble, dries in transparent plates of an orange-red colour; the salt of lead, which is slightly soluble in alcohol, contains 32·8 to 33·4 of lead.

These numbers indicate the following formula:—

| | | |
|---|---|---|
| $C^{40}$ | 3000 | 56·87 |
| $H^{13}$ | 325 | 6·15 |
| $N^4$ | 350 | 6·60 |
| $O^{16}$ | 1600 | 30·38 |
| | 5275 | 100·00 |

Salt of Lead.

| | | |
|---|---|---|
| $C^{40} H^{13} N^4 O^{16}$ | 5250 | 66·88 |
| $Pb^4$ | 2600 | 33·12 |
| | 7850 | 100·00 |

As the salt of lead deflagrates slightly when heated, and as the nitromarates are yellow, the nitrogen must be in the state of hyponitric acid $NO^4 = X$. Nitromaric acid then becomes $C^{40} H^{12} X^4 O^8$, derived from $C^{40} H^{16} O^8$.

Comparing it with pimaric acid..  $C^{40} H^{30} O^4$ monobasic,
we have             Maric acid  .. $C^{40} H^{30} O^3 + O^4$ bibasic.
            Nitromaric acid $C^{40} H^{12} X^4 O^4 + O^5$ bibasic.

It appears that under the influence of nitric acid, pimaric acid first exchanges $H^4$ for $O^2$, then absorbs two more atoms of oxygen, becoming bibasic maric acid (hypothetical). The latter afterwards exchanges $H^4$ for its equivalent $X^4$, and is converted into nitromaric acid. The preceding formulæ, unfolded, become

Pinic, sylvic and pimaric acid..  $C^{40} H^{30} + O^2$.
Salts  ........................ $C^{40} H^{30} M + O^2$.
Nitromaric acid ............. $C^{40} H^{30} X^2 O + O^3$.
Salts ........................... $C^{40} H^{30} M^2 X^2 O + O^1$.

*Annales de Ch. et de Phys.*, Avril 1848.

### ACTION OF ZINC ON SELENIOUS ACID.

M. Wœhler remarks, that zinc does not act with selenious acid as it does with sulphurous; some selenium is reduced, and there is obtained an acidulous selenite of zinc. The solution of this salt, when evaporated *in vacuo*, yields large yellow crystals, which are modified rhombic prisms. It yielded by analysis,—

| | |
|---|---|
| Selenious acid | 76·03 |
| Oxide of zinc | 14·86 |
| Water | 9·10 |
| | 99·99 |

This salt is unalterable by the air, very soluble in water, and has a strong acid reaction: when heated the solution becomes turbid, selenious acid is disengaged, and a colourless neutral powder of selenite of zinc is deposited, which by long boiling redissolves.—*Journ. de Ph. et de Ch.*, Mars 1848.

### LIEBENERITE—A NEW MINERAL.

This name has been given to a mineral of a greenish-gray colour, crystallized in hexahedral prisms, and found disseminated in a red felspar porphyry at Monte Viesena, near Forno, in the valley of Flems (Vallé de Fassa).

M. Marignac has submitted this mineral to analysis, and has determined its mineralogical characters. Its density is 2·814; its hardness between that of carbonate of lime and fluor-spar. Its composition, taking the mean of three experiments, was found to be—

| | |
|---|---|
| Silica | 44·66 |
| Alumina | 36·51 |
| Protoxide of iron | 1·75 |
| Magnesia | 1·40 |
| Potash | 9·90 |
| Soda | 0·92 |
| Water and carbonic acid | 4·49 |
| | 99·63 |

*Journ. de Ph. et de Ch.*, Mars 1848.

## METEOROLOGICAL OBSERVATIONS FOR APRIL 1848.

*Chiswick.*—April 1. Foggy: very fine: clear. 2. Foggy in the morning: very fine. 3, 4. Slight fog: fine. 5. Fine. 6. Overcast: very fine. 7. Cloudy: rain at night. 8, 9. Rain. 10. Fine: rain at night. 11. Cloudy: rain. 12. Showery. 13. Overcast: heavy rain at night. 14. Clear and cold. 15. Foggy: rain. 16. Hazy and damp: cloudy: rain. 17. Showery. 18. Rain. 19. Cloudy: fine. 20. Fine: rain. 21. Drizzly: overcast: rain at night. 22. Rain: drizzly: partially overcast. 23. Fine: cloudy: slight rain. 24. Overcast: drizzly. 25. Densely clouded. 26. Fine. 27. Clear: shower: clear. 28. Cold rain: overcast: clear. 29. Overcast: fine. 30. Fine throughout.

| | |
|---|---|
| Mean temperature of the month | 47°·33 |
| Mean temperature of April 1847 | 44 ·28 |
| Mean temperature of April for the last twenty years | 47 ·06 |
| Average amount of rain in April | 1·47 inch. |

*Boston.*—April 1. Foggy. 2. Fine: thunder and lightning P.M. 3, 4. Fine. 5. Cloudy: rain P.M. 6. Fine: rain early A.M. 7. Fine. 8. Rain: rain A.M. and P.M. 9. Cloudy: rain A.M. 10. Cloudy: rain P.M. 11. Fine. 12. Cloudy: rain A.M. and P.M. 13. Rain: rain A.M. 14. Fine. 15. Cloudy. 16. Cloudy: rain P.M. 17. Cloudy: rain early A.M. 18. Cloudy: rain P.M. 19, 20. Fine: rain P.M. 21. Cloudy. 22. Cloudy: rain early A.M. 23. Cloudy: brisk wind: rain P.M. 24. Rain: rain A.M. 25. Rain: rain early A.M.: rain P.M. 26. Cloudy: hail and rain A.M. 27. Fine. 28. Cloudy. 29, 30. Fine.

*Applegarth Manse, Dumfries-shire.*—April 1. Fine spring day. 2. Fine spring day: one slight shower. 3. Fine spring day: rain P.M. 4. Fair, but cloudy. 5. Fair A.M.: rain P.M. 6. Fair A.M.: rain: hail. 7. Rain: frost A.M. 8. Showers: snow preceding night. 9. Fair: cloudy P.M. 10, 11. Frost A.M. 12. Cloudy: cleared. 13. Frost A.M. 14. Frost: one shower. 15. Frost: very cold. 16. Cloudy and threatening. 17. Rain early A.M. 18. Slight rain early. 19. Fair and fine: thunder. 20. Fine: showers. 21. Rain early A.M. 22. Slight shower: rain P.M. 23. Fair and droughty. 24. Fair: rain P.M. 25. Showery. 26. Slight hail. 27. Frost, keen: rain P.M. 28. Hail: frequent showers. 29. Hail: frost. 30. Hard frost.

| | |
|---|---|
| Mean temperature of the month | 42°·2 |
| Mean temperature of April 1847 | 43 ·4 |
| Mean temperature of April for twenty-five years | 44 ·2 |
| Mean rain in April for twenty years | 1·76 inch. |

*Sandwick Manse, Orkney.*—April 1. Bright: cloudy. 2. Bright: drops. 3. Damp: drops. 4. Bright: showers. 5. Showers: aurora. 6. Sleet-showers: showers: sleet. 7. Clear: frost: aurora. 8. Clear: frost: snow-showers. 9. Snow-showers: clear: frost. 10—13. Clear. 14. Cloudy. 15. Bright: cloudy. 16. Bright: cloudy: drops. 17, 18. Damp. 19. Cloudy. 20. Damp. 21. Cloudy. 22. Clear: cloudy. 23, 24. Damp. 25. Cloudy: drops. 26. Snow-showers: clear. 27. Bright: cloudy. 28. Hail-showers. 29. Sleet-showers: hail-showers: aurora. 30. Bright: hail-showers: aurora.

*Meteorological Observations made by* Mr. Thompson *at the Garden of the Horticultural Society at* CHISWICK, *near London; by* Mr. Veall, *at* BOSTON; *by the* Rev. W. Dunbar, *at Applegarth Manse,* DUMFRIES-SHIRE; *and by the* Rev. C. Clouston, *at Sandwick Manse,* ORKNEY.

| Days of Month. | Barometer. | | | | | | | Thermometer. | | | | | | | | Wind. | | | | Rain. | | | |
|---|---|---|---|---|---|---|---|---|---|---|---|---|---|---|---|---|---|---|---|---|---|---|---|
| | Chiswick. | | Boston 8½ a.m. | Dumfries-shire. | | Orkney, Sandwick. | | Chiswick. | | Boston 8½ a.m. | Dumfries-shire. | | Orkney, Sandwick. | | | Chiswick 1 p.m. | Boston. | Dumfries-shire. | Orkney, Sandwick. | Chiswick. | Boston. | Dumfries-shire. | Orkney, Sandwick. |
| 1818. April. | Max. | Min. | | 9 a.m. | 9 p.m. | 9¼ a.m. | 8¾ p.m. | Max. | Min. | | Max. | Min. | 9¼ a.m. | 8¾ p.m. | | | | | | | | | |
| 1. | 30·024 | 30·002 | 29·64 | 29·90 | 29·90 | 29·77 | 29·85 | 72 | 38 | 51 | 58 | 35 | 50½ | 49 | | ne. | calm | sw. | calm | ...... | ...... | ...... | ·05 |
| 2. | 29·984 | 29·881 | 29·56 | 29·85 | 29·80 | 29·81 | 29·84 | 75 | 40 | 58 | 60 | 34 | 52 | 45 | | e. | calm | s. | w. | ...... | ...... | ...... | ...... |
| ● 3. | 29·991 | 29·948 | 29·54 | 29·85 | 29·83 | 29·83 | 29·69 | 78 | 36 | 57 | ... | ... | 50 | 46½ | | s. | nnw. | s. | w. | ...... | ...... | ...... | ...... |
| 4. | 30·033 | 30·015 | 29·55 | 29·88 | 29·80 | 29·62 | 29·52 | 75 | 41 | 57 | ... | ... | 46½ | 41½ | | w. | w. | sw. | wsw. | ...... | ...... | ...... | ·04 |
| 5. | 29·989 | 29·736 | 29·47 | 29·74 | 29·59 | 29·47 | 29·53 | 61 | 40 | 53 | ... | ... | 42½ | 41 | | w. | w. | w. | nw. | ·01 | ...... | ...... | ·20 |
| 6. | 29·653 | 29·633 | 29·27 | 29·60 | 29·62 | 29·72 | 29·70 | 53 | 31 | 46 | ... | ... | 40½ | 36½ | | ne. | n. | n. | nw. | ...... | ·16 | ...... | ·10 |
| 7. | 29·591 | 29·440 | 29·24 | 29·56 | 29·40 | 29·59 | 29·70 | 47 | 36 | 46 | ... | ... | 37 | 35 | | ne. | n. | e. | calm | ·04 | ...... | ...... | ·15 |
| 8. | 29·460 | 29·334 | 29·08 | 29·50 | 29·58 | 29·79 | 29·84 | 45 | 38 | 40 | 40 | 32 | 41 | 36 | | ne. | e. | e. | nne. | ·04 | ·04 | 0·45 | ·06 |
| 9. | 29·515 | 29·539 | 29·32 | 29·61 | 29·46 | 29·71 | 29·58 | 53 | 34 | 42 | 45½ | 30 | 37 | 33½ | | ne. | ne. | e. | calm | ·14 | ·23 | ...... | ...... |
| ☽ 10. | 29·483 | 29·328 | 29·13 | 29·27 | 29·29 | 29·50 | 29·54 | 53 | 30 | 39·5 | 42 | 32 | 41 | 36 | | s. | ne. | ese. | calm | ·27 | ...... | ...... | ...... |
| 11. | 29·759 | 29·453 | 29·28 | 29·53 | 29·48 | 29·57 | 29·54 | 59 | 42 | 42 | 39 | 29 | 41 | 36 | | nw. | n. | sw. | calm | ·12 | ·32 | ...... | ...... |
| 12. | 29·540 | 29·432 | 29·00 | 29·25 | 29·33 | 29·41 | 29·47 | 60 | 43 | 50 | 49 | 34 | 41 | 38½ | | sw. | wsw. | ne. | w. | ·16 | ·25 | ...... | ...... |
| 13. | 29·675 | 29·540 | 29·20 | 29·52 | 29·55 | 29·53 | 29·57 | 57 | 35 | 47 | 45 | 31½ | 38 | 40 | | w. | nw. | nw. | w. | ·45 | ·40 | ...... | ...... |
| 14. | 30·069 | 29·853 | 29·43 | 29·72 | 29·91 | 29·77 | 30·03 | 55 | 29 | 42 | 50 | 31 | 40½ | 38 | | nw. | nnw. | w.n.w. | n. | ...... | ·05 | ...... | ...... |
| 15. | 29·994 | 29·881 | 29·60 | 29·81 | 29·73 | 29·94 | 29·87 | 55 | 43 | 44·5 | 51½ | 33 | 42½ | 40 | | sw. | se. | e. | se. | ·28 | ...... | ...... | ...... |
| 16. | 29·980 | 29·733 | 29·50 | 29·75 | 29·47 | 29·76 | 29·58 | 58 | 46 | 48 | 52 | 38½ | 47 | 44 | | s. | sse. | e. | se. | ·29 | ...... | 0·05 | ...... |
| 17. | 29·693 | 29·619 | 29·22 | 29·35 | 29·39 | 29·41 | 29·46 | 61 | 32 | 52 | 55 | 45 | 47 | 44 | | sw. | calm | sw. | se. | ·11 | ·10 | ...... | ·17 |
| ○ 18. | 29·695 | 29·308 | 29·95 | 29·39 | 29·14 | 29·56 | 29·58 | 57 | 35 | 48 | 57 | 42½ | 44 | 43 | | s. | calm | se.–e | ese. | ·31 | ...... | ...... | ...... |
| 19. | 29·231 | 29·292 | 28·94 | 29·13 | 29·21 | 29·58 | 29·57 | 61 | 36 | 53 | 55½ | 45 | 45 | 43 | | s. | s. | ne. | ne. | ...... | ·15 | ...... | ...... |
| 20. | 29·389 | 29·304 | 29·00 | 29·39 | 29·48 | 29·62 | 29·79 | 59 | 46 | 55 | 58 | 42 | 44 | 44½ | | ne. | ene. | ne. | e. | ·39 | ·05 | ...... | ·07 |
| 21. | 29·507 | 29·442 | 29·10 | 29·50 | 29·60 | 29·81 | 29·89 | 51 | 46 | 51·5 | 55½ | 43½ | 50½ | 47 | | nw. | calm | nne. | e. | ·09 | ·31 | ...... | ·07 |
| 22. | 29·583 | 29·447 | 29·11 | 29·61 | 29·68 | 29·94 | 30·00 | 54 | 44 | 50 | 54 | 44 | 51 | 45 | | nw. | e. | nne. | ene. | ·02 | ·04 | ...... | ...... |
| 23. | 29·679 | 29·652 | 29·35 | 29·75 | 29·77 | 29·97 | 30·03 | 60 | 44 | 52 | 51 | 41½ | 43½ | 45 | | ne. | ne. | ne. | ne. | ·03 | ...... | 0·32 | ...... |
| 24. | 29·823 | 29·619 | 29·35 | 29·82 | 29·85 | 30·04 | 30·01 | 50 | 39 | 45·5 | 54 | 41½ | 45½ | 43 | | ne. | ene. | ne. | n. | ·08 | ·20 | ...... | ...... |
| 25. | 29·862 | 29·827 | 29·50 | 29·81 | 29·80 | 29·98 | 29·98 | 50 | 29 | 41 | 53 | 43 | 43½ | 39½ | | n. | e. | ne. | n. | ·01 | ·10 | ...... | ...... |
| ☾ 26. | 29·923 | 29·761 | 29·48 | 29·83 | 29·79 | 29·89 | 29·81 | 54 | 26 | 45 | 51 | 35½ | 41½ | 38 | | ne. | nw. | n. | nne. | ...... | ·01 | ...... | ·07 |
| 27. | 29·899 | 29·793 | 29·54 | 29·70 | 29·50 | 29·67 | 29·63 | 57 | 30 | 47 | 52 | 29½ | 41 | 39 | | sw. | calm | n.-sw. | calm | ·10 | ·07 | ...... | ...... |
| 28. | 29·844 | 29·694 | 29·30 | 29·40 | 29·60 | 29·51 | 29·53 | 56 | 28 | 46 | 48 | 34 | 38 | 39 | | sw. | nw. | wnw. | wnw. | ·12 | ...... | ...... | ·06 |
| 29. | 30·034 | 29·989 | 29·56 | 29·75 | 29·86 | 29·56 | 29·74 | 58 | 27 | 48 | 48½ | 32 | 41 | 39 | | sw. | n. | nw. | wnw. | ...... | ...... | ...... | ·11 |
| 30. | 30·171 | 30·001 | 29·73 | 29·95 | 30·00 | 29·94 | 30·06 | 63 | 29 | 51 | 53 | 28 | 41 | 41½ | | n. | n. | nnw. | w. | ...... | ...... | 0·45 | ...... |
| Mean. | 29·772 | 29·649 | 29·36 | 29·624 | 29·613 | 29·710 | 29·731 | 58·26 | 36·40 | 46·7 | 50·7 | 36·2 | 43·48 | 40·83 | | | | | | 3·06 | 2·78 | 1·27 | 1·15 |

# INDEX to VOL. XXXII.

ABEL (F. A.) on some of the products of oxidation of cumol by nitric acid, 63.
Acids :—toluylic, 15; nitrotoluylic, 25; nitrobenzoic, 67; phenylic, 151; propionic, 156; metacetonic and butyro-acetic, *ib.*; chrysammic, 236; orsellic, 301; erythric, 302; evernic, 303; aspartic, 317; arsenious, 398; pinic, sylvic and pimaric, 542; nitromaric, 543.
Airy (Prof.) on the occultation of stars and planets by the moon, observed at Cambridge Observatory from 1830 to 1835, 146; on Prof. Challis's theoretical determination of the velocity of sound, 339.
Alcohol, on the preparation of absolute, 123.
Algebraic equations of the fifth degree, observations on, 50.
Alumina, analysis of a hydrated silicate of, 149.
Ampère, objections to the theory of, 461.
Andrews (T.) on the heat disengaged during the combination of bodies with oxygen and chlorine, 321, 426; on the heat disengaged during metallic substitutions, 392.
Animals, on the law of the nutrition of, 456.
Annular eclipses, on beads in, 145.
Anthracite coal, on the fossil vegetation of, 78.
Antimony, on a new method of estimating, 394.
Arsenic, on a new method of estimating, 394.
Arsenious acid, on the transparent and opake modifications of, 398.
Asia Minor, on the present state of knowledge of the geology of, 137.
Asparagin, researches on, 233, 317.
Aspartic acid, on the preparation and composition of, 317.
Astronomical observations made at the Cape of Good Hope, results of, 378, 518.
Baggs (I.) on the disruptive discharge of accumulated electricity, and the proximate cause of lightning, 391.
Barlow (W. H.) on alternating diurnal currents of electricity at the terrestrial surface, 389.
Barometric wave, on the great symmetrical, 38.
Barral (M.) on the composition and properties of nicotina, 158.
Beechey (Capt. W. F.) on the tides of the Irish sea, 538.
Bell's (A.) Elements of Plane Geometry, reviewed, 526.
Benzoate of potash, action of chlorine on, 151.
Birt (W. R.) on the great symmetrical barometric wave, 38.
Blood, on the existence of several metals in the human, 310; on galvanic currents in the, 229.
Bodies, incandescent, on the radiations of, 262.
Bone-caverns, on the geological age of, 119.
Books, new, notices respecting. R. Pott's Euclid's Elements of Geometry, 69; Gaskin's Solutions of Trigonometrical Problems, *ib.*; Solutions of Geometrical Problems, *ib.*; Daubeny's Description of Active and Extinct Volcanos, 216, 296; Capt. Yolland's Account of the Measurement of the Lough Foyle Base in Ireland, 287; Sir John Herschel's Results of Astronomical Observations made at the Cape of Good Hope, 378, 518; Bell's Elements of Plane Geometry, 526; Tate's Principles of Geometry, 535.
Boole (G.) on the solution of a particular differential equation, 413.
Bouis (J.) on the action of chlorine on cyanide of mercury, 152.
Brewster (Sir D.) on the optical phænomena, nature and locality of *Muscæ volitantes*, 1; on the distinctness of vision produced by the use of the polarizing apparatus in microscopes, 161; on the phæ-

nomena of thin plates of solid and fluid substances exposed to polarized light, 181; on the decomposition and dispersion of light within solid and fluid bodies, 401; on the elementary colours of the spectrum, in reply to M. Melloni, 489.

Brongniart (A.) notice of the late, 228.

Bronwin (Rev. B.) on the solution of a particular differential equation, 256.

Brooke (C.) on a remarkable magnetic disturbance, 35.

Brucia, action of nitric acid on, 392.

Bussy (M.) on transparent and opake arsenious acid, 398.

Butyro-acetic and metacetonic acids, on the identity of, 156.

Cacothelin, on the composition of, 393.

Cadmium, on the hydrate of, 317.

Cambridge Philosophical Society, proceedings of the, 141.

Carbon, on some properties of, 76.

Challis (Rev. J.) on the course of a ray of light from a celestial body to the earth's surface, 168; on the velocity of sound, 276, 494.

Chapman (E. J.) on a new method of distinguishing the protoxide of iron from the peroxide by the blowpipe, 309.

Chlorine, on the heat disengaged during the combination of bodies with, 321, 426.

Christianite, analysis of, 155.

Chrysammic acid, experiments on, 236.

Claudet (A.) on different properties of solar radiation modified by coloured glass media, 88; on photographic phænomena referring to the various actions of the red and yellow rays on Daguerreotype plates when they have been affected by daylight, 199; on the priority respecting the discovery of the accelerating process in the Daguereotype operation, 215.

Clouds, on an easy method of measuring the distance and height of, 375.

Cockle (J.) on algebraic equations of the fifth degree, 50; on the method of vanishing groups, 114; on the theory of equations, 351; on certain researches of Murphy, 421.

Cutton (Dr. R. P.) on the geological age of bone-caverns, 119.

Cumol, action of nitric acid upon, 63.

Cyanide of mercury, on the action of chlorine on, 152.

Cymol, on the action of nitric acid on, 15.

Daguerreotype plates, on the advantage of electrotyping, 541.

Damour (M. A.) on phosphate of iron, manganese and soda, 74; on a hydrated silicate of alumina, 149.

Davies (T. S.) on the theory of equations, 351; on geometry and geometers, 419.

Daubeny's (Dr. C.) Description of Active and Extinct Volcanos, of Earthquakes and of Thermal Springs, notice of, 216, 297.

De Morgan (Prof.) on the speculations of Thomas Wright of Durham, 241; on the additions made to the second edition of the *Commercium Epistolicum*, 446.

Descloizeaux (M.) on christianite, a new mineral, 155.

Draper (Dr. J. W.) on the production of light by chemical action, 100.

Drinkwater (J.) on the preparation of absolute alcohol, and the composition of "proof-spirit," 123.

Dufay, objections to the theory of, 461.

Dumas (M.) on the identity of metacetonic and butyro-acetic acids, 156.

Ebelmen (M.) on the artificial formation of crystallized minerals, 312.

Eclipse of October 8, 1847, observations on the, 144.

Electrical insulation, on the use of gutta percha in, 165.

Electrical phænomena, observations on, 466.

Electricity, magnetism, light and heat, researches into the identity of, 172; on alternating diurnal currents of, at the terrestrial surface, 389; on the disruptive discharge of accumulated, 391.

Equation, differential, on the solution of a particular, 256, 413.

# INDEX.

Equations, analysis of the theory of, 351.
Erythric acid, 303.
Evernic acid, on the preparation and constitution of, 303.
Faraday (Prof.) on the use of gutta percha in electrical insulation, 165.
Figures of equilibrium of a liquid mass withdrawn from the action of gravity, researches on, 61.
Flames, on the constitution of, 104.
Fordos (M.) on the acids of sulphur, 75.
Franklin, objections to the theory of, 461.
Fraunhofer's dark lines, on the physical cause of, 113.
Frigorific mixture, 153.
Functions of the form $F(x+x)$, on the development of, 284.
Galvanic currents in the blood, observations on, 229.
Garbett (E. L.) on some parhelia seen at Portsea on the 29th of March 1848, 434.
Gases, prismatic analysis of the flames of various, 101.
Gaskin's (T.) Solutions of the Trigonometrical Problems proposed at St. John's College from 1829 to 1836, notice of, 69; Solutions of Geometrical Problems, notice of, ib.
Gelis (M.) on the acids of sulphur, 75.
Geology of Asia Minor, on the present state of knowledge of the, 137.
Geometry and geometers, notes on, 419.
Glaisher (J.) on the weather during the quarters ending December 31, 1847, and March 31, 1848, 130, 506; on the corrections necessary to be applied to meteorological observations, 537.
Goodman (J.) on the identity of light, heat, electricity and magnetism, 172.
Gravity, researches on figures of equilibrium of a liquid mass withdrawn from the action of, 61.
Gutta percha, on the use of, in electrical insulation, 165.
Hailstone (Rev. J.), notice of the late, 221.
Hamilton (Sir W. R.) on quaternions, 367.

Hare (Dr. R.) on the theories severally of Franklin, Dufay and Ampère, with an attempt to explain electrical phænomena by statical or undulatory polarization, 461.
Heale (J. N.) on galvanic currents existing in the blood, 229.
Heat, light, electricity and magnetism, researches into the identity of, 172.
Heat disengaged during the combination of bodies with oxygen and chlorine, on the, 321, 426.
Henwood (W. J.), abstract of meteorological observations made during 1847, in the interior of Brazil, 422.
Herschel's (Sir J. F. W.) Results of Astronomical Observations made during the years 1834, 1835, 1836, 1837, 1838, at the Cape of Good Hope, notice of, 378, 518.
Hop-ash, analysis of, 54.
Hopkins (W.) on the internal pressure to which rock masses may be subjected, 141.
Hunt (R.) on the supposed influence of magnetism on chemical action, 252.
Iodine, on some remarkable properties of, 206.
Iron, method of distinguishing the peroxide from the protoxide of, by the blowpipe, 309.
Jacob (Capt.) on the annular eclipse of October, 8, 9, 1847, 144.
Johnson (Capt. E.) on some magnetical experiments, 389.
Joule (J. P.) on shooting stars, 349.
Jourdan (M. B. F.) on a frigorific mixture, 153.
Kane (Sir R.) on the occurrence of a deposit of native earthy carbonate of manganese in Ireland, 37.
Kilburn (W. E.) on the advantage of electrotyping Daguerreotype plates, 541.
Knapp (Dr. F.) on the law of the nutrition of animals, 456.
Lassaigne (M.) on the detection of free sulphuric acid added to wines, 77.
Laurent (M. Aug.) on the action of nitric acid on brucia, 392; on cacotheline, 393; on the acids of pines, 542.
Lazowski (M.) on some properties of carbon, 76.

Leblanc (M. F.) on the identity of metacetonic and butyro-acetic acids, 156.
Lichens, on the proximate principles of the, 300.
Liebenerite, analysis of, 544.
Light, on the production of, by chemical action, 100; on the course of a ray of, from a celestial body to the earth's surface, 168; heat, electricity and magnetism, researches into the identity of, 172; on the aberration of, 343; on the decomposition and dispersion of, within solid and fluid bodies, 401; researches on, 501.
——, polarized, on the phænomena of thin plates of solid and fluid substances exposed to, 181; on the influence of magnetism on, 306.
Lightning, on the proximate cause of, 391.
Lubbock (Sir J. W.) on shooting stars, 81, 170.
Luminiferous æther, on the constitution of the, 343.
MacCullagh (Prof.), notice of the late, 222.
Maclaurin's theorem, observations on, 98.
Magnetic disturbance, account of a remarkable, 35.
Magnetism, electricity, heat and light, researches into the identity of, 172; on the supposed influence of, on chemical action, 252; on the influence of, on polarized light, 306.
——, terrestrial, researches on, 390.
Malaguti (M.) on the identity of metacetonic and butyro-acetic acids, 156.
Manganese, on the occurrence of a deposit of native carbonate of, in Ireland, 37.
Marchand (M.) on a reagent for strychnia, 396.
Marignac (M.) on liebenerite—a new mineral, 544.
Matteucci (Prof. C.) on the influence of magnetism on polarized light, 306.
Melloni (M.) on the radiations of incandescent bodies, and on the elementary colours of the solar spectrum, 262.
Metacetonic and butyro-acetic acids, on the identity of, 156.

Metals, on the existence of several in the human blood, 311.
Meteorological observations, 79, 130, 159, 239, 319, 399, 422, 506, 537.
Millon (M.) on the existence of several metals in the human blood, and the fixed salt it contains, 310.
Minerals, on the artificial formation of crystallized, 312.
Mineralogy:—native carbonate of manganese, 37; analysis of phosphate of iron, manganese and soda, 74; of columbite, ib.; urancotantalite, 77; samarskite, ib.; hydrated silicate of alumina, 149; christianite, 155; liebenerite, 544.
Mulder (M.) on chrysammic acid, 236.
Murphy, on certain researches of, 421.
Muscæ volitantes, on the optical phænomena, nature and locality of the, 1.
Napier (Mr. M.), notice of the late, 220.
Nicklès (M. J.) on the crystalline form of metallic zinc, 314; on the crystallized monohydrate of zinc, 315; on the hydrate of cadmium, 317.
Nicotina, on the composition and properties of, 159.
Niépce de Saint-Victor (M.) on some remarkable properties of iodine, phosphorus, nitric acid, &c., 206.
Nitro-toluylic acid, on the formation and composition of, 15.
Nitromaric acid, on the composition of, 543.
Noad (H. M.) on the action of nitric acid on cymol, 15.
Norton (W. A.) on terrestrial magnetism, 390.
Orsellic acid, 301.
Oxygen, on the heat disengaged during the combination of bodies with, 321, 426.
Parhelia, description of some, with remarks on the phænomena, 434.
Pentathionic acid, 75.
Phenylic acid, 151.
Phosphorus, researches on, 153; on some remarkable properties of, 206.
Photographic phænomena, observations on some, 199, 206, 213, 215.
Photography, observations on, 88.

# INDEX.

Picro-erythrine, on the composition of, 302.
Pimaric acid, on the constitution of, 542.
Pinic acid, researches on, 542.
Piria (M.) on the preparation and chemical constitution of asparagin, 233; on the action of acids and alkalies on asparagin and aspartic acid, 317.
Planets, results deduced from the occultations of, 146.
Plateau (M.) on figures of equilibrium of a liquid mass withdrawn from the action of gravity, 61.
Polarizing microscope, on the distinctness of vision produced by, 161.
Potts' (R.) Euclid's Elements of Geometry, notice of, 69.
Powell (Rev. Prof. B.) on beads in annular eclipses, 145.
Pringle (W.) on a remarkable solar spot, 232, 308.
Propionic acid, 156.
Pseudo-orcine, on the preparation and composition of, 302.
Quaternions, a new system of imaginaries in algebra, on, 367.
Ragona-Scinà (Prof.) on the solar spectrum, 505.
Reviews:—Potts' Euclid's Elements of Geometry, 69; Gaskin's Solutions of Trigonometrical Problems, *ib.*; Solutions of Geometrical Problems, *ib.*; Dr. Daubeny's Description of Active and Extinct Volcanos, 216, 296; Capt. Yolland's Account of the Measurement of the Lough Foyle Base in Ireland, 287; Sir John Herschel's Results of Astronomical Observations made at the Cape of Good Hope, 367, 518; Bell's Elements of Plane Geometry, 526; Tate's Principles of Geometry, 535.
Roberts (S.) on the development of functions of the form $F(z+x)$, 284.
Roccellinine, on the composition of, 301.
Rocks, influence of internal pressure on the production of laminated structure in, 141.
Rose (Prof. H.) on the composition of urano-tantalite and columbite, 77; on a new method of estimating arsenic, antimony and tin, 394.

Royal Astronomical Society, proceedings of the, 144.
Royal Society, proceedings of the, 139, 219, 300, 389, 537.
Saint-Evre (M.) on the action of chlorine on benzoate of potash, 149.
Salvetat (M.) on a hydrated silicate of alumina, 149.
Selenium, on the presence of, in iodide of potassium, 397.
Shooting stars, researches on, 81, 170, 349.
Shortrede (Capt.) on a formula for the elastic force of vapour, at different temperatures, 303; on the moist-bulb problem, 305.
Solar radiation, on different properties of, 88.
Solar spot, notice of a remarkable, 232, 308.
Solar spectrum, on the elementary colours of the, 262, 489; on some new lines in the, 499.
Sound, theoretical determination of the velocity of, 276, 339, 494.
Spectrum, on the elementary colours of the, 489.
Stars, results deduced from the occultations of, 146; double, of the southern hemisphere, on the, 518.
Stenhouse (Dr. J.) on the proximate principles of the lichens, 300.
Stokes (G. G.) on the constitution of the luminiferous æther, 343.
Strickland (H. E.) on the present state of knowledge of the geology of Asia Minor, 137.
Strychnia, on a reagent for, 396.
Sulphur, on the acids of, 75.
Sylvic acid, on the constitution of, 542.
Tate's (Thomas) Principles of Geometry, &c., reviewed, 535.
Taylor's theorem, observations on, 98.
Teschemacher (J. E.) on the fossil vegetation of anthracite coal, 78.
Thenard (M. P.) on phosphorus, 153.
Theorems of Maclaurin and Taylor, on the combination of the, 98.
Thomson (Dr. R. D.) on the law of the nutrition of animals, 456.
Tides, researches on, 139; report on experiments made on the, in the Irish Sea, 538.
Tin, on a new method of estimating, 394.

Toluol, on the formation and composition of, 31.
Toluylic acid, on the formation and composition of, 15.
Trez (M. de) on the presence of selenium in the iodide of potassium, 397.
Vanishing groups, account of the method of, 114.
Vapour, on a formula for the elastic force of, 303.
Vapours, prismatic analysis of the flames of various, 101.
Vision, on the distinctness of, produced in certain cases by the use of the polarizing microscope, 161.
Vitreous humour, on the structure of the, 1.
Volcanic geology, observations on, 216, 296.
Wartmann (Prof. E.) on an easy method of measuring the distance and height of an elevated point, 375; on some new lines in the solar spectrum, 499.

Watts (Henry) on the analysis of hop-ash, 54.
Weather, remarks on the, 130, 506.
Whewell (Dr.), researches on tides, 139.
Wöhler (M.), on the action of zinc on selenious acid, 544.
Wright (T.), an account of the speculations of, 241.
Yollond's (Capt. W.) Account of the Measurement of the Lough Foyle Base in Ireland, noticed, 287.
Young (Prof. J. R.) on the integral $\int \frac{dx}{x}$, 11; on the combination of the theorems of Maclaurin and Taylor, 98.
Zantedeschi (M.), physico-chemical researches of, 501.
Zinc, on the crystalline form of metallic, 314; on the crystallized monohydrate of, 315; action of, on selenious acid, 544.

END OF THE THIRTY-SECOND VOLUME.

PRINTED BY RICHARD AND JOHN E. TAYLOR,
RED LION COURT, FLEET STREET.

www.ingramcontent.com/pod-product-compliance
Lightning Source LLC
Chambersburg PA
CBHW031938290426
44108CB00011B/599